# DILBERT™

## A Treasury of Sunday Strips:
### Version 00

## Other DILBERT books from Andrews McMeel Publishing

**Random Acts of Management**
ISBN: 0-7407-0453-2

**Dilbert Gives You the Business**
ISBN: 0-7407-0338-2 hardcover
ISBN: 0-7407-0003-0 paperback

**Don't Step in the Leadership**
ISBN: 0-8362-7844-5

**Journey to Cubeville**
ISBN: 0-8362-7175-0 hardcover
ISBN: 0-8362-6745-1 paperback

**I'm Not Anti-Business, I'm Anti-Idiot**
ISBN: 0-8362-5182-2

**Seven Years of Highly Defective People**
ISBN: 0-8362-5129-6 hardcover
ISBN: 0-8362-3668-8 paperback

**Casual Day Has Gone Too Far**
ISBN: 0-8362-2899-5

**Fugitive from the Cubicle Police**
ISBN: 0-8362-2119-2

**Still Pumped from Using the Mouse**
ISBN: 0-8362-1026-3

**It's Obvious You Won't Survive by Your Wits Alone**
ISBN: 0-8362-0415-8

**Bring Me the Head of Willy the Mailboy!**
ISBN: 0-8362-1779-9

**Shave the Whales**
ISBN: 0-8362-1740-3

**Dogbert's Clues for the Clueless**
ISBN: 0-8362-1737-3

**Build a Better Life by Stealing Office Supplies**
ISBN: 0-8362-1757-8

**Always Postpone Meetings with Time-Wasting Morons**
ISBN: 0-8362-1758-6

**For ordering information, call 1-800-642-6480.**

# DILBERT™

## A Treasury of Sunday Strips: Version 00   by SCOTT ADAMS

Andrews McMeel
Publishing

Kansas City

*Dilbert—A Treasury of Sunday Strips: Version 00* copyright © 2000 by United Feature Syndicate, Inc. All rights reserved. Printed in the United States of America. No part of this book may be used or reproduced in any manner whatsoever without written permission except in the case of reprints in the context of reviews. For information, write Andrews McMeel Publishing, an Andrews McMeel Universal company, 4520 Main Street, Kansas City, Missouri 64111.

00 01 02 03 04 BAM 10 9 8 7 6 5 4 3 2 1

ISBN: 0-7407-0531-8

Library of Congress Catalog Card Number: 00-103471

**What the heck is a finial and why do we need one?**

# Introduction

Have you ever noticed that crazy people don't think they're crazy? I'm talking about the run-of-the-mill wackos who populate your day. They think they're "quirky" or "high maintenance" or "perfectionists," but they rarely realize they are nuts. This got me to thinking, what if I'm nuts and I don't know it?

I started a list of all the things I do that could be construed as crazy by an unkind observer. Number one on the list is "creating a list of all the things I do that could be construed as crazy by an unkind observer." Number two was wondering if writing "number one" is redundant, since "one" is obviously a number. Number three, or as I call it now, just "three," was overanalyzing everything. Soon I had over forty items that were about the list itself. I decided those don't count.

Sometimes I ask questions and then I don't listen to the answers. It's not entirely my fault. If I ask a simple question and someone launches into a background story with charts and graphs and samples of DNA, I start thinking about other things. Sometimes I get hungry and wander away. That probably looks crazy.

For five years I couldn't sleep if I lay on my left side. It felt like my guts weren't in the right place. It didn't hurt, it just felt weird knowing my internal organs might not be where they belonged. When I lay on my other side everything was fine. I don't know what changed, but now both sides work and my guts feel okay. I credit my spleen for fixing the problem because I don't know what else it's supposed to do and it rarely gets credit.

I'm a vegetarian. Some people think that's crazy. Every now and then a slow-witted carnivore will engage me in a philosophical debate on the question of whether humans are meant to eat meat. I point out that a live cow makes a lion salivate, whereas a human just wants to say "moo" and see if the cow responds. I suppose if you were really, really, hungry, a cow might make you salivate, too. But by then you'd be willing to eat your sneakers, your relatives, dirt, and just about anything else. If you were meant to eat cows, you'd see ol' Bessie in a pasture and think how satisfying it would be to tackle her from behind and start gnawing on her thigh. All of my arguments make perfect sense to me, but other people just shake their heads and walk away muttering.

I also have a habit of changing the subject without warning. This book is full of Sunday-sized color cartoons. Most people think it's my best work. I think they're crazy, but only in general—not on that specific point. I hope you like it.

Speaking of crazy, it's not too late to join Dogbert's New Ruling Class (DNRC) and be a part of the elite when Dogbert conquers the world and makes everyone else our domestic servants. All you have to do is sign up for the totally free *Dilbert* newsletter that comes out whenever I feel like it, usually four times a year.

To subscribe, send a blank E-mail to dilbert-text-on@list.unitedmedia.com.
To unsubscribe, send a blank E-mail to dilbert-off@list.unitedmedia.com.
If you have problems with the automated subscription method, write to newsletter@united-media.com.

You can also subscribe via snail mail:

Dilbert Mailing List
United Media
200 Madison Ave.
New York, NY 10016


Sometimes the sun makes me sneeze, but that's a fascinating story for another day.

S.Adams

Scott Adams

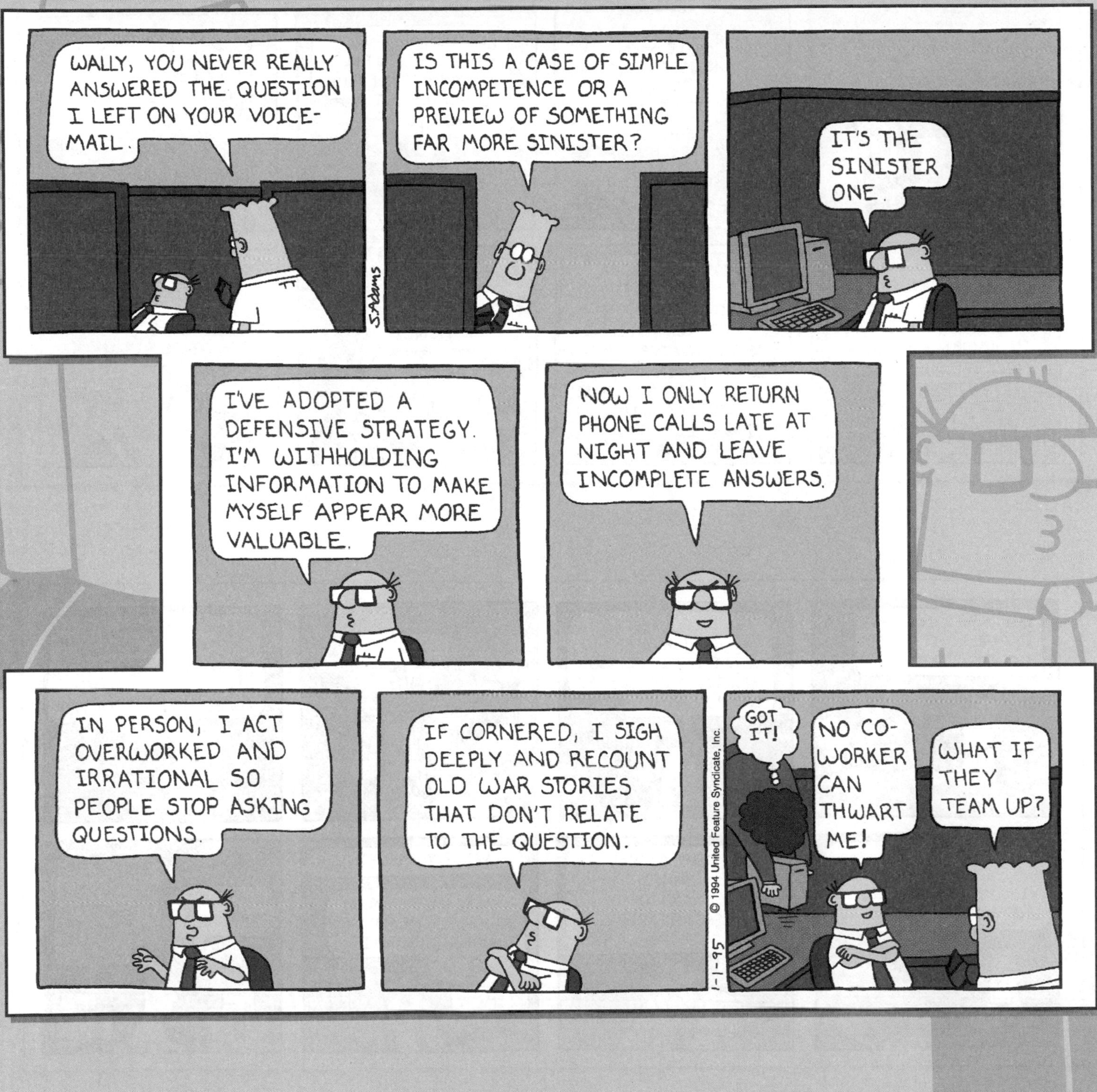
WALLY, YOU NEVER REALLY ANSWERED THE QUESTION I LEFT ON YOUR VOICE-MAIL.
S.Adams
IS THIS A CASE OF SIMPLE INCOMPETENCE OR A PREVIEW OF SOMETHING FAR MORE SINISTER?
IT'S THE SINISTER ONE.
I'VE ADOPTED A DEFENSIVE STRATEGY. I'M WITHHOLDING INFORMATION TO MAKE MYSELF APPEAR MORE VALUABLE.
NOW I ONLY RETURN PHONE CALLS LATE AT NIGHT AND LEAVE INCOMPLETE ANSWERS.
IN PERSON, I ACT OVERWORKED AND IRRATIONAL SO PEOPLE STOP ASKING QUESTIONS.
IF CORNERED, I SIGH DEEPLY AND RECOUNT OLD WAR STORIES THAT DON'T RELATE TO THE QUESTION.
1-1-95
© 1994 United Feature Syndicate, Inc.
GOT IT!
NO CO-WORKER CAN THWART ME!
WHAT IF THEY TEAM UP?

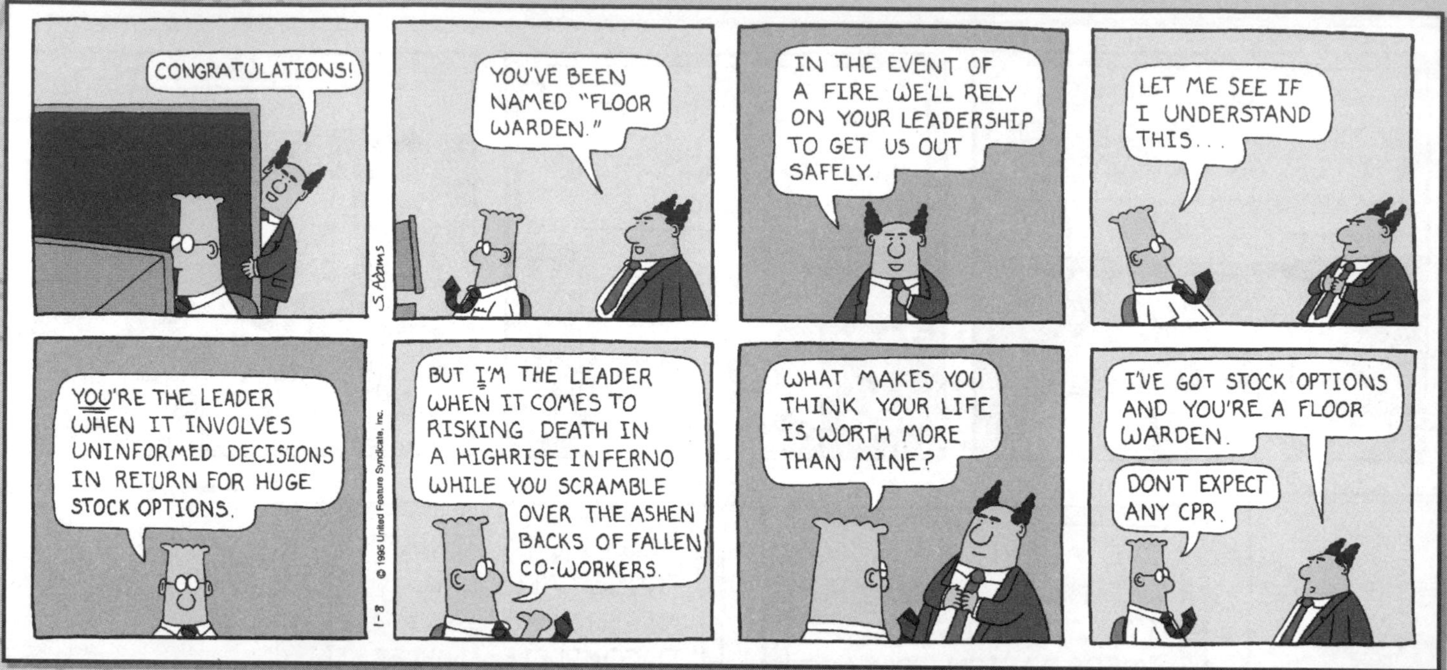
CONGRATULATIONS!
YOU'VE BEEN NAMED "FLOOR WARDEN."
IN THE EVENT OF A FIRE WE'LL RELY ON YOUR LEADERSHIP TO GET US OUT SAFELY.
LET ME SEE IF I UNDERSTAND THIS...
YOU'RE THE LEADER WHEN IT INVOLVES UNINFORMED DECISIONS IN RETURN FOR HUGE STOCK OPTIONS.
BUT I'M THE LEADER WHEN IT COMES TO RISKING DEATH IN A HIGHRISE INFERNO WHILE YOU SCRAMBLE OVER THE ASHEN BACKS OF FALLEN CO-WORKERS.
WHAT MAKES YOU THINK YOUR LIFE IS WORTH MORE THAN MINE?
I'VE GOT STOCK OPTIONS AND YOU'RE A FLOOR WARDEN.
DON'T EXPECT ANY CPR.
S. Adams
© 1995 United Feature Syndicate, Inc.
1-8

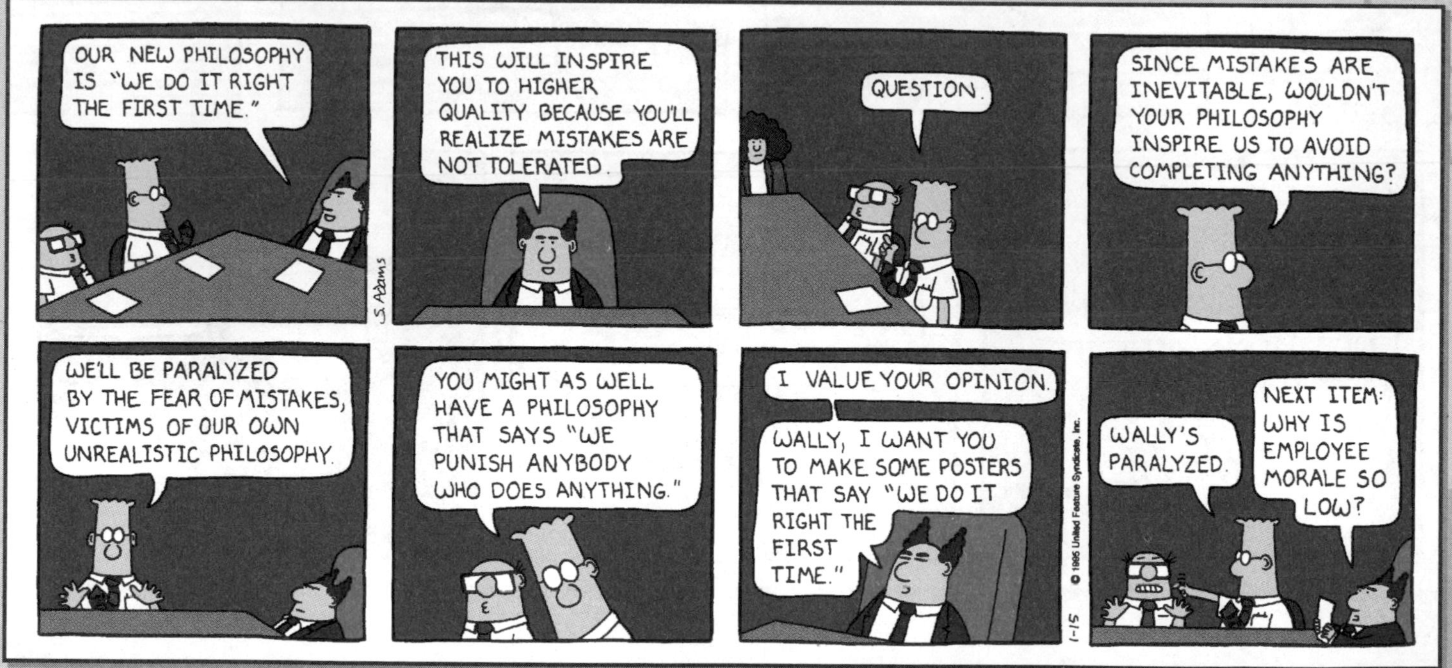
OUR NEW PHILOSOPHY IS "WE DO IT RIGHT THE FIRST TIME."
THIS WILL INSPIRE YOU TO HIGHER QUALITY BECAUSE YOU'LL REALIZE MISTAKES ARE NOT TOLERATED.
QUESTION.
SINCE MISTAKES ARE INEVITABLE, WOULDN'T YOUR PHILOSOPHY INSPIRE US TO AVOID COMPLETING ANYTHING?
WE'LL BE PARALYZED BY THE FEAR OF MISTAKES, VICTIMS OF OUR OWN UNREALISTIC PHILOSOPHY.
YOU MIGHT AS WELL HAVE A PHILOSOPHY THAT SAYS "WE PUNISH ANYBODY WHO DOES ANYTHING."
I VALUE YOUR OPINION.
WALLY, I WANT YOU TO MAKE SOME POSTERS THAT SAY "WE DO IT RIGHT THE FIRST TIME."
WALLY'S PARALYZED.
NEXT ITEM: WHY IS EMPLOYEE MORALE SO LOW?
S. Adams
© 1995 United Feature Syndicate, Inc.
1-15

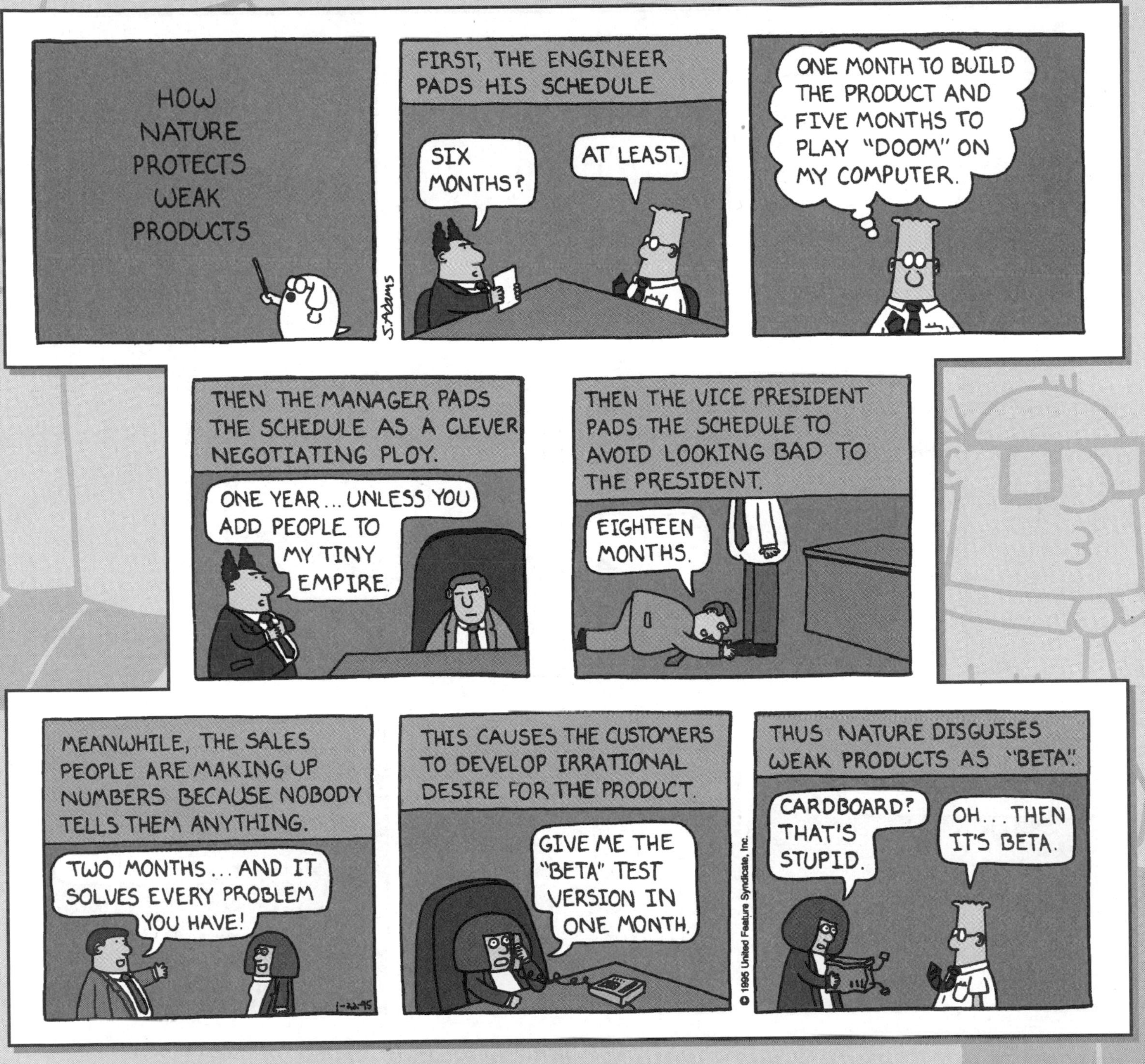
HOW NATURE PROTECTS WEAK PRODUCTS
S.Adams
FIRST, THE ENGINEER PADS HIS SCHEDULE
SIX MONTHS?
AT LEAST.
ONE MONTH TO BUILD THE PRODUCT AND FIVE MONTHS TO PLAY "DOOM" ON MY COMPUTER.
THEN THE MANAGER PADS THE SCHEDULE AS A CLEVER NEGOTIATING PLOY.
ONE YEAR... UNLESS YOU ADD PEOPLE TO MY TINY EMPIRE.
THEN THE VICE PRESIDENT PADS THE SCHEDULE TO AVOID LOOKING BAD TO THE PRESIDENT.
EIGHTEEN MONTHS.
MEANWHILE, THE SALES PEOPLE ARE MAKING UP NUMBERS BECAUSE NOBODY TELLS THEM ANYTHING.
TWO MONTHS... AND IT SOLVES EVERY PROBLEM YOU HAVE!
1-22-95
THIS CAUSES THE CUSTOMERS TO DEVELOP IRRATIONAL DESIRE FOR THE PRODUCT.
GIVE ME THE "BETA" TEST VERSION IN ONE MONTH.
© 1995 United Feature Syndicate, Inc.
THUS NATURE DISGUISES WEAK PRODUCTS AS "BETA".
CARDBOARD? THAT'S STUPID.
OH... THEN IT'S BETA.

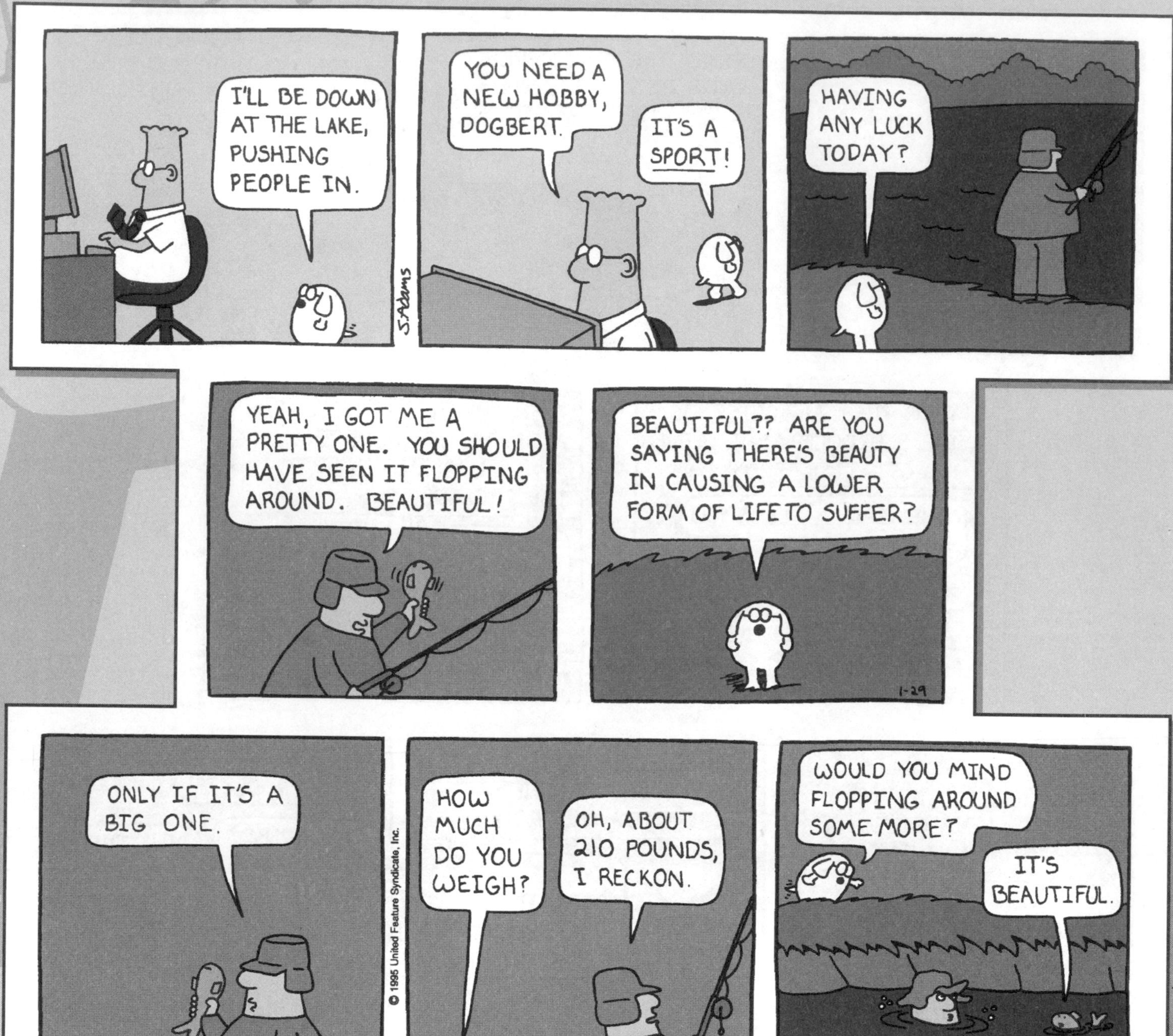
I'LL BE DOWN AT THE LAKE, PUSHING PEOPLE IN.
S. Adams
YOU NEED A NEW HOBBY, DOGBERT.
IT'S A SPORT!
HAVING ANY LUCK TODAY?
YEAH, I GOT ME A PRETTY ONE. YOU SHOULD HAVE SEEN IT FLOPPING AROUND. BEAUTIFUL!
BEAUTIFUL?? ARE YOU SAYING THERE'S BEAUTY IN CAUSING A LOWER FORM OF LIFE TO SUFFER?
1-29
ONLY IF IT'S A BIG ONE.
© 1995 United Feature Syndicate, Inc.
HOW MUCH DO YOU WEIGH?
OH, ABOUT 210 POUNDS, I RECKON.
WOULD YOU MIND FLOPPING AROUND SOME MORE?
IT'S BEAUTIFUL.

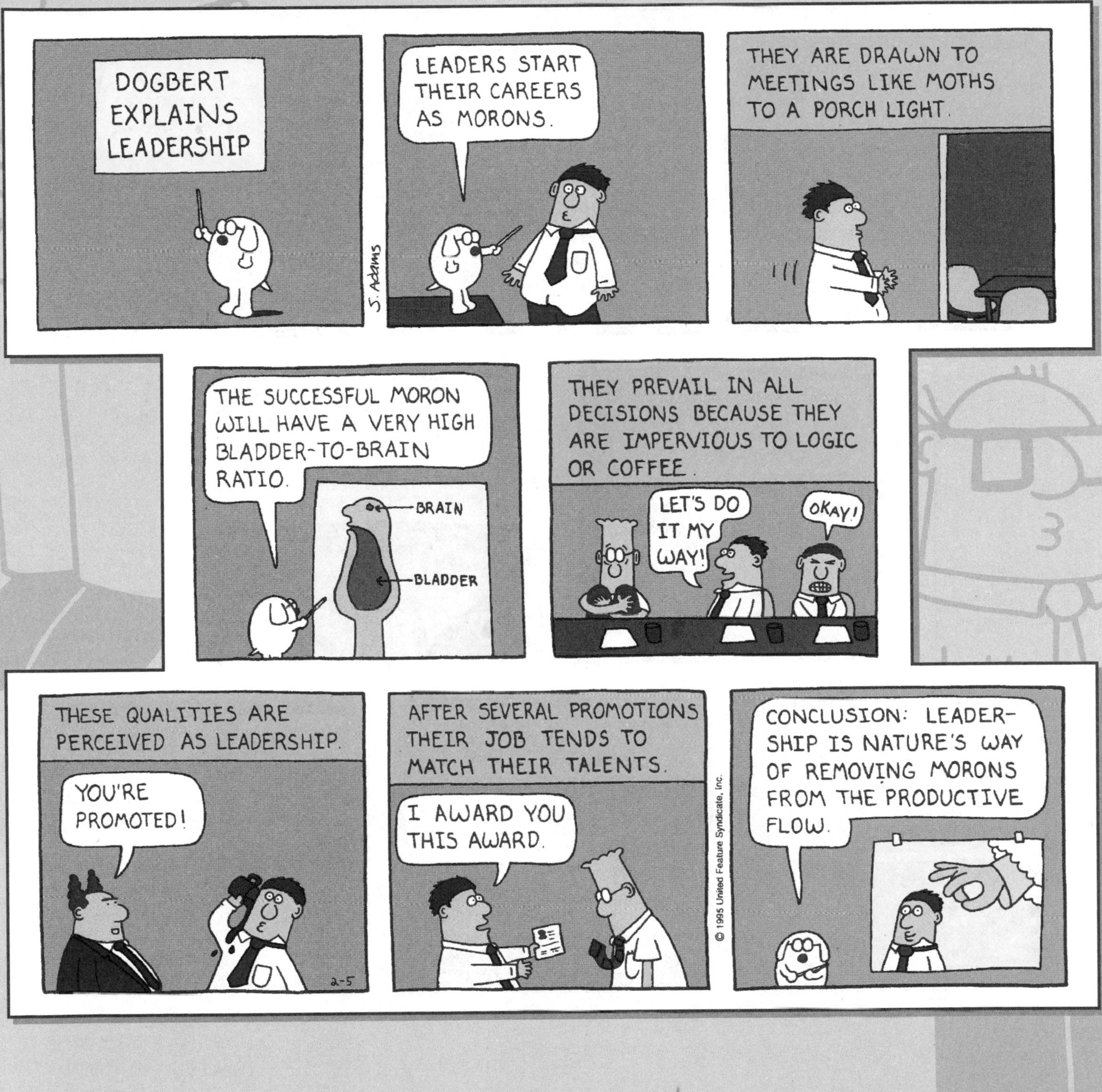
DOGBERT EXPLAINS LEADERSHIP
LEADERS START THEIR CAREERS AS MORONS.
S. Adams
THEY ARE DRAWN TO MEETINGS LIKE MOTHS TO A PORCH LIGHT.
THE SUCCESSFUL MORON WILL HAVE A VERY HIGH BLADDER-TO-BRAIN RATIO.
BRAIN
BLADDER
THEY PREVAIL IN ALL DECISIONS BECAUSE THEY ARE IMPERVIOUS TO LOGIC OR COFFEE.
LET'S DO IT MY WAY!
OKAY!
THESE QUALITIES ARE PERCEIVED AS LEADERSHIP.
YOU'RE PROMOTED!
2-5
AFTER SEVERAL PROMOTIONS THEIR JOB TENDS TO MATCH THEIR TALENTS.
I AWARD YOU THIS AWARD.
© 1995 United Feature Syndicate, Inc.
CONCLUSION: LEADERSHIP IS NATURE'S WAY OF REMOVING MORONS FROM THE PRODUCTIVE FLOW.

I'M PUTTING YOU ON THE STRATEGIC PLANNING TEAM.
S. Adams
IT'S LIKE WORK BUT WITHOUT THE SATISFACTION OF ACCOMPLISHING ANYTHING.
YOU'RE NEW, SO LET ME EXPLAIN HOW THIS WORKS.
WE HAVE MEETINGS AND TALK ABOUT THE COMPANY'S STRATEGY IN VAGUE EMOTIONAL TERMS.
IN TIME, WE CONVINCE OURSELVES THAT WE'RE MORE THAN MEDIOCRE THINKERS WHO SIT AROUND COMPLAINING.
2-12
WE START BELIEVING OUR OPINIONS WILL STEER THE COMPANY. WE FEEL IMPORTANT. WE FEEL ALIVE!!
THEN WE SNAP OUT OF IT AND MAKE VIEWGRAPHS THAT SAY WE SHOULD KEEP DOING WHAT WE'RE DOING.
© 1995 United Feature Syndicate, Inc.
I LIKE MAKING VIEW-GRAPHS.
ACTUALLY, WE USE LAST YEAR'S VIEWGRAPH.

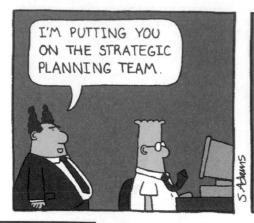

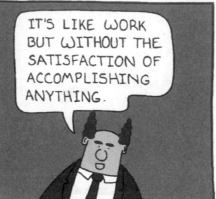

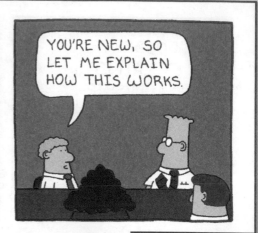

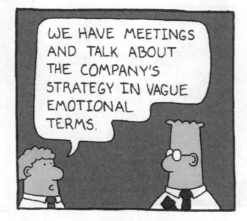

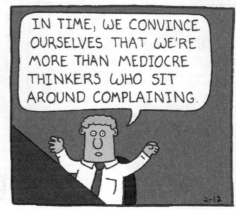

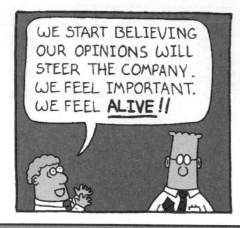

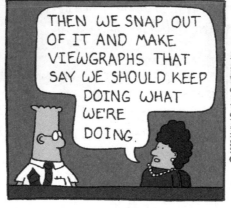

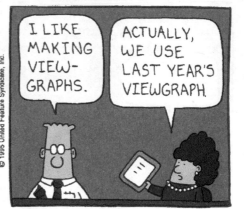

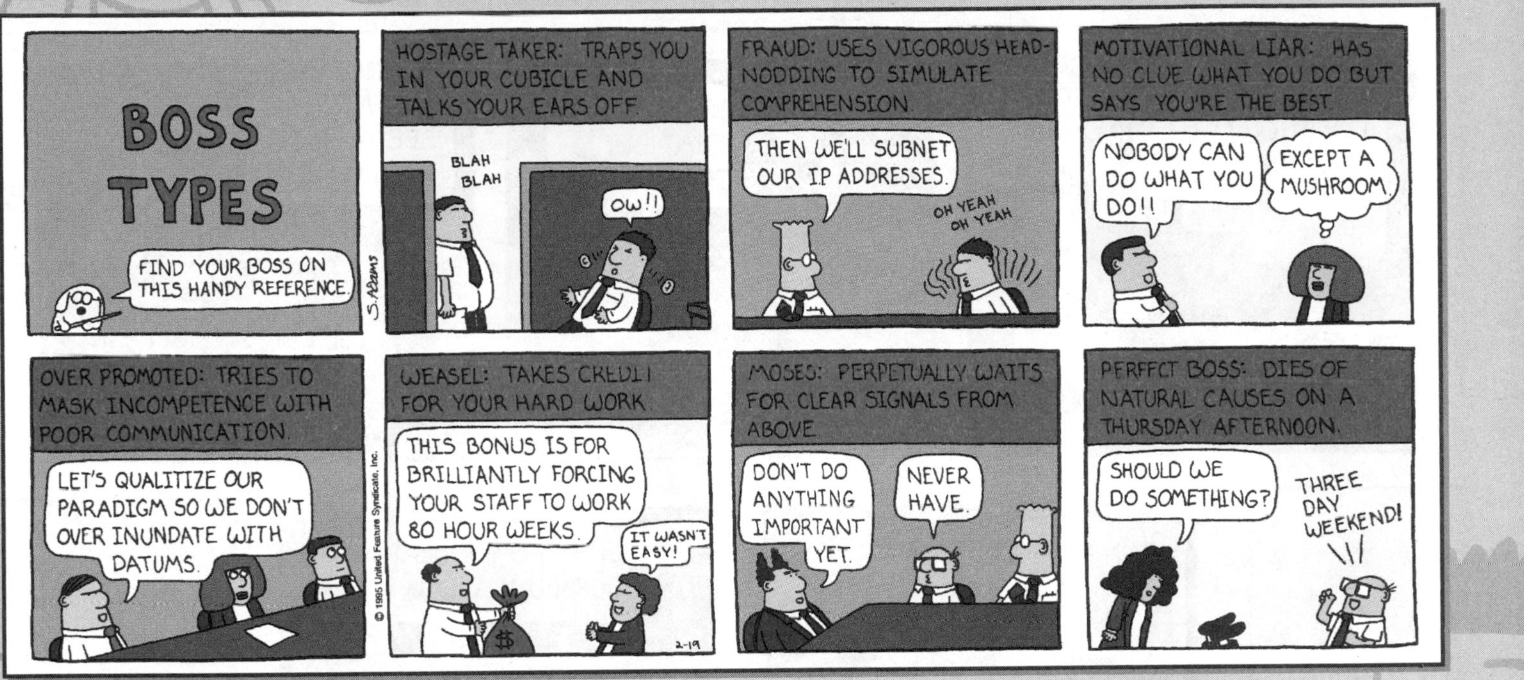
BOSS TYPES
FIND YOUR BOSS ON THIS HANDY REFERENCE.
HOSTAGE TAKER: TRAPS YOU IN YOUR CUBICLE AND TALKS YOUR EARS OFF.
BLAH BLAH
OW!!
FRAUD: USES VIGOROUS HEAD-NODDING TO SIMULATE COMPREHENSION.
THEN WE'LL SUBNET OUR IP ADDRESSES.
OH YEAH OH YEAH
MOTIVATIONAL LIAR: HAS NO CLUE WHAT YOU DO BUT SAYS YOU'RE THE BEST.
NOBODY CAN DO WHAT YOU DO!!
EXCEPT A MUSHROOM.
OVER PROMOTED: TRIES TO MASK INCOMPETENCE WITH POOR COMMUNICATION.
LET'S QUALITIZE OUR PARADIGM SO WE DON'T OVER INUNDATE WITH DATUMS.
WEASEL: TAKES CREDIT FOR YOUR HARD WORK.
THIS BONUS IS FOR BRILLIANTLY FORCING YOUR STAFF TO WORK 80 HOUR WEEKS.
IT WASN'T EASY!
MOSES: PERPETUALLY WAITS FOR CLEAR SIGNALS FROM ABOVE.
DON'T DO ANYTHING IMPORTANT YET.
NEVER HAVE.
PERFECT BOSS: DIES OF NATURAL CAUSES ON A THURSDAY AFTERNOON.
SHOULD WE DO SOMETHING?
THREE DAY WEEKEND!
© 1995 United Feature Syndicate, Inc.

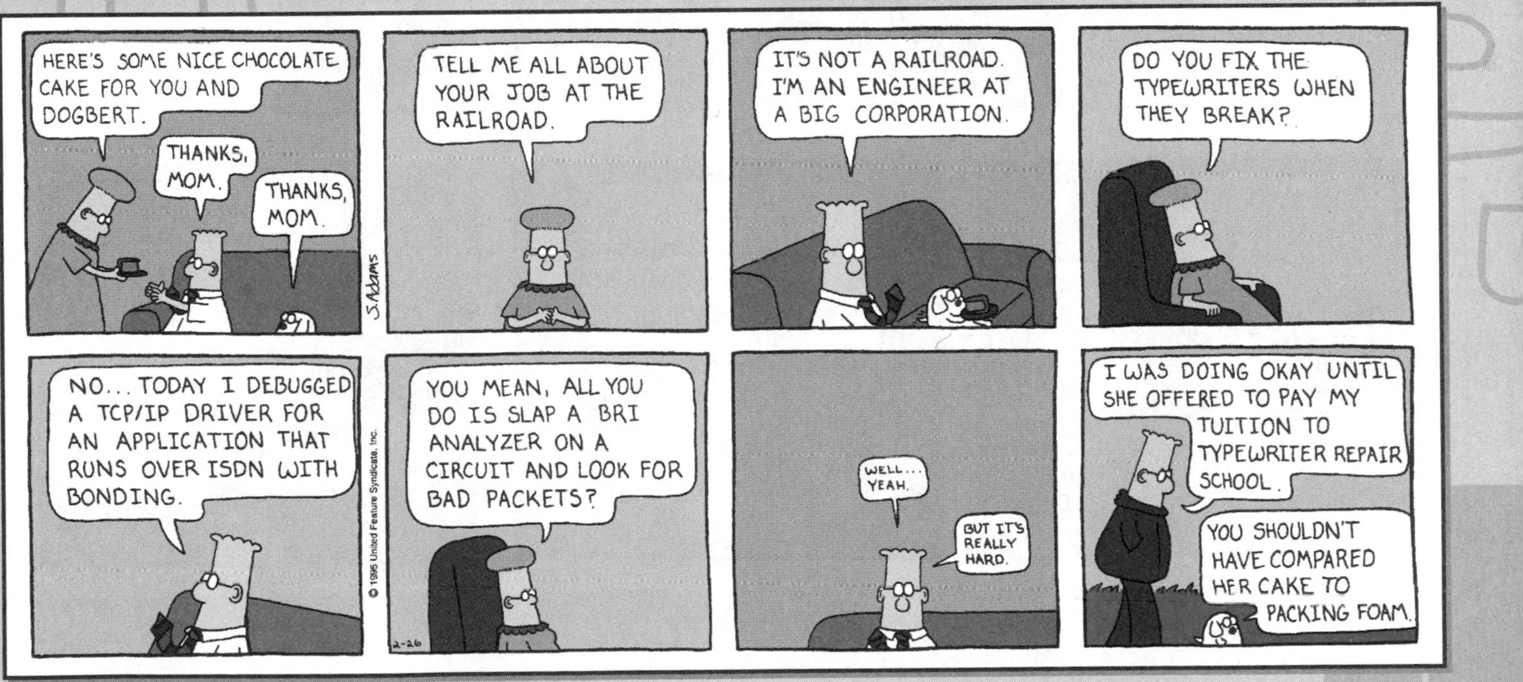
HERE'S SOME NICE CHOCOLATE CAKE FOR YOU AND DOGBERT.
THANKS, MOM.
THANKS, MOM.
TELL ME ALL ABOUT YOUR JOB AT THE RAILROAD.
IT'S NOT A RAILROAD. I'M AN ENGINEER AT A BIG CORPORATION.
DO YOU FIX THE TYPEWRITERS WHEN THEY BREAK?
NO... TODAY I DEBUGGED A TCP/IP DRIVER FOR AN APPLICATION THAT RUNS OVER ISDN WITH BONDING.
YOU MEAN, ALL YOU DO IS SLAP A BRI ANALYZER ON A CIRCUIT AND LOOK FOR BAD PACKETS?
WELL... YEAH.
BUT IT'S REALLY HARD.
I WAS DOING OKAY UNTIL SHE OFFERED TO PAY MY TUITION TO TYPEWRITER REPAIR SCHOOL.
YOU SHOULDN'T HAVE COMPARED HER CAKE TO PACKING FOAM.
© 1995 United Feature Syndicate, Inc.

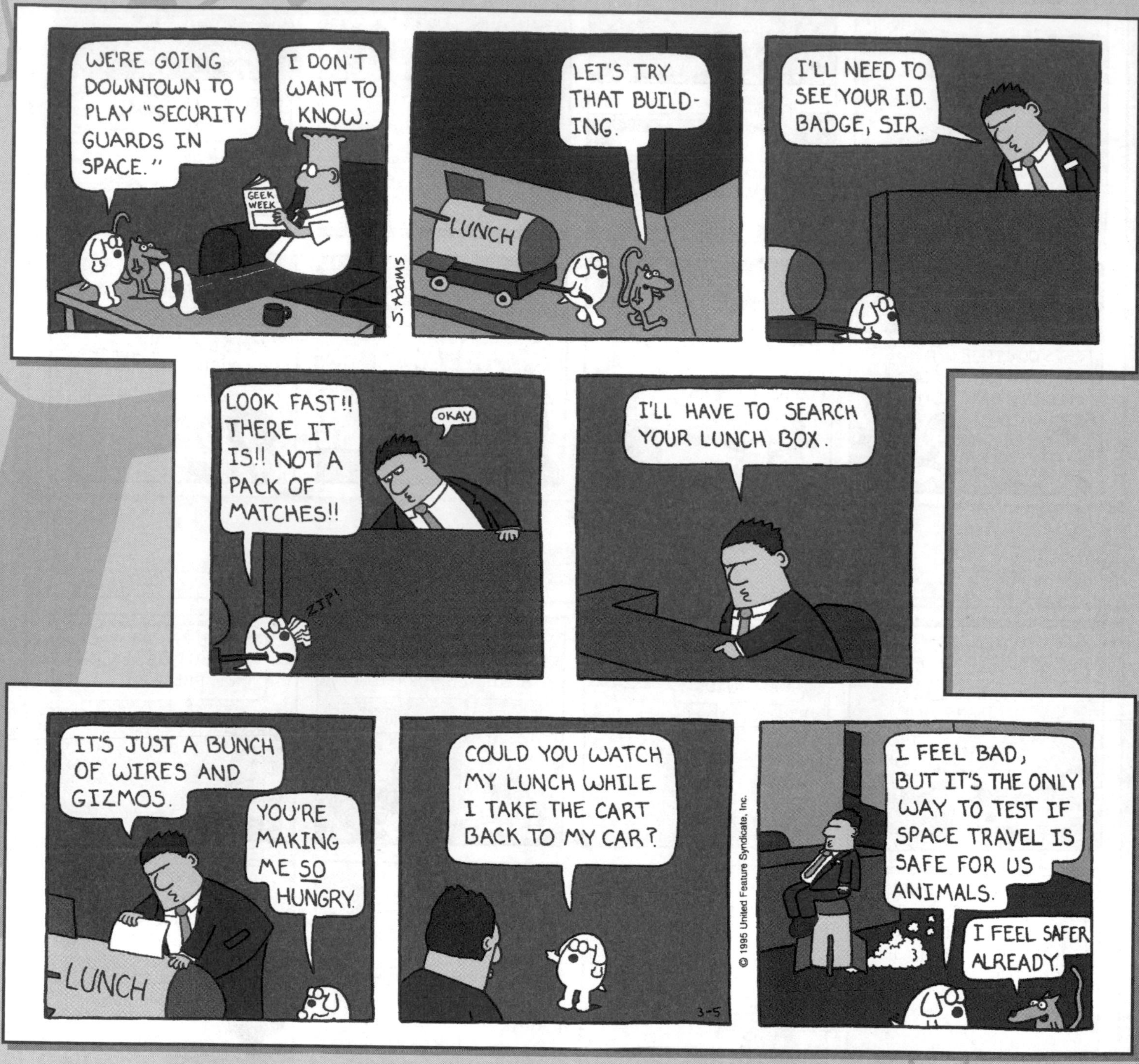
WE'RE GOING DOWNTOWN TO PLAY "SECURITY GUARDS IN SPACE."
I DON'T WANT TO KNOW.
GEEK WEEK
S. Adams
LET'S TRY THAT BUILD-ING.
LUNCH
I'LL NEED TO SEE YOUR I.D. BADGE, SIR.
LOOK FAST!! THERE IT IS!! NOT A PACK OF MATCHES!!
OKAY
ZIP!
I'LL HAVE TO SEARCH YOUR LUNCH BOX.
IT'S JUST A BUNCH OF WIRES AND GIZMOS.
YOU'RE MAKING ME SO HUNGRY.
LUNCH
COULD YOU WATCH MY LUNCH WHILE I TAKE THE CART BACK TO MY CAR?
© 1995 United Feature Syndicate, Inc.
3-5
I FEEL BAD, BUT IT'S THE ONLY WAY TO TEST IF SPACE TRAVEL IS SAFE FOR US ANIMALS.
I FEEL SAFER ALREADY.

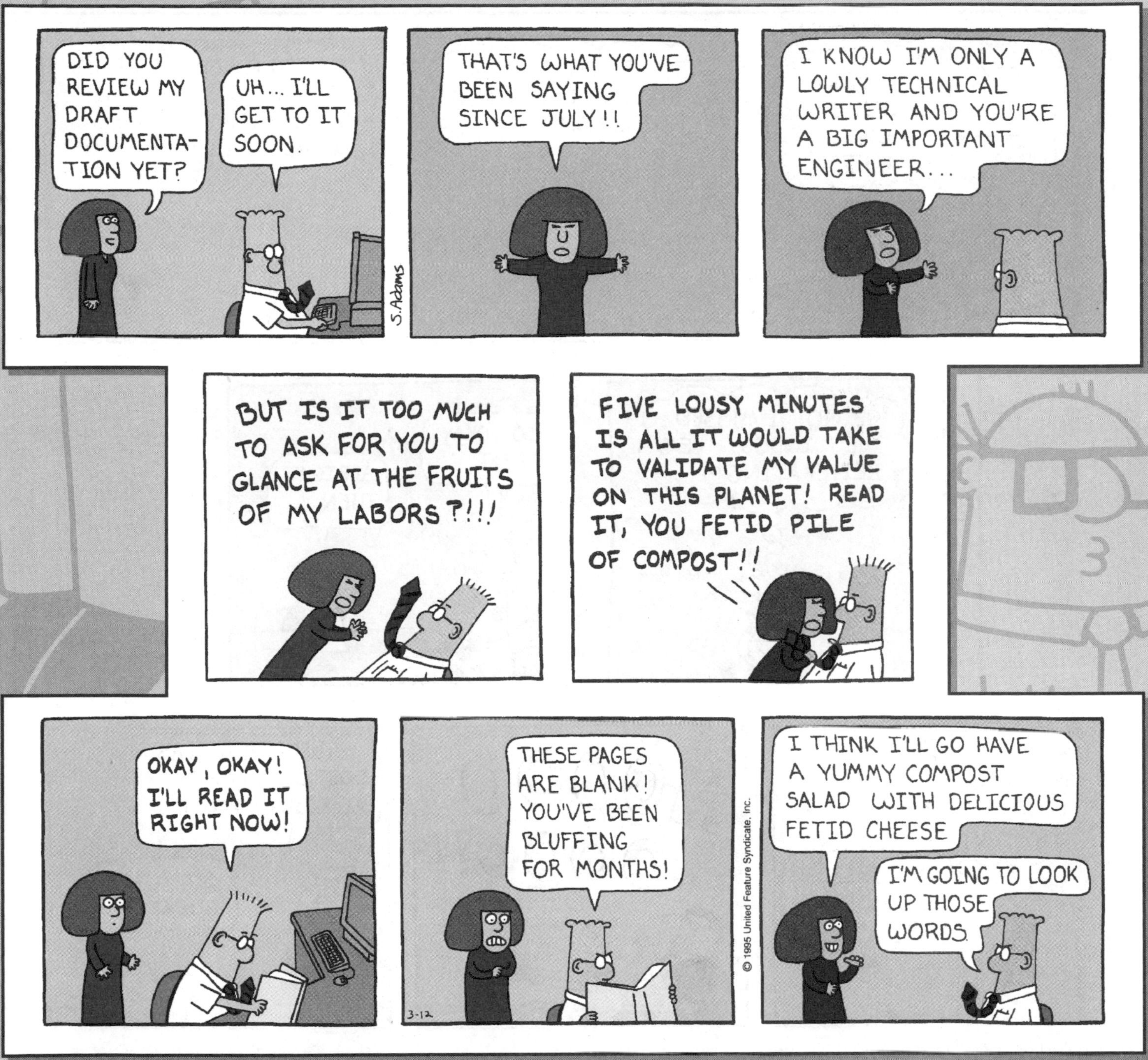
DID YOU REVIEW MY DRAFT DOCUMENTATION YET?
UH... I'LL GET TO IT SOON.
S. Adams
THAT'S WHAT YOU'VE BEEN SAYING SINCE JULY!!
I KNOW I'M ONLY A LOWLY TECHNICAL WRITER AND YOU'RE A BIG IMPORTANT ENGINEER...
BUT IS IT TOO MUCH TO ASK FOR YOU TO GLANCE AT THE FRUITS OF MY LABORS?!!!
FIVE LOUSY MINUTES IS ALL IT WOULD TAKE TO VALIDATE MY VALUE ON THIS PLANET! READ IT, YOU FETID PILE OF COMPOST!!
OKAY, OKAY! I'LL READ IT RIGHT NOW!
THESE PAGES ARE BLANK! YOU'VE BEEN BLUFFING FOR MONTHS!
3-12
© 1995 United Feature Syndicate, Inc.
I THINK I'LL GO HAVE A YUMMY COMPOST SALAD WITH DELICIOUS FETID CHEESE
I'M GOING TO LOOK UP THOSE WORDS.

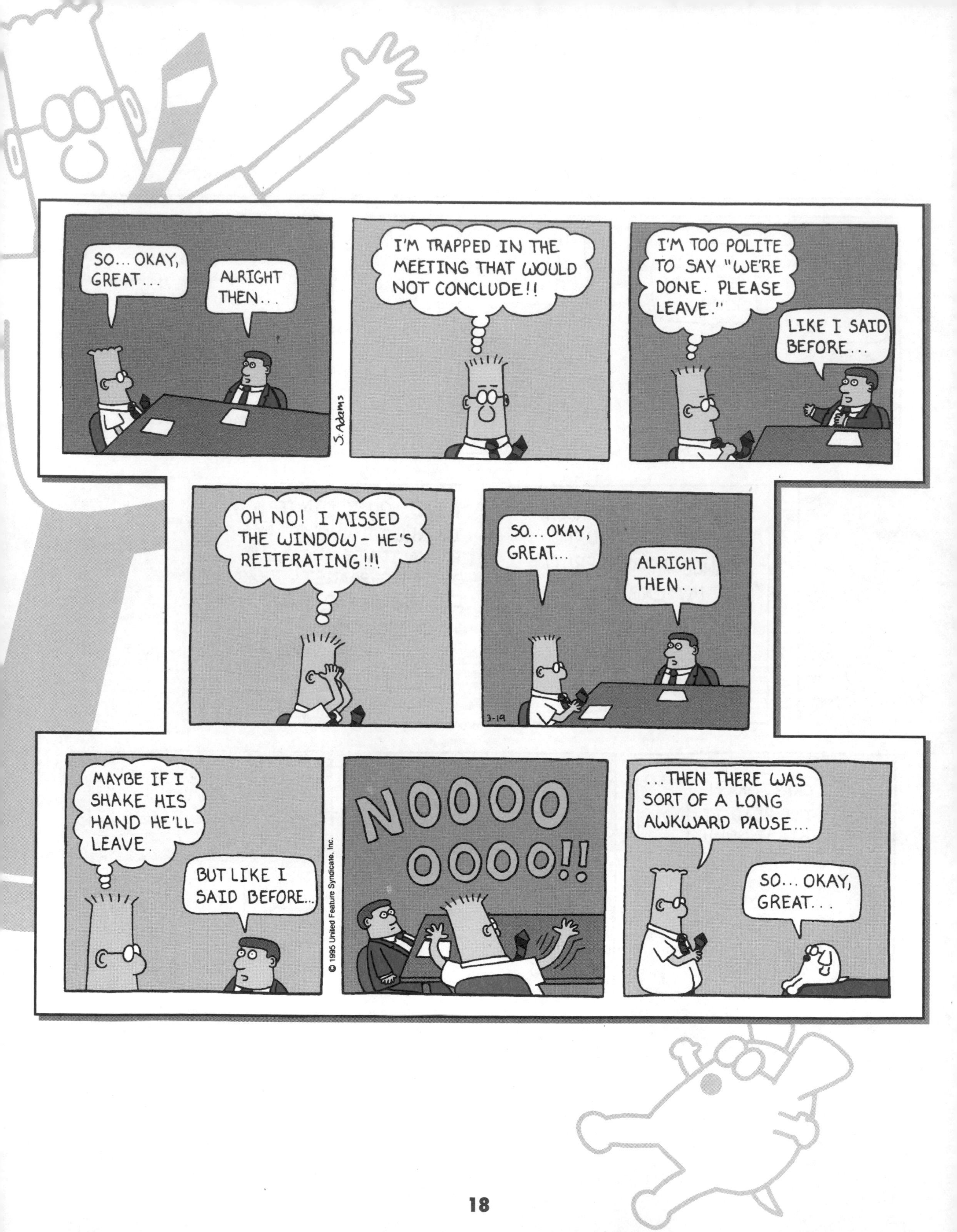
SO... OKAY, GREAT...
ALRIGHT THEN...
S. Adams
I'M TRAPPED IN THE MEETING THAT WOULD NOT CONCLUDE!!
I'M TOO POLITE TO SAY "WE'RE DONE. PLEASE LEAVE."
LIKE I SAID BEFORE...
OH NO! I MISSED THE WINDOW – HE'S REITERATING!!!
SO... OKAY, GREAT...
ALRIGHT THEN...
3-19
MAYBE IF I SHAKE HIS HAND HE'LL LEAVE.
BUT LIKE I SAID BEFORE...
© 1995 United Feature Syndicate, Inc.
NOOOO OOOO!!
...THEN THERE WAS SORT OF A LONG AWKWARD PAUSE...
SO... OKAY, GREAT...

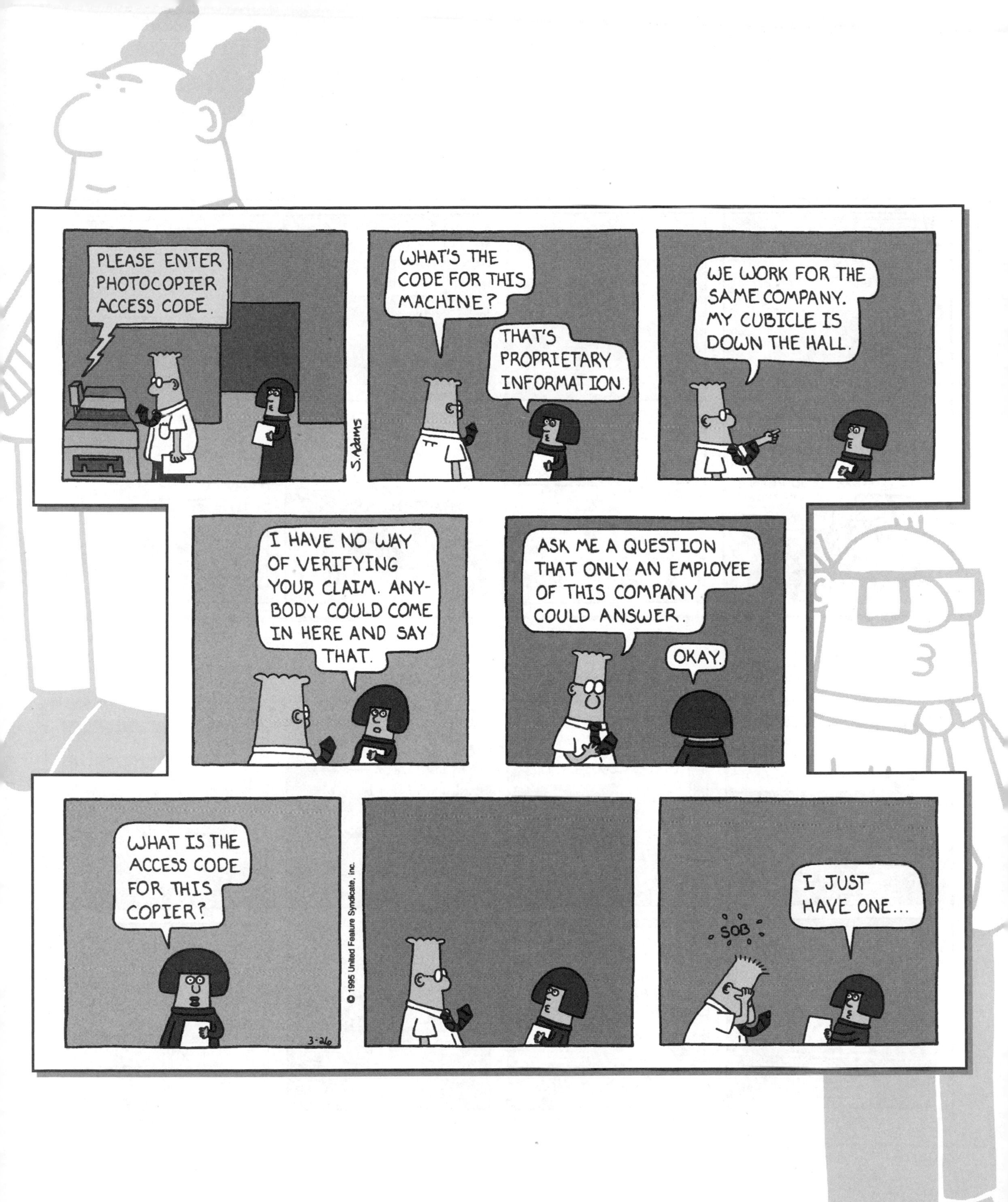
PLEASE ENTER PHOTOCOPIER ACCESS CODE.
S. Adams
WHAT'S THE CODE FOR THIS MACHINE?
THAT'S PROPRIETARY INFORMATION.
WE WORK FOR THE SAME COMPANY. MY CUBICLE IS DOWN THE HALL.
I HAVE NO WAY OF VERIFYING YOUR CLAIM. ANY-BODY COULD COME IN HERE AND SAY THAT.
ASK ME A QUESTION THAT ONLY AN EMPLOYEE OF THIS COMPANY COULD ANSWER.
OKAY.
WHAT IS THE ACCESS CODE FOR THIS COPIER?
© 1995 United Feature Syndicate, Inc.
3-26
SOB
I JUST HAVE ONE...

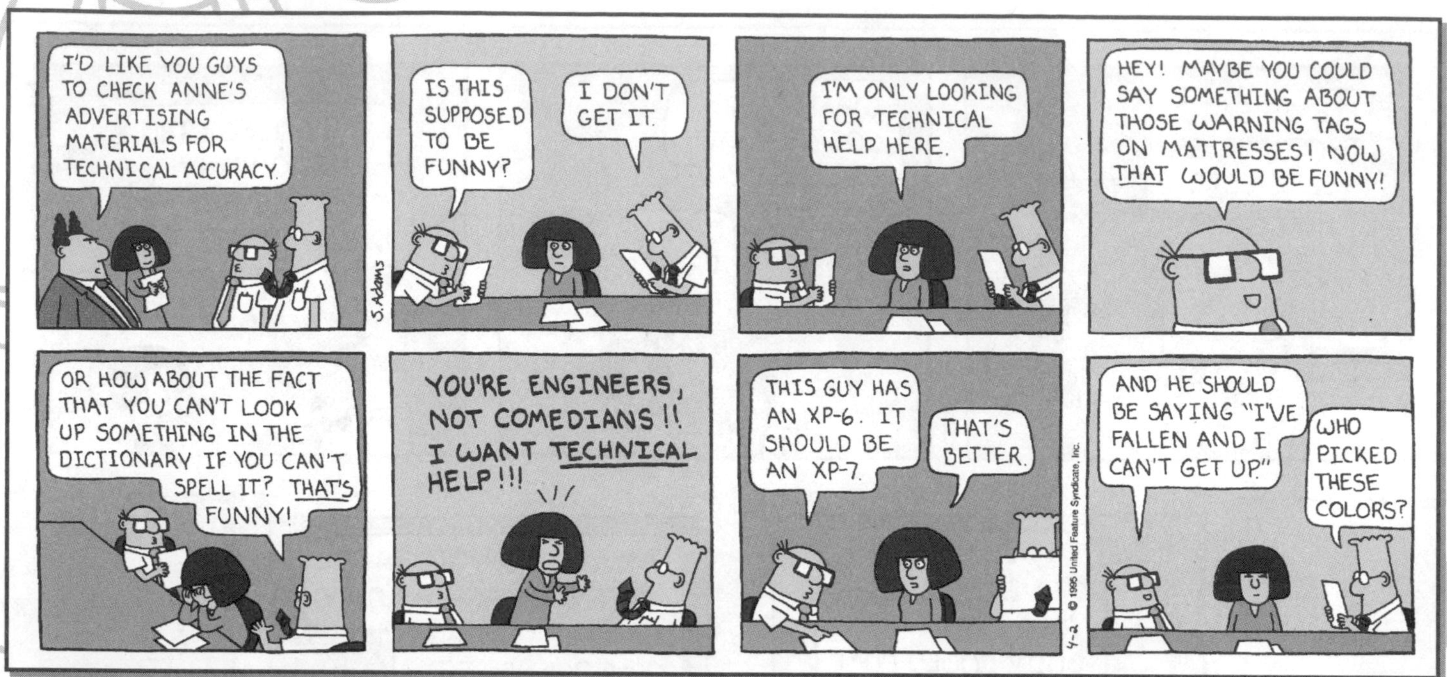
I'D LIKE YOU GUYS TO CHECK ANNE'S ADVERTISING MATERIALS FOR TECHNICAL ACCURACY.
S. Adams
IS THIS SUPPOSED TO BE FUNNY?
I DON'T GET IT.
I'M ONLY LOOKING FOR TECHNICAL HELP HERE.
HEY! MAYBE YOU COULD SAY SOMETHING ABOUT THOSE WARNING TAGS ON MATTRESSES! NOW THAT WOULD BE FUNNY!
OR HOW ABOUT THE FACT THAT YOU CAN'T LOOK UP SOMETHING IN THE DICTIONARY IF YOU CAN'T SPELL IT? THAT'S FUNNY!
YOU'RE ENGINEERS, NOT COMEDIANS!! I WANT TECHNICAL HELP!!!
THIS GUY HAS AN XP-6. IT SHOULD BE AN XP-7.
THAT'S BETTER.
4-2 © 1995 United Feature Syndicate, Inc.
AND HE SHOULD BE SAYING "I'VE FALLEN AND I CAN'T GET UP."
WHO PICKED THESE COLORS?

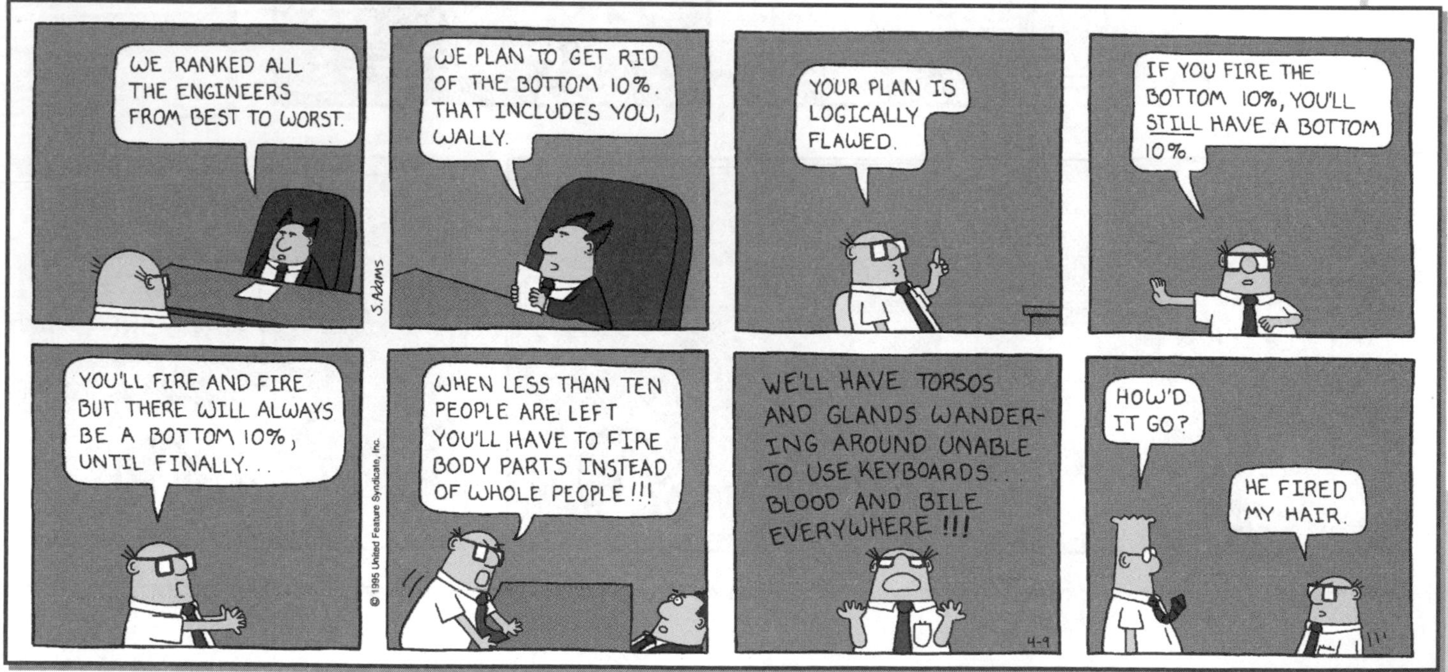
WE RANKED ALL THE ENGINEERS FROM BEST TO WORST.
S. Adams
WE PLAN TO GET RID OF THE BOTTOM 10%. THAT INCLUDES YOU, WALLY.
YOUR PLAN IS LOGICALLY FLAWED.
IF YOU FIRE THE BOTTOM 10%, YOU'LL STILL HAVE A BOTTOM 10%.
YOU'LL FIRE AND FIRE BUT THERE WILL ALWAYS BE A BOTTOM 10%, UNTIL FINALLY...
© 1995 United Feature Syndicate, Inc.
WHEN LESS THAN TEN PEOPLE ARE LEFT YOU'LL HAVE TO FIRE BODY PARTS INSTEAD OF WHOLE PEOPLE!!!
WE'LL HAVE TORSOS AND GLANDS WANDERING AROUND UNABLE TO USE KEYBOARDS... BLOOD AND BILE EVERYWHERE!!!
4-9
HOW'D IT GO?
HE FIRED MY HAIR.

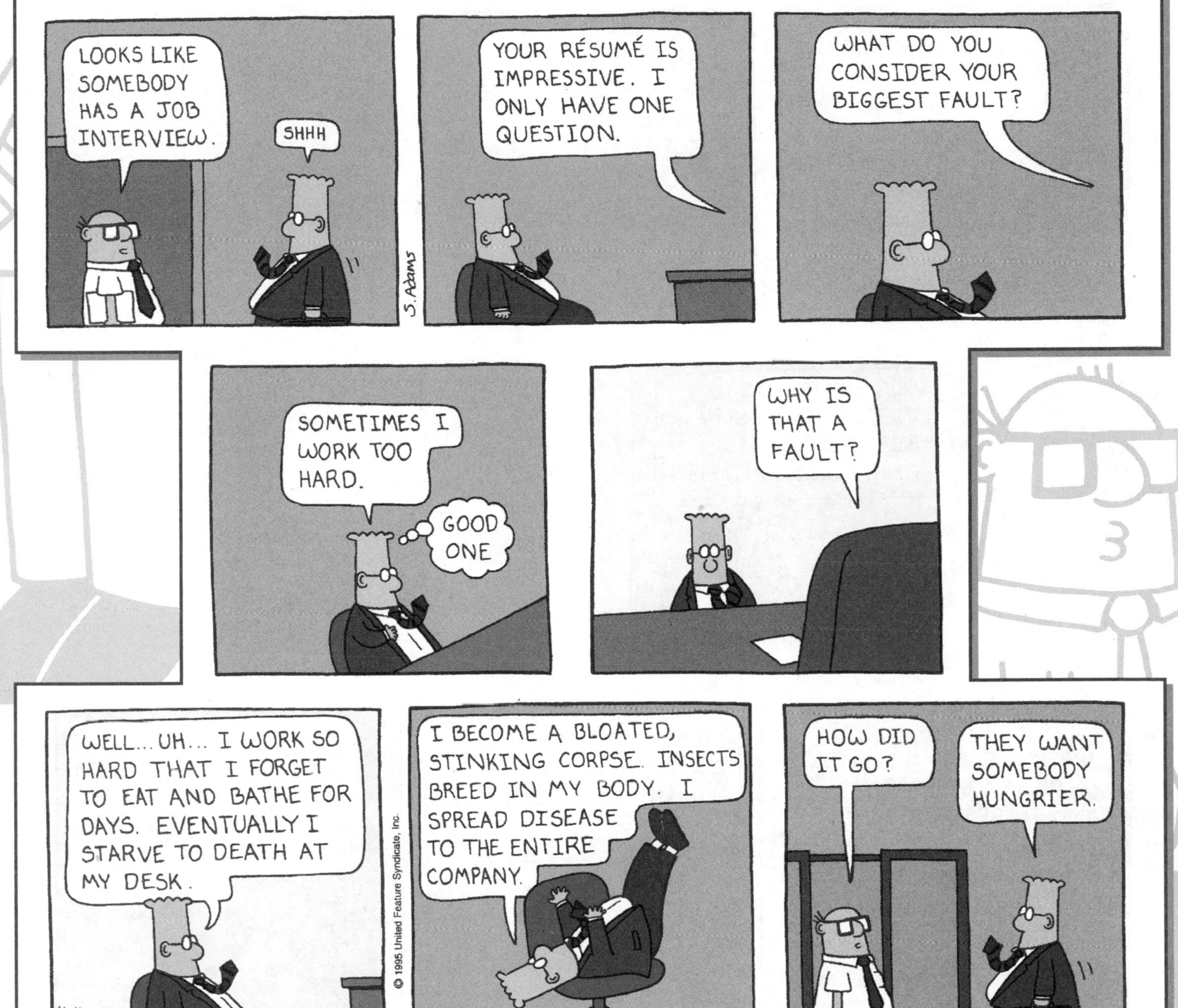
LOOKS LIKE SOMEBODY HAS A JOB INTERVIEW.
SHHH
S. Adams
YOUR RÉSUMÉ IS IMPRESSIVE. I ONLY HAVE ONE QUESTION.
WHAT DO YOU CONSIDER YOUR BIGGEST FAULT?
SOMETIMES I WORK TOO HARD.
GOOD ONE
WHY IS THAT A FAULT?
WELL... UH... I WORK SO HARD THAT I FORGET TO EAT AND BATHE FOR DAYS. EVENTUALLY I STARVE TO DEATH AT MY DESK.
4-16
© 1995 United Feature Syndicate, Inc.
I BECOME A BLOATED, STINKING CORPSE. INSECTS BREED IN MY BODY. I SPREAD DISEASE TO THE ENTIRE COMPANY.
HOW DID IT GO?
THEY WANT SOMEBODY HUNGRIER.

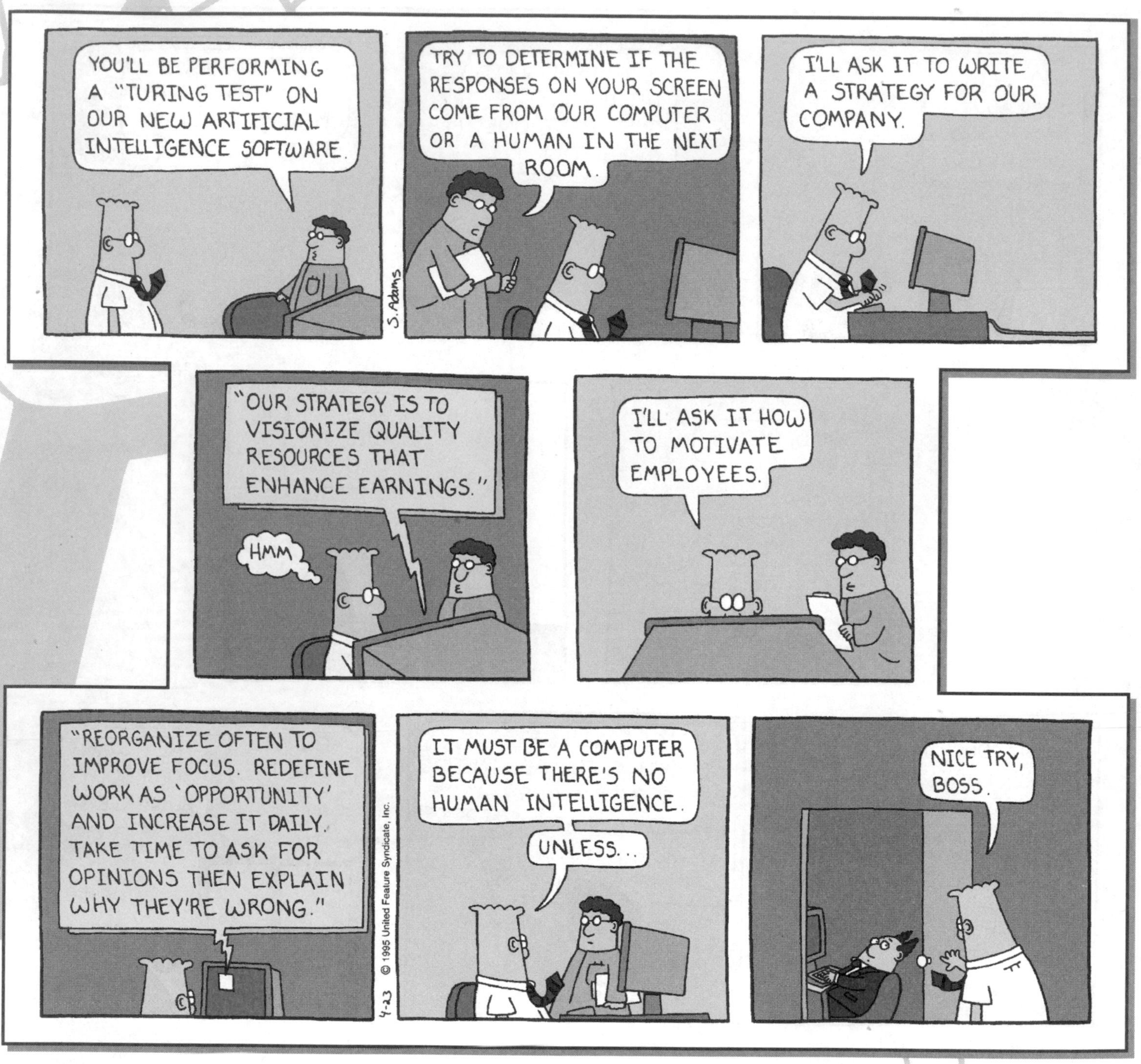
YOU'LL BE PERFORMING A "TURING TEST" ON OUR NEW ARTIFICIAL INTELLIGENCE SOFTWARE.
S. Adams
TRY TO DETERMINE IF THE RESPONSES ON YOUR SCREEN COME FROM OUR COMPUTER OR A HUMAN IN THE NEXT ROOM.
I'LL ASK IT TO WRITE A STRATEGY FOR OUR COMPANY.
"OUR STRATEGY IS TO VISIONIZE QUALITY RESOURCES THAT ENHANCE EARNINGS."
HMM
I'LL ASK IT HOW TO MOTIVATE EMPLOYEES.
"REORGANIZE OFTEN TO IMPROVE FOCUS. REDEFINE WORK AS 'OPPORTUNITY' AND INCREASE IT DAILY. TAKE TIME TO ASK FOR OPINIONS THEN EXPLAIN WHY THEY'RE WRONG."
© 1995 United Feature Syndicate, Inc.
4-23
IT MUST BE A COMPUTER BECAUSE THERE'S NO HUMAN INTELLIGENCE.
UNLESS...
NICE TRY, BOSS.

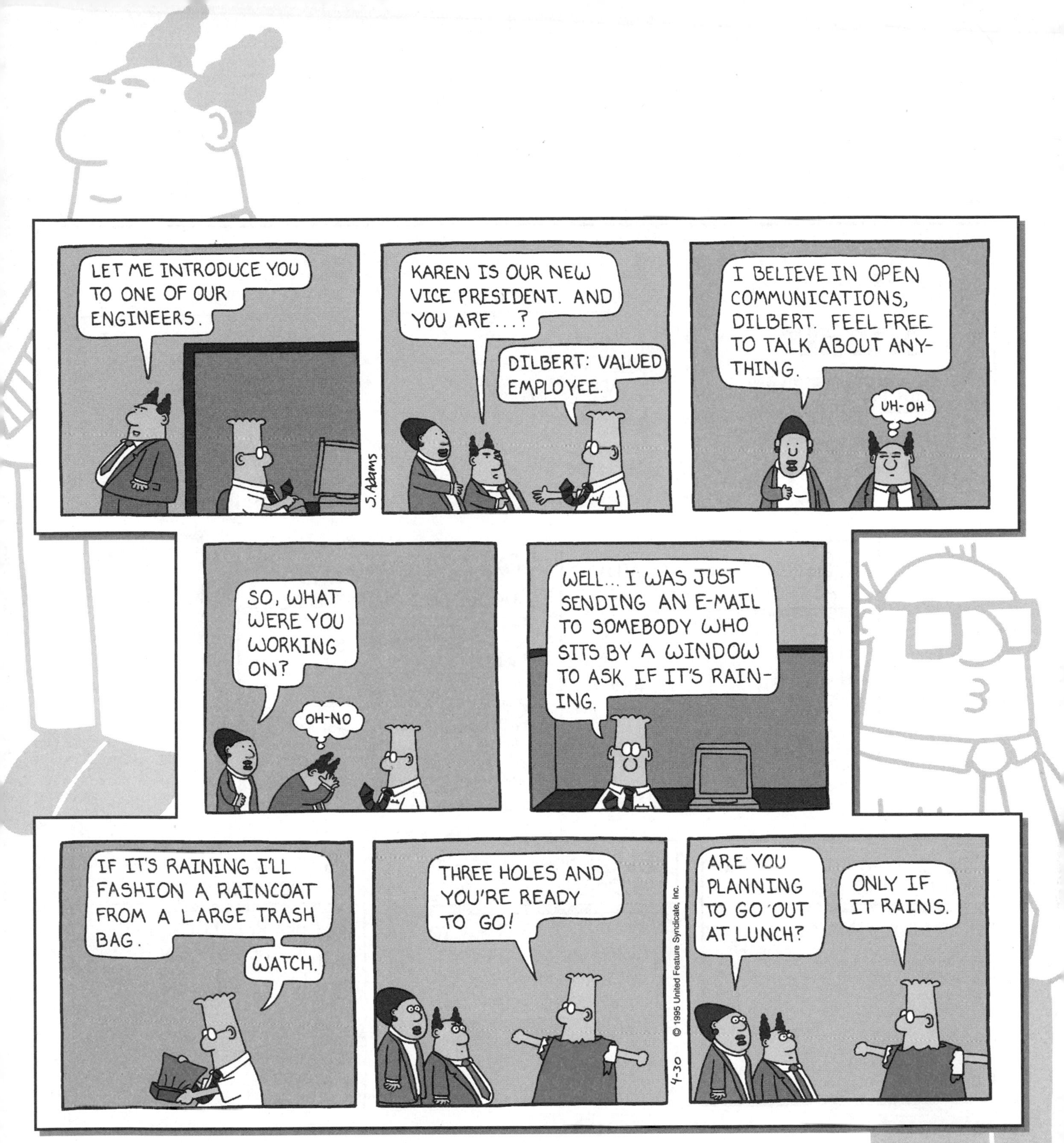

LET ME INTRODUCE YOU TO ONE OF OUR ENGINEERS.
S. Adams
KAREN IS OUR NEW VICE PRESIDENT. AND YOU ARE...?
DILBERT: VALUED EMPLOYEE.
I BELIEVE IN OPEN COMMUNICATIONS, DILBERT. FEEL FREE TO TALK ABOUT ANYTHING.
UH-OH
SO, WHAT WERE YOU WORKING ON?
OH-NO
WELL... I WAS JUST SENDING AN E-MAIL TO SOMEBODY WHO SITS BY A WINDOW TO ASK IF IT'S RAINING.
IF IT'S RAINING I'LL FASHION A RAINCOAT FROM A LARGE TRASH BAG.
WATCH.
THREE HOLES AND YOU'RE READY TO GO!
© 1995 United Feature Syndicate, Inc.
4-30
ARE YOU PLANNING TO GO OUT AT LUNCH?
ONLY IF IT RAINS.

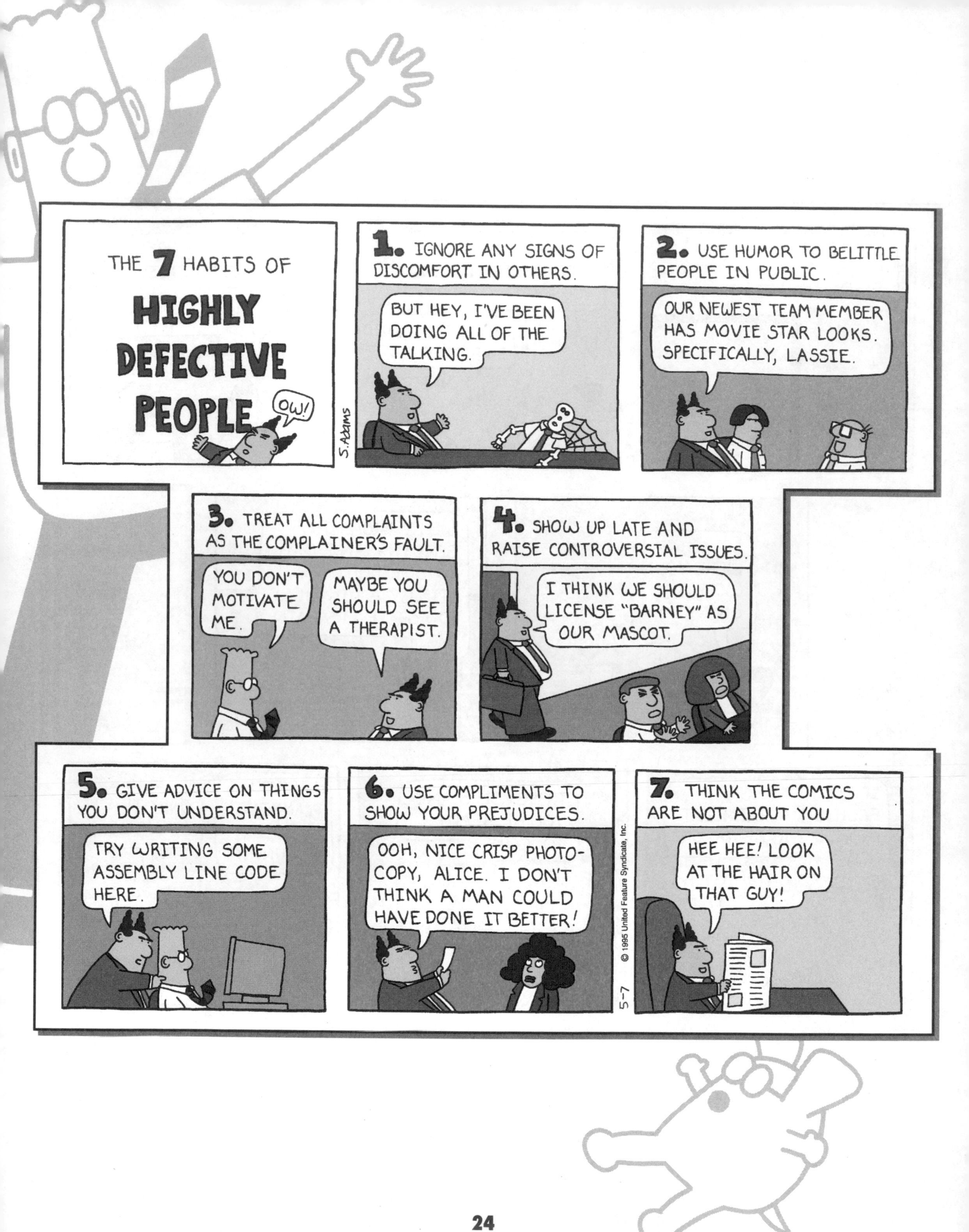
THE 7 HABITS OF
HIGHLY DEFECTIVE PEOPLE
OW!
S. Adams
1. IGNORE ANY SIGNS OF DISCOMFORT IN OTHERS.
BUT HEY, I'VE BEEN DOING ALL OF THE TALKING.
2. USE HUMOR TO BELITTLE PEOPLE IN PUBLIC.
OUR NEWEST TEAM MEMBER HAS MOVIE STAR LOOKS. SPECIFICALLY, LASSIE.
3. TREAT ALL COMPLAINTS AS THE COMPLAINER'S FAULT.
YOU DON'T MOTIVATE ME.
MAYBE YOU SHOULD SEE A THERAPIST.
4. SHOW UP LATE AND RAISE CONTROVERSIAL ISSUES.
I THINK WE SHOULD LICENSE "BARNEY" AS OUR MASCOT.
5. GIVE ADVICE ON THINGS YOU DON'T UNDERSTAND.
TRY WRITING SOME ASSEMBLY LINE CODE HERE.
6. USE COMPLIMENTS TO SHOW YOUR PREJUDICES.
OOH, NICE CRISP PHOTO-COPY, ALICE. I DON'T THINK A MAN COULD HAVE DONE IT BETTER!
© 1995 United Feature Syndicate, Inc.
5-7
7. THINK THE COMICS ARE NOT ABOUT YOU
HEE HEE! LOOK AT THE HAIR ON THAT GUY!

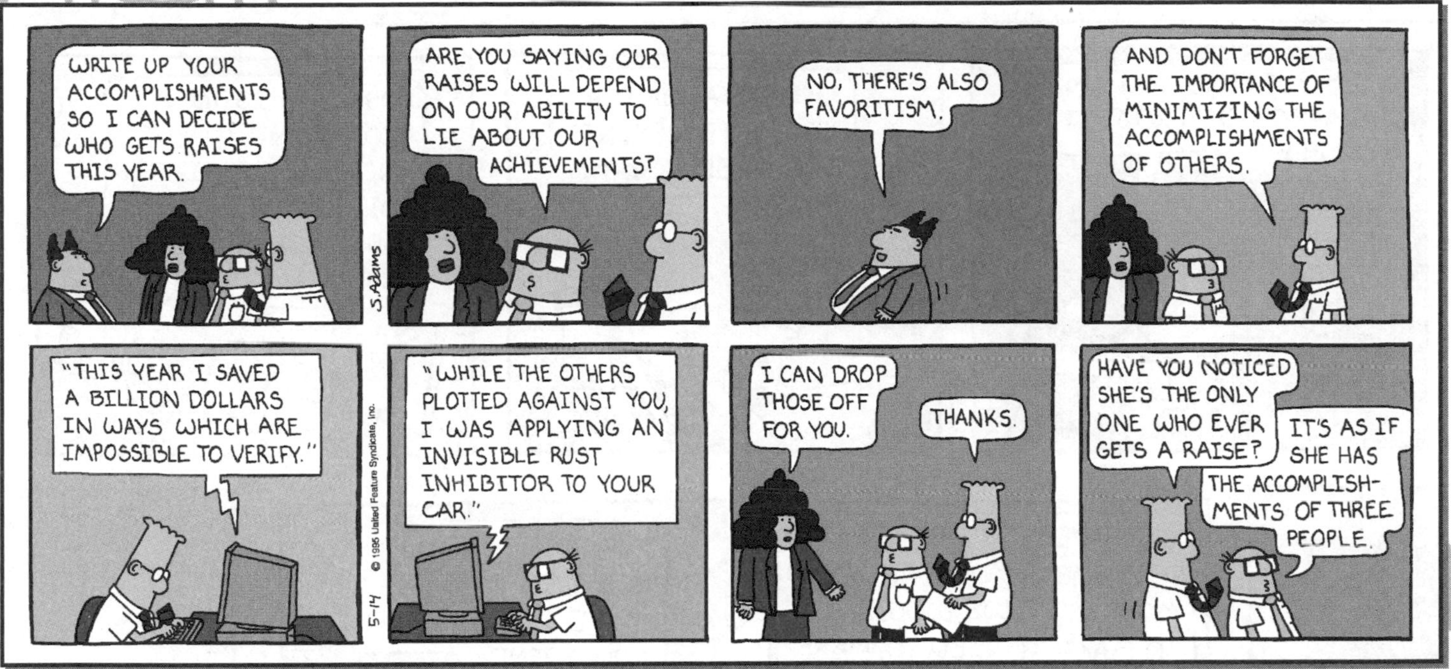
WRITE UP YOUR ACCOMPLISHMENTS SO I CAN DECIDE WHO GETS RAISES THIS YEAR.
ARE YOU SAYING OUR RAISES WILL DEPEND ON OUR ABILITY TO LIE ABOUT OUR ACHIEVEMENTS?
NO, THERE'S ALSO FAVORITISM.
AND DON'T FORGET THE IMPORTANCE OF MINIMIZING THE ACCOMPLISHMENTS OF OTHERS.
S. Adams
5-14
© 1995 United Feature Syndicate, Inc.
"THIS YEAR I SAVED A BILLION DOLLARS IN WAYS WHICH ARE IMPOSSIBLE TO VERIFY."
"WHILE THE OTHERS PLOTTED AGAINST YOU, I WAS APPLYING AN INVISIBLE RUST INHIBITOR TO YOUR CAR."
I CAN DROP THOSE OFF FOR YOU.
THANKS.
HAVE YOU NOTICED SHE'S THE ONLY ONE WHO EVER GETS A RAISE?
IT'S AS IF SHE HAS THE ACCOMPLISHMENTS OF THREE PEOPLE.

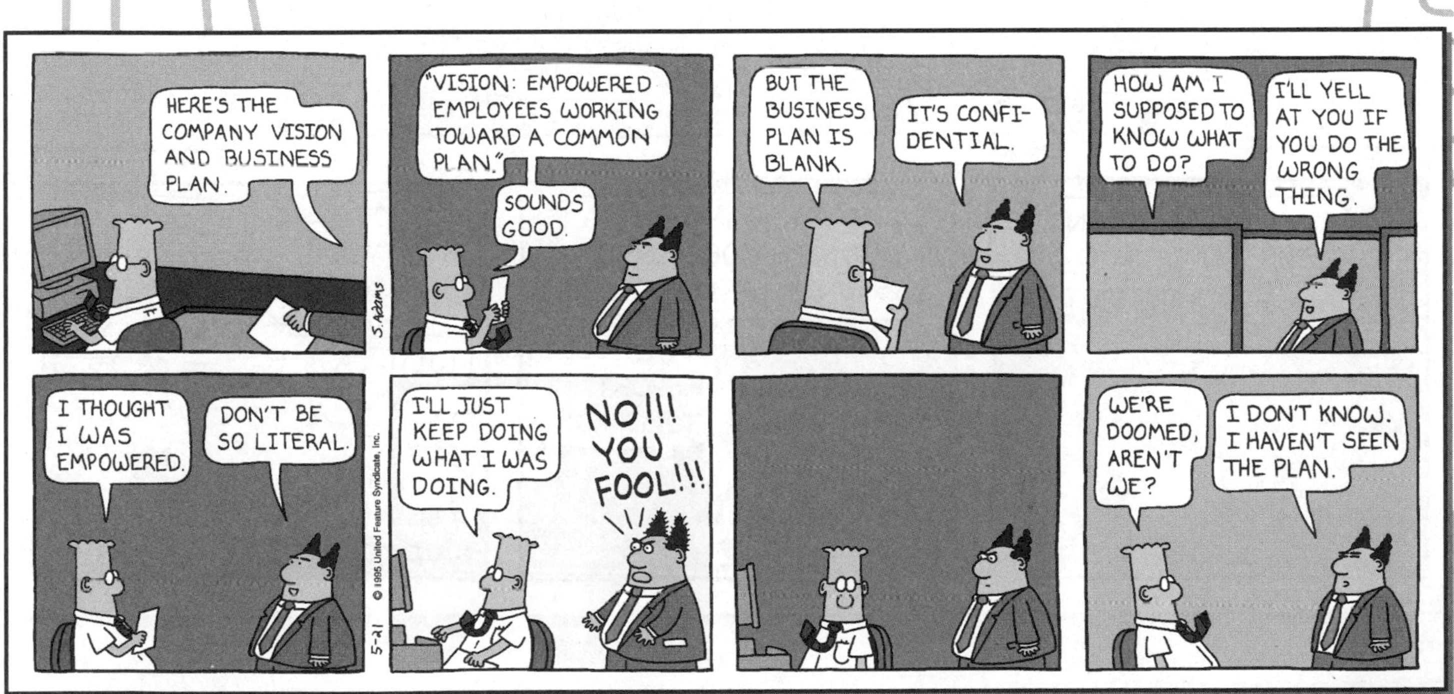
HERE'S THE COMPANY VISION AND BUSINESS PLAN.
"VISION: EMPOWERED EMPLOYEES WORKING TOWARD A COMMON PLAN."
SOUNDS GOOD.
BUT THE BUSINESS PLAN IS BLANK.
IT'S CONFI-DENTIAL.
HOW AM I SUPPOSED TO KNOW WHAT TO DO?
I'LL YELL AT YOU IF YOU DO THE WRONG THING.
S. Adams
5-21
© 1995 United Feature Syndicate, Inc.
I THOUGHT I WAS EMPOWERED.
DON'T BE SO LITERAL.
I'LL JUST KEEP DOING WHAT I WAS DOING.
NO!!! YOU FOOL!!!
WE'RE DOOMED, AREN'T WE?
I DON'T KNOW. I HAVEN'T SEEN THE PLAN.

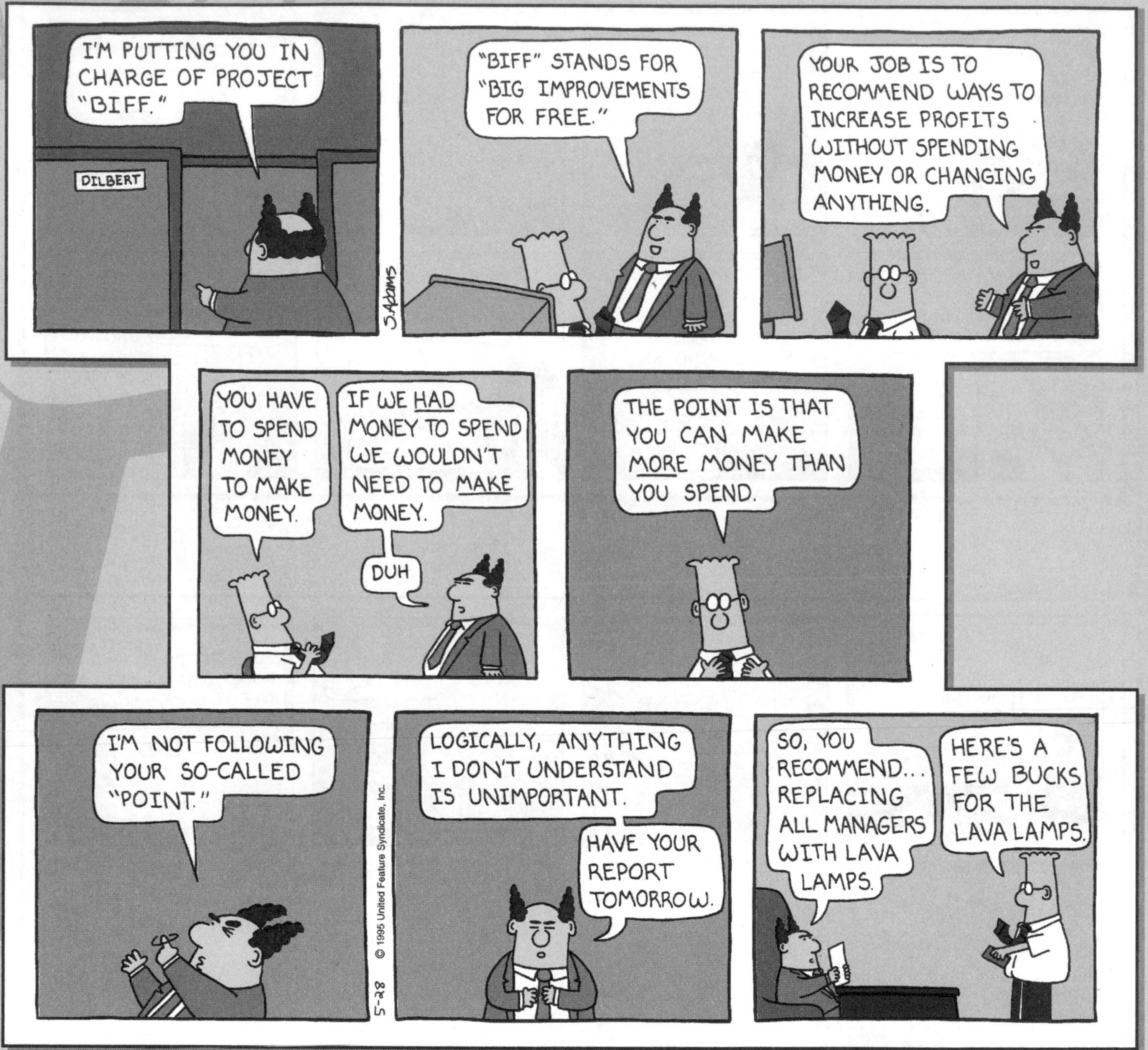
I'M PUTTING YOU IN CHARGE OF PROJECT "BIFF."
DILBERT
S.Adams
"BIFF" STANDS FOR "BIG IMPROVEMENTS FOR FREE."
YOUR JOB IS TO RECOMMEND WAYS TO INCREASE PROFITS WITHOUT SPENDING MONEY OR CHANGING ANYTHING.
YOU HAVE TO SPEND MONEY TO MAKE MONEY.
IF WE HAD MONEY TO SPEND WE WOULDN'T NEED TO MAKE MONEY.
DUH
THE POINT IS THAT YOU CAN MAKE MORE MONEY THAN YOU SPEND.
I'M NOT FOLLOWING YOUR SO-CALLED "POINT."
5-28
© 1995 United Feature Syndicate, Inc.
LOGICALLY, ANYTHING I DON'T UNDERSTAND IS UNIMPORTANT.
HAVE YOUR REPORT TOMORROW.
SO, YOU RECOMMEND... REPLACING ALL MANAGERS WITH LAVA LAMPS.
HERE'S A FEW BUCKS FOR THE LAVA LAMPS.

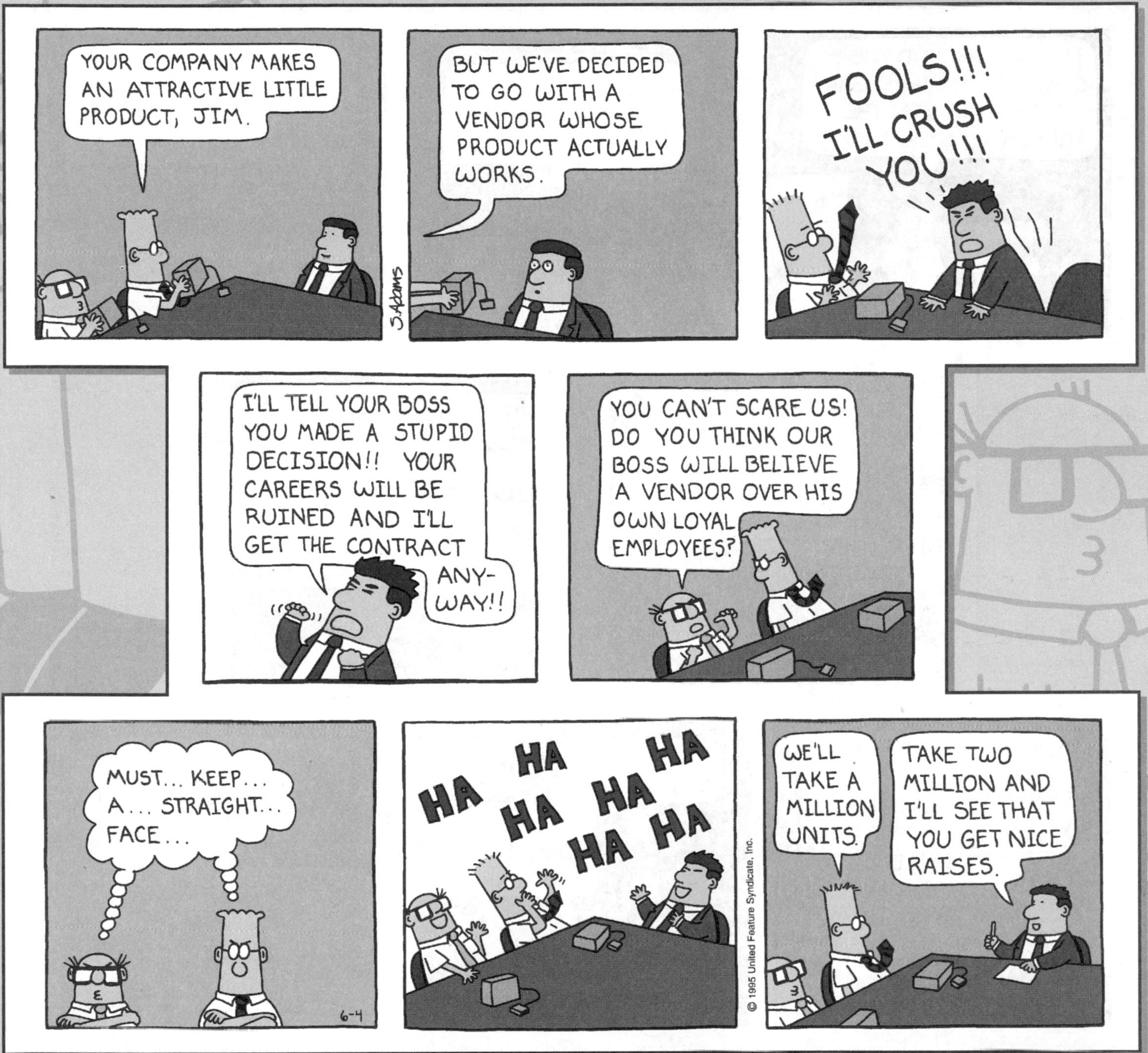
YOUR COMPANY MAKES AN ATTRACTIVE LITTLE PRODUCT, JIM.
S.Adams
BUT WE'VE DECIDED TO GO WITH A VENDOR WHOSE PRODUCT ACTUALLY WORKS.
FOOLS!!! I'LL CRUSH YOU!!!
I'LL TELL YOUR BOSS YOU MADE A STUPID DECISION!! YOUR CAREERS WILL BE RUINED AND I'LL GET THE CONTRACT ANY-WAY!!
YOU CAN'T SCARE US! DO YOU THINK OUR BOSS WILL BELIEVE A VENDOR OVER HIS OWN LOYAL EMPLOYEES?
MUST... KEEP... A... STRAIGHT... FACE...
6-4
HA HA HA HA HA HA HA HA
© 1995 United Feature Syndicate, Inc.
WE'LL TAKE A MILLION UNITS.
TAKE TWO MILLION AND I'LL SEE THAT YOU GET NICE RAISES.

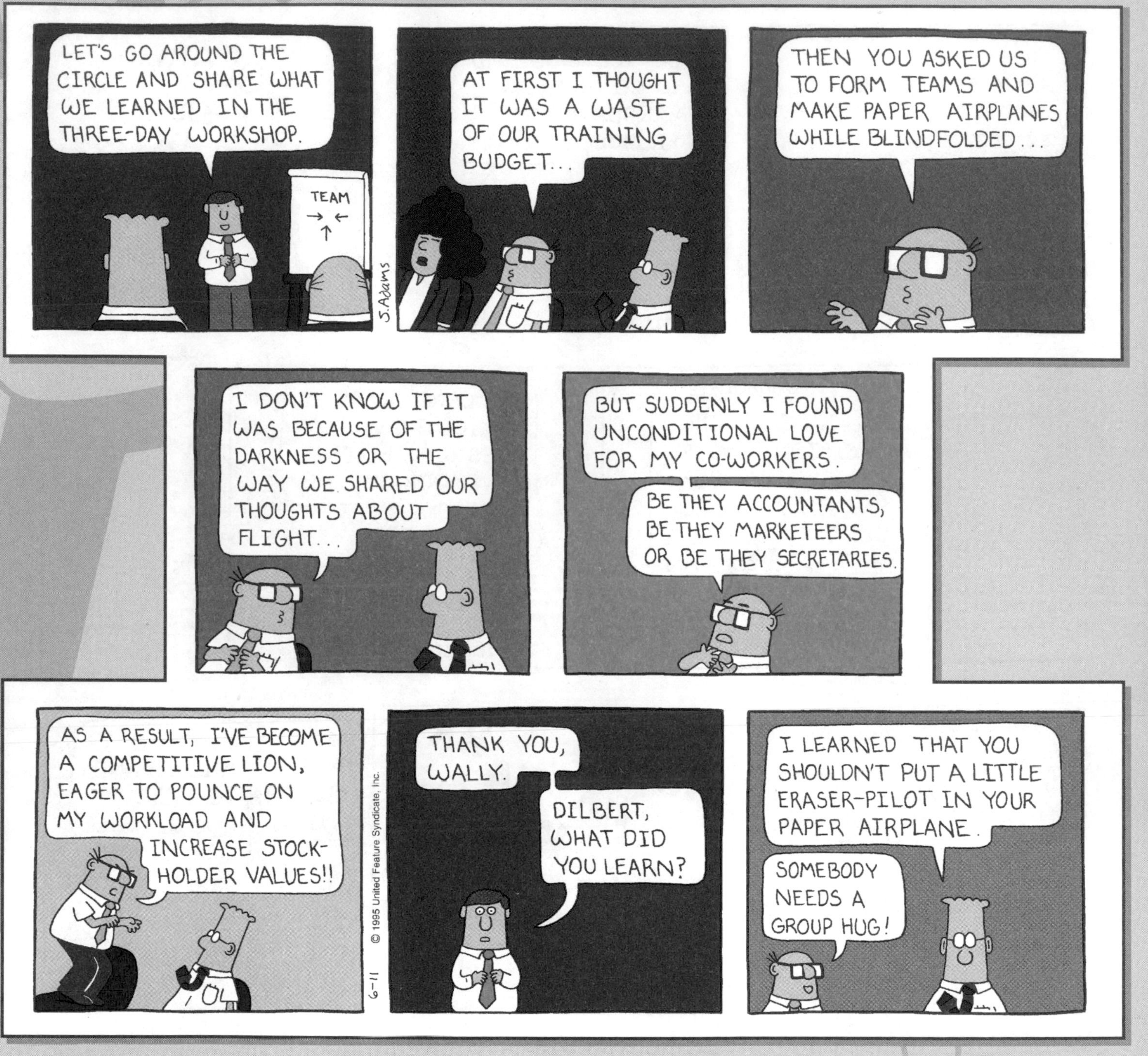
LET'S GO AROUND THE CIRCLE AND SHARE WHAT WE LEARNED IN THE THREE-DAY WORKSHOP.
TEAM
S. Adams
AT FIRST I THOUGHT IT WAS A WASTE OF OUR TRAINING BUDGET...
THEN YOU ASKED US TO FORM TEAMS AND MAKE PAPER AIRPLANES WHILE BLINDFOLDED...
I DON'T KNOW IF IT WAS BECAUSE OF THE DARKNESS OR THE WAY WE SHARED OUR THOUGHTS ABOUT FLIGHT...
BUT SUDDENLY I FOUND UNCONDITIONAL LOVE FOR MY CO-WORKERS.
BE THEY ACCOUNTANTS, BE THEY MARKETEERS OR BE THEY SECRETARIES.
AS A RESULT, I'VE BECOME A COMPETITIVE LION, EAGER TO POUNCE ON MY WORKLOAD AND
INCREASE STOCK-HOLDER VALUES!!
© 1995 United Feature Syndicate, Inc.
6-11
THANK YOU, WALLY.
DILBERT, WHAT DID YOU LEARN?
I LEARNED THAT YOU SHOULDN'T PUT A LITTLE ERASER-PILOT IN YOUR PAPER AIRPLANE.
SOMEBODY NEEDS A GROUP HUG!

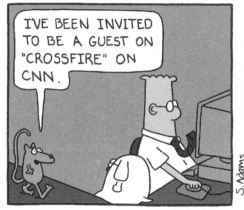

I'VE BEEN INVITED TO BE A GUEST ON "CROSSFIRE" ON CNN.
S. Adams
I'M THE ONLY CREATURE ON EARTH WHO HASN'T ALREADY BEEN ON TELEVISION.
CAN YOU TEACH ME HOW TO DEBATE ON TELEVISION, DOGBERT?
OKAY
FIRST, RATBERT, ASSUME EVERYBODY HAS THE SAME DESIRES AND EXPERIENCES AS YOU.
ABSORB ABSORB
THEREFORE, IF THEY DISAGREE WITH YOU THEY MUST BE STUPID.
I THINK YOU'RE OVER-SIMPLIFYING, DOGBERT.
WHAT WAS THAT OPINION, RATBERT?
STUPID!
© 1995 United Feature Syndicate, Inc.
6-18
YOU'RE READY FOR "CROSSFIRE," RATBERT.
I USUALLY LIKE THE SAME MOVIES AS THE FAT ONE.

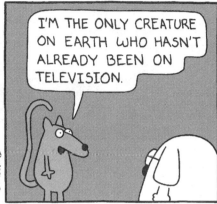

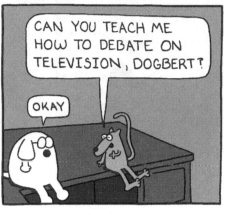

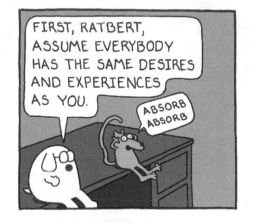

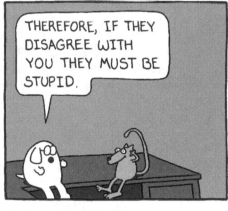

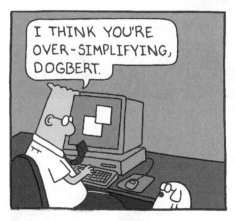

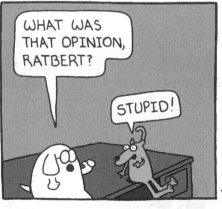

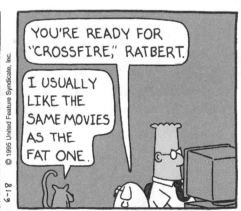

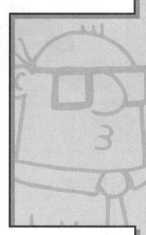

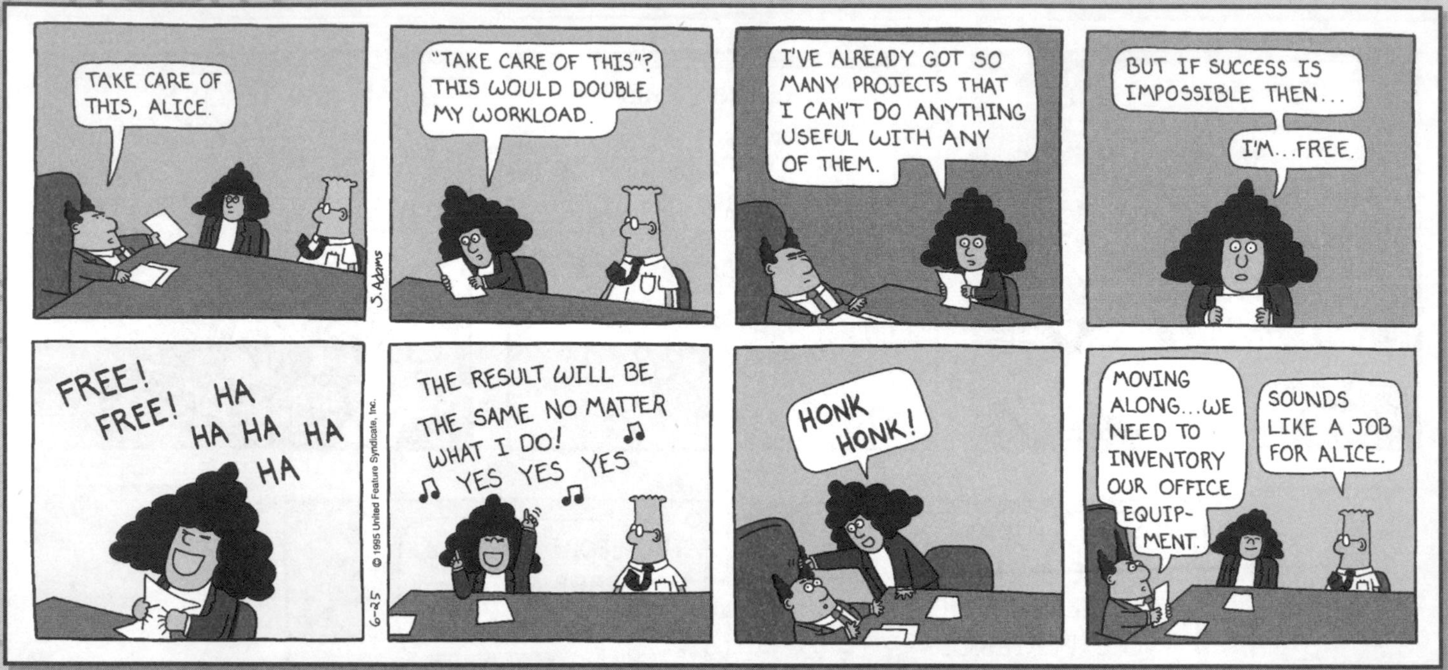
TAKE CARE OF THIS, ALICE.
"TAKE CARE OF THIS"? THIS WOULD DOUBLE MY WORKLOAD.
I'VE ALREADY GOT SO MANY PROJECTS THAT I CAN'T DO ANYTHING USEFUL WITH ANY OF THEM.
BUT IF SUCCESS IS IMPOSSIBLE THEN...
I'M...FREE.
FREE! FREE! HA HA HA HA HA
THE RESULT WILL BE THE SAME NO MATTER WHAT I DO! YES YES YES
HONK HONK!
MOVING ALONG...WE NEED TO INVENTORY OUR OFFICE EQUIP-MENT.
SOUNDS LIKE A JOB FOR ALICE.
S. Adams
6-25
© 1995 United Feature Syndicate, Inc.

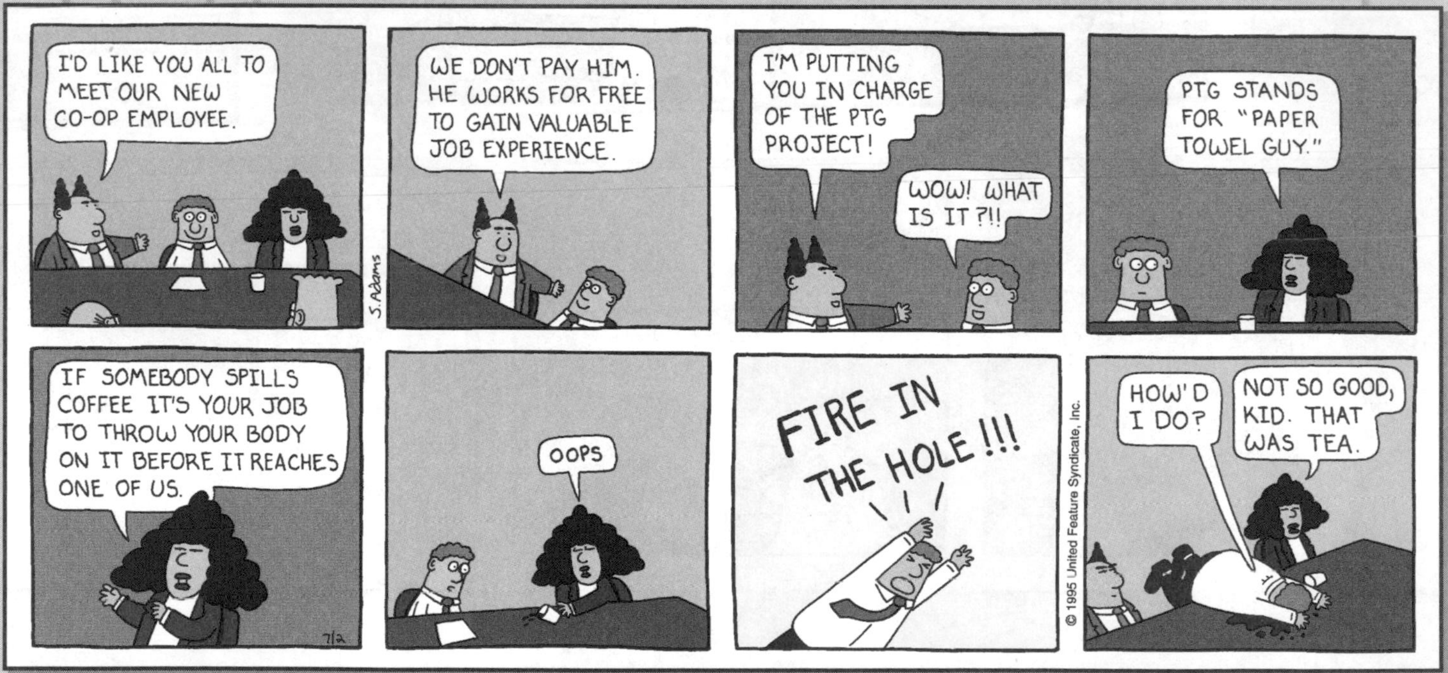
I'D LIKE YOU ALL TO MEET OUR NEW CO-OP EMPLOYEE.
WE DON'T PAY HIM. HE WORKS FOR FREE TO GAIN VALUABLE JOB EXPERIENCE.
I'M PUTTING YOU IN CHARGE OF THE PTG PROJECT!
WOW! WHAT IS IT?!!
PTG STANDS FOR "PAPER TOWEL GUY."
IF SOMEBODY SPILLS COFFEE IT'S YOUR JOB TO THROW YOUR BODY ON IT BEFORE IT REACHES ONE OF US.
OOPS
FIRE IN THE HOLE!!!
HOW'D I DO?
NOT SO GOOD, KID. THAT WAS TEA.
S. Adams
7/2
© 1995 United Feature Syndicate, Inc.

WE DESPERATELY NEED ANOTHER PERSON ON MY PROJECT!
S. Adams
WE'RE ALREADY OVER HEADCOUNT. GET A CONTRACT EMPLOYEE.
OKAY, BUT THEY COST TWICE AS MUCH.
PLUS WE NEED TO BUY A COMPUTER.
RENT ONE. WE'RE OVER OUR CAPITAL BUDGET.
RENTING IS EXPENSIVE. WE'LL GO OVER OUR EXPENSE BUDGET.
I'LL FIRE WALLY. THAT WILL FREE UP SOME CASH.
WALLY'S ON MY PROJECT!
7/9
FORGET IT! I'LL JUST WORK SIXTEEN HOURS A DAY!!
THAT WORKED OUT PERFECTLY. I THINK I MIGHT BE A GENIUS OR SOMETHING.
© 1995 United Feature Syndicate, Inc.
I WONDER IF I SHOULD HAVE TOLD HIM THE PROJECT WAS CANCELLED LAST WEEK.

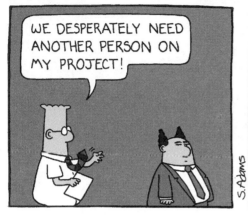

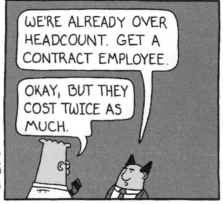

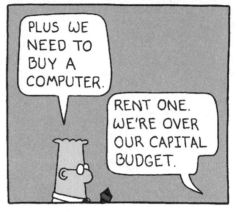

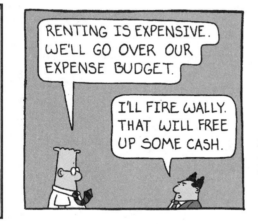

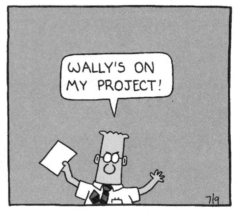

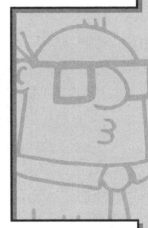

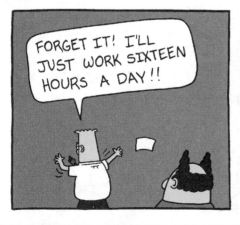

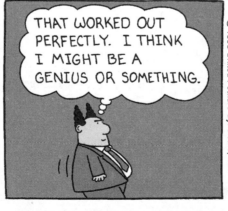

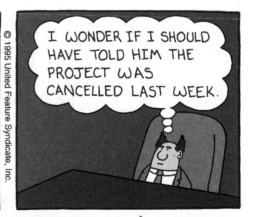

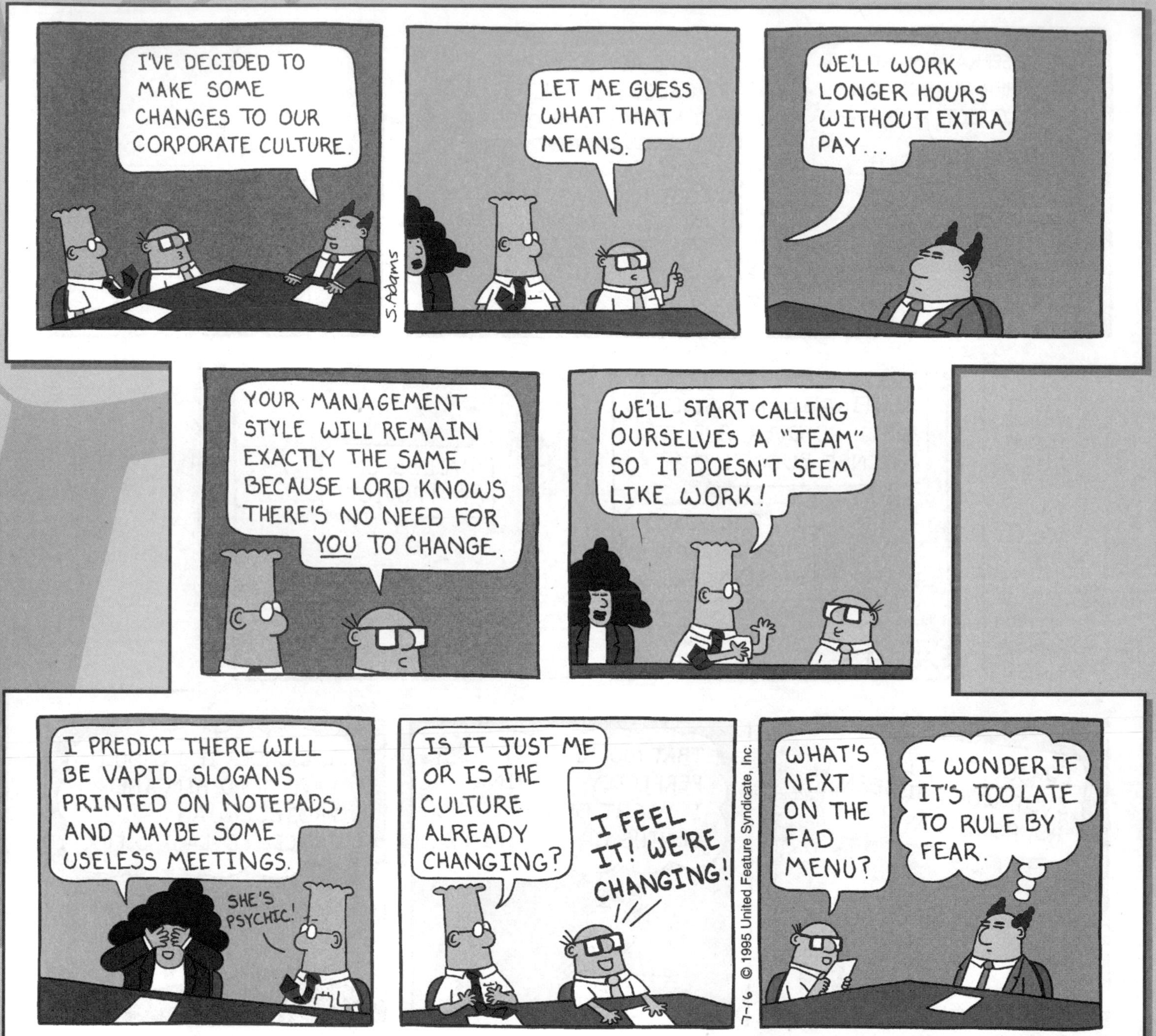
I'VE DECIDED TO MAKE SOME CHANGES TO OUR CORPORATE CULTURE.
S. Adams
LET ME GUESS WHAT THAT MEANS.
WE'LL WORK LONGER HOURS WITHOUT EXTRA PAY...
YOUR MANAGEMENT STYLE WILL REMAIN EXACTLY THE SAME BECAUSE LORD KNOWS THERE'S NO NEED FOR YOU TO CHANGE.
WE'LL START CALLING OURSELVES A "TEAM" SO IT DOESN'T SEEM LIKE WORK!
I PREDICT THERE WILL BE VAPID SLOGANS PRINTED ON NOTEPADS, AND MAYBE SOME USELESS MEETINGS.
SHE'S PSYCHIC!
IS IT JUST ME OR IS THE CULTURE ALREADY CHANGING?
I FEEL IT! WE'RE CHANGING!
7-16 © 1995 United Feature Syndicate, Inc.
WHAT'S NEXT ON THE FAD MENU?
I WONDER IF IT'S TOO LATE TO RULE BY FEAR.

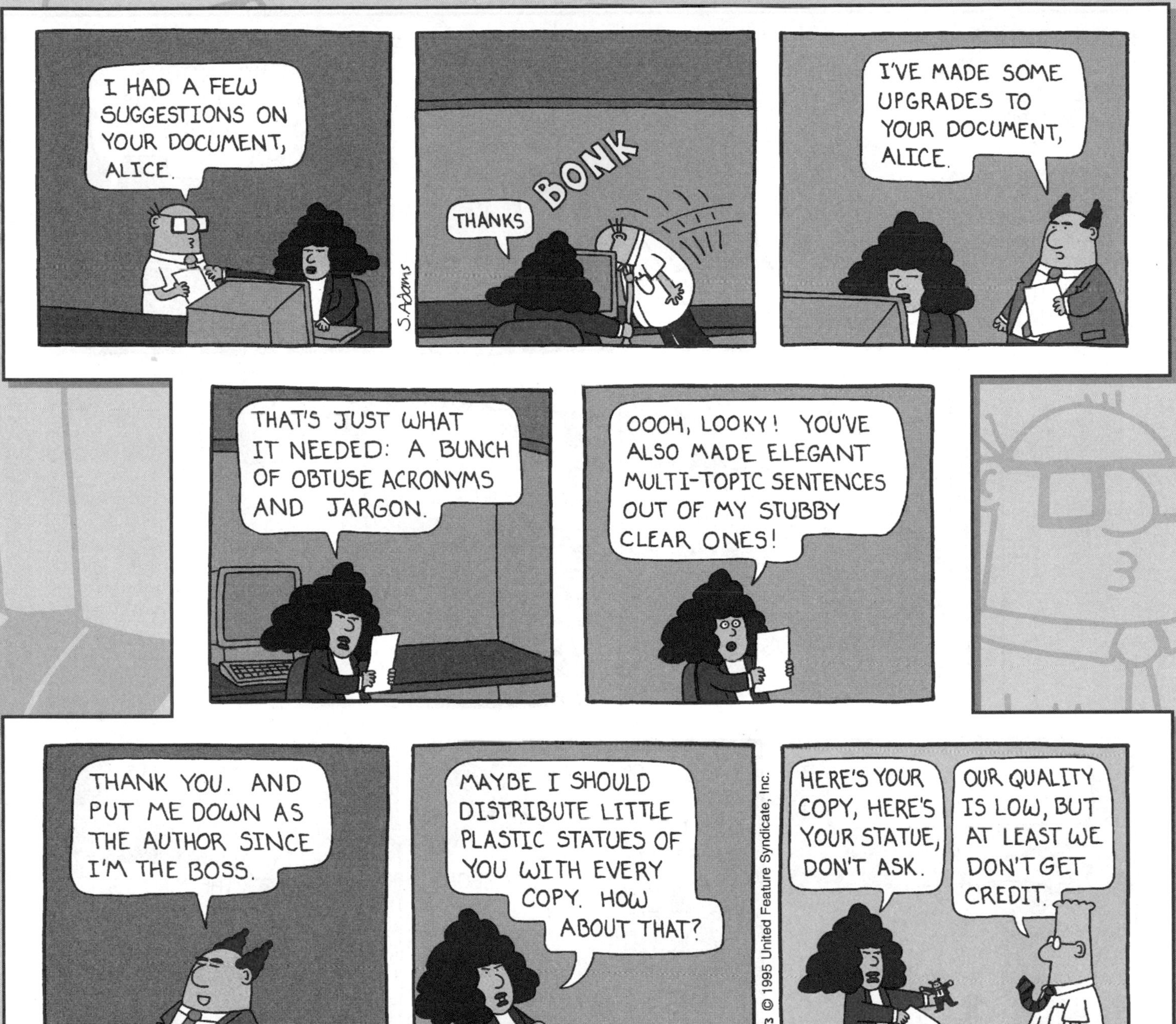
I HAD A FEW SUGGESTIONS ON YOUR DOCUMENT, ALICE.
THANKS
BONK
S. Adams
I'VE MADE SOME UPGRADES TO YOUR DOCUMENT, ALICE.
THAT'S JUST WHAT IT NEEDED: A BUNCH OF OBTUSE ACRONYMS AND JARGON.
OOOH, LOOKY! YOU'VE ALSO MADE ELEGANT MULTI-TOPIC SENTENCES OUT OF MY STUBBY CLEAR ONES!
THANK YOU. AND PUT ME DOWN AS THE AUTHOR SINCE I'M THE BOSS.
MAYBE I SHOULD DISTRIBUTE LITTLE PLASTIC STATUES OF YOU WITH EVERY COPY. HOW ABOUT THAT?
7/23 © 1995 United Feature Syndicate, Inc.
HERE'S YOUR COPY, HERE'S YOUR STATUE, DON'T ASK.
OUR QUALITY IS LOW, BUT AT LEAST WE DON'T GET CREDIT.

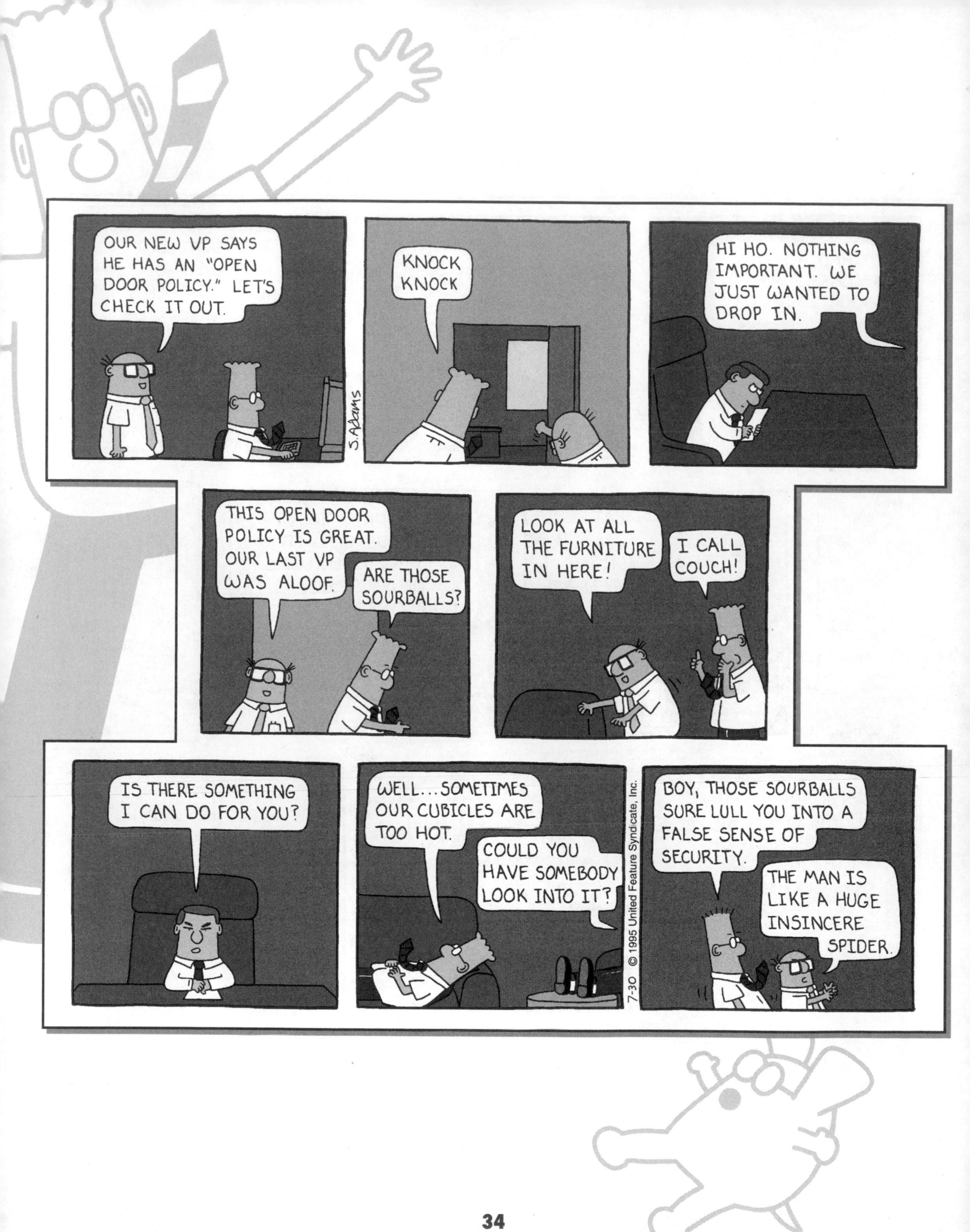

OUR NEW VP SAYS HE HAS AN "OPEN DOOR POLICY." LET'S CHECK IT OUT.
S. ADAMS
KNOCK KNOCK
HI HO. NOTHING IMPORTANT. WE JUST WANTED TO DROP IN.
THIS OPEN DOOR POLICY IS GREAT. OUR LAST VP WAS ALOOF.
ARE THOSE SOURBALLS?
LOOK AT ALL THE FURNITURE IN HERE!
I CALL COUCH!
IS THERE SOMETHING I CAN DO FOR YOU?
WELL... SOMETIMES OUR CUBICLES ARE TOO HOT.
COULD YOU HAVE SOMEBODY LOOK INTO IT?
7-30 © 1995 United Feature Syndicate, Inc.
BOY, THOSE SOURBALLS SURE LULL YOU INTO A FALSE SENSE OF SECURITY.
THE MAN IS LIKE A HUGE INSINCERE SPIDER.

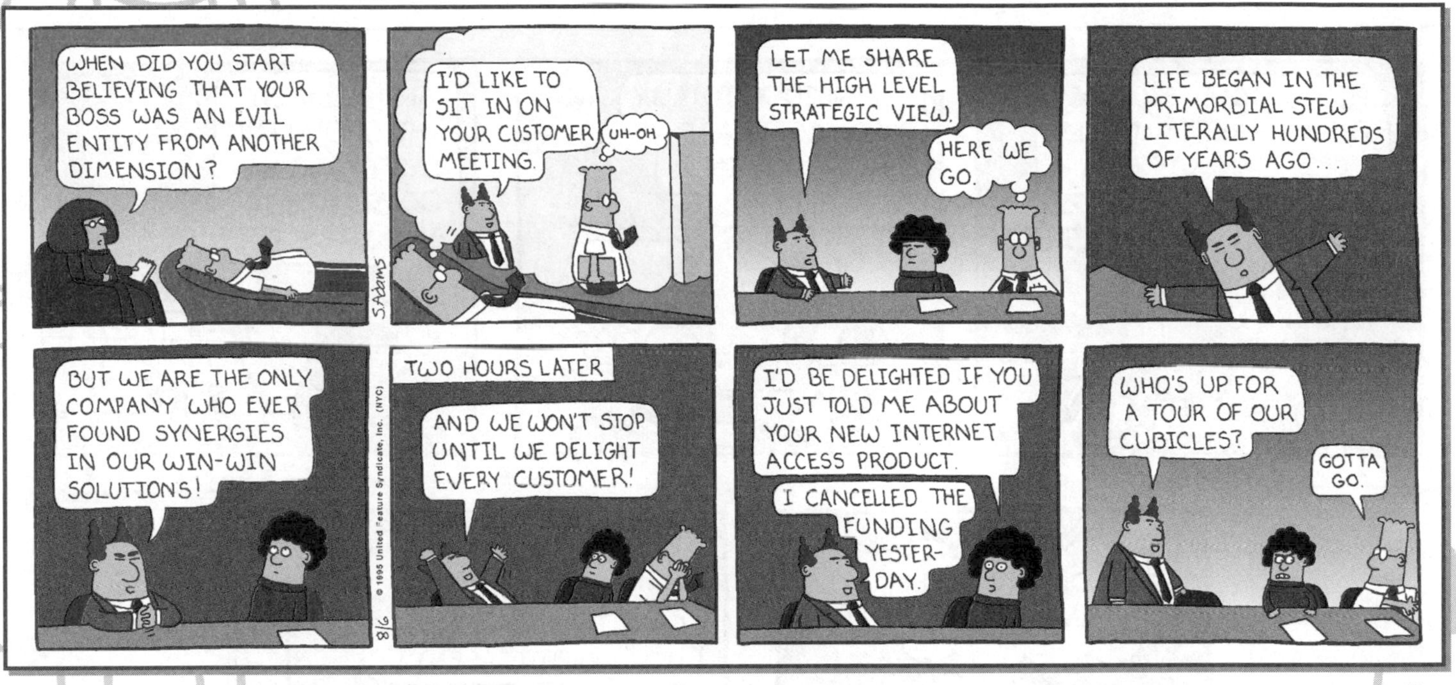
WHEN DID YOU START BELIEVING THAT YOUR BOSS WAS AN EVIL ENTITY FROM ANOTHER DIMENSION?
I'D LIKE TO SIT IN ON YOUR CUSTOMER MEETING.
UH-OH.
LET ME SHARE THE HIGH LEVEL STRATEGIC VIEW.
HERE WE GO.
LIFE BEGAN IN THE PRIMORDIAL STEW LITERALLY HUNDREDS OF YEARS AGO...
S.Adams
© 1995 United Feature Syndicate, Inc. (NYC)
8/6
BUT WE ARE THE ONLY COMPANY WHO EVER FOUND SYNERGIES IN OUR WIN-WIN SOLUTIONS!
TWO HOURS LATER
AND WE WON'T STOP UNTIL WE DELIGHT EVERY CUSTOMER!
I'D BE DELIGHTED IF YOU JUST TOLD ME ABOUT YOUR NEW INTERNET ACCESS PRODUCT.
I CANCELLED THE FUNDING YESTER-DAY.
WHO'S UP FOR A TOUR OF OUR CUBICLES?
GOTTA GO.

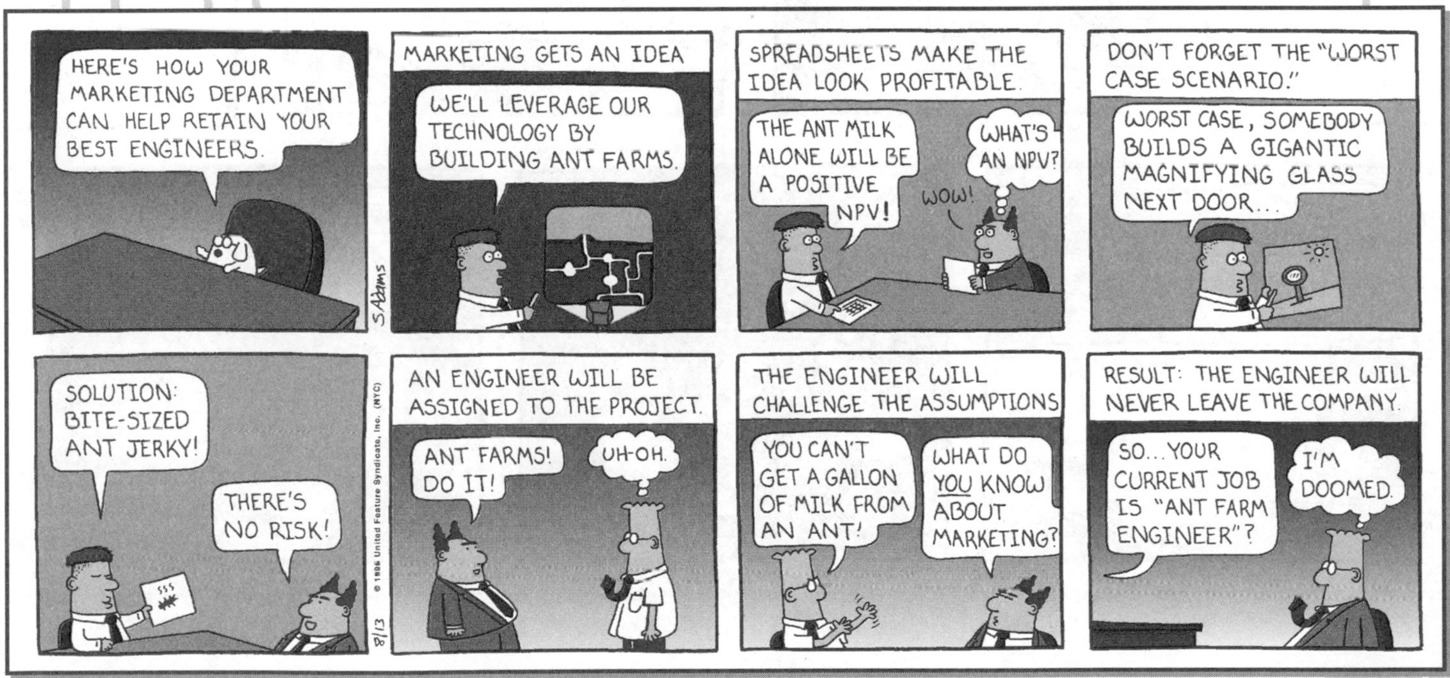
HERE'S HOW YOUR MARKETING DEPARTMENT CAN HELP RETAIN YOUR BEST ENGINEERS.
MARKETING GETS AN IDEA
WE'LL LEVERAGE OUR TECHNOLOGY BY BUILDING ANT FARMS.
SPREADSHEETS MAKE THE IDEA LOOK PROFITABLE.
THE ANT MILK ALONE WILL BE A POSITIVE NPV!
WHAT'S AN NPV?
WOW!
DON'T FORGET THE "WORST CASE SCENARIO."
WORST CASE, SOMEBODY BUILDS A GIGANTIC MAGNIFYING GLASS NEXT DOOR...
S.Adams
© 1996 United Feature Syndicate, Inc. (NYC)
8/13
SOLUTION: BITE-SIZED ANT JERKY!
THERE'S NO RISK!
AN ENGINEER WILL BE ASSIGNED TO THE PROJECT.
ANT FARMS! DO IT!
UH-OH.
THE ENGINEER WILL CHALLENGE THE ASSUMPTIONS
YOU CAN'T GET A GALLON OF MILK FROM AN ANT!
WHAT DO YOU KNOW ABOUT MARKETING?
RESULT: THE ENGINEER WILL NEVER LEAVE THE COMPANY.
SO... YOUR CURRENT JOB IS "ANT FARM ENGINEER"?
I'M DOOMED.

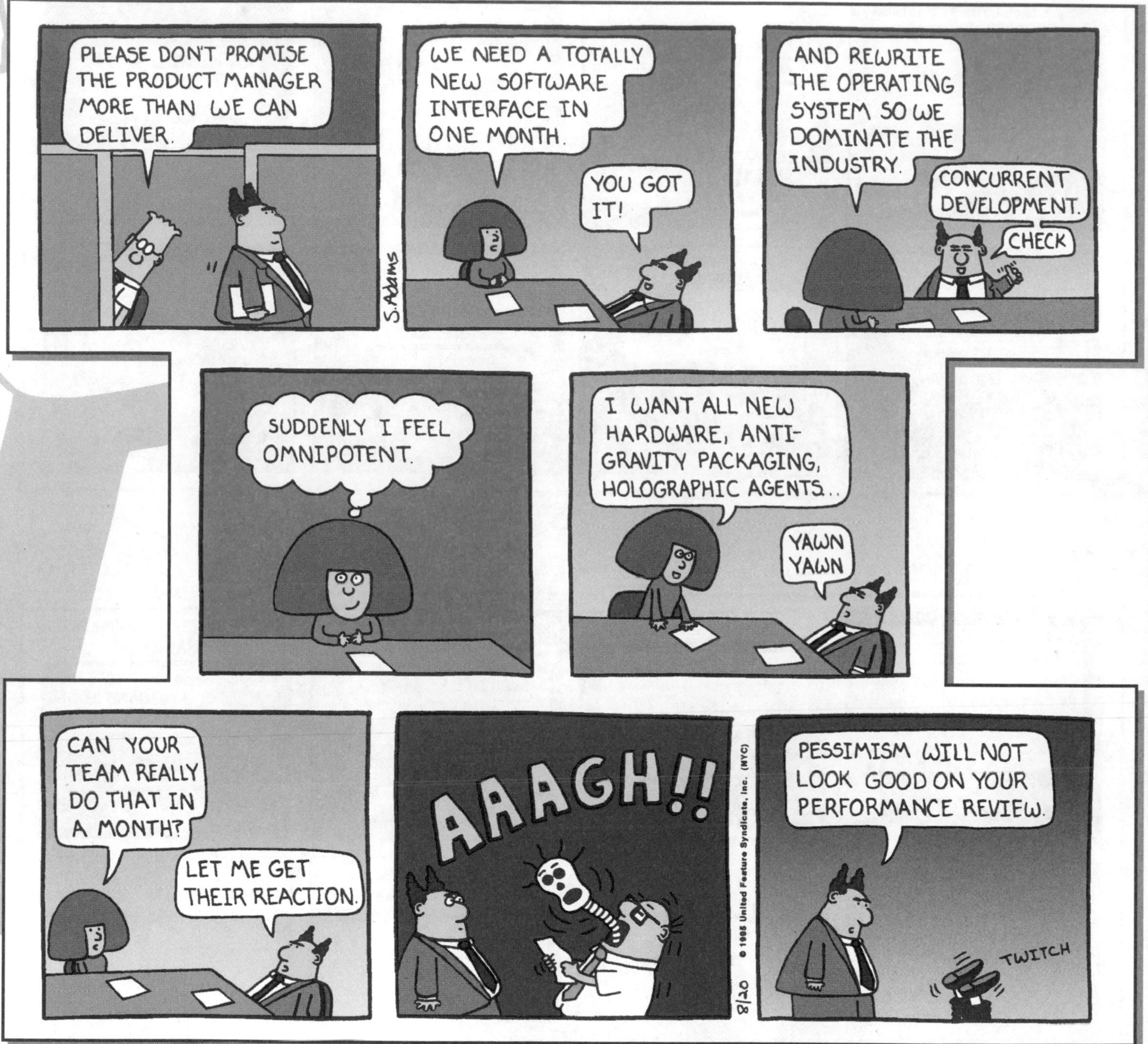
PLEASE DON'T PROMISE THE PRODUCT MANAGER MORE THAN WE CAN DELIVER.
S. Adams
WE NEED A TOTALLY NEW SOFTWARE INTERFACE IN ONE MONTH.
YOU GOT IT!
AND REWRITE THE OPERATING SYSTEM SO WE DOMINATE THE INDUSTRY.
CONCURRENT DEVELOPMENT.
CHECK
SUDDENLY I FEEL OMNIPOTENT.
I WANT ALL NEW HARDWARE, ANTI-GRAVITY PACKAGING, HOLOGRAPHIC AGENTS...
YAWN YAWN
CAN YOUR TEAM REALLY DO THAT IN A MONTH?
LET ME GET THEIR REACTION.
AAAGH!!
© 1995 United Feature Syndicate, Inc. (NYC)
8/20
PESSIMISM WILL NOT LOOK GOOD ON YOUR PERFORMANCE REVIEW.
TWITCH

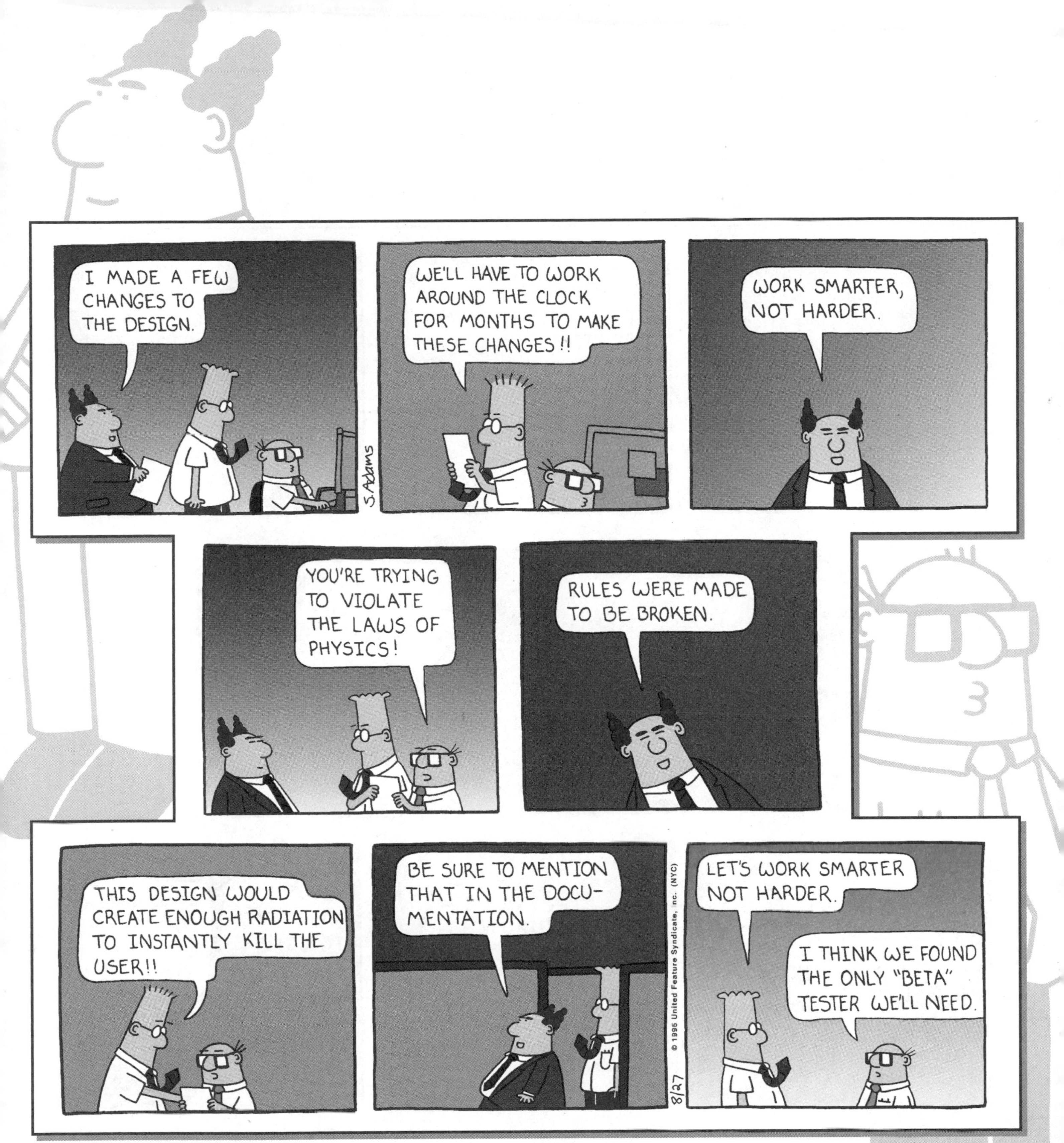
I MADE A FEW CHANGES TO THE DESIGN.
S. Adams
WE'LL HAVE TO WORK AROUND THE CLOCK FOR MONTHS TO MAKE THESE CHANGES !!
WORK SMARTER, NOT HARDER.
YOU'RE TRYING TO VIOLATE THE LAWS OF PHYSICS!
RULES WERE MADE TO BE BROKEN.
THIS DESIGN WOULD CREATE ENOUGH RADIATION TO INSTANTLY KILL THE USER!!
BE SURE TO MENTION THAT IN THE DOCU-MENTATION.
© 1995 United Feature Syndicate, Inc. (NYC)
8/27
LET'S WORK SMARTER NOT HARDER.
I THINK WE FOUND THE ONLY "BETA" TESTER WE'LL NEED.

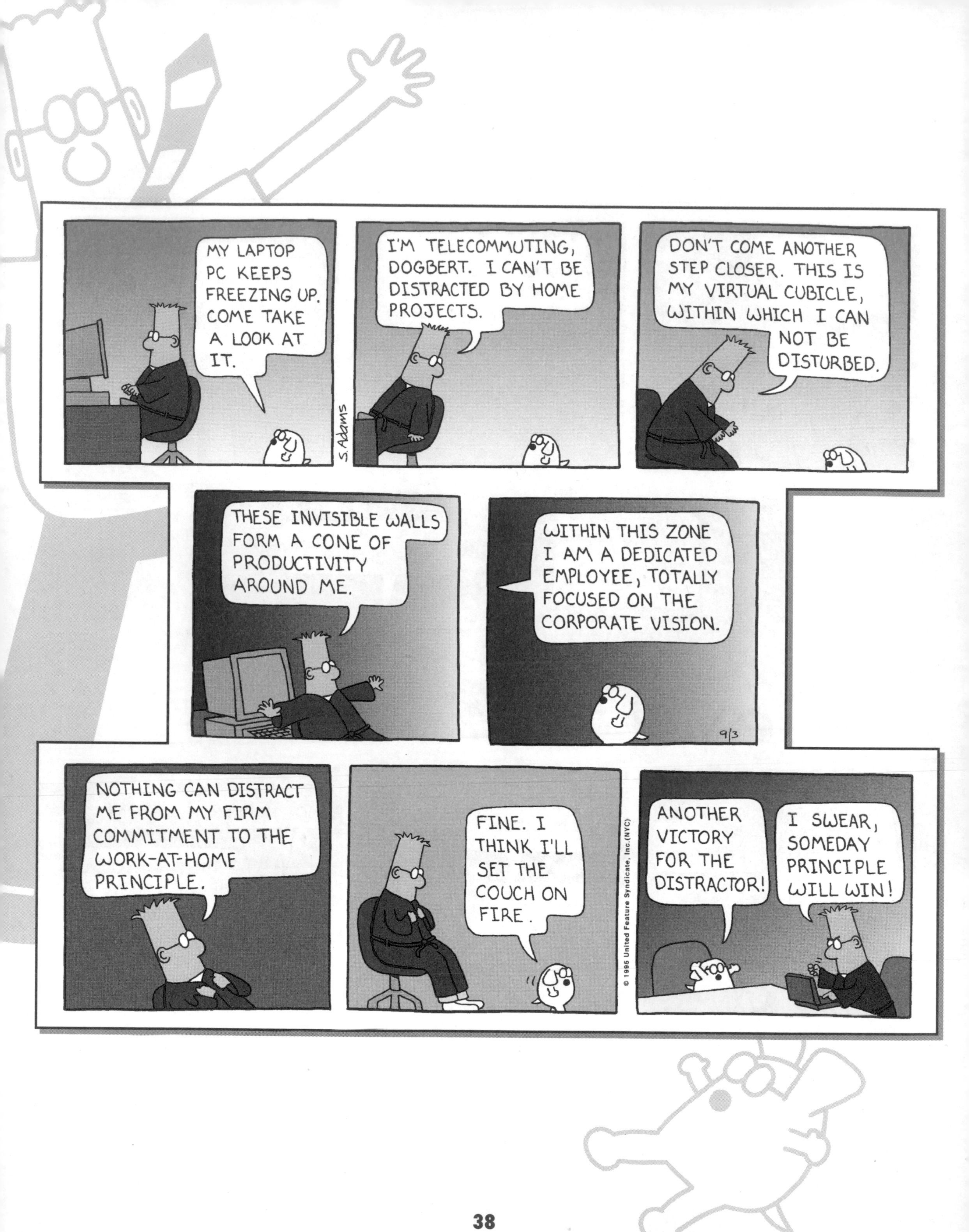
MY LAPTOP PC KEEPS FREEZING UP. COME TAKE A LOOK AT IT.
S. Adams
I'M TELECOMMUTING, DOGBERT. I CAN'T BE DISTRACTED BY HOME PROJECTS.
DON'T COME ANOTHER STEP CLOSER. THIS IS MY VIRTUAL CUBICLE, WITHIN WHICH I CAN NOT BE DISTURBED.
THESE INVISIBLE WALLS FORM A CONE OF PRODUCTIVITY AROUND ME.
WITHIN THIS ZONE I AM A DEDICATED EMPLOYEE, TOTALLY FOCUSED ON THE CORPORATE VISION.
9/3
NOTHING CAN DISTRACT ME FROM MY FIRM COMMITMENT TO THE WORK-AT-HOME PRINCIPLE.
FINE. I THINK I'LL SET THE COUCH ON FIRE.
© 1995 United Feature Syndicate, Inc.(NYC)
ANOTHER VICTORY FOR THE DISTRACTOR!
I SWEAR, SOMEDAY PRINCIPLE WILL WIN!

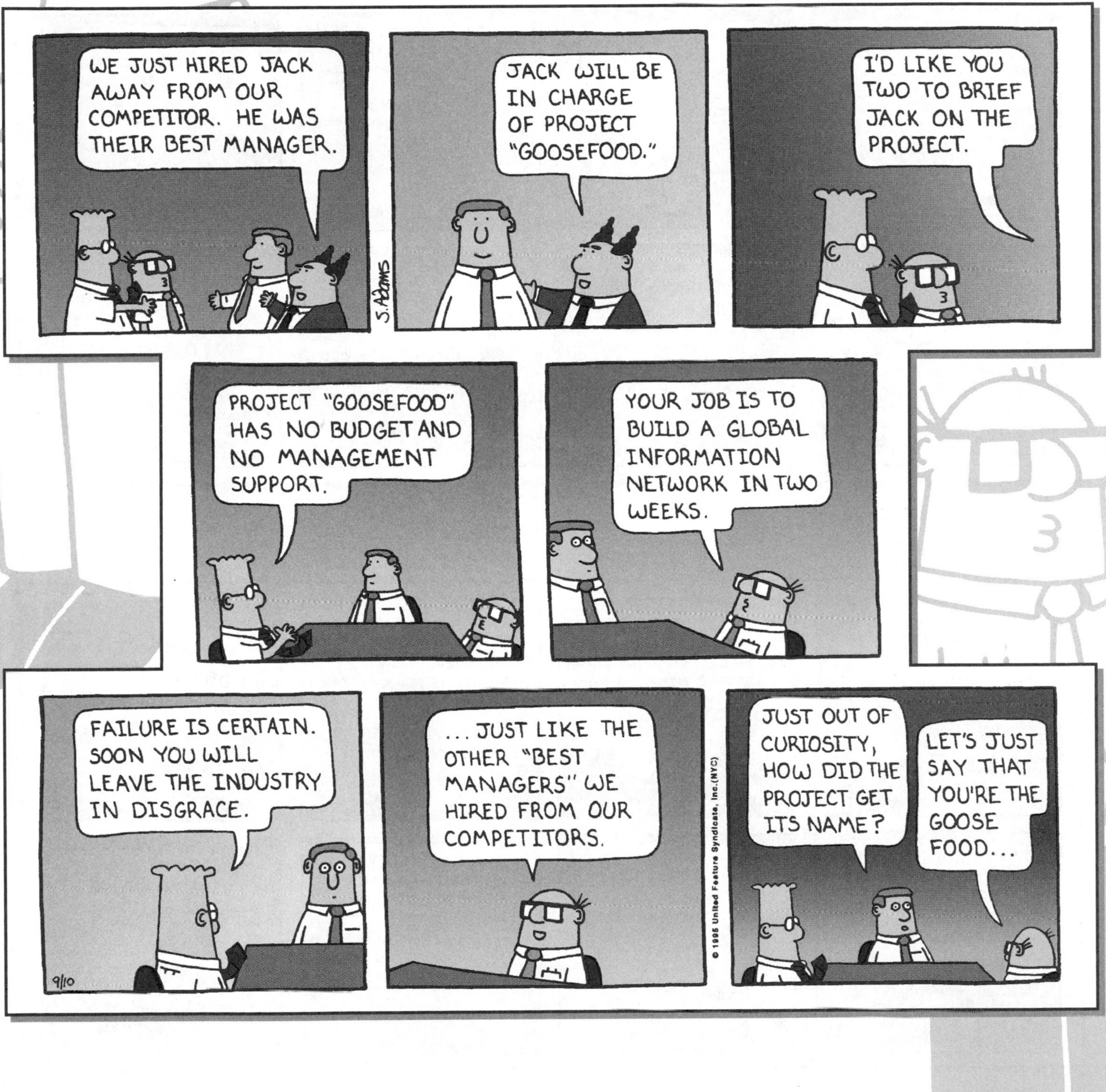
WE JUST HIRED JACK AWAY FROM OUR COMPETITOR. HE WAS THEIR BEST MANAGER.
S. ADAMS
JACK WILL BE IN CHARGE OF PROJECT "GOOSEFOOD."
I'D LIKE YOU TWO TO BRIEF JACK ON THE PROJECT.
PROJECT "GOOSEFOOD" HAS NO BUDGET AND NO MANAGEMENT SUPPORT.
YOUR JOB IS TO BUILD A GLOBAL INFORMATION NETWORK IN TWO WEEKS.
FAILURE IS CERTAIN. SOON YOU WILL LEAVE THE INDUSTRY IN DISGRACE.
9/10
. . . JUST LIKE THE OTHER "BEST MANAGERS" WE HIRED FROM OUR COMPETITORS.
© 1995 United Feature Syndicate, Inc.(NYC)
JUST OUT OF CURIOSITY, HOW DID THE PROJECT GET ITS NAME?
LET'S JUST SAY THAT YOU'RE THE GOOSE FOOD . . .

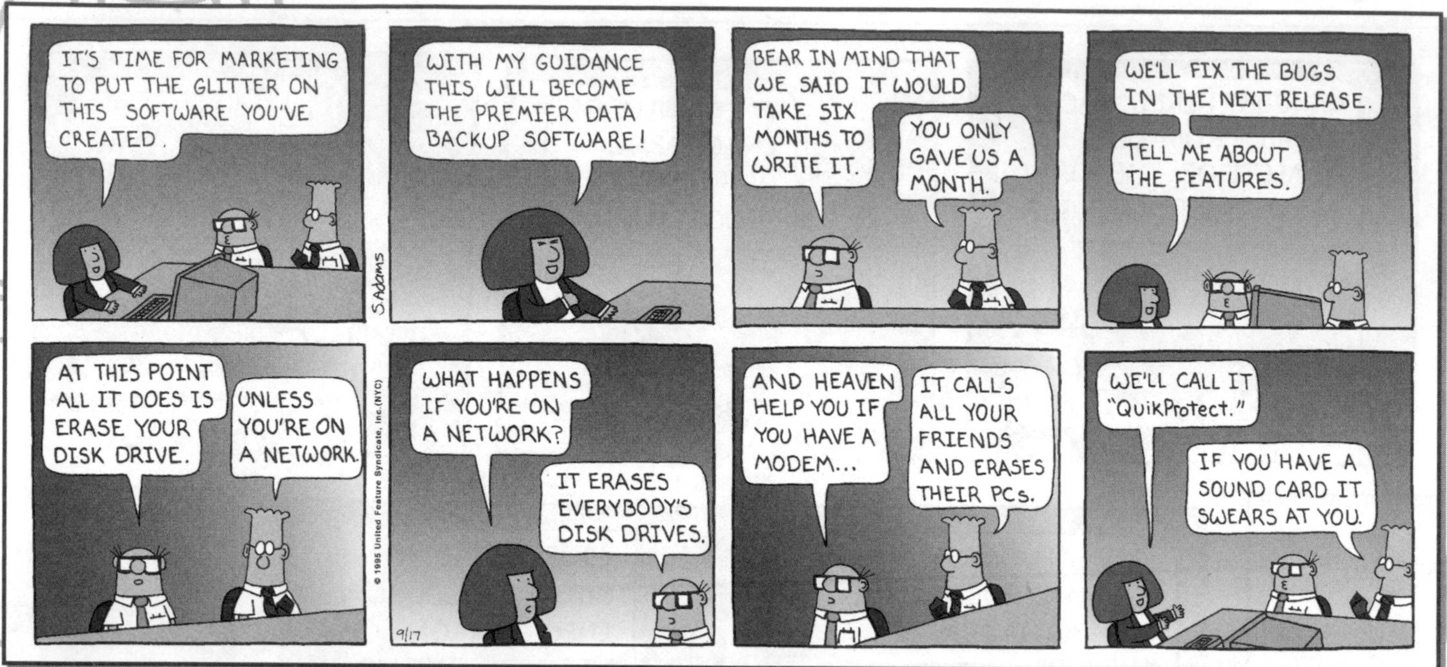
IT'S TIME FOR MARKETING TO PUT THE GLITTER ON THIS SOFTWARE YOU'VE CREATED.
WITH MY GUIDANCE THIS WILL BECOME THE PREMIER DATA BACKUP SOFTWARE!
BEAR IN MIND THAT WE SAID IT WOULD TAKE SIX MONTHS TO WRITE IT.
YOU ONLY GAVE US A MONTH.
WE'LL FIX THE BUGS IN THE NEXT RELEASE.
TELL ME ABOUT THE FEATURES.
AT THIS POINT ALL IT DOES IS ERASE YOUR DISK DRIVE.
UNLESS YOU'RE ON A NETWORK.
WHAT HAPPENS IF YOU'RE ON A NETWORK?
IT ERASES EVERYBODY'S DISK DRIVES.
AND HEAVEN HELP YOU IF YOU HAVE A MODEM...
IT CALLS ALL YOUR FRIENDS AND ERASES THEIR PCs.
WE'LL CALL IT "QuikProtect."
IF YOU HAVE A SOUND CARD IT SWEARS AT YOU.
S. Adams
© 1995 United Feature Syndicate, Inc.(NYC)
9/17

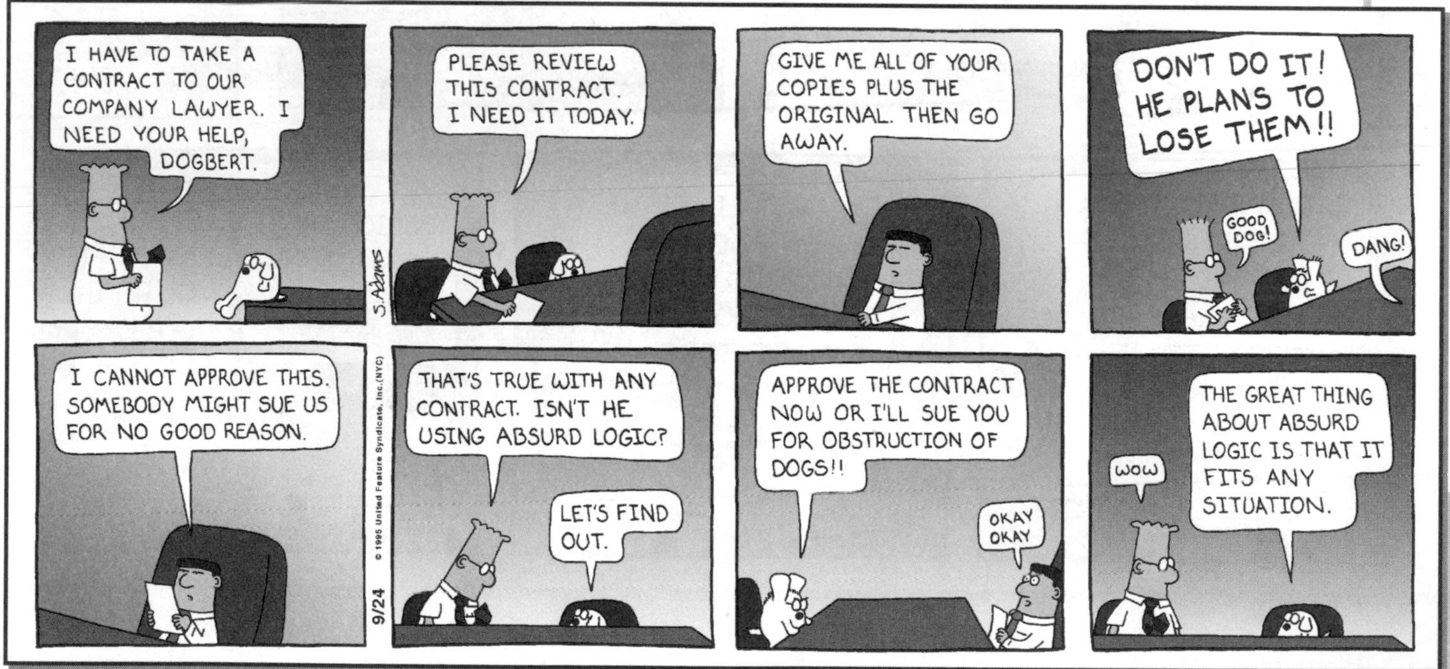
I HAVE TO TAKE A CONTRACT TO OUR COMPANY LAWYER. I NEED YOUR HELP, DOGBERT.
PLEASE REVIEW THIS CONTRACT. I NEED IT TODAY.
GIVE ME ALL OF YOUR COPIES PLUS THE ORIGINAL. THEN GO AWAY.
DON'T DO IT! HE PLANS TO LOSE THEM!!
GOOD DOG!
DANG!
I CANNOT APPROVE THIS. SOMEBODY MIGHT SUE US FOR NO GOOD REASON.
THAT'S TRUE WITH ANY CONTRACT. ISN'T HE USING ABSURD LOGIC?
LET'S FIND OUT.
APPROVE THE CONTRACT NOW OR I'LL SUE YOU FOR OBSTRUCTION OF DOGS!!
OKAY OKAY
WOW
THE GREAT THING ABOUT ABSURD LOGIC IS THAT IT FITS ANY SITUATION.
S. Adams
© 1995 United Feature Syndicate, Inc.(NYC)
9/24

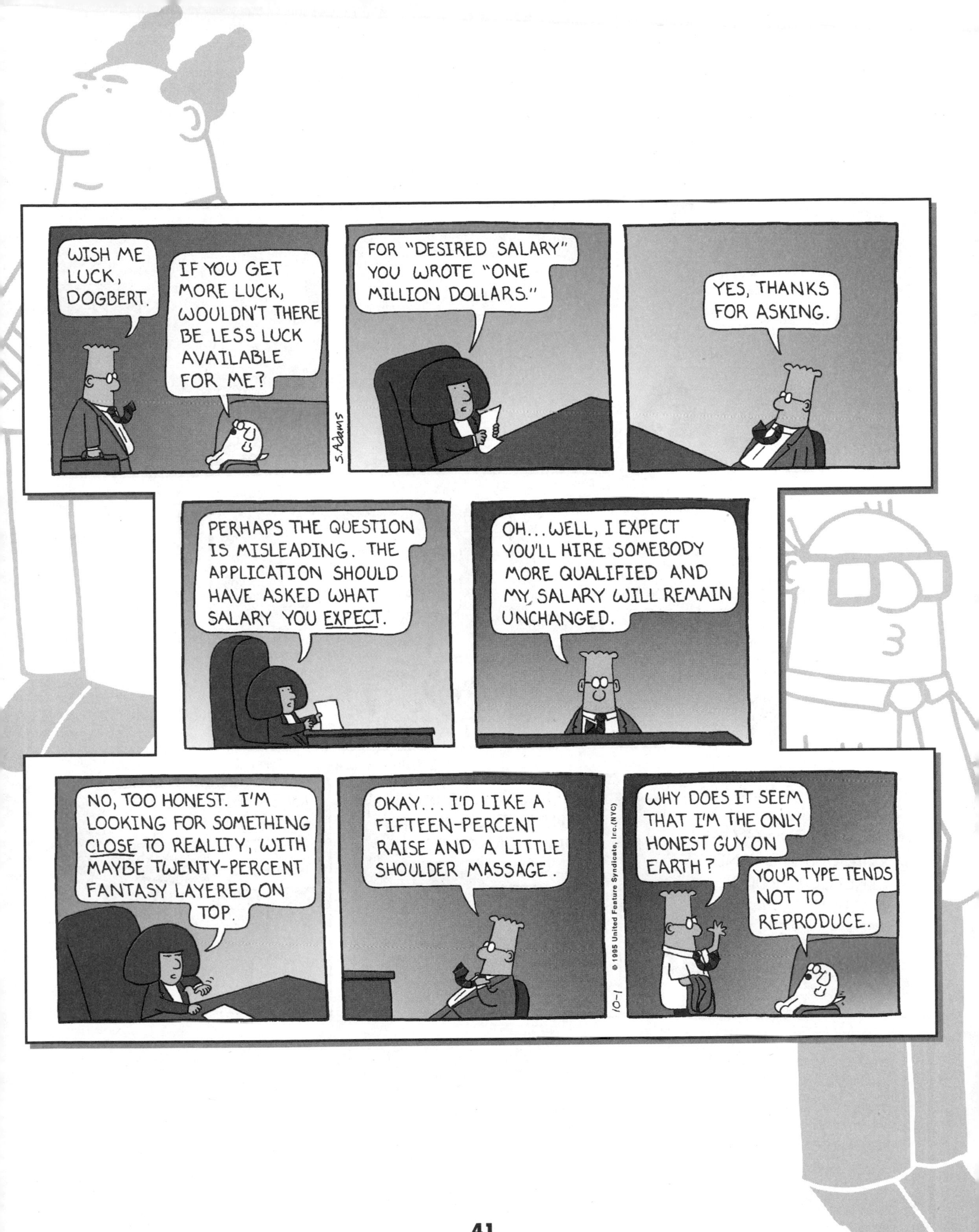
WISH ME LUCK, DOGBERT.
IF YOU GET MORE LUCK, WOULDN'T THERE BE LESS LUCK AVAILABLE FOR ME?
S. Adams
FOR "DESIRED SALARY" YOU WROTE "ONE MILLION DOLLARS."
YES, THANKS FOR ASKING.
PERHAPS THE QUESTION IS MISLEADING. THE APPLICATION SHOULD HAVE ASKED WHAT SALARY YOU EXPECT.
OH... WELL, I EXPECT YOU'LL HIRE SOMEBODY MORE QUALIFIED AND MY SALARY WILL REMAIN UNCHANGED.
NO, TOO HONEST. I'M LOOKING FOR SOMETHING CLOSE TO REALITY, WITH MAYBE TWENTY-PERCENT FANTASY LAYERED ON TOP.
OKAY... I'D LIKE A FIFTEEN-PERCENT RAISE AND A LITTLE SHOULDER MASSAGE.
© 1995 United Feature Syndicate, Inc.(NYC)
10-1
WHY DOES IT SEEM THAT I'M THE ONLY HONEST GUY ON EARTH?
YOUR TYPE TENDS NOT TO REPRODUCE.

THAT'S FOUR HOURS THAT I'D LIKE TO HAVE BACK.
WHO CALLED THAT MEETING ANYWAY?
S. Adams
I MUST HAVE LEFT MY CALENDAR IN THERE.
OOOH
?
I'VE DISCOVERED A PRIMITIVE DONUT-SCAVENGING MAN CLAD ONLY IN YELLOW STICKY NOTES!!
I WAS ONCE LIKE YOU, BEFORE THE GREAT RIF.
BUT RATHER THAN LEAVE IN HUMILIATION I DECIDED TO STAY AND LIVE OFF THE LAND LIKE OUR PROUD ANCESTORS.
TO ENSURE A BOUNTIFUL HARVEST I DO MY DONUT DANCE TO THE GODS.
© 1995 United Feature Syndicate, Inc.(NYC)
10-8
WHEN THAT DOESN'T WORK I DISTRIBUTE MEETING NOTICES.
YOU'RE THE ONE!!

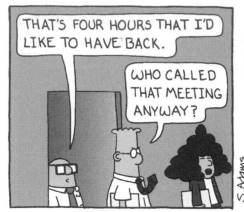

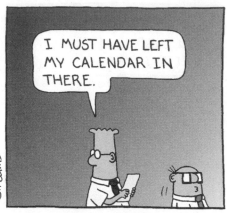

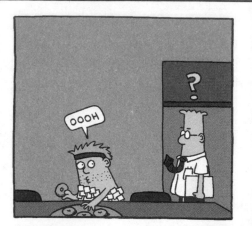

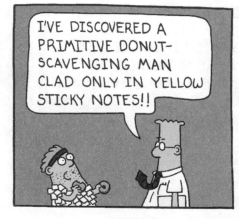

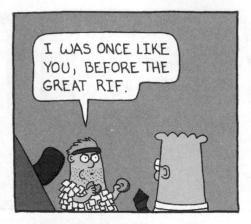

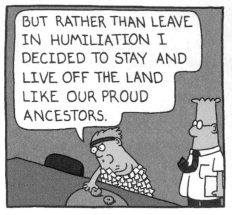

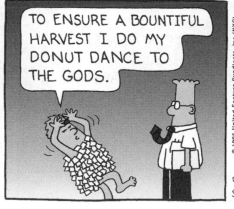

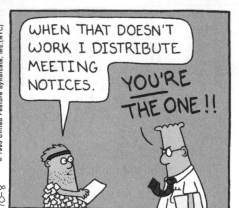

WHY DO YOU WANT TO BE OUR NEW "LONG RANGE PLANNER," MISTER DOGBERT?
S. Adams
BECAUSE "LONG RANGE" IS VERY FAR AWAY . . .
. . . THEREFORE IT WILL BE IMPOSSIBLE TO EVALUATE MY PERFORMANCE.
IF IT'S NOT TOO MUCH TO ASK, I'D LIKE TO BE ON FLEX-TIME SO YOU'LL NEVER KNOW IF I'M SUPPOSED TO BE AT WORK.
I'LL NEED AN INTERNET CONNECTION AT HOME SO I CAN TELECOMMUTE AND NOT POLLUTE.
BECAUSE I GIVE A HOOT.
ALSO, I'D LIKE TO BE IN A GROUP WITH LOTS OF LOSERS. THAT WAY I'LL GET THE BIGGEST RAISE WHEN WE'RE RANKED.
YOU'RE HIRED. ALL OF THE OTHER APPLICANTS DEMANDED RELOCATION EXPENSES AND I HAVE NO BUDGET FOR THAT.
10-15
© 1995 United Feature Syndicate, Inc.(NYC)
WHY DO I HAVE TO WORK WHILE YOU JUST LOOK FOR POODLE GRAPHICS ON THE INTERNET?
DON'T WORK TOO HARD; I'D LIKE A BIG RAISE.

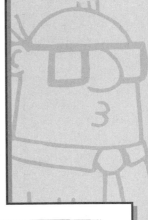

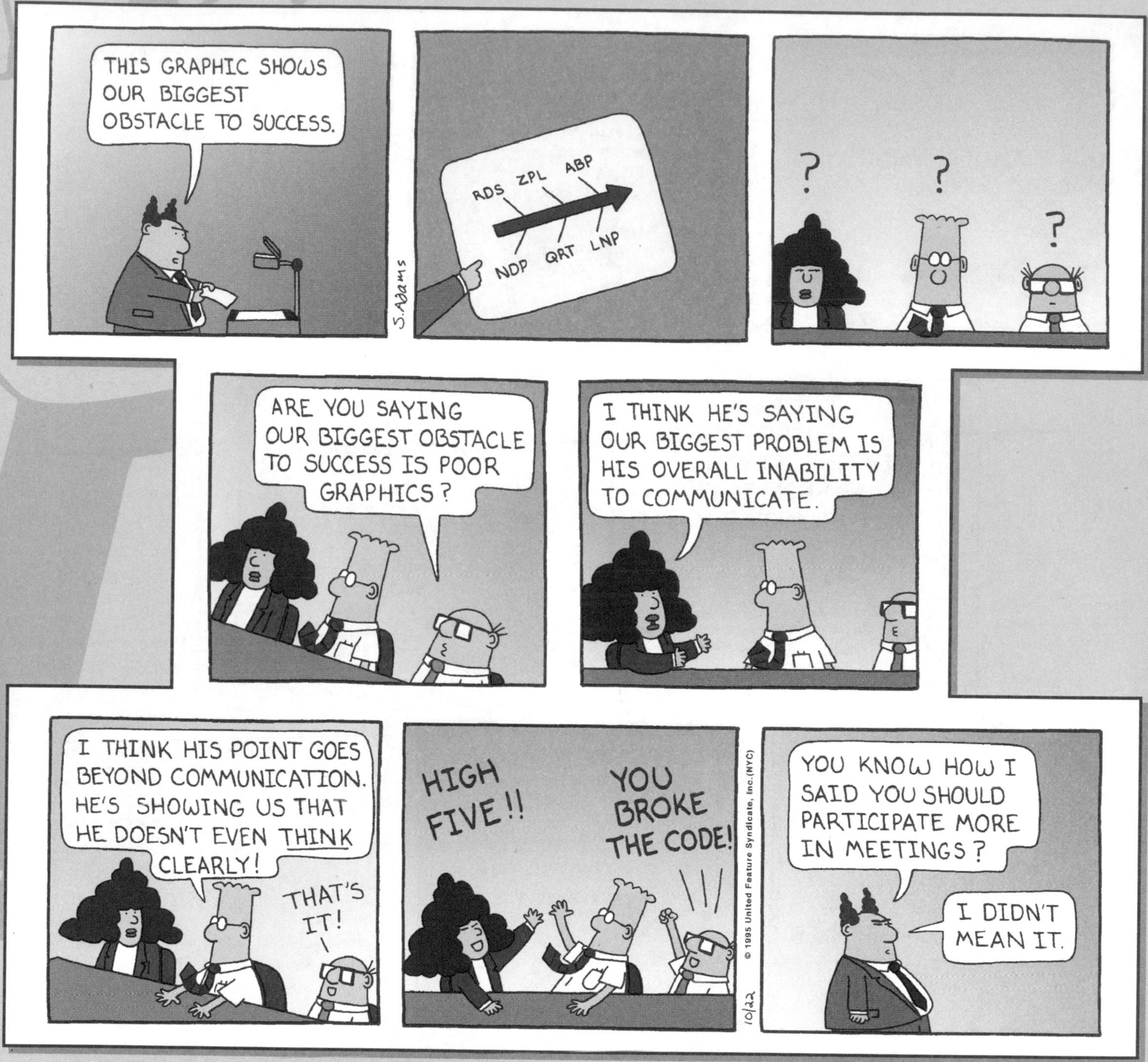

THIS GRAPHIC SHOWS OUR BIGGEST OBSTACLE TO SUCCESS.
RDS ZPL ABP NDP QRT LNP
S. Adams
?
?
?
ARE YOU SAYING OUR BIGGEST OBSTACLE TO SUCCESS IS POOR GRAPHICS?
I THINK HE'S SAYING OUR BIGGEST PROBLEM IS HIS OVERALL INABILITY TO COMMUNICATE.
I THINK HIS POINT GOES BEYOND COMMUNICATION. HE'S SHOWING US THAT HE DOESN'T EVEN THINK CLEARLY!
THAT'S IT!
HIGH FIVE!!
YOU BROKE THE CODE!
© 1995 United Feature Syndicate, Inc.(NYC)
10/22
YOU KNOW HOW I SAID YOU SHOULD PARTICIPATE MORE IN MEETINGS?
I DIDN'T MEAN IT.

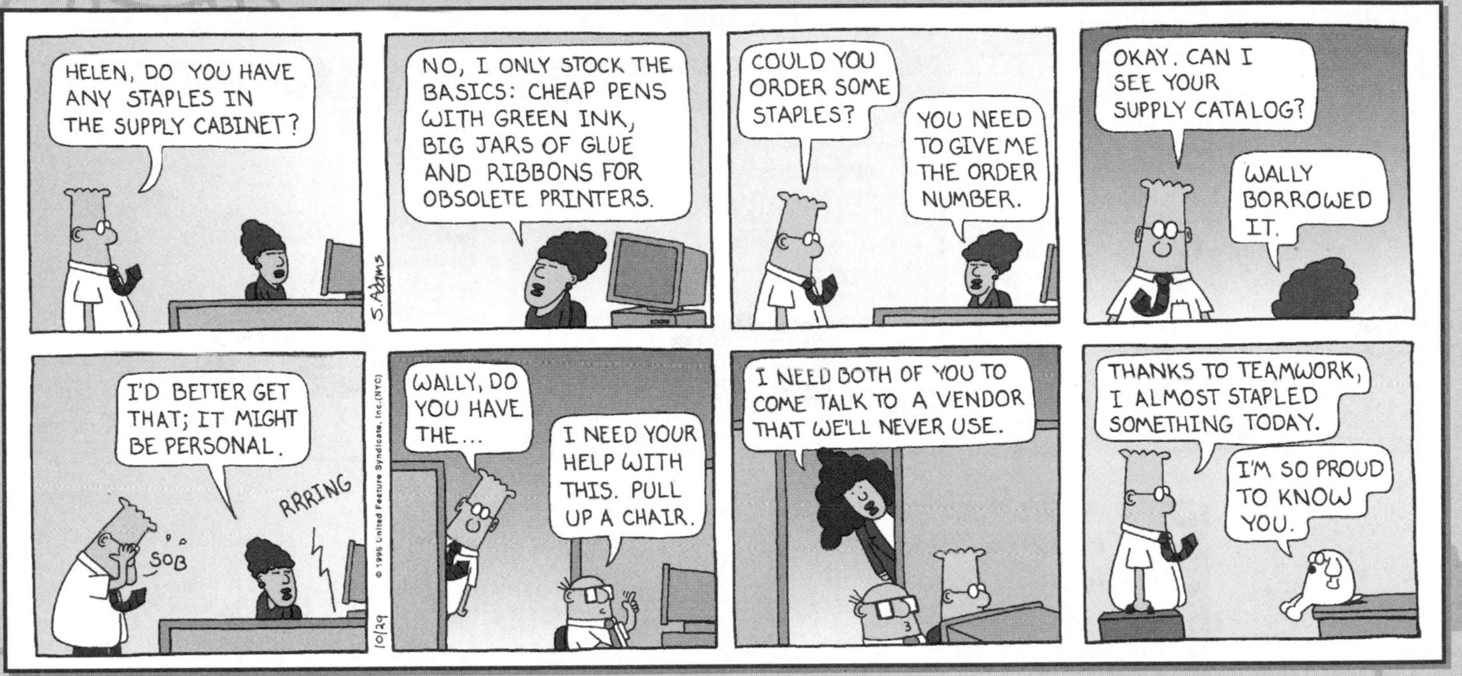
HELEN, DO YOU HAVE ANY STAPLES IN THE SUPPLY CABINET?
NO, I ONLY STOCK THE BASICS: CHEAP PENS WITH GREEN INK, BIG JARS OF GLUE AND RIBBONS FOR OBSOLETE PRINTERS.
COULD YOU ORDER SOME STAPLES?
YOU NEED TO GIVE ME THE ORDER NUMBER.
OKAY. CAN I SEE YOUR SUPPLY CATALOG?
WALLY BORROWED IT.
I'D BETTER GET THAT; IT MIGHT BE PERSONAL.
SOB
RRRING
WALLY, DO YOU HAVE THE...
I NEED YOUR HELP WITH THIS. PULL UP A CHAIR.
I NEED BOTH OF YOU TO COME TALK TO A VENDOR THAT WE'LL NEVER USE.
THANKS TO TEAMWORK, I ALMOST STAPLED SOMETHING TODAY.
I'M SO PROUD TO KNOW YOU.

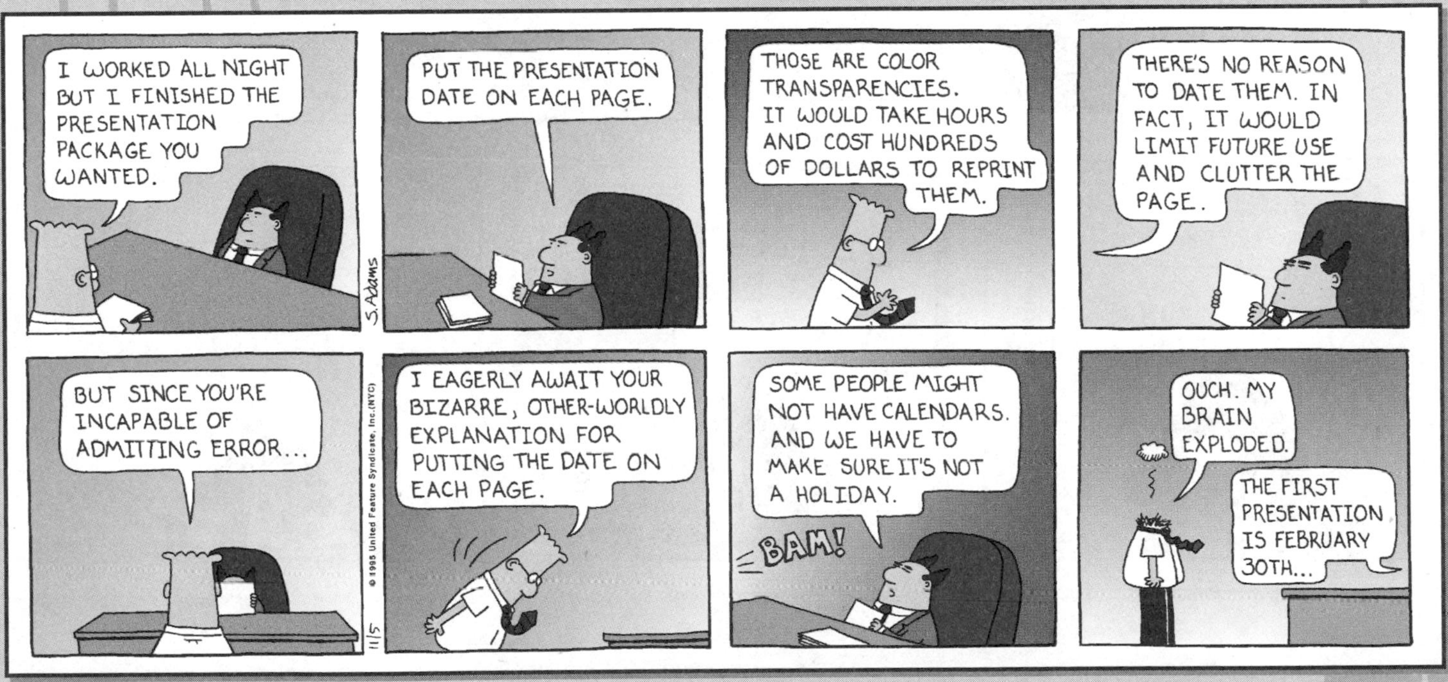
I WORKED ALL NIGHT BUT I FINISHED THE PRESENTATION PACKAGE YOU WANTED.
PUT THE PRESENTATION DATE ON EACH PAGE.
THOSE ARE COLOR TRANSPARENCIES. IT WOULD TAKE HOURS AND COST HUNDREDS OF DOLLARS TO REPRINT THEM.
THERE'S NO REASON TO DATE THEM. IN FACT, IT WOULD LIMIT FUTURE USE AND CLUTTER THE PAGE.
BUT SINCE YOU'RE INCAPABLE OF ADMITTING ERROR...
I EAGERLY AWAIT YOUR BIZARRE, OTHER-WORLDLY EXPLANATION FOR PUTTING THE DATE ON EACH PAGE.
SOME PEOPLE MIGHT NOT HAVE CALENDARS. AND WE HAVE TO MAKE SURE IT'S NOT A HOLIDAY.
BAM!
OUCH. MY BRAIN EXPLODED.
THE FIRST PRESENTATION IS FEBRUARY 30TH...

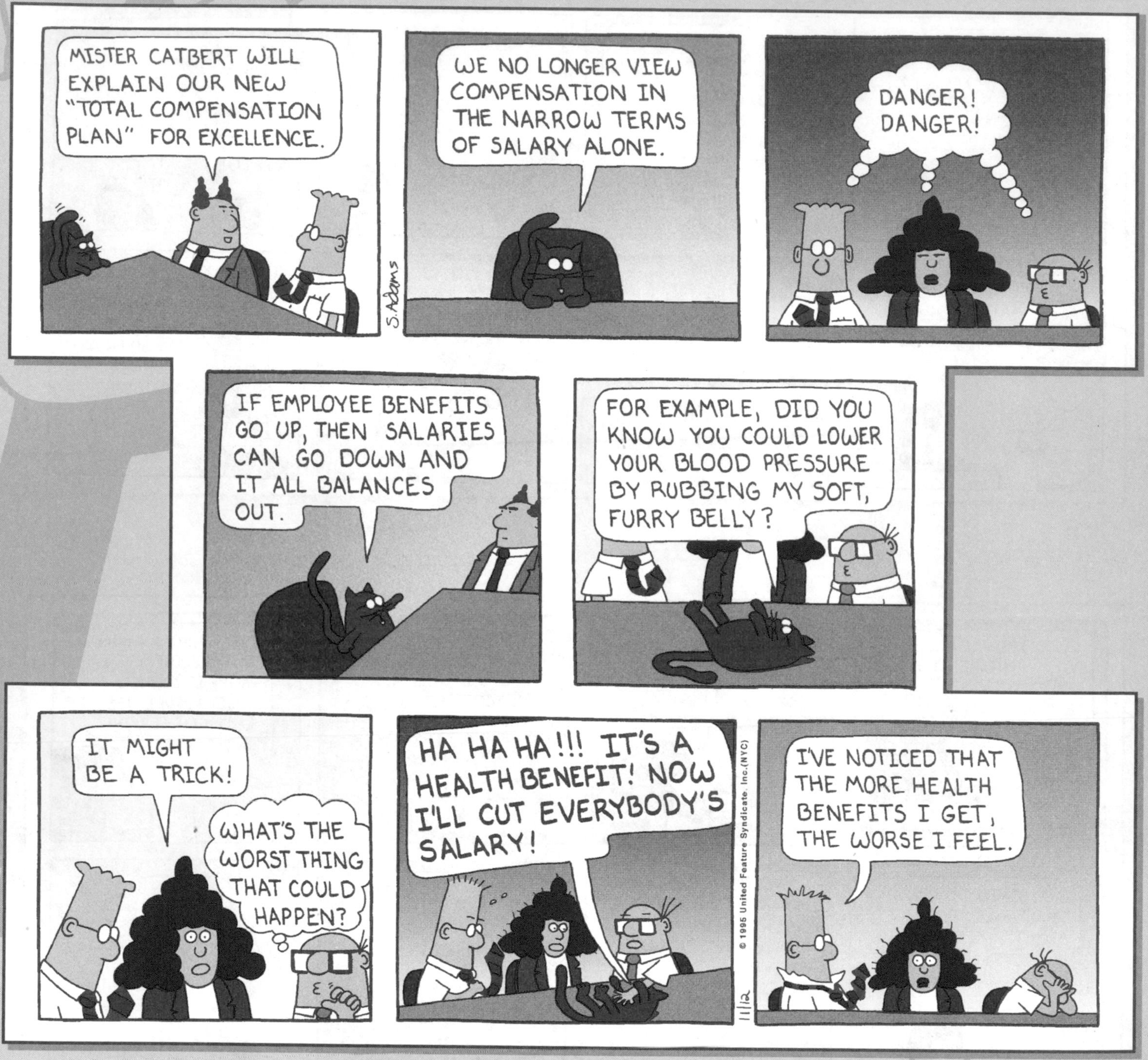
MISTER CATBERT WILL EXPLAIN OUR NEW "TOTAL COMPENSATION PLAN" FOR EXCELLENCE.
S. Adams
WE NO LONGER VIEW COMPENSATION IN THE NARROW TERMS OF SALARY ALONE.
DANGER! DANGER!
IF EMPLOYEE BENEFITS GO UP, THEN SALARIES CAN GO DOWN AND IT ALL BALANCES OUT.
FOR EXAMPLE, DID YOU KNOW YOU COULD LOWER YOUR BLOOD PRESSURE BY RUBBING MY SOFT, FURRY BELLY?
IT MIGHT BE A TRICK!
WHAT'S THE WORST THING THAT COULD HAPPEN?
HA HA HA!!! IT'S A HEALTH BENEFIT! NOW I'LL CUT EVERYBODY'S SALARY!
© 1995 United Feature Syndicate, Inc.(NYC)
11/12
I'VE NOTICED THAT THE MORE HEALTH BENEFITS I GET, THE WORSE I FEEL.

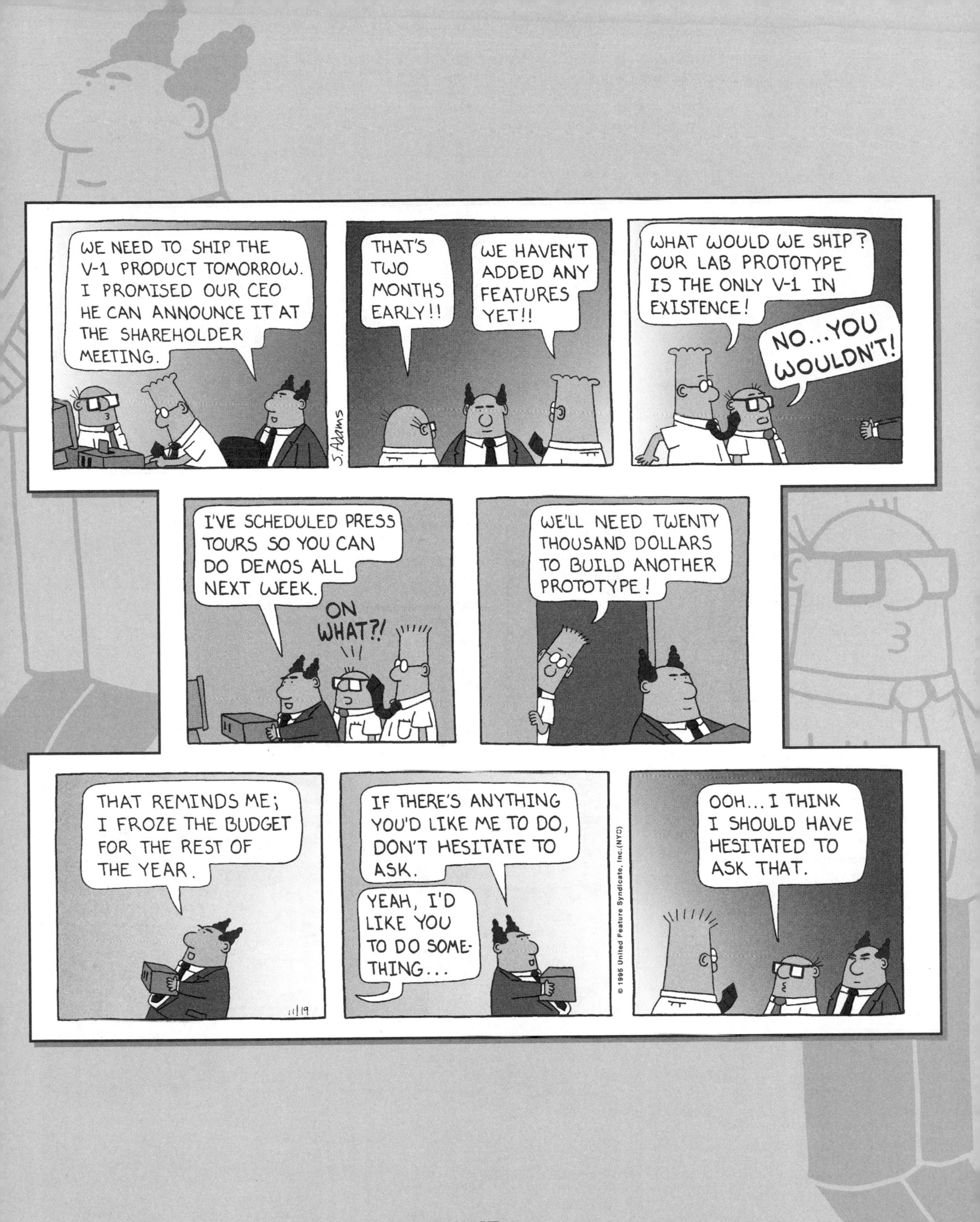
WE NEED TO SHIP THE V-1 PRODUCT TOMORROW. I PROMISED OUR CEO HE CAN ANNOUNCE IT AT THE SHAREHOLDER MEETING.
S. Adams
THAT'S TWO MONTHS EARLY!!
WE HAVEN'T ADDED ANY FEATURES YET!!
WHAT WOULD WE SHIP? OUR LAB PROTOTYPE IS THE ONLY V-1 IN EXISTENCE!
NO...YOU WOULDN'T!
I'VE SCHEDULED PRESS TOURS SO YOU CAN DO DEMOS ALL NEXT WEEK.
ON WHAT?!
WE'LL NEED TWENTY THOUSAND DOLLARS TO BUILD ANOTHER PROTOTYPE!
THAT REMINDS ME; I FROZE THE BUDGET FOR THE REST OF THE YEAR.
11/19
IF THERE'S ANYTHING YOU'D LIKE ME TO DO, DON'T HESITATE TO ASK.
YEAH, I'D LIKE YOU TO DO SOME-THING...
© 1995 United Feature Syndicate, Inc.(NYC)
OOH... I THINK I SHOULD HAVE HESITATED TO ASK THAT.

THE CLEVER SALES-MAN EVALUATES HIS PREY.
BADGE
VISITORS SIGN IN
S. Adams
I HOPE HE'S AN IMPORTANT DECISION-MAKER.
TAKE ANY SEAT. I CALL THE GOOD CHAIR.
WARNING! CUBICLE! LOW-RANKING EMPLOYEE!
HERE'S OUR ORGANIZATION CHART: PRESIDENT... SENIOR VICE PRESIDENT... VICE PRESIDENT...
OKAY, LIFT YOUR FOOT. DO YOU SEE THAT COFFEE STAIN ON THE CARPET?
THAT'S YOU?
NO, THAT'S MY BOSS. I WOULD BE UNDER THE CARPET.
11/26
DO I HAVE ANY HOPE OF TALKING TO SOME-BODY WHO CAN MAKE A DECISION?
LET ME CHECK.
© 1995 United Feature Syndicate, Inc.(NYC)
HEY, WALLY. WHAT'S A "DECISION"?
IT SOUNDS LIKE SOMETHING OUR COMPETITORS DO.
SOB

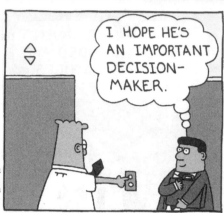

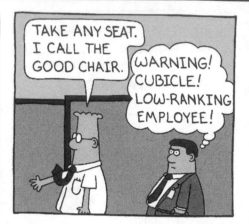

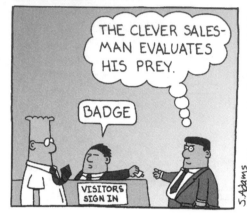

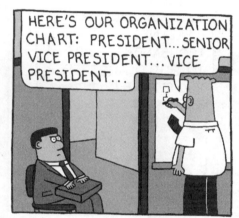

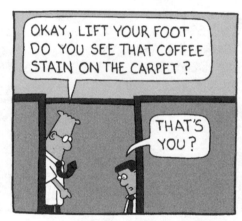

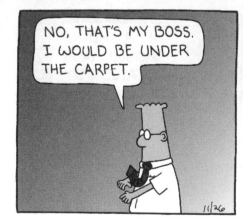

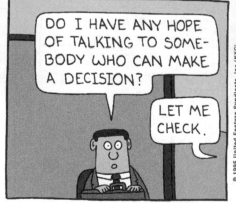

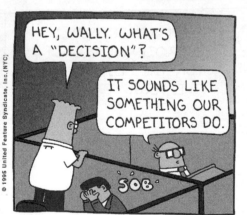

WORKING LATE AGAIN, HUH, ALICE?
S. Adams
SEVENTY HOURS THIS WEEK...
ME TOO. THANK GOODNESS FOR OVERTIME PAY!
OVERTIME PAY?
ALLOW ME TO EXPLAIN.
UNLIKE YOU SO-CALLED "EXEMPT" EMPLOYEES, MY INCOME INCREASES IF I WORK ADDITIONAL HOURS.
$
Hours
I'M PULLING IN SEVENTY-FIVE THOUSAND A YEAR. AND HALF THE TIME I JUST HIDE IN THE BASEMENT READING "FISHING" MAGAZINE.
THE ONLY DOWN SIDE IS THAT I DON'T GET TO ENJOY THE INTELLECTUAL STIMULATION OF MY CO-WORKERS THE WAY YOU DO.
12/3
© 1995 United Feature Syndicate, Inc.(NYC)
I DON'T KNOW WHAT I LIKE BETTER — DEEP SEA FISHING OR CUBICLE FISHING.
FISH

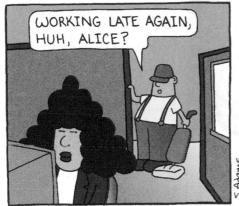

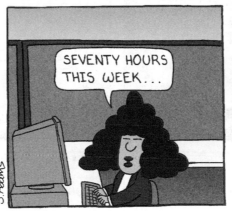

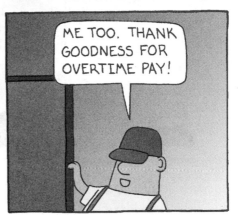

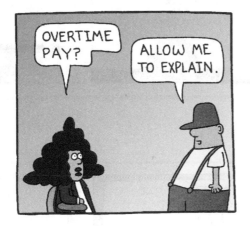

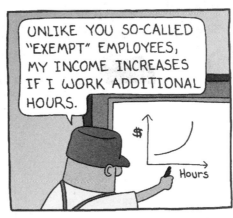

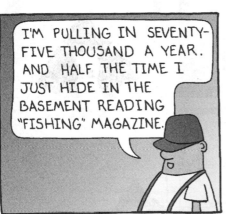

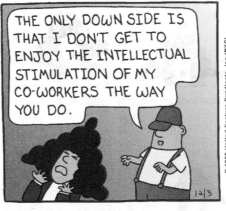

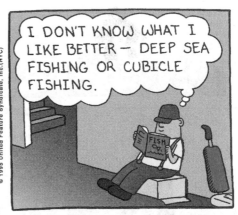

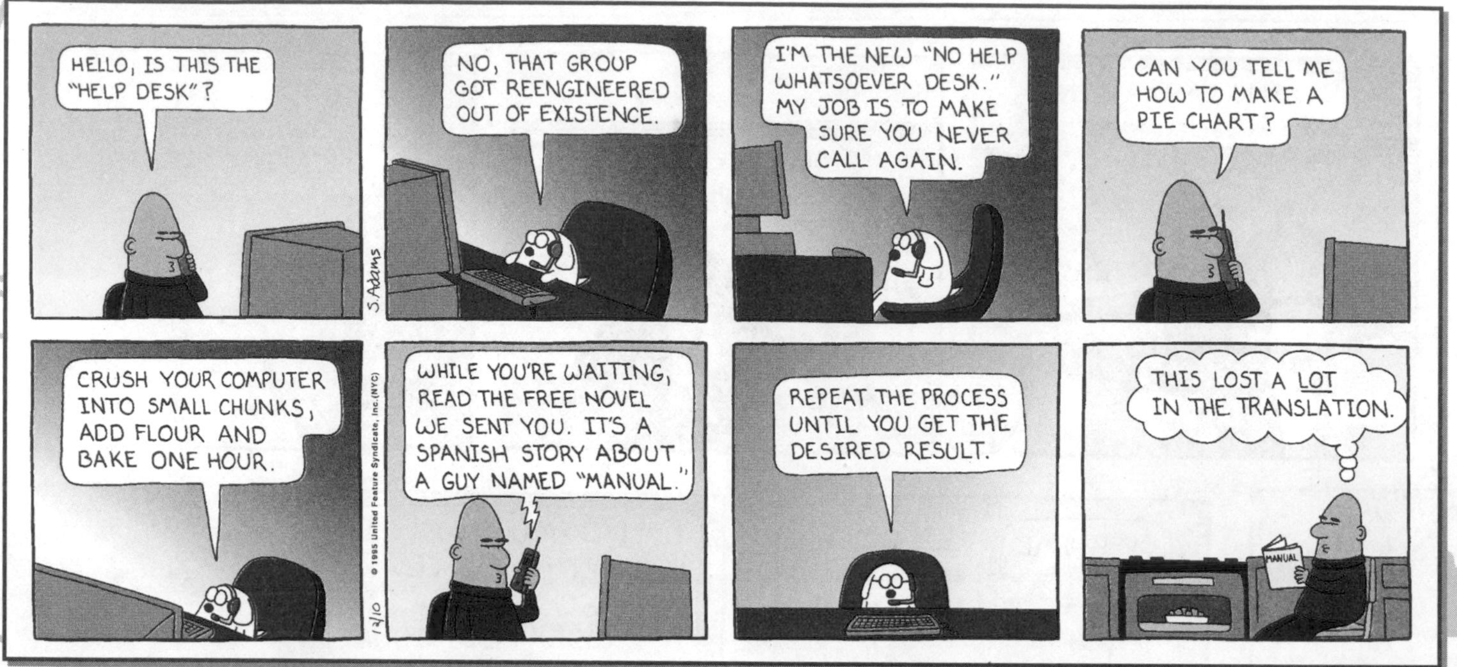
HELLO, IS THIS THE "HELP DESK"?
NO, THAT GROUP GOT REENGINEERED OUT OF EXISTENCE.
S. Adams
I'M THE NEW "NO HELP WHATSOEVER DESK." MY JOB IS TO MAKE SURE YOU NEVER CALL AGAIN.
CAN YOU TELL ME HOW TO MAKE A PIE CHART?
CRUSH YOUR COMPUTER INTO SMALL CHUNKS, ADD FLOUR AND BAKE ONE HOUR.
© 1995 United Feature Syndicate, Inc.(NYC)
12/10
WHILE YOU'RE WAITING, READ THE FREE NOVEL WE SENT YOU. IT'S A SPANISH STORY ABOUT A GUY NAMED "MANUAL."
REPEAT THE PROCESS UNTIL YOU GET THE DESIRED RESULT.
THIS LOST A LOT IN THE TRANSLATION.
MANUAL

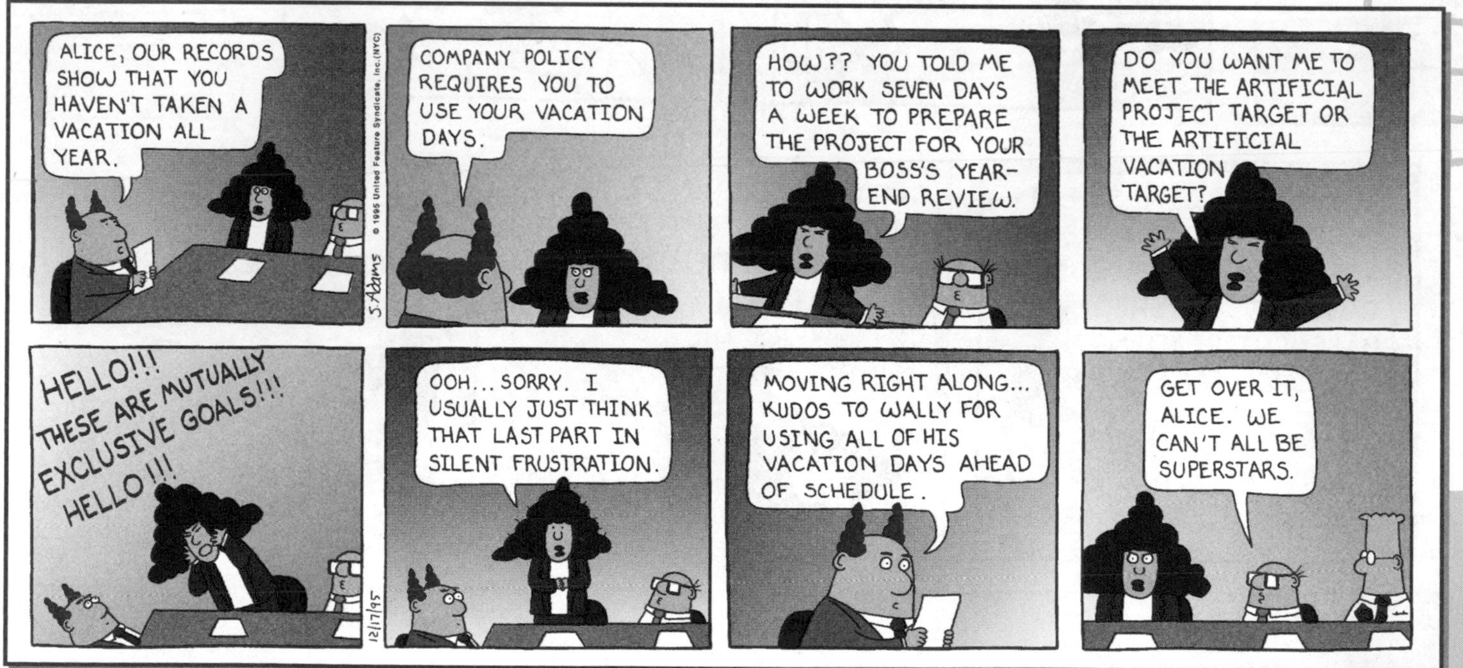
ALICE, OUR RECORDS SHOW THAT YOU HAVEN'T TAKEN A VACATION ALL YEAR.
© 1995 United Feature Syndicate, Inc.(NYC)
S. Adams
COMPANY POLICY REQUIRES YOU TO USE YOUR VACATION DAYS.
HOW?? YOU TOLD ME TO WORK SEVEN DAYS A WEEK TO PREPARE THE PROJECT FOR YOUR BOSS'S YEAR-END REVIEW.
DO YOU WANT ME TO MEET THE ARTIFICIAL PROJECT TARGET OR THE ARTIFICIAL VACATION TARGET?
HELLO!!! THESE ARE MUTUALLY EXCLUSIVE GOALS!!! HELLO!!!
12/17/95
OOH... SORRY. I USUALLY JUST THINK THAT LAST PART IN SILENT FRUSTRATION.
MOVING RIGHT ALONG... KUDOS TO WALLY FOR USING ALL OF HIS VACATION DAYS AHEAD OF SCHEDULE.
GET OVER IT, ALICE. WE CAN'T ALL BE SUPERSTARS.

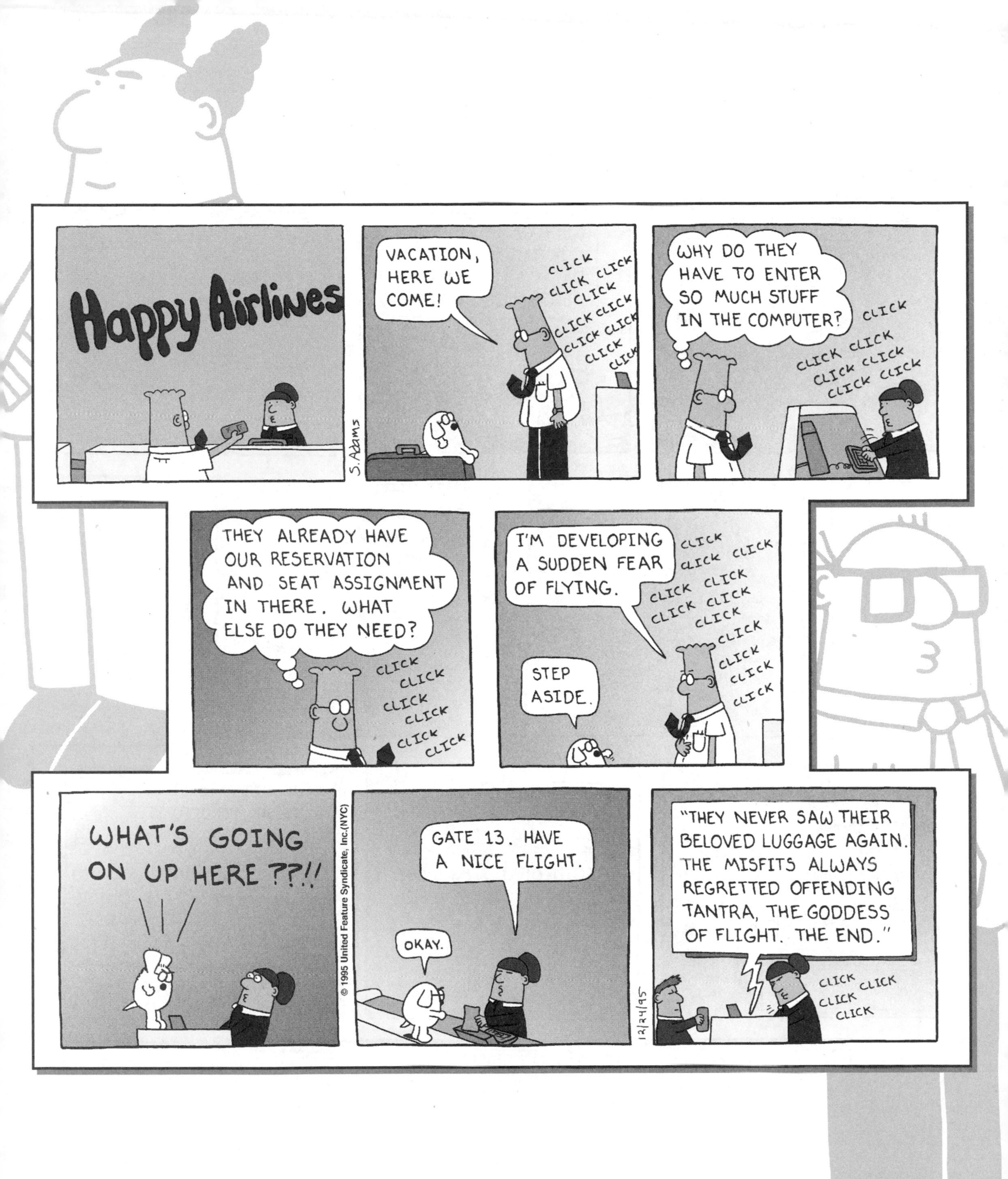

Happy Airlines
S. Adams
VACATION, HERE WE COME!
CLICK CLICK CLICK CLICK CLICK CLICK CLICK CLICK CLICK CLICK CLICK
WHY DO THEY HAVE TO ENTER SO MUCH STUFF IN THE COMPUTER?
CLICK CLICK CLICK CLICK CLICK CLICK CLICK
THEY ALREADY HAVE OUR RESERVATION AND SEAT ASSIGNMENT IN THERE. WHAT ELSE DO THEY NEED?
CLICK CLICK CLICK CLICK CLICK CLICK
I'M DEVELOPING A SUDDEN FEAR OF FLYING.
CLICK CLICK CLICK CLICK CLICK CLICK CLICK CLICK CLICK CLICK CLICK CLICK
STEP ASIDE.
WHAT'S GOING ON UP HERE ??!!
© 1995 United Feature Syndicate, Inc.(NYC)
GATE 13. HAVE A NICE FLIGHT.
OKAY.
12/24/95
"THEY NEVER SAW THEIR BELOVED LUGGAGE AGAIN. THE MISFITS ALWAYS REGRETTED OFFENDING TANTRA, THE GODDESS OF FLIGHT. THE END."
CLICK CLICK CLICK CLICK

I'VE GOT AN IDEA!
WE'RE DOOMED.
S. Adams
WHY CAN'T WE RUN OUR INVENTORY DATABASE OVER OUR E-MAIL SYSTEM?
FACT: THAT IS THE STUPIDEST IDEA IN THE UNIVERSE.
FACT: HIS COMPREHENSION IS SO LIMITED THAT DEBATE IS FUTILE.
FACT: WE COULD SPEND HOURS UNSUCCESSFULLY EXPLAINING WHY IT'S A STUPID IDEA.
FACT: HE WOULD NEVER KNOW IF WE USED HIS IDEA OR NOT.
NO PROBLEM.
WE'LL GET RIGHT ON IT.
MY WORK IS DONE.
12/31/95 © 1995 United Feature Syndicate, Inc.(NYC)
STUPIDITY IS LIKE NUCLEAR POWER; IT CAN BE USED FOR GOOD OR EVIL.
AND YOU DON'T WANT TO GET ANY ON YOU.

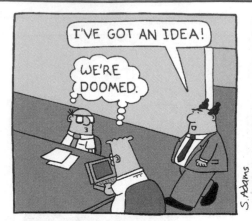

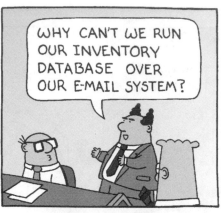

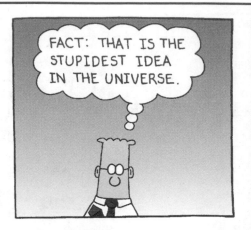

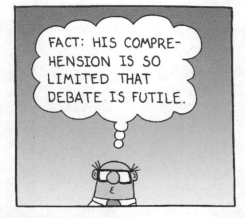

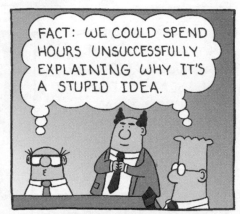

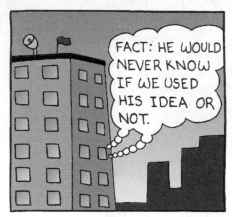

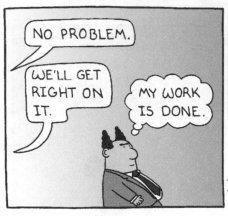

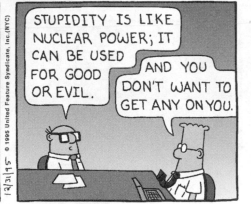

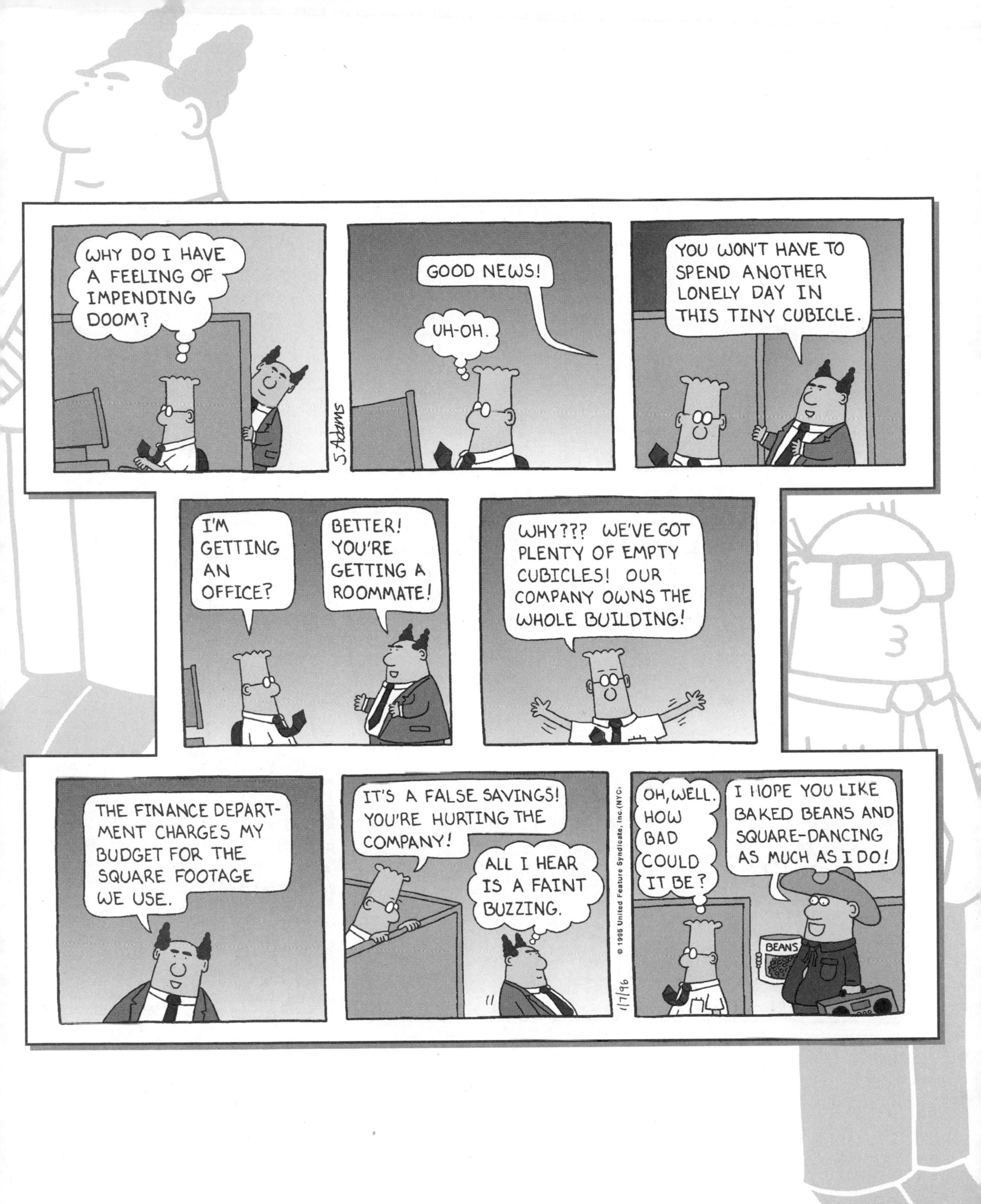
WHY DO I HAVE A FEELING OF IMPENDING DOOM?
S. Adams
GOOD NEWS!
UH-OH.
YOU WON'T HAVE TO SPEND ANOTHER LONELY DAY IN THIS TINY CUBICLE.
I'M GETTING AN OFFICE?
BETTER! YOU'RE GETTING A ROOMMATE!
WHY??? WE'VE GOT PLENTY OF EMPTY CUBICLES! OUR COMPANY OWNS THE WHOLE BUILDING!
THE FINANCE DEPARTMENT CHARGES MY BUDGET FOR THE SQUARE FOOTAGE WE USE.
IT'S A FALSE SAVINGS! YOU'RE HURTING THE COMPANY!
ALL I HEAR IS A FAINT BUZZING.
© 1995 United Feature Syndicate, Inc.(NYC)
1/7/96
OH, WELL. HOW BAD COULD IT BE?
I HOPE YOU LIKE BAKED BEANS AND SQUARE-DANCING AS MUCH AS I DO!
BEANS

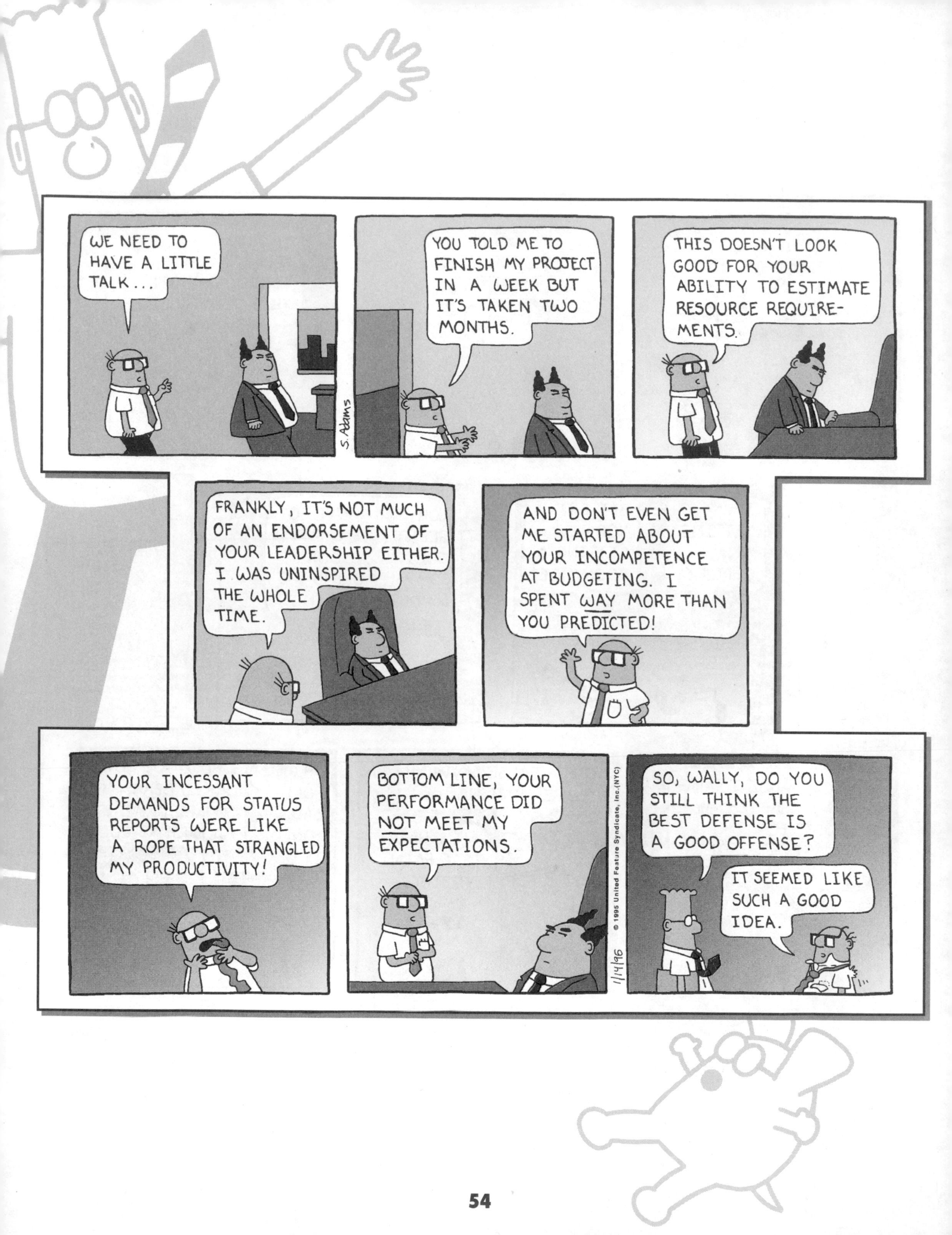
WE NEED TO HAVE A LITTLE TALK...
YOU TOLD ME TO FINISH MY PROJECT IN A WEEK BUT IT'S TAKEN TWO MONTHS.
THIS DOESN'T LOOK GOOD FOR YOUR ABILITY TO ESTIMATE RESOURCE REQUIREMENTS.
FRANKLY, IT'S NOT MUCH OF AN ENDORSEMENT OF YOUR LEADERSHIP EITHER. I WAS UNINSPIRED THE WHOLE TIME.
AND DON'T EVEN GET ME STARTED ABOUT YOUR INCOMPETENCE AT BUDGETING. I SPENT WAY MORE THAN YOU PREDICTED!
YOUR INCESSANT DEMANDS FOR STATUS REPORTS WERE LIKE A ROPE THAT STRANGLED MY PRODUCTIVITY!
BOTTOM LINE, YOUR PERFORMANCE DID NOT MEET MY EXPECTATIONS.
SO, WALLY, DO YOU STILL THINK THE BEST DEFENSE IS A GOOD OFFENSE?
IT SEEMED LIKE SUCH A GOOD IDEA.
S. Adams
© 1995 United Feature Syndicate, Inc.(NYC)
1/14/96

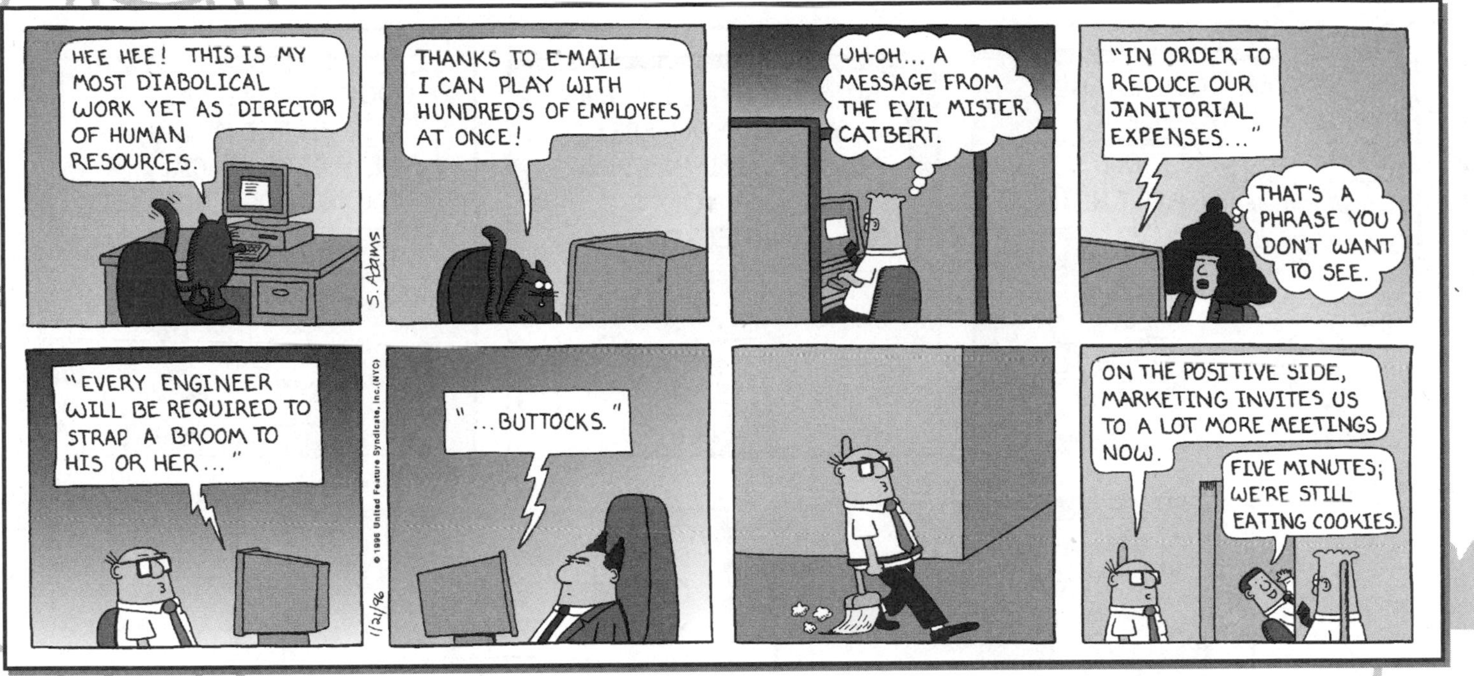
HEE HEE! THIS IS MY MOST DIABOLICAL WORK YET AS DIRECTOR OF HUMAN RESOURCES.
THANKS TO E-MAIL I CAN PLAY WITH HUNDREDS OF EMPLOYEES AT ONCE!
UH-OH... A MESSAGE FROM THE EVIL MISTER CATBERT.
"IN ORDER TO REDUCE OUR JANITORIAL EXPENSES..."
THAT'S A PHRASE YOU DON'T WANT TO SEE.
"EVERY ENGINEER WILL BE REQUIRED TO STRAP A BROOM TO HIS OR HER..."
"...BUTTOCKS."
ON THE POSITIVE SIDE, MARKETING INVITES US TO A LOT MORE MEETINGS NOW.
FIVE MINUTES; WE'RE STILL EATING COOKIES.
S. Adams
1/21/96
© 1996 United Feature Syndicate, Inc.(NYC)

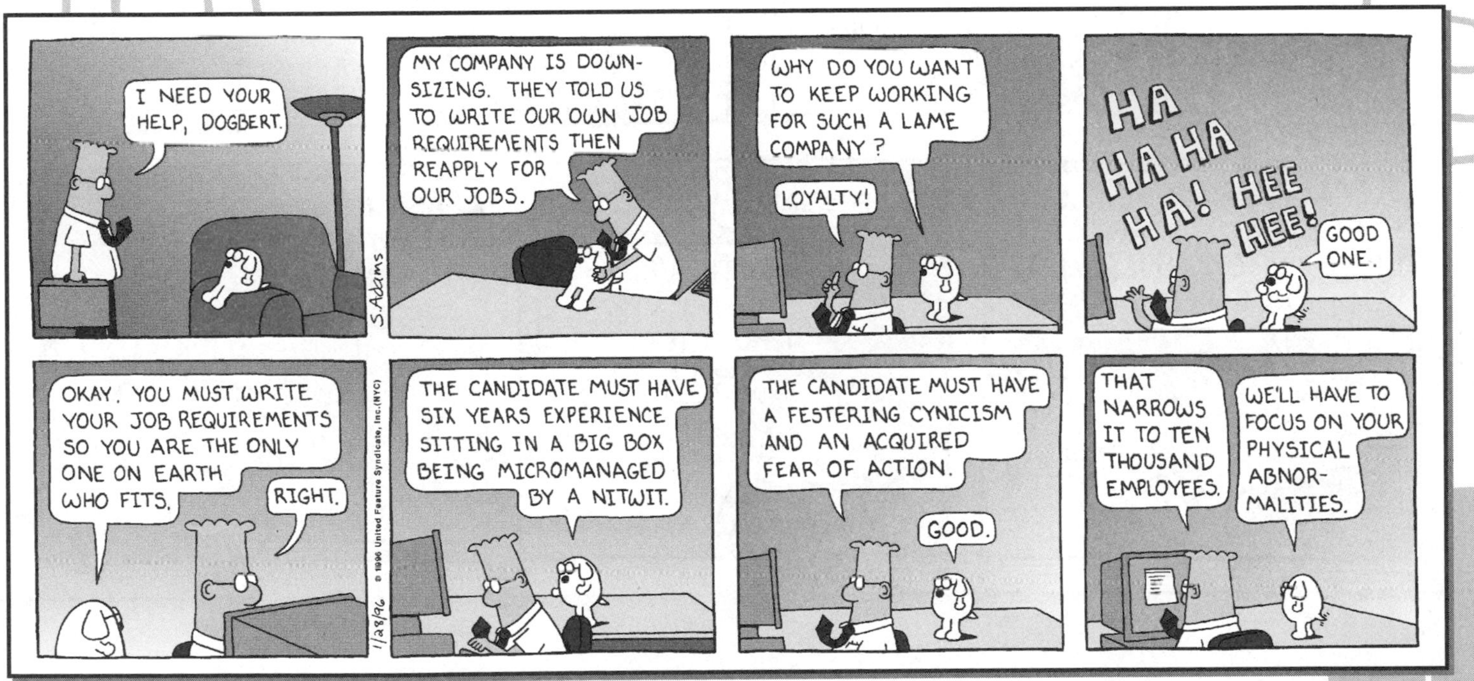
I NEED YOUR HELP, DOGBERT.
MY COMPANY IS DOWNSIZING. THEY TOLD US TO WRITE OUR OWN JOB REQUIREMENTS THEN REAPPLY FOR OUR JOBS.
WHY DO YOU WANT TO KEEP WORKING FOR SUCH A LAME COMPANY?
LOYALTY!
HA HA HA HA! HEE HEE!
GOOD ONE.
OKAY. YOU MUST WRITE YOUR JOB REQUIREMENTS SO YOU ARE THE ONLY ONE ON EARTH WHO FITS.
RIGHT.
THE CANDIDATE MUST HAVE SIX YEARS EXPERIENCE SITTING IN A BIG BOX BEING MICROMANAGED BY A NITWIT.
THE CANDIDATE MUST HAVE A FESTERING CYNICISM AND AN ACQUIRED FEAR OF ACTION.
GOOD.
THAT NARROWS IT TO TEN THOUSAND EMPLOYEES.
WE'LL HAVE TO FOCUS ON YOUR PHYSICAL ABNORMALITIES.
S. Adams
1/28/96
© 1996 United Feature Syndicate, Inc.(NYC)

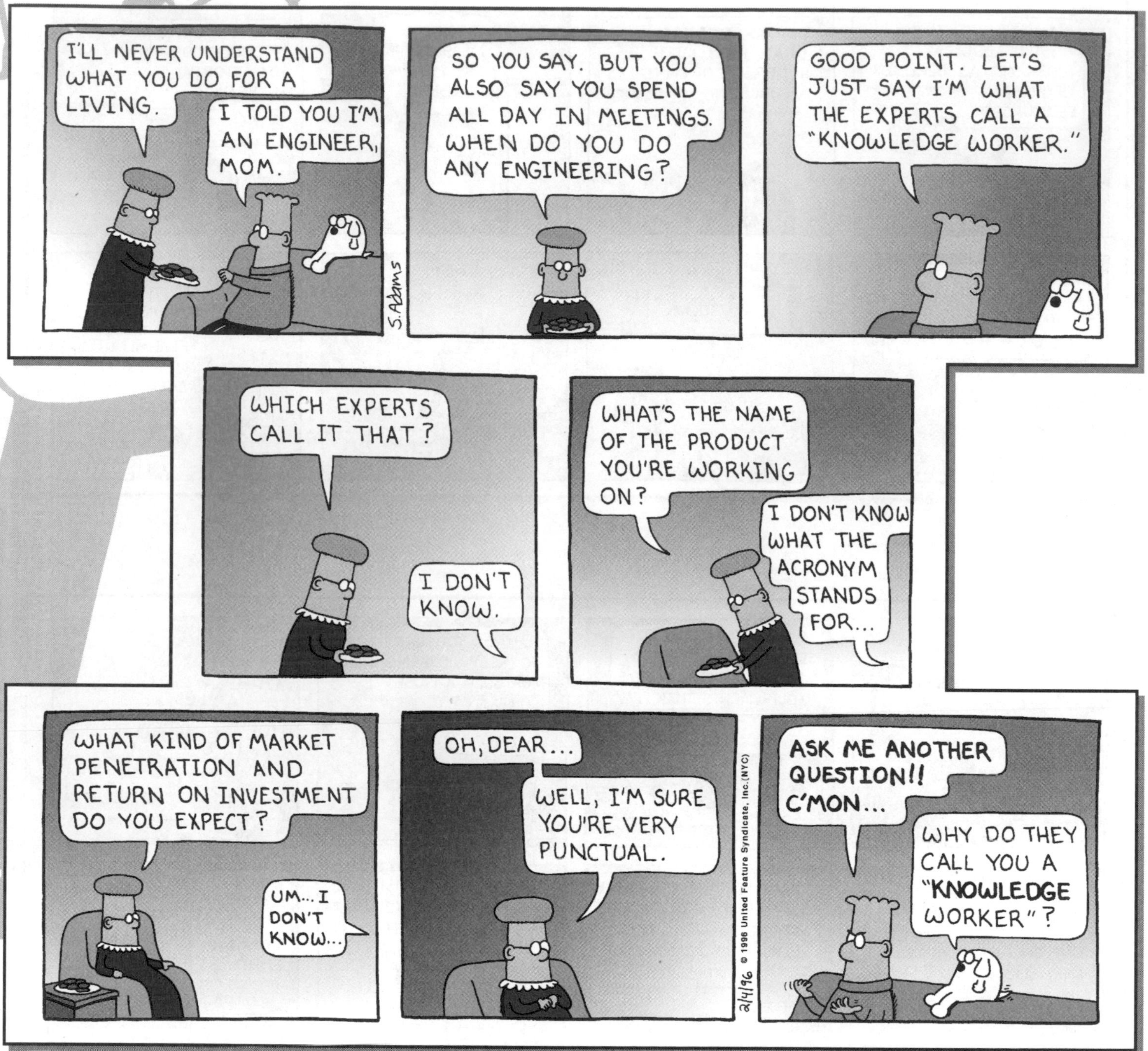
I'LL NEVER UNDERSTAND WHAT YOU DO FOR A LIVING.
I TOLD YOU I'M AN ENGINEER, MOM.
S. Adams
SO YOU SAY. BUT YOU ALSO SAY YOU SPEND ALL DAY IN MEETINGS. WHEN DO YOU DO ANY ENGINEERING?
GOOD POINT. LET'S JUST SAY I'M WHAT THE EXPERTS CALL A "KNOWLEDGE WORKER."
WHICH EXPERTS CALL IT THAT?
I DON'T KNOW.
WHAT'S THE NAME OF THE PRODUCT YOU'RE WORKING ON?
I DON'T KNOW WHAT THE ACRONYM STANDS FOR...
WHAT KIND OF MARKET PENETRATION AND RETURN ON INVESTMENT DO YOU EXPECT?
UM... I DON'T KNOW...
OH, DEAR...
WELL, I'M SURE YOU'RE VERY PUNCTUAL.
2/4/96 © 1996 United Feature Syndicate, Inc.(NYC)
ASK ME ANOTHER QUESTION!! C'MON...
WHY DO THEY CALL YOU A "KNOWLEDGE WORKER"?

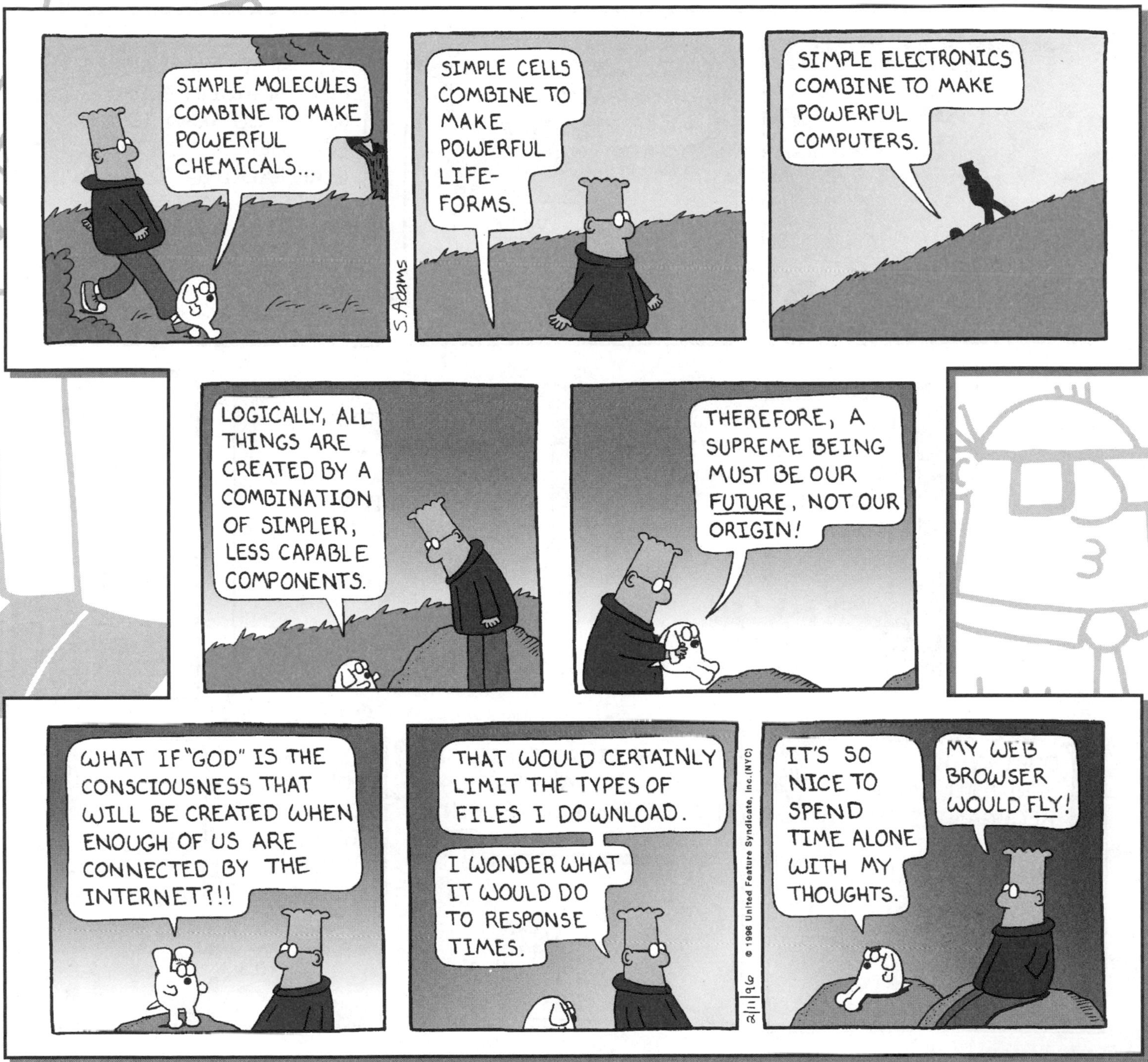
SIMPLE MOLECULES COMBINE TO MAKE POWERFUL CHEMICALS...
S. Adams
SIMPLE CELLS COMBINE TO MAKE POWERFUL LIFE-FORMS.
SIMPLE ELECTRONICS COMBINE TO MAKE POWERFUL COMPUTERS.
LOGICALLY, ALL THINGS ARE CREATED BY A COMBINATION OF SIMPLER, LESS CAPABLE COMPONENTS.
THEREFORE, A SUPREME BEING MUST BE OUR FUTURE, NOT OUR ORIGIN!
WHAT IF "GOD" IS THE CONSCIOUSNESS THAT WILL BE CREATED WHEN ENOUGH OF US ARE CONNECTED BY THE INTERNET?!!
THAT WOULD CERTAINLY LIMIT THE TYPES OF FILES I DOWNLOAD.
I WONDER WHAT IT WOULD DO TO RESPONSE TIMES.
© 1996 United Feature Syndicate, Inc.(NYC)
2/11/96
IT'S SO NICE TO SPEND TIME ALONE WITH MY THOUGHTS.
MY WEB BROWSER WOULD FLY!

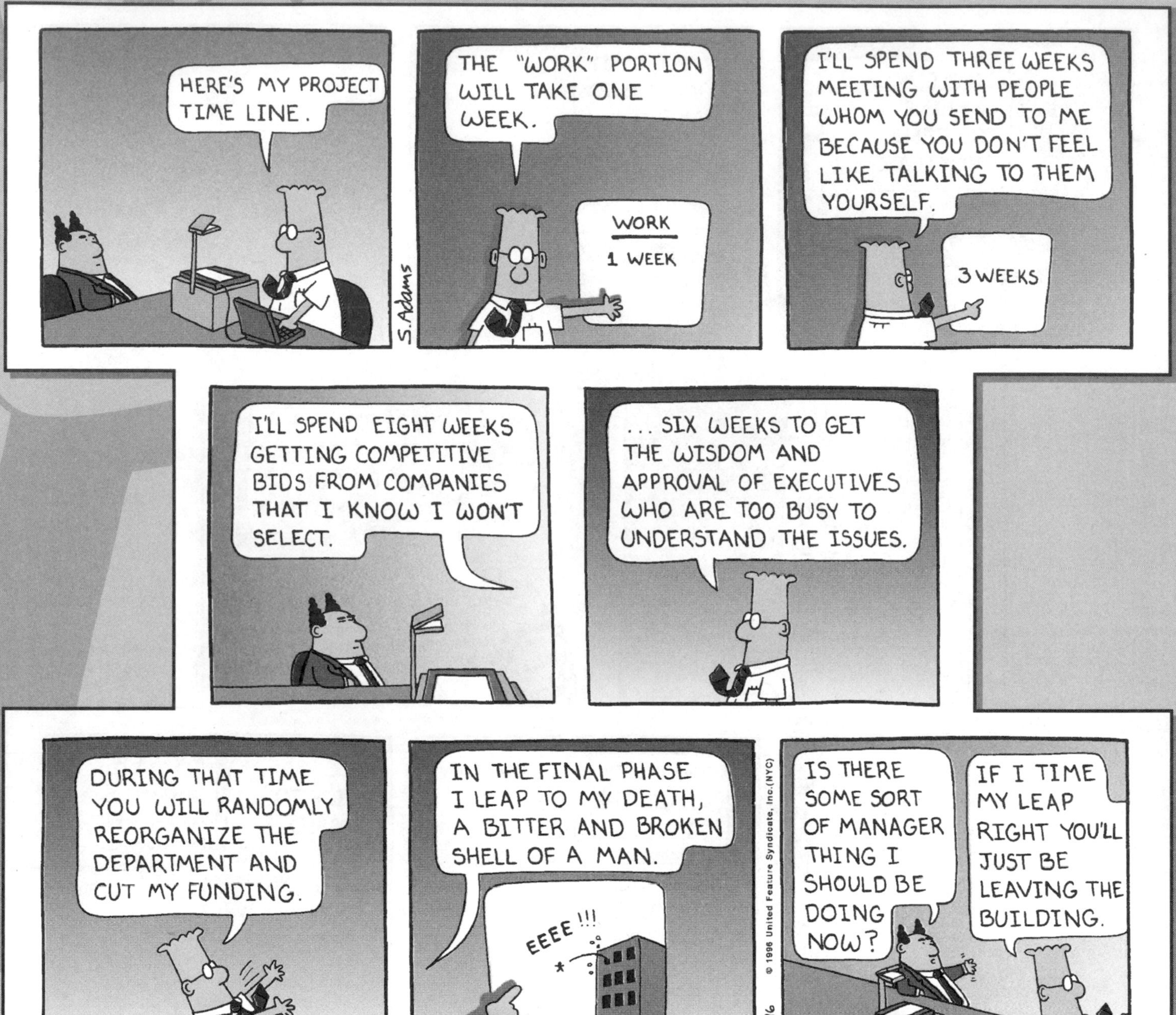
HERE'S MY PROJECT TIME LINE.
S. Adams
THE "WORK" PORTION WILL TAKE ONE WEEK.
WORK
1 WEEK
I'LL SPEND THREE WEEKS MEETING WITH PEOPLE WHOM YOU SEND TO ME BECAUSE YOU DON'T FEEL LIKE TALKING TO THEM YOURSELF.
3 WEEKS
I'LL SPEND EIGHT WEEKS GETTING COMPETITIVE BIDS FROM COMPANIES THAT I KNOW I WON'T SELECT.
. . . SIX WEEKS TO GET THE WISDOM AND APPROVAL OF EXECUTIVES WHO ARE TOO BUSY TO UNDERSTAND THE ISSUES.
DURING THAT TIME YOU WILL RANDOMLY REORGANIZE THE DEPARTMENT AND CUT MY FUNDING.
IN THE FINAL PHASE I LEAP TO MY DEATH, A BITTER AND BROKEN SHELL OF A MAN.
EEEE!!!
© 1996 United Feature Syndicate, Inc.(NYC)
2/18/96
IS THERE SOME SORT OF MANAGER THING I SHOULD BE DOING NOW?
IF I TIME MY LEAP RIGHT YOU'LL JUST BE LEAVING THE BUILDING.

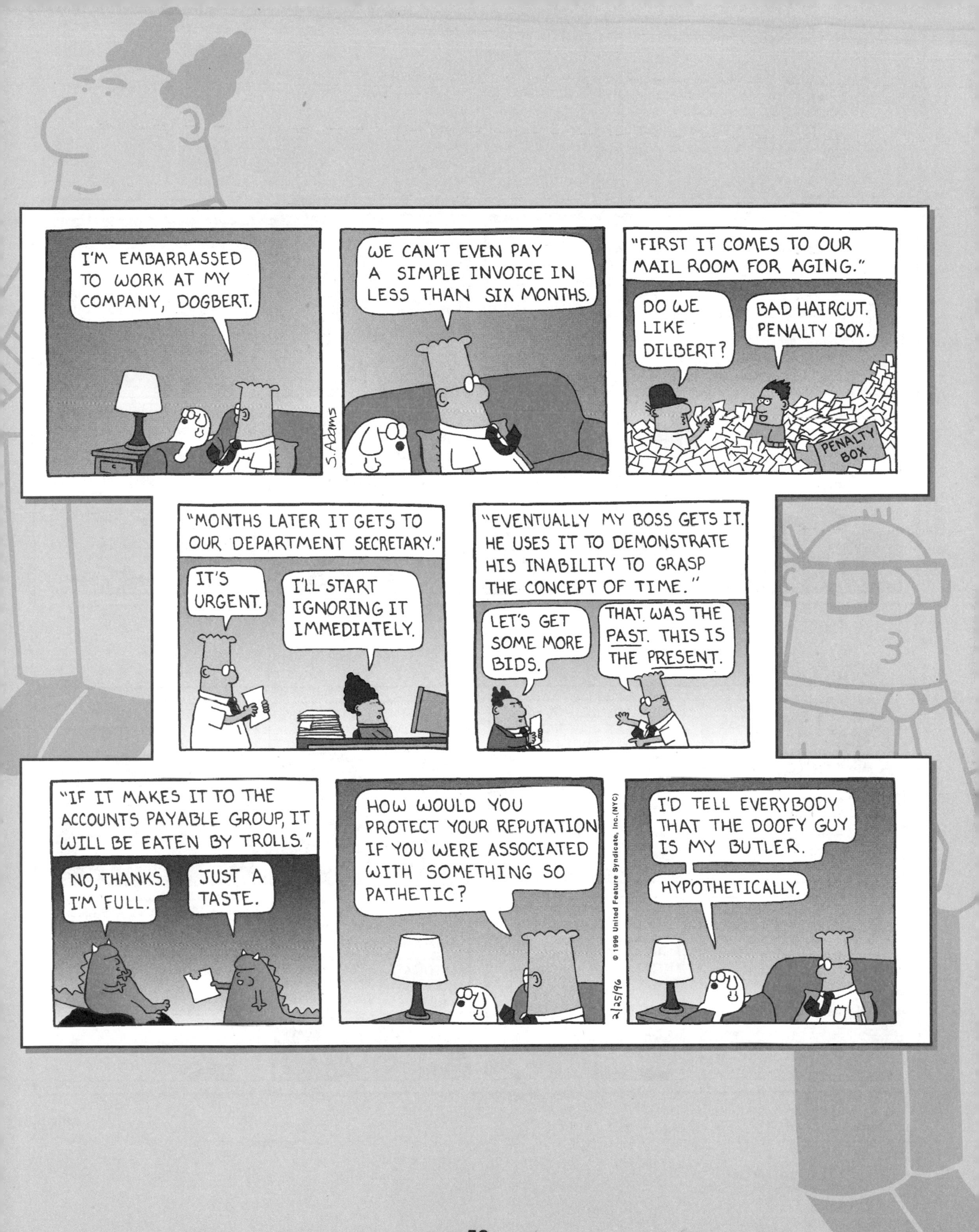

I'M EMBARRASSED TO WORK AT MY COMPANY, DOGBERT.
S. Adams
WE CAN'T EVEN PAY A SIMPLE INVOICE IN LESS THAN SIX MONTHS.
"FIRST IT COMES TO OUR MAIL ROOM FOR AGING."
DO WE LIKE DILBERT?
BAD HAIRCUT. PENALTY BOX.
PENALTY BOX
"MONTHS LATER IT GETS TO OUR DEPARTMENT SECRETARY."
IT'S URGENT.
I'LL START IGNORING IT IMMEDIATELY.
"EVENTUALLY MY BOSS GETS IT. HE USES IT TO DEMONSTRATE HIS INABILITY TO GRASP THE CONCEPT OF TIME."
LET'S GET SOME MORE BIDS.
THAT WAS THE PAST. THIS IS THE PRESENT.
"IF IT MAKES IT TO THE ACCOUNTS PAYABLE GROUP, IT WILL BE EATEN BY TROLLS."
NO, THANKS. I'M FULL.
JUST A TASTE.
HOW WOULD YOU PROTECT YOUR REPUTATION IF YOU WERE ASSOCIATED WITH SOMETHING SO PATHETIC?
2/25/96
© 1996 United Feature Syndicate, Inc.(NYC)
I'D TELL EVERYBODY THAT THE DOOFY GUY IS MY BUTLER.
HYPOTHETICALLY.

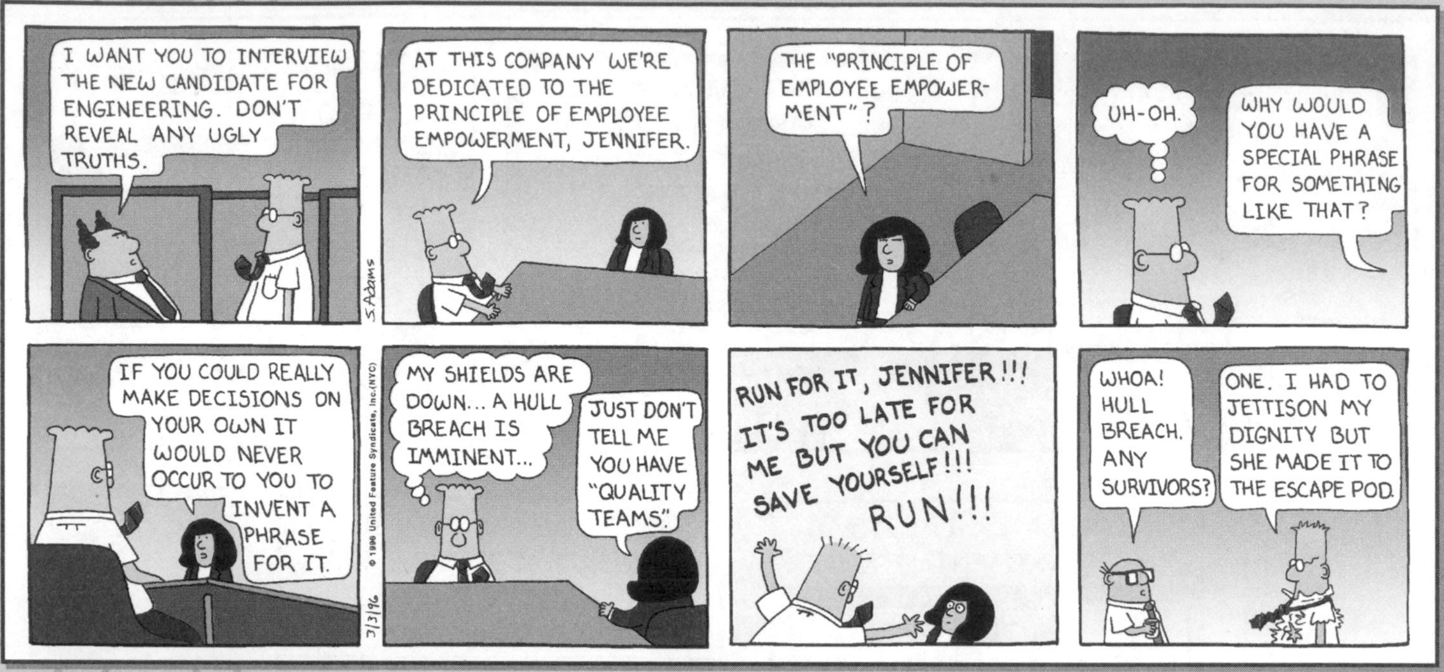
I WANT YOU TO INTERVIEW THE NEW CANDIDATE FOR ENGINEERING. DON'T REVEAL ANY UGLY TRUTHS.
AT THIS COMPANY WE'RE DEDICATED TO THE PRINCIPLE OF EMPLOYEE EMPOWERMENT, JENNIFER.
THE "PRINCIPLE OF EMPLOYEE EMPOWERMENT"?
UH-OH.
WHY WOULD YOU HAVE A SPECIAL PHRASE FOR SOMETHING LIKE THAT?
IF YOU COULD REALLY MAKE DECISIONS ON YOUR OWN IT WOULD NEVER OCCUR TO YOU TO INVENT A PHRASE FOR IT.
MY SHIELDS ARE DOWN... A HULL BREACH IS IMMINENT...
JUST DON'T TELL ME YOU HAVE "QUALITY TEAMS."
RUN FOR IT, JENNIFER!!! IT'S TOO LATE FOR ME BUT YOU CAN SAVE YOURSELF!!!
RUN!!!
WHOA! HULL BREACH. ANY SURVIVORS?
ONE. I HAD TO JETTISON MY DIGNITY BUT SHE MADE IT TO THE ESCAPE POD.
S. Adams
© 1996 United Feature Syndicate, Inc.(NYC)
3/3/96

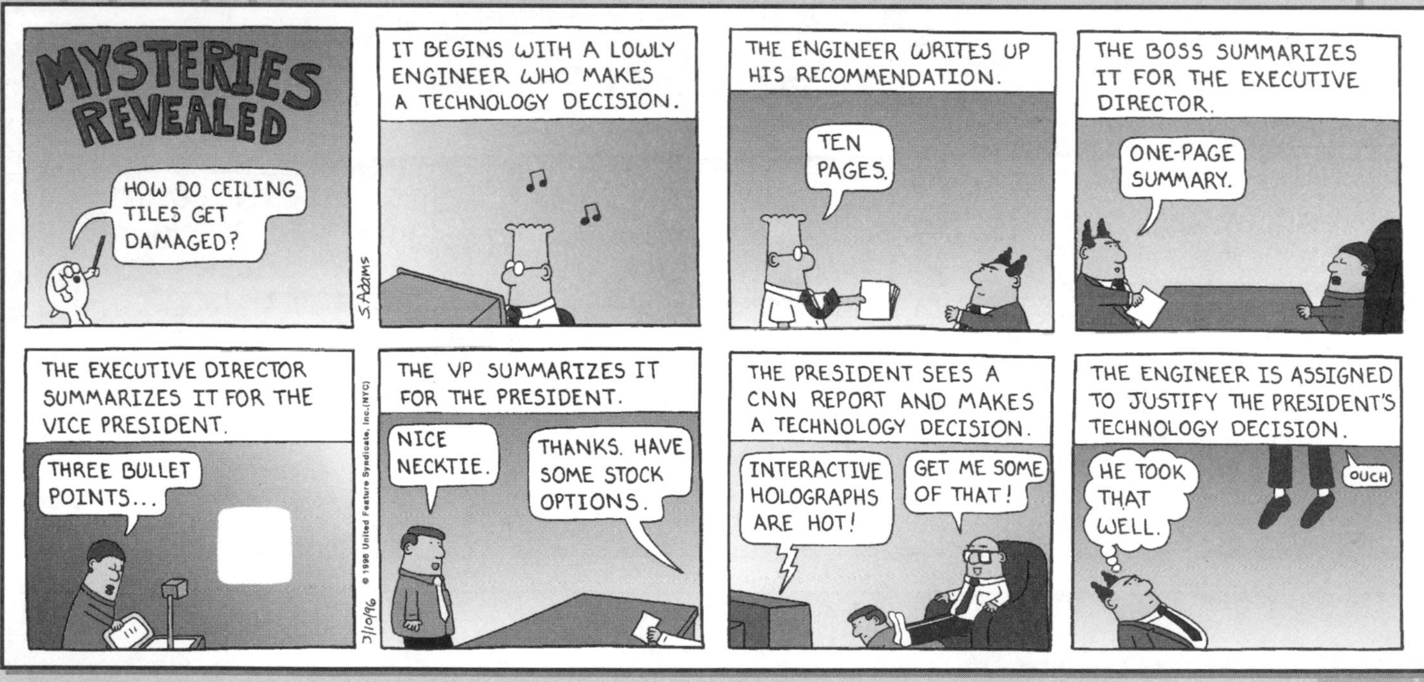
MYSTERIES REVEALED
HOW DO CEILING TILES GET DAMAGED?
IT BEGINS WITH A LOWLY ENGINEER WHO MAKES A TECHNOLOGY DECISION.
THE ENGINEER WRITES UP HIS RECOMMENDATION.
TEN PAGES.
THE BOSS SUMMARIZES IT FOR THE EXECUTIVE DIRECTOR.
ONE-PAGE SUMMARY.
THE EXECUTIVE DIRECTOR SUMMARIZES IT FOR THE VICE PRESIDENT.
THREE BULLET POINTS...
THE VP SUMMARIZES IT FOR THE PRESIDENT.
NICE NECKTIE.
THANKS. HAVE SOME STOCK OPTIONS.
THE PRESIDENT SEES A CNN REPORT AND MAKES A TECHNOLOGY DECISION.
INTERACTIVE HOLOGRAPHS ARE HOT!
GET ME SOME OF THAT!
THE ENGINEER IS ASSIGNED TO JUSTIFY THE PRESIDENT'S TECHNOLOGY DECISION.
HE TOOK THAT WELL.
OUCH
S. Adams
© 1996 United Feature Syndicate, Inc.(NYC)
3/10/96

I HAVE AN ETHICAL QUESTION, DOGBERT.
I'M HERE TO HELP.
S. Adams
IS IT BETTER TO GIVE CUSTOMERS A LOW QUALITY PRODUCT IN A TIMELY FASHION...
OR IS IT BETTER TO LIE ABOUT PRODUCT AVAILABILITY UNTIL THE BUGS ARE FIXED?
I WILL NEED MY ASSISTANT, RATBERT, TO ADDRESS YOUR ETHICAL QUESTION.
SNAP
LET'S SAY RATBERT IS A TRUSTING AND INNOCENT CUSTOMER.
SUPPOSE SOMEBODY ABUSES HIS TRUST LIKE THIS...
SMACK
3/17/96 © 1996 United Feature Syndicate, Inc.(NYC)
HOW DOES THIS RELATE TO MY SITUATION?
TO BE HONEST, I WASN'T LISTENING TO YOU.

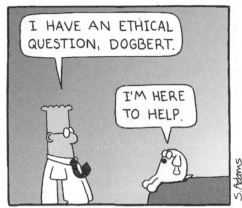

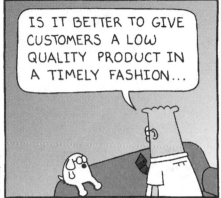

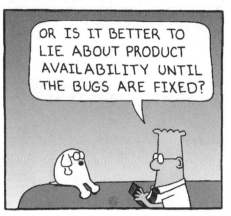

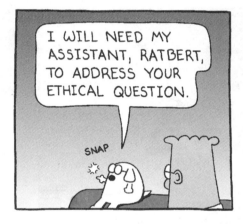

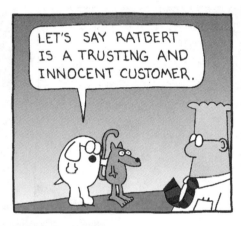

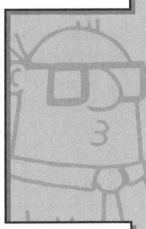

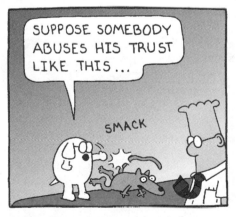

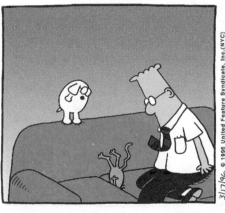

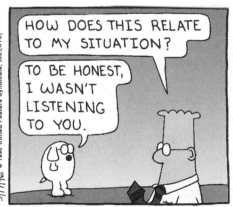

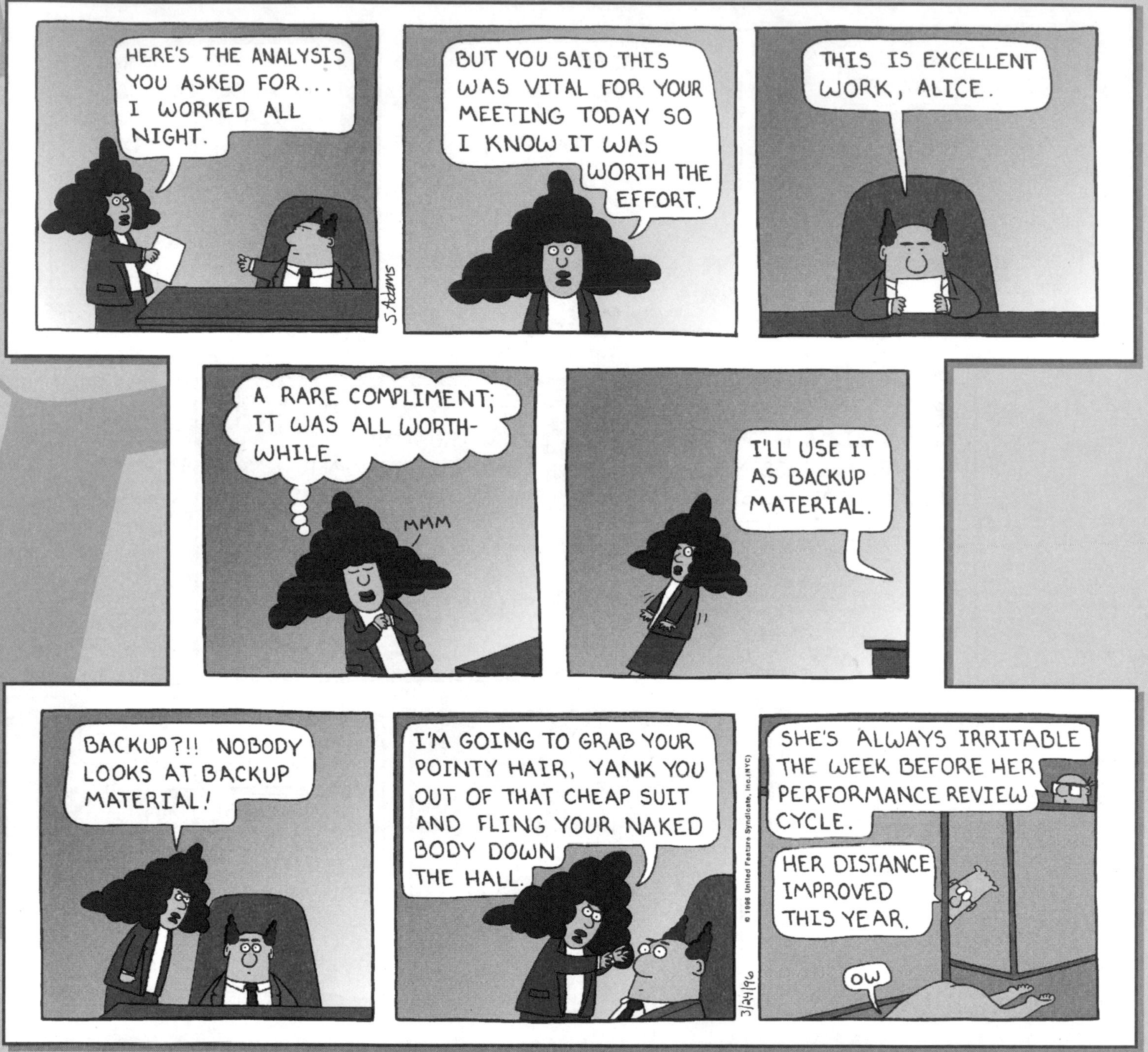
HERE'S THE ANALYSIS YOU ASKED FOR... I WORKED ALL NIGHT.
S. Adams
BUT YOU SAID THIS WAS VITAL FOR YOUR MEETING TODAY SO I KNOW IT WAS WORTH THE EFFORT.
THIS IS EXCELLENT WORK, ALICE.
A RARE COMPLIMENT; IT WAS ALL WORTH-WHILE.
MMM
I'LL USE IT AS BACKUP MATERIAL.
BACKUP?!! NOBODY LOOKS AT BACKUP MATERIAL!
I'M GOING TO GRAB YOUR POINTY HAIR, YANK YOU OUT OF THAT CHEAP SUIT AND FLING YOUR NAKED BODY DOWN THE HALL.
© 1996 United Feature Syndicate, Inc.(NYC)
3/24/96
SHE'S ALWAYS IRRITABLE THE WEEK BEFORE HER PERFORMANCE REVIEW CYCLE.
HER DISTANCE IMPROVED THIS YEAR.
OW

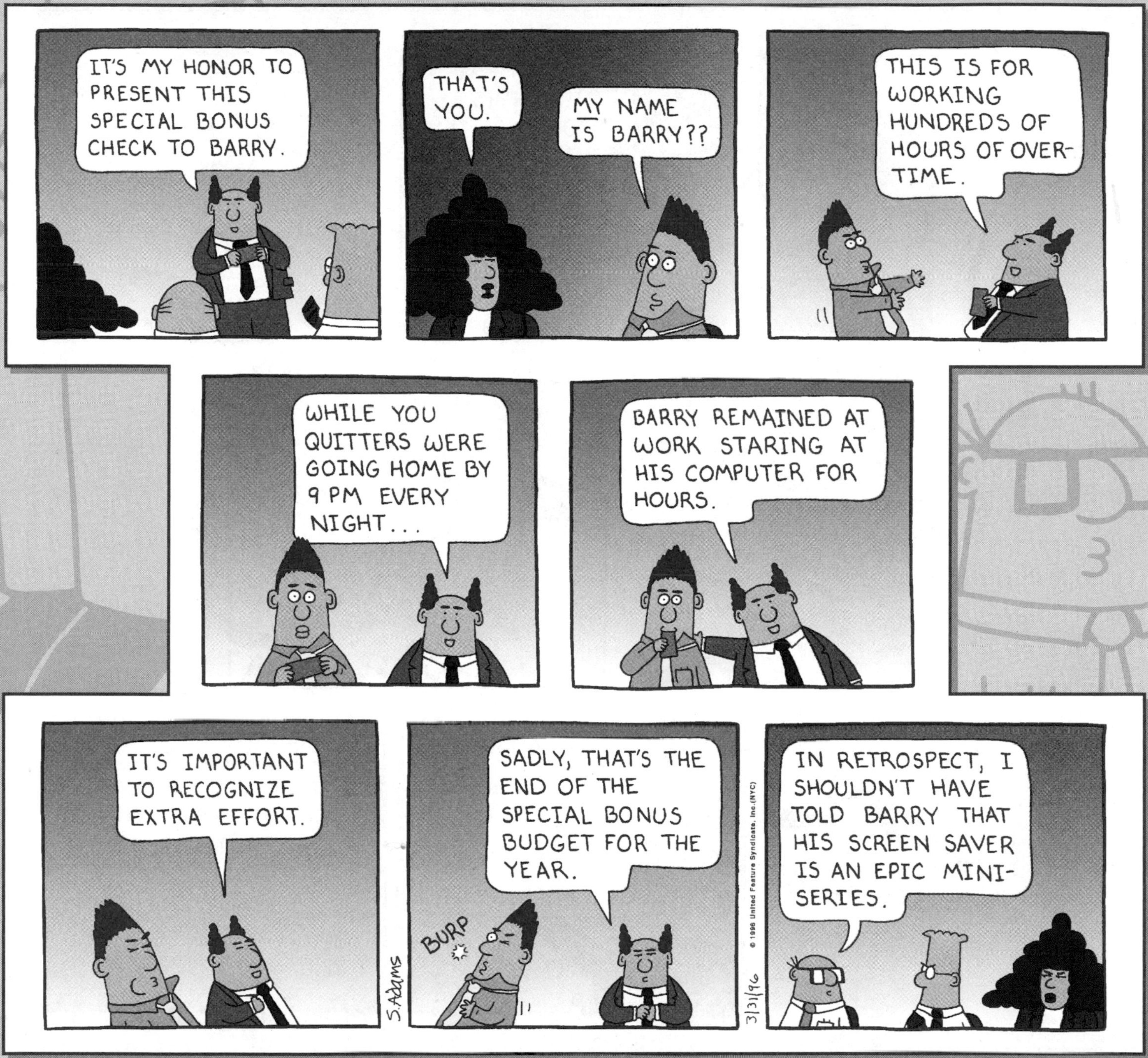
IT'S MY HONOR TO PRESENT THIS SPECIAL BONUS CHECK TO BARRY.
THAT'S YOU.
MY NAME IS BARRY??
THIS IS FOR WORKING HUNDREDS OF HOURS OF OVER-TIME.
WHILE YOU QUITTERS WERE GOING HOME BY 9 PM EVERY NIGHT...
BARRY REMAINED AT WORK STARING AT HIS COMPUTER FOR HOURS.
IT'S IMPORTANT TO RECOGNIZE EXTRA EFFORT.
S.Adams
BURP
SADLY, THAT'S THE END OF THE SPECIAL BONUS BUDGET FOR THE YEAR.
3/31/96
© 1996 United Feature Syndicate, Inc.(NYC)
IN RETROSPECT, I SHOULDN'T HAVE TOLD BARRY THAT HIS SCREEN SAVER IS AN EPIC MINI-SERIES.

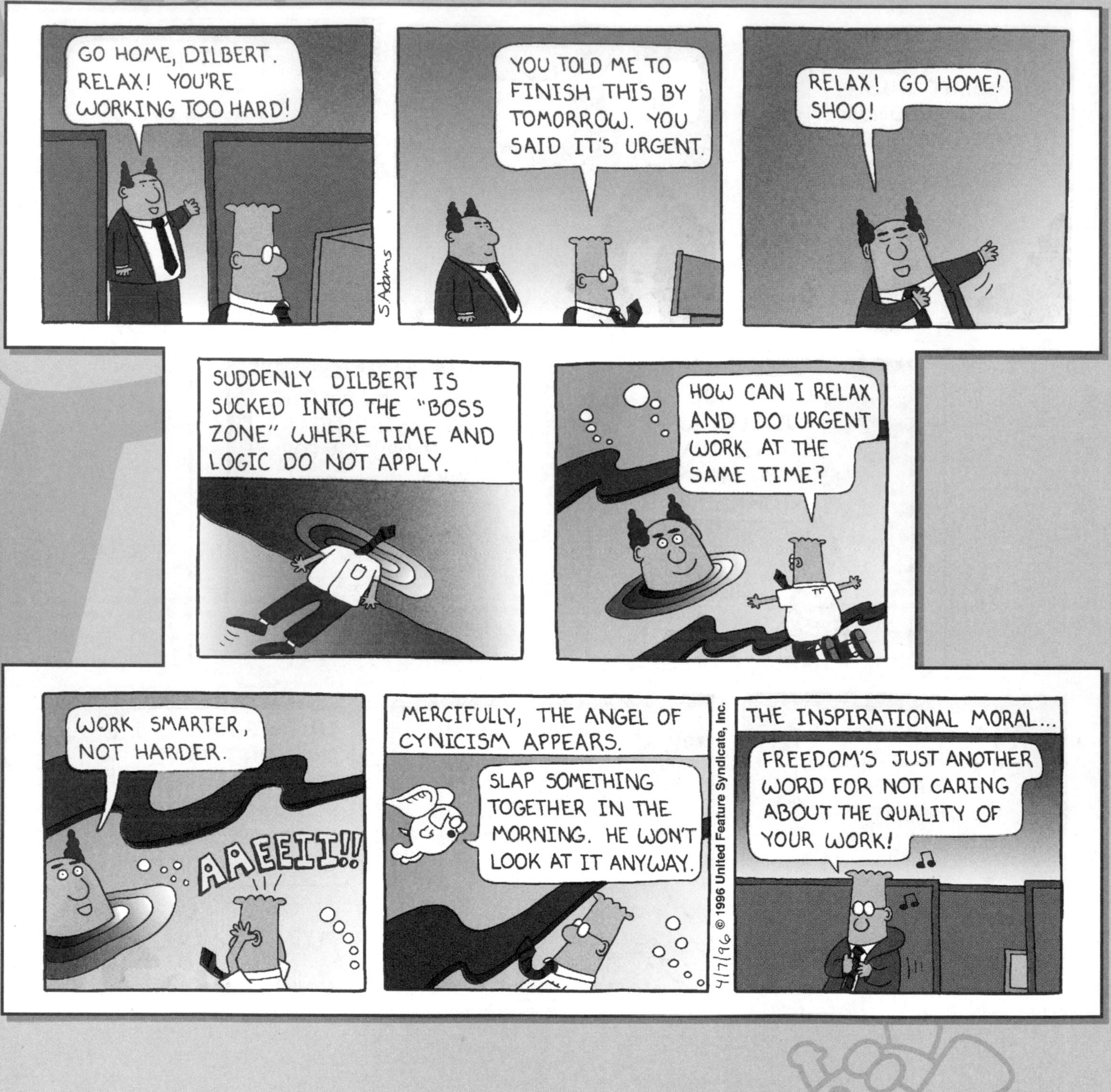

GO HOME, DILBERT. RELAX! YOU'RE WORKING TOO HARD!
S. Adams
YOU TOLD ME TO FINISH THIS BY TOMORROW. YOU SAID IT'S URGENT.
RELAX! GO HOME! SHOO!
SUDDENLY DILBERT IS SUCKED INTO THE "BOSS ZONE" WHERE TIME AND LOGIC DO NOT APPLY.
HOW CAN I RELAX AND DO URGENT WORK AT THE SAME TIME?
WORK SMARTER, NOT HARDER.
AAEEEII!!
MERCIFULLY, THE ANGEL OF CYNICISM APPEARS.
SLAP SOMETHING TOGETHER IN THE MORNING. HE WON'T LOOK AT IT ANYWAY.
4/7/96 © 1996 United Feature Syndicate, Inc.
THE INSPIRATIONAL MORAL...
FREEDOM'S JUST ANOTHER WORD FOR NOT CARING ABOUT THE QUALITY OF YOUR WORK!

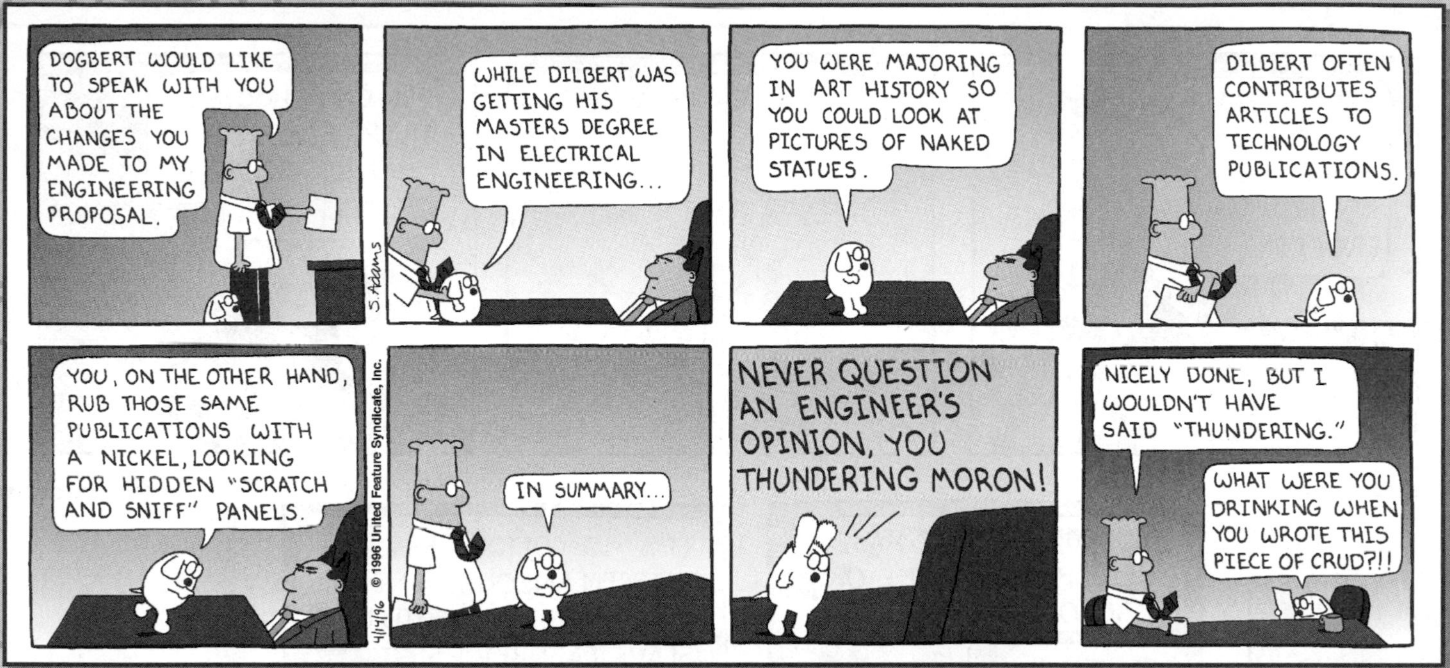
DOGBERT WOULD LIKE TO SPEAK WITH YOU ABOUT THE CHANGES YOU MADE TO MY ENGINEERING PROPOSAL.
S. Adams
WHILE DILBERT WAS GETTING HIS MASTERS DEGREE IN ELECTRICAL ENGINEERING...
YOU WERE MAJORING IN ART HISTORY SO YOU COULD LOOK AT PICTURES OF NAKED STATUES.
DILBERT OFTEN CONTRIBUTES ARTICLES TO TECHNOLOGY PUBLICATIONS.
YOU, ON THE OTHER HAND, RUB THOSE SAME PUBLICATIONS WITH A NICKEL, LOOKING FOR HIDDEN "SCRATCH AND SNIFF" PANELS.
4/14/96 © 1996 United Feature Syndicate, Inc.
IN SUMMARY...
NEVER QUESTION AN ENGINEER'S OPINION, YOU THUNDERING MORON!
NICELY DONE, BUT I WOULDN'T HAVE SAID "THUNDERING."
WHAT WERE YOU DRINKING WHEN YOU WROTE THIS PIECE OF CRUD?!!

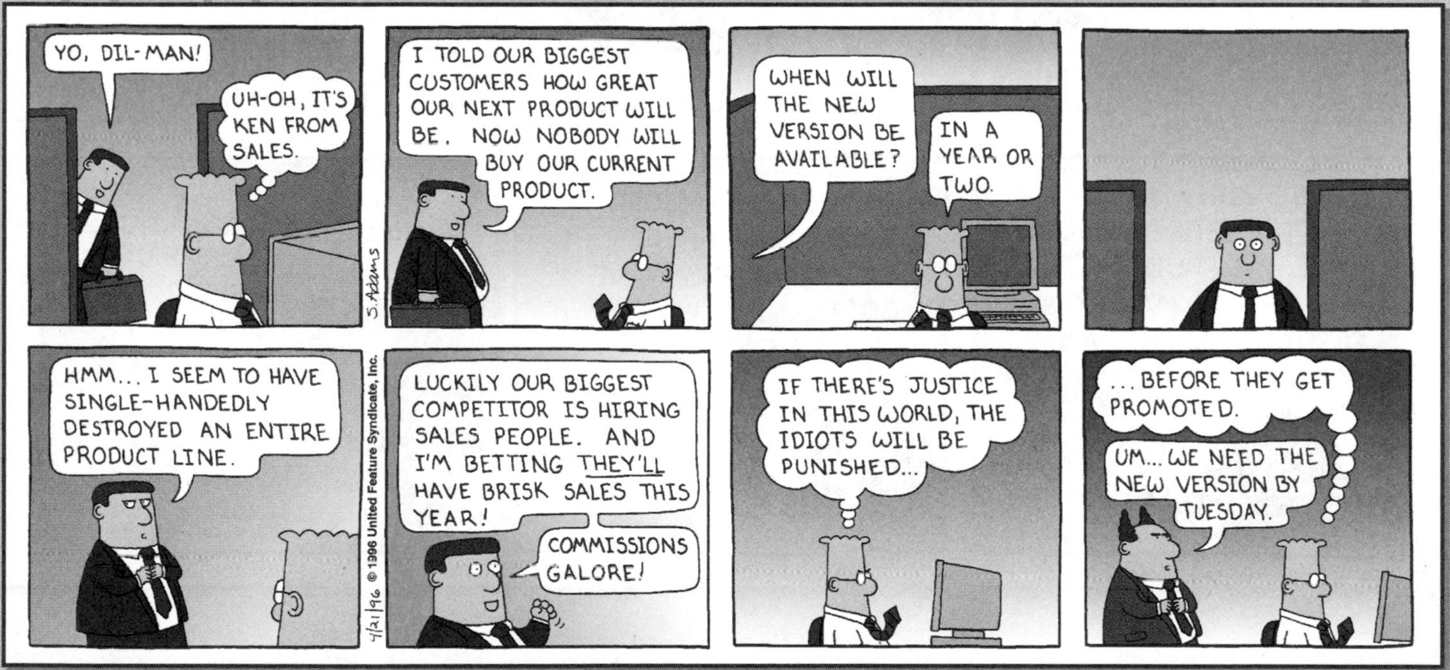
YO, DIL-MAN!
UH-OH, IT'S KEN FROM SALES.
S. Adams
I TOLD OUR BIGGEST CUSTOMERS HOW GREAT OUR NEXT PRODUCT WILL BE. NOW NOBODY WILL BUY OUR CURRENT PRODUCT.
WHEN WILL THE NEW VERSION BE AVAILABLE?
IN A YEAR OR TWO.
HMM... I SEEM TO HAVE SINGLE-HANDEDLY DESTROYED AN ENTIRE PRODUCT LINE.
4/21/96 © 1996 United Feature Syndicate, Inc.
LUCKILY OUR BIGGEST COMPETITOR IS HIRING SALES PEOPLE. AND I'M BETTING THEY'LL HAVE BRISK SALES THIS YEAR!
COMMISSIONS GALORE!
IF THERE'S JUSTICE IN THIS WORLD, THE IDIOTS WILL BE PUNISHED...
...BEFORE THEY GET PROMOTED.
UM... WE NEED THE NEW VERSION BY TUESDAY.

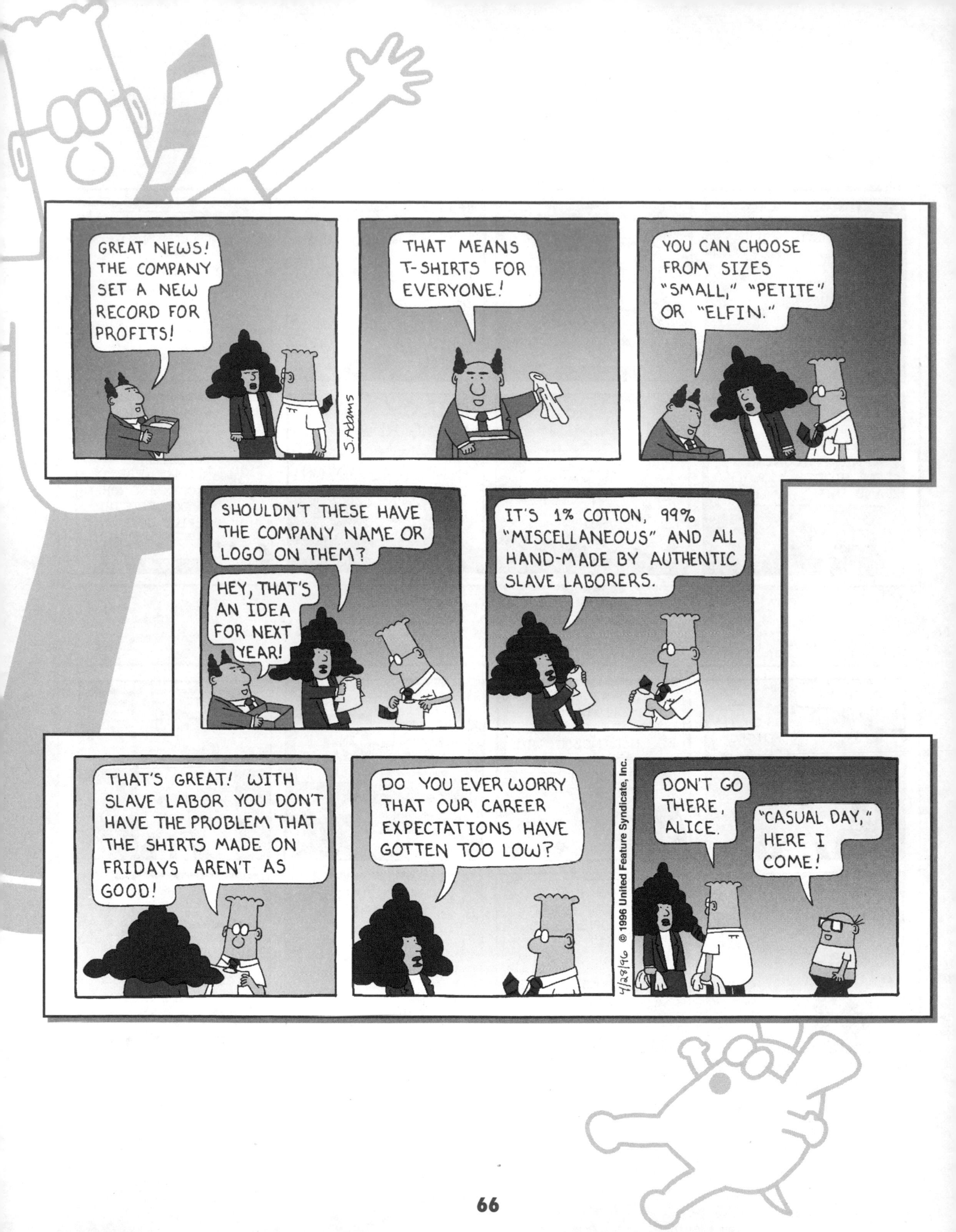

GREAT NEWS! THE COMPANY SET A NEW RECORD FOR PROFITS!
S. Adams
THAT MEANS T-SHIRTS FOR EVERYONE!
YOU CAN CHOOSE FROM SIZES "SMALL," "PETITE" OR "ELFIN."
SHOULDN'T THESE HAVE THE COMPANY NAME OR LOGO ON THEM?
HEY, THAT'S AN IDEA FOR NEXT YEAR!
IT'S 1% COTTON, 99% "MISCELLANEOUS" AND ALL HAND-MADE BY AUTHENTIC SLAVE LABORERS.
THAT'S GREAT! WITH SLAVE LABOR YOU DON'T HAVE THE PROBLEM THAT THE SHIRTS MADE ON FRIDAYS AREN'T AS GOOD!
DO YOU EVER WORRY THAT OUR CAREER EXPECTATIONS HAVE GOTTEN TOO LOW?
4/28/96 © 1996 United Feature Syndicate, Inc.
DON'T GO THERE, ALICE.
"CASUAL DAY," HERE I COME!

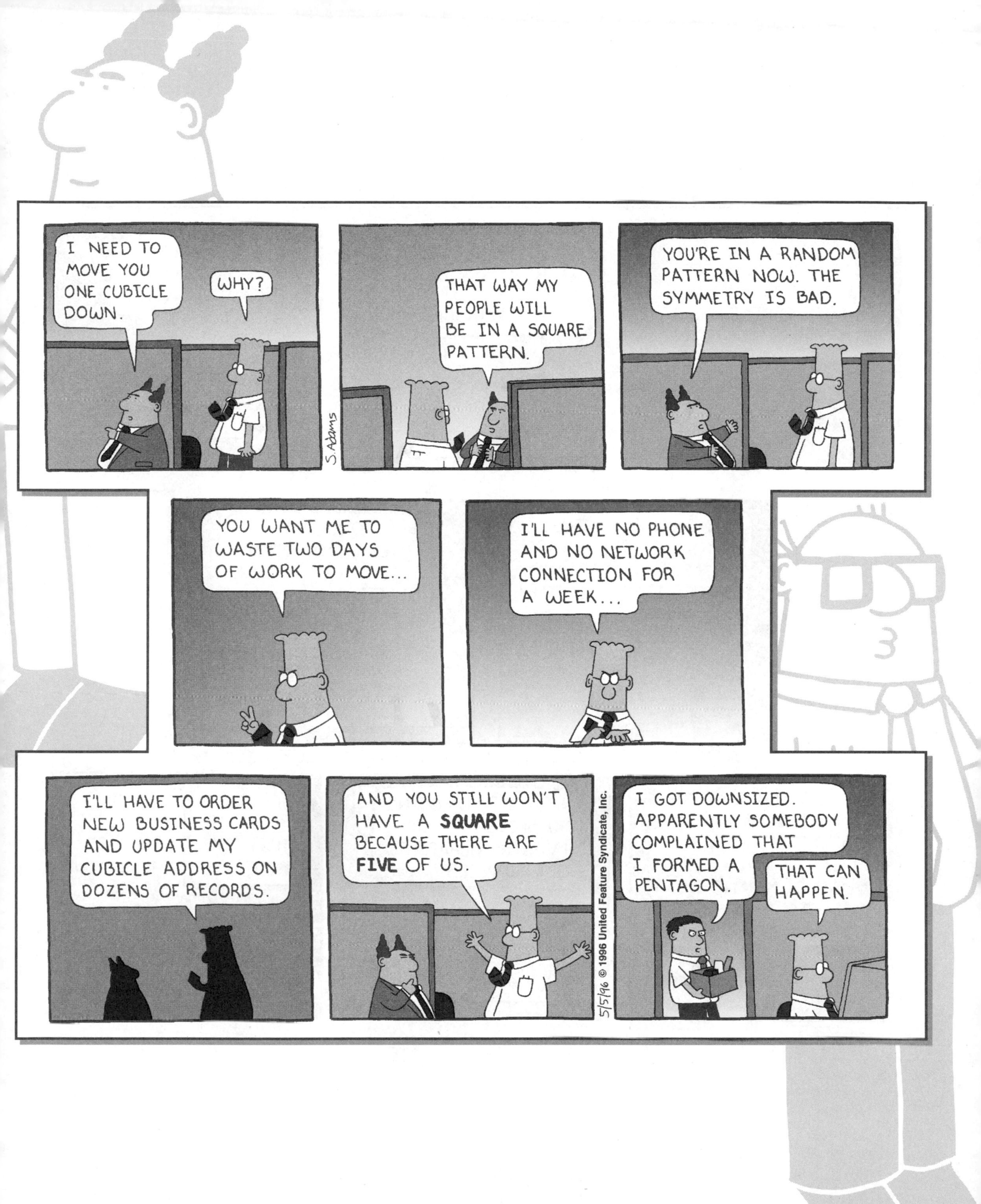
I NEED TO MOVE YOU ONE CUBICLE DOWN.
WHY?
S. Adams
THAT WAY MY PEOPLE WILL BE IN A SQUARE PATTERN.
YOU'RE IN A RANDOM PATTERN NOW. THE SYMMETRY IS BAD.
YOU WANT ME TO WASTE TWO DAYS OF WORK TO MOVE...
I'LL HAVE NO PHONE AND NO NETWORK CONNECTION FOR A WEEK...
I'LL HAVE TO ORDER NEW BUSINESS CARDS AND UPDATE MY CUBICLE ADDRESS ON DOZENS OF RECORDS.
AND YOU STILL WON'T HAVE A **SQUARE** BECAUSE THERE ARE **FIVE** OF US.
5/5/96 © 1996 United Feature Syndicate, Inc.
I GOT DOWNSIZED. APPARENTLY SOMEBODY COMPLAINED THAT I FORMED A PENTAGON.
THAT CAN HAPPEN.

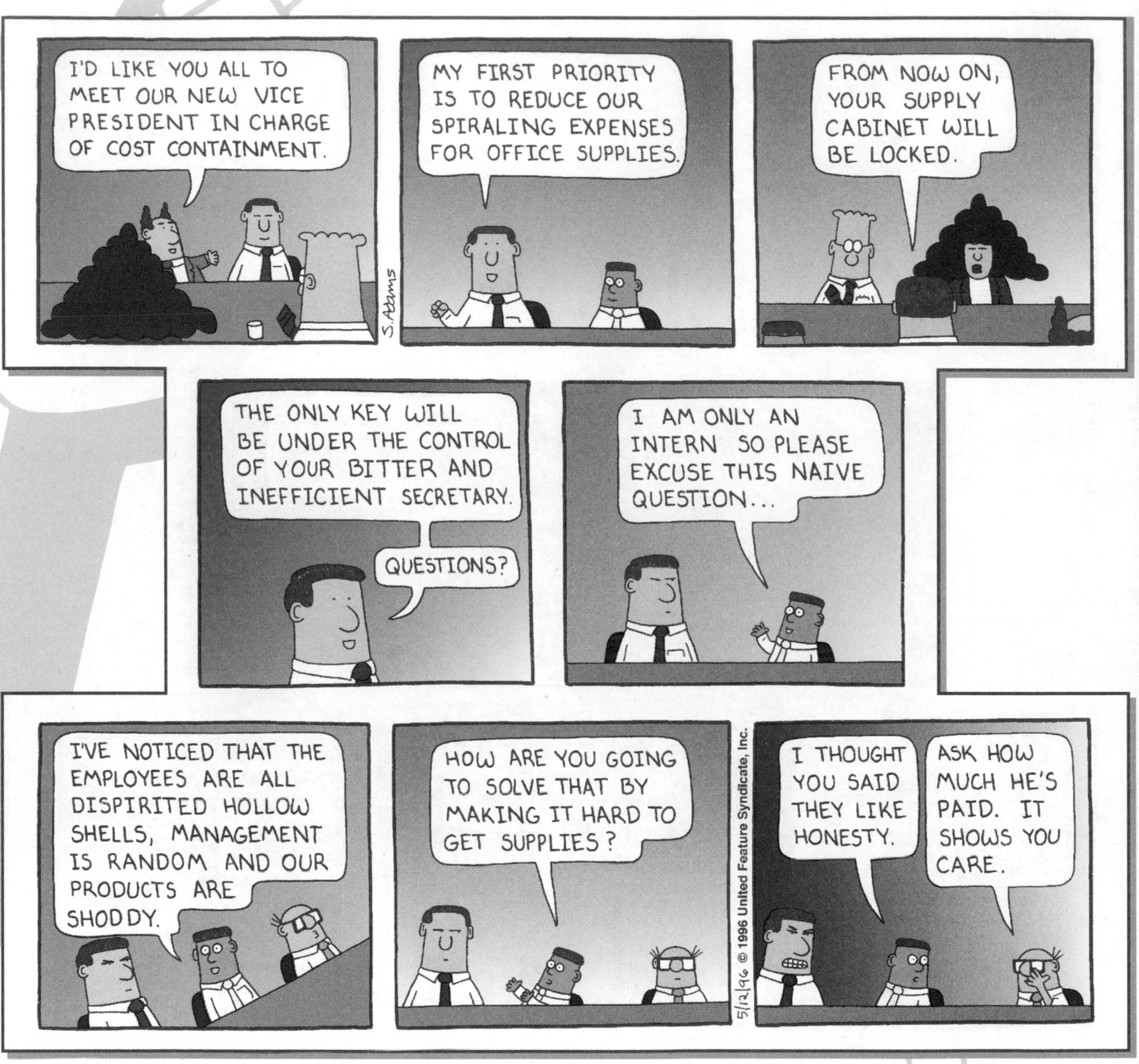
I'D LIKE YOU ALL TO MEET OUR NEW VICE PRESIDENT IN CHARGE OF COST CONTAINMENT.
S. Adams
MY FIRST PRIORITY IS TO REDUCE OUR SPIRALING EXPENSES FOR OFFICE SUPPLIES.
FROM NOW ON, YOUR SUPPLY CABINET WILL BE LOCKED.
THE ONLY KEY WILL BE UNDER THE CONTROL OF YOUR BITTER AND INEFFICIENT SECRETARY.
QUESTIONS?
I AM ONLY AN INTERN SO PLEASE EXCUSE THIS NAIVE QUESTION...
I'VE NOTICED THAT THE EMPLOYEES ARE ALL DISPIRITED HOLLOW SHELLS, MANAGEMENT IS RANDOM AND OUR PRODUCTS ARE SHODDY.
HOW ARE YOU GOING TO SOLVE THAT BY MAKING IT HARD TO GET SUPPLIES?
5/12/96 © 1996 United Feature Syndicate, Inc.
I THOUGHT YOU SAID THEY LIKE HONESTY.
ASK HOW MUCH HE'S PAID. IT SHOWS YOU CARE.

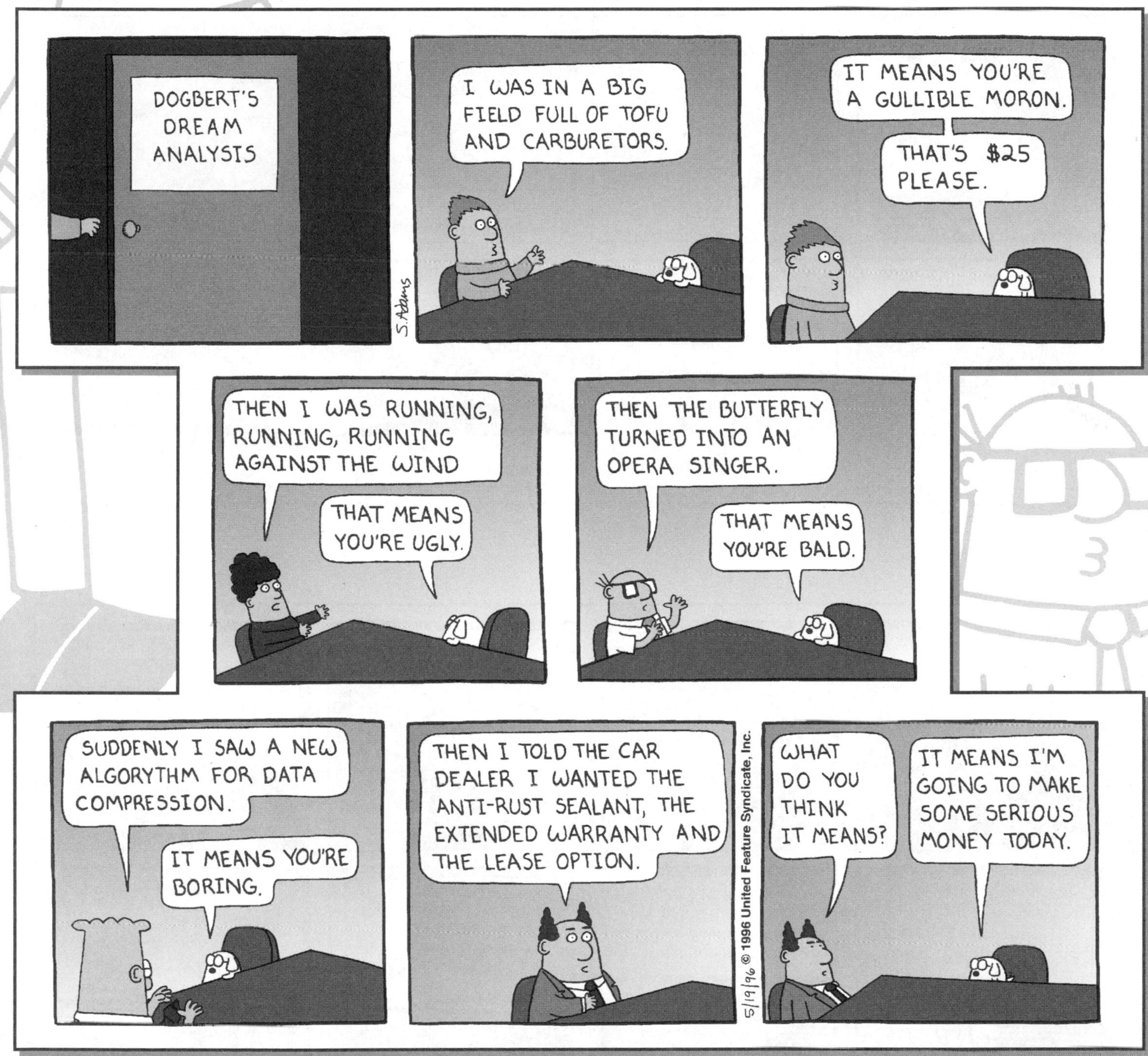
DOGBERT'S DREAM ANALYSIS
S. Adams
I WAS IN A BIG FIELD FULL OF TOFU AND CARBURETORS.
IT MEANS YOU'RE A GULLIBLE MORON.
THAT'S $25 PLEASE.
THEN I WAS RUNNING, RUNNING, RUNNING AGAINST THE WIND
THAT MEANS YOU'RE UGLY.
THEN THE BUTTERFLY TURNED INTO AN OPERA SINGER.
THAT MEANS YOU'RE BALD.
SUDDENLY I SAW A NEW ALGORYTHM FOR DATA COMPRESSION.
IT MEANS YOU'RE BORING.
THEN I TOLD THE CAR DEALER I WANTED THE ANTI-RUST SEALANT, THE EXTENDED WARRANTY AND THE LEASE OPTION.
5/19/96 © 1996 United Feature Syndicate, Inc.
WHAT DO YOU THINK IT MEANS?
IT MEANS I'M GOING TO MAKE SOME SERIOUS MONEY TODAY.

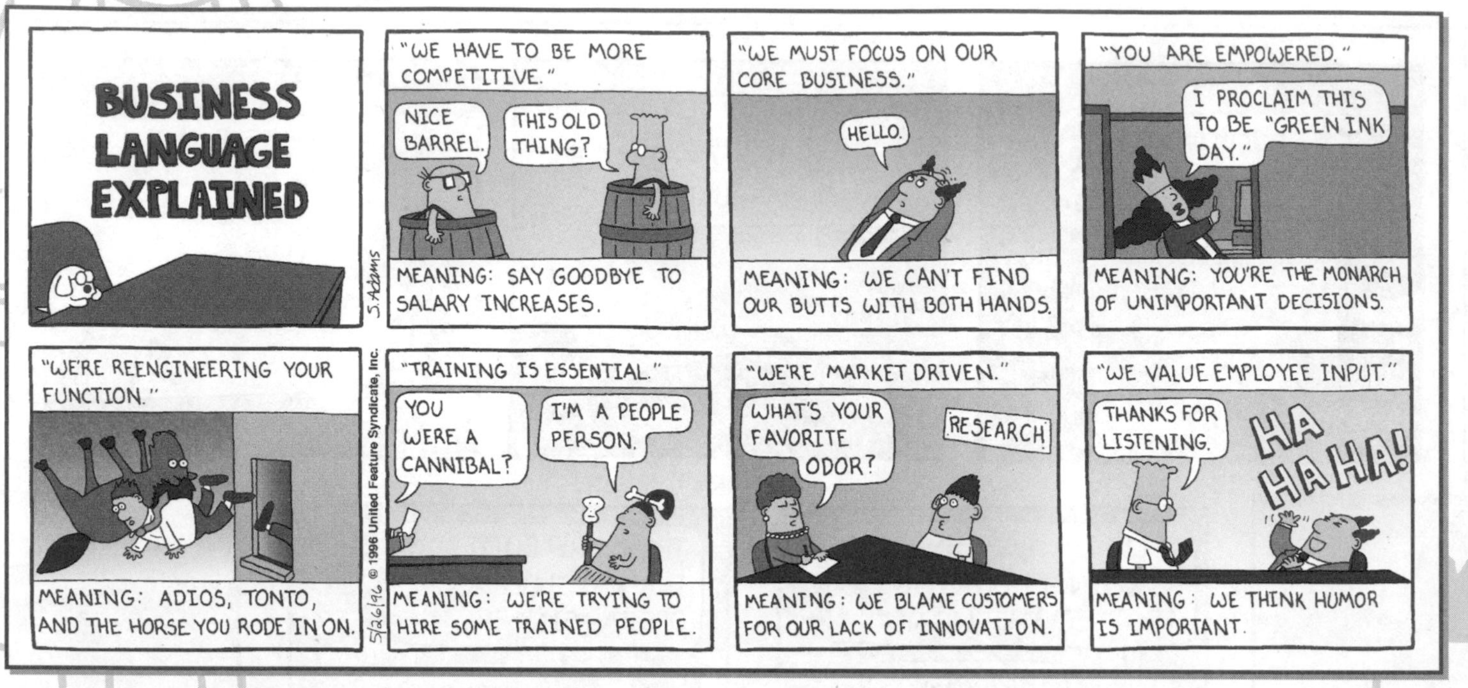
BUSINESS LANGUAGE EXPLAINED
S. Adams
"WE HAVE TO BE MORE COMPETITIVE."
NICE BARREL.
THIS OLD THING?
MEANING: SAY GOODBYE TO SALARY INCREASES.
"WE MUST FOCUS ON OUR CORE BUSINESS."
HELLO.
MEANING: WE CAN'T FIND OUR BUTTS WITH BOTH HANDS.
"YOU ARE EMPOWERED."
I PROCLAIM THIS TO BE "GREEN INK DAY."
MEANING: YOU'RE THE MONARCH OF UNIMPORTANT DECISIONS.
"WE'RE REENGINEERING YOUR FUNCTION."
MEANING: ADIOS, TONTO, AND THE HORSE YOU RODE IN ON.
5/26/96 © 1996 United Feature Syndicate, Inc.
"TRAINING IS ESSENTIAL."
YOU WERE A CANNIBAL?
I'M A PEOPLE PERSON.
MEANING: WE'RE TRYING TO HIRE SOME TRAINED PEOPLE.
"WE'RE MARKET DRIVEN."
WHAT'S YOUR FAVORITE ODOR?
RESEARCH
MEANING: WE BLAME CUSTOMERS FOR OUR LACK OF INNOVATION.
"WE VALUE EMPLOYEE INPUT."
THANKS FOR LISTENING.
HA HA HA!
MEANING: WE THINK HUMOR IS IMPORTANT.

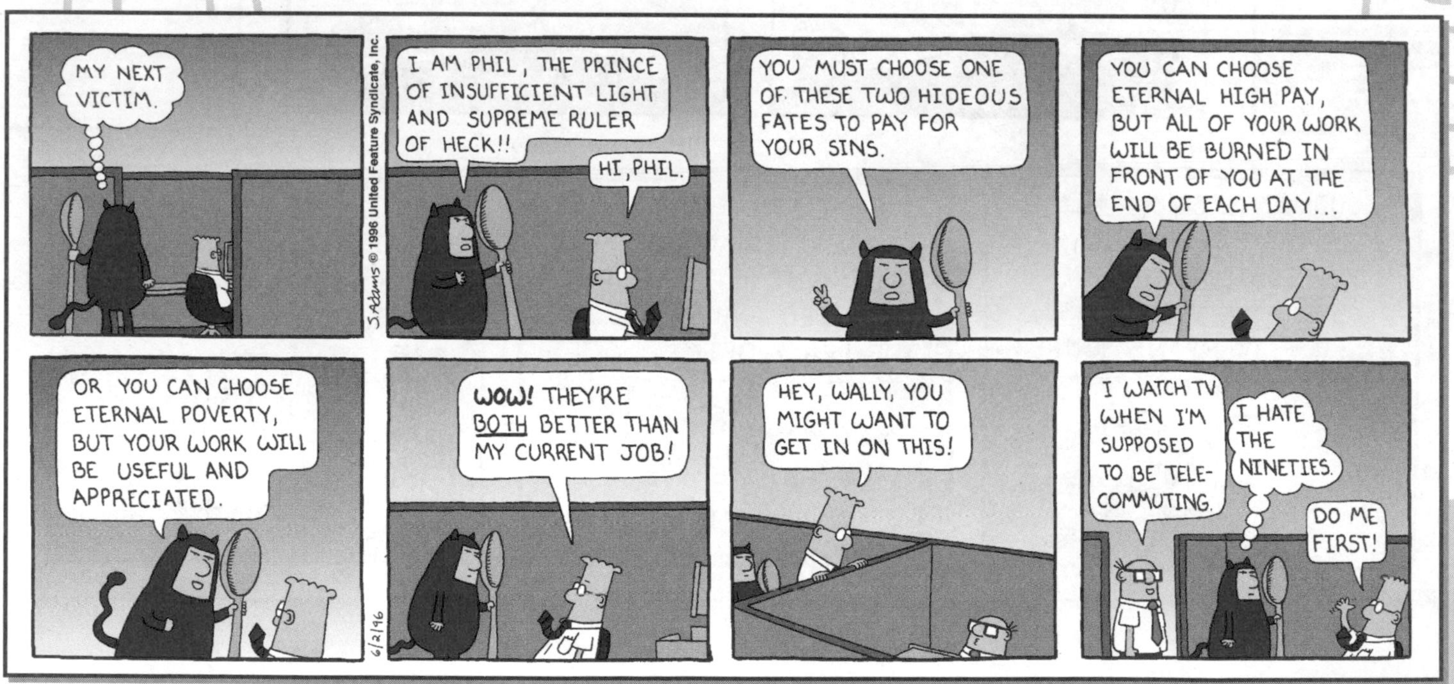
MY NEXT VICTIM.
S. Adams © 1996 United Feature Syndicate, Inc.
I AM PHIL, THE PRINCE OF INSUFFICIENT LIGHT AND SUPREME RULER OF HECK!!
HI, PHIL.
YOU MUST CHOOSE ONE OF THESE TWO HIDEOUS FATES TO PAY FOR YOUR SINS.
YOU CAN CHOOSE ETERNAL HIGH PAY, BUT ALL OF YOUR WORK WILL BE BURNED IN FRONT OF YOU AT THE END OF EACH DAY...
OR YOU CAN CHOOSE ETERNAL POVERTY, BUT YOUR WORK WILL BE USEFUL AND APPRECIATED.
6/2/96
WOW! THEY'RE BOTH BETTER THAN MY CURRENT JOB!
HEY, WALLY, YOU MIGHT WANT TO GET IN ON THIS!
I WATCH TV WHEN I'M SUPPOSED TO BE TELE-COMMUTING.
I HATE THE NINETIES.
DO ME FIRST!

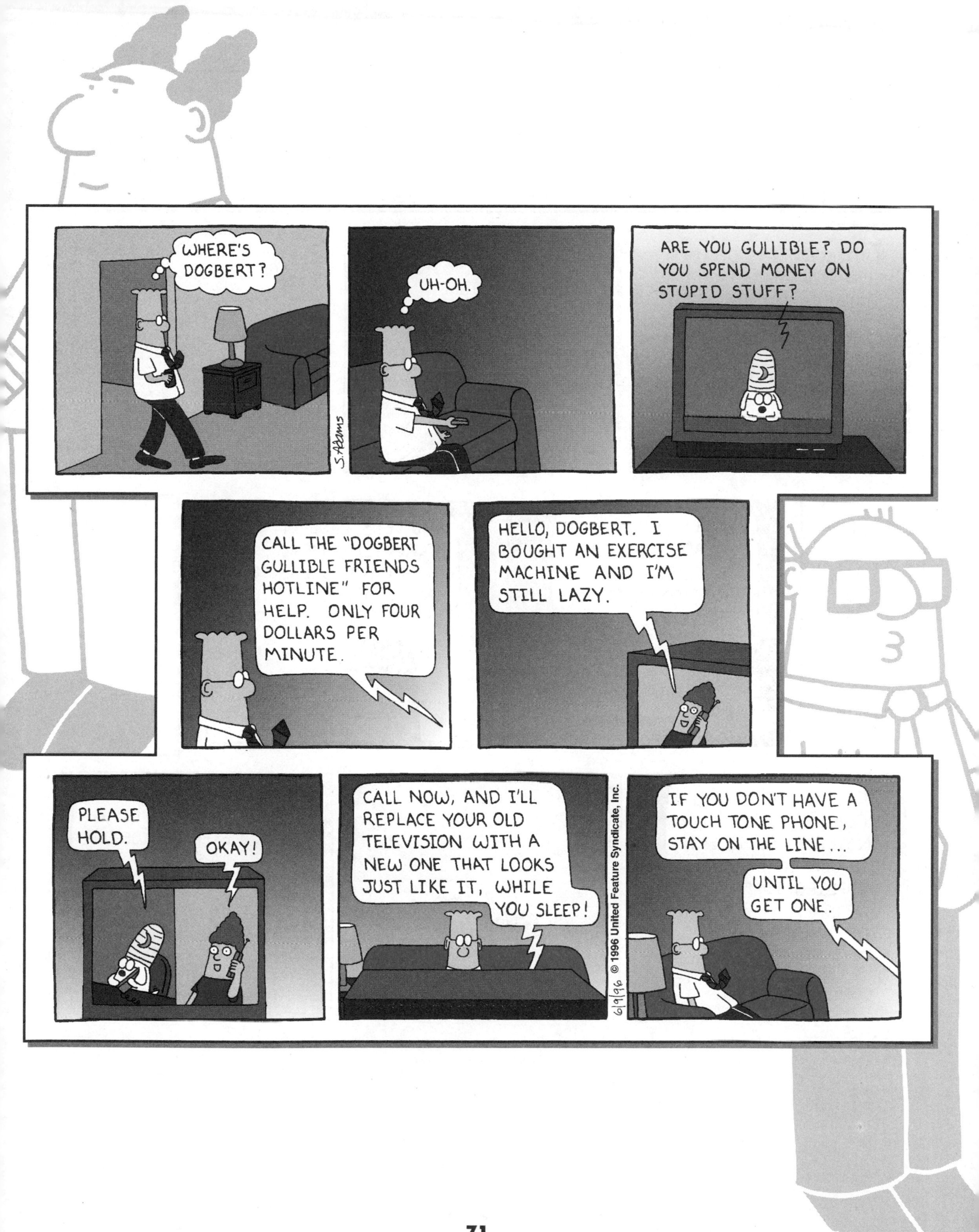

WHERE'S DOGBERT?
S. Adams
UH-OH.
ARE YOU GULLIBLE? DO YOU SPEND MONEY ON STUPID STUFF?
CALL THE "DOGBERT GULLIBLE FRIENDS HOTLINE" FOR HELP. ONLY FOUR DOLLARS PER MINUTE.
HELLO, DOGBERT. I BOUGHT AN EXERCISE MACHINE AND I'M STILL LAZY.
PLEASE HOLD.
OKAY!
CALL NOW, AND I'LL REPLACE YOUR OLD TELEVISION WITH A NEW ONE THAT LOOKS JUST LIKE IT, WHILE YOU SLEEP!
6/9/96 © 1996 United Feature Syndicate, Inc.
IF YOU DON'T HAVE A TOUCH TONE PHONE, STAY ON THE LINE...
UNTIL YOU GET ONE.

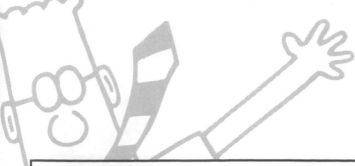

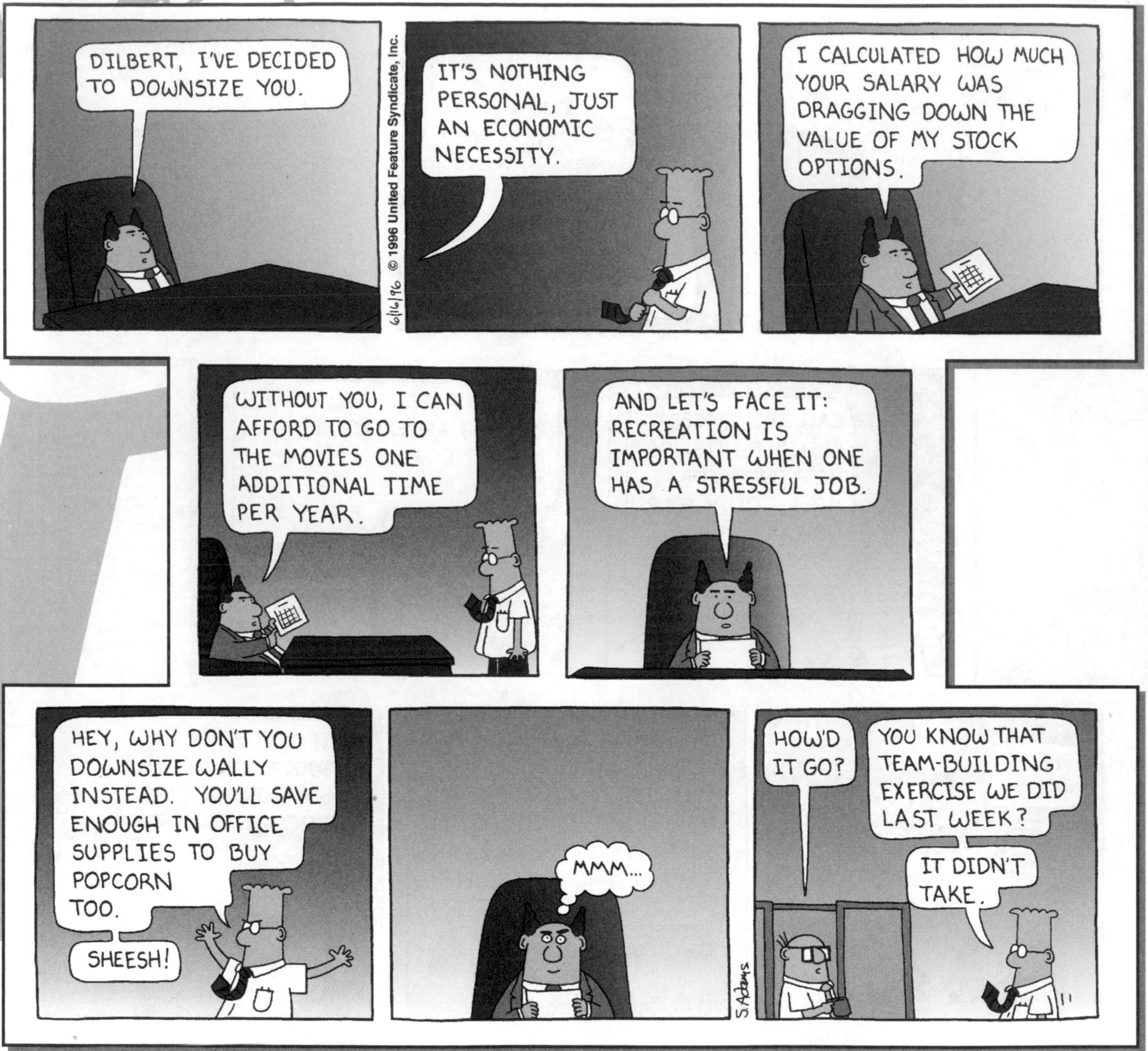
DILBERT, I'VE DECIDED TO DOWNSIZE YOU.
6/16/96 © 1996 United Feature Syndicate, Inc.
IT'S NOTHING PERSONAL, JUST AN ECONOMIC NECESSITY.
I CALCULATED HOW MUCH YOUR SALARY WAS DRAGGING DOWN THE VALUE OF MY STOCK OPTIONS.
WITHOUT YOU, I CAN AFFORD TO GO TO THE MOVIES ONE ADDITIONAL TIME PER YEAR.
AND LET'S FACE IT: RECREATION IS IMPORTANT WHEN ONE HAS A STRESSFUL JOB.
HEY, WHY DON'T YOU DOWNSIZE WALLY INSTEAD. YOU'LL SAVE ENOUGH IN OFFICE SUPPLIES TO BUY POPCORN TOO.
SHEESH!
MMM...
S. Adams
HOW'D IT GO?
YOU KNOW THAT TEAM-BUILDING EXERCISE WE DID LAST WEEK?
IT DIDN'T TAKE.

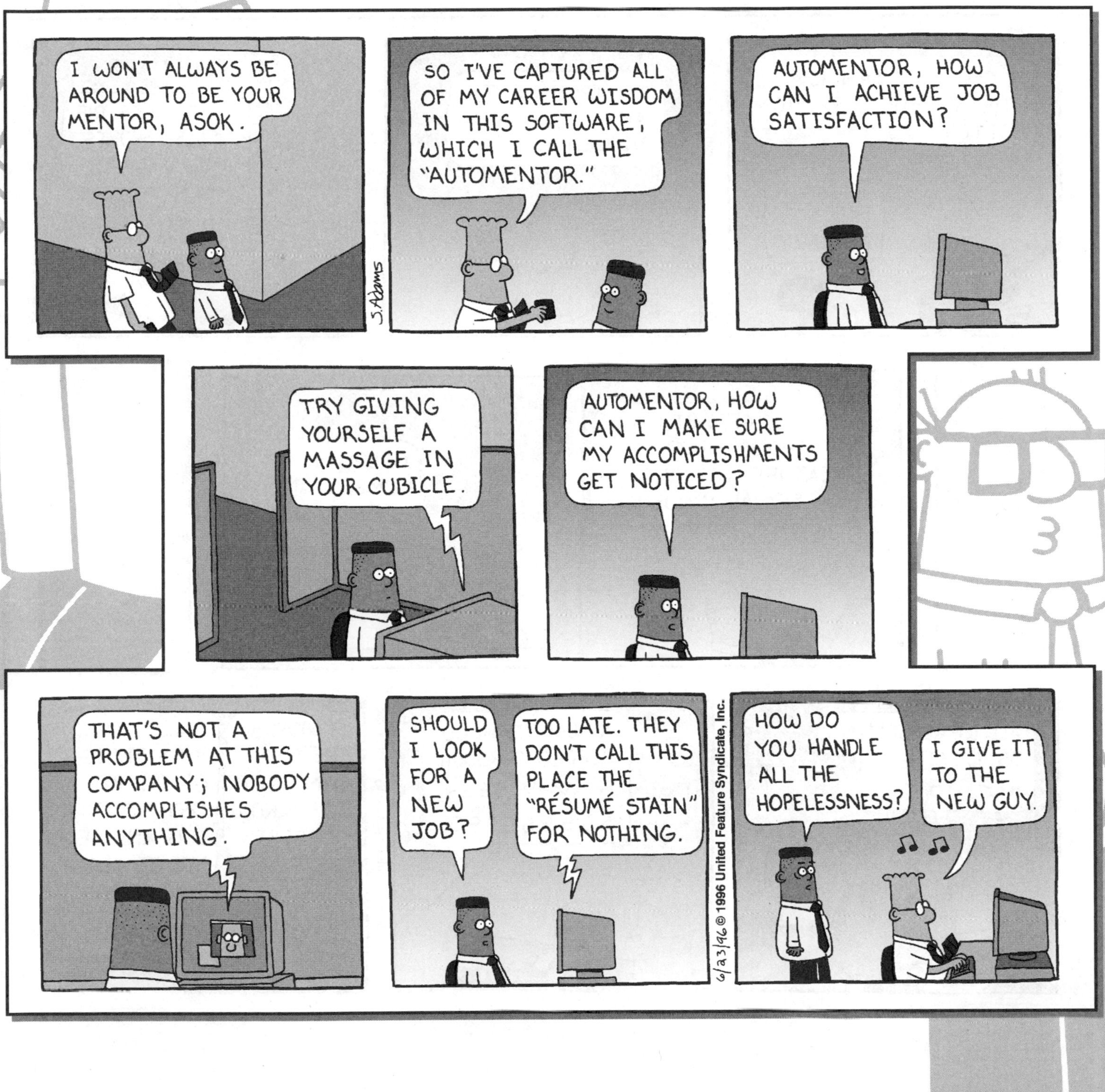
I WON'T ALWAYS BE AROUND TO BE YOUR MENTOR, ASOK.
SO I'VE CAPTURED ALL OF MY CAREER WISDOM IN THIS SOFTWARE, WHICH I CALL THE "AUTOMENTOR."
AUTOMENTOR, HOW CAN I ACHIEVE JOB SATISFACTION?
TRY GIVING YOURSELF A MASSAGE IN YOUR CUBICLE.
AUTOMENTOR, HOW CAN I MAKE SURE MY ACCOMPLISHMENTS GET NOTICED?
THAT'S NOT A PROBLEM AT THIS COMPANY; NOBODY ACCOMPLISHES ANYTHING.
SHOULD I LOOK FOR A NEW JOB?
TOO LATE. THEY DON'T CALL THIS PLACE THE "RÉSUMÉ STAIN" FOR NOTHING.
HOW DO YOU HANDLE ALL THE HOPELESSNESS?
I GIVE IT TO THE NEW GUY.
S. Adams
6/23/96 © 1996 United Feature Syndicate, Inc.

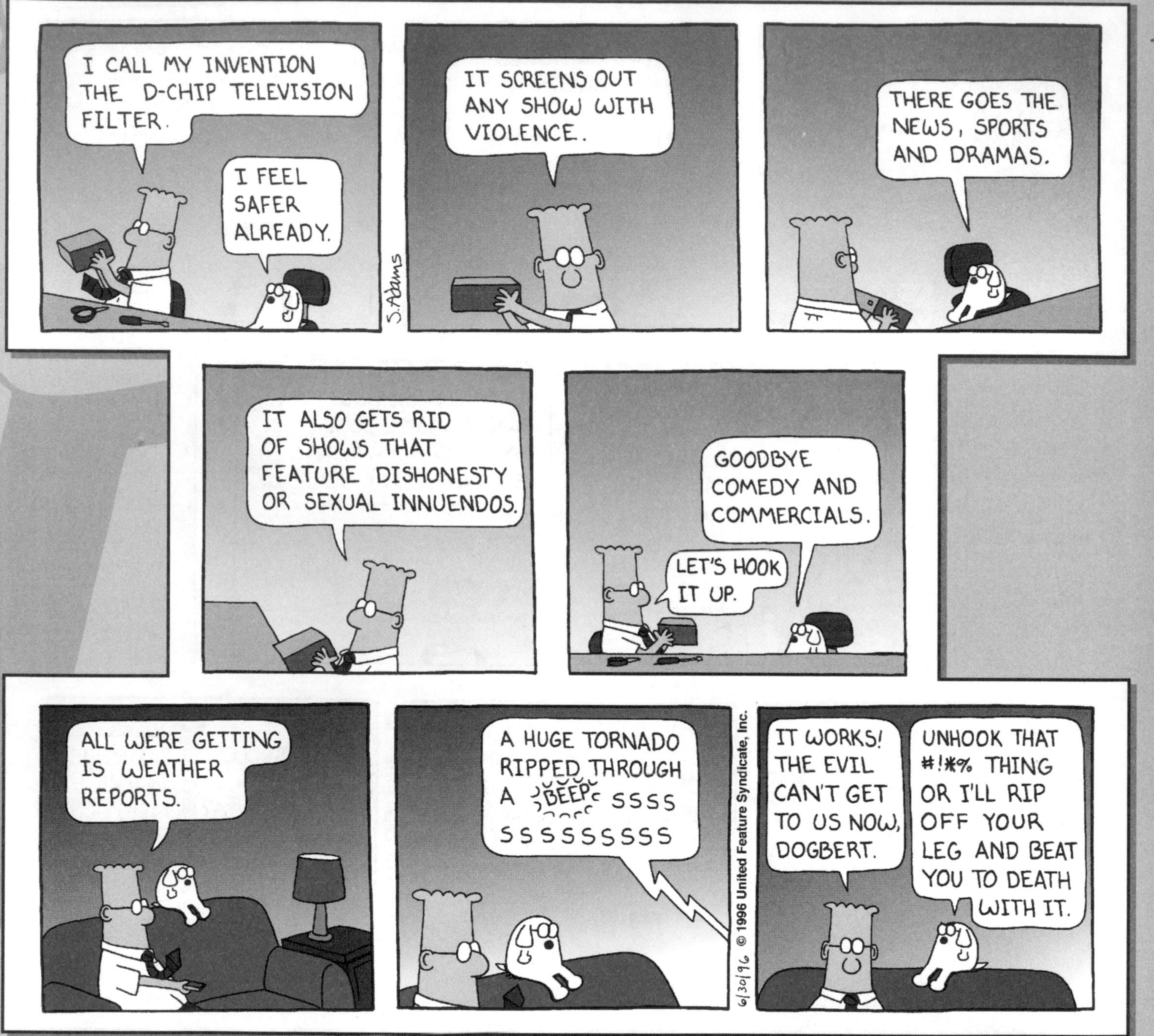
I CALL MY INVENTION THE D-CHIP TELEVISION FILTER.
I FEEL SAFER ALREADY.
S. Adams
IT SCREENS OUT ANY SHOW WITH VIOLENCE.
THERE GOES THE NEWS, SPORTS AND DRAMAS.
IT ALSO GETS RID OF SHOWS THAT FEATURE DISHONESTY OR SEXUAL INNUENDOS.
GOODBYE COMEDY AND COMMERCIALS.
LET'S HOOK IT UP.
ALL WE'RE GETTING IS WEATHER REPORTS.
A HUGE TORNADO RIPPED THROUGH A BEEP SSSS SSSSSSSSS
6/30/96 © 1996 United Feature Syndicate, Inc.
IT WORKS! THE EVIL CAN'T GET TO US NOW, DOGBERT.
UNHOOK THAT #!*% THING OR I'LL RIP OFF YOUR LEG AND BEAT YOU TO DEATH WITH IT.

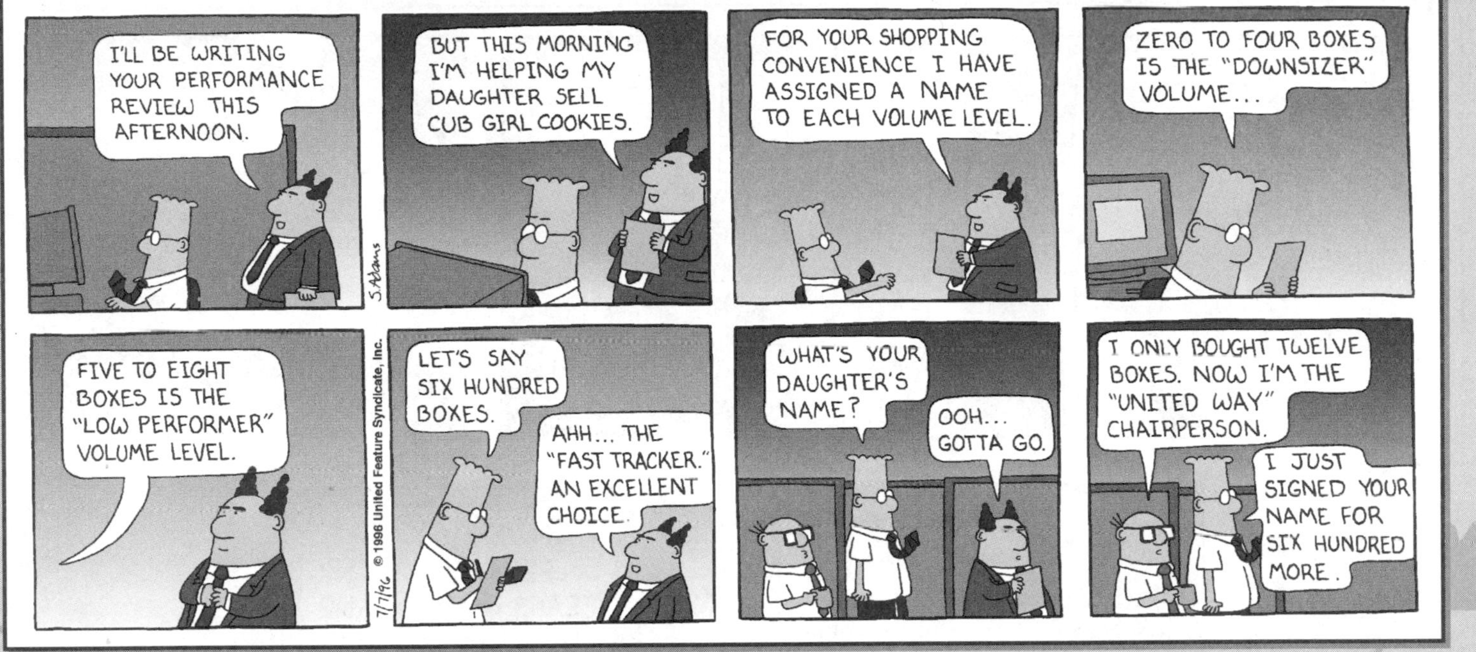
I'LL BE WRITING YOUR PERFORMANCE REVIEW THIS AFTERNOON.
BUT THIS MORNING I'M HELPING MY DAUGHTER SELL CUB GIRL COOKIES.
FOR YOUR SHOPPING CONVENIENCE I HAVE ASSIGNED A NAME TO EACH VOLUME LEVEL.
ZERO TO FOUR BOXES IS THE "DOWNSIZER" VOLUME...
FIVE TO EIGHT BOXES IS THE "LOW PERFORMER" VOLUME LEVEL.
LET'S SAY SIX HUNDRED BOXES.
AHH... THE "FAST TRACKER." AN EXCELLENT CHOICE.
WHAT'S YOUR DAUGHTER'S NAME?
OOH... GOTTA GO.
I ONLY BOUGHT TWELVE BOXES. NOW I'M THE "UNITED WAY" CHAIRPERSON.
I JUST SIGNED YOUR NAME FOR SIX HUNDRED MORE.
S. Adams
7/7/96 © 1996 United Feature Syndicate, Inc.

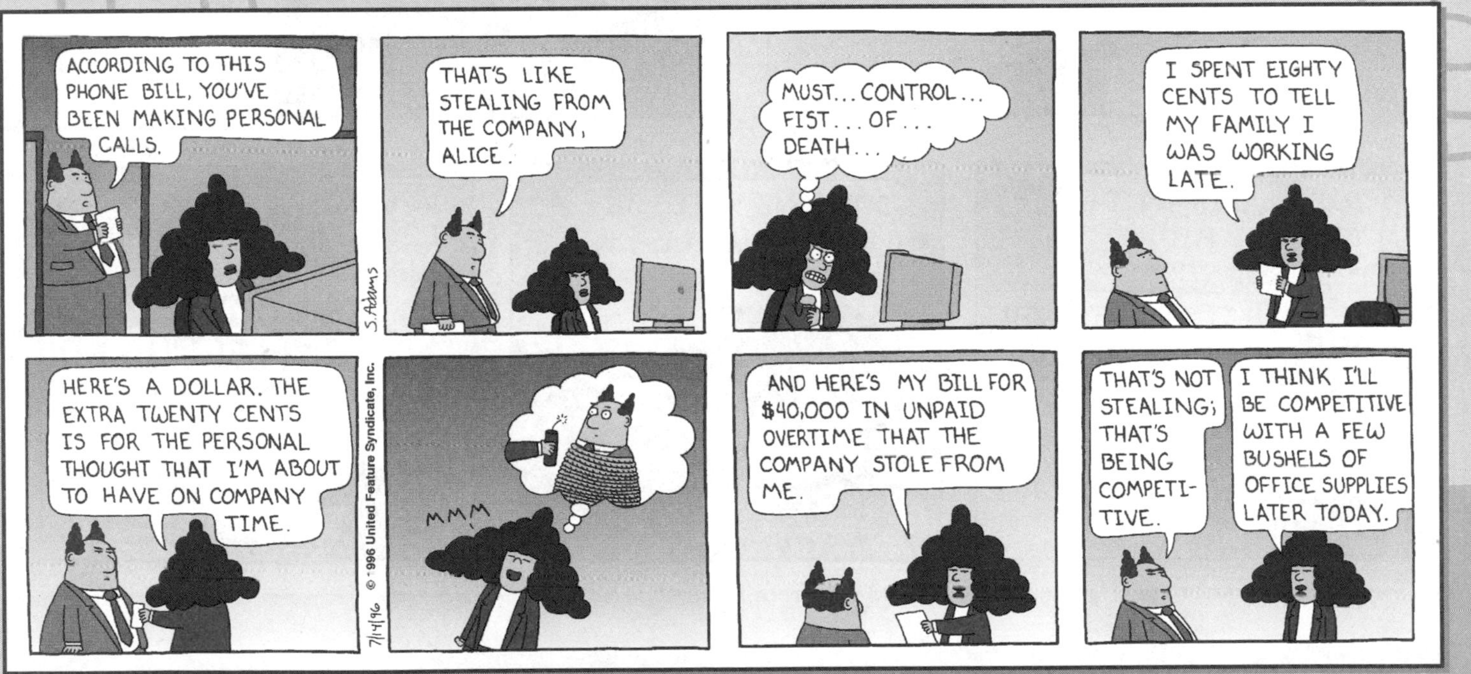
ACCORDING TO THIS PHONE BILL, YOU'VE BEEN MAKING PERSONAL CALLS.
THAT'S LIKE STEALING FROM THE COMPANY, ALICE.
MUST... CONTROL... FIST... OF... DEATH...
I SPENT EIGHTY CENTS TO TELL MY FAMILY I WAS WORKING LATE.
HERE'S A DOLLAR. THE EXTRA TWENTY CENTS IS FOR THE PERSONAL THOUGHT THAT I'M ABOUT TO HAVE ON COMPANY TIME.
MMM
AND HERE'S MY BILL FOR $40,000 IN UNPAID OVERTIME THAT THE COMPANY STOLE FROM ME.
THAT'S NOT STEALING; THAT'S BEING COMPETI-TIVE.
I THINK I'LL BE COMPETITIVE WITH A FEW BUSHELS OF OFFICE SUPPLIES LATER TODAY.
S. Adams
7/14/96 © 1996 United Feature Syndicate, Inc.

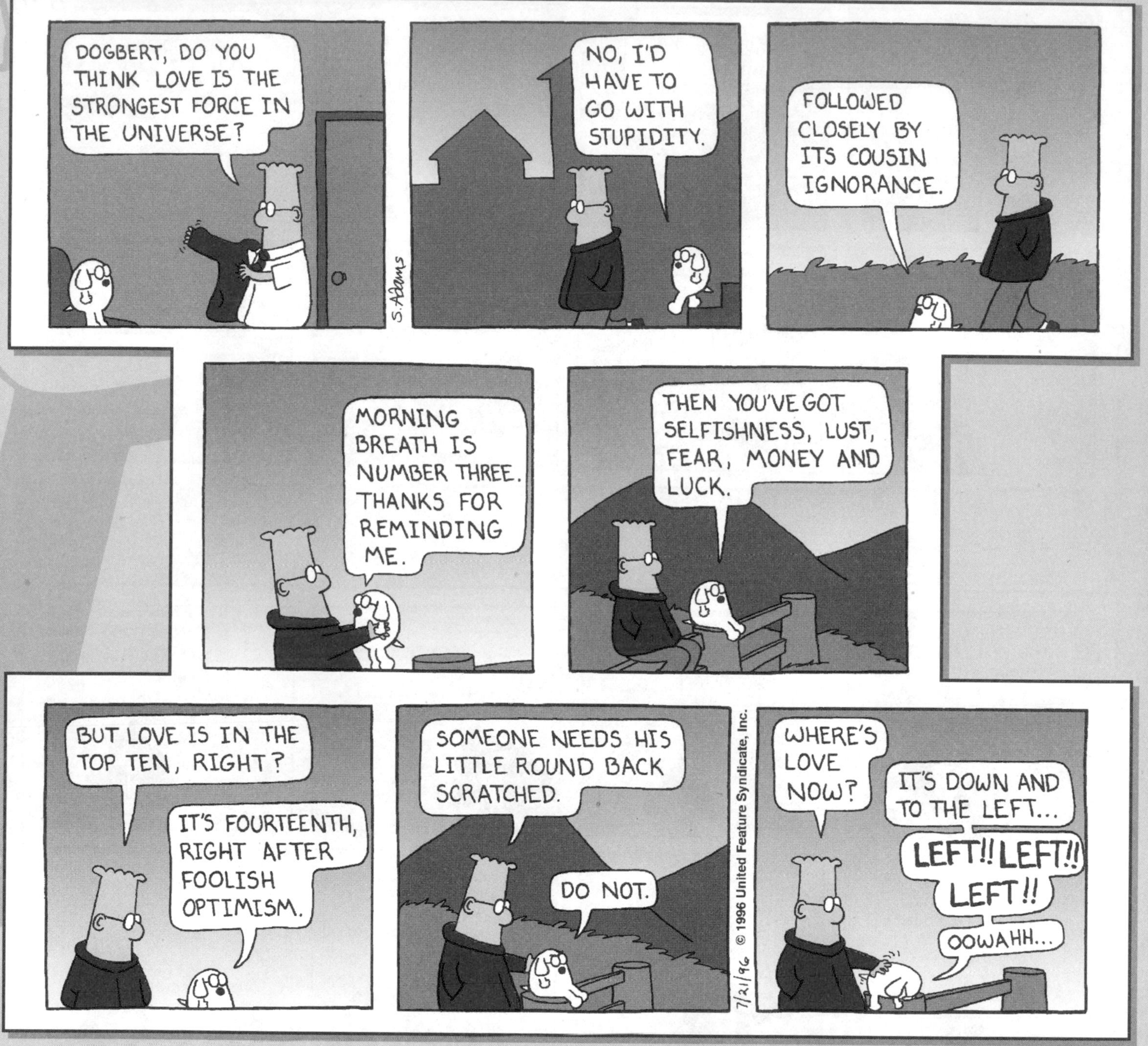

DOGBERT, DO YOU THINK LOVE IS THE STRONGEST FORCE IN THE UNIVERSE?
S. Adams
NO, I'D HAVE TO GO WITH STUPIDITY.
FOLLOWED CLOSELY BY ITS COUSIN IGNORANCE.
MORNING BREATH IS NUMBER THREE. THANKS FOR REMINDING ME.
THEN YOU'VE GOT SELFISHNESS, LUST, FEAR, MONEY AND LUCK.
BUT LOVE IS IN THE TOP TEN, RIGHT?
IT'S FOURTEENTH, RIGHT AFTER FOOLISH OPTIMISM.
SOMEONE NEEDS HIS LITTLE ROUND BACK SCRATCHED.
DO NOT.
7/21/96 © 1996 United Feature Syndicate, Inc.
WHERE'S LOVE NOW?
IT'S DOWN AND TO THE LEFT...
LEFT!! LEFT!! LEFT!!
OOWAHH...

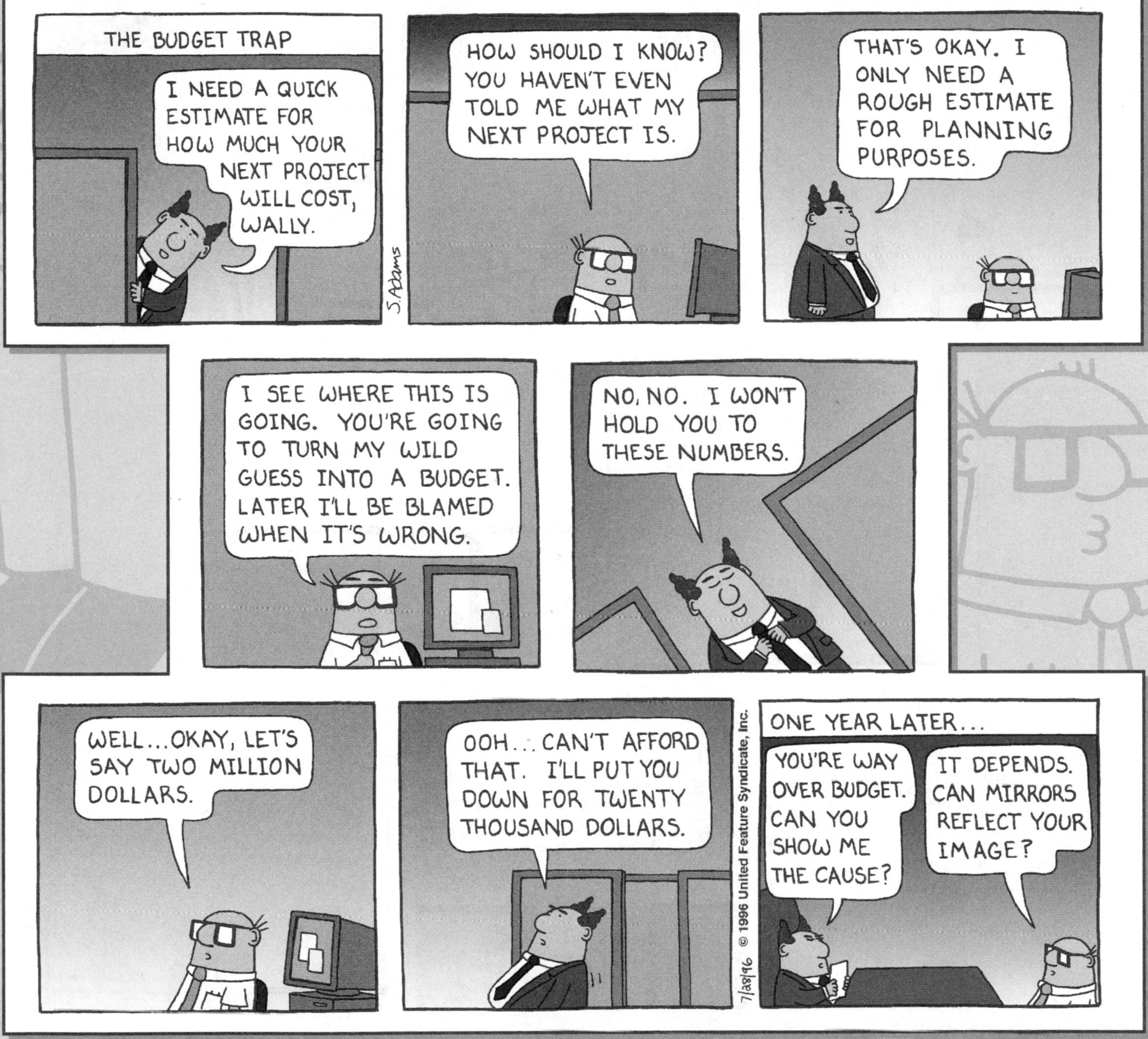
THE BUDGET TRAP
I NEED A QUICK ESTIMATE FOR HOW MUCH YOUR NEXT PROJECT WILL COST, WALLY.
S. Adams
HOW SHOULD I KNOW? YOU HAVEN'T EVEN TOLD ME WHAT MY NEXT PROJECT IS.
THAT'S OKAY. I ONLY NEED A ROUGH ESTIMATE FOR PLANNING PURPOSES.
I SEE WHERE THIS IS GOING. YOU'RE GOING TO TURN MY WILD GUESS INTO A BUDGET. LATER I'LL BE BLAMED WHEN IT'S WRONG.
NO, NO. I WON'T HOLD YOU TO THESE NUMBERS.
WELL...OKAY, LET'S SAY TWO MILLION DOLLARS.
OOH... CAN'T AFFORD THAT. I'LL PUT YOU DOWN FOR TWENTY THOUSAND DOLLARS.
7/28/96 © 1996 United Feature Syndicate, Inc.
ONE YEAR LATER...
YOU'RE WAY OVER BUDGET. CAN YOU SHOW ME THE CAUSE?
IT DEPENDS. CAN MIRRORS REFLECT YOUR IMAGE?

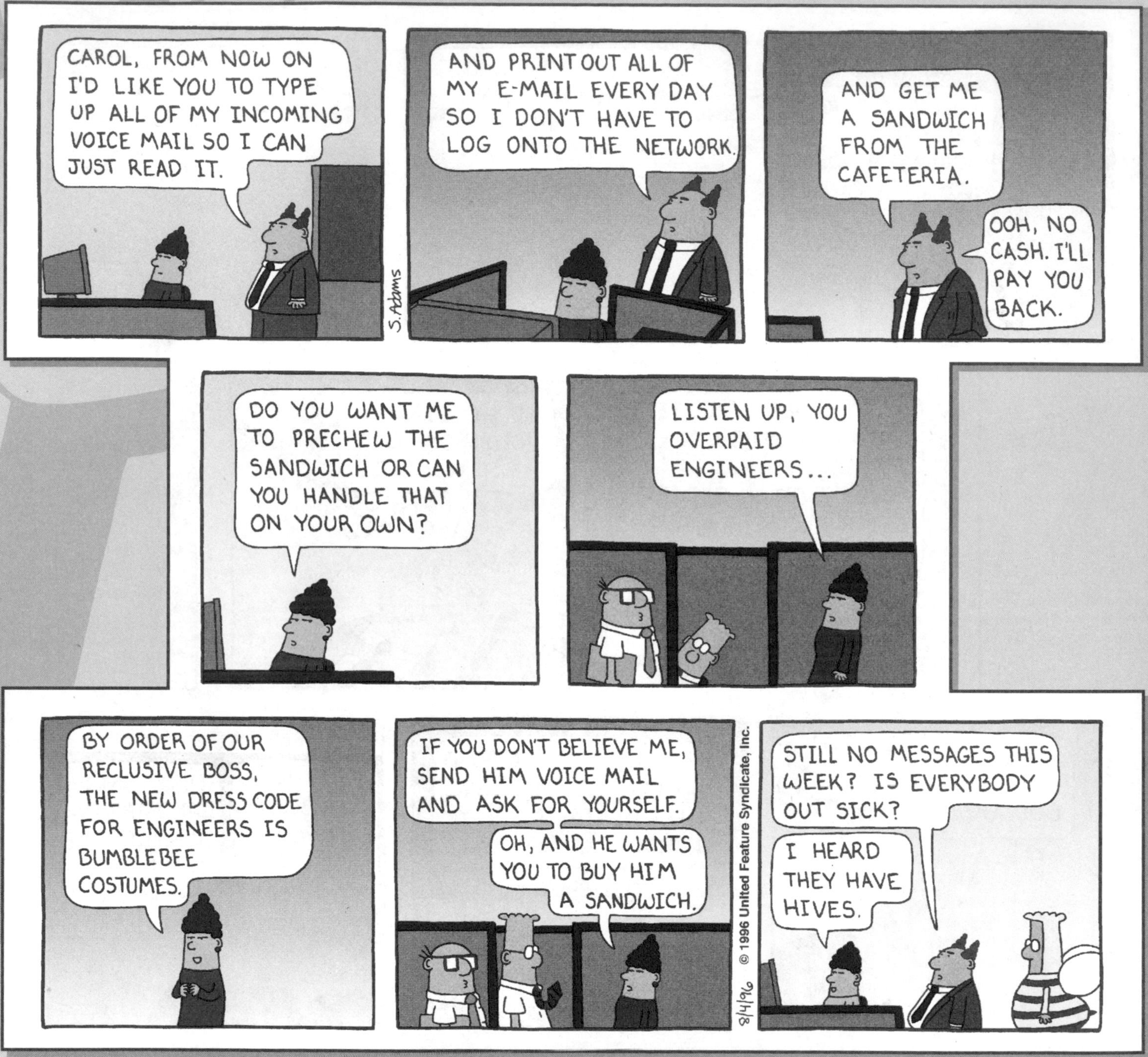
CAROL, FROM NOW ON I'D LIKE YOU TO TYPE UP ALL OF MY INCOMING VOICE MAIL SO I CAN JUST READ IT.
S. Adams
AND PRINT OUT ALL OF MY E-MAIL EVERY DAY SO I DON'T HAVE TO LOG ONTO THE NETWORK.
AND GET ME A SANDWICH FROM THE CAFETERIA.
OOH, NO CASH. I'LL PAY YOU BACK.
DO YOU WANT ME TO PRECHEW THE SANDWICH OR CAN YOU HANDLE THAT ON YOUR OWN?
LISTEN UP, YOU OVERPAID ENGINEERS...
BY ORDER OF OUR RECLUSIVE BOSS, THE NEW DRESS CODE FOR ENGINEERS IS BUMBLEBEE COSTUMES.
IF YOU DON'T BELIEVE ME, SEND HIM VOICE MAIL AND ASK FOR YOURSELF.
OH, AND HE WANTS YOU TO BUY HIM A SANDWICH.
8/4/96 © 1996 United Feature Syndicate, Inc.
STILL NO MESSAGES THIS WEEK? IS EVERYBODY OUT SICK?
I HEARD THEY HAVE HIVES.

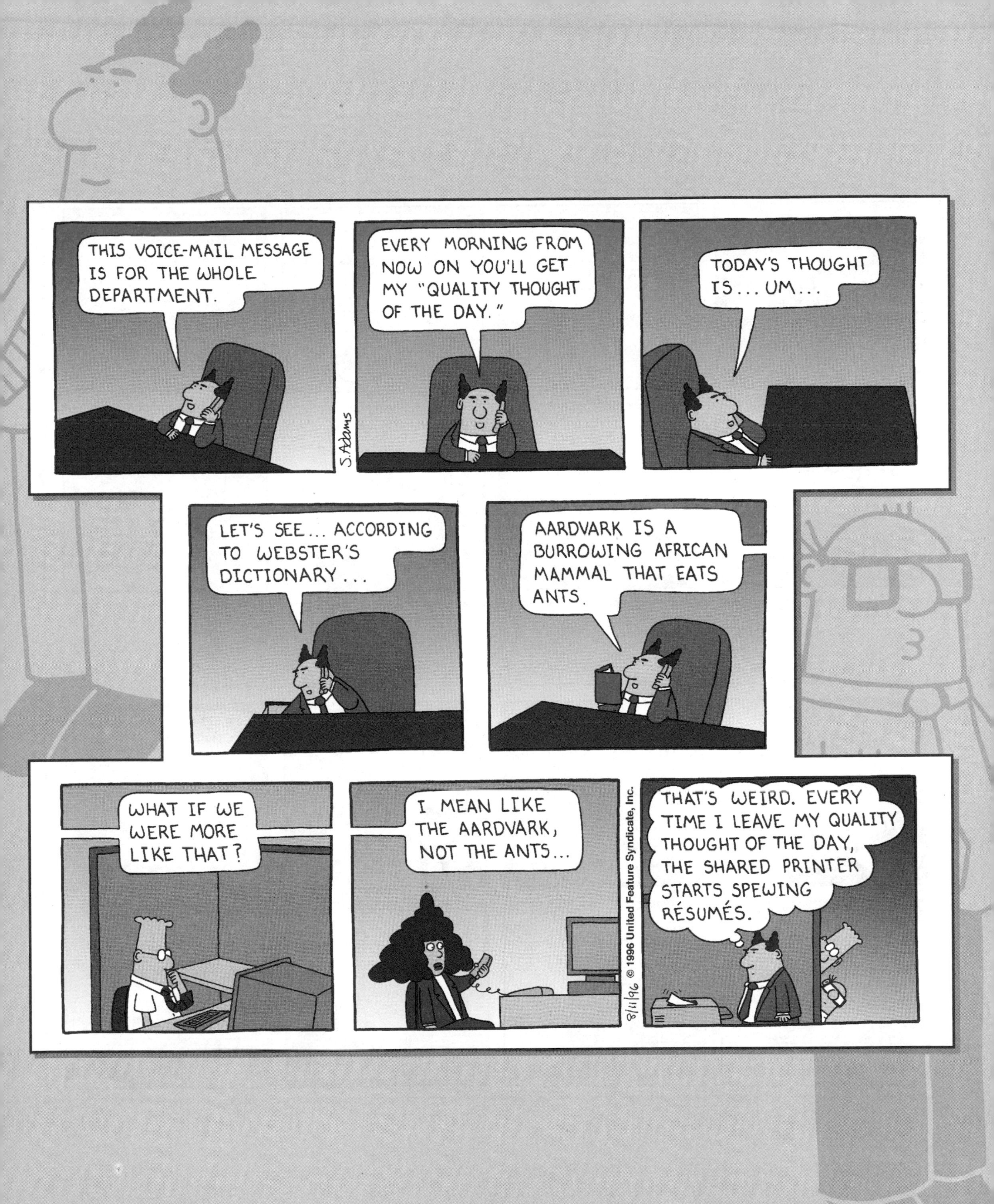

THIS VOICE-MAIL MESSAGE IS FOR THE WHOLE DEPARTMENT.
EVERY MORNING FROM NOW ON YOU'LL GET MY "QUALITY THOUGHT OF THE DAY."
S. Adams
TODAY'S THOUGHT IS... UM...
LET'S SEE... ACCORDING TO WEBSTER'S DICTIONARY...
AARDVARK IS A BURROWING AFRICAN MAMMAL THAT EATS ANTS.
WHAT IF WE WERE MORE LIKE THAT?
I MEAN LIKE THE AARDVARK, NOT THE ANTS...
8/11/96 © 1996 United Feature Syndicate, Inc.
THAT'S WEIRD. EVERY TIME I LEAVE MY QUALITY THOUGHT OF THE DAY, THE SHARED PRINTER STARTS SPEWING RÉSUMÉS.

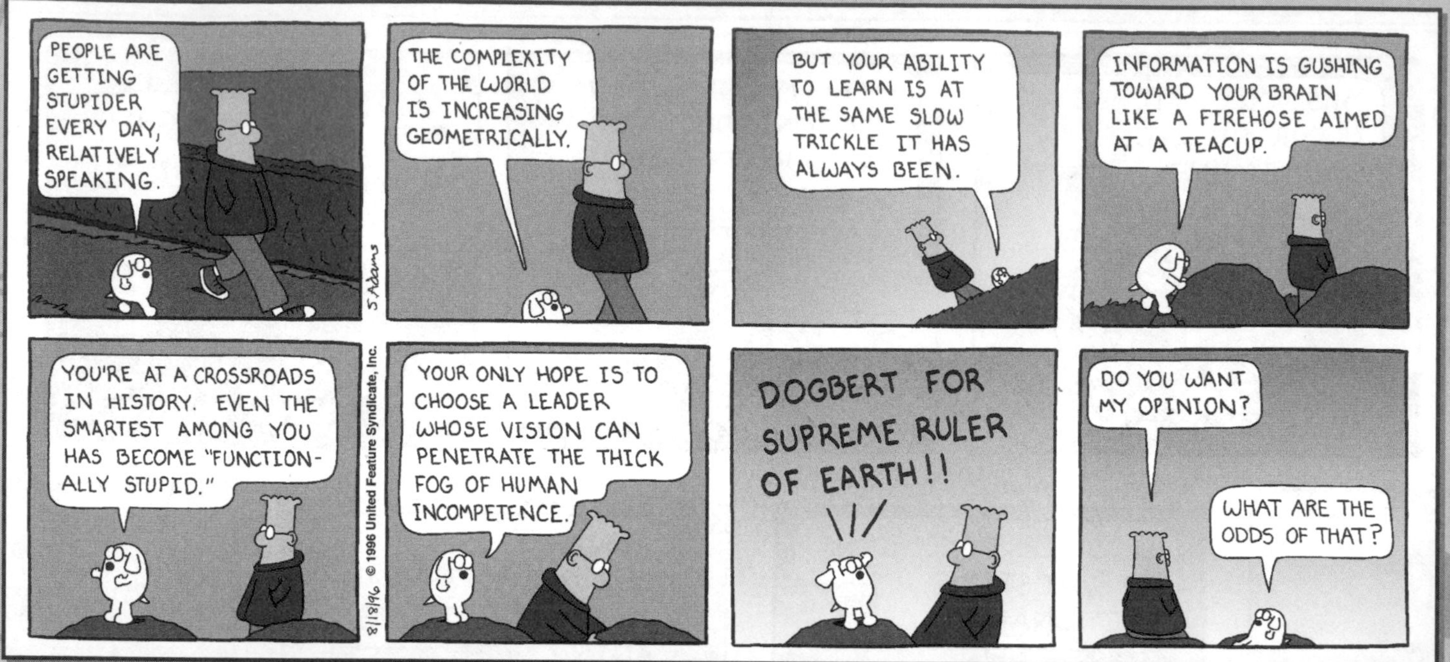
PEOPLE ARE GETTING STUPIDER EVERY DAY, RELATIVELY SPEAKING.
THE COMPLEXITY OF THE WORLD IS INCREASING GEOMETRICALLY.
BUT YOUR ABILITY TO LEARN IS AT THE SAME SLOW TRICKLE IT HAS ALWAYS BEEN.
INFORMATION IS GUSHING TOWARD YOUR BRAIN LIKE A FIREHOSE AIMED AT A TEACUP.
YOU'RE AT A CROSSROADS IN HISTORY. EVEN THE SMARTEST AMONG YOU HAS BECOME "FUNCTIONALLY STUPID."
YOUR ONLY HOPE IS TO CHOOSE A LEADER WHOSE VISION CAN PENETRATE THE THICK FOG OF HUMAN INCOMPETENCE.
DOGBERT FOR SUPREME RULER OF EARTH!!
DO YOU WANT MY OPINION?
WHAT ARE THE ODDS OF THAT?
8/18/96 © 1996 United Feature Syndicate, Inc.
S. Adams

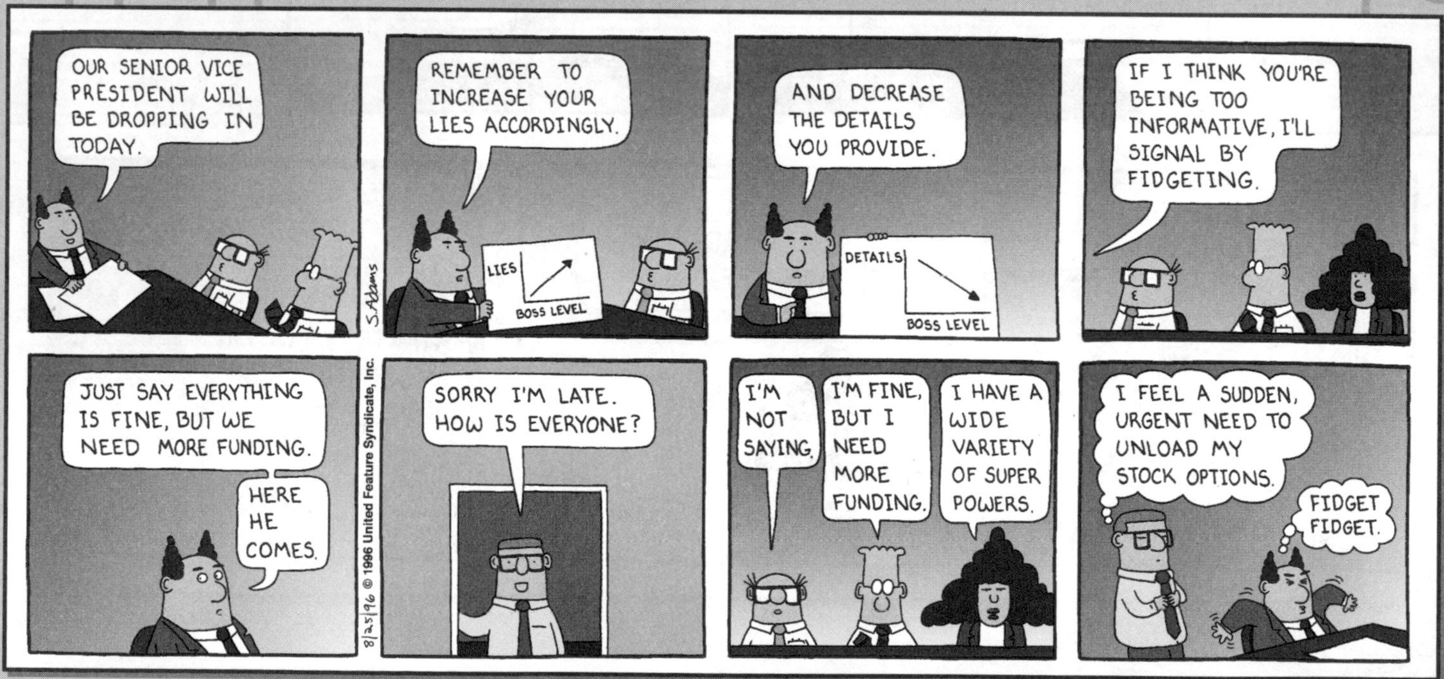
OUR SENIOR VICE PRESIDENT WILL BE DROPPING IN TODAY.
REMEMBER TO INCREASE YOUR LIES ACCORDINGLY.
LIES
BOSS LEVEL
AND DECREASE THE DETAILS YOU PROVIDE.
DETAILS
BOSS LEVEL
IF I THINK YOU'RE BEING TOO INFORMATIVE, I'LL SIGNAL BY FIDGETING.
JUST SAY EVERYTHING IS FINE, BUT WE NEED MORE FUNDING.
HERE HE COMES.
SORRY I'M LATE. HOW IS EVERYONE?
I'M NOT SAYING.
I'M FINE, BUT I NEED MORE FUNDING.
I HAVE A WIDE VARIETY OF SUPER POWERS.
I FEEL A SUDDEN, URGENT NEED TO UNLOAD MY STOCK OPTIONS.
FIDGET FIDGET.
8/25/96 © 1996 United Feature Syndicate, Inc.
S. Adams

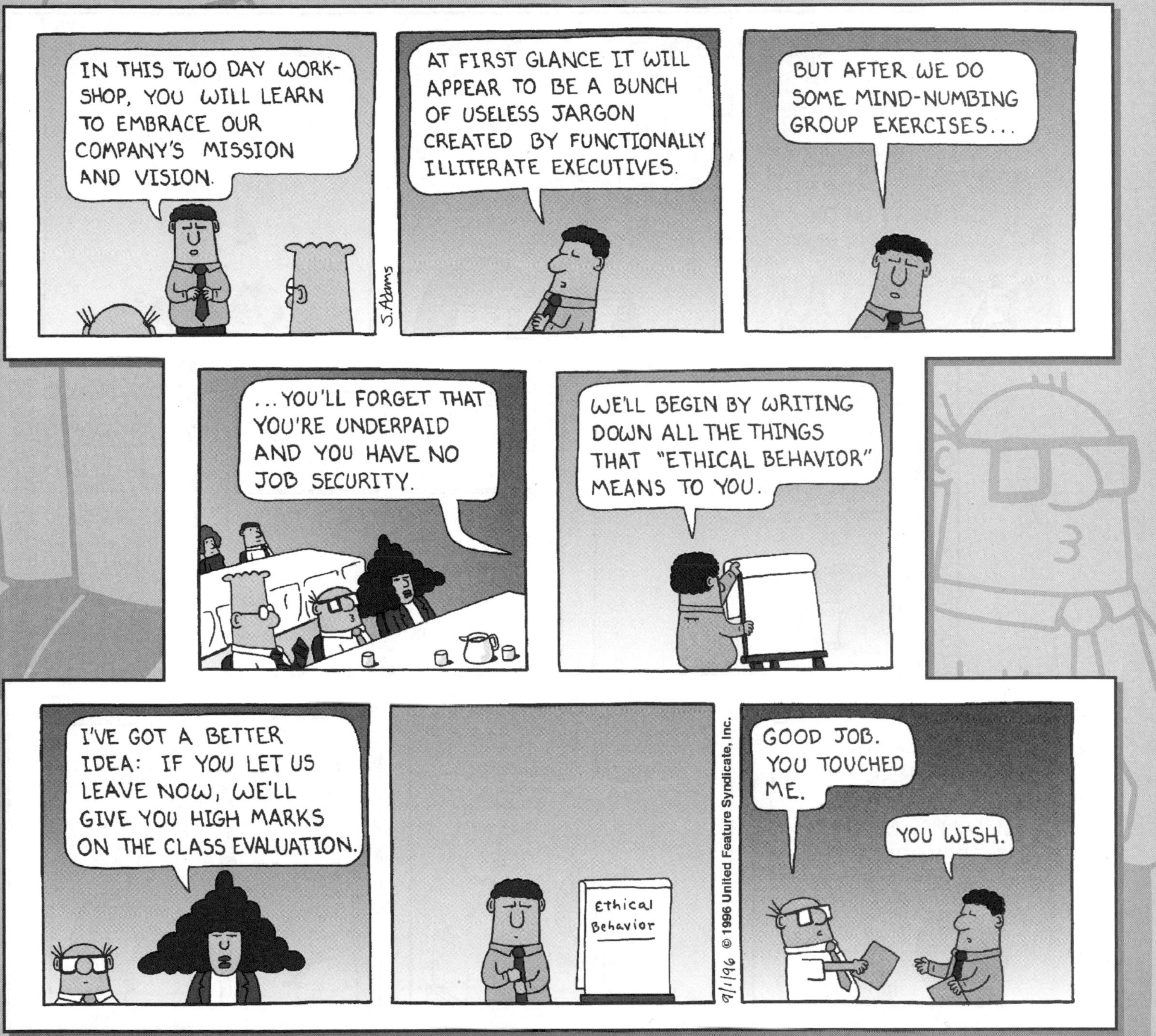
IN THIS TWO DAY WORK-SHOP, YOU WILL LEARN TO EMBRACE OUR COMPANY'S MISSION AND VISION.
S. Adams
AT FIRST GLANCE IT WILL APPEAR TO BE A BUNCH OF USELESS JARGON CREATED BY FUNCTIONALLY ILLITERATE EXECUTIVES.
BUT AFTER WE DO SOME MIND-NUMBING GROUP EXERCISES...
...YOU'LL FORGET THAT YOU'RE UNDERPAID AND YOU HAVE NO JOB SECURITY.
WE'LL BEGIN BY WRITING DOWN ALL THE THINGS THAT "ETHICAL BEHAVIOR" MEANS TO YOU.
I'VE GOT A BETTER IDEA: IF YOU LET US LEAVE NOW, WE'LL GIVE YOU HIGH MARKS ON THE CLASS EVALUATION.
Ethical Behavior
9/1/96 © 1996 United Feature Syndicate, Inc.
GOOD JOB. YOU TOUCHED ME.
YOU WISH.

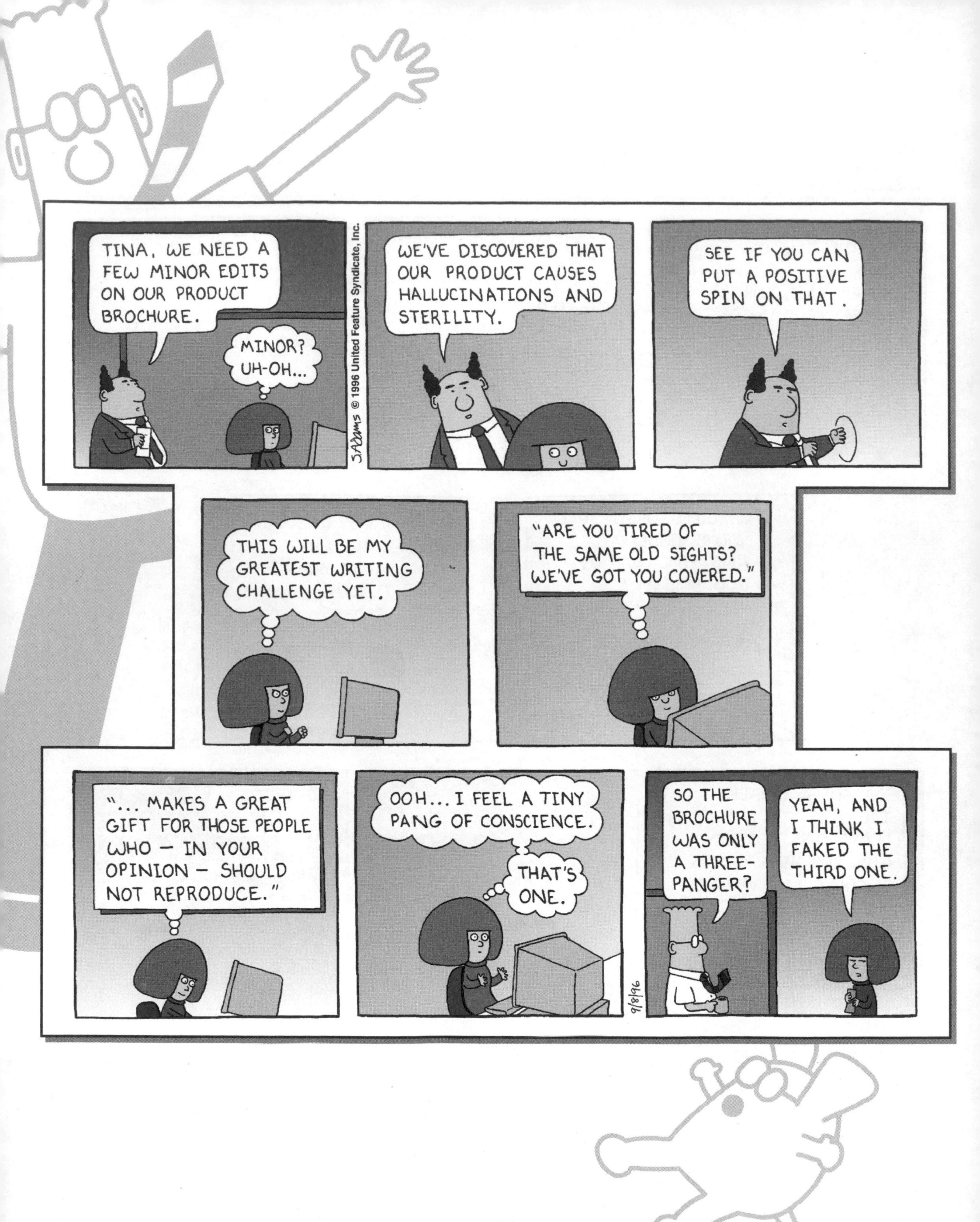
TINA, WE NEED A FEW MINOR EDITS ON OUR PRODUCT BROCHURE.
MINOR? UH-OH...
S.ADAMS © 1996 United Feature Syndicate, Inc.
WE'VE DISCOVERED THAT OUR PRODUCT CAUSES HALLUCINATIONS AND STERILITY.
SEE IF YOU CAN PUT A POSITIVE SPIN ON THAT.
THIS WILL BE MY GREATEST WRITING CHALLENGE YET.
"ARE YOU TIRED OF THE SAME OLD SIGHTS? WE'VE GOT YOU COVERED."
"... MAKES A GREAT GIFT FOR THOSE PEOPLE WHO – IN YOUR OPINION – SHOULD NOT REPRODUCE."
OOH... I FEEL A TINY PANG OF CONSCIENCE.
THAT'S ONE.
9/8/96
SO THE BROCHURE WAS ONLY A THREE-PANGER?
YEAH, AND I THINK I FAKED THE THIRD ONE.

MR. CATBERT, OUR EVIL DIRECTOR OF HUMAN RESOURCES, WILL DESCRIBE OUR NEW CUBICLE PLAN.
S. Adams
LAST YEAR WE REDUCED THE SIZE OF CUBICLES IN THE DENSIFICATION PROJECT.
WE DIDN'T SAVE MUCH MONEY, BUT WE DID LOWER MORALE.
THIS YEAR WE'LL BUILD ON THAT SUCCESS...
WITH THE PATENTED "HEAD CUBICLE."
HOLD STILL, WALLY.
AND THE HEAD CUBICLE CAN BE RECYCLED AFTER YOU'RE DOWNSIZED!
9/15/96 © 1996 United Feature Syndicate, Inc.
WE REALLY NEED TO DRAW THE LINE AT SOME POINT.
WHILE WE STILL HAVE OUR DIGNITY.

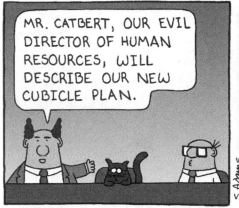

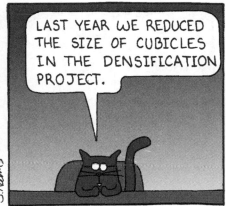

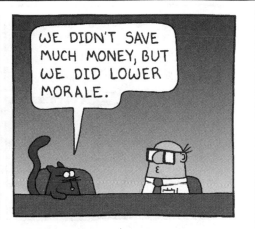

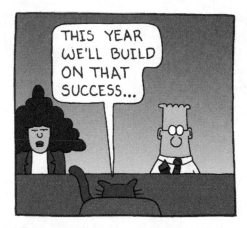

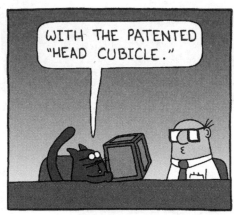

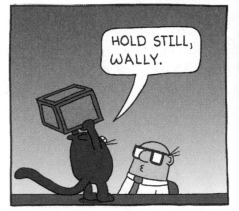

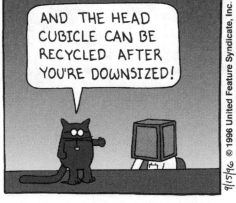

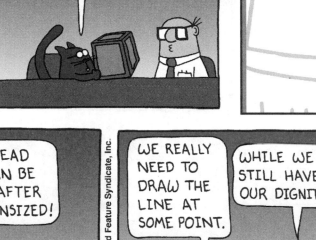

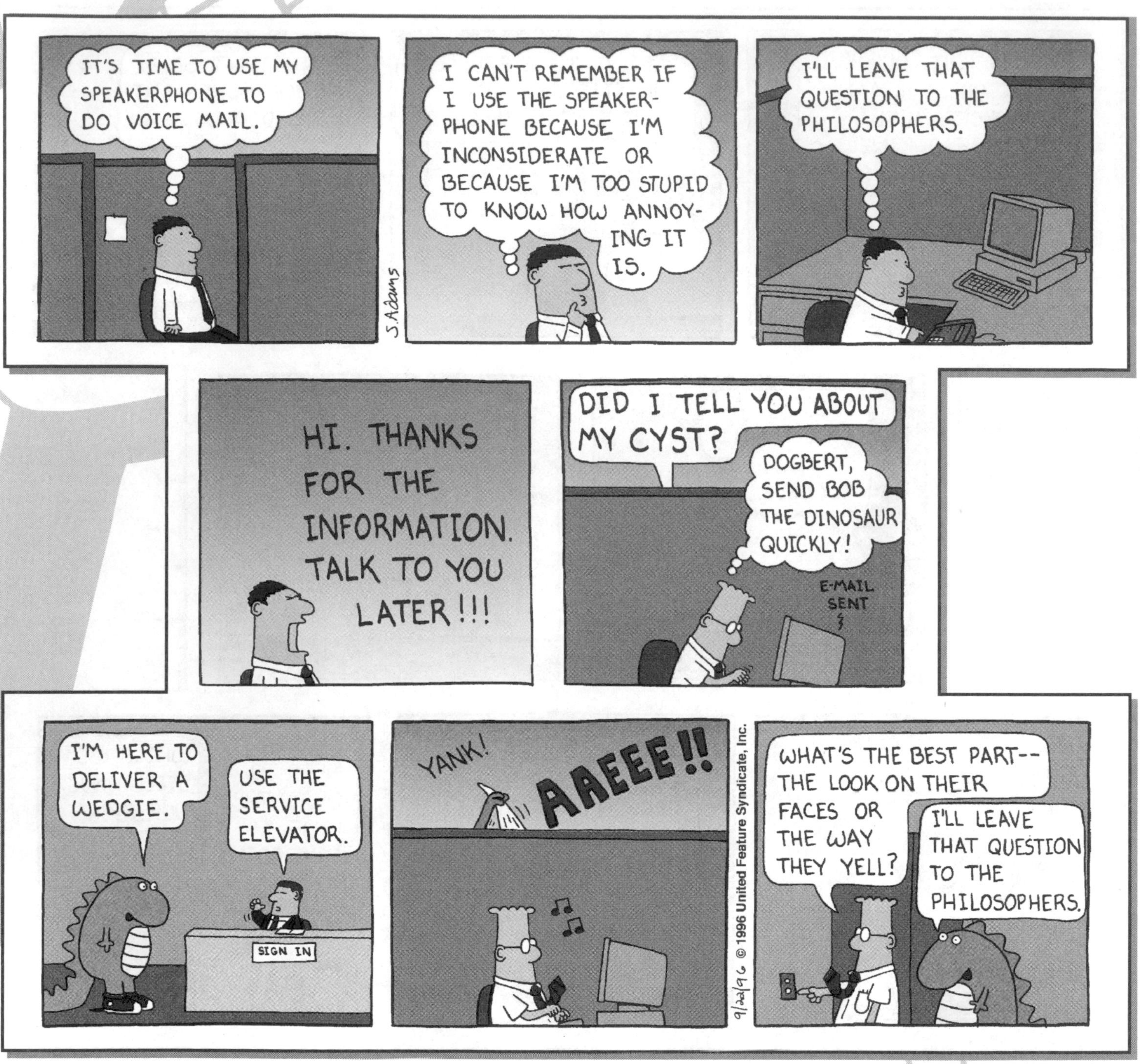

IT'S TIME TO USE MY SPEAKERPHONE TO DO VOICE MAIL.
S. Adams
I CAN'T REMEMBER IF I USE THE SPEAKER-PHONE BECAUSE I'M INCONSIDERATE OR BECAUSE I'M TOO STUPID TO KNOW HOW ANNOY-ING IT IS.
I'LL LEAVE THAT QUESTION TO THE PHILOSOPHERS.
HI. THANKS FOR THE INFORMATION. TALK TO YOU LATER!!!
DID I TELL YOU ABOUT MY CYST?
DOGBERT, SEND BOB THE DINOSAUR QUICKLY!
E-MAIL SENT
I'M HERE TO DELIVER A WEDGIE.
USE THE SERVICE ELEVATOR.
SIGN IN
YANK!
AAEEE!!
9/22/96 © 1996 United Feature Syndicate, Inc.
WHAT'S THE BEST PART-- THE LOOK ON THEIR FACES OR THE WAY THEY YELL?
I'LL LEAVE THAT QUESTION TO THE PHILOSOPHERS.

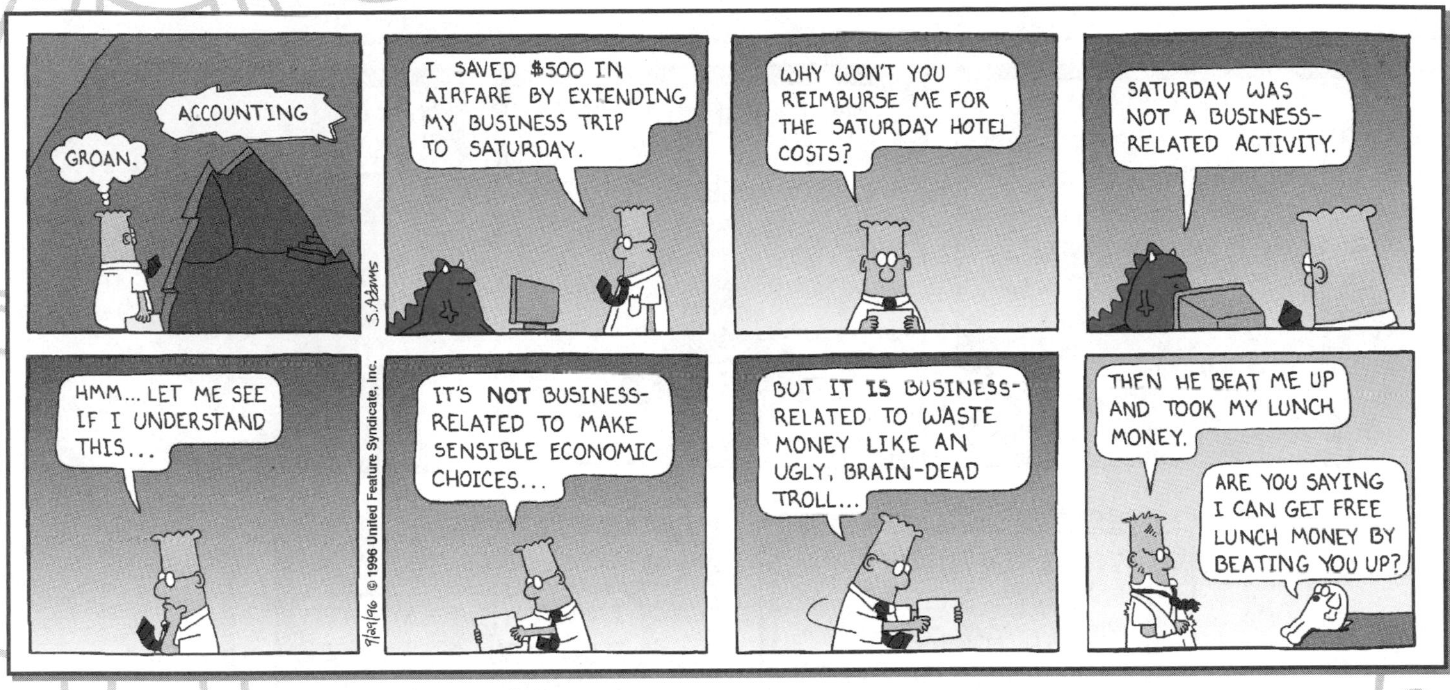
GROAN.
ACCOUNTING
S. Adams
I SAVED $500 IN AIRFARE BY EXTENDING MY BUSINESS TRIP TO SATURDAY.
WHY WON'T YOU REIMBURSE ME FOR THE SATURDAY HOTEL COSTS?
SATURDAY WAS NOT A BUSINESS-RELATED ACTIVITY.
HMM... LET ME SEE IF I UNDERSTAND THIS...
9/29/96 © 1996 United Feature Syndicate, Inc.
IT'S NOT BUSINESS-RELATED TO MAKE SENSIBLE ECONOMIC CHOICES...
BUT IT IS BUSINESS-RELATED TO WASTE MONEY LIKE AN UGLY, BRAIN-DEAD TROLL...
THEN HE BEAT ME UP AND TOOK MY LUNCH MONEY.
ARE YOU SAYING I CAN GET FREE LUNCH MONEY BY BEATING YOU UP?

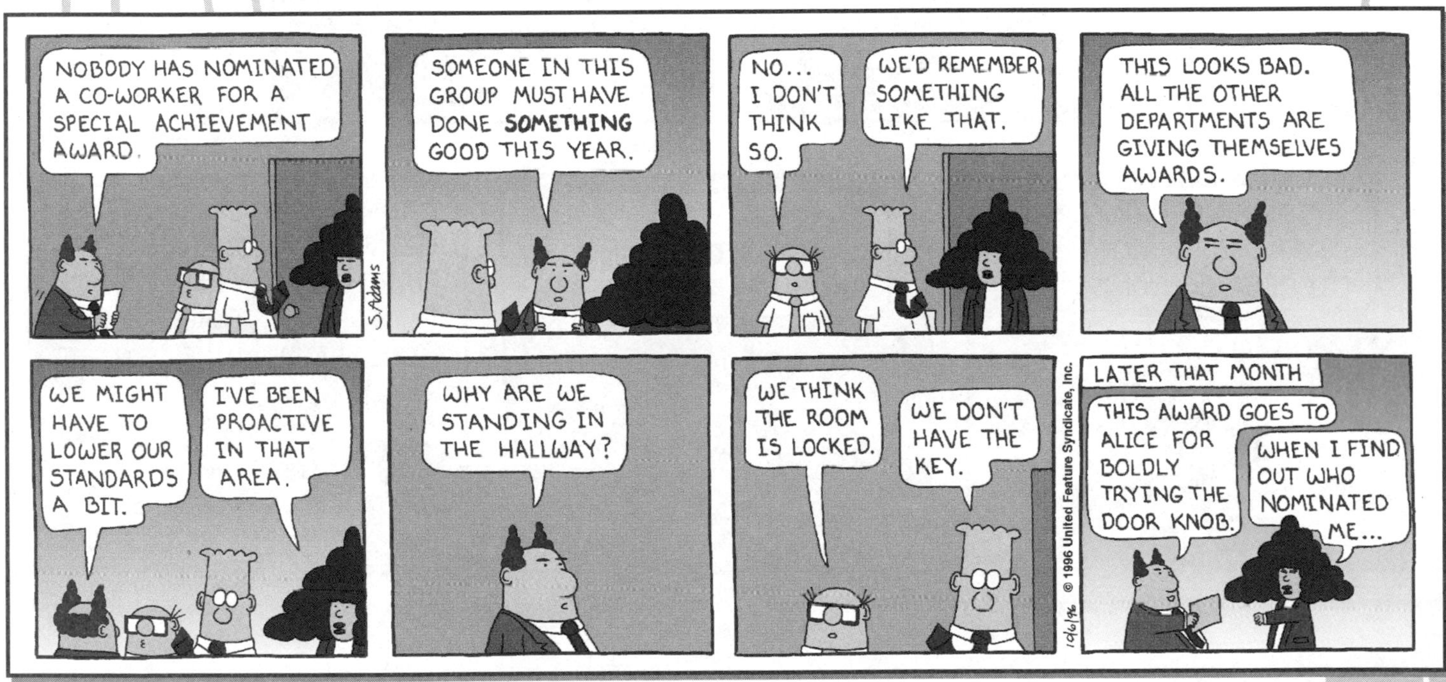
NOBODY HAS NOMINATED A CO-WORKER FOR A SPECIAL ACHIEVEMENT AWARD.
S. Adams
SOMEONE IN THIS GROUP MUST HAVE DONE SOMETHING GOOD THIS YEAR.
NO... I DON'T THINK SO.
WE'D REMEMBER SOMETHING LIKE THAT.
THIS LOOKS BAD. ALL THE OTHER DEPARTMENTS ARE GIVING THEMSELVES AWARDS.
WE MIGHT HAVE TO LOWER OUR STANDARDS A BIT.
I'VE BEEN PROACTIVE IN THAT AREA.
WHY ARE WE STANDING IN THE HALLWAY?
WE THINK THE ROOM IS LOCKED.
WE DON'T HAVE THE KEY.
10/6/96 © 1996 United Feature Syndicate, Inc.
LATER THAT MONTH
THIS AWARD GOES TO ALICE FOR BOLDLY TRYING THE DOOR KNOB.
WHEN I FIND OUT WHO NOMINATED ME...

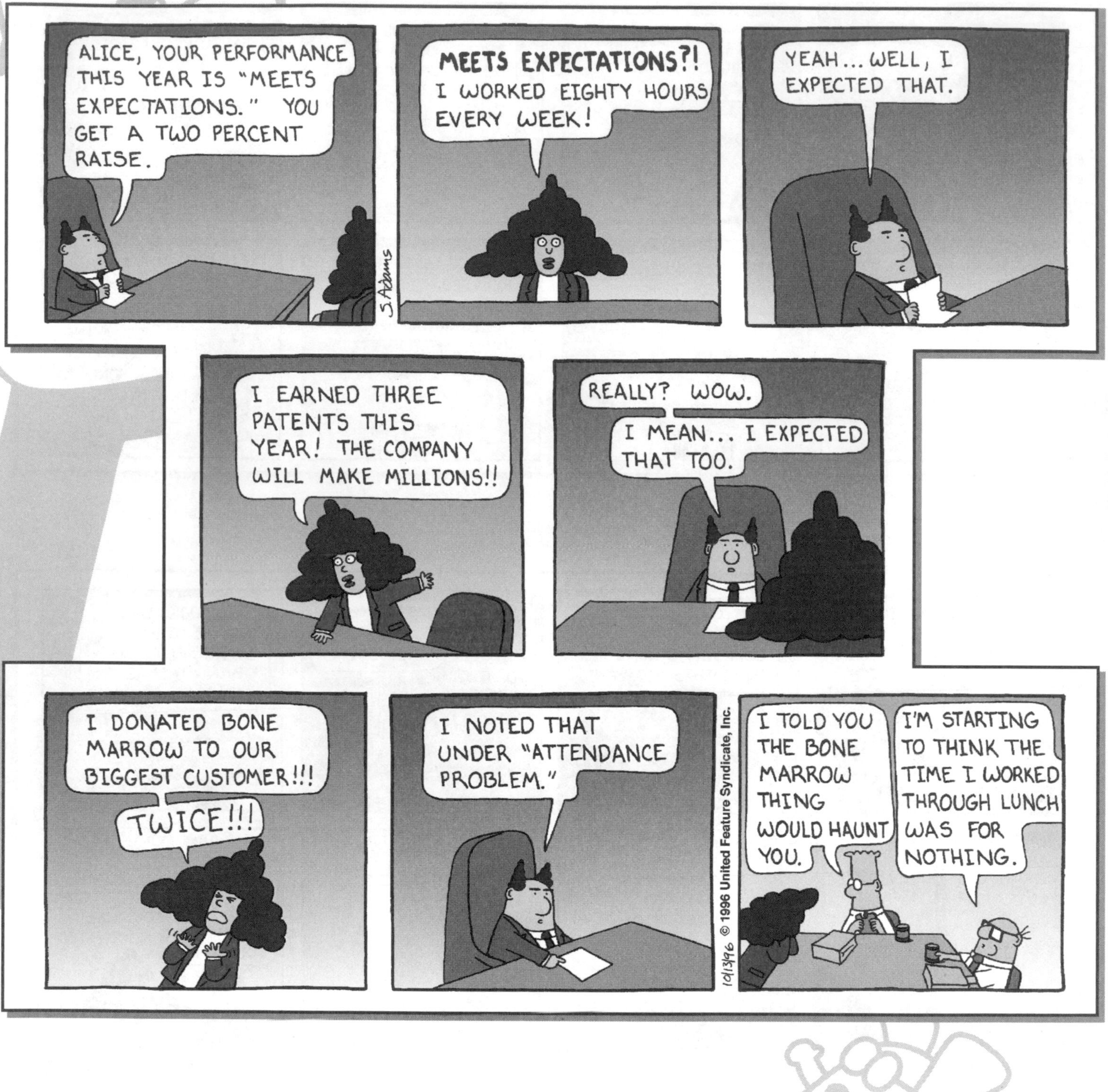
ALICE, YOUR PERFORMANCE THIS YEAR IS "MEETS EXPECTATIONS." YOU GET A TWO PERCENT RAISE.
S. Adams
MEETS EXPECTATIONS?! I WORKED EIGHTY HOURS EVERY WEEK!
YEAH... WELL, I EXPECTED THAT.
I EARNED THREE PATENTS THIS YEAR! THE COMPANY WILL MAKE MILLIONS!!
REALLY? WOW.
I MEAN... I EXPECTED THAT TOO.
I DONATED BONE MARROW TO OUR BIGGEST CUSTOMER!!!
TWICE!!!
I NOTED THAT UNDER "ATTENDANCE PROBLEM."
10/13/96 © 1996 United Feature Syndicate, Inc.
I TOLD YOU THE BONE MARROW THING WOULD HAUNT YOU.
I'M STARTING TO THINK THE TIME I WORKED THROUGH LUNCH WAS FOR NOTHING.

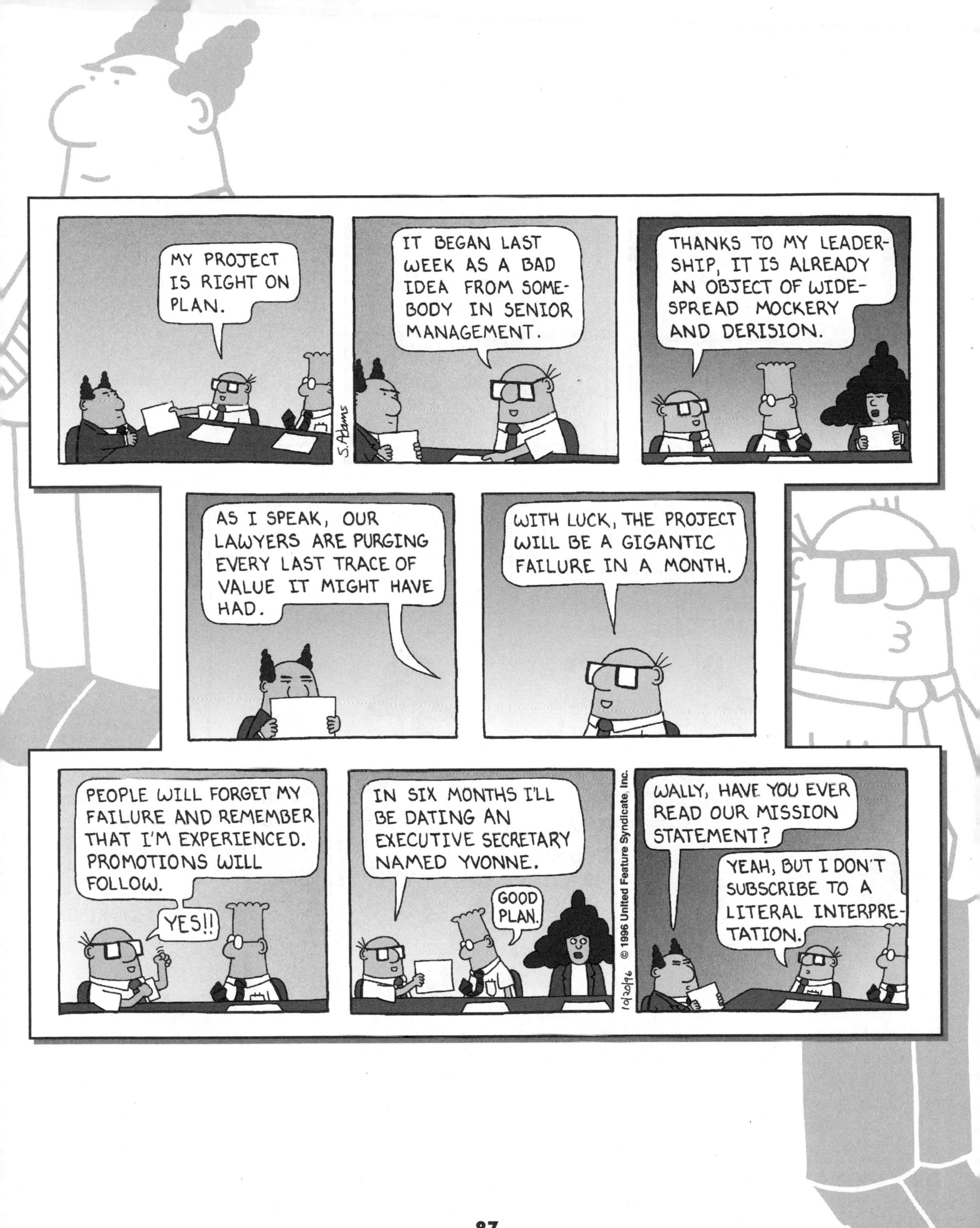

MY PROJECT IS RIGHT ON PLAN.
S. Adams
IT BEGAN LAST WEEK AS A BAD IDEA FROM SOMEBODY IN SENIOR MANAGEMENT.
THANKS TO MY LEADERSHIP, IT IS ALREADY AN OBJECT OF WIDESPREAD MOCKERY AND DERISION.
AS I SPEAK, OUR LAWYERS ARE PURGING EVERY LAST TRACE OF VALUE IT MIGHT HAVE HAD.
WITH LUCK, THE PROJECT WILL BE A GIGANTIC FAILURE IN A MONTH.
PEOPLE WILL FORGET MY FAILURE AND REMEMBER THAT I'M EXPERIENCED. PROMOTIONS WILL FOLLOW.
YES!!
IN SIX MONTHS I'LL BE DATING AN EXECUTIVE SECRETARY NAMED YVONNE.
GOOD PLAN.
10/20/96 © 1996 United Feature Syndicate, Inc.
WALLY, HAVE YOU EVER READ OUR MISSION STATEMENT?
YEAH, BUT I DON'T SUBSCRIBE TO A LITERAL INTERPRETATION.

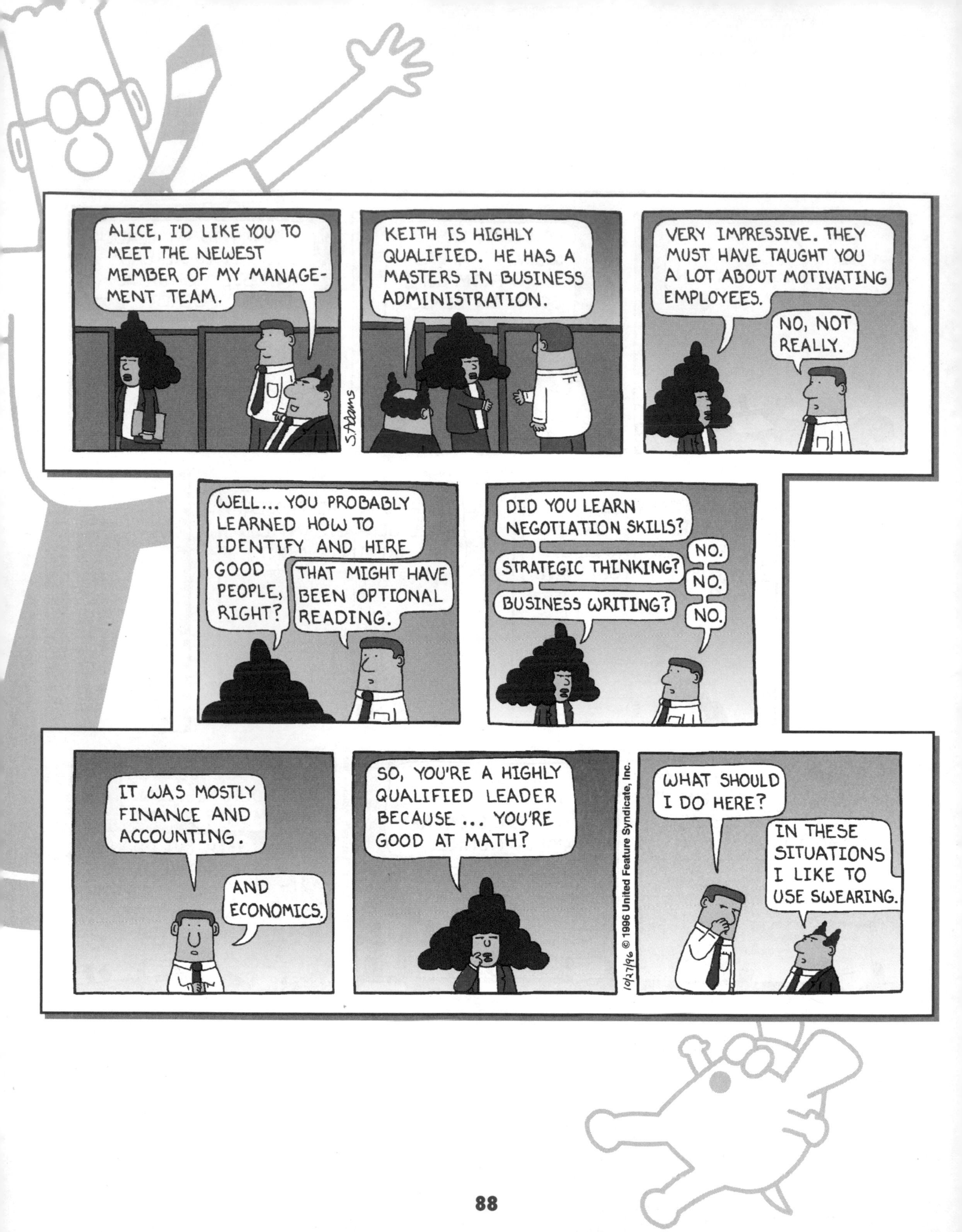
ALICE, I'D LIKE YOU TO MEET THE NEWEST MEMBER OF MY MANAGEMENT TEAM.
S. Adams
KEITH IS HIGHLY QUALIFIED. HE HAS A MASTERS IN BUSINESS ADMINISTRATION.
VERY IMPRESSIVE. THEY MUST HAVE TAUGHT YOU A LOT ABOUT MOTIVATING EMPLOYEES.
NO, NOT REALLY.
WELL... YOU PROBABLY LEARNED HOW TO IDENTIFY AND HIRE GOOD PEOPLE, RIGHT?
THAT MIGHT HAVE BEEN OPTIONAL READING.
DID YOU LEARN NEGOTIATION SKILLS?
NO.
STRATEGIC THINKING?
NO.
BUSINESS WRITING?
NO.
IT WAS MOSTLY FINANCE AND ACCOUNTING.
AND ECONOMICS.
SO, YOU'RE A HIGHLY QUALIFIED LEADER BECAUSE ... YOU'RE GOOD AT MATH?
10/27/96 © 1996 United Feature Syndicate, Inc.
WHAT SHOULD I DO HERE?
IN THESE SITUATIONS I LIKE TO USE SWEARING.

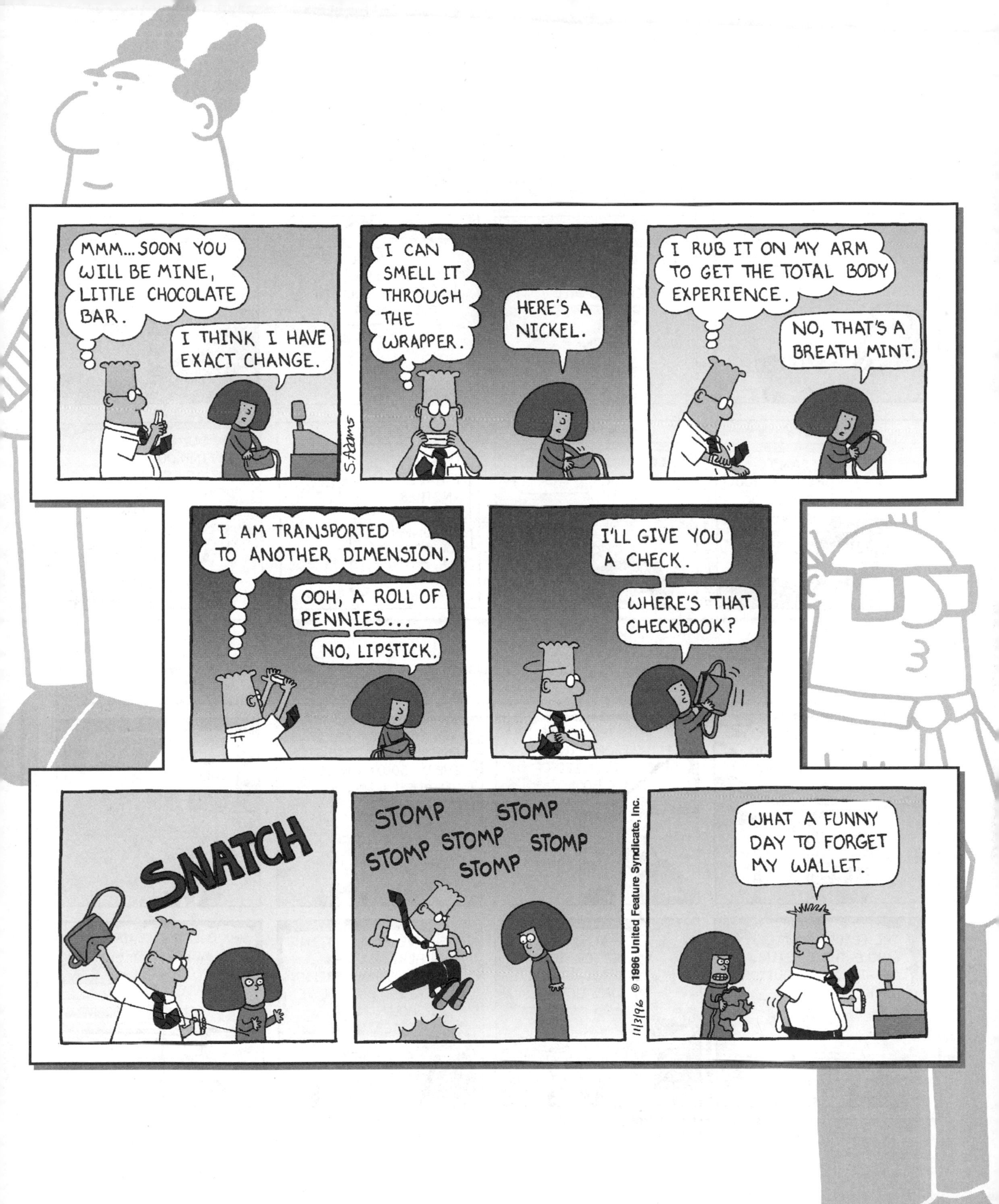
MMM...SOON YOU WILL BE MINE, LITTLE CHOCOLATE BAR.
I THINK I HAVE EXACT CHANGE.
S. Adams
I CAN SMELL IT THROUGH THE WRAPPER.
HERE'S A NICKEL.
I RUB IT ON MY ARM TO GET THE TOTAL BODY EXPERIENCE.
NO, THAT'S A BREATH MINT.
I AM TRANSPORTED TO ANOTHER DIMENSION.
OOH, A ROLL OF PENNIES...
NO, LIPSTICK.
I'LL GIVE YOU A CHECK.
WHERE'S THAT CHECKBOOK?
SNATCH
STOMP STOMP STOMP STOMP STOMP STOMP
11/3/96 © 1996 United Feature Syndicate, Inc.
WHAT A FUNNY DAY TO FORGET MY WALLET.

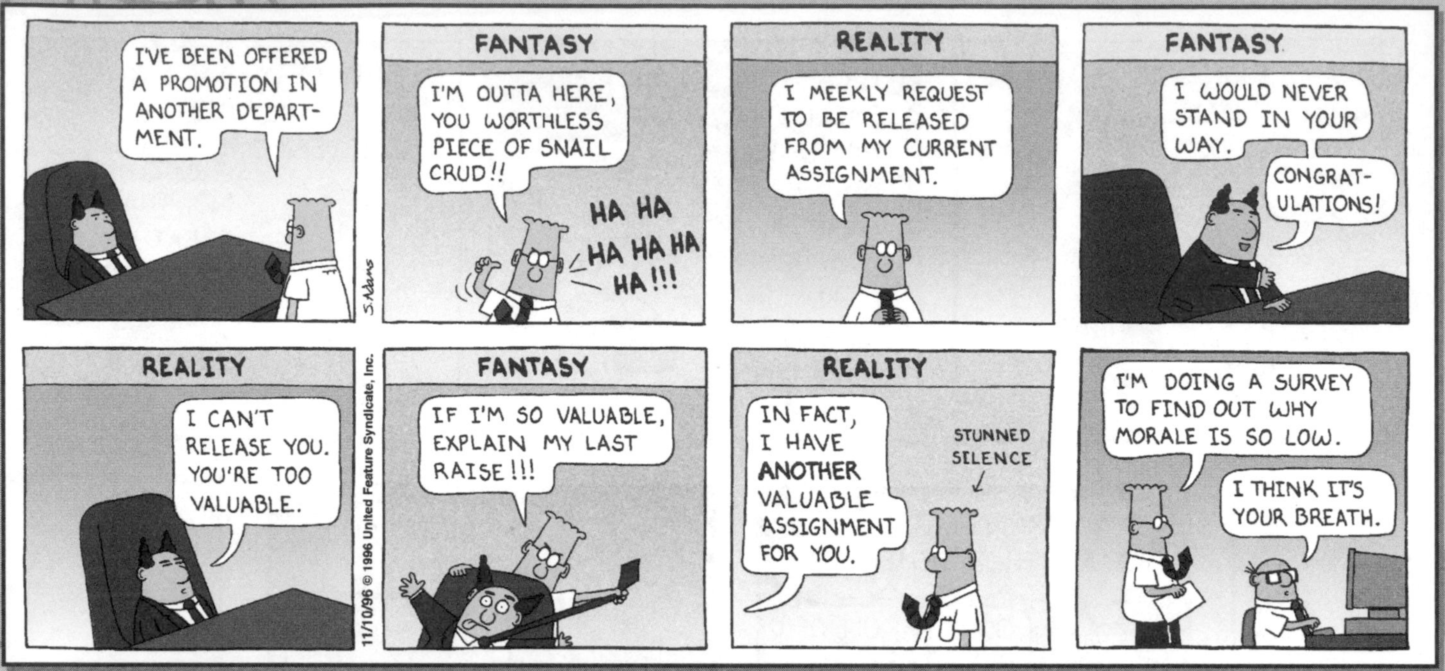
I'VE BEEN OFFERED A PROMOTION IN ANOTHER DEPARTMENT.
S. Adams
FANTASY
I'M OUTTA HERE, YOU WORTHLESS PIECE OF SNAIL CRUD!!
HA HA HA HA HA HA!!!
REALITY
I MEEKLY REQUEST TO BE RELEASED FROM MY CURRENT ASSIGNMENT.
FANTASY
I WOULD NEVER STAND IN YOUR WAY.
CONGRATULATIONS!
REALITY
I CAN'T RELEASE YOU. YOU'RE TOO VALUABLE.
11/10/96 © 1996 United Feature Syndicate, Inc.
FANTASY
IF I'M SO VALUABLE, EXPLAIN MY LAST RAISE!!!
REALITY
IN FACT, I HAVE ANOTHER VALUABLE ASSIGNMENT FOR YOU.
STUNNED SILENCE
I'M DOING A SURVEY TO FIND OUT WHY MORALE IS SO LOW.
I THINK IT'S YOUR BREATH.

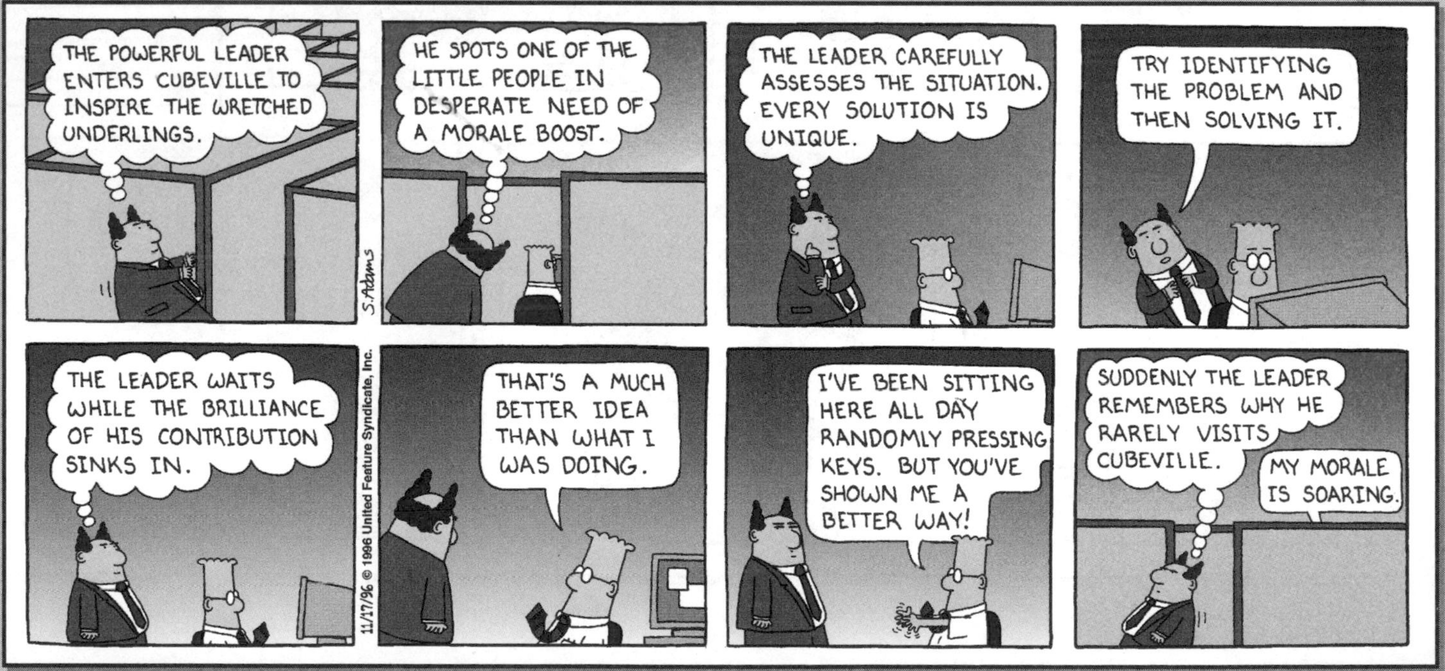
THE POWERFUL LEADER ENTERS CUBEVILLE TO INSPIRE THE WRETCHED UNDERLINGS.
S. Adams
HE SPOTS ONE OF THE LITTLE PEOPLE IN DESPERATE NEED OF A MORALE BOOST.
THE LEADER CAREFULLY ASSESSES THE SITUATION. EVERY SOLUTION IS UNIQUE.
TRY IDENTIFYING THE PROBLEM AND THEN SOLVING IT.
THE LEADER WAITS WHILE THE BRILLIANCE OF HIS CONTRIBUTION SINKS IN.
11/17/96 © 1996 United Feature Syndicate, Inc.
THAT'S A MUCH BETTER IDEA THAN WHAT I WAS DOING.
I'VE BEEN SITTING HERE ALL DAY RANDOMLY PRESSING KEYS. BUT YOU'VE SHOWN ME A BETTER WAY!
SUDDENLY THE LEADER REMEMBERS WHY HE RARELY VISITS CUBEVILLE.
MY MORALE IS SOARING.

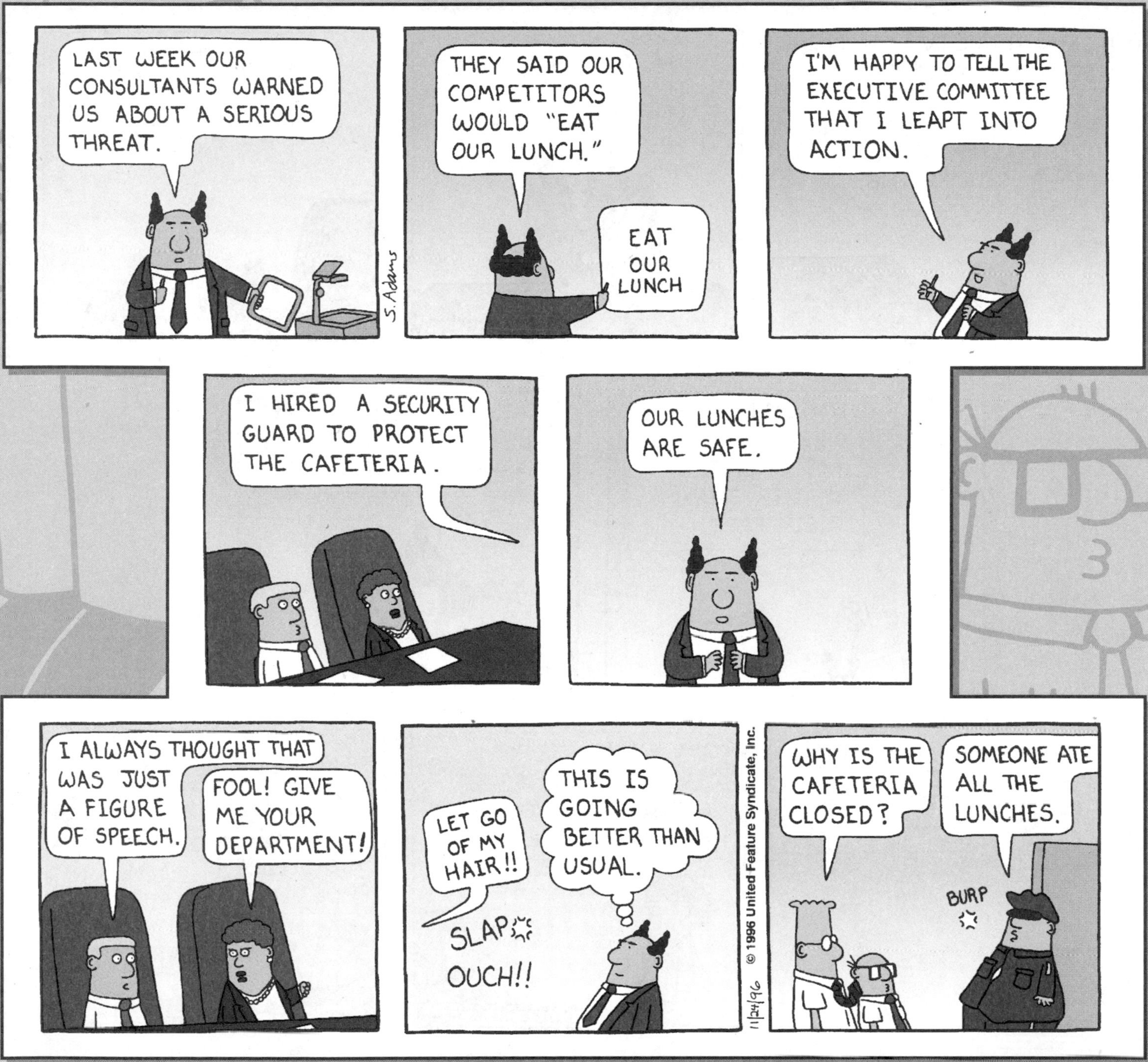
LAST WEEK OUR CONSULTANTS WARNED US ABOUT A SERIOUS THREAT.
S. Adams
THEY SAID OUR COMPETITORS WOULD "EAT OUR LUNCH."
EAT OUR LUNCH
I'M HAPPY TO TELL THE EXECUTIVE COMMITTEE THAT I LEAPT INTO ACTION.
I HIRED A SECURITY GUARD TO PROTECT THE CAFETERIA.
OUR LUNCHES ARE SAFE.
I ALWAYS THOUGHT THAT WAS JUST A FIGURE OF SPEECH.
FOOL! GIVE ME YOUR DEPARTMENT!
LET GO OF MY HAIR!!
SLAP
OUCH!!
THIS IS GOING BETTER THAN USUAL.
© 1996 United Feature Syndicate, Inc.
11/24/96
WHY IS THE CAFETERIA CLOSED?
SOMEONE ATE ALL THE LUNCHES.
BURP

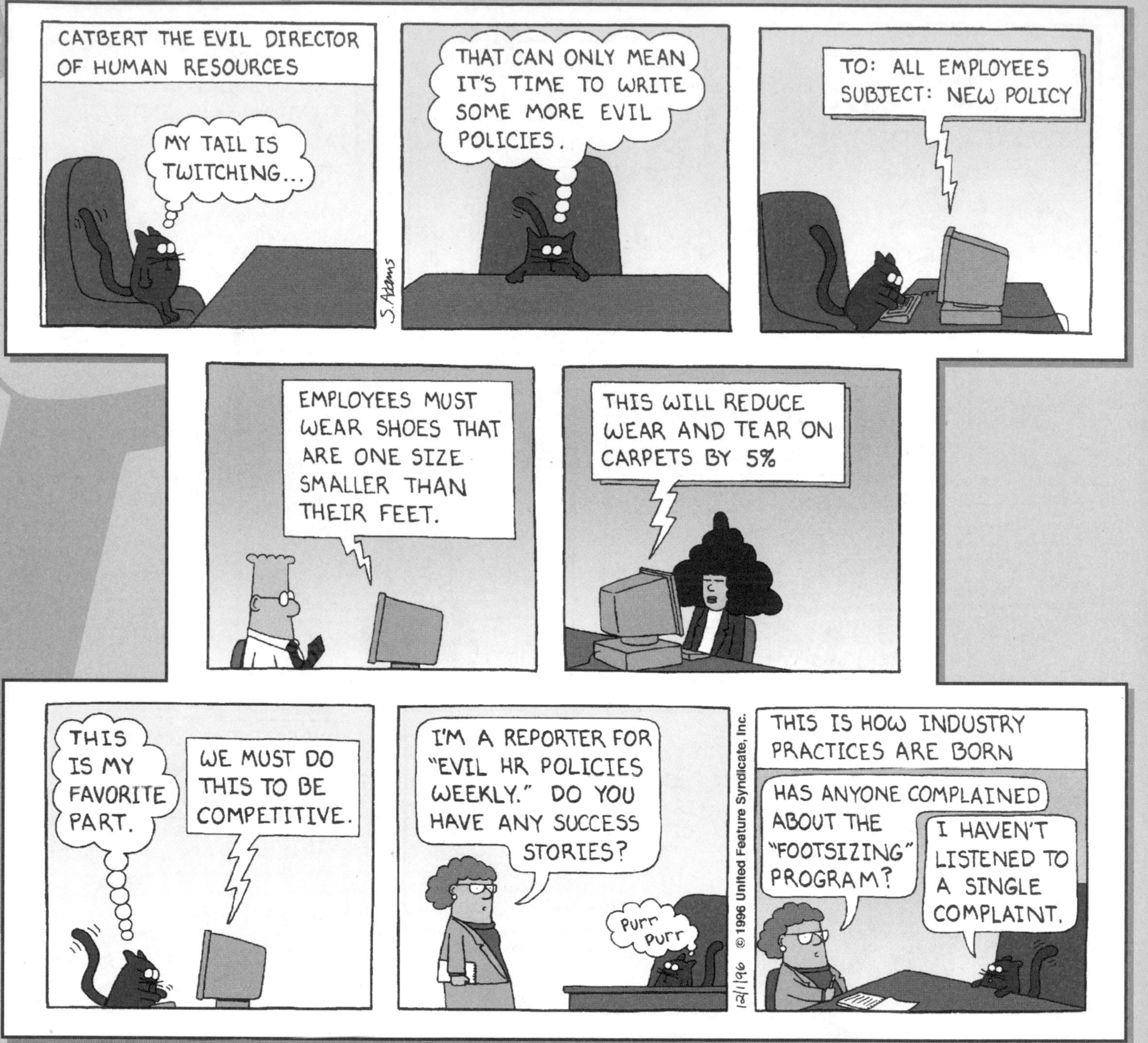
CATBERT THE EVIL DIRECTOR OF HUMAN RESOURCES
MY TAIL IS TWITCHING...
S. Adams
THAT CAN ONLY MEAN IT'S TIME TO WRITE SOME MORE EVIL POLICIES.
TO: ALL EMPLOYEES SUBJECT: NEW POLICY
EMPLOYEES MUST WEAR SHOES THAT ARE ONE SIZE SMALLER THAN THEIR FEET.
THIS WILL REDUCE WEAR AND TEAR ON CARPETS BY 5%
THIS IS MY FAVORITE PART.
WE MUST DO THIS TO BE COMPETITIVE.
I'M A REPORTER FOR "EVIL HR POLICIES WEEKLY." DO YOU HAVE ANY SUCCESS STORIES?
Purr Purr
© 1996 United Feature Syndicate, Inc.
12/1/96
THIS IS HOW INDUSTRY PRACTICES ARE BORN
HAS ANYONE COMPLAINED ABOUT THE "FOOTSIZING" PROGRAM?
I HAVEN'T LISTENED TO A SINGLE COMPLAINT.

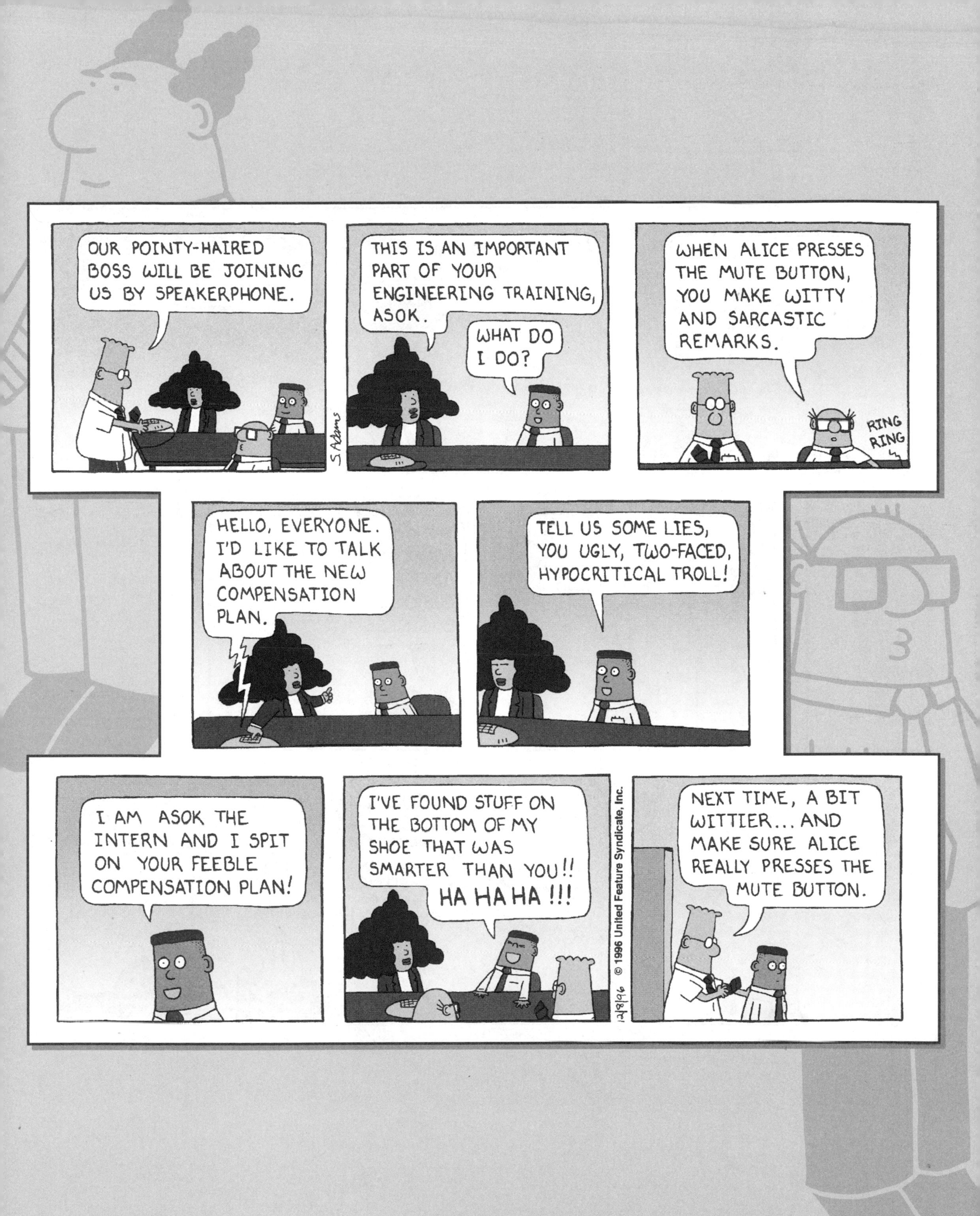
OUR POINTY-HAIRED BOSS WILL BE JOINING US BY SPEAKERPHONE.
S. Adams
THIS IS AN IMPORTANT PART OF YOUR ENGINEERING TRAINING, ASOK.
WHAT DO I DO?
WHEN ALICE PRESSES THE MUTE BUTTON, YOU MAKE WITTY AND SARCASTIC REMARKS.
RING RING
HELLO, EVERYONE. I'D LIKE TO TALK ABOUT THE NEW COMPENSATION PLAN.
TELL US SOME LIES, YOU UGLY, TWO-FACED, HYPOCRITICAL TROLL!
I AM ASOK THE INTERN AND I SPIT ON YOUR FEEBLE COMPENSATION PLAN!
I'VE FOUND STUFF ON THE BOTTOM OF MY SHOE THAT WAS SMARTER THAN YOU!!
HA HA HA !!!
12/8/96 © 1996 United Feature Syndicate, Inc.
NEXT TIME, A BIT WITTIER... AND MAKE SURE ALICE REALLY PRESSES THE MUTE BUTTON.

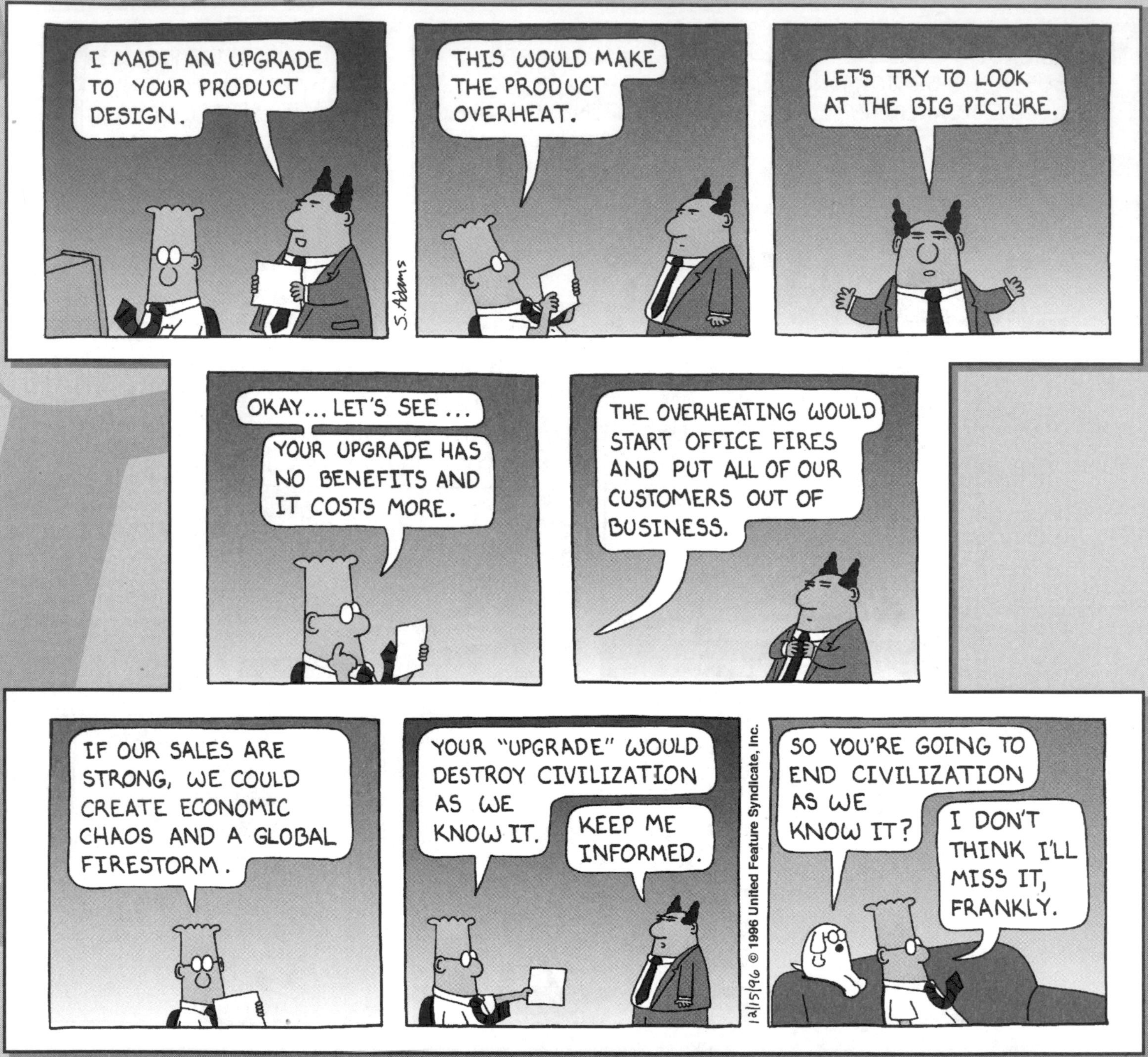
I MADE AN UPGRADE TO YOUR PRODUCT DESIGN.
THIS WOULD MAKE THE PRODUCT OVERHEAT.
S. Adams
LET'S TRY TO LOOK AT THE BIG PICTURE.
OKAY... LET'S SEE ...
YOUR UPGRADE HAS NO BENEFITS AND IT COSTS MORE.
THE OVERHEATING WOULD START OFFICE FIRES AND PUT ALL OF OUR CUSTOMERS OUT OF BUSINESS.
IF OUR SALES ARE STRONG, WE COULD CREATE ECONOMIC CHAOS AND A GLOBAL FIRESTORM.
YOUR "UPGRADE" WOULD DESTROY CIVILIZATION AS WE KNOW IT.
KEEP ME INFORMED.
12/5/96 © 1996 United Feature Syndicate, Inc.
SO YOU'RE GOING TO END CIVILIZATION AS WE KNOW IT?
I DON'T THINK I'LL MISS IT, FRANKLY.

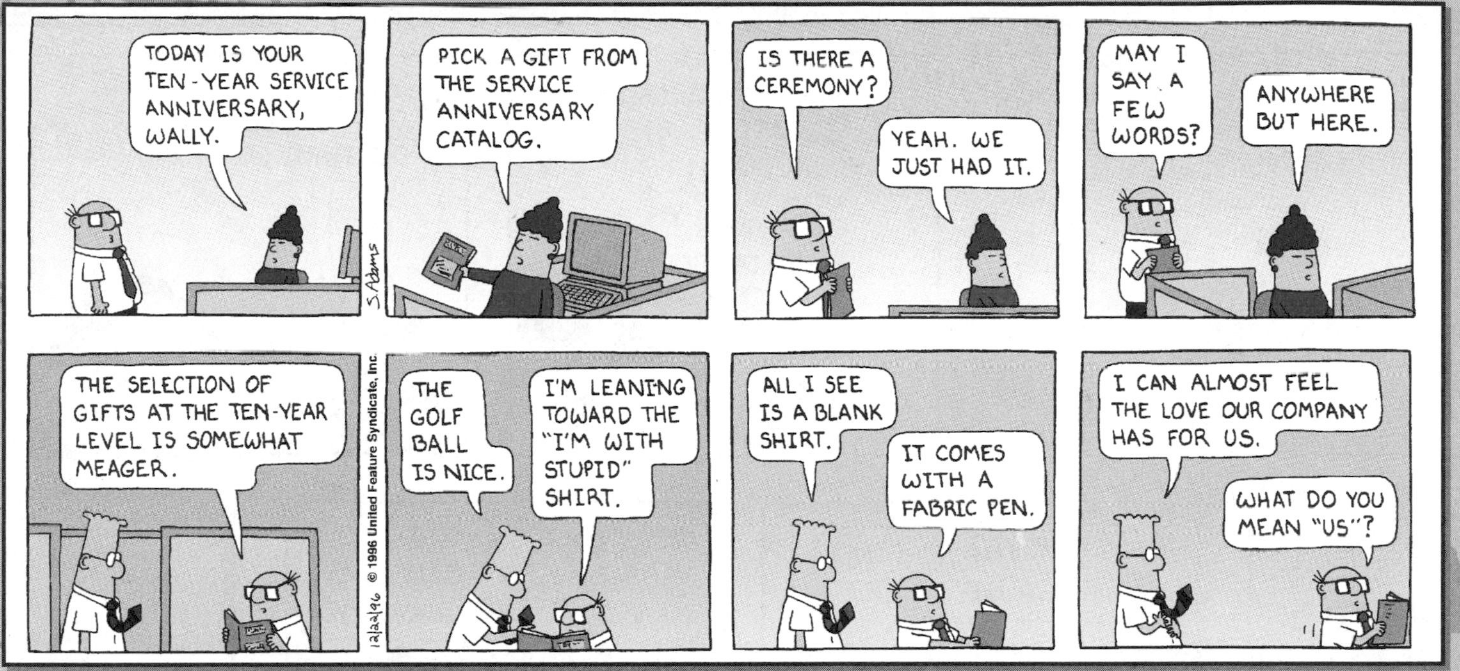
TODAY IS YOUR TEN-YEAR SERVICE ANNIVERSARY, WALLY.
S. Adams
PICK A GIFT FROM THE SERVICE ANNIVERSARY CATALOG.
IS THERE A CEREMONY?
YEAH. WE JUST HAD IT.
MAY I SAY A FEW WORDS?
ANYWHERE BUT HERE.
THE SELECTION OF GIFTS AT THE TEN-YEAR LEVEL IS SOMEWHAT MEAGER.
12/22/96 © 1996 United Feature Syndicate, Inc.
THE GOLF BALL IS NICE.
I'M LEANING TOWARD THE "I'M WITH STUPID" SHIRT.
ALL I SEE IS A BLANK SHIRT.
IT COMES WITH A FABRIC PEN.
I CAN ALMOST FEEL THE LOVE OUR COMPANY HAS FOR US.
WHAT DO YOU MEAN "US"?

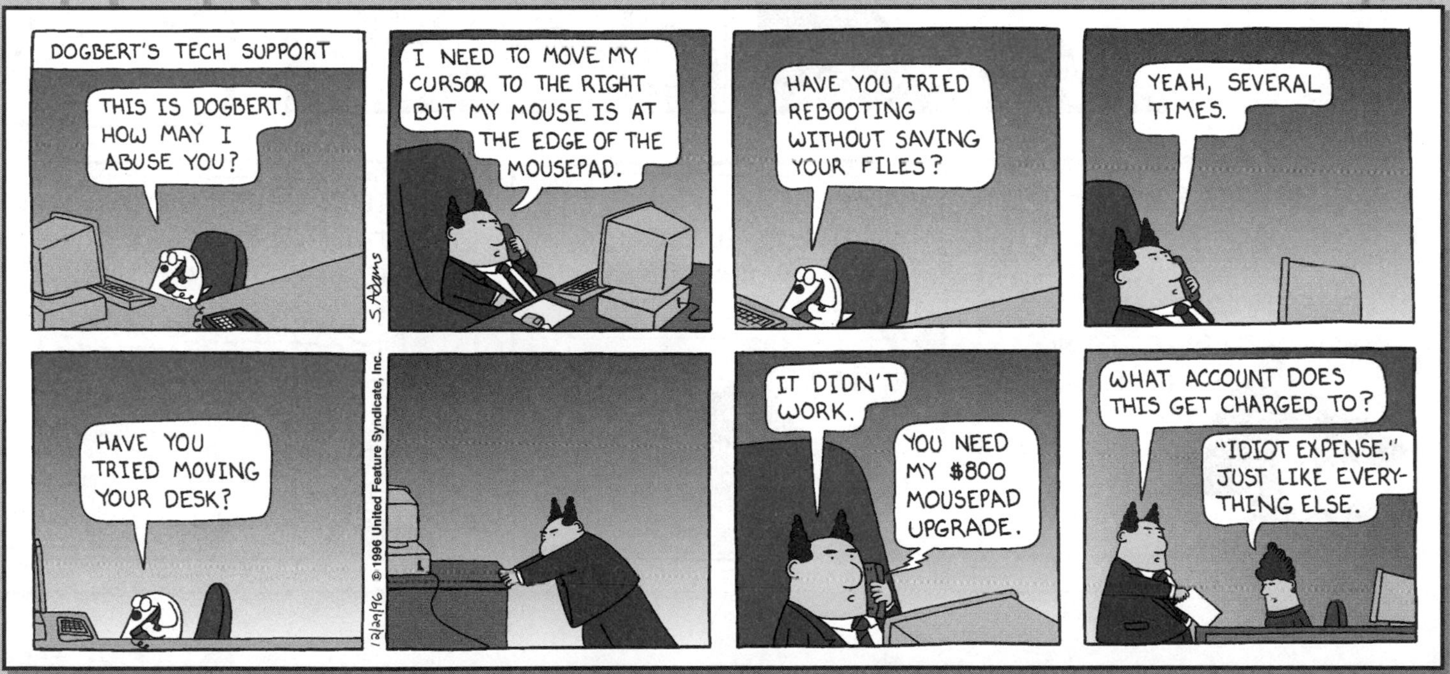
DOGBERT'S TECH SUPPORT
THIS IS DOGBERT. HOW MAY I ABUSE YOU?
S. Adams
I NEED TO MOVE MY CURSOR TO THE RIGHT BUT MY MOUSE IS AT THE EDGE OF THE MOUSEPAD.
HAVE YOU TRIED REBOOTING WITHOUT SAVING YOUR FILES?
YEAH, SEVERAL TIMES.
HAVE YOU TRIED MOVING YOUR DESK?
12/29/96 © 1996 United Feature Syndicate, Inc.
IT DIDN'T WORK.
YOU NEED MY $800 MOUSEPAD UPGRADE.
WHAT ACCOUNT DOES THIS GET CHARGED TO?
"IDIOT EXPENSE," JUST LIKE EVERYTHING ELSE.

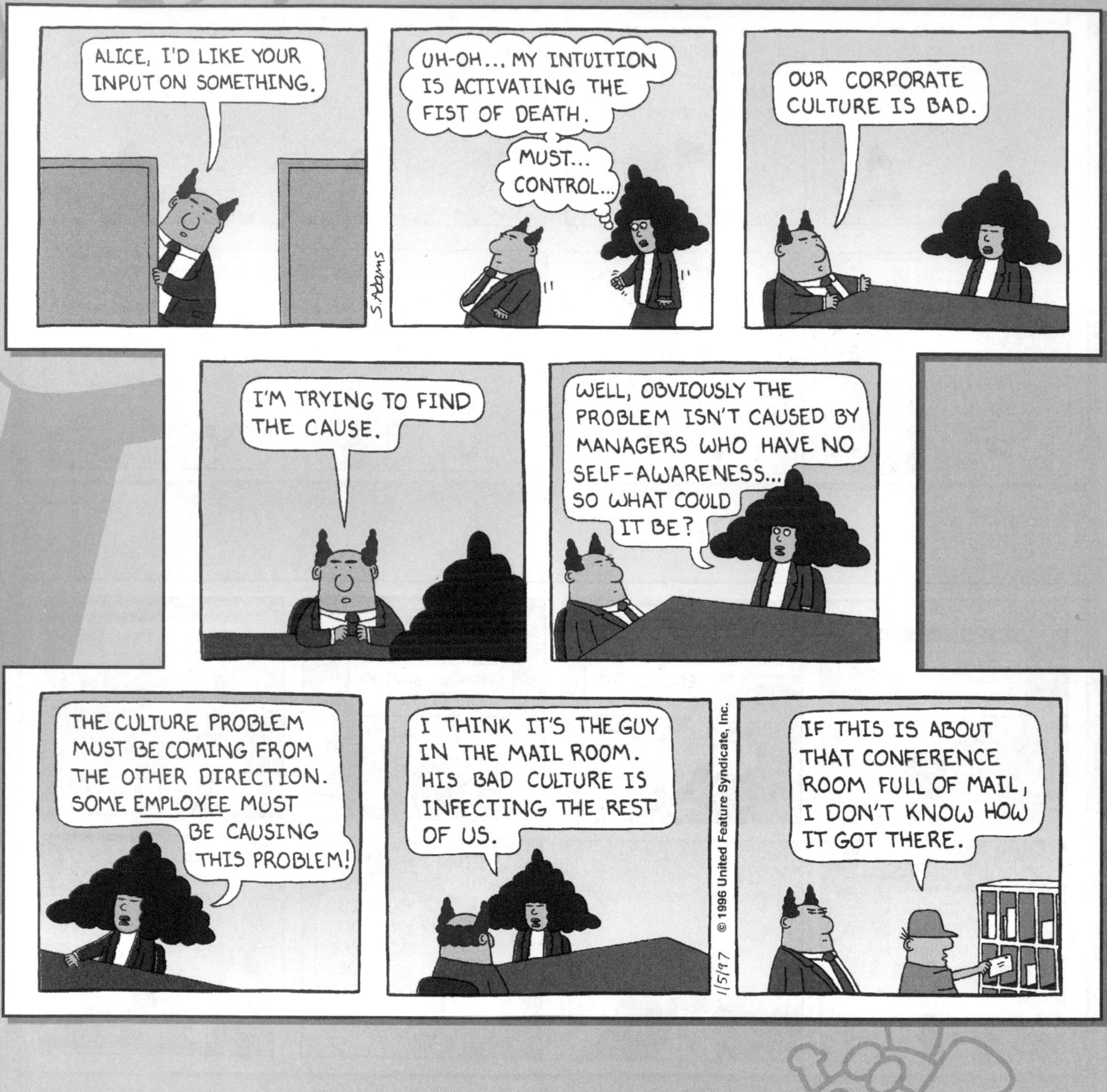

ALICE, I'D LIKE YOUR INPUT ON SOMETHING.
S. Adams
UH-OH... MY INTUITION IS ACTIVATING THE FIST OF DEATH.
MUST... CONTROL...
OUR CORPORATE CULTURE IS BAD.
I'M TRYING TO FIND THE CAUSE.
WELL, OBVIOUSLY THE PROBLEM ISN'T CAUSED BY MANAGERS WHO HAVE NO SELF-AWARENESS... SO WHAT COULD IT BE?
THE CULTURE PROBLEM MUST BE COMING FROM THE OTHER DIRECTION. SOME EMPLOYEE MUST BE CAUSING THIS PROBLEM!
I THINK IT'S THE GUY IN THE MAIL ROOM. HIS BAD CULTURE IS INFECTING THE REST OF US.
© 1996 United Feature Syndicate, Inc.
1/5/97
IF THIS IS ABOUT THAT CONFERENCE ROOM FULL OF MAIL, I DON'T KNOW HOW IT GOT THERE.

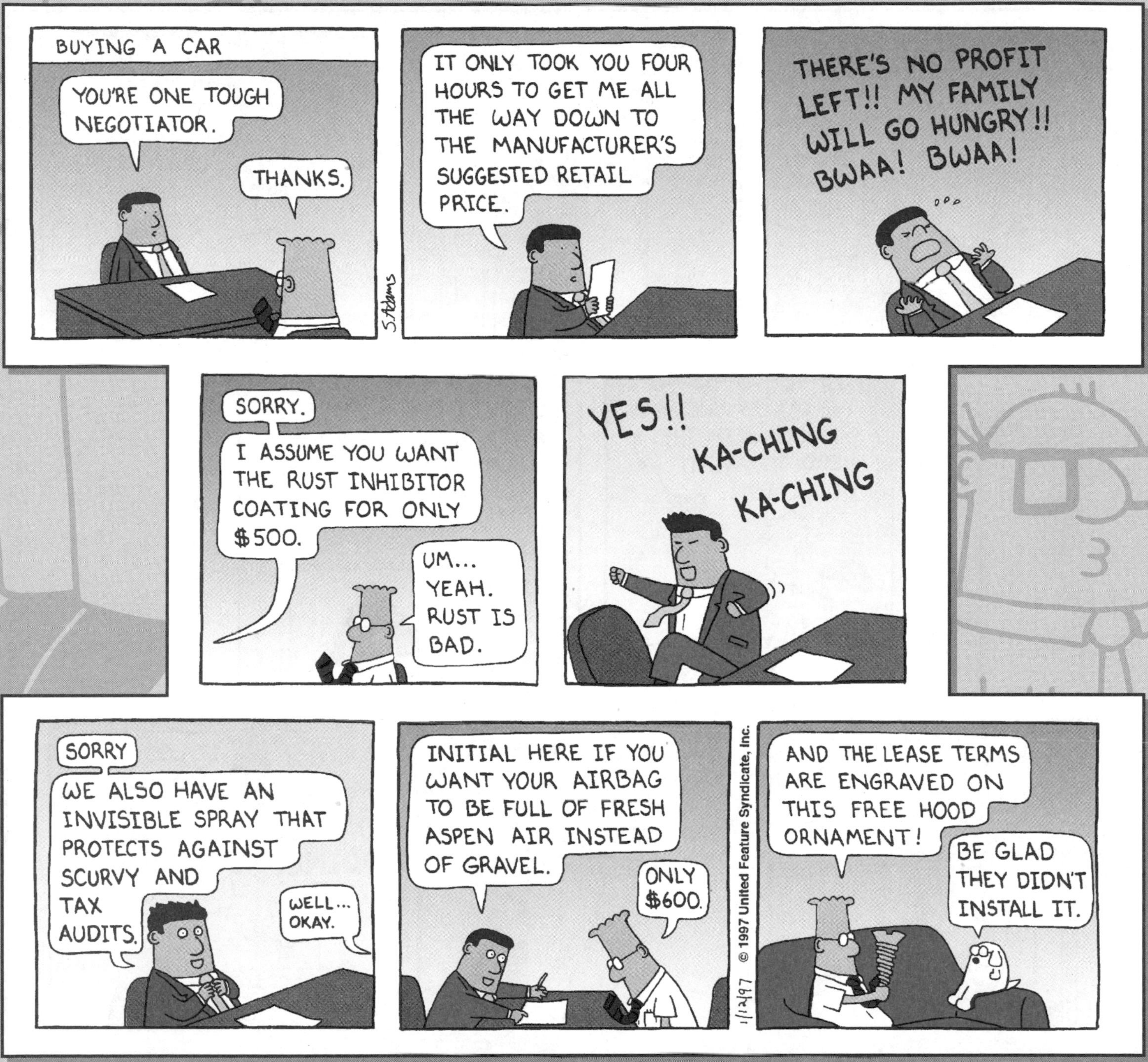
BUYING A CAR
YOU'RE ONE TOUGH NEGOTIATOR.
THANKS.
S. Adams
IT ONLY TOOK YOU FOUR HOURS TO GET ME ALL THE WAY DOWN TO THE MANUFACTURER'S SUGGESTED RETAIL PRICE.
THERE'S NO PROFIT LEFT!! MY FAMILY WILL GO HUNGRY!! BWAA! BWAA!
SORRY.
I ASSUME YOU WANT THE RUST INHIBITOR COATING FOR ONLY $500.
UM... YEAH. RUST IS BAD.
YES!!
KA-CHING
KA-CHING
SORRY
WE ALSO HAVE AN INVISIBLE SPRAY THAT PROTECTS AGAINST SCURVY AND TAX AUDITS.
WELL... OKAY.
INITIAL HERE IF YOU WANT YOUR AIRBAG TO BE FULL OF FRESH ASPEN AIR INSTEAD OF GRAVEL.
ONLY $600.
© 1997 United Feature Syndicate, Inc.
1/12/97
AND THE LEASE TERMS ARE ENGRAVED ON THIS FREE HOOD ORNAMENT!
BE GLAD THEY DIDN'T INSTALL IT.

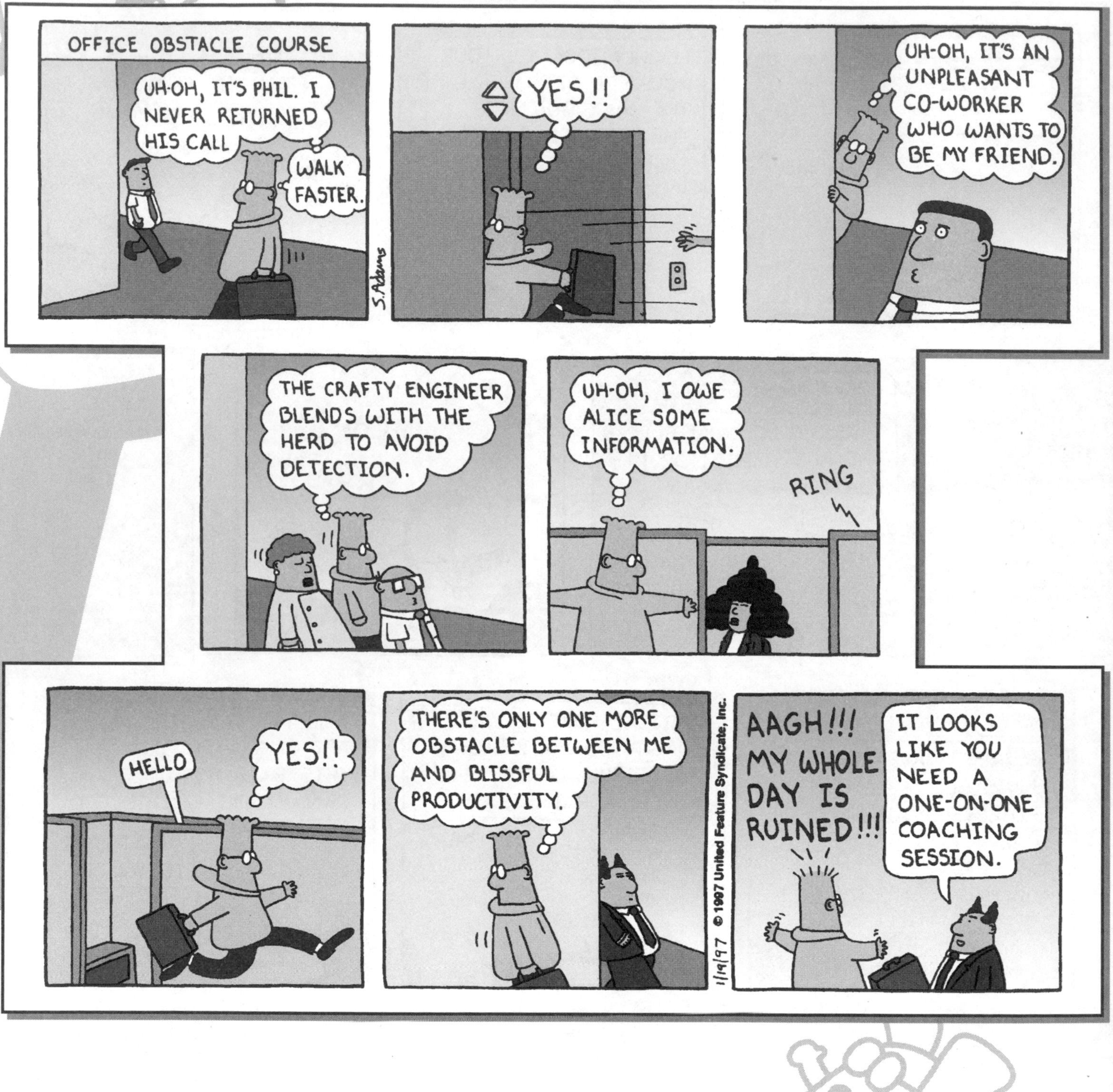
OFFICE OBSTACLE COURSE
UH-OH, IT'S PHIL. I NEVER RETURNED HIS CALL
WALK FASTER.
S. Adams
YES!!
UH-OH, IT'S AN UNPLEASANT CO-WORKER WHO WANTS TO BE MY FRIEND.
THE CRAFTY ENGINEER BLENDS WITH THE HERD TO AVOID DETECTION.
UH-OH, I OWE ALICE SOME INFORMATION.
RING
HELLO
YES!!
THERE'S ONLY ONE MORE OBSTACLE BETWEEN ME AND BLISSFUL PRODUCTIVITY.
1/19/97 © 1997 United Feature Syndicate, Inc.
AAGH!!! MY WHOLE DAY IS RUINED!!!
IT LOOKS LIKE YOU NEED A ONE-ON-ONE COACHING SESSION.

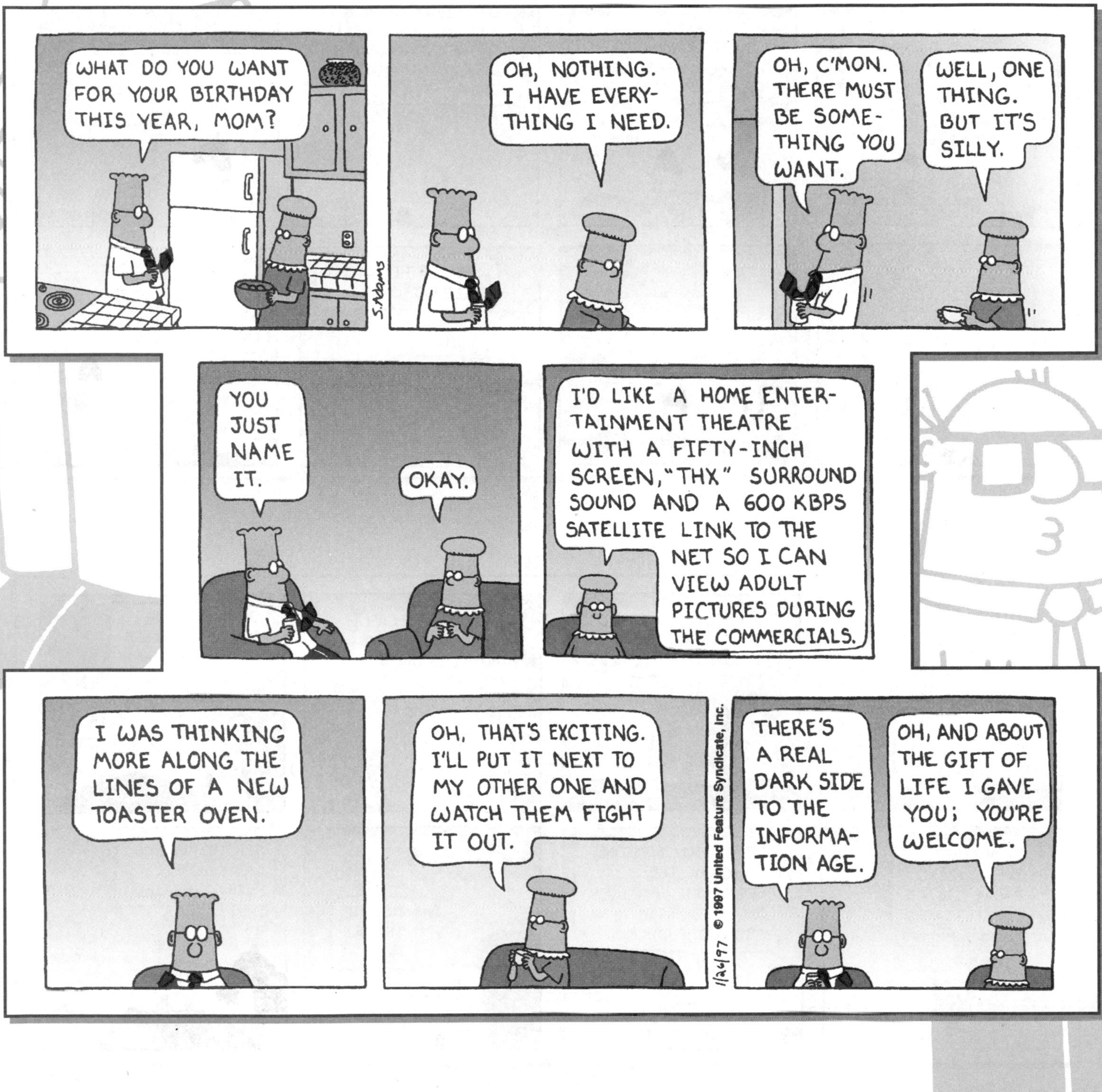
WHAT DO YOU WANT FOR YOUR BIRTHDAY THIS YEAR, MOM?
S. Adams
OH, NOTHING. I HAVE EVERYTHING I NEED.
OH, C'MON. THERE MUST BE SOMETHING YOU WANT.
WELL, ONE THING. BUT IT'S SILLY.
YOU JUST NAME IT.
OKAY.
I'D LIKE A HOME ENTERTAINMENT THEATRE WITH A FIFTY-INCH SCREEN, "THX" SURROUND SOUND AND A 600 KBPS SATELLITE LINK TO THE NET SO I CAN VIEW ADULT PICTURES DURING THE COMMERCIALS.
I WAS THINKING MORE ALONG THE LINES OF A NEW TOASTER OVEN.
OH, THAT'S EXCITING. I'LL PUT IT NEXT TO MY OTHER ONE AND WATCH THEM FIGHT IT OUT.
1/26/97 © 1997 United Feature Syndicate, Inc.
THERE'S A REAL DARK SIDE TO THE INFORMATION AGE.
OH, AND ABOUT THE GIFT OF LIFE I GAVE YOU; YOU'RE WELCOME.

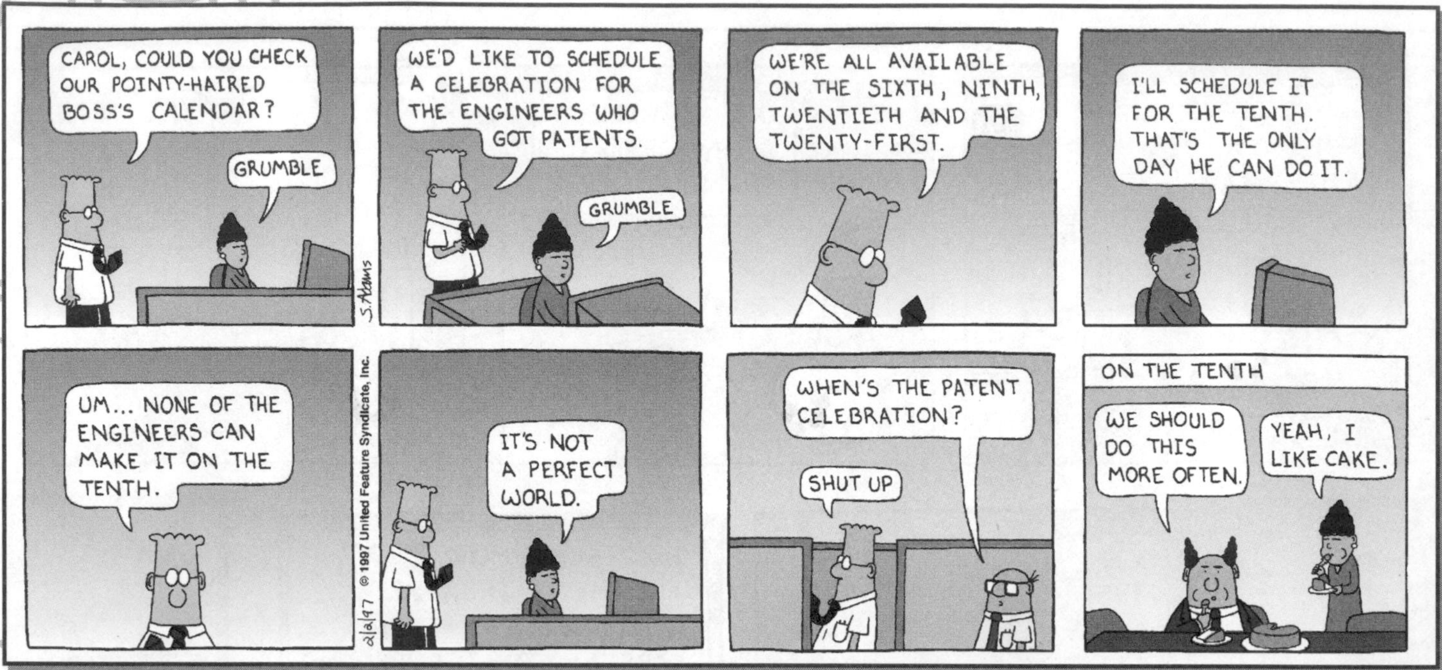
CAROL, COULD YOU CHECK OUR POINTY-HAIRED BOSS'S CALENDAR?
GRUMBLE
S. Adams
WE'D LIKE TO SCHEDULE A CELEBRATION FOR THE ENGINEERS WHO GOT PATENTS.
GRUMBLE
WE'RE ALL AVAILABLE ON THE SIXTH, NINTH, TWENTIETH AND THE TWENTY-FIRST.
I'LL SCHEDULE IT FOR THE TENTH. THAT'S THE ONLY DAY HE CAN DO IT.
UM... NONE OF THE ENGINEERS CAN MAKE IT ON THE TENTH.
© 1997 United Feature Syndicate, Inc.
IT'S NOT A PERFECT WORLD.
WHEN'S THE PATENT CELEBRATION?
SHUT UP
ON THE TENTH
WE SHOULD DO THIS MORE OFTEN.
YEAH, I LIKE CAKE.

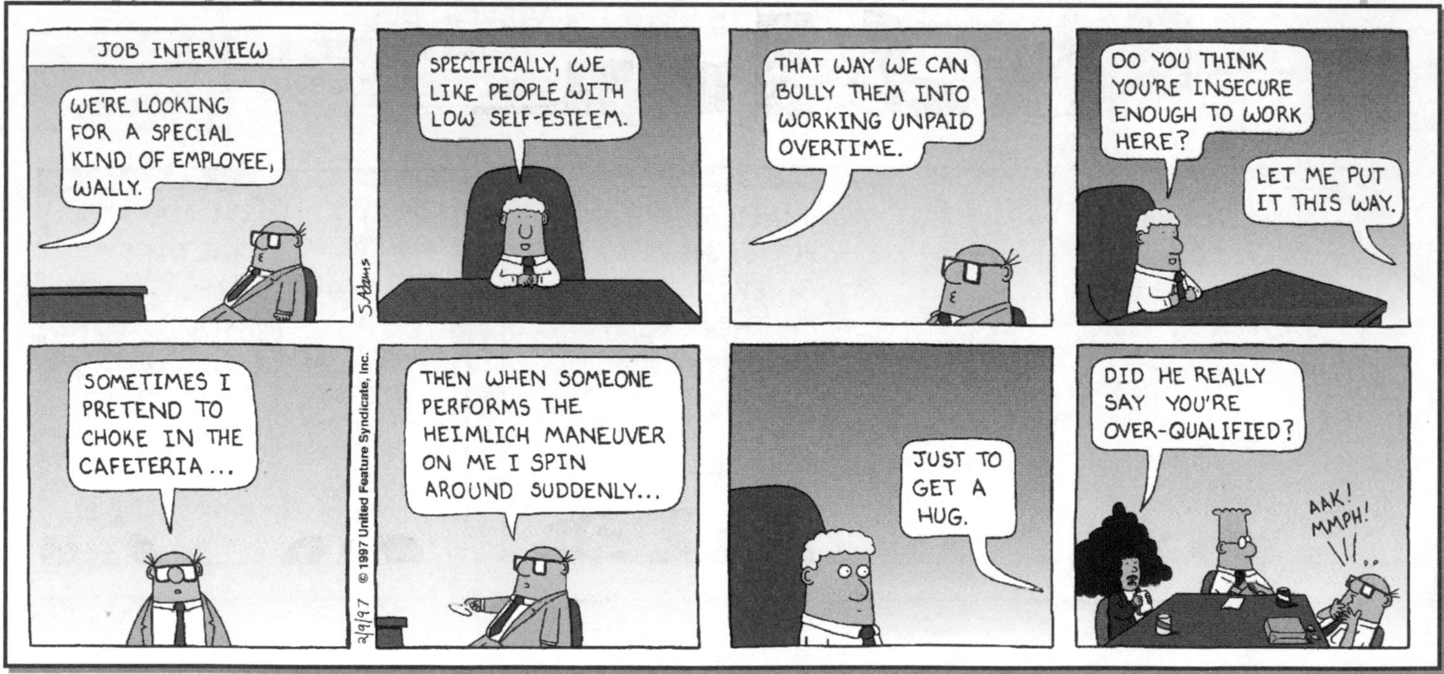
JOB INTERVIEW
WE'RE LOOKING FOR A SPECIAL KIND OF EMPLOYEE, WALLY.
S. Adams
SPECIFICALLY, WE LIKE PEOPLE WITH LOW SELF-ESTEEM.
THAT WAY WE CAN BULLY THEM INTO WORKING UNPAID OVERTIME.
DO YOU THINK YOU'RE INSECURE ENOUGH TO WORK HERE?
LET ME PUT IT THIS WAY.
SOMETIMES I PRETEND TO CHOKE IN THE CAFETERIA...
© 1997 United Feature Syndicate, Inc.
THEN WHEN SOMEONE PERFORMS THE HEIMLICH MANEUVER ON ME I SPIN AROUND SUDDENLY...
JUST TO GET A HUG.
DID HE REALLY SAY YOU'RE OVER-QUALIFIED?
AAK! MMPH!

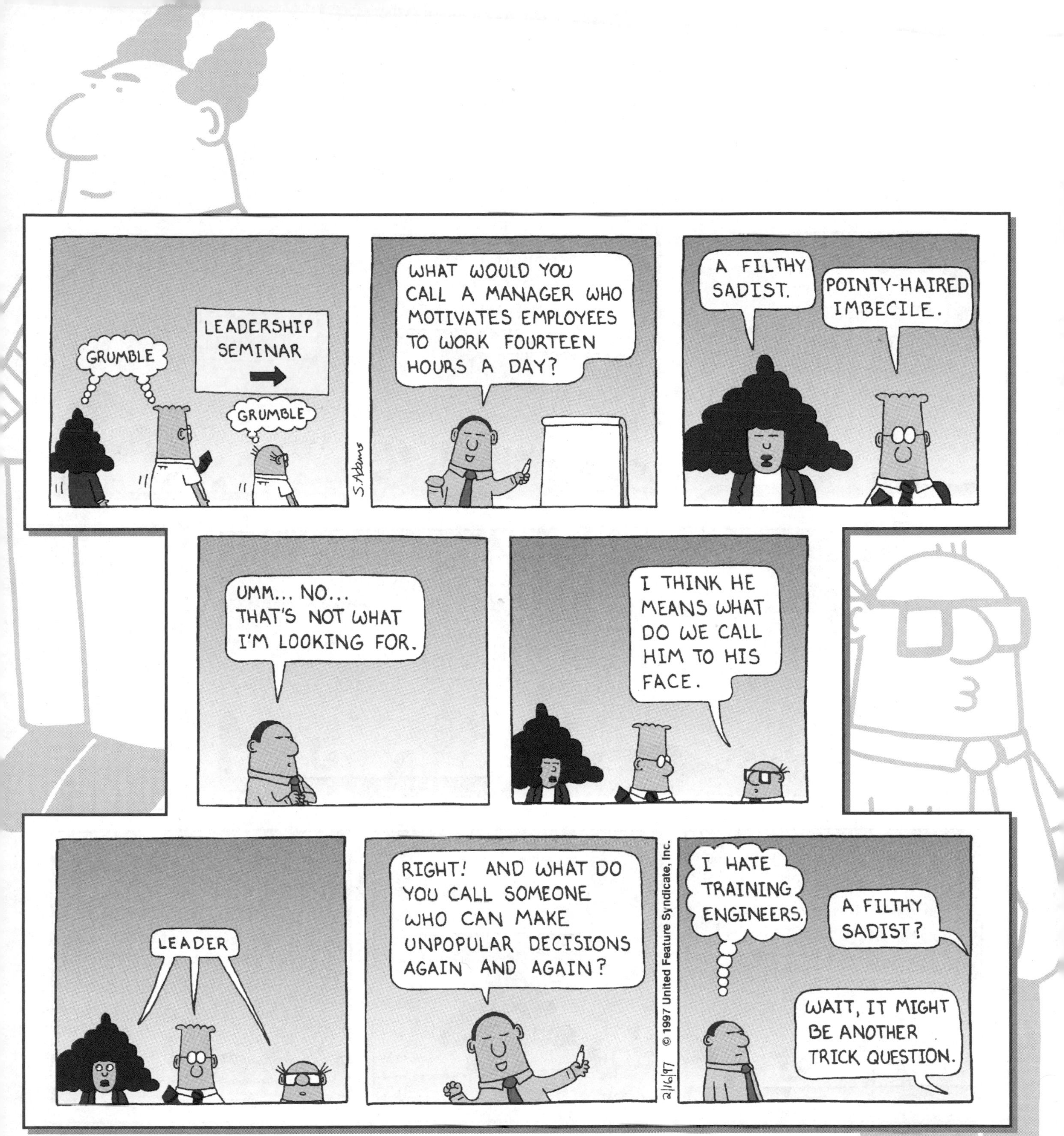
GRUMBLE
LEADERSHIP SEMINAR
GRUMBLE
S. Adams
WHAT WOULD YOU CALL A MANAGER WHO MOTIVATES EMPLOYEES TO WORK FOURTEEN HOURS A DAY?
A FILTHY SADIST.
POINTY-HAIRED IMBECILE.
UMM... NO... THAT'S NOT WHAT I'M LOOKING FOR.
I THINK HE MEANS WHAT DO WE CALL HIM TO HIS FACE.
LEADER
RIGHT! AND WHAT DO YOU CALL SOMEONE WHO CAN MAKE UNPOPULAR DECISIONS AGAIN AND AGAIN?
2/16/97 © 1997 United Feature Syndicate, Inc.
I HATE TRAINING ENGINEERS.
A FILTHY SADIST?
WAIT, IT MIGHT BE ANOTHER TRICK QUESTION.

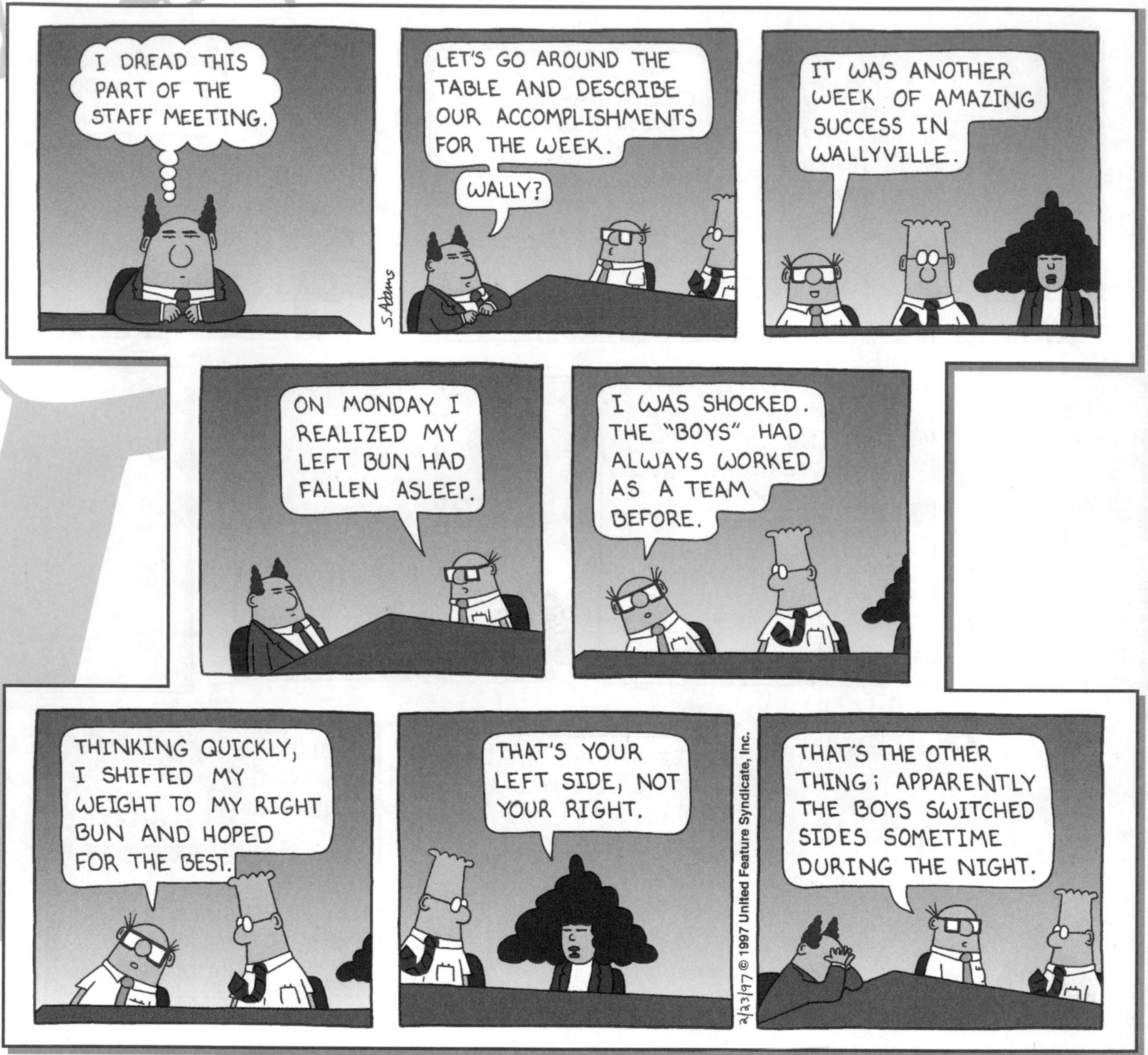
I DREAD THIS PART OF THE STAFF MEETING.
LET'S GO AROUND THE TABLE AND DESCRIBE OUR ACCOMPLISHMENTS FOR THE WEEK.
WALLY?
S. Adams
IT WAS ANOTHER WEEK OF AMAZING SUCCESS IN WALLYVILLE.
ON MONDAY I REALIZED MY LEFT BUN HAD FALLEN ASLEEP.
I WAS SHOCKED. THE "BOYS" HAD ALWAYS WORKED AS A TEAM BEFORE.
THINKING QUICKLY, I SHIFTED MY WEIGHT TO MY RIGHT BUN AND HOPED FOR THE BEST.
THAT'S YOUR LEFT SIDE, NOT YOUR RIGHT.
2/23/97 © 1997 United Feature Syndicate, Inc.
THAT'S THE OTHER THING; APPARENTLY THE BOYS SWITCHED SIDES SOMETIME DURING THE NIGHT.

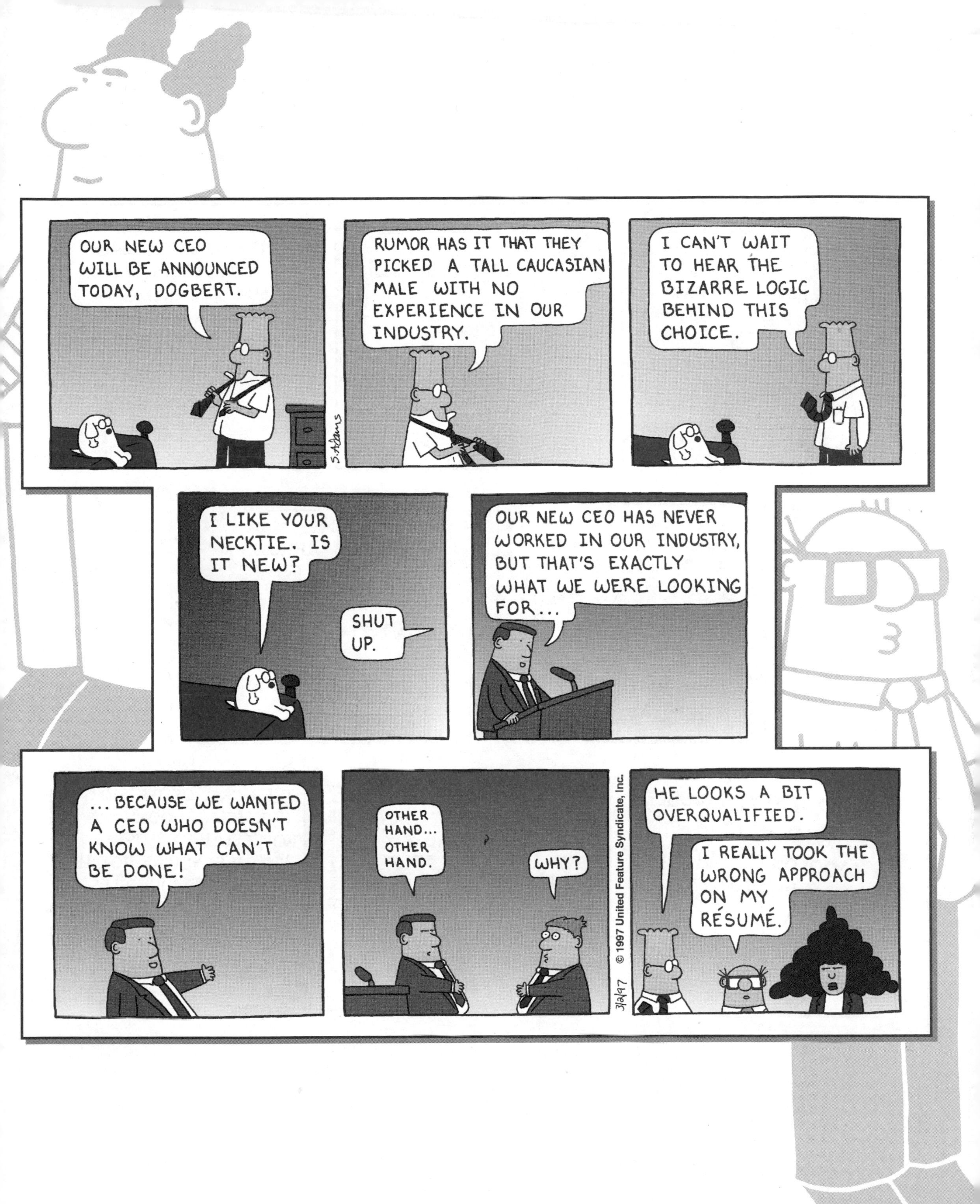
OUR NEW CEO WILL BE ANNOUNCED TODAY, DOGBERT.
S. Adams
RUMOR HAS IT THAT THEY PICKED A TALL CAUCASIAN MALE WITH NO EXPERIENCE IN OUR INDUSTRY.
I CAN'T WAIT TO HEAR THE BIZARRE LOGIC BEHIND THIS CHOICE.
I LIKE YOUR NECKTIE. IS IT NEW?
SHUT UP.
OUR NEW CEO HAS NEVER WORKED IN OUR INDUSTRY, BUT THAT'S EXACTLY WHAT WE WERE LOOKING FOR...
... BECAUSE WE WANTED A CEO WHO DOESN'T KNOW WHAT CAN'T BE DONE!
OTHER HAND... OTHER HAND.
WHY?
3/2/97 © 1997 United Feature Syndicate, Inc.
HE LOOKS A BIT OVERQUALIFIED.
I REALLY TOOK THE WRONG APPROACH ON MY RÉSUMÉ.

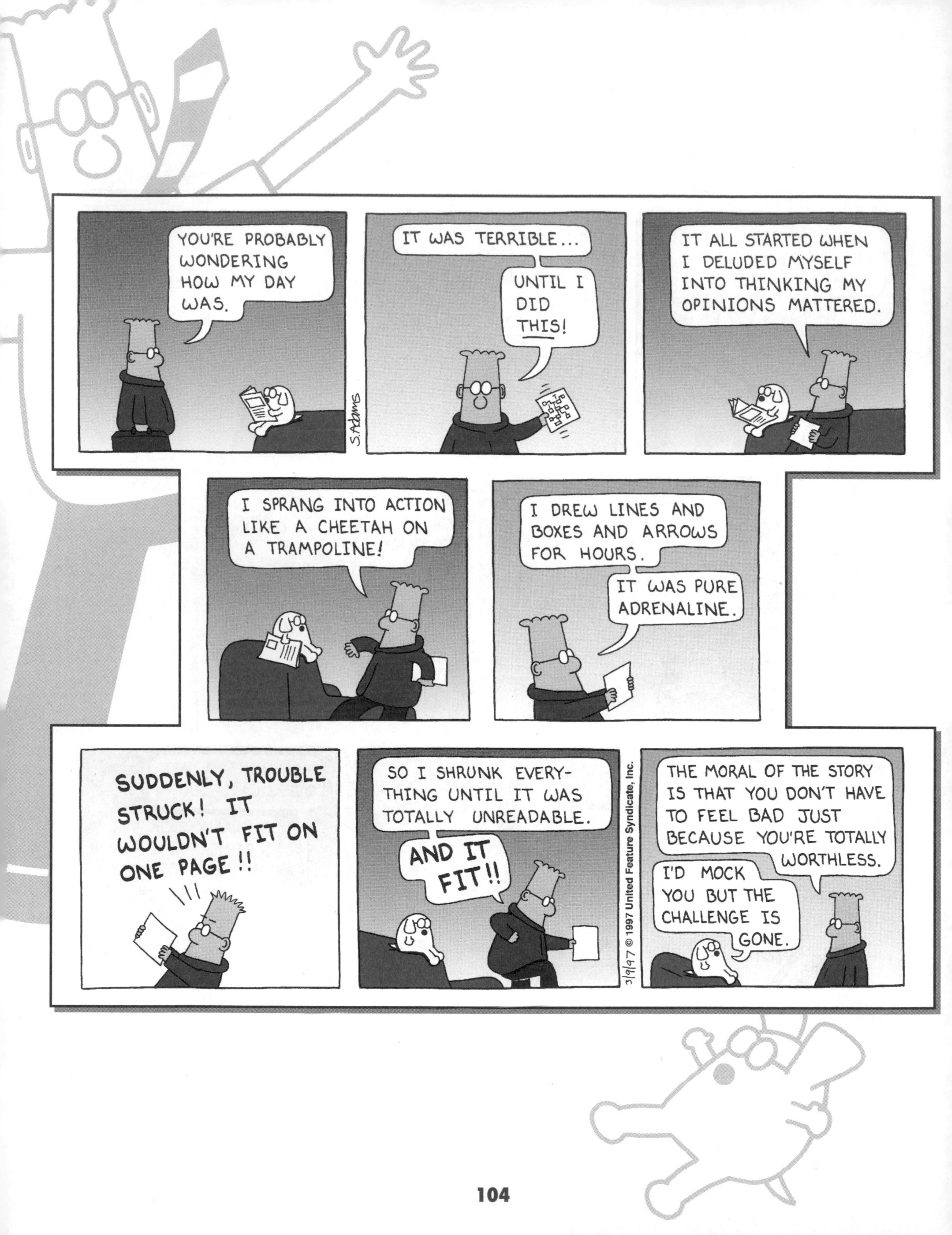

YOU'RE PROBABLY WONDERING HOW MY DAY WAS.
S. Adams
IT WAS TERRIBLE...
UNTIL I DID THIS!
IT ALL STARTED WHEN I DELUDED MYSELF INTO THINKING MY OPINIONS MATTERED.
I SPRANG INTO ACTION LIKE A CHEETAH ON A TRAMPOLINE!
I DREW LINES AND BOXES AND ARROWS FOR HOURS.
IT WAS PURE ADRENALINE.
SUDDENLY, TROUBLE STRUCK! IT WOULDN'T FIT ON ONE PAGE!!
SO I SHRUNK EVERYTHING UNTIL IT WAS TOTALLY UNREADABLE.
AND IT FIT!!
3/9/97 © 1997 United Feature Syndicate, Inc.
THE MORAL OF THE STORY IS THAT YOU DON'T HAVE TO FEEL BAD JUST BECAUSE YOU'RE TOTALLY WORTHLESS.
I'D MOCK YOU BUT THE CHALLENGE IS GONE.

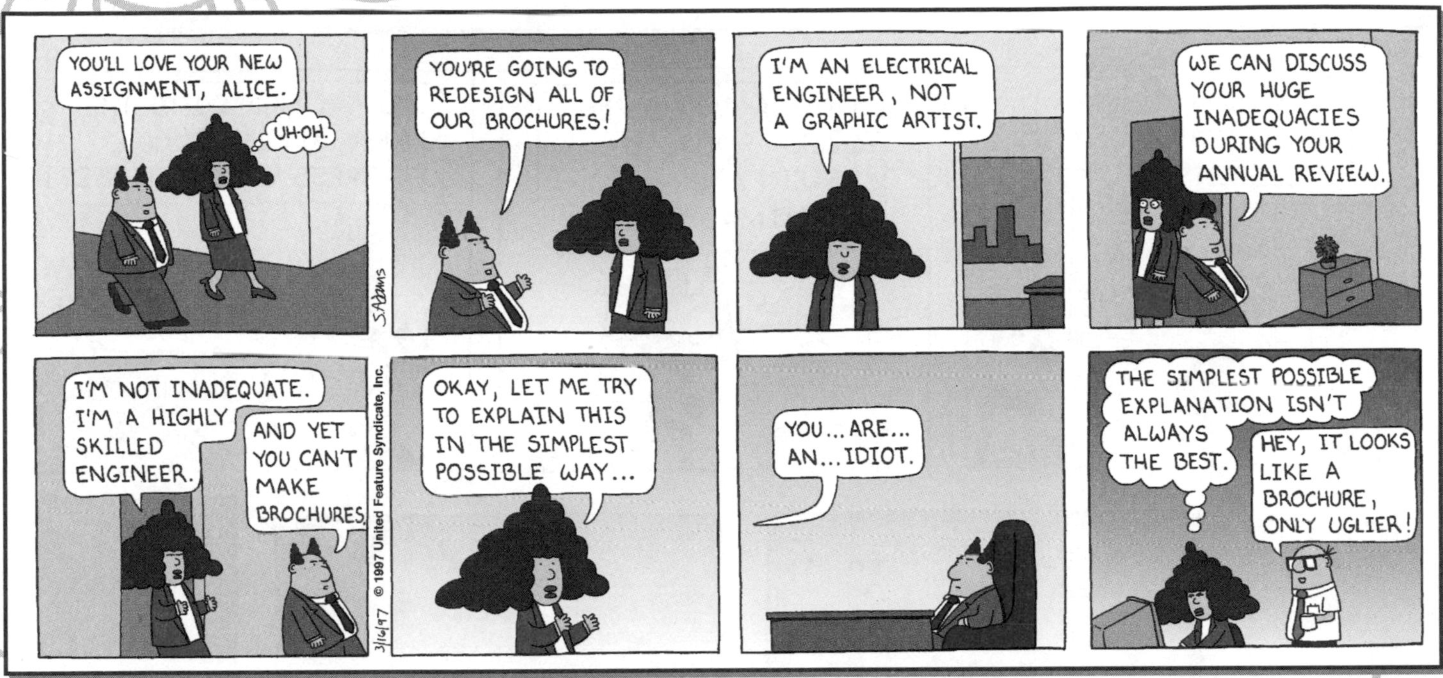
YOU'LL LOVE YOUR NEW ASSIGNMENT, ALICE.
UH-OH.
YOU'RE GOING TO REDESIGN ALL OF OUR BROCHURES!
I'M AN ELECTRICAL ENGINEER, NOT A GRAPHIC ARTIST.
WE CAN DISCUSS YOUR HUGE INADEQUACIES DURING YOUR ANNUAL REVIEW.
S.Adams
I'M NOT INADEQUATE. I'M A HIGHLY SKILLED ENGINEER.
AND YET YOU CAN'T MAKE BROCHURES.
3/16/97 © 1997 United Feature Syndicate, Inc.
OKAY, LET ME TRY TO EXPLAIN THIS IN THE SIMPLEST POSSIBLE WAY...
YOU... ARE... AN... IDIOT.
THE SIMPLEST POSSIBLE EXPLANATION ISN'T ALWAYS THE BEST.
HEY, IT LOOKS LIKE A BROCHURE, ONLY UGLIER!

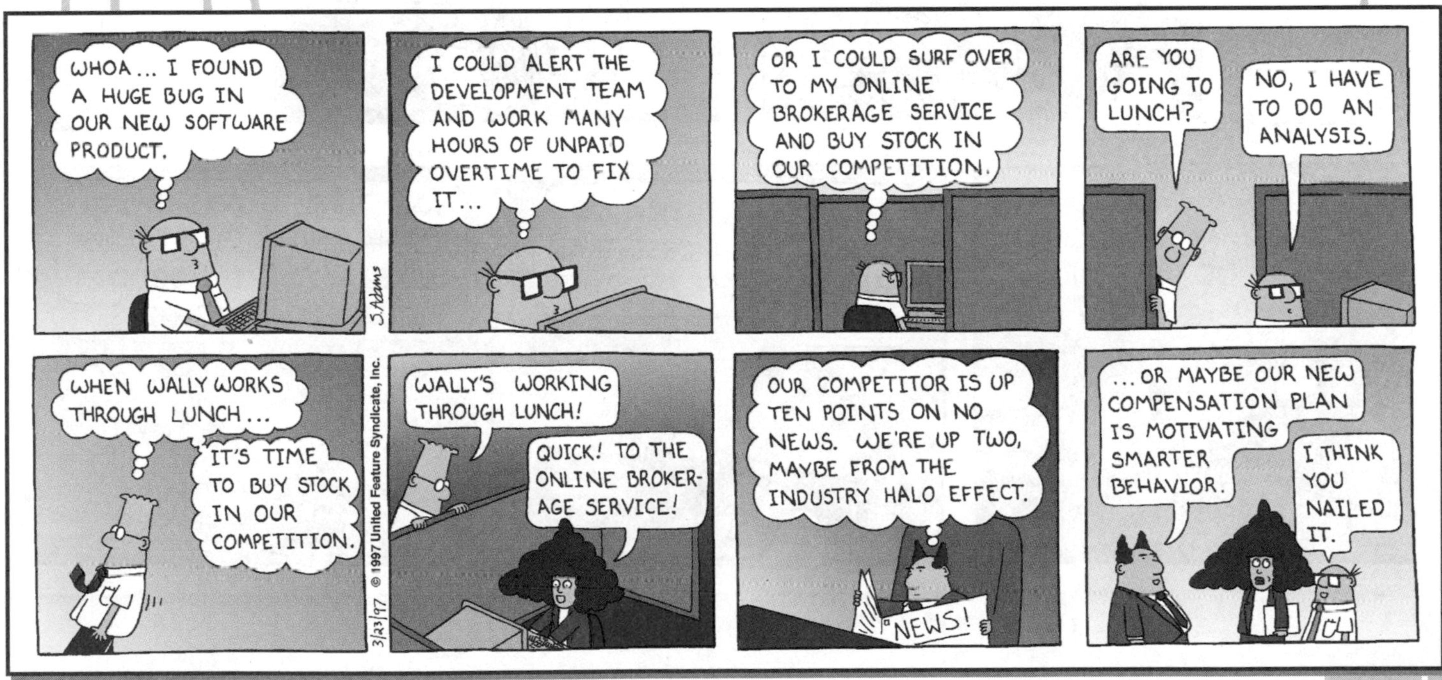
WHOA... I FOUND A HUGE BUG IN OUR NEW SOFTWARE PRODUCT.
I COULD ALERT THE DEVELOPMENT TEAM AND WORK MANY HOURS OF UNPAID OVERTIME TO FIX IT...
OR I COULD SURF OVER TO MY ONLINE BROKERAGE SERVICE AND BUY STOCK IN OUR COMPETITION.
ARE YOU GOING TO LUNCH?
NO, I HAVE TO DO AN ANALYSIS.
S.Adams
WHEN WALLY WORKS THROUGH LUNCH...
IT'S TIME TO BUY STOCK IN OUR COMPETITION.
3/23/97 © 1997 United Feature Syndicate, Inc.
WALLY'S WORKING THROUGH LUNCH!
QUICK! TO THE ONLINE BROKERAGE SERVICE!
OUR COMPETITOR IS UP TEN POINTS ON NO NEWS. WE'RE UP TWO, MAYBE FROM THE INDUSTRY HALO EFFECT.
NEWS!
...OR MAYBE OUR NEW COMPENSATION PLAN IS MOTIVATING SMARTER BEHAVIOR.
I THINK YOU NAILED IT.

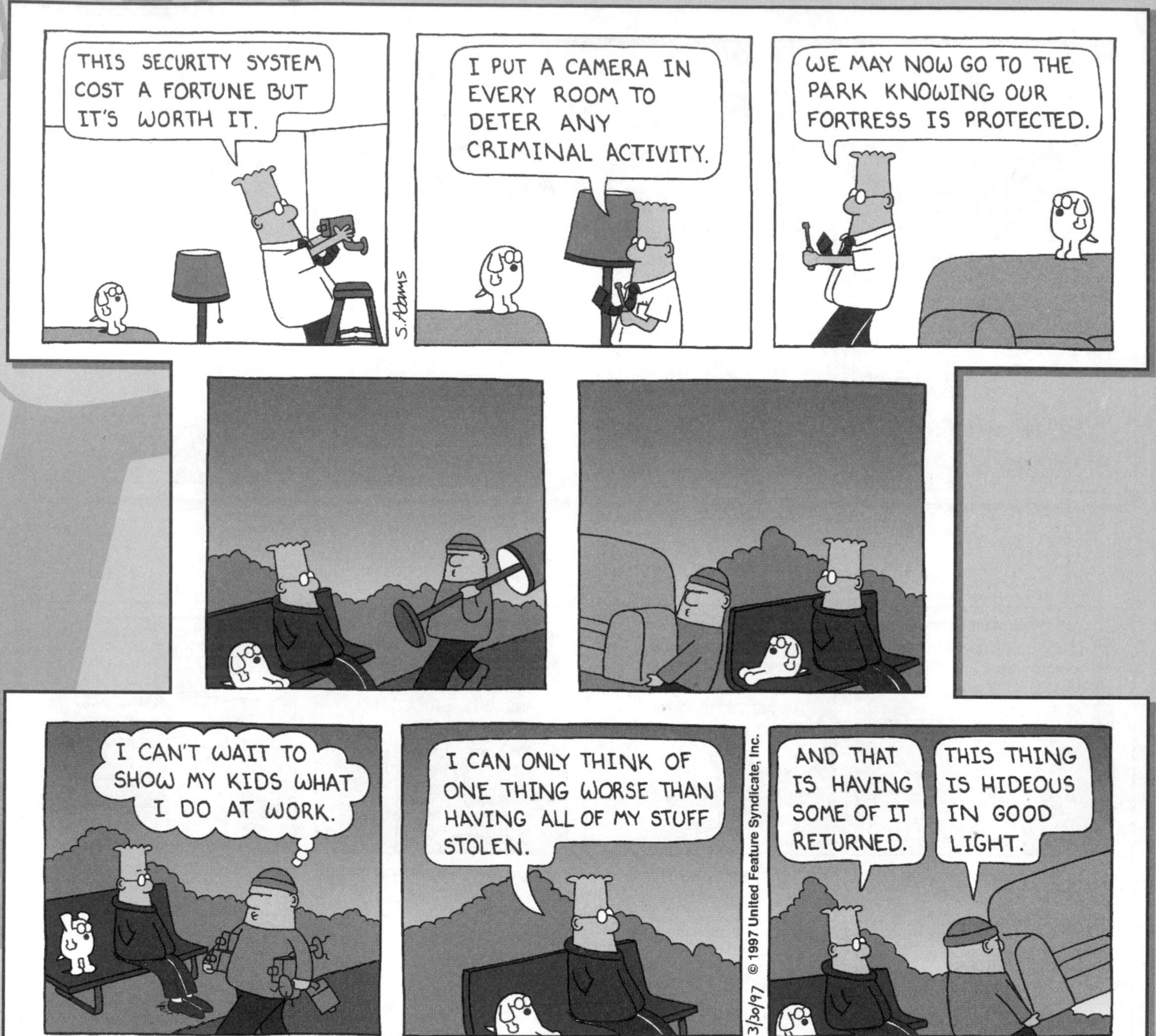

THIS SECURITY SYSTEM COST A FORTUNE BUT IT'S WORTH IT.
S. Adams
I PUT A CAMERA IN EVERY ROOM TO DETER ANY CRIMINAL ACTIVITY.
WE MAY NOW GO TO THE PARK KNOWING OUR FORTRESS IS PROTECTED.
I CAN'T WAIT TO SHOW MY KIDS WHAT I DO AT WORK.
I CAN ONLY THINK OF ONE THING WORSE THAN HAVING ALL OF MY STUFF STOLEN.
3/30/97 © 1997 United Feature Syndicate, Inc.
AND THAT IS HAVING SOME OF IT RETURNED.
THIS THING IS HIDEOUS IN GOOD LIGHT.

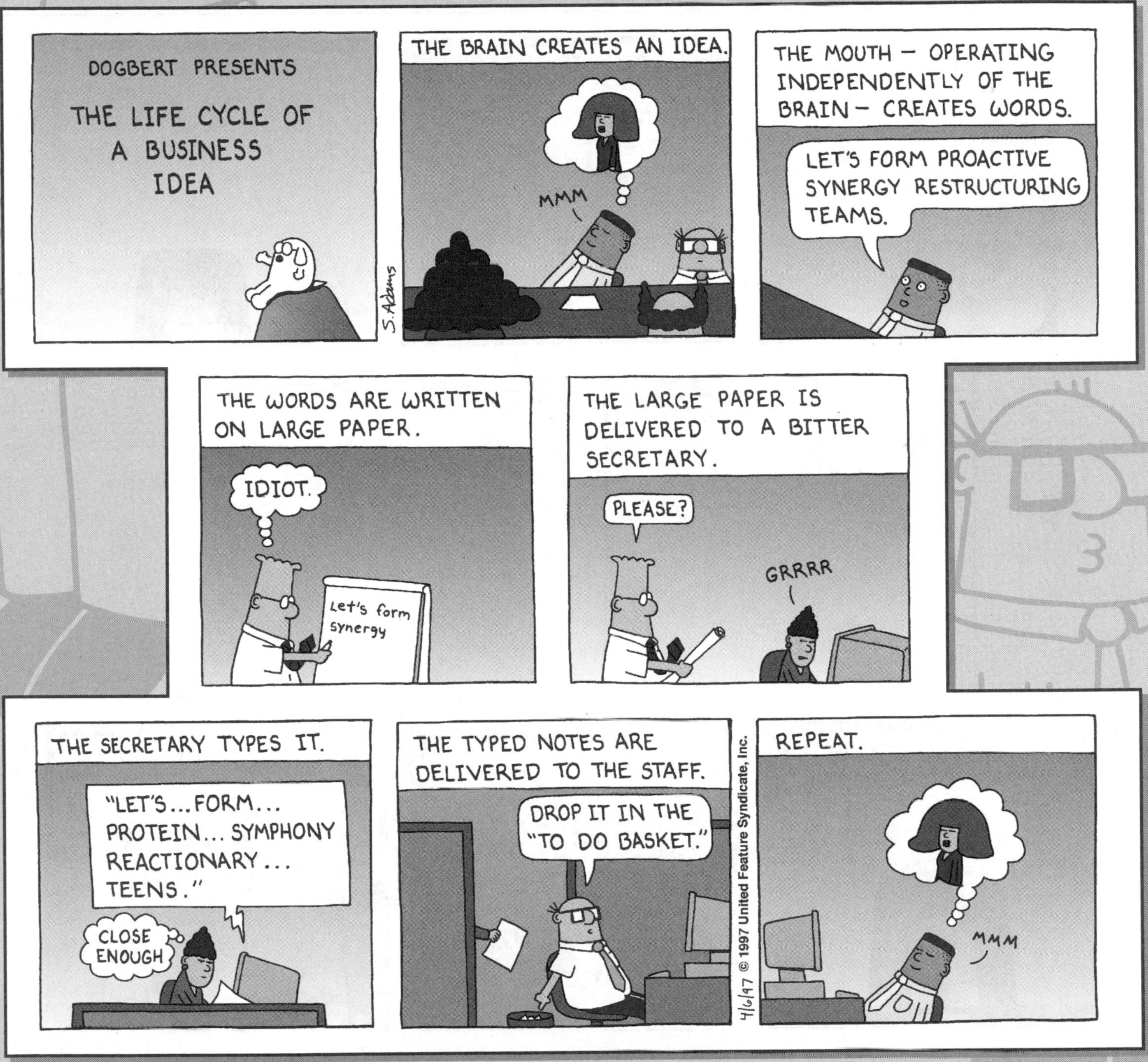
DOGBERT PRESENTS
THE LIFE CYCLE OF A BUSINESS IDEA
S. Adams
THE BRAIN CREATES AN IDEA.
MMM
THE MOUTH – OPERATING INDEPENDENTLY OF THE BRAIN – CREATES WORDS.
LET'S FORM PROACTIVE SYNERGY RESTRUCTURING TEAMS.
THE WORDS ARE WRITTEN ON LARGE PAPER.
IDIOT.
Let's form synergy
THE LARGE PAPER IS DELIVERED TO A BITTER SECRETARY.
PLEASE?
GRRRR
THE SECRETARY TYPES IT.
"LET'S ... FORM ... PROTEIN ... SYMPHONY REACTIONARY ... TEENS."
CLOSE ENOUGH
THE TYPED NOTES ARE DELIVERED TO THE STAFF.
DROP IT IN THE "TO DO BASKET."
4/6/97 © 1997 United Feature Syndicate, Inc.
REPEAT.
MMM

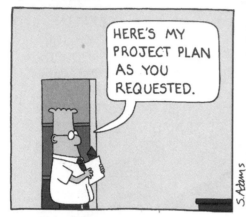

HERE'S MY PROJECT PLAN AS YOU REQUESTED.
S. Adams
OUR TEAM IS ALREADY WORKING DAY AND NIGHT ON OTHER PROJECTS.
I ASSUMED WE'D GIVE UP EATING, SLEEPING AND BATHING TO FIT THIS IN.
BY THE SECOND WEEK WE'LL BE STARVING, DELIRIOUS AND STINKING.
WE'LL BE LIKE WILD, UNPREDICTABLE ANIMALS.
SPECIFICALLY, WE'D BE LIKE WILD CHIPMUNKS. NONE OF US ARE VERY AGGRESSIVE.
THIS CLIP-ART REPRESENTS US IN WEEK THREE AS A PILE OF DEAD CHIPMUNKS.
4/13/97 © 1997 United Feature Syndicate, Inc.
NOW HE WANTS IT IN TWO WEEKS?
NEVER MIX SARCASM WITH GOOD CLIP-ART.

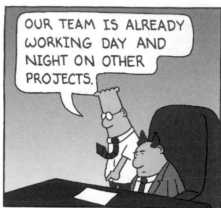

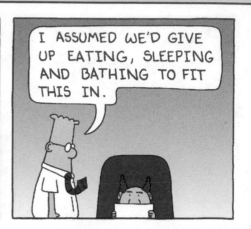

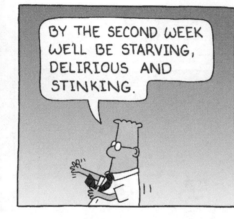

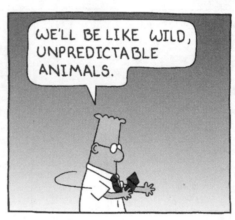

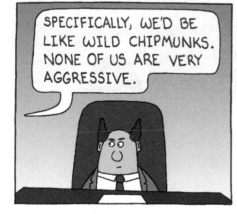

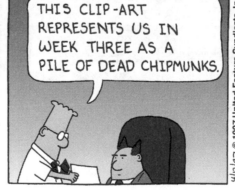

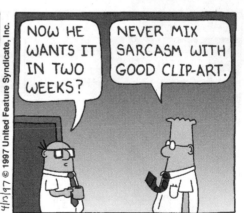

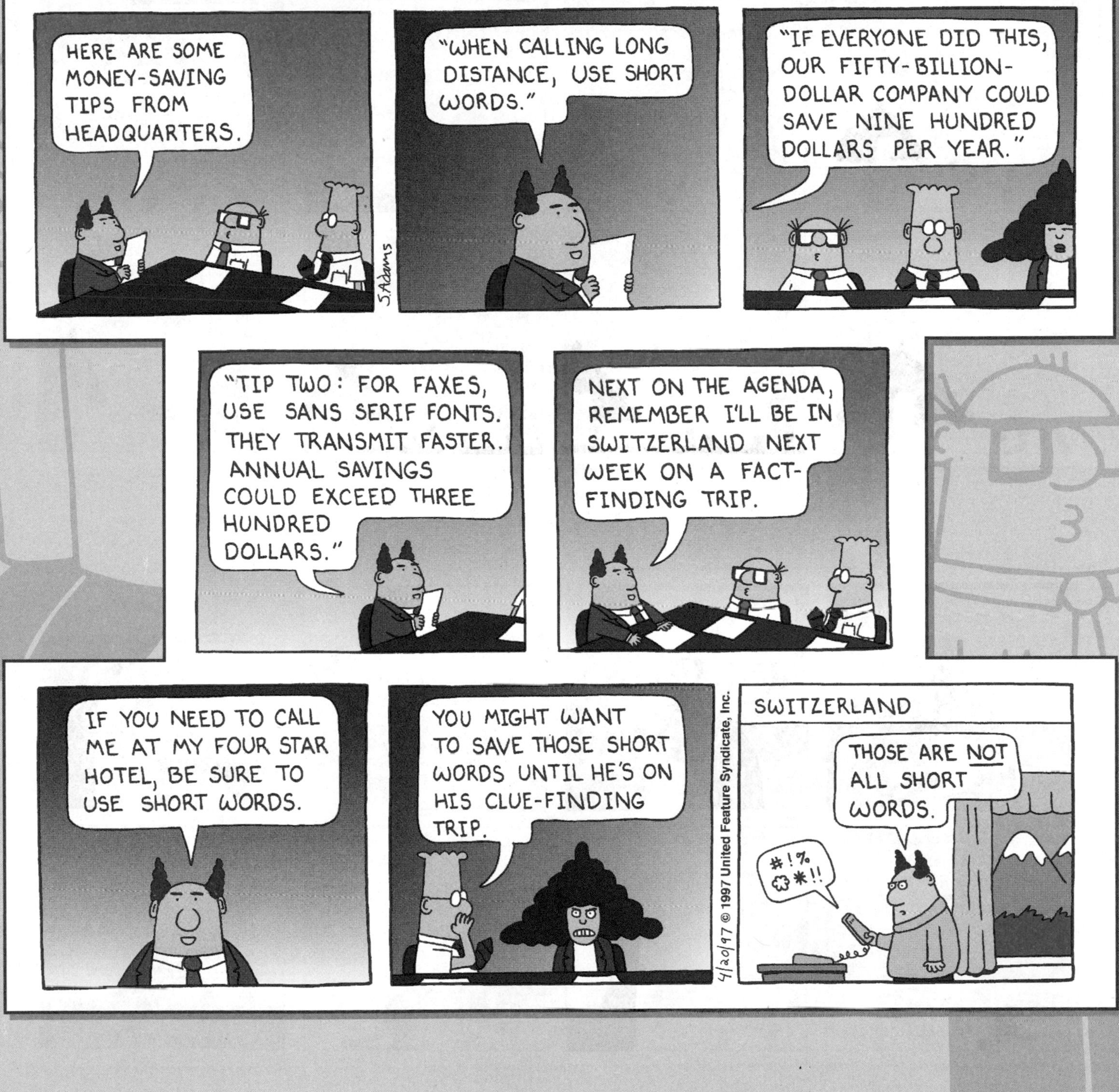
HERE ARE SOME MONEY-SAVING TIPS FROM HEADQUARTERS.
S.Adams
"WHEN CALLING LONG DISTANCE, USE SHORT WORDS."
"IF EVERYONE DID THIS, OUR FIFTY-BILLION-DOLLAR COMPANY COULD SAVE NINE HUNDRED DOLLARS PER YEAR."
"TIP TWO: FOR FAXES, USE SANS SERIF FONTS. THEY TRANSMIT FASTER. ANNUAL SAVINGS COULD EXCEED THREE HUNDRED DOLLARS."
NEXT ON THE AGENDA, REMEMBER I'LL BE IN SWITZERLAND NEXT WEEK ON A FACT-FINDING TRIP.
IF YOU NEED TO CALL ME AT MY FOUR STAR HOTEL, BE SURE TO USE SHORT WORDS.
YOU MIGHT WANT TO SAVE THOSE SHORT WORDS UNTIL HE'S ON HIS CLUE-FINDING TRIP.
4/20/97 © 1997 United Feature Syndicate, Inc.
SWITZERLAND
THOSE ARE NOT ALL SHORT WORDS.

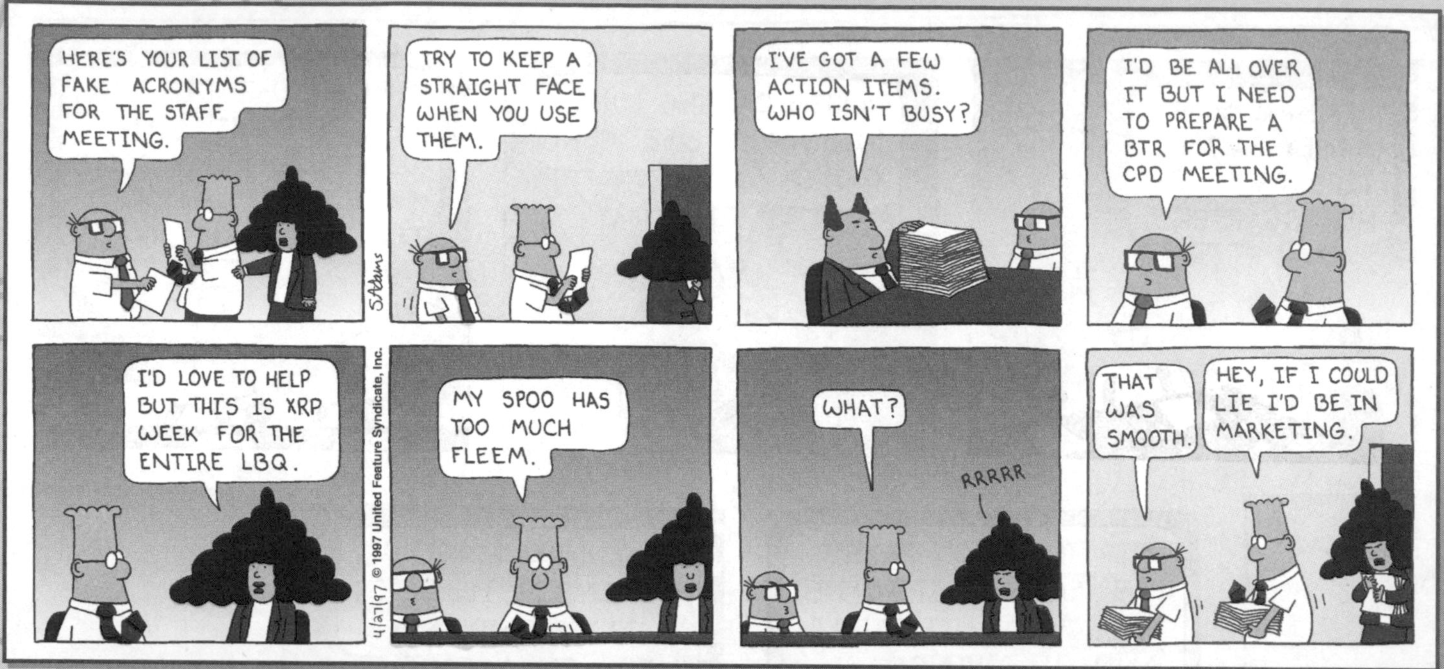
HERE'S YOUR LIST OF FAKE ACRONYMS FOR THE STAFF MEETING.
TRY TO KEEP A STRAIGHT FACE WHEN YOU USE THEM.
I'VE GOT A FEW ACTION ITEMS. WHO ISN'T BUSY?
I'D BE ALL OVER IT BUT I NEED TO PREPARE A BTR FOR THE CPD MEETING.
I'D LOVE TO HELP BUT THIS IS XRP WEEK FOR THE ENTIRE LBQ.
MY SPOO HAS TOO MUCH FLEEM.
WHAT?
RRRRR
THAT WAS SMOOTH.
HEY, IF I COULD LIE I'D BE IN MARKETING.
S. Adams
4/27/97 © 1997 United Feature Syndicate, Inc.

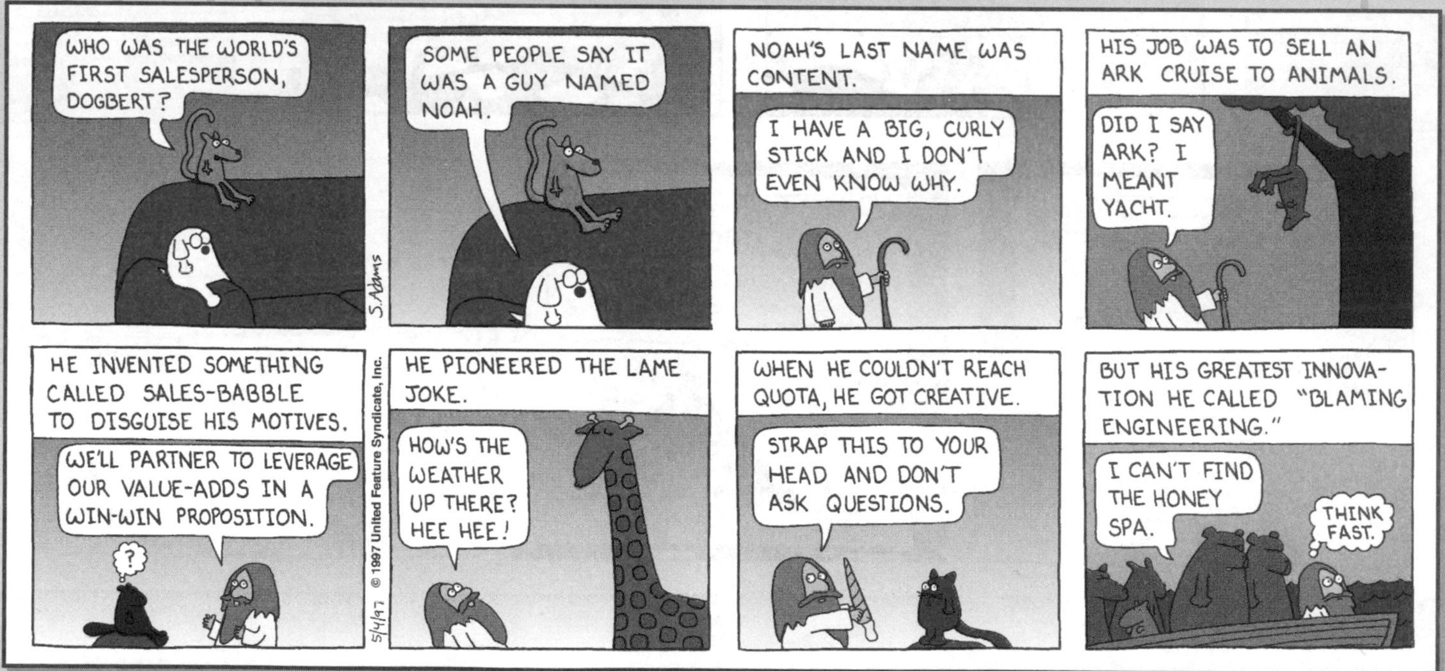
WHO WAS THE WORLD'S FIRST SALESPERSON, DOGBERT?
SOME PEOPLE SAY IT WAS A GUY NAMED NOAH.
NOAH'S LAST NAME WAS CONTENT.
I HAVE A BIG, CURLY STICK AND I DON'T EVEN KNOW WHY.
HIS JOB WAS TO SELL AN ARK CRUISE TO ANIMALS.
DID I SAY ARK? I MEANT YACHT.
HE INVENTED SOMETHING CALLED SALES-BABBLE TO DISGUISE HIS MOTIVES.
WE'LL PARTNER TO LEVERAGE OUR VALUE-ADDS IN A WIN-WIN PROPOSITION.
?
HE PIONEERED THE LAME JOKE.
HOW'S THE WEATHER UP THERE? HEE HEE!
WHEN HE COULDN'T REACH QUOTA, HE GOT CREATIVE.
STRAP THIS TO YOUR HEAD AND DON'T ASK QUESTIONS.
BUT HIS GREATEST INNOVATION HE CALLED "BLAMING ENGINEERING."
I CAN'T FIND THE HONEY SPA.
THINK FAST.
S. Adams
5/4/97 © 1997 United Feature Syndicate, Inc.

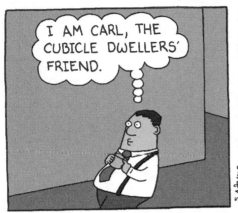

I AM CARL, THE CUBICLE DWELLERS' FRIEND.
I TRAVEL FROM CUBICLE TO CUBICLE TO TELL PEOPLE HOW HARD I'M WORKING.
I AM WORKING SO-O-O-O HARD. WORK, WORK, WORK. IT'S ALL I DO.
HOW IS THAT POSSIBLE?
YOU WALK AROUND ALL DAY WITH THAT COFFEE CUP RESTING ON YOUR BELLY.
DOES YOUR JOB DESCRIPTION SAY "TRANSPORT COFFEE CUP ON BELLY"?
HE'S A TERRIBLE CONVERSATIONALIST.
HOW MANY MILES PER GALLON DO YOU GET?
HYPOTHETICALLY, IF YOU WERE DOWNSIZED, HOW WOULD THE CUP GET AROUND?
WHAT'S WRONG WITH THESE PEOPLE?
S. Adams
5/11/97
© 1997 United Feature Syndicate, Inc.

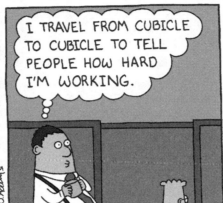

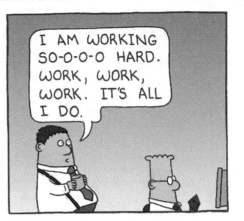

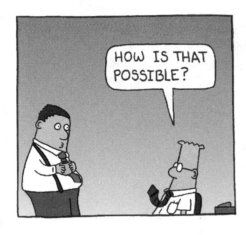

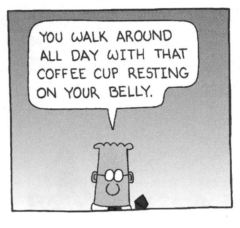

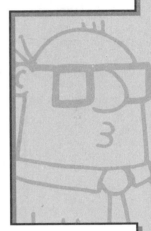

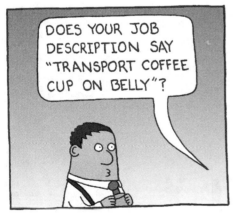

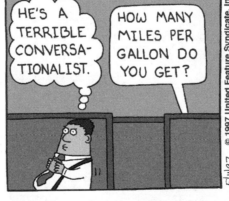

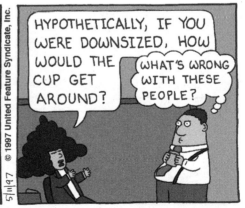

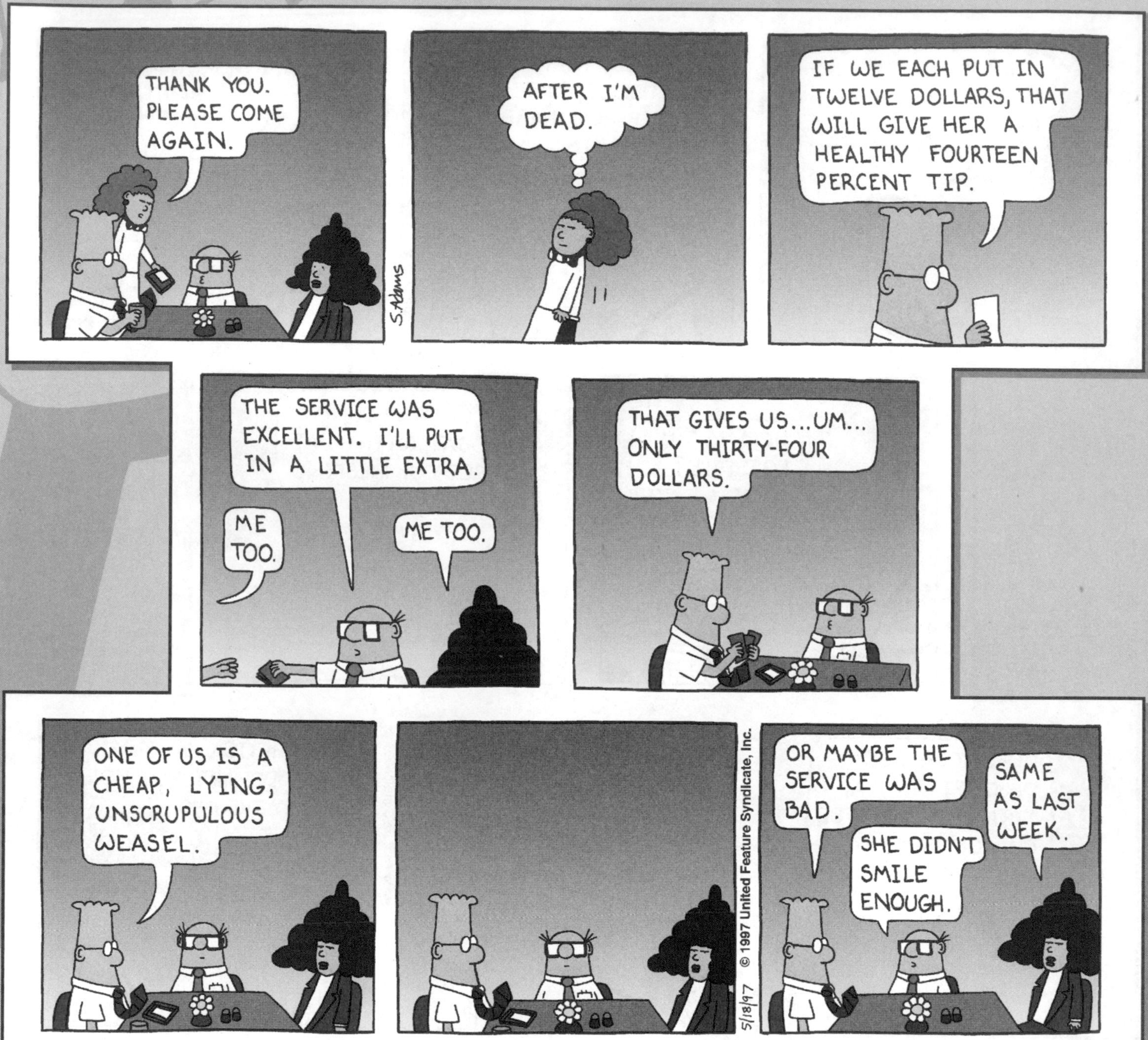
THANK YOU. PLEASE COME AGAIN.
AFTER I'M DEAD.
S.Adams
IF WE EACH PUT IN TWELVE DOLLARS, THAT WILL GIVE HER A HEALTHY FOURTEEN PERCENT TIP.
THE SERVICE WAS EXCELLENT. I'LL PUT IN A LITTLE EXTRA.
ME TOO.
ME TOO.
THAT GIVES US...UM... ONLY THIRTY-FOUR DOLLARS.
ONE OF US IS A CHEAP, LYING, UNSCRUPULOUS WEASEL.
5/18/97 © 1997 United Feature Syndicate, Inc.
OR MAYBE THE SERVICE WAS BAD.
SHE DIDN'T SMILE ENOUGH.
SAME AS LAST WEEK.

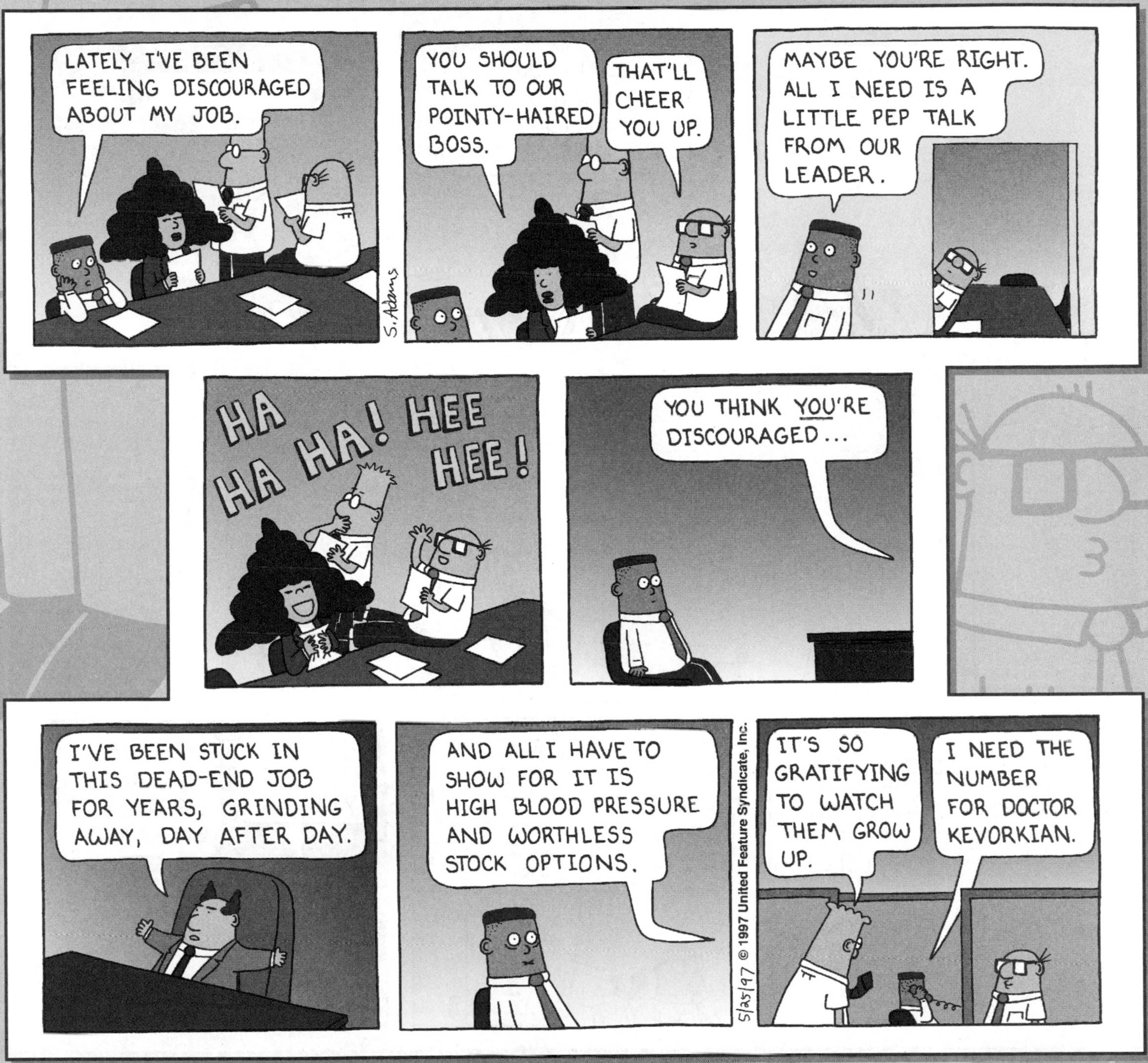
LATELY I'VE BEEN FEELING DISCOURAGED ABOUT MY JOB.
YOU SHOULD TALK TO OUR POINTY-HAIRED BOSS.
THAT'LL CHEER YOU UP.
S. Adams
MAYBE YOU'RE RIGHT. ALL I NEED IS A LITTLE PEP TALK FROM OUR LEADER.
HA HA HA! HEE HEE!
YOU THINK YOU'RE DISCOURAGED...
I'VE BEEN STUCK IN THIS DEAD-END JOB FOR YEARS, GRINDING AWAY, DAY AFTER DAY.
AND ALL I HAVE TO SHOW FOR IT IS HIGH BLOOD PRESSURE AND WORTHLESS STOCK OPTIONS.
5/25/97 © 1997 United Feature Syndicate, Inc.
IT'S SO GRATIFYING TO WATCH THEM GROW UP.
I NEED THE NUMBER FOR DOCTOR KEVORKIAN.

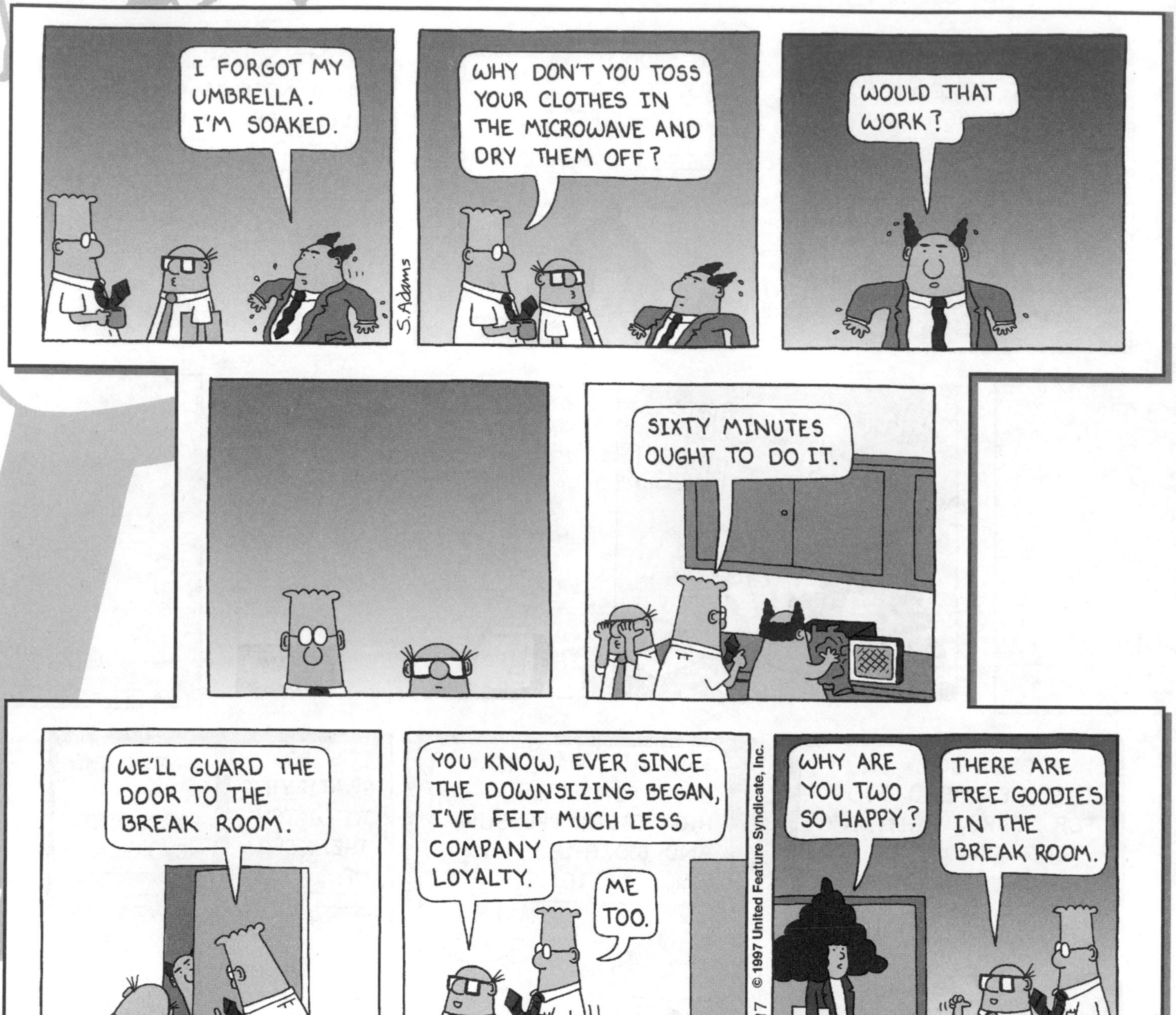
I FORGOT MY UMBRELLA. I'M SOAKED.
S. Adams
WHY DON'T YOU TOSS YOUR CLOTHES IN THE MICROWAVE AND DRY THEM OFF?
WOULD THAT WORK?
SIXTY MINUTES OUGHT TO DO IT.
WE'LL GUARD THE DOOR TO THE BREAK ROOM.
YOU KNOW, EVER SINCE THE DOWNSIZING BEGAN, I'VE FELT MUCH LESS COMPANY LOYALTY.
ME TOO.
6/1/97 © 1997 United Feature Syndicate, Inc.
WHY ARE YOU TWO SO HAPPY?
THERE ARE FREE GOODIES IN THE BREAK ROOM.

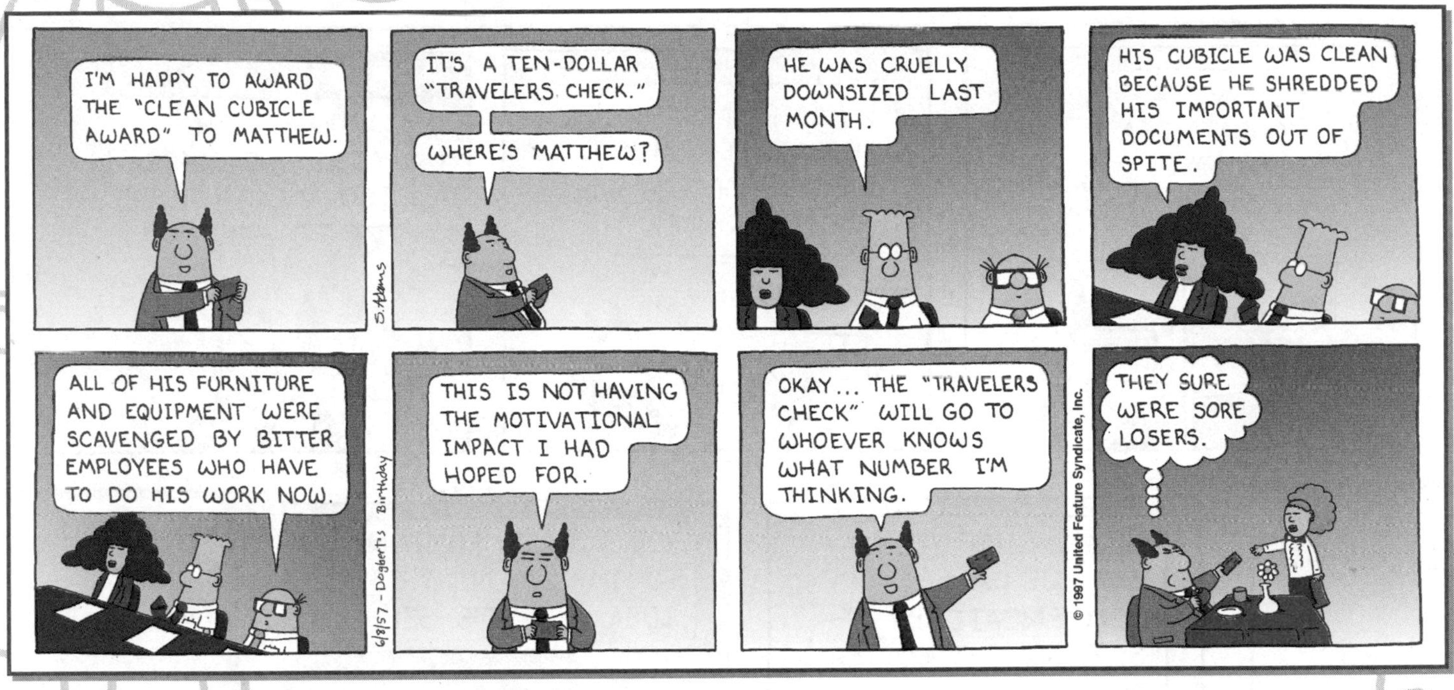
I'M HAPPY TO AWARD THE "CLEAN CUBICLE AWARD" TO MATTHEW.
IT'S A TEN-DOLLAR "TRAVELERS CHECK."
WHERE'S MATTHEW?
HE WAS CRUELLY DOWNSIZED LAST MONTH.
HIS CUBICLE WAS CLEAN BECAUSE HE SHREDDED HIS IMPORTANT DOCUMENTS OUT OF SPITE.
ALL OF HIS FURNITURE AND EQUIPMENT WERE SCAVENGED BY BITTER EMPLOYEES WHO HAVE TO DO HIS WORK NOW.
THIS IS NOT HAVING THE MOTIVATIONAL IMPACT I HAD HOPED FOR.
OKAY... THE "TRAVELERS CHECK" WILL GO TO WHOEVER KNOWS WHAT NUMBER I'M THINKING.
THEY SURE WERE SORE LOSERS.
S. Adams
6/8/57 - Dogbert's Birthday
© 1997 United Feature Syndicate, Inc.

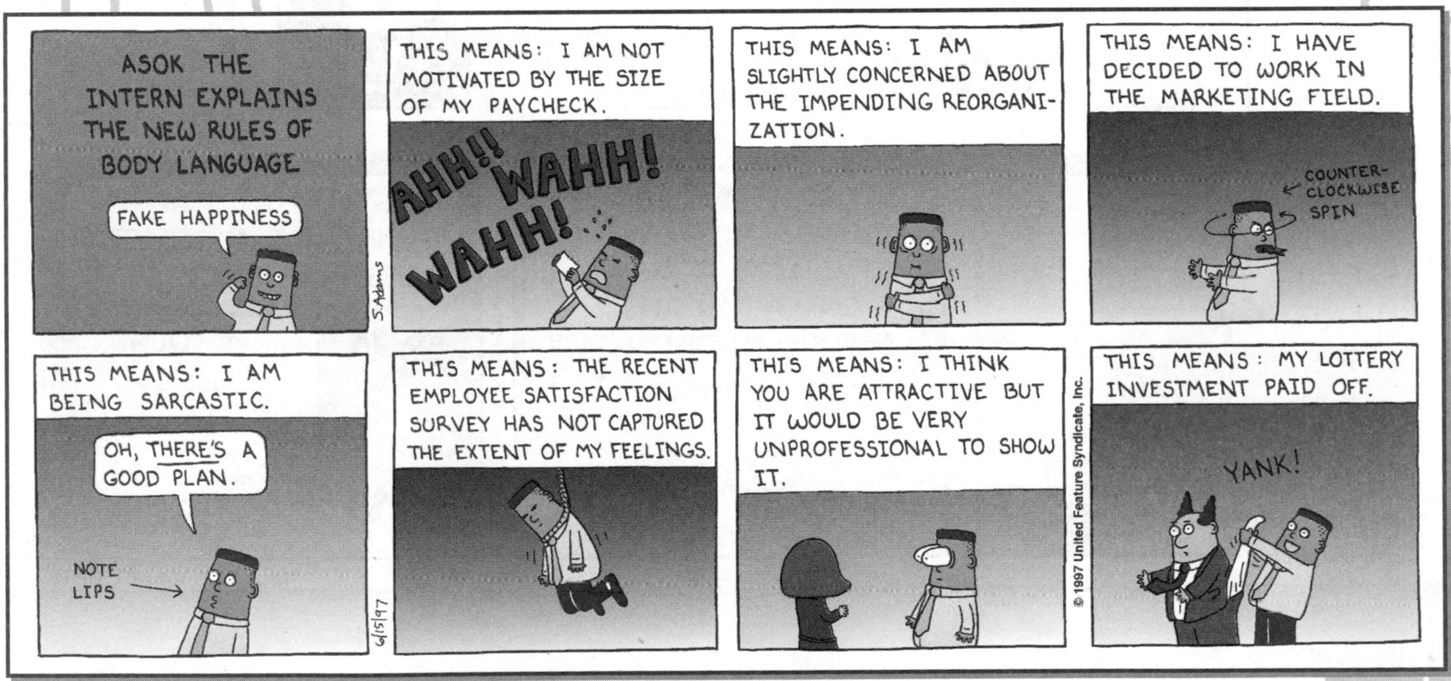
ASOK THE INTERN EXPLAINS THE NEW RULES OF BODY LANGUAGE
FAKE HAPPINESS
THIS MEANS: I AM NOT MOTIVATED BY THE SIZE OF MY PAYCHECK.
AHH!! WAHH! WAHH!
THIS MEANS: I AM SLIGHTLY CONCERNED ABOUT THE IMPENDING REORGANIZATION.
THIS MEANS: I HAVE DECIDED TO WORK IN THE MARKETING FIELD.
COUNTER-CLOCKWISE SPIN
THIS MEANS: I AM BEING SARCASTIC.
OH, THERE'S A GOOD PLAN.
NOTE LIPS
THIS MEANS: THE RECENT EMPLOYEE SATISFACTION SURVEY HAS NOT CAPTURED THE EXTENT OF MY FEELINGS.
THIS MEANS: I THINK YOU ARE ATTRACTIVE BUT IT WOULD BE VERY UNPROFESSIONAL TO SHOW IT.
THIS MEANS: MY LOTTERY INVESTMENT PAID OFF.
YANK!
S. Adams
6/5/97
© 1997 United Feature Syndicate, Inc.

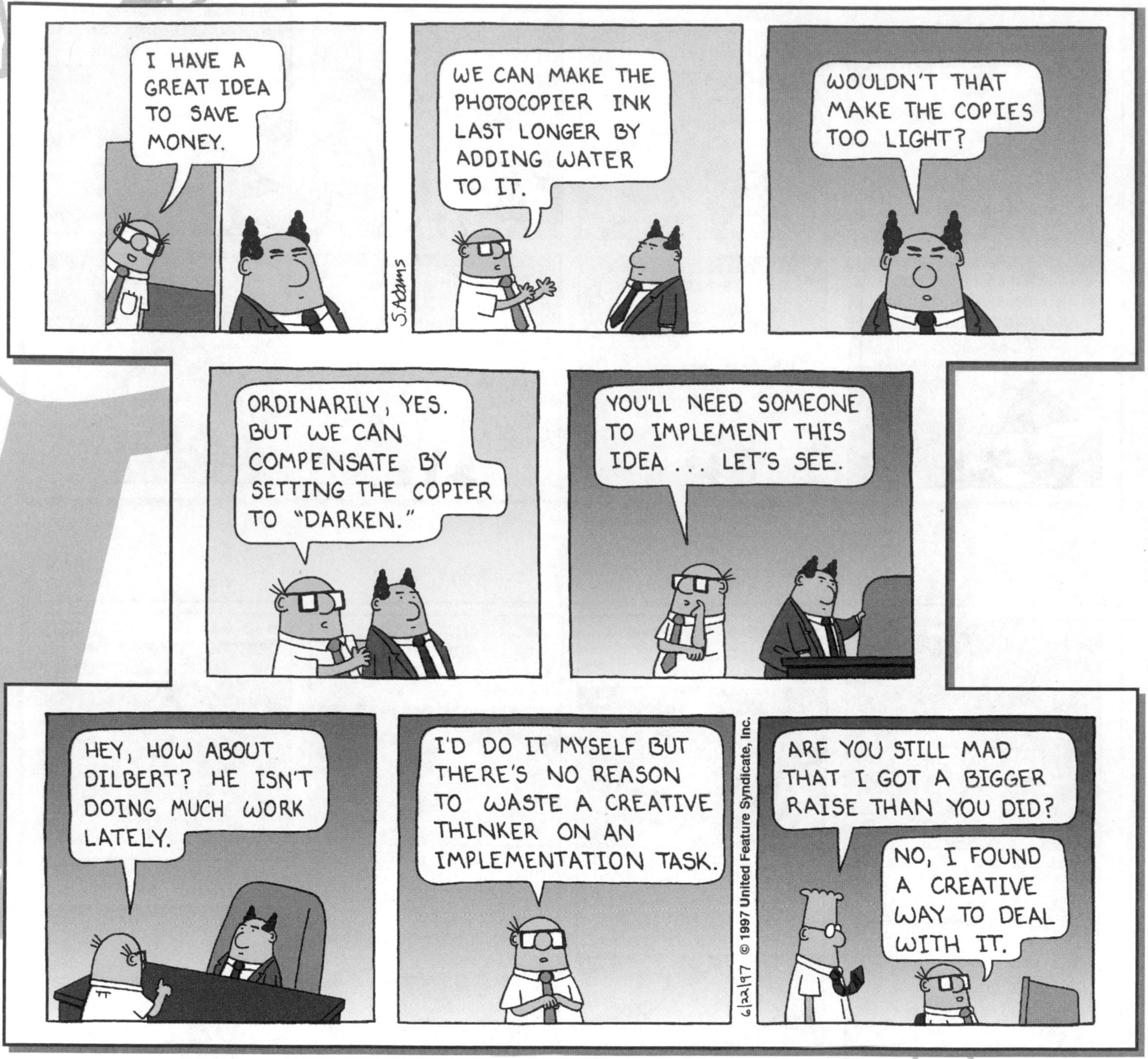
I HAVE A GREAT IDEA TO SAVE MONEY.
S. Adams
WE CAN MAKE THE PHOTOCOPIER INK LAST LONGER BY ADDING WATER TO IT.
WOULDN'T THAT MAKE THE COPIES TOO LIGHT?
ORDINARILY, YES. BUT WE CAN COMPENSATE BY SETTING THE COPIER TO "DARKEN."
YOU'LL NEED SOMEONE TO IMPLEMENT THIS IDEA . . . LET'S SEE.
HEY, HOW ABOUT DILBERT? HE ISN'T DOING MUCH WORK LATELY.
I'D DO IT MYSELF BUT THERE'S NO REASON TO WASTE A CREATIVE THINKER ON AN IMPLEMENTATION TASK.
6/22/97 © 1997 United Feature Syndicate, Inc.
ARE YOU STILL MAD THAT I GOT A BIGGER RAISE THAN YOU DID?
NO, I FOUND A CREATIVE WAY TO DEAL WITH IT.

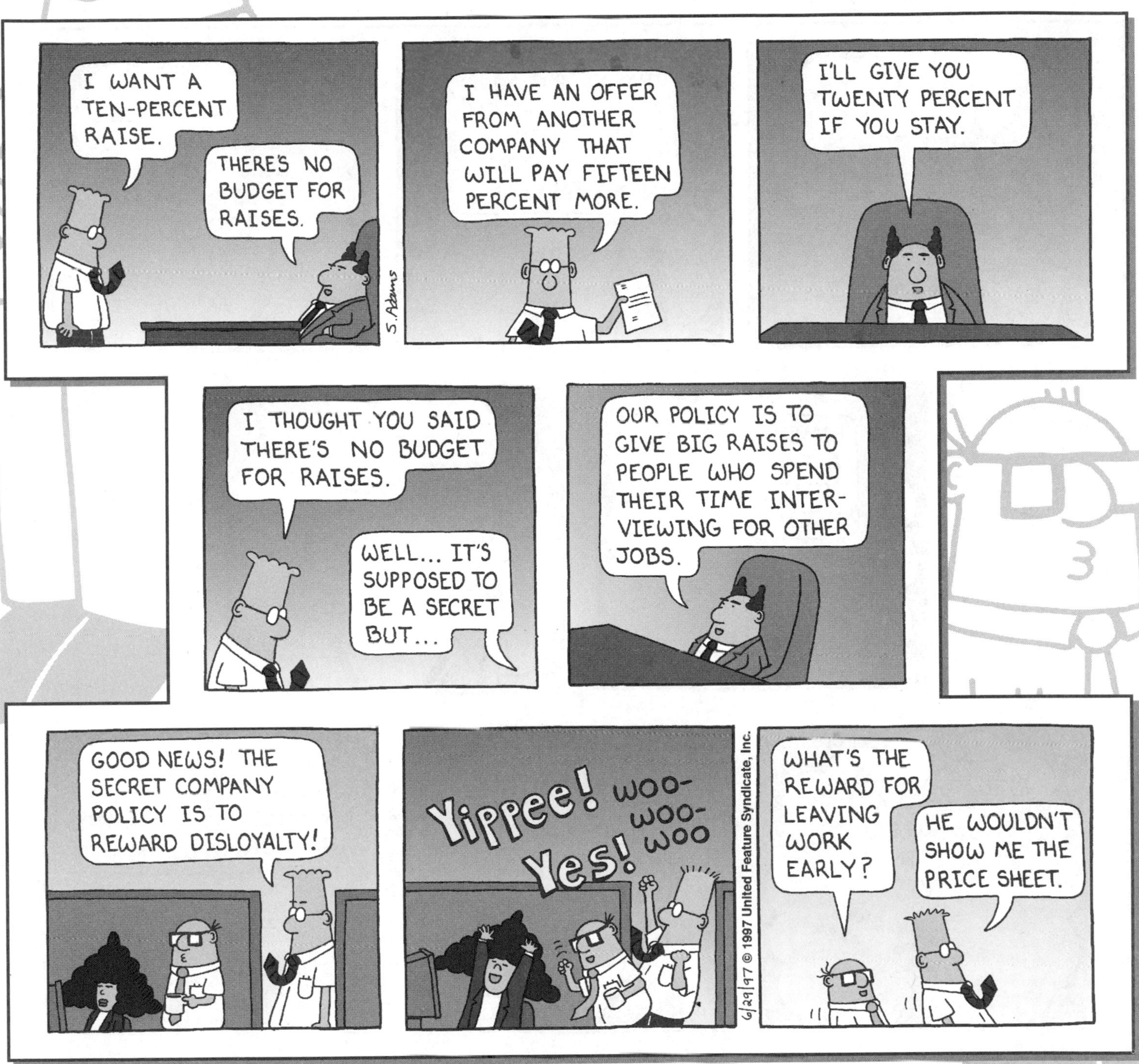

I WANT A TEN-PERCENT RAISE.
THERE'S NO BUDGET FOR RAISES.
S. Adams
I HAVE AN OFFER FROM ANOTHER COMPANY THAT WILL PAY FIFTEEN PERCENT MORE.
I'LL GIVE YOU TWENTY PERCENT IF YOU STAY.
I THOUGHT YOU SAID THERE'S NO BUDGET FOR RAISES.
WELL... IT'S SUPPOSED TO BE A SECRET BUT...
OUR POLICY IS TO GIVE BIG RAISES TO PEOPLE WHO SPEND THEIR TIME INTER-VIEWING FOR OTHER JOBS.
GOOD NEWS! THE SECRET COMPANY POLICY IS TO REWARD DISLOYALTY!
Yippee! Yes! WOO-WOO-WOO
6/29/97 © 1997 United Feature Syndicate, Inc.
WHAT'S THE REWARD FOR LEAVING WORK EARLY?
HE WOULDN'T SHOW ME THE PRICE SHEET.

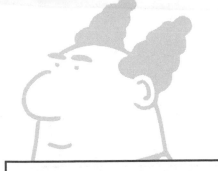

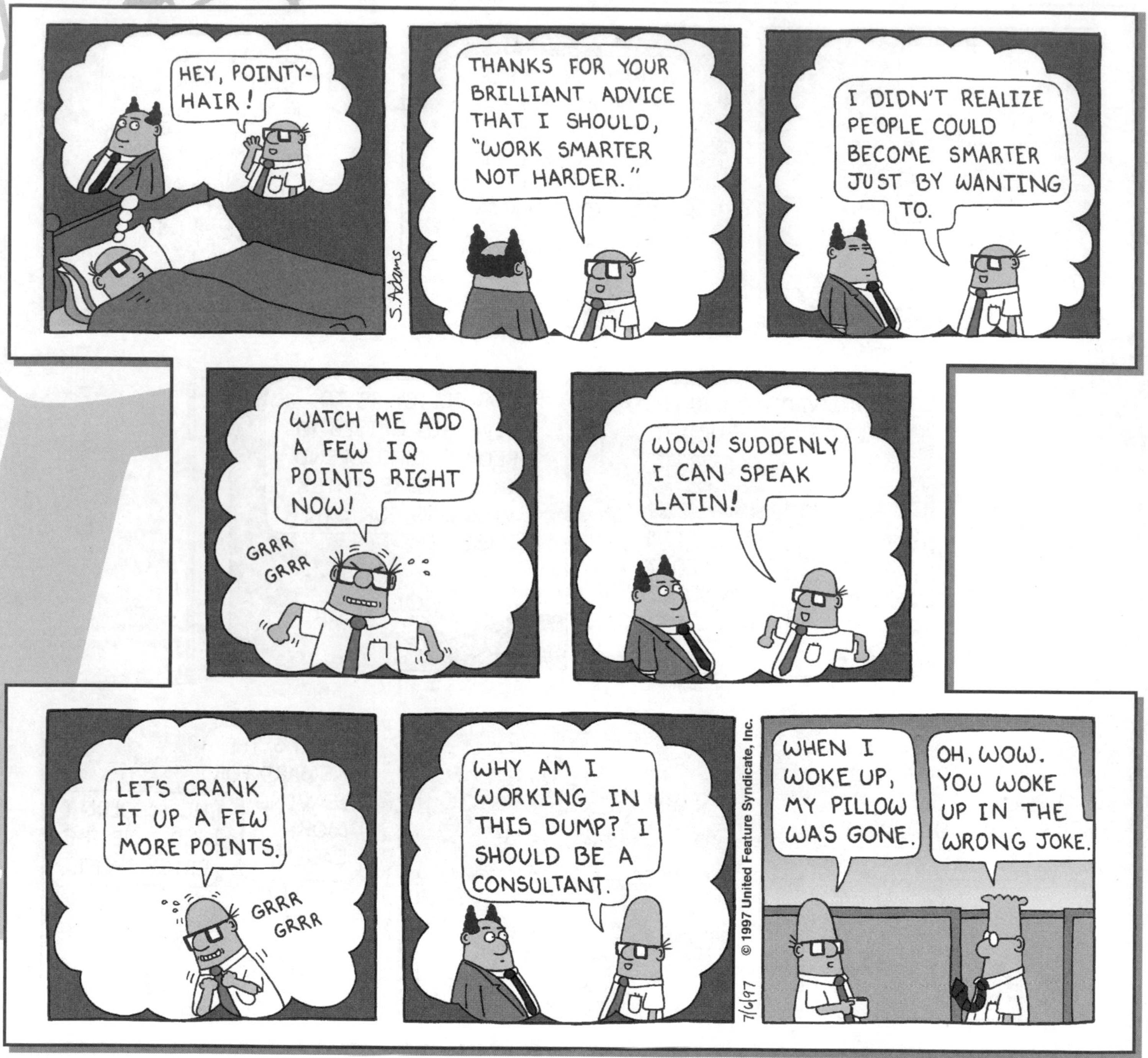
HEY, POINTY-HAIR!
S. Adams
THANKS FOR YOUR BRILLIANT ADVICE THAT I SHOULD, "WORK SMARTER NOT HARDER."
I DIDN'T REALIZE PEOPLE COULD BECOME SMARTER JUST BY WANTING TO.
WATCH ME ADD A FEW IQ POINTS RIGHT NOW!
GRRR GRRR
WOW! SUDDENLY I CAN SPEAK LATIN!
LET'S CRANK IT UP A FEW MORE POINTS.
GRRR GRRR
WHY AM I WORKING IN THIS DUMP? I SHOULD BE A CONSULTANT.
© 1997 United Feature Syndicate, Inc.
7/6/97
WHEN I WOKE UP, MY PILLOW WAS GONE.
OH, WOW. YOU WOKE UP IN THE WRONG JOKE.

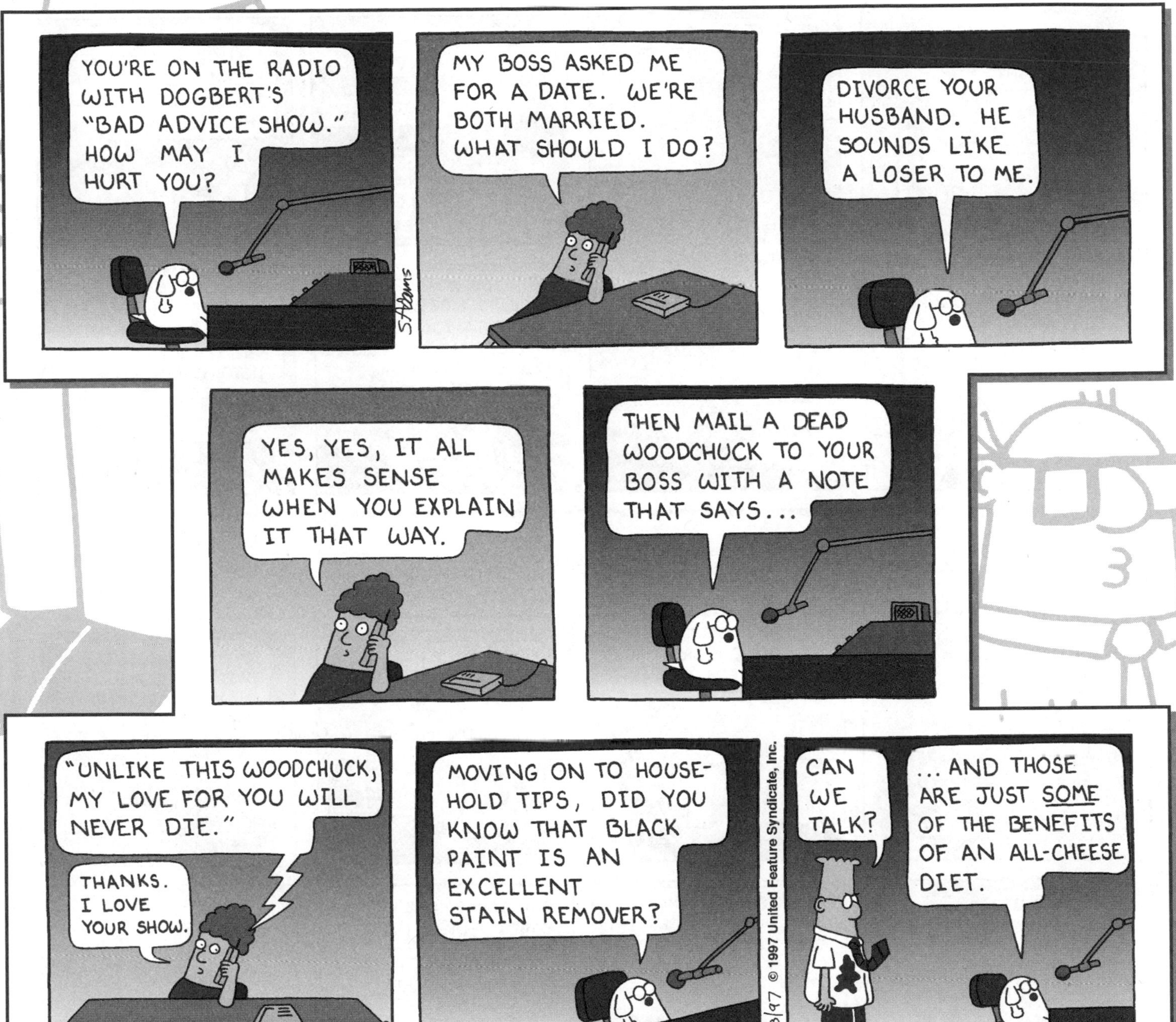

YOU'RE ON THE RADIO WITH DOGBERT'S "BAD ADVICE SHOW." HOW MAY I HURT YOU?
S.Adams
MY BOSS ASKED ME FOR A DATE. WE'RE BOTH MARRIED. WHAT SHOULD I DO?
DIVORCE YOUR HUSBAND. HE SOUNDS LIKE A LOSER TO ME.
YES, YES, IT ALL MAKES SENSE WHEN YOU EXPLAIN IT THAT WAY.
THEN MAIL A DEAD WOODCHUCK TO YOUR BOSS WITH A NOTE THAT SAYS...
"UNLIKE THIS WOODCHUCK, MY LOVE FOR YOU WILL NEVER DIE."
THANKS. I LOVE YOUR SHOW.
MOVING ON TO HOUSE-HOLD TIPS, DID YOU KNOW THAT BLACK PAINT IS AN EXCELLENT STAIN REMOVER?
7/13/97 © 1997 United Feature Syndicate, Inc.
CAN WE TALK?
... AND THOSE ARE JUST SOME OF THE BENEFITS OF AN ALL-CHEESE DIET.

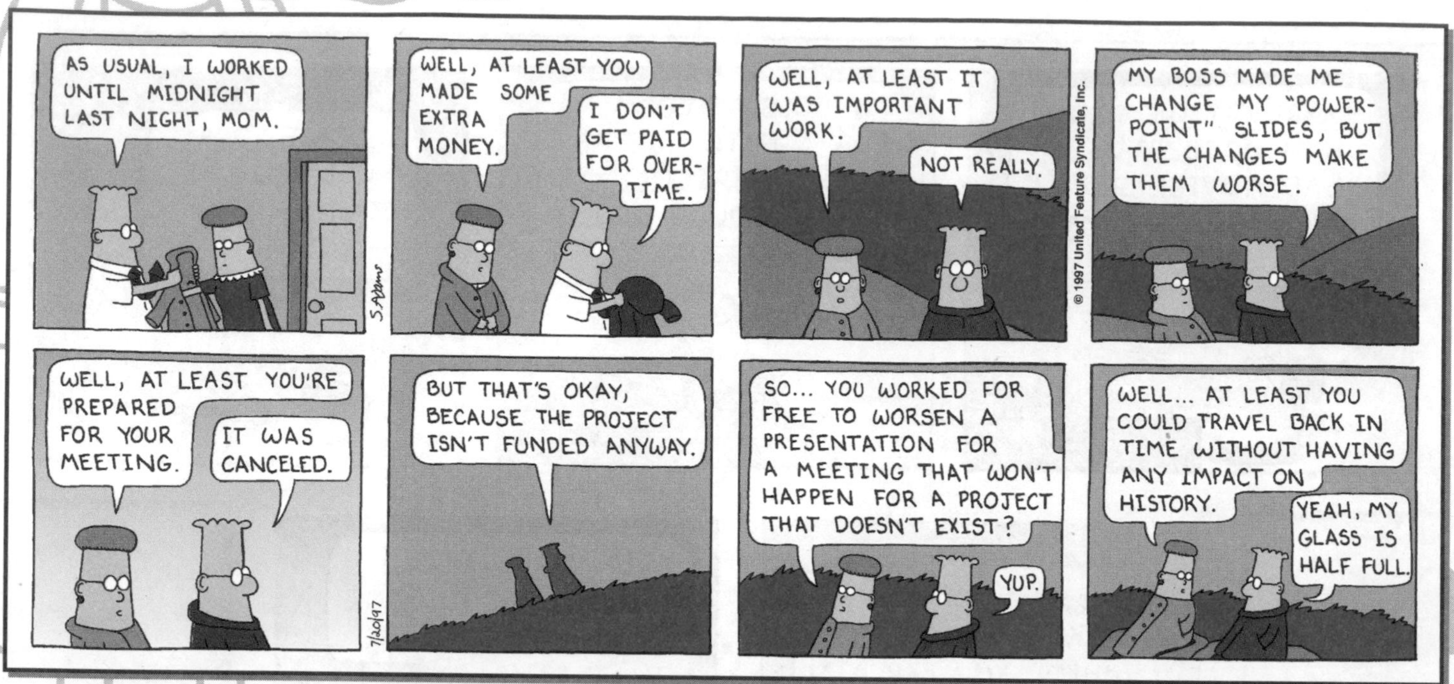
AS USUAL, I WORKED UNTIL MIDNIGHT LAST NIGHT, MOM.
WELL, AT LEAST YOU MADE SOME EXTRA MONEY.
I DON'T GET PAID FOR OVER-TIME.
WELL, AT LEAST IT WAS IMPORTANT WORK.
NOT REALLY.
MY BOSS MADE ME CHANGE MY "POWER-POINT" SLIDES, BUT THE CHANGES MAKE THEM WORSE.
WELL, AT LEAST YOU'RE PREPARED FOR YOUR MEETING.
IT WAS CANCELED.
BUT THAT'S OKAY, BECAUSE THE PROJECT ISN'T FUNDED ANYWAY.
SO... YOU WORKED FOR FREE TO WORSEN A PRESENTATION FOR A MEETING THAT WON'T HAPPEN FOR A PROJECT THAT DOESN'T EXIST?
YUP.
WELL... AT LEAST YOU COULD TRAVEL BACK IN TIME WITHOUT HAVING ANY IMPACT ON HISTORY.
YEAH, MY GLASS IS HALF FULL.
© 1997 United Feature Syndicate, Inc.
7/20/97

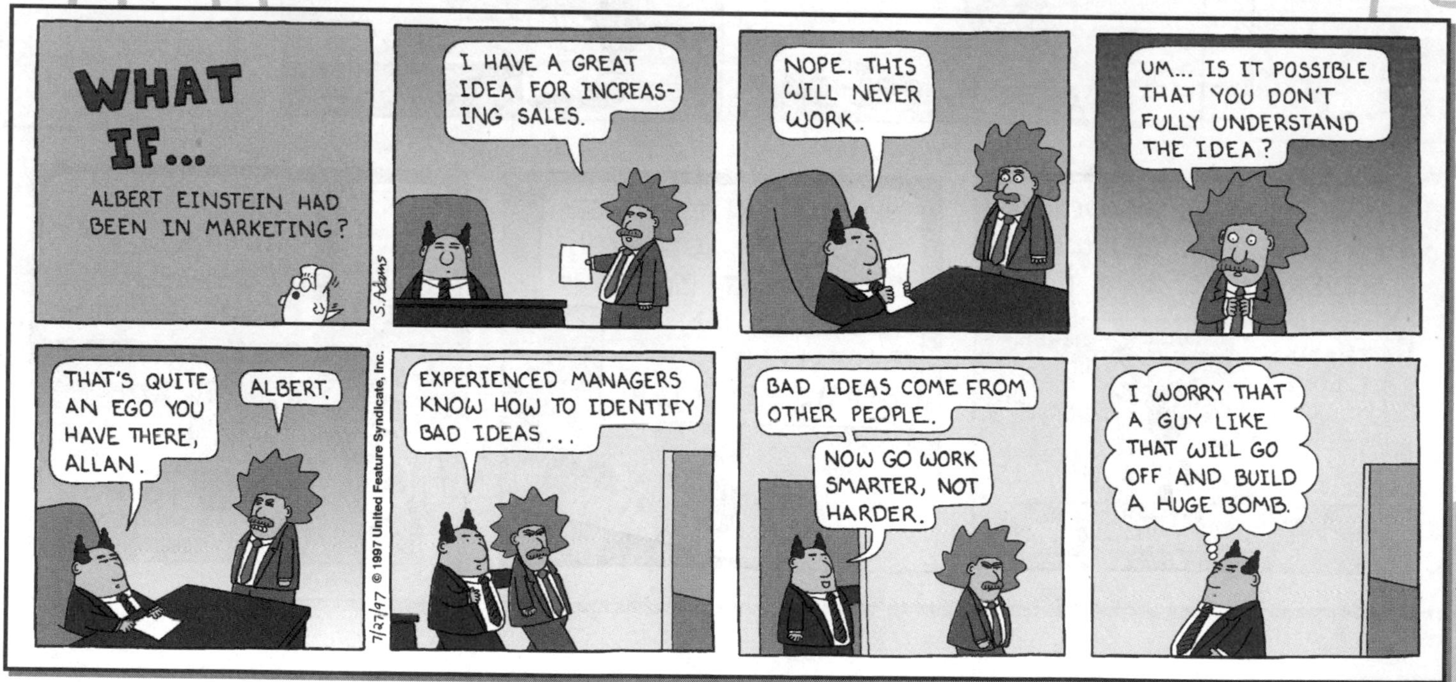
WHAT IF...
ALBERT EINSTEIN HAD BEEN IN MARKETING?
I HAVE A GREAT IDEA FOR INCREAS-ING SALES.
NOPE. THIS WILL NEVER WORK.
UM... IS IT POSSIBLE THAT YOU DON'T FULLY UNDERSTAND THE IDEA?
THAT'S QUITE AN EGO YOU HAVE THERE, ALLAN.
ALBERT.
EXPERIENCED MANAGERS KNOW HOW TO IDENTIFY BAD IDEAS...
BAD IDEAS COME FROM OTHER PEOPLE.
NOW GO WORK SMARTER, NOT HARDER.
I WORRY THAT A GUY LIKE THAT WILL GO OFF AND BUILD A HUGE BOMB.
© 1997 United Feature Syndicate, Inc.
7/27/97

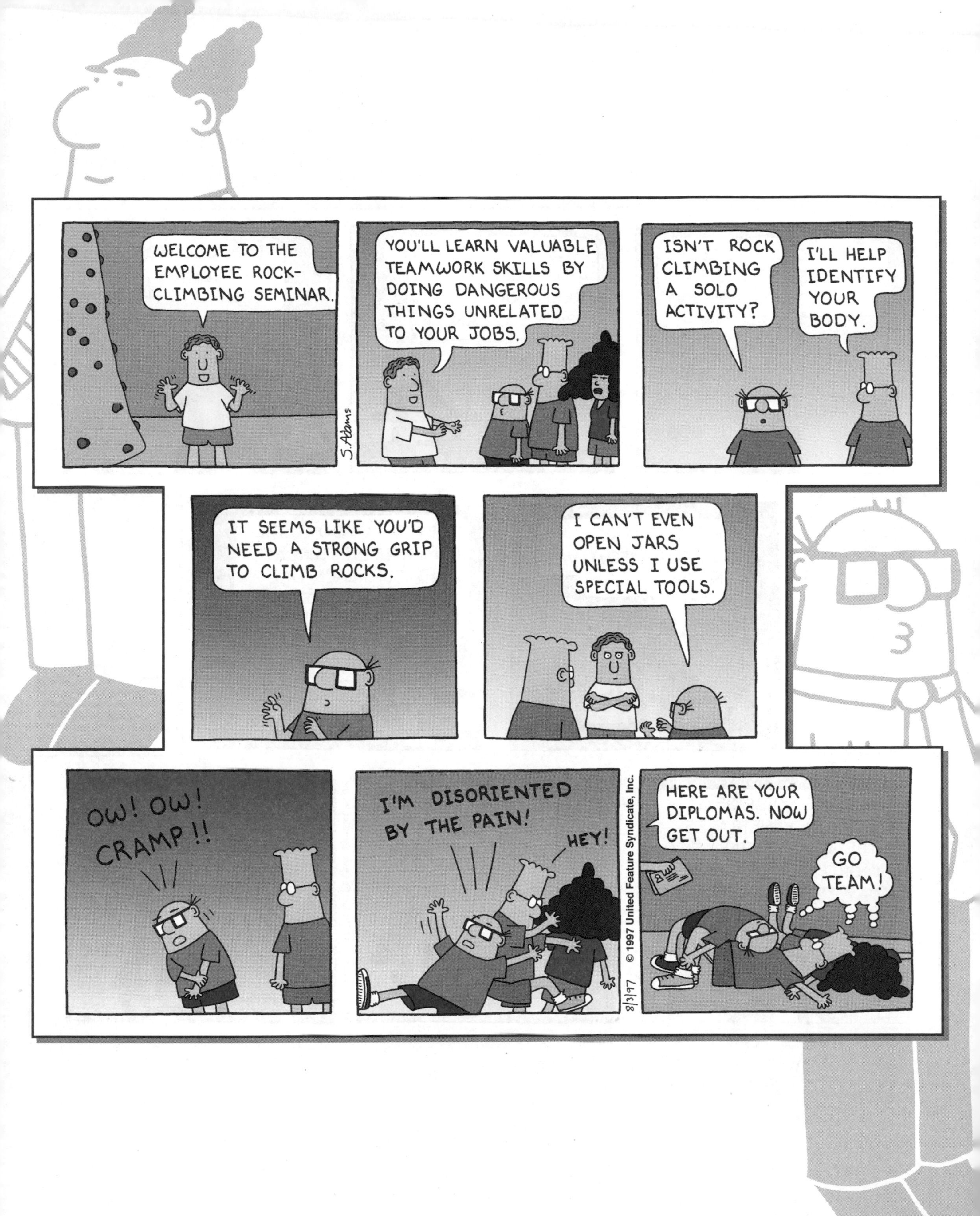
WELCOME TO THE EMPLOYEE ROCK-CLIMBING SEMINAR.
S. Adams
YOU'LL LEARN VALUABLE TEAMWORK SKILLS BY DOING DANGEROUS THINGS UNRELATED TO YOUR JOBS.
ISN'T ROCK CLIMBING A SOLO ACTIVITY?
I'LL HELP IDENTIFY YOUR BODY.
IT SEEMS LIKE YOU'D NEED A STRONG GRIP TO CLIMB ROCKS.
I CAN'T EVEN OPEN JARS UNLESS I USE SPECIAL TOOLS.
OW! OW! CRAMP!!
I'M DISORIENTED BY THE PAIN!
HEY!
© 1997 United Feature Syndicate, Inc.
8/3/97
HERE ARE YOUR DIPLOMAS. NOW GET OUT.
GO TEAM!

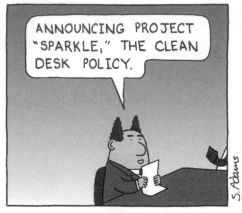

ANNOUNCING PROJECT "SPARKLE," THE CLEAN DESK POLICY.
S. Adams
THIS IS A COMPANY-WIDE EFFORT TO KEEP OUR WORK SPACES CLEAN.
TINY QUESTION. I'M CURIOUS ABOUT ONE THING.
I'M PICTURING OUR TOP EXECUTIVES IN THE "WAR ROOM."
THEY TALK ABOUT THE COMPETITIVE THREAT AND OUR LACK OF RESOURCES. SUDDENLY, PANIC SETS IN!!
A LONE VOICE OF REASON PENETRATES THE CONFUSION. TWO WORDS: "PAPER TOWELS."
IS THAT PRETTY MUCH HOW IT WENT?
8/10/97 © 1997 United Feature Syndicate, Inc.
MOVING ALONG, YOU EACH GET A LAMINATED CARD WITH OUR MISSION STATEMENT.
LET ME DO THIS ONE.

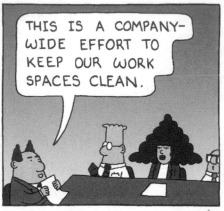

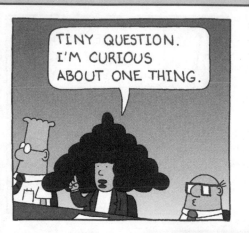

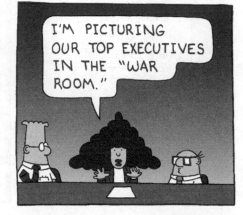

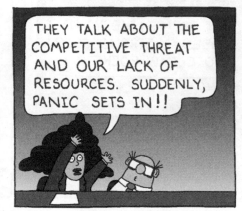

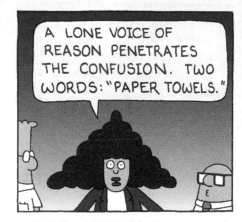

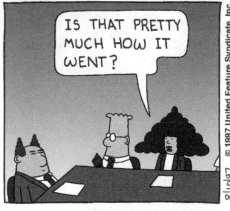

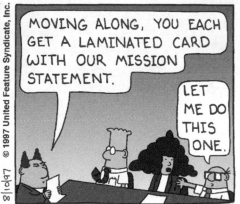

I HAVE A VAGUE FEELING OF UNCERTAINTY.
S. Adams
IT GETS STRONGER AT THE OFFICE.
THE UNCERTAINTY SAPS MY STRENGTH. MY BRIEFCASE IS GETTING HEAVIER.
MUST... GET... TO... CUBICLE.
THE UNCERTAINTY FEELS LIKE A PIANO UPON MY CHEST.
I DECIDED TO REORGANIZE. OR MAYBE DOWNSIZE. UNLESS THERE'S A MERGER.
MMPH MMPH
I SUMMON THE UNHOLY DEMONS OF APATHY, SARCASM AND CYNICISM!!
8/17/97
© 1997 United Feature Syndicate, Inc.
GOOD THINKING! REORGANIZATIONS ALWAYS INCREASE PROFITS!
WOW. THIRD TIME TODAY.

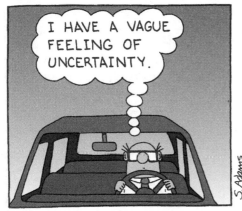

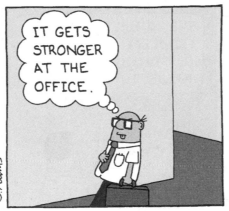

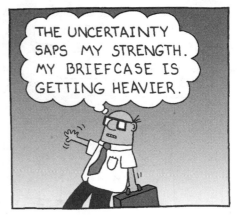

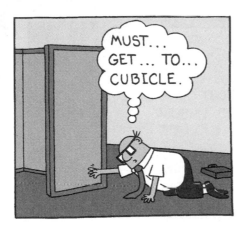

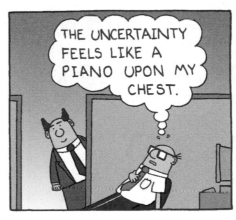

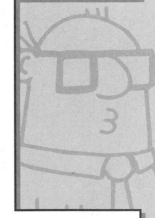

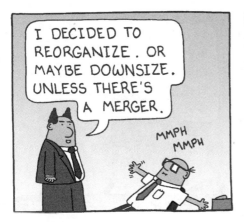

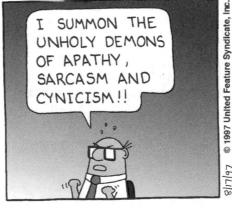

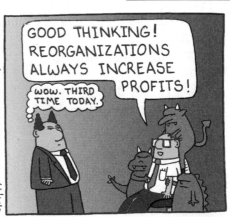

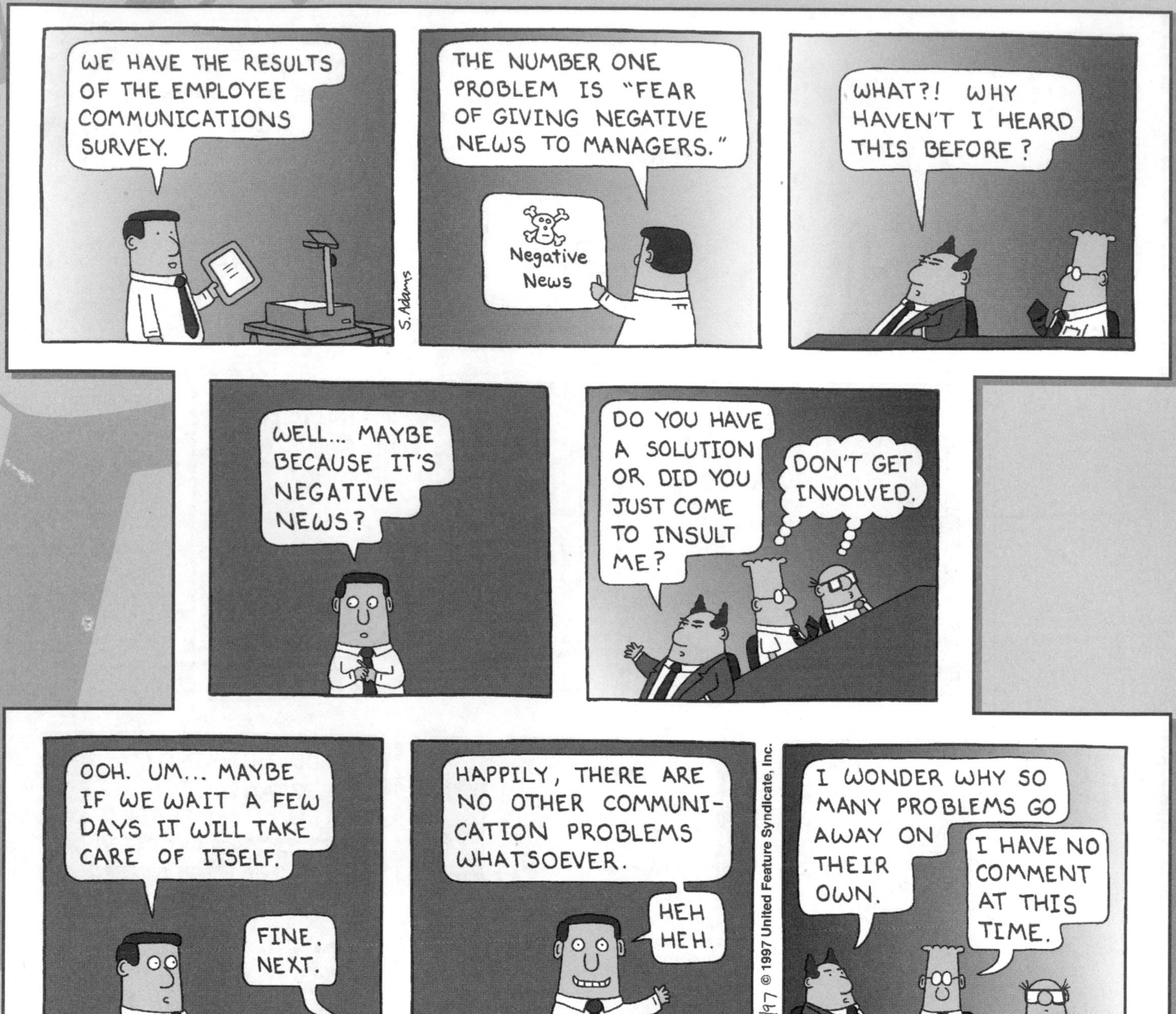

WE HAVE THE RESULTS OF THE EMPLOYEE COMMUNICATIONS SURVEY.
THE NUMBER ONE PROBLEM IS "FEAR OF GIVING NEGATIVE NEWS TO MANAGERS."
Negative News
S. Adams
WHAT?! WHY HAVEN'T I HEARD THIS BEFORE?
WELL... MAYBE BECAUSE IT'S NEGATIVE NEWS?
DO YOU HAVE A SOLUTION OR DID YOU JUST COME TO INSULT ME?
DON'T GET INVOLVED.
OOH. UM... MAYBE IF WE WAIT A FEW DAYS IT WILL TAKE CARE OF ITSELF.
FINE. NEXT.
HAPPILY, THERE ARE NO OTHER COMMUNI-CATION PROBLEMS WHATSOEVER.
HEH HEH.
8/24/97 © 1997 United Feature Syndicate, Inc.
I WONDER WHY SO MANY PROBLEMS GO AWAY ON THEIR OWN.
I HAVE NO COMMENT AT THIS TIME.

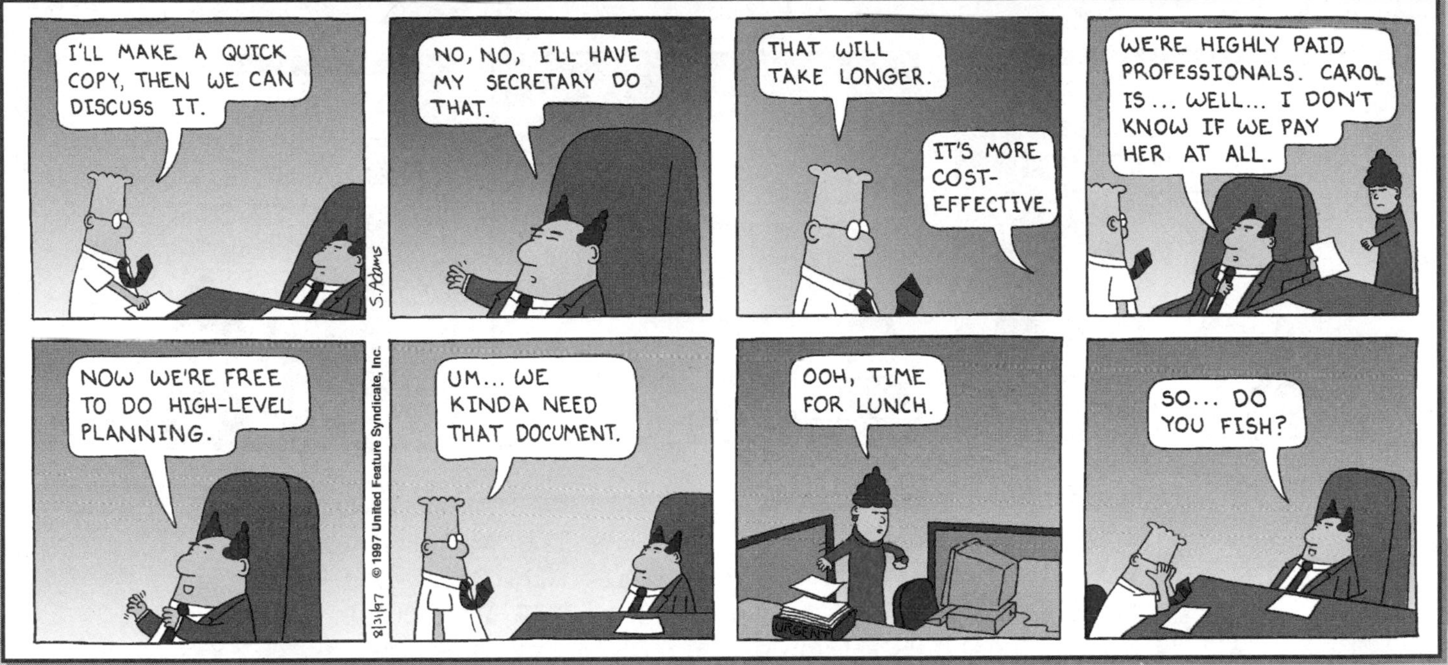
I'LL MAKE A QUICK COPY, THEN WE CAN DISCUSS IT.
NO, NO, I'LL HAVE MY SECRETARY DO THAT.
THAT WILL TAKE LONGER.
IT'S MORE COST-EFFECTIVE.
WE'RE HIGHLY PAID PROFESSIONALS. CAROL IS ... WELL ... I DON'T KNOW IF WE PAY HER AT ALL.
NOW WE'RE FREE TO DO HIGH-LEVEL PLANNING.
UM ... WE KINDA NEED THAT DOCUMENT.
OOH, TIME FOR LUNCH.
URGENT
SO ... DO YOU FISH?
S. Adams
8/31/97 © 1997 United Feature Syndicate, Inc.

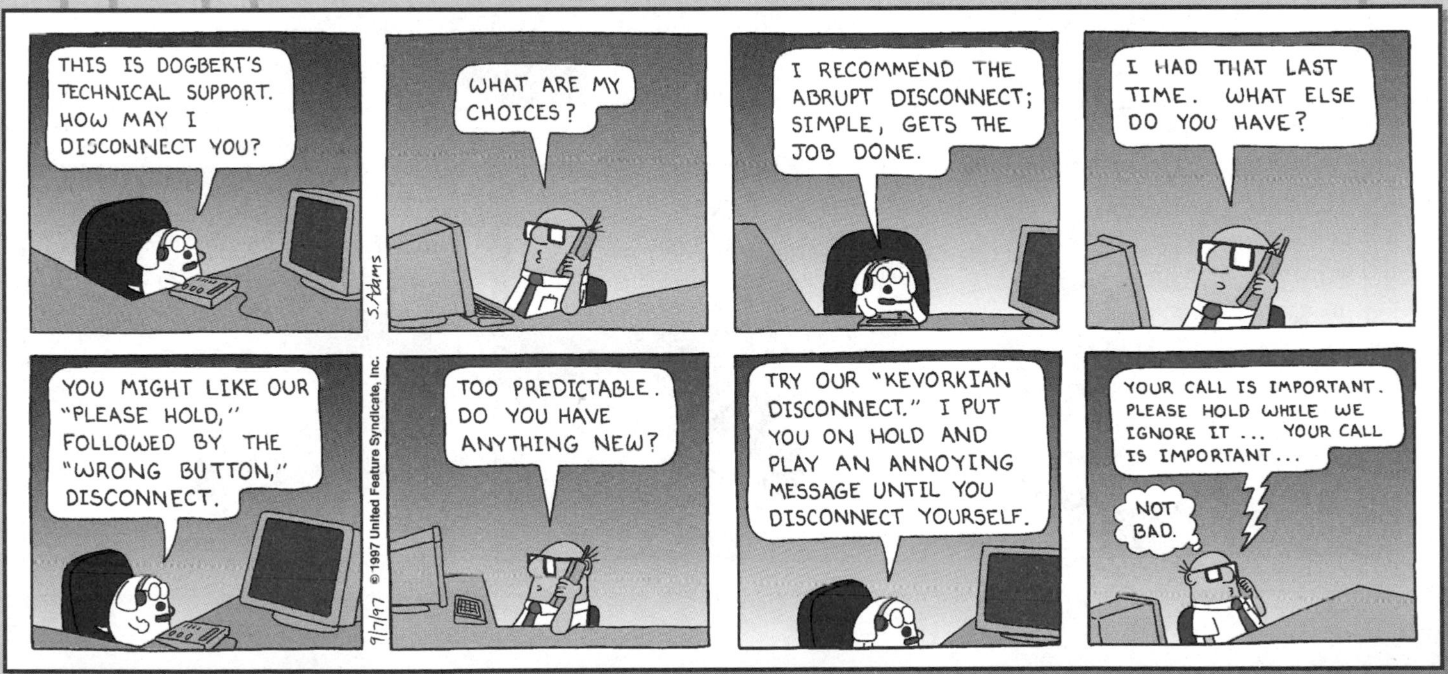
THIS IS DOGBERT'S TECHNICAL SUPPORT. HOW MAY I DISCONNECT YOU?
WHAT ARE MY CHOICES?
I RECOMMEND THE ABRUPT DISCONNECT; SIMPLE, GETS THE JOB DONE.
I HAD THAT LAST TIME. WHAT ELSE DO YOU HAVE?
YOU MIGHT LIKE OUR "PLEASE HOLD," FOLLOWED BY THE "WRONG BUTTON," DISCONNECT.
TOO PREDICTABLE. DO YOU HAVE ANYTHING NEW?
TRY OUR "KEVORKIAN DISCONNECT." I PUT YOU ON HOLD AND PLAY AN ANNOYING MESSAGE UNTIL YOU DISCONNECT YOURSELF.
YOUR CALL IS IMPORTANT. PLEASE HOLD WHILE WE IGNORE IT ... YOUR CALL IS IMPORTANT ...
NOT BAD.
S. Adams
9/7/97 © 1997 United Feature Syndicate, Inc.

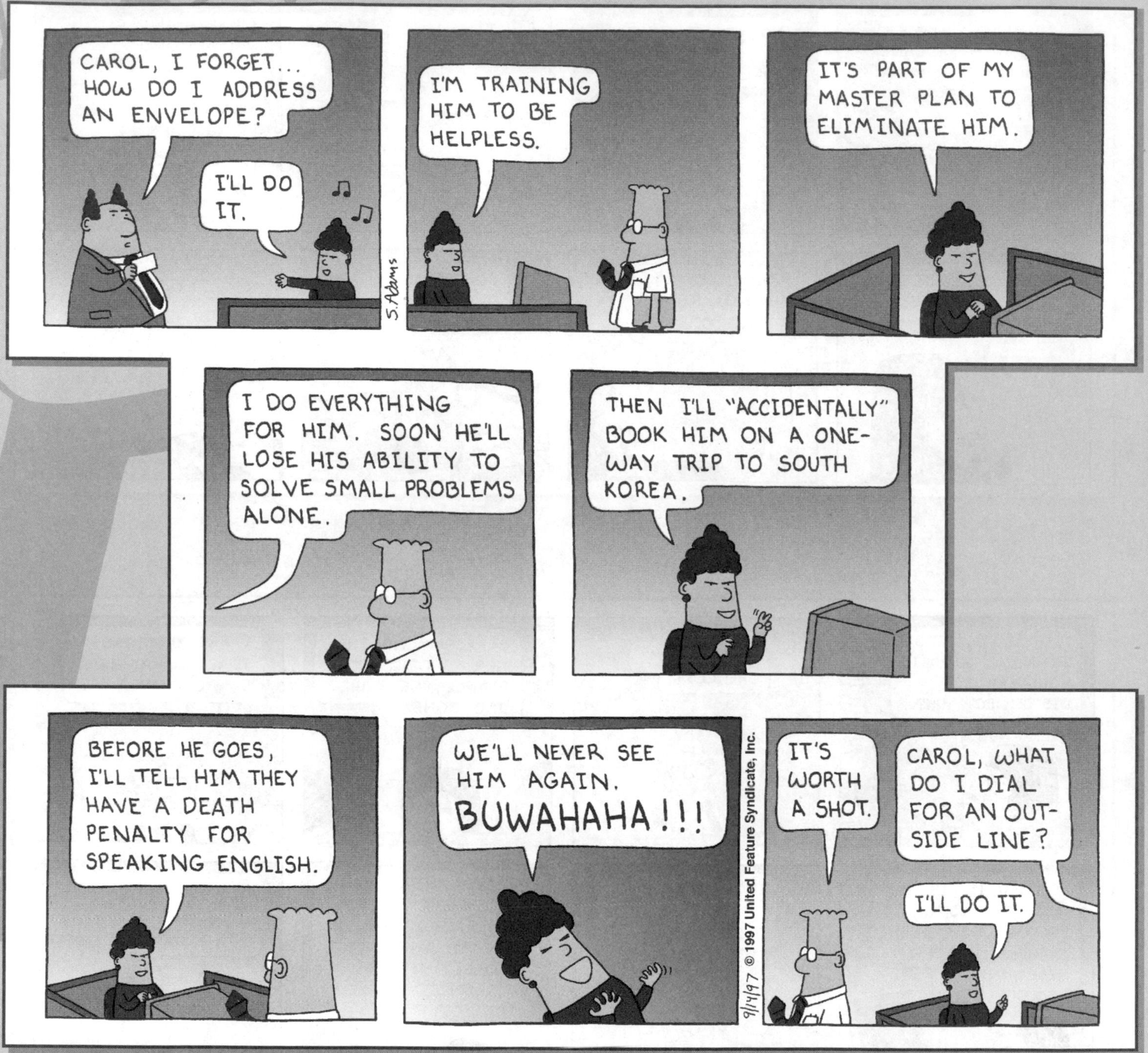
CAROL, I FORGET... HOW DO I ADDRESS AN ENVELOPE?
I'LL DO IT.
S. Adams
I'M TRAINING HIM TO BE HELPLESS.
IT'S PART OF MY MASTER PLAN TO ELIMINATE HIM.
I DO EVERYTHING FOR HIM. SOON HE'LL LOSE HIS ABILITY TO SOLVE SMALL PROBLEMS ALONE.
THEN I'LL "ACCIDENTALLY" BOOK HIM ON A ONE-WAY TRIP TO SOUTH KOREA.
BEFORE HE GOES, I'LL TELL HIM THEY HAVE A DEATH PENALTY FOR SPEAKING ENGLISH.
WE'LL NEVER SEE HIM AGAIN. BUWAHAHA!!!
9/14/97 © 1997 United Feature Syndicate, Inc.
IT'S WORTH A SHOT.
CAROL, WHAT DO I DIAL FOR AN OUT-SIDE LINE?
I'LL DO IT.

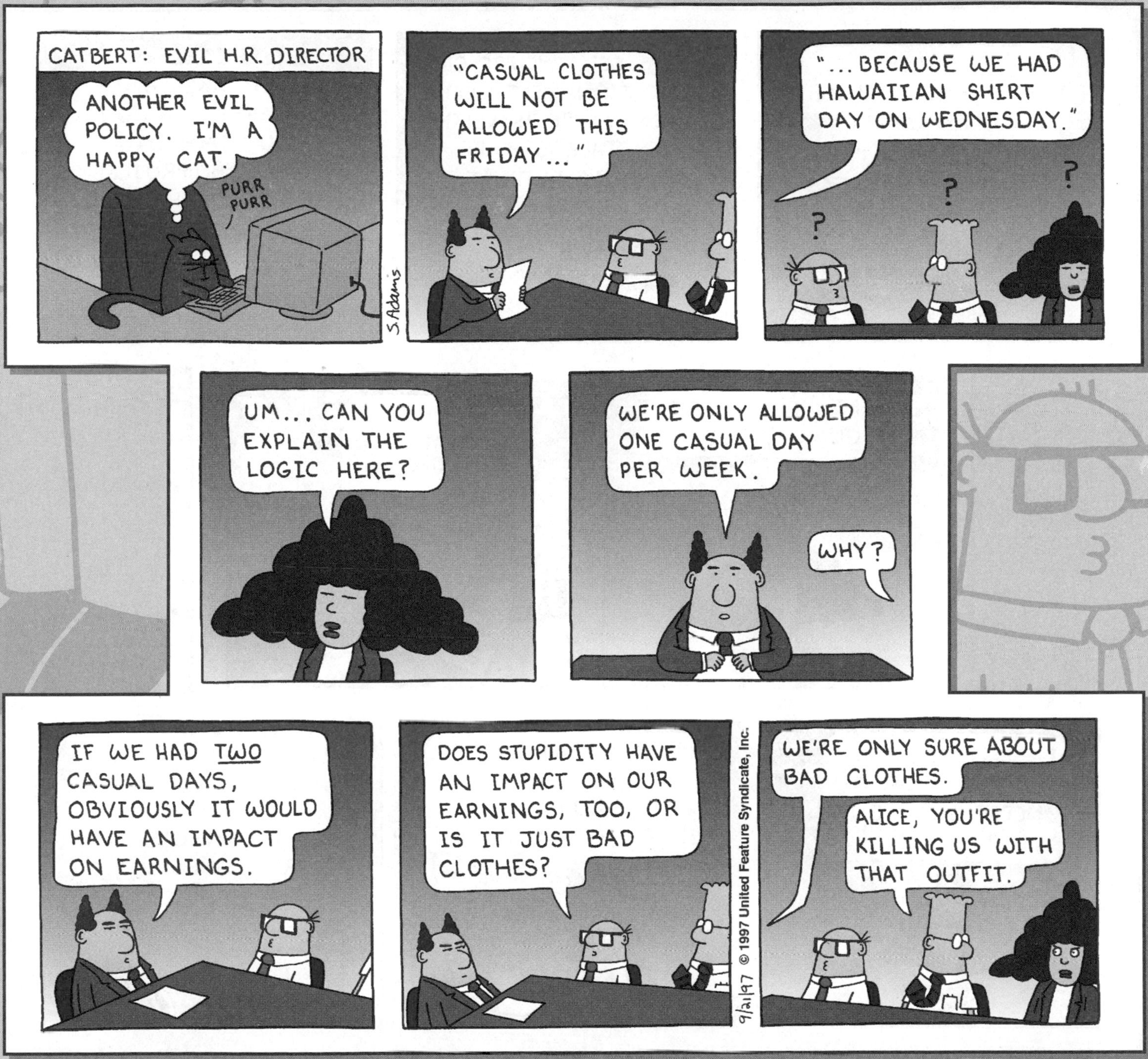
CATBERT: EVIL H.R. DIRECTOR
ANOTHER EVIL POLICY. I'M A HAPPY CAT.
PURR PURR
S. Adams
"CASUAL CLOTHES WILL NOT BE ALLOWED THIS FRIDAY ..."
"... BECAUSE WE HAD HAWAIIAN SHIRT DAY ON WEDNESDAY."
?
?
?
UM... CAN YOU EXPLAIN THE LOGIC HERE?
WE'RE ONLY ALLOWED ONE CASUAL DAY PER WEEK.
WHY?
IF WE HAD TWO CASUAL DAYS, OBVIOUSLY IT WOULD HAVE AN IMPACT ON EARNINGS.
DOES STUPIDITY HAVE AN IMPACT ON OUR EARNINGS, TOO, OR IS IT JUST BAD CLOTHES?
9/21/97 © 1997 United Feature Syndicate, Inc.
WE'RE ONLY SURE ABOUT BAD CLOTHES.
ALICE, YOU'RE KILLING US WITH THAT OUTFIT.

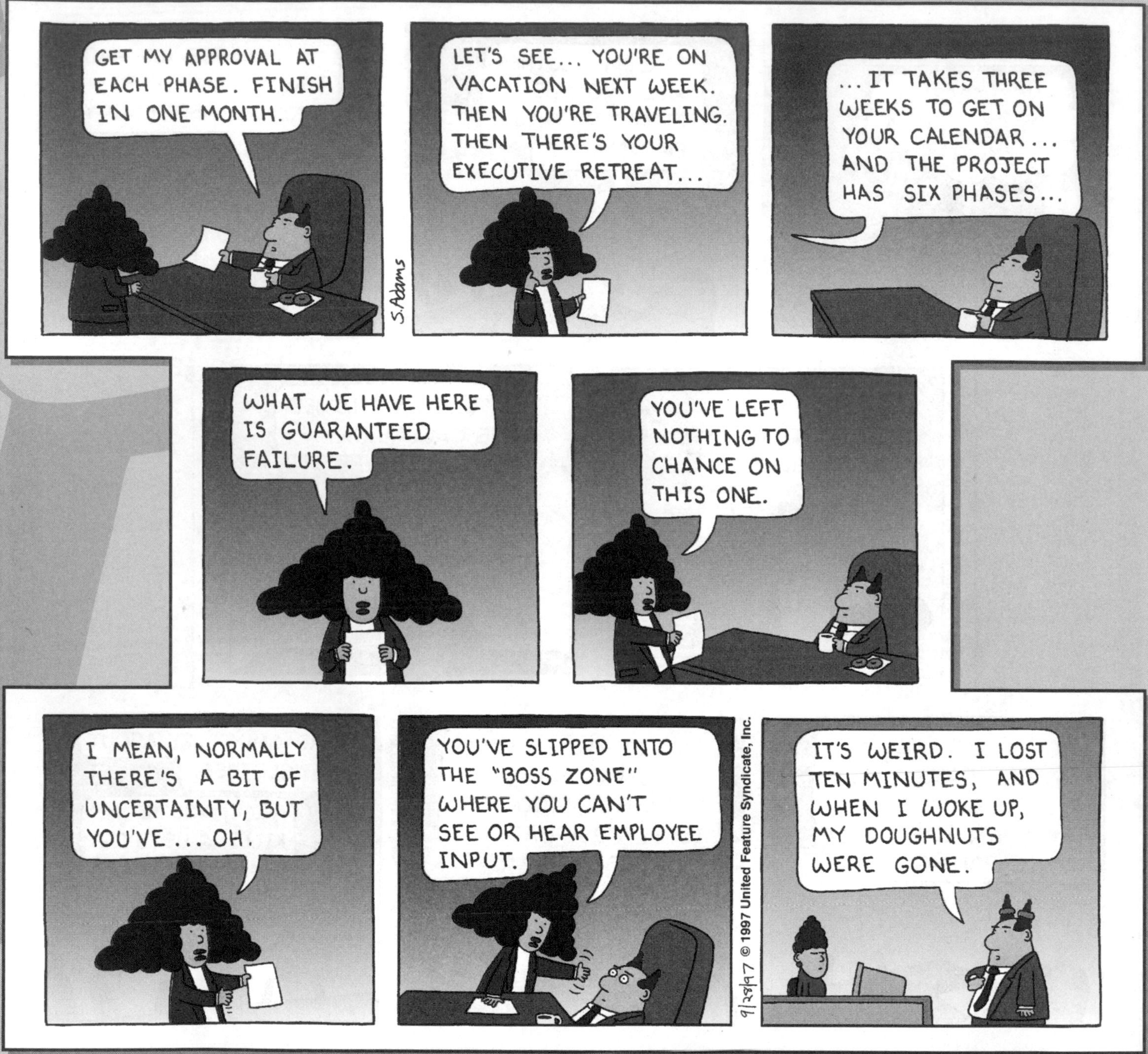
GET MY APPROVAL AT EACH PHASE. FINISH IN ONE MONTH.
S. Adams
LET'S SEE... YOU'RE ON VACATION NEXT WEEK. THEN YOU'RE TRAVELING. THEN THERE'S YOUR EXECUTIVE RETREAT...
... IT TAKES THREE WEEKS TO GET ON YOUR CALENDAR ... AND THE PROJECT HAS SIX PHASES ...
WHAT WE HAVE HERE IS GUARANTEED FAILURE.
YOU'VE LEFT NOTHING TO CHANCE ON THIS ONE.
I MEAN, NORMALLY THERE'S A BIT OF UNCERTAINTY, BUT YOU'VE ... OH.
YOU'VE SLIPPED INTO THE "BOSS ZONE" WHERE YOU CAN'T SEE OR HEAR EMPLOYEE INPUT.
9/28/97 © 1997 United Feature Syndicate, Inc.
IT'S WEIRD. I LOST TEN MINUTES, AND WHEN I WOKE UP, MY DOUGHNUTS WERE GONE.

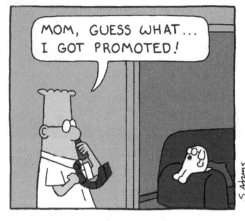

MOM, GUESS WHAT... I GOT PROMOTED!
S. Adams
YOU'RE TALKING TO THE NEW "EXECUTIVE ENGINEER."
NO... NOBODY REPORTS TO ME.
NO... IT'S THE SAME PAY AS BEFORE.
BUT I DO GET A LOT MORE RESPONSIBILITY!
SHE'S GOING TO THROW A PARTY FOR ME!
NO... NO GIFTS.
NO... NO MUSIC.
NO... NO FOOD.
NO... NO GUESTS.
I GUESS IT'S JUST YOU AND ME.
I'M BUSY THAT DAY.
10/5/97 © 1997 United Feature Syndicate, Inc.
I'M NOT ALLOWED TO GET NEW BUSINESS CARDS, BUT I CAN WRITE MY NEW TITLE ON THE OLD ONES!
ZZZZ

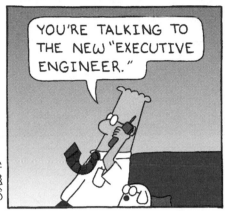

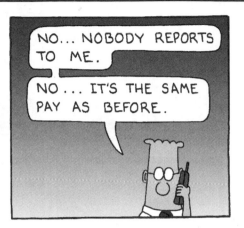

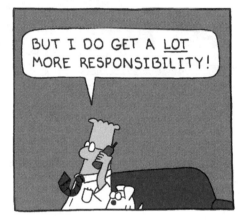

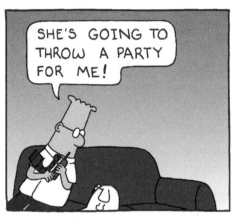

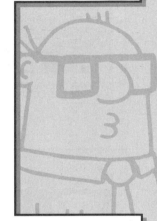

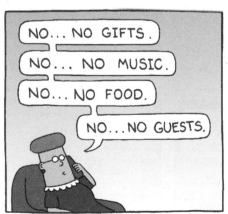

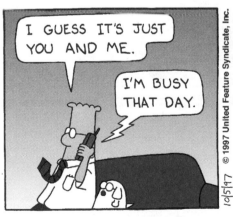

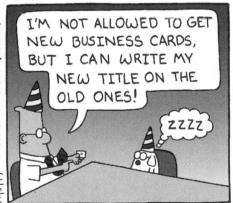

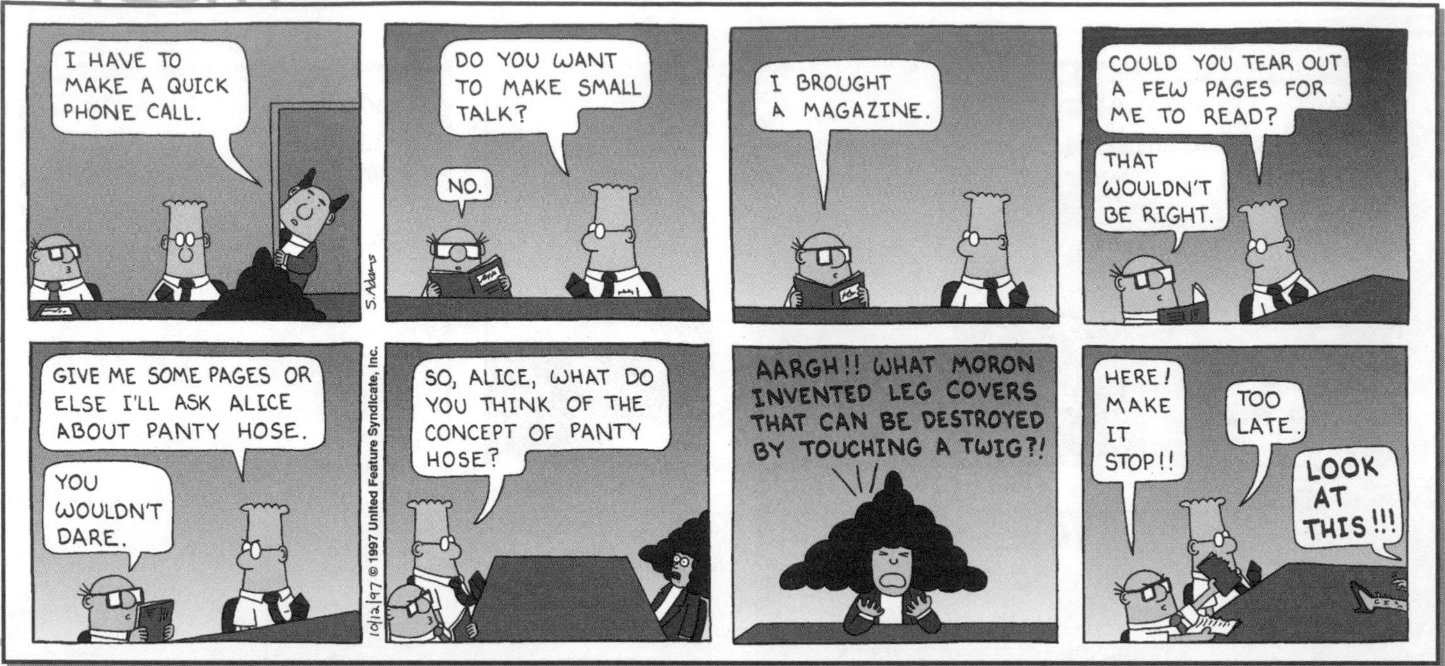
I HAVE TO MAKE A QUICK PHONE CALL.
S. Adams
DO YOU WANT TO MAKE SMALL TALK?
NO.
I BROUGHT A MAGAZINE.
COULD YOU TEAR OUT A FEW PAGES FOR ME TO READ?
THAT WOULDN'T BE RIGHT.
GIVE ME SOME PAGES OR ELSE I'LL ASK ALICE ABOUT PANTY HOSE.
YOU WOULDN'T DARE.
10/12/97 © 1997 United Feature Syndicate, Inc.
SO, ALICE, WHAT DO YOU THINK OF THE CONCEPT OF PANTY HOSE?
AARGH!! WHAT MORON INVENTED LEG COVERS THAT CAN BE DESTROYED BY TOUCHING A TWIG?!
HERE! MAKE IT STOP!!
TOO LATE.
LOOK AT THIS!!!

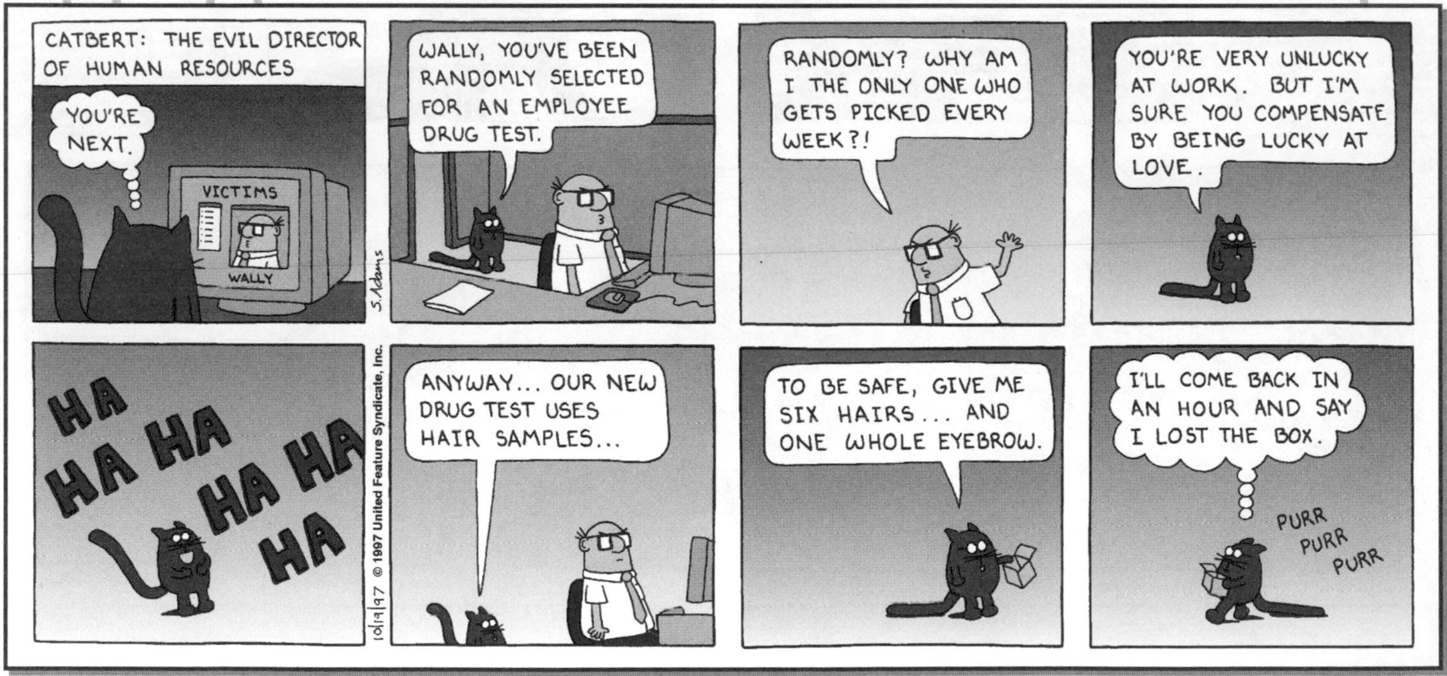
CATBERT: THE EVIL DIRECTOR OF HUMAN RESOURCES
YOU'RE NEXT.
VICTIMS
WALLY
S. Adams
WALLY, YOU'VE BEEN RANDOMLY SELECTED FOR AN EMPLOYEE DRUG TEST.
RANDOMLY? WHY AM I THE ONLY ONE WHO GETS PICKED EVERY WEEK?!
YOU'RE VERY UNLUCKY AT WORK. BUT I'M SURE YOU COMPENSATE BY BEING LUCKY AT LOVE.
HA HA HA HA HA HA
10/19/97 © 1997 United Feature Syndicate, Inc.
ANYWAY... OUR NEW DRUG TEST USES HAIR SAMPLES...
TO BE SAFE, GIVE ME SIX HAIRS... AND ONE WHOLE EYEBROW.
I'LL COME BACK IN AN HOUR AND SAY I LOST THE BOX.
PURR PURR PURR

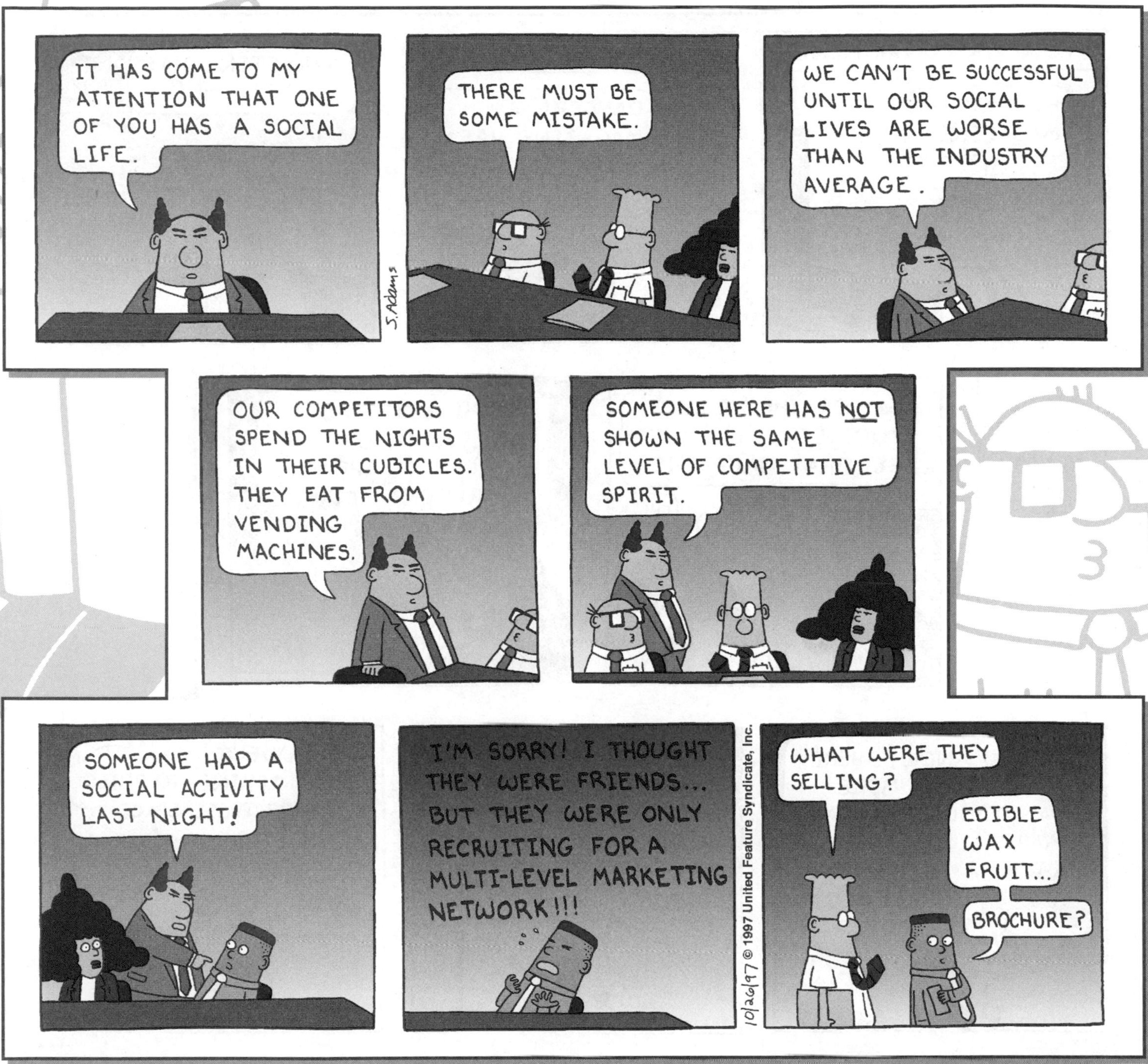
IT HAS COME TO MY ATTENTION THAT ONE OF YOU HAS A SOCIAL LIFE.
S. Adams
THERE MUST BE SOME MISTAKE.
WE CAN'T BE SUCCESSFUL UNTIL OUR SOCIAL LIVES ARE WORSE THAN THE INDUSTRY AVERAGE.
OUR COMPETITORS SPEND THE NIGHTS IN THEIR CUBICLES. THEY EAT FROM VENDING MACHINES.
SOMEONE HERE HAS NOT SHOWN THE SAME LEVEL OF COMPETITIVE SPIRIT.
SOMEONE HAD A SOCIAL ACTIVITY LAST NIGHT!
I'M SORRY! I THOUGHT THEY WERE FRIENDS... BUT THEY WERE ONLY RECRUITING FOR A MULTI-LEVEL MARKETING NETWORK!!!
10/26/97 © 1997 United Feature Syndicate, Inc.
WHAT WERE THEY SELLING?
EDIBLE WAX FRUIT...
BROCHURE?

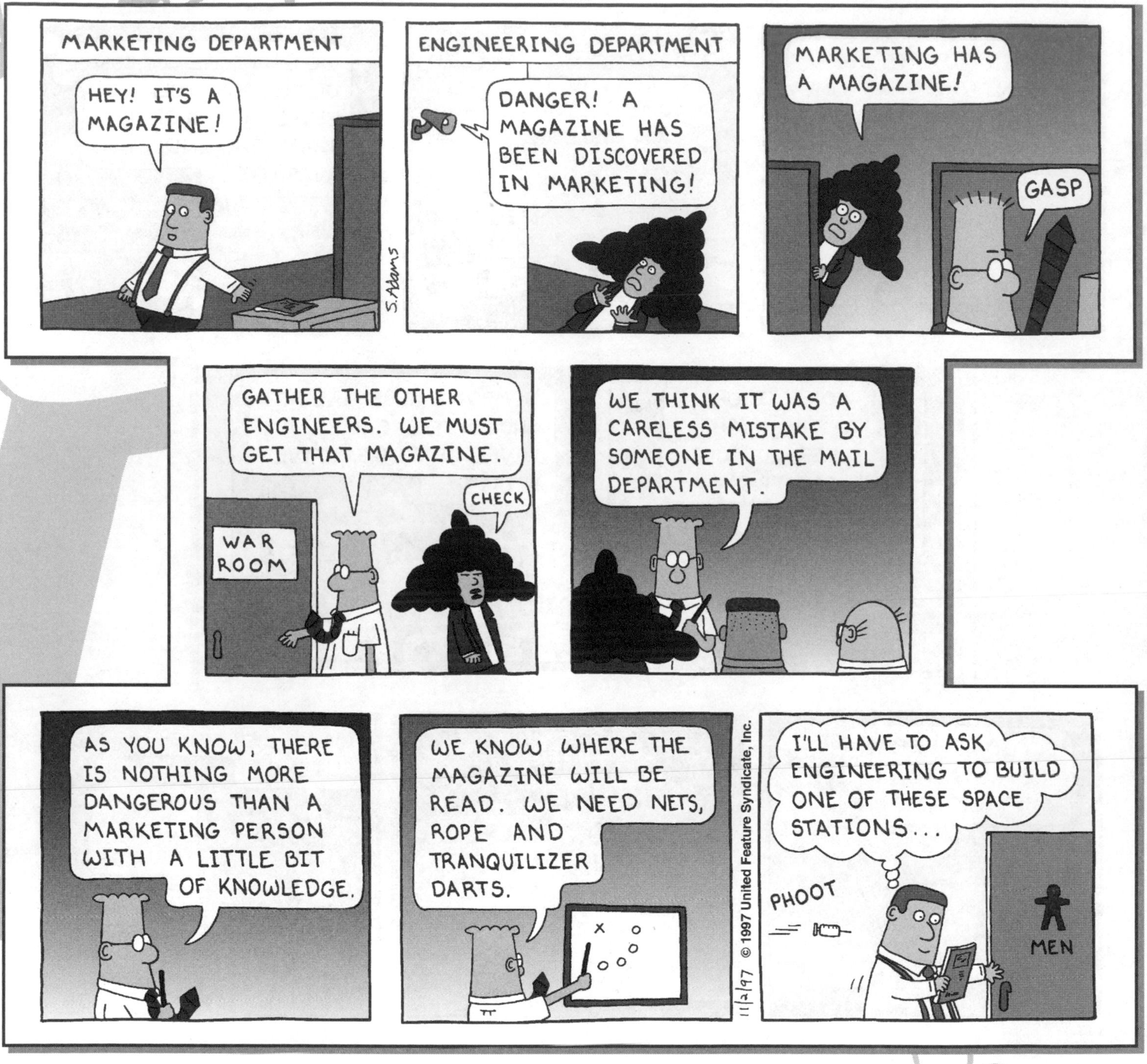
MARKETING DEPARTMENT
HEY! IT'S A MAGAZINE!
S. Adams
ENGINEERING DEPARTMENT
DANGER! A MAGAZINE HAS BEEN DISCOVERED IN MARKETING!
MARKETING HAS A MAGAZINE!
GASP
GATHER THE OTHER ENGINEERS. WE MUST GET THAT MAGAZINE.
WAR ROOM
CHECK
WE THINK IT WAS A CARELESS MISTAKE BY SOMEONE IN THE MAIL DEPARTMENT.
AS YOU KNOW, THERE IS NOTHING MORE DANGEROUS THAN A MARKETING PERSON WITH A LITTLE BIT OF KNOWLEDGE.
WE KNOW WHERE THE MAGAZINE WILL BE READ. WE NEED NETS, ROPE AND TRANQUILIZER DARTS.
11/2/97 © 1997 United Feature Syndicate, Inc.
I'LL HAVE TO ASK ENGINEERING TO BUILD ONE OF THESE SPACE STATIONS...
PHOOT
MEN

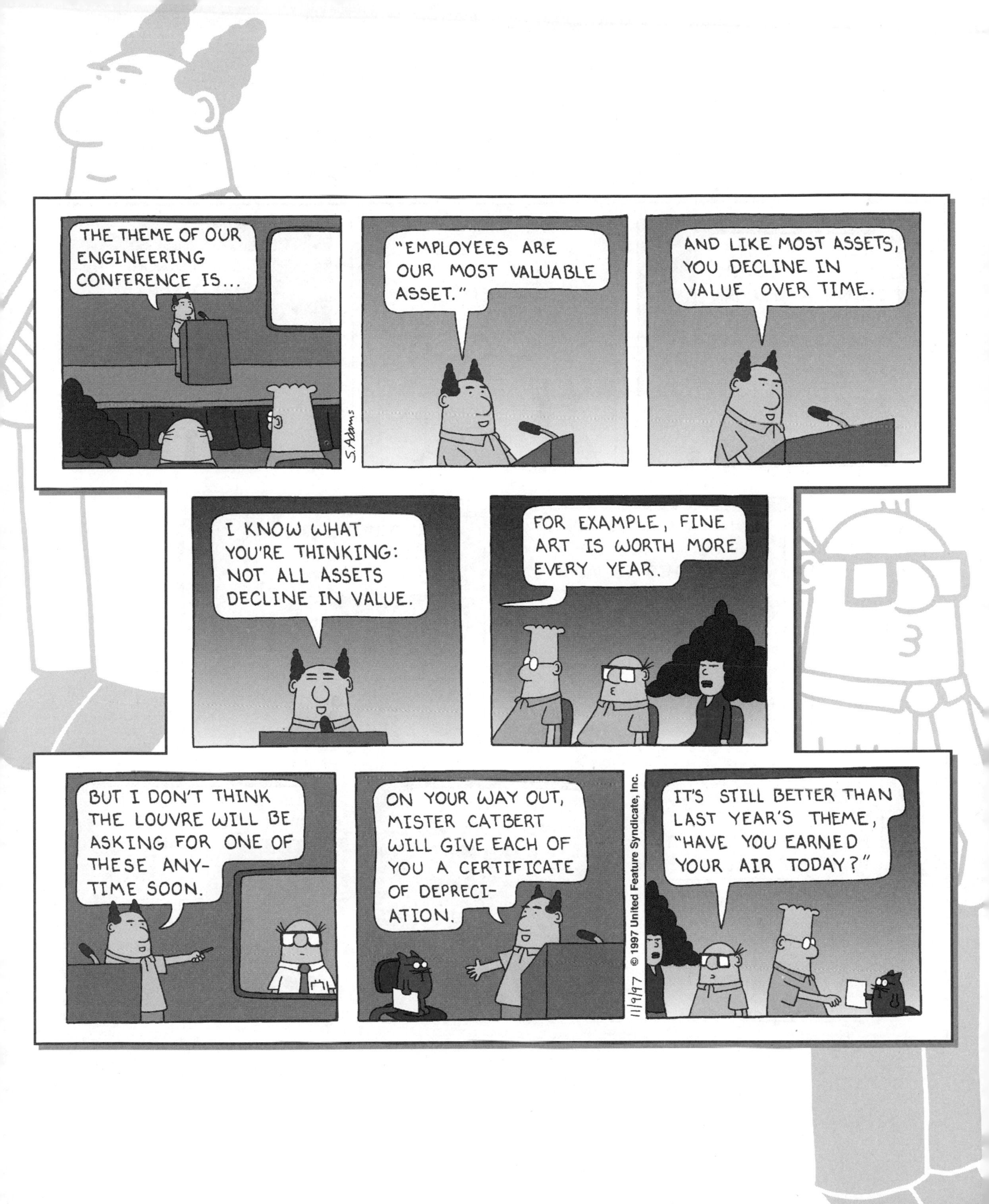

THE THEME OF OUR ENGINEERING CONFERENCE IS...
S. Adams
"EMPLOYEES ARE OUR MOST VALUABLE ASSET."
AND LIKE MOST ASSETS, YOU DECLINE IN VALUE OVER TIME.
I KNOW WHAT YOU'RE THINKING: NOT ALL ASSETS DECLINE IN VALUE.
FOR EXAMPLE, FINE ART IS WORTH MORE EVERY YEAR.
BUT I DON'T THINK THE LOUVRE WILL BE ASKING FOR ONE OF THESE ANY-TIME SOON.
ON YOUR WAY OUT, MISTER CATBERT WILL GIVE EACH OF YOU A CERTIFICATE OF DEPRECI-ATION.
11/9/97 © 1997 United Feature Syndicate, Inc.
IT'S STILL BETTER THAN LAST YEAR'S THEME, "HAVE YOU EARNED YOUR AIR TODAY?"

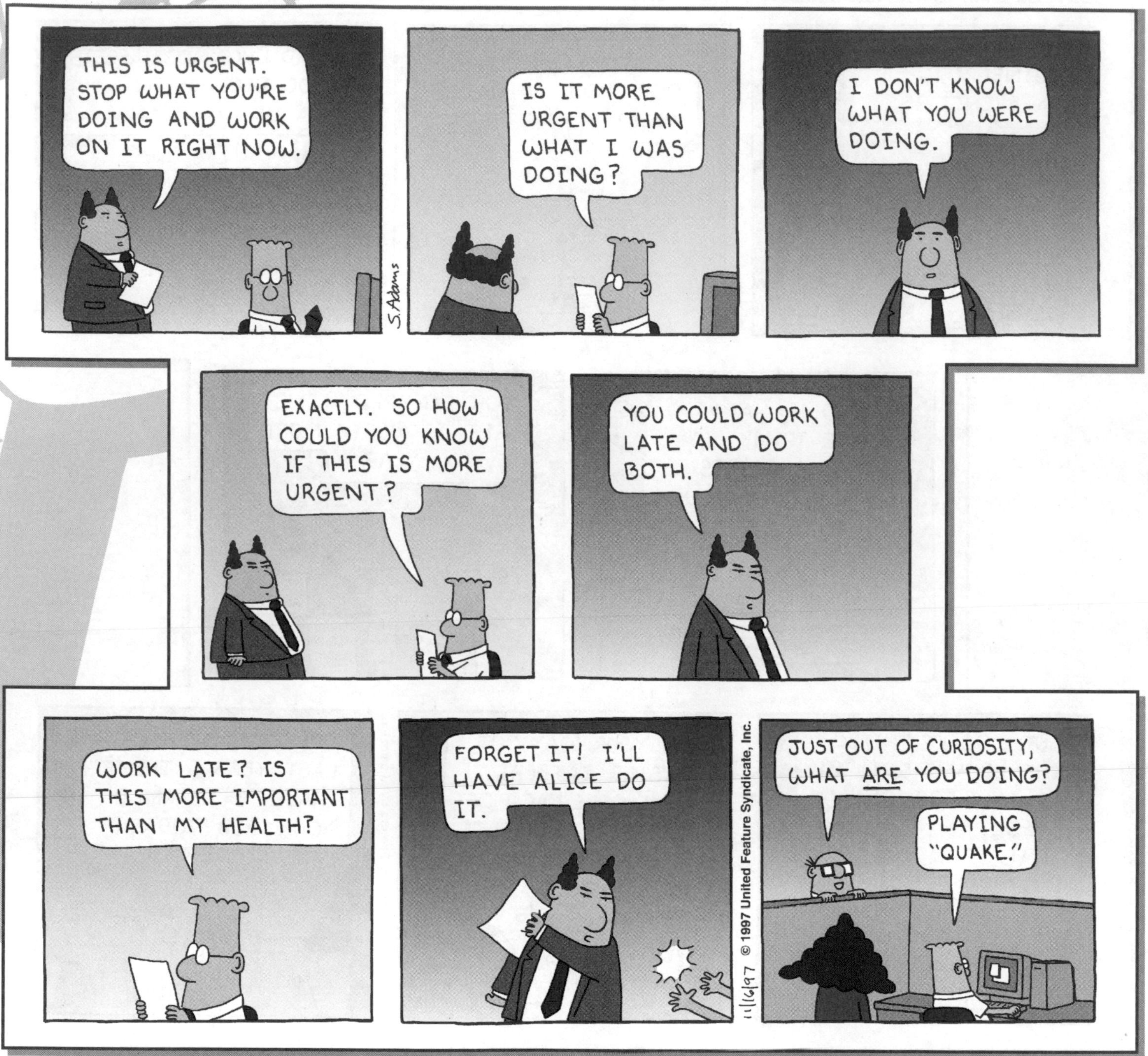
THIS IS URGENT. STOP WHAT YOU'RE DOING AND WORK ON IT RIGHT NOW.
S. Adams
IS IT MORE URGENT THAN WHAT I WAS DOING?
I DON'T KNOW WHAT YOU WERE DOING.
EXACTLY. SO HOW COULD YOU KNOW IF THIS IS MORE URGENT?
YOU COULD WORK LATE AND DO BOTH.
WORK LATE? IS THIS MORE IMPORTANT THAN MY HEALTH?
FORGET IT! I'LL HAVE ALICE DO IT.
11/16/97 © 1997 United Feature Syndicate, Inc.
JUST OUT OF CURIOSITY, WHAT ARE YOU DOING?
PLAYING "QUAKE."

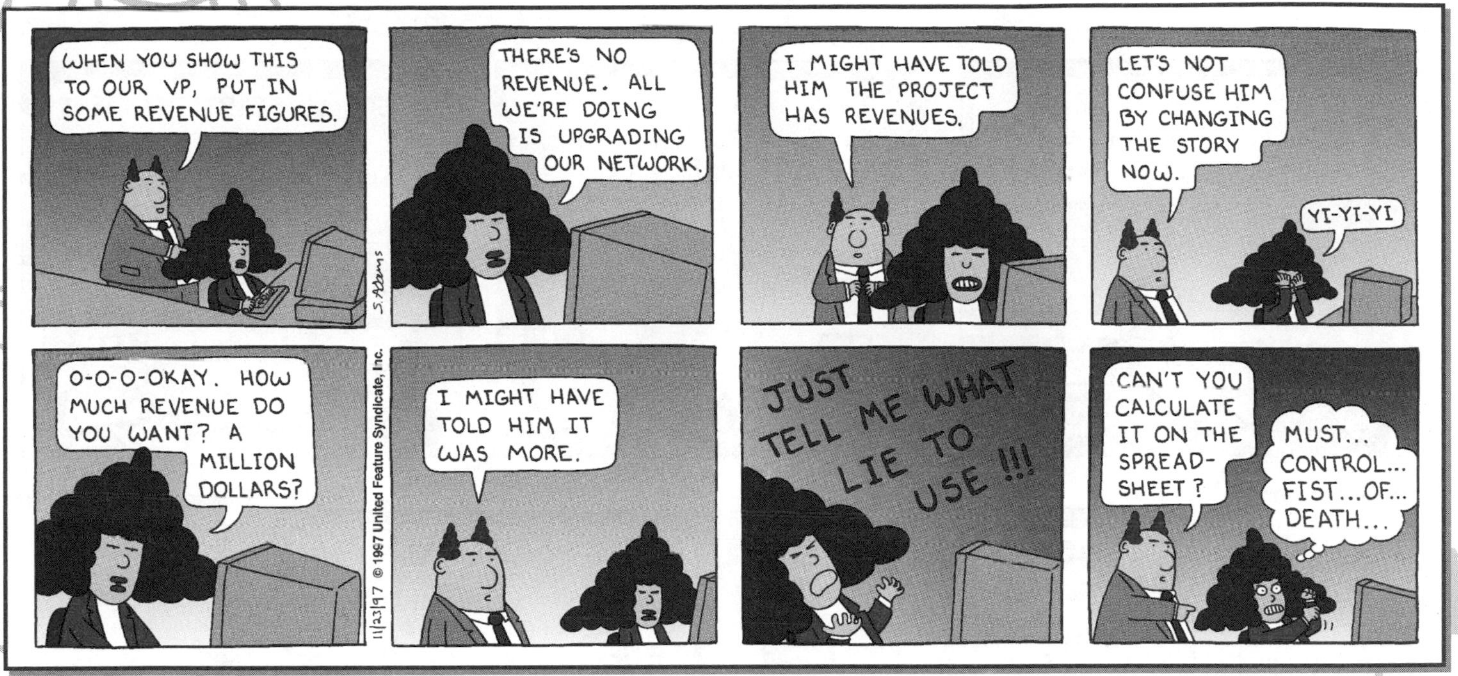
WHEN YOU SHOW THIS TO OUR VP, PUT IN SOME REVENUE FIGURES.
THERE'S NO REVENUE. ALL WE'RE DOING IS UPGRADING OUR NETWORK.
I MIGHT HAVE TOLD HIM THE PROJECT HAS REVENUES.
LET'S NOT CONFUSE HIM BY CHANGING THE STORY NOW.
YI-YI-YI
O-O-O-OKAY. HOW MUCH REVENUE DO YOU WANT? A MILLION DOLLARS?
I MIGHT HAVE TOLD HIM IT WAS MORE.
JUST TELL ME WHAT LIE TO USE !!!
CAN'T YOU CALCULATE IT ON THE SPREAD-SHEET?
MUST... CONTROL... FIST...OF... DEATH...
S. Adams
11/23/97 © 1997 United Feature Syndicate, Inc.

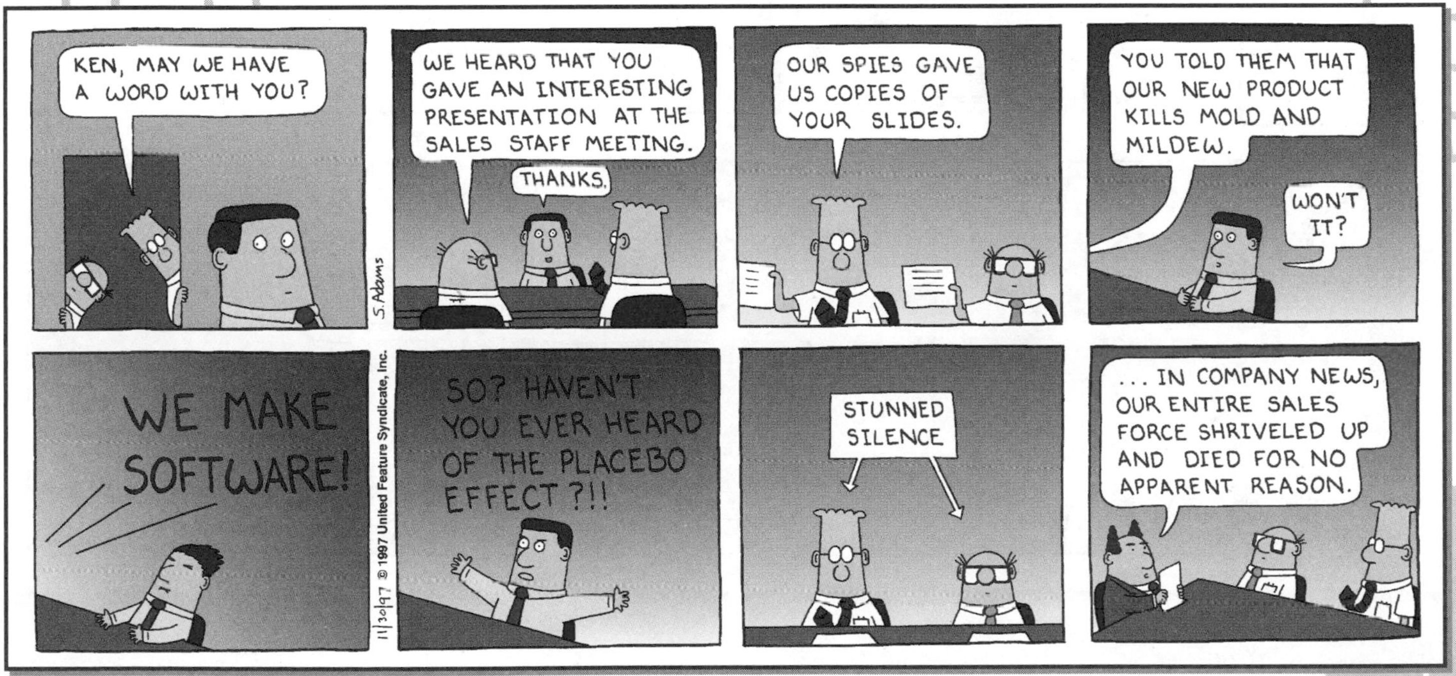
KEN, MAY WE HAVE A WORD WITH YOU?
WE HEARD THAT YOU GAVE AN INTERESTING PRESENTATION AT THE SALES STAFF MEETING.
THANKS.
OUR SPIES GAVE US COPIES OF YOUR SLIDES.
YOU TOLD THEM THAT OUR NEW PRODUCT KILLS MOLD AND MILDEW.
WON'T IT?
WE MAKE SOFTWARE!
SO? HAVEN'T YOU EVER HEARD OF THE PLACEBO EFFECT?!!
STUNNED SILENCE
... IN COMPANY NEWS, OUR ENTIRE SALES FORCE SHRIVELED UP AND DIED FOR NO APPARENT REASON.
S. Adams
11/30/97 © 1997 United Feature Syndicate, Inc.

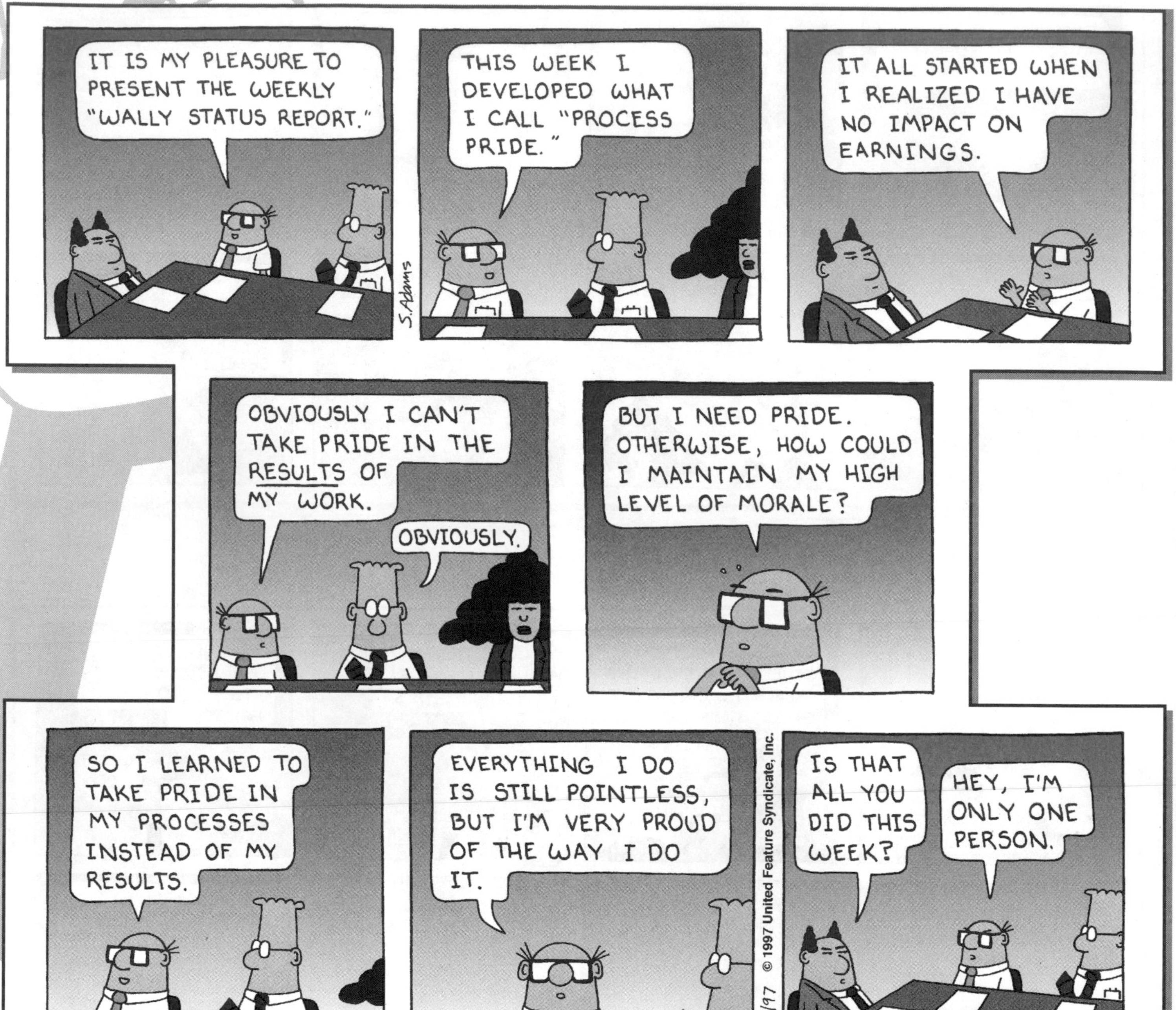
IT IS MY PLEASURE TO PRESENT THE WEEKLY "WALLY STATUS REPORT."
S. Adams
THIS WEEK I DEVELOPED WHAT I CALL "PROCESS PRIDE."
IT ALL STARTED WHEN I REALIZED I HAVE NO IMPACT ON EARNINGS.
OBVIOUSLY I CAN'T TAKE PRIDE IN THE RESULTS OF MY WORK.
OBVIOUSLY.
BUT I NEED PRIDE. OTHERWISE, HOW COULD I MAINTAIN MY HIGH LEVEL OF MORALE?
SO I LEARNED TO TAKE PRIDE IN MY PROCESSES INSTEAD OF MY RESULTS.
EVERYTHING I DO IS STILL POINTLESS, BUT I'M VERY PROUD OF THE WAY I DO IT.
12/7/97 © 1997 United Feature Syndicate, Inc.
IS THAT ALL YOU DID THIS WEEK?
HEY, I'M ONLY ONE PERSON.

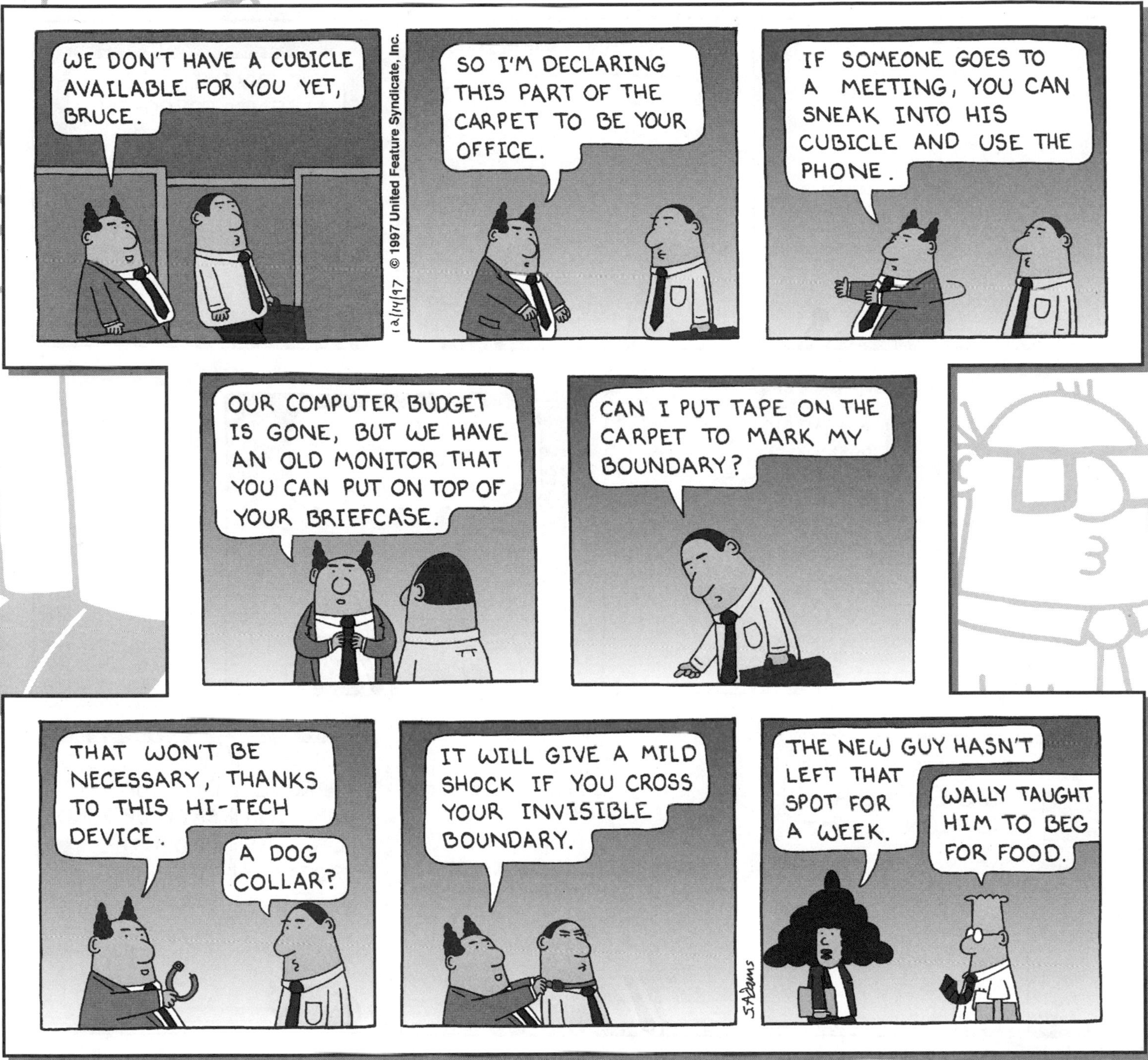
WE DON'T HAVE A CUBICLE AVAILABLE FOR YOU YET, BRUCE.
12/14/97 © 1997 United Feature Syndicate, Inc.
SO I'M DECLARING THIS PART OF THE CARPET TO BE YOUR OFFICE.
IF SOMEONE GOES TO A MEETING, YOU CAN SNEAK INTO HIS CUBICLE AND USE THE PHONE.
OUR COMPUTER BUDGET IS GONE, BUT WE HAVE AN OLD MONITOR THAT YOU CAN PUT ON TOP OF YOUR BRIEFCASE.
CAN I PUT TAPE ON THE CARPET TO MARK MY BOUNDARY?
THAT WON'T BE NECESSARY, THANKS TO THIS HI-TECH DEVICE.
A DOG COLLAR?
IT WILL GIVE A MILD SHOCK IF YOU CROSS YOUR INVISIBLE BOUNDARY.
THE NEW GUY HASN'T LEFT THAT SPOT FOR A WEEK.
WALLY TAUGHT HIM TO BEG FOR FOOD.
S.ADAMS

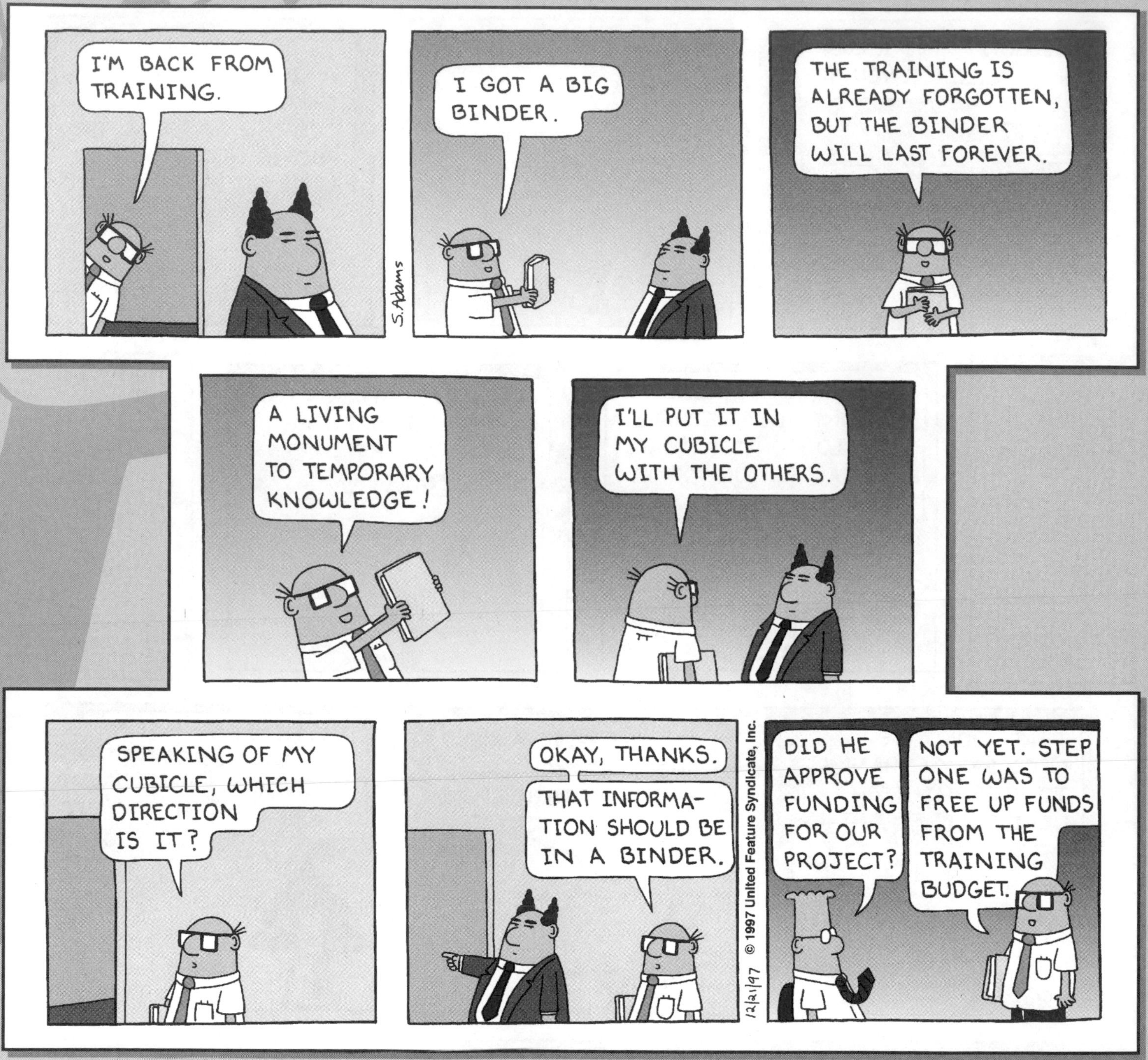

I'M BACK FROM TRAINING.
I GOT A BIG BINDER.
S. Adams
THE TRAINING IS ALREADY FORGOTTEN, BUT THE BINDER WILL LAST FOREVER.
A LIVING MONUMENT TO TEMPORARY KNOWLEDGE!
I'LL PUT IT IN MY CUBICLE WITH THE OTHERS.
SPEAKING OF MY CUBICLE, WHICH DIRECTION IS IT?
OKAY, THANKS.
THAT INFORMATION SHOULD BE IN A BINDER.
12/21/97 © 1997 United Feature Syndicate, Inc.
DID HE APPROVE FUNDING FOR OUR PROJECT?
NOT YET. STEP ONE WAS TO FREE UP FUNDS FROM THE TRAINING BUDGET.

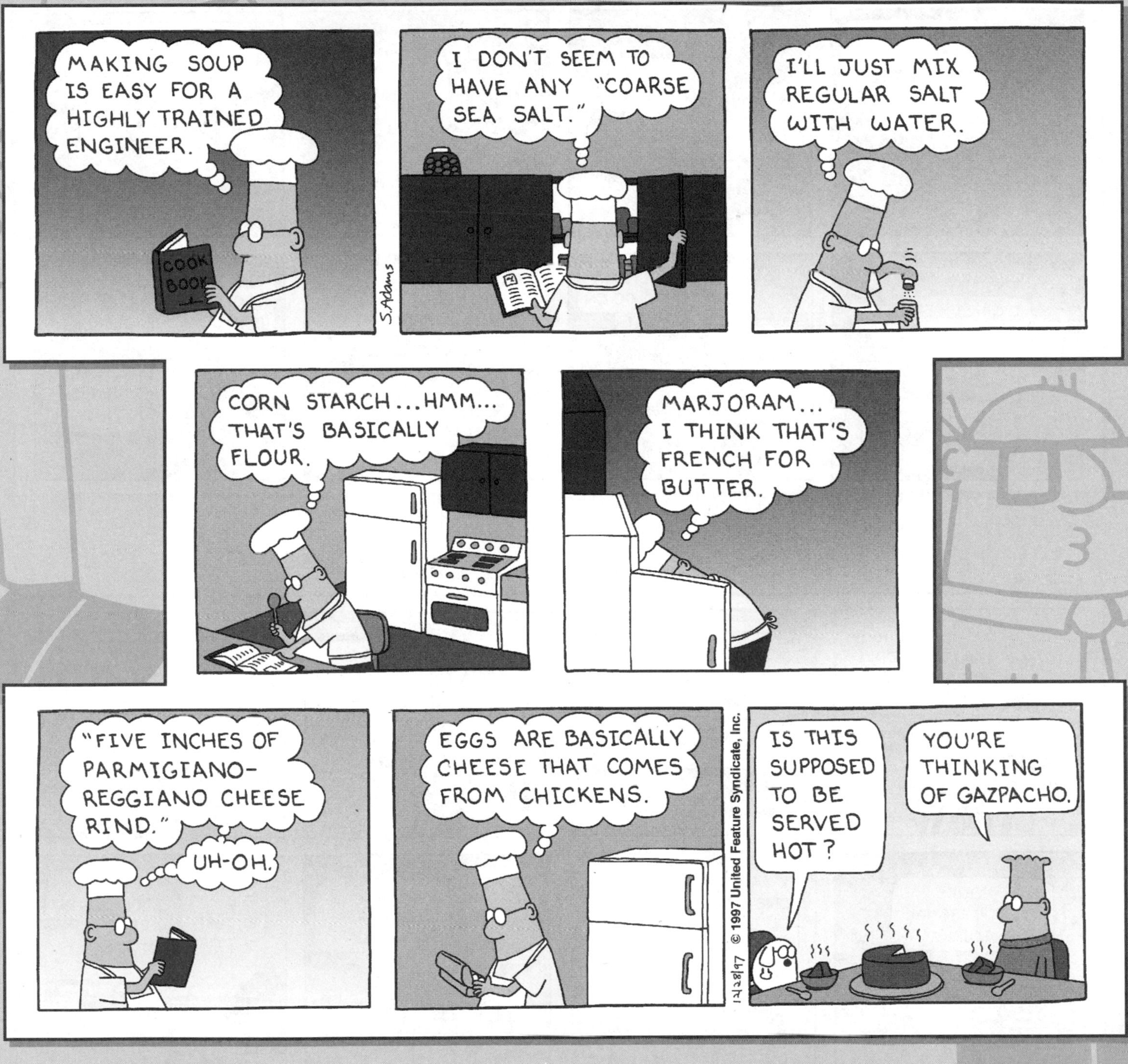
MAKING SOUP IS EASY FOR A HIGHLY TRAINED ENGINEER.
COOK BOOK
S. Adams
I DON'T SEEM TO HAVE ANY "COARSE SEA SALT."
I'LL JUST MIX REGULAR SALT WITH WATER.
CORN STARCH...HMM... THAT'S BASICALLY FLOUR.
MARJORAM... I THINK THAT'S FRENCH FOR BUTTER.
"FIVE INCHES OF PARMIGIANO-REGGIANO CHEESE RIND."
UH-OH.
EGGS ARE BASICALLY CHEESE THAT COMES FROM CHICKENS.
12/28/97 © 1997 United Feature Syndicate, Inc.
IS THIS SUPPOSED TO BE SERVED HOT?
YOU'RE THINKING OF GAZPACHO.

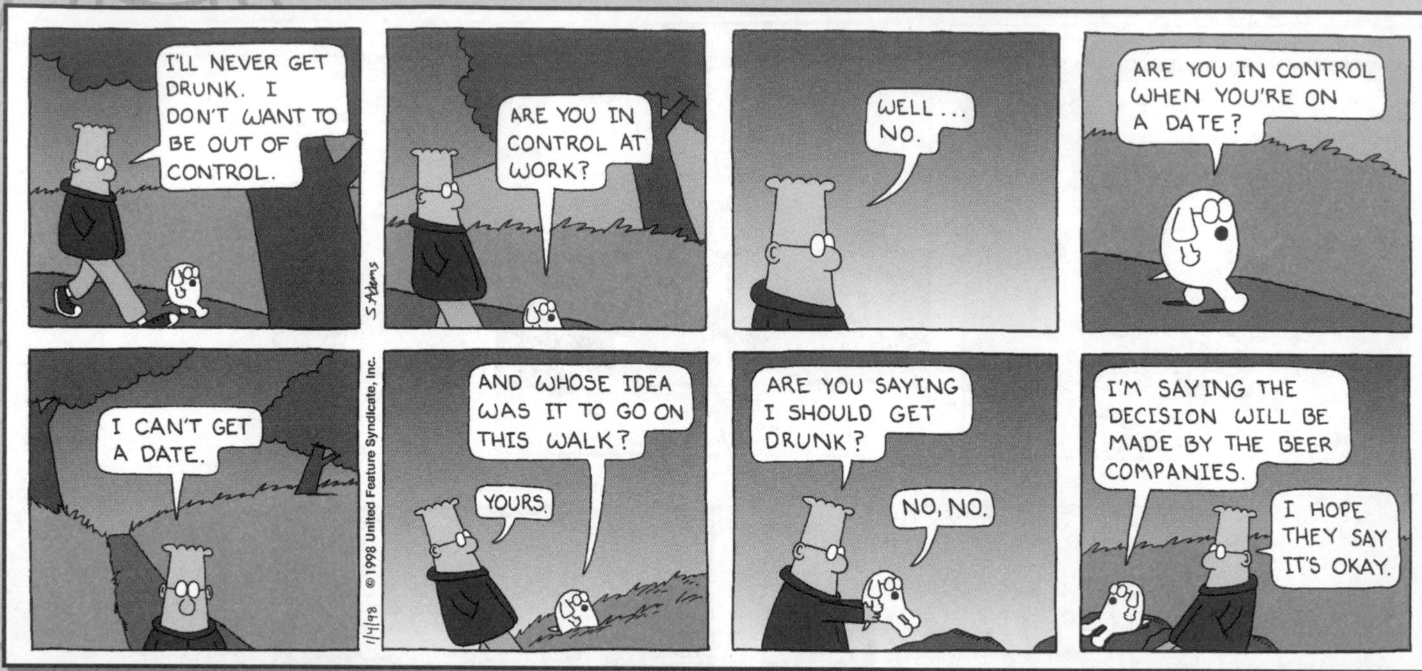
I'LL NEVER GET DRUNK. I DON'T WANT TO BE OUT OF CONTROL.
ARE YOU IN CONTROL AT WORK?
WELL... NO.
ARE YOU IN CONTROL WHEN YOU'RE ON A DATE?
I CAN'T GET A DATE.
AND WHOSE IDEA WAS IT TO GO ON THIS WALK?
YOURS.
ARE YOU SAYING I SHOULD GET DRUNK?
NO, NO.
I'M SAYING THE DECISION WILL BE MADE BY THE BEER COMPANIES.
I HOPE THEY SAY IT'S OKAY.
S.Adams
1/4/98
© 1998 United Feature Syndicate, Inc.

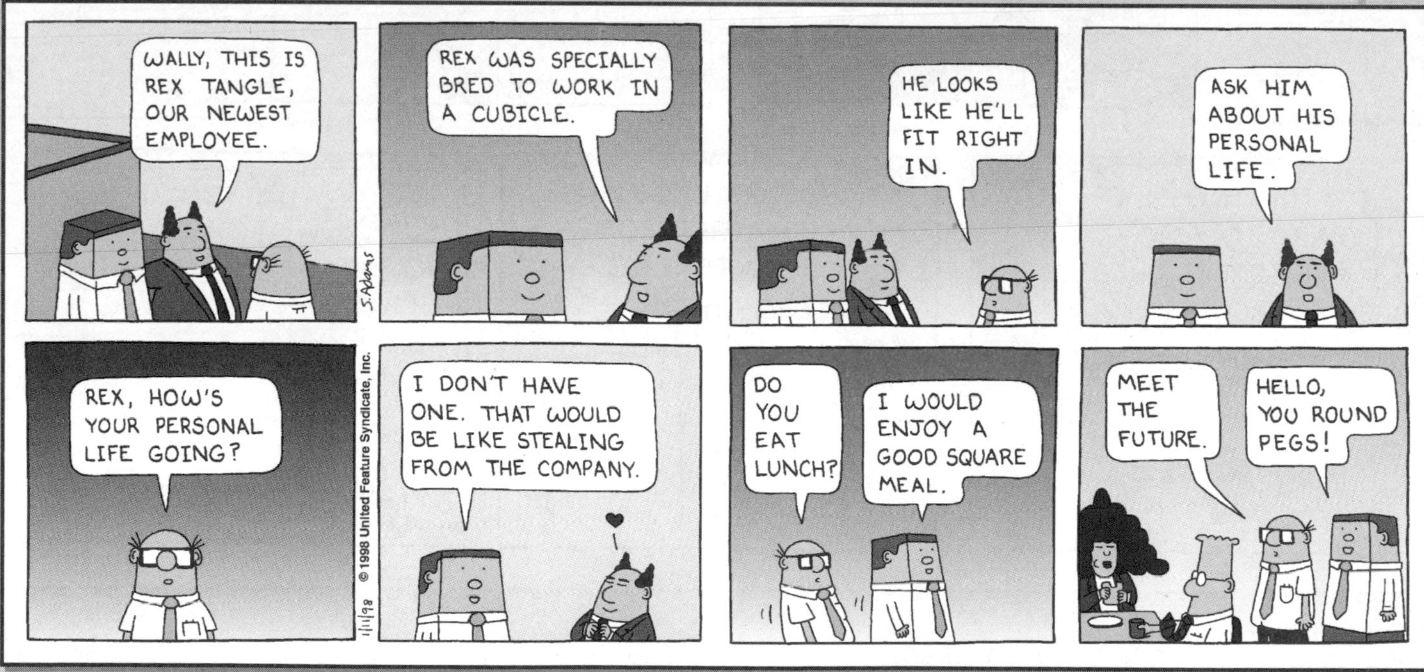
WALLY, THIS IS REX TANGLE, OUR NEWEST EMPLOYEE.
REX WAS SPECIALLY BRED TO WORK IN A CUBICLE.
HE LOOKS LIKE HE'LL FIT RIGHT IN.
ASK HIM ABOUT HIS PERSONAL LIFE.
REX, HOW'S YOUR PERSONAL LIFE GOING?
I DON'T HAVE ONE. THAT WOULD BE LIKE STEALING FROM THE COMPANY.
DO YOU EAT LUNCH?
I WOULD ENJOY A GOOD SQUARE MEAL.
MEET THE FUTURE.
HELLO, YOU ROUND PEGS!
S.Adams
1/11/98
© 1998 United Feature Syndicate, Inc.

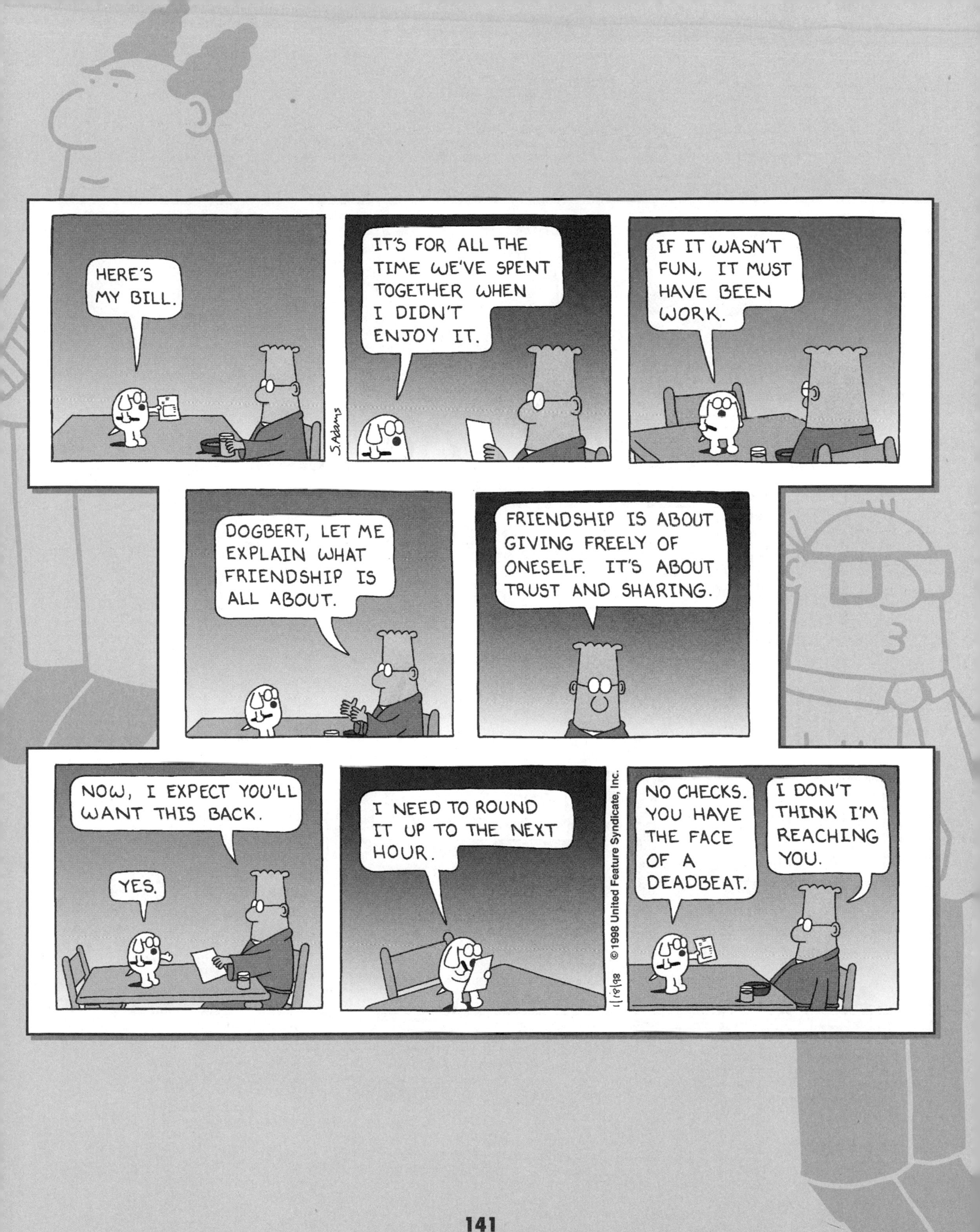
HERE'S MY BILL.
S. Adams
IT'S FOR ALL THE TIME WE'VE SPENT TOGETHER WHEN I DIDN'T ENJOY IT.
IF IT WASN'T FUN, IT MUST HAVE BEEN WORK.
DOGBERT, LET ME EXPLAIN WHAT FRIENDSHIP IS ALL ABOUT.
FRIENDSHIP IS ABOUT GIVING FREELY OF ONESELF. IT'S ABOUT TRUST AND SHARING.
NOW, I EXPECT YOU'LL WANT THIS BACK.
YES.
I NEED TO ROUND IT UP TO THE NEXT HOUR.
1/18/98 © 1998 United Feature Syndicate, Inc.
NO CHECKS. YOU HAVE THE FACE OF A DEADBEAT.
I DON'T THINK I'M REACHING YOU.

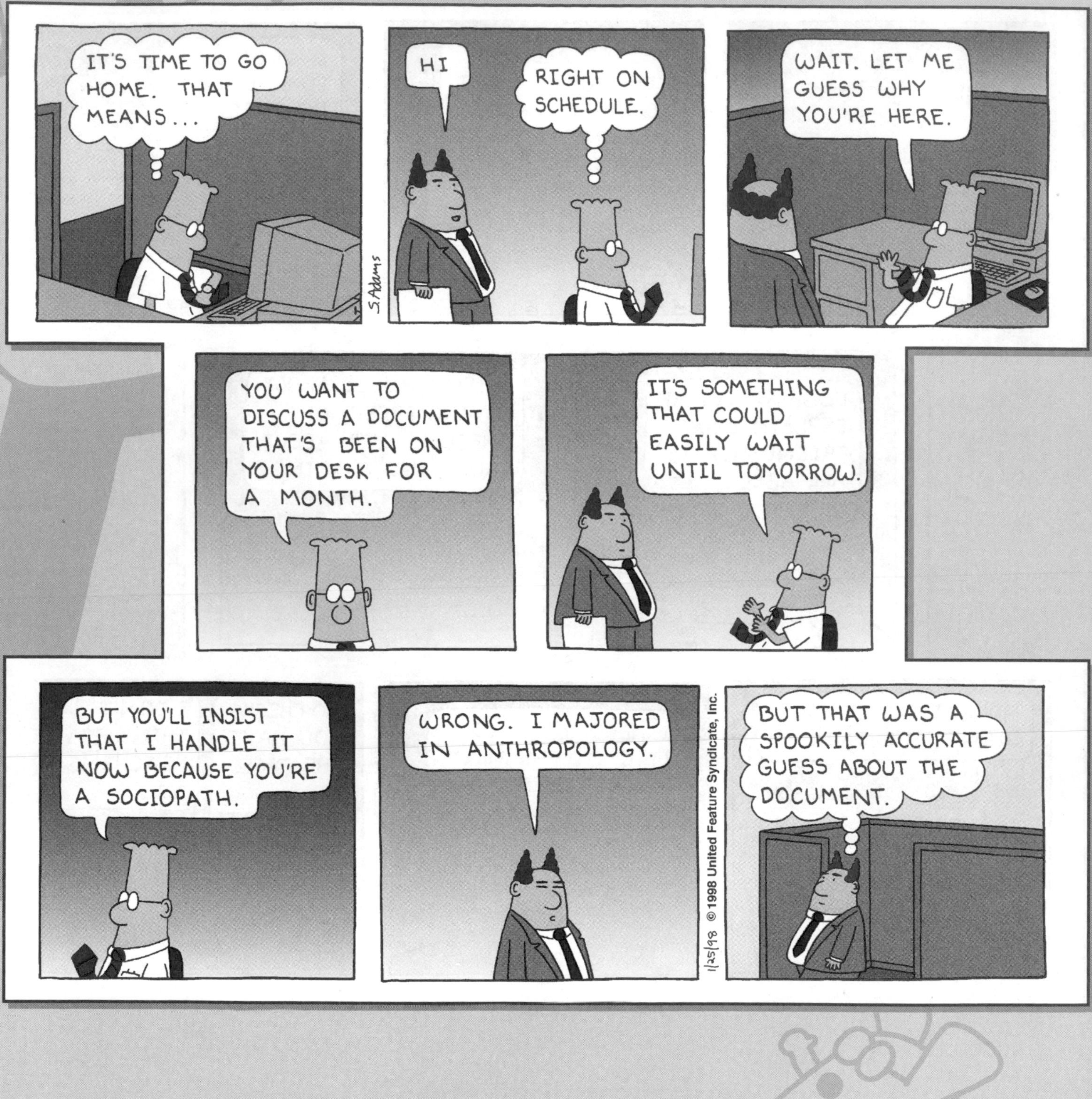
IT'S TIME TO GO HOME. THAT MEANS...
HI
RIGHT ON SCHEDULE.
S. Adams
WAIT. LET ME GUESS WHY YOU'RE HERE.
YOU WANT TO DISCUSS A DOCUMENT THAT'S BEEN ON YOUR DESK FOR A MONTH.
IT'S SOMETHING THAT COULD EASILY WAIT UNTIL TOMORROW.
BUT YOU'LL INSIST THAT I HANDLE IT NOW BECAUSE YOU'RE A SOCIOPATH.
WRONG. I MAJORED IN ANTHROPOLOGY.
1/25/98 © 1998 United Feature Syndicate, Inc.
BUT THAT WAS A SPOOKILY ACCURATE GUESS ABOUT THE DOCUMENT.

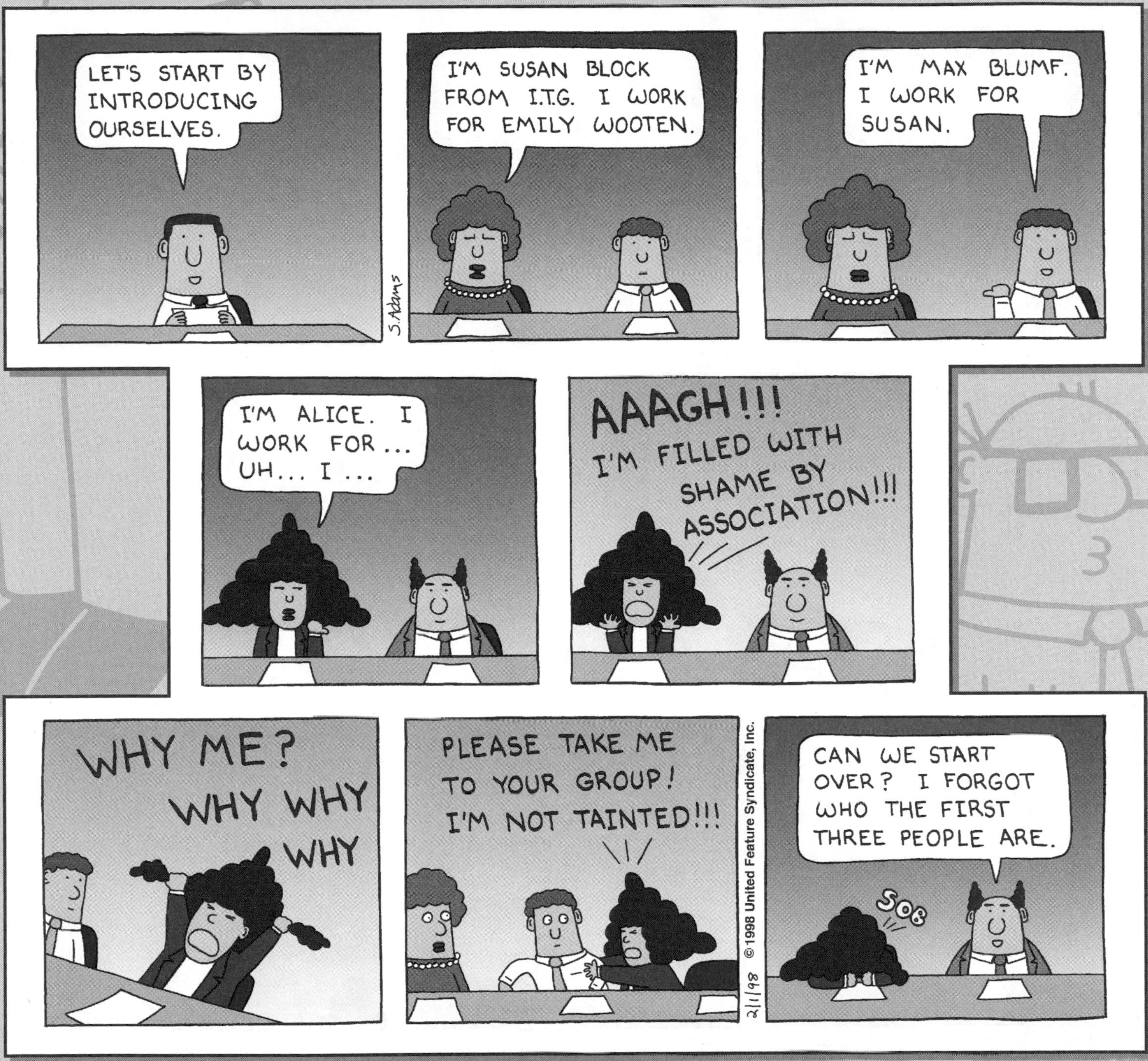
LET'S START BY INTRODUCING OURSELVES.
S. Adams
I'M SUSAN BLOCK FROM I.T.G. I WORK FOR EMILY WOOTEN.
I'M MAX BLUMF. I WORK FOR SUSAN.
I'M ALICE. I WORK FOR... UH... I...
AAAGH!!! I'M FILLED WITH SHAME BY ASSOCIATION!!!
WHY ME? WHY WHY WHY
PLEASE TAKE ME TO YOUR GROUP! I'M NOT TAINTED!!!
2/1/98 © 1998 United Feature Syndicate, Inc.
CAN WE START OVER? I FORGOT WHO THE FIRST THREE PEOPLE ARE.
SOB

I'VE BEEN HIRED BY AN EMPLOYEE WHO JUST RESIGNED.

© 1998 United Feature Syndicate, Inc.

2/8/98

I'LL BE HIS STAND-IN FOR THE EXIT INTERVIEW.

I'D LIKE TO BEGIN BY DISCUSSING YOUR SENSELESS SLAUGHTER OF THE ENGLISH LANGUAGE.

... AND ON APRIL 8TH, YOU WERE HEARD SAYING, "WE HAVE TO NIP THAT PROBLEM IN THE BUTT."

NOW LET'S TALK ABOUT YOUR STELLAR LEADERSHIP.

YOUR INSPIRATIONAL MOTTO IS ...

"IF I WANT YOU TO DO SOMETHING THAT'S A WASTE OF TIME, IT'S MY PREROGATIVE!"

S. Adams

MOVING ON TO HYGIENE...

I'M PROBABLY ONE OF THOSE MISUNDERSTOOD GENIUSES.

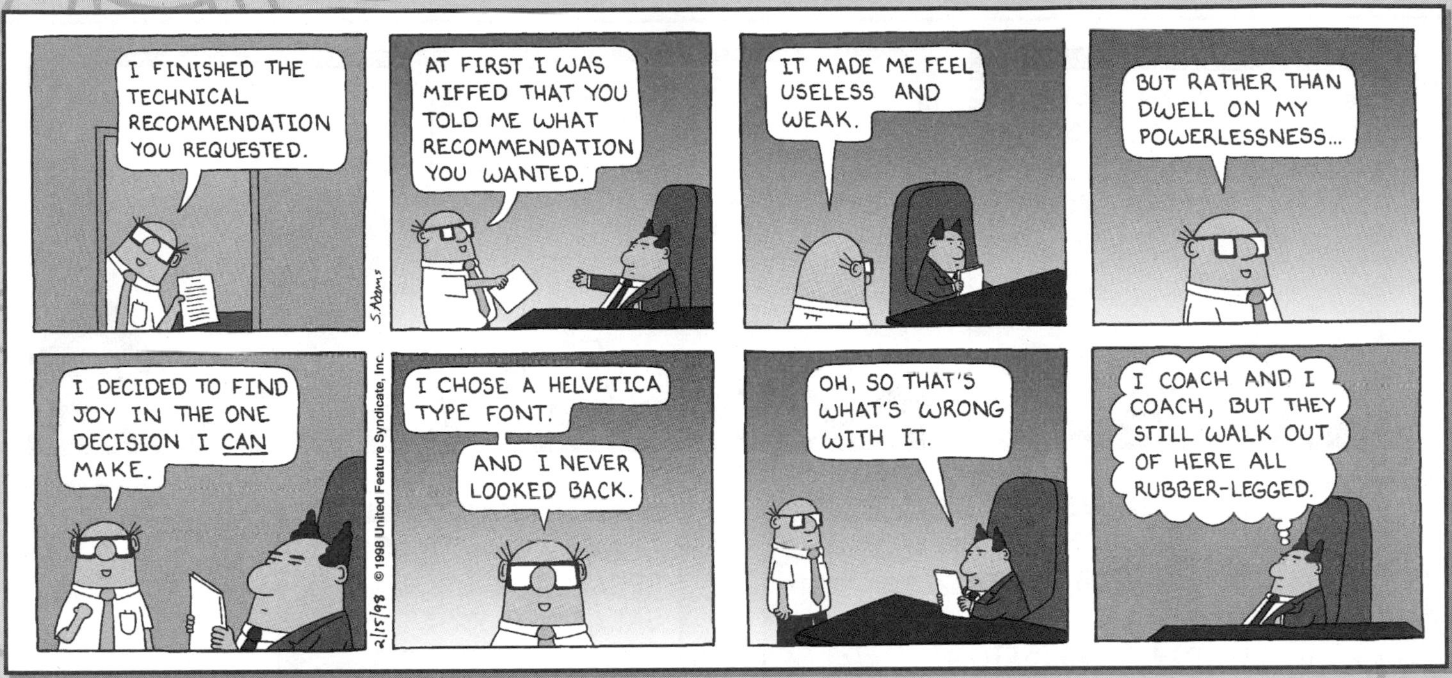
I FINISHED THE TECHNICAL RECOMMENDATION YOU REQUESTED.
AT FIRST I WAS MIFFED THAT YOU TOLD ME WHAT RECOMMENDATION YOU WANTED.
IT MADE ME FEEL USELESS AND WEAK.
BUT RATHER THAN DWELL ON MY POWERLESSNESS...
I DECIDED TO FIND JOY IN THE ONE DECISION I CAN MAKE.
I CHOSE A HELVETICA TYPE FONT.
AND I NEVER LOOKED BACK.
OH, SO THAT'S WHAT'S WRONG WITH IT.
I COACH AND I COACH, BUT THEY STILL WALK OUT OF HERE ALL RUBBER-LEGGED.
S.Adams
2/15/98 © 1998 United Feature Syndicate, Inc.

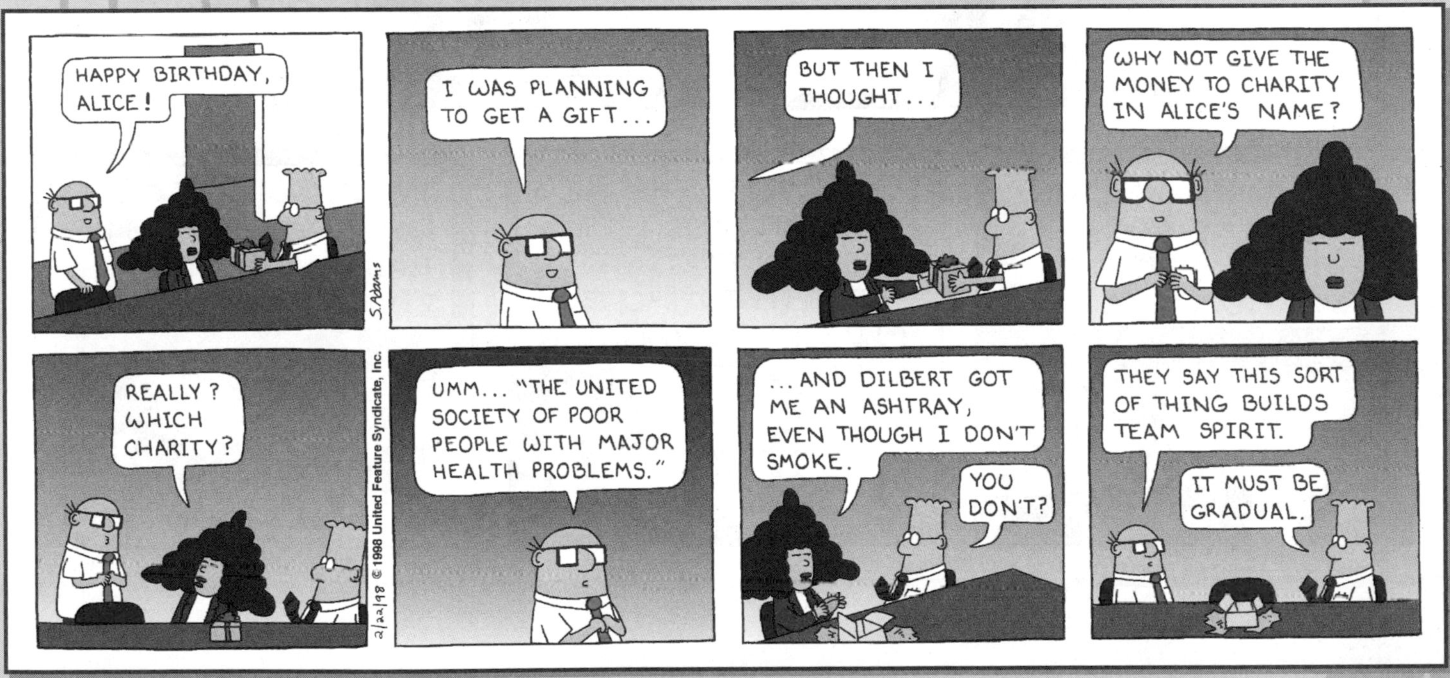
HAPPY BIRTHDAY, ALICE!
I WAS PLANNING TO GET A GIFT...
BUT THEN I THOUGHT...
WHY NOT GIVE THE MONEY TO CHARITY IN ALICE'S NAME?
REALLY? WHICH CHARITY?
UMM... "THE UNITED SOCIETY OF POOR PEOPLE WITH MAJOR HEALTH PROBLEMS."
...AND DILBERT GOT ME AN ASHTRAY, EVEN THOUGH I DON'T SMOKE.
YOU DON'T?
THEY SAY THIS SORT OF THING BUILDS TEAM SPIRIT.
IT MUST BE GRADUAL.
S.Adams
2/22/98 © 1998 United Feature Syndicate, Inc.

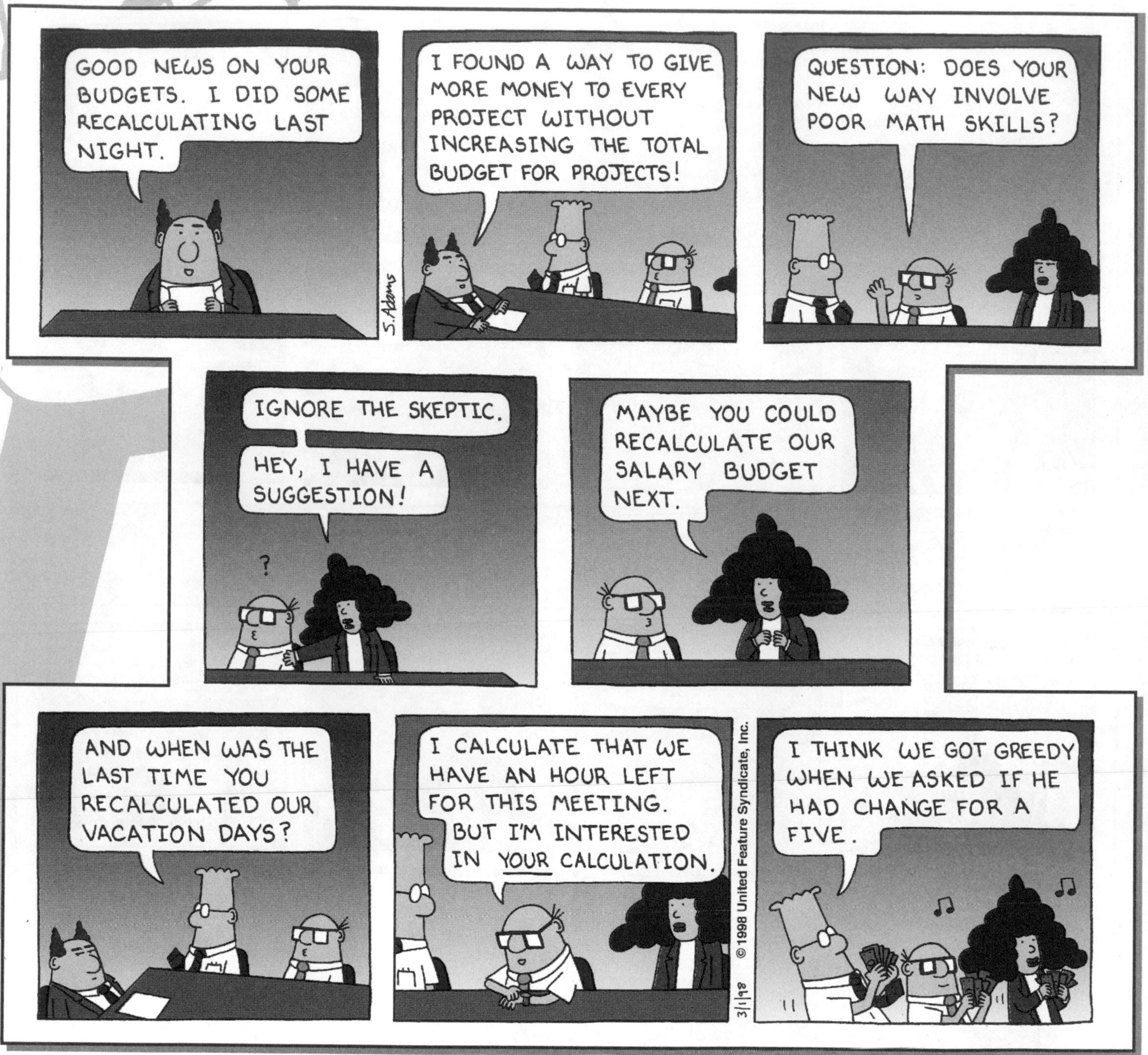
GOOD NEWS ON YOUR BUDGETS. I DID SOME RECALCULATING LAST NIGHT.
S. Adams
I FOUND A WAY TO GIVE MORE MONEY TO EVERY PROJECT WITHOUT INCREASING THE TOTAL BUDGET FOR PROJECTS!
QUESTION: DOES YOUR NEW WAY INVOLVE POOR MATH SKILLS?
IGNORE THE SKEPTIC.
HEY, I HAVE A SUGGESTION!
?
MAYBE YOU COULD RECALCULATE OUR SALARY BUDGET NEXT.
AND WHEN WAS THE LAST TIME YOU RECALCULATED OUR VACATION DAYS?
I CALCULATE THAT WE HAVE AN HOUR LEFT FOR THIS MEETING.
BUT I'M INTERESTED IN YOUR CALCULATION.
© 1998 United Feature Syndicate, Inc.
3/1/98
I THINK WE GOT GREEDY WHEN WE ASKED IF HE HAD CHANGE FOR A FIVE.

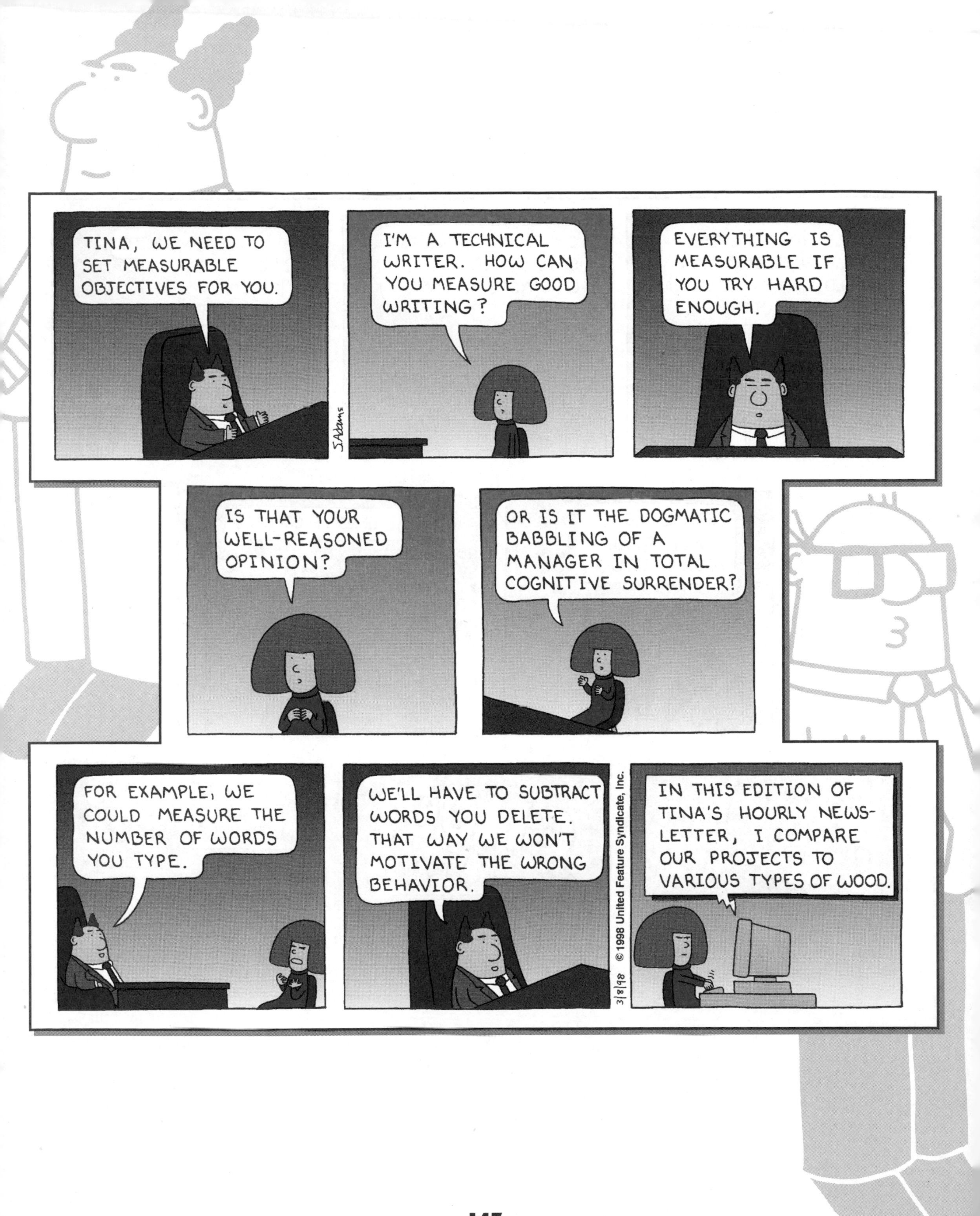
TINA, WE NEED TO SET MEASURABLE OBJECTIVES FOR YOU.
S.Adams
I'M A TECHNICAL WRITER. HOW CAN YOU MEASURE GOOD WRITING?
EVERYTHING IS MEASURABLE IF YOU TRY HARD ENOUGH.
IS THAT YOUR WELL-REASONED OPINION?
OR IS IT THE DOGMATIC BABBLING OF A MANAGER IN TOTAL COGNITIVE SURRENDER?
FOR EXAMPLE, WE COULD MEASURE THE NUMBER OF WORDS YOU TYPE.
WE'LL HAVE TO SUBTRACT WORDS YOU DELETE. THAT WAY WE WON'T MOTIVATE THE WRONG BEHAVIOR.
3/8/98 © 1998 United Feature Syndicate, Inc.
IN THIS EDITION OF TINA'S HOURLY NEWS-LETTER, I COMPARE OUR PROJECTS TO VARIOUS TYPES OF WOOD.

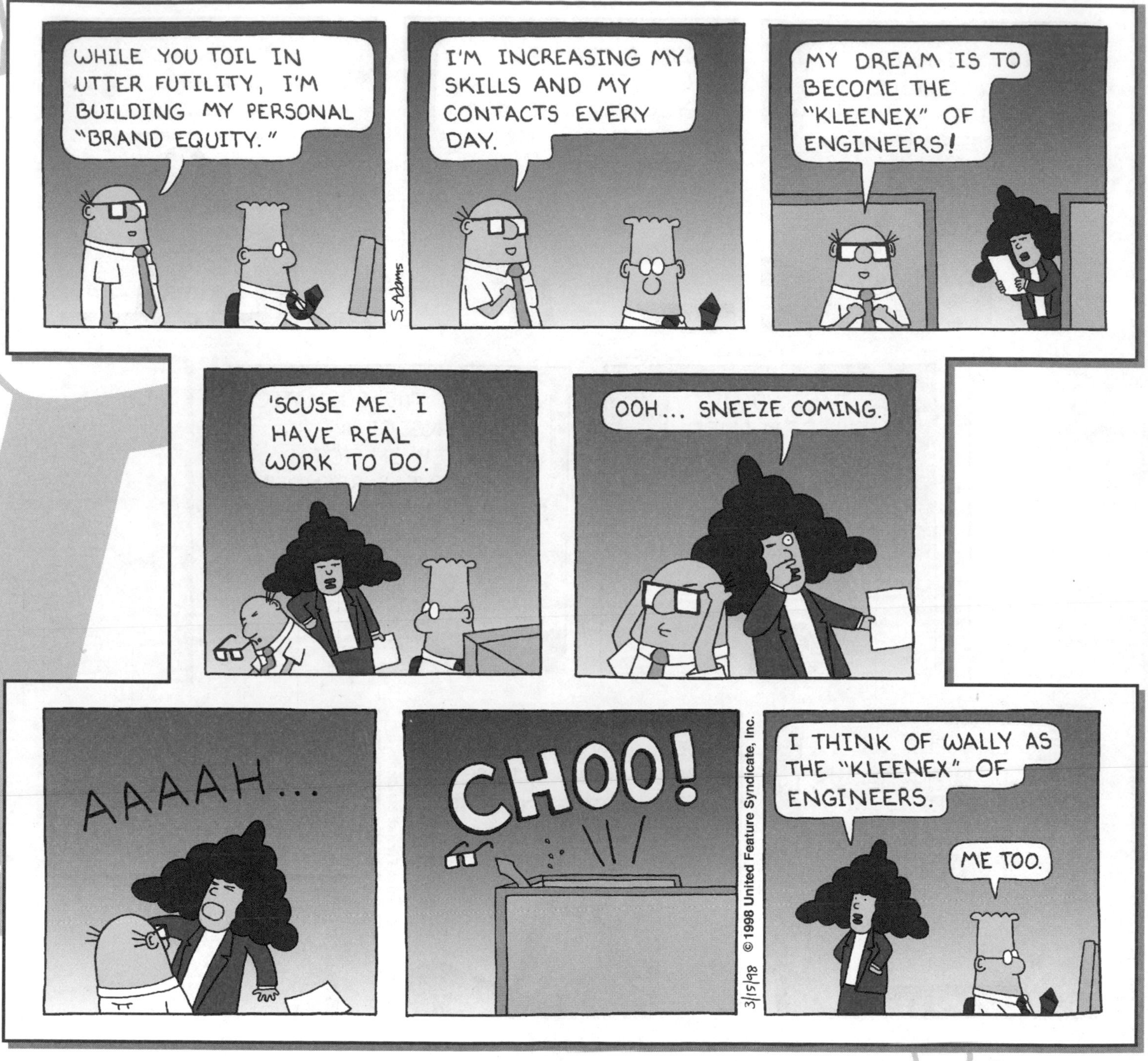
WHILE YOU TOIL IN UTTER FUTILITY, I'M BUILDING MY PERSONAL "BRAND EQUITY."
S.ADAMS
I'M INCREASING MY SKILLS AND MY CONTACTS EVERY DAY.
MY DREAM IS TO BECOME THE "KLEENEX" OF ENGINEERS!
'SCUSE ME. I HAVE REAL WORK TO DO.
OOH... SNEEZE COMING.
AAAAH...
CHOO!
3/15/98 © 1998 United Feature Syndicate, Inc.
I THINK OF WALLY AS THE "KLEENEX" OF ENGINEERS.
ME TOO.

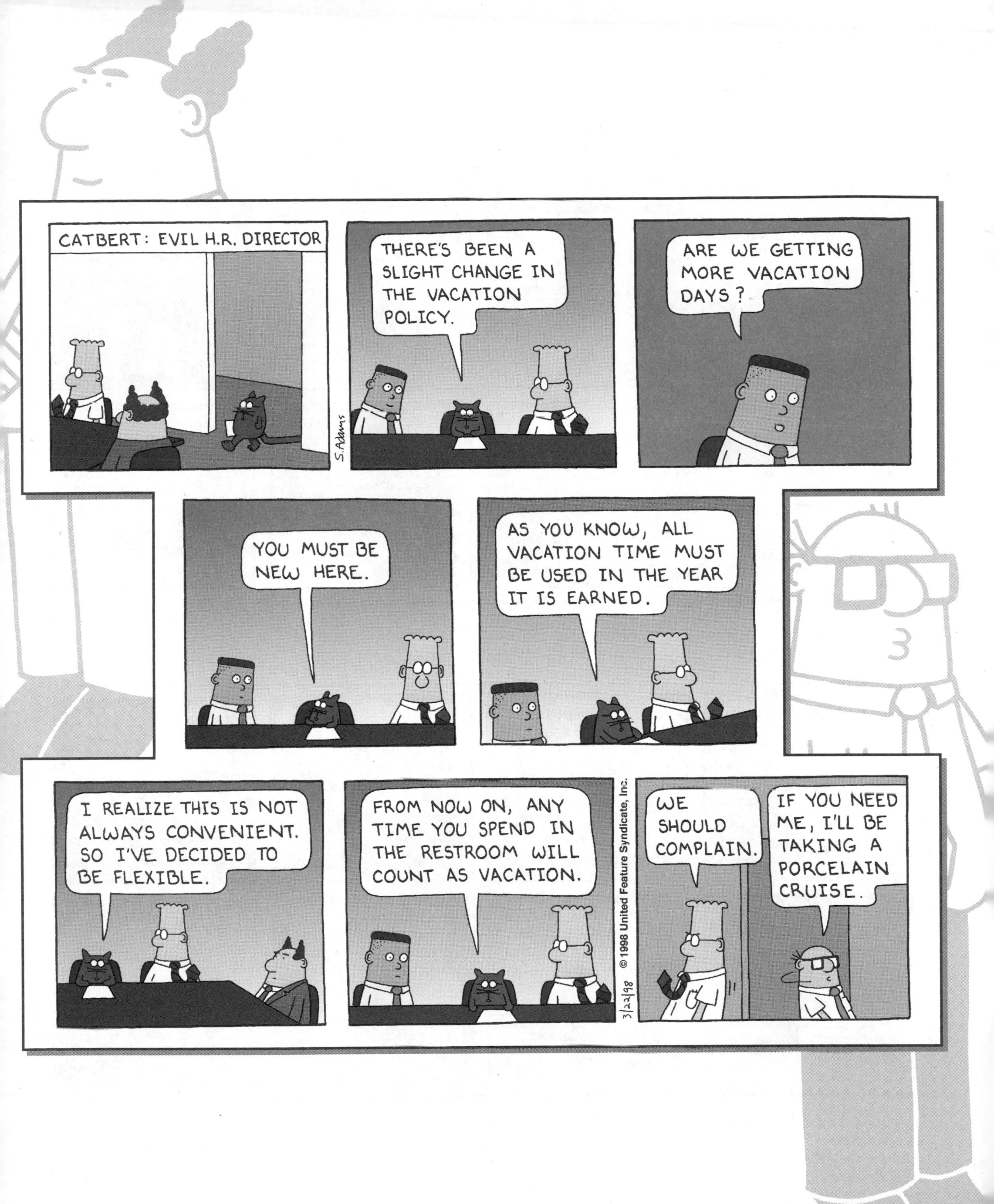
CATBERT: EVIL H.R. DIRECTOR
S. Adams
THERE'S BEEN A SLIGHT CHANGE IN THE VACATION POLICY.
ARE WE GETTING MORE VACATION DAYS?
YOU MUST BE NEW HERE.
AS YOU KNOW, ALL VACATION TIME MUST BE USED IN THE YEAR IT IS EARNED.
I REALIZE THIS IS NOT ALWAYS CONVENIENT. SO I'VE DECIDED TO BE FLEXIBLE.
FROM NOW ON, ANY TIME YOU SPEND IN THE RESTROOM WILL COUNT AS VACATION.
© 1998 United Feature Syndicate, Inc.
3/22/98
WE SHOULD COMPLAIN.
IF YOU NEED ME, I'LL BE TAKING A PORCELAIN CRUISE.

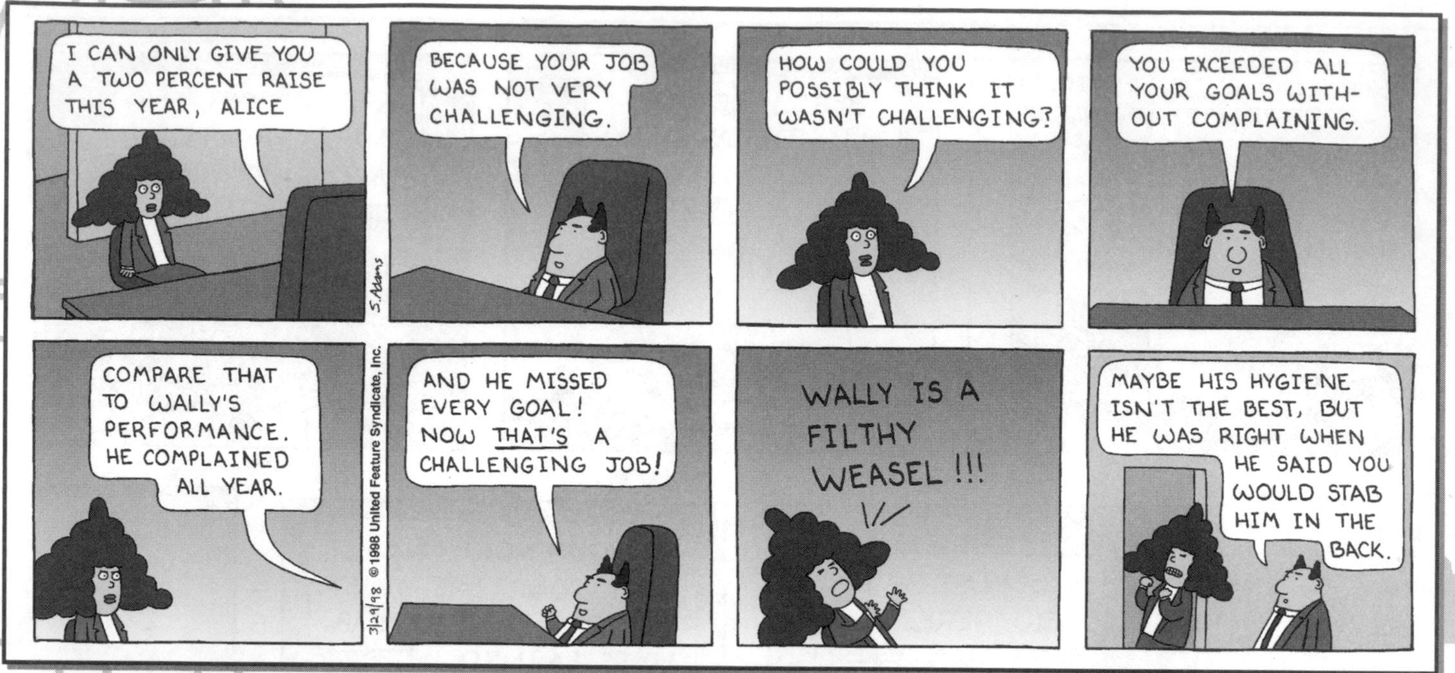
I CAN ONLY GIVE YOU A TWO PERCENT RAISE THIS YEAR, ALICE
BECAUSE YOUR JOB WAS NOT VERY CHALLENGING.
HOW COULD YOU POSSIBLY THINK IT WASN'T CHALLENGING?
YOU EXCEEDED ALL YOUR GOALS WITHOUT COMPLAINING.
COMPARE THAT TO WALLY'S PERFORMANCE. HE COMPLAINED ALL YEAR.
AND HE MISSED EVERY GOAL! NOW THAT'S A CHALLENGING JOB!
WALLY IS A FILTHY WEASEL !!!
MAYBE HIS HYGIENE ISN'T THE BEST, BUT HE WAS RIGHT WHEN HE SAID YOU WOULD STAB HIM IN THE BACK.
S. Adams
3/29/98 © 1998 United Feature Syndicate, Inc.

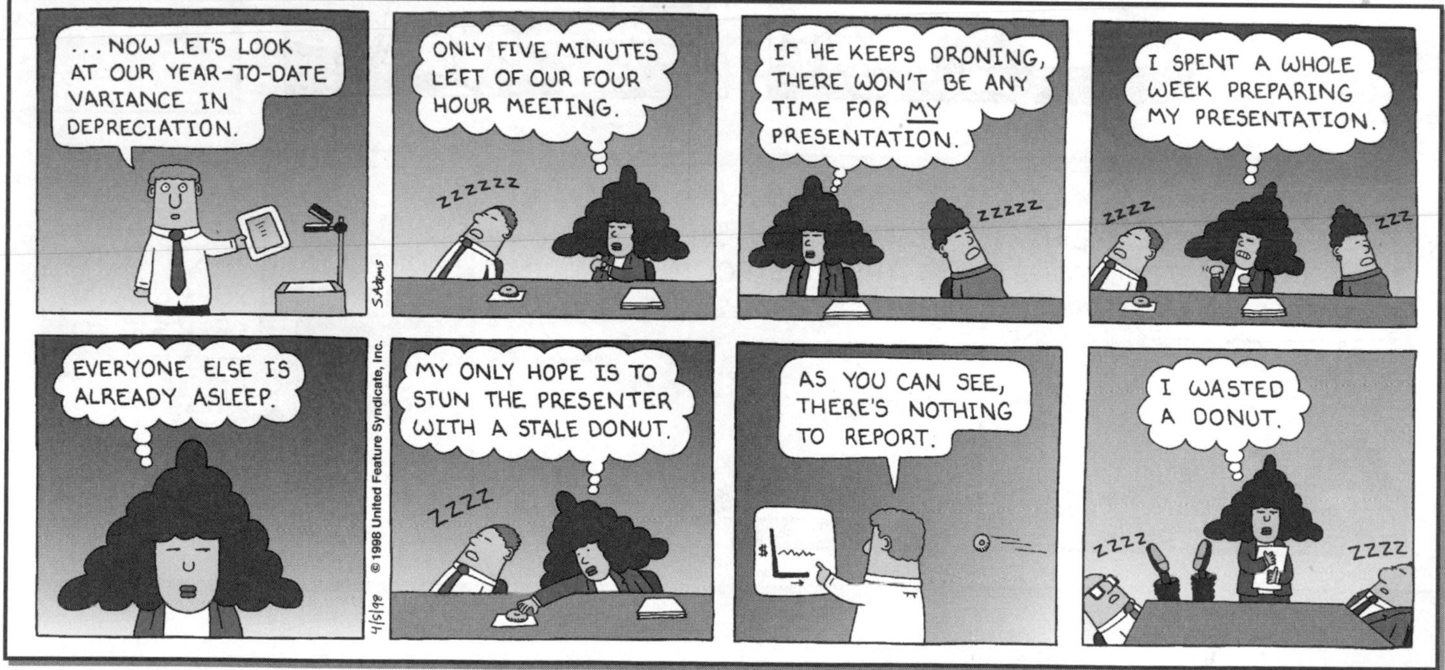
...NOW LET'S LOOK AT OUR YEAR-TO-DATE VARIANCE IN DEPRECIATION.
ONLY FIVE MINUTES LEFT OF OUR FOUR HOUR MEETING.
ZZZZZZ
IF HE KEEPS DRONING, THERE WON'T BE ANY TIME FOR MY PRESENTATION.
ZZZZZ
I SPENT A WHOLE WEEK PREPARING MY PRESENTATION.
ZZZZ
ZZZ
EVERYONE ELSE IS ALREADY ASLEEP.
MY ONLY HOPE IS TO STUN THE PRESENTER WITH A STALE DONUT.
ZZZZ
AS YOU CAN SEE, THERE'S NOTHING TO REPORT.
$
I WASTED A DONUT.
ZZZZ
ZZZZ
S. Adams
4/5/98 © 1998 United Feature Syndicate, Inc.

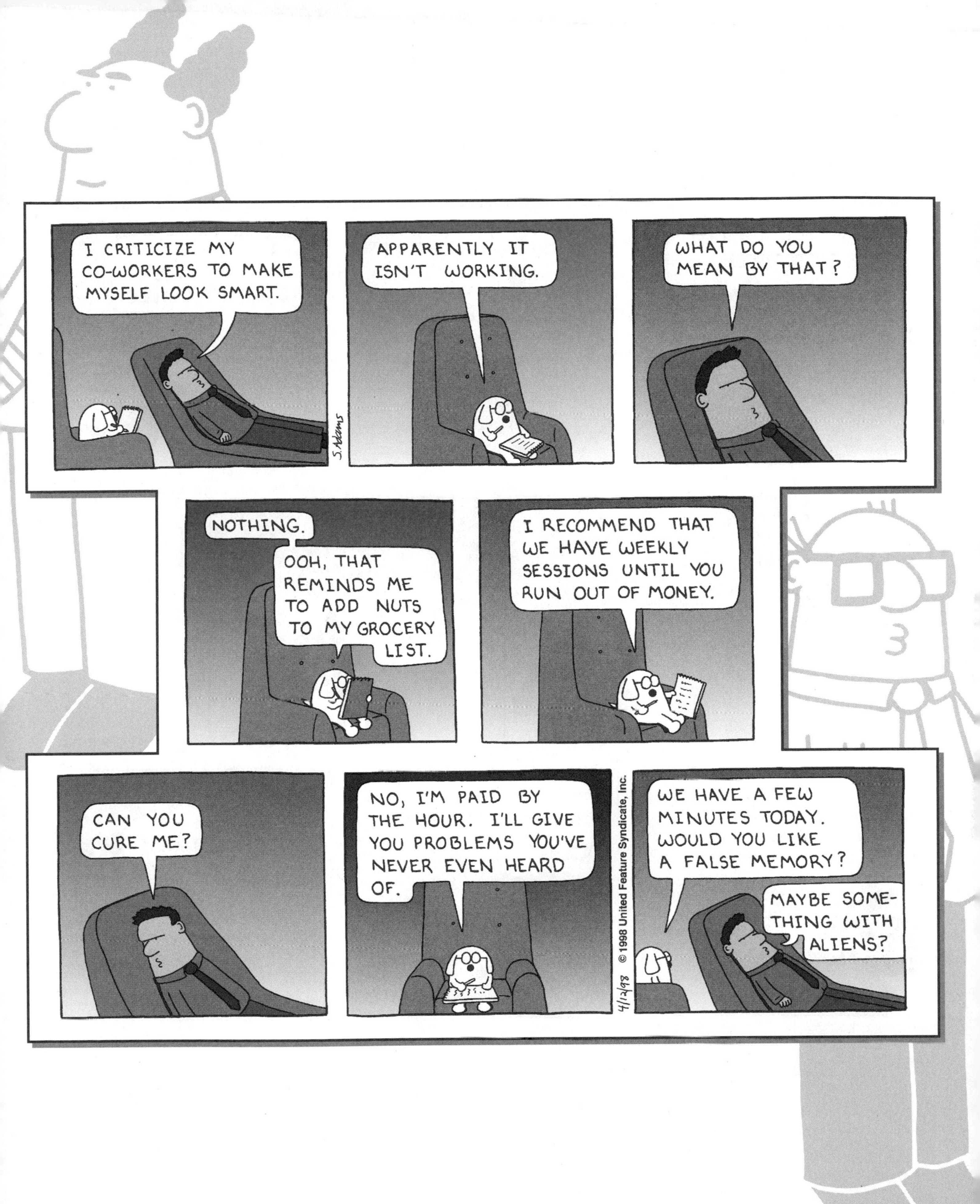
I CRITICIZE MY CO-WORKERS TO MAKE MYSELF LOOK SMART.
S. Adams
APPARENTLY IT ISN'T WORKING.
WHAT DO YOU MEAN BY THAT?
NOTHING.
OOH, THAT REMINDS ME TO ADD NUTS TO MY GROCERY LIST.
I RECOMMEND THAT WE HAVE WEEKLY SESSIONS UNTIL YOU RUN OUT OF MONEY.
CAN YOU CURE ME?
NO, I'M PAID BY THE HOUR. I'LL GIVE YOU PROBLEMS YOU'VE NEVER EVEN HEARD OF.
4/12/98 © 1998 United Feature Syndicate, Inc.
WE HAVE A FEW MINUTES TODAY. WOULD YOU LIKE A FALSE MEMORY?
MAYBE SOMETHING WITH ALIENS?

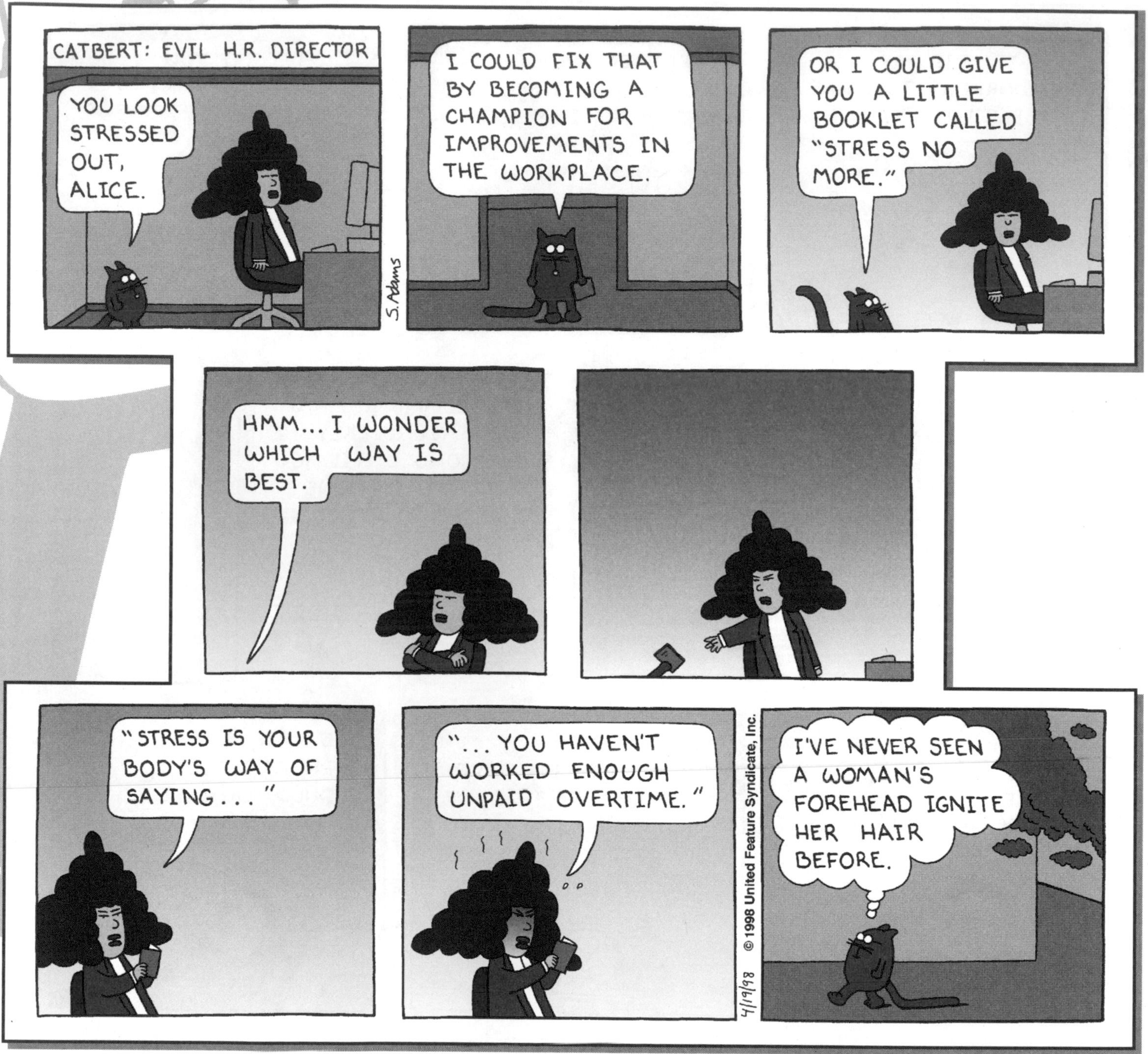
CATBERT: EVIL H.R. DIRECTOR
YOU LOOK STRESSED OUT, ALICE.
S. Adams
I COULD FIX THAT BY BECOMING A CHAMPION FOR IMPROVEMENTS IN THE WORKPLACE.
OR I COULD GIVE YOU A LITTLE BOOKLET CALLED "STRESS NO MORE."
HMM... I WONDER WHICH WAY IS BEST.
"STRESS IS YOUR BODY'S WAY OF SAYING..."
"...YOU HAVEN'T WORKED ENOUGH UNPAID OVERTIME."
© 1998 United Feature Syndicate, Inc.
4/19/98
I'VE NEVER SEEN A WOMAN'S FOREHEAD IGNITE HER HAIR BEFORE.

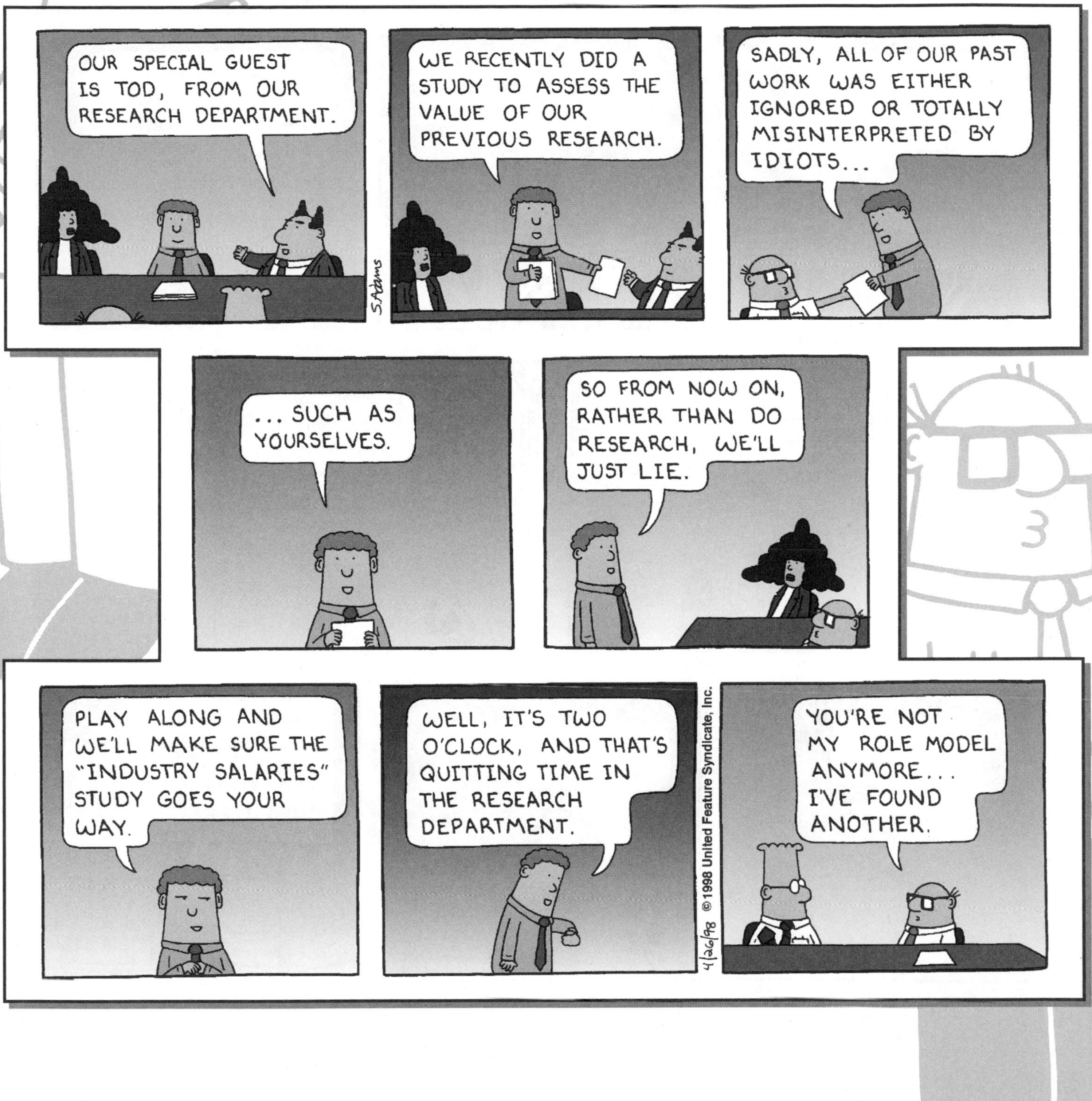
OUR SPECIAL GUEST IS TOD, FROM OUR RESEARCH DEPARTMENT.
S. Adams
WE RECENTLY DID A STUDY TO ASSESS THE VALUE OF OUR PREVIOUS RESEARCH.
SADLY, ALL OF OUR PAST WORK WAS EITHER IGNORED OR TOTALLY MISINTERPRETED BY IDIOTS...
... SUCH AS YOURSELVES.
SO FROM NOW ON, RATHER THAN DO RESEARCH, WE'LL JUST LIE.
PLAY ALONG AND WE'LL MAKE SURE THE "INDUSTRY SALARIES" STUDY GOES YOUR WAY.
WELL, IT'S TWO O'CLOCK, AND THAT'S QUITTING TIME IN THE RESEARCH DEPARTMENT.
4/26/98 © 1998 United Feature Syndicate, Inc.
YOU'RE NOT MY ROLE MODEL ANYMORE... I'VE FOUND ANOTHER.

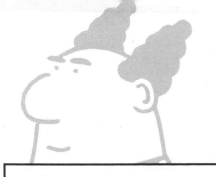

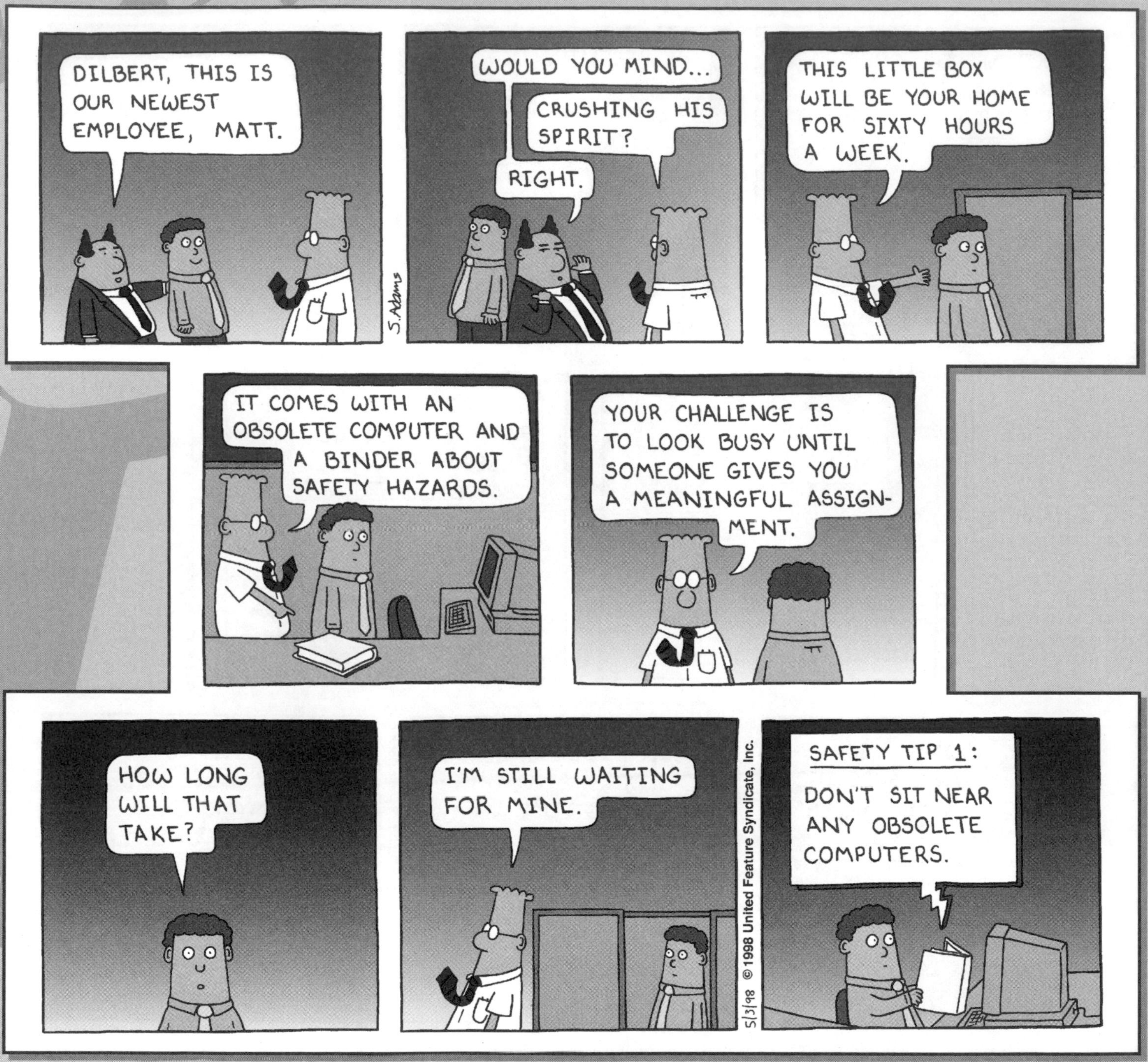
DILBERT, THIS IS OUR NEWEST EMPLOYEE, MATT.
S. Adams
WOULD YOU MIND...
RIGHT.
CRUSHING HIS SPIRIT?
THIS LITTLE BOX WILL BE YOUR HOME FOR SIXTY HOURS A WEEK.
IT COMES WITH AN OBSOLETE COMPUTER AND A BINDER ABOUT SAFETY HAZARDS.
YOUR CHALLENGE IS TO LOOK BUSY UNTIL SOMEONE GIVES YOU A MEANINGFUL ASSIGNMENT.
HOW LONG WILL THAT TAKE?
I'M STILL WAITING FOR MINE.
5/3/98 © 1998 United Feature Syndicate, Inc.
SAFETY TIP 1:
DON'T SIT NEAR ANY OBSOLETE COMPUTERS.

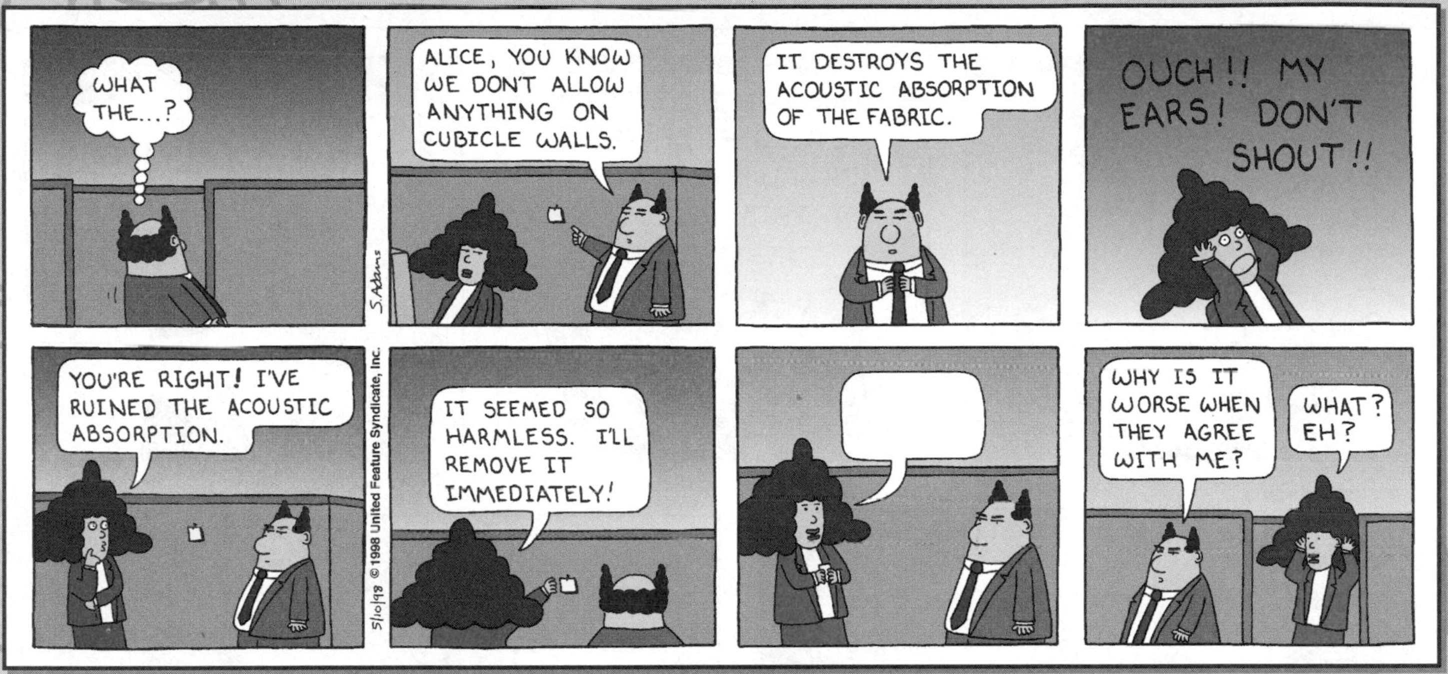
WHAT THE...?
ALICE, YOU KNOW WE DON'T ALLOW ANYTHING ON CUBICLE WALLS.
IT DESTROYS THE ACOUSTIC ABSORPTION OF THE FABRIC.
OUCH!! MY EARS! DON'T SHOUT!!
YOU'RE RIGHT! I'VE RUINED THE ACOUSTIC ABSORPTION.
IT SEEMED SO HARMLESS. I'LL REMOVE IT IMMEDIATELY!
WHY IS IT WORSE WHEN THEY AGREE WITH ME?
WHAT? EH?
S. Adams
5/10/98 © 1998 United Feature Syndicate, Inc.

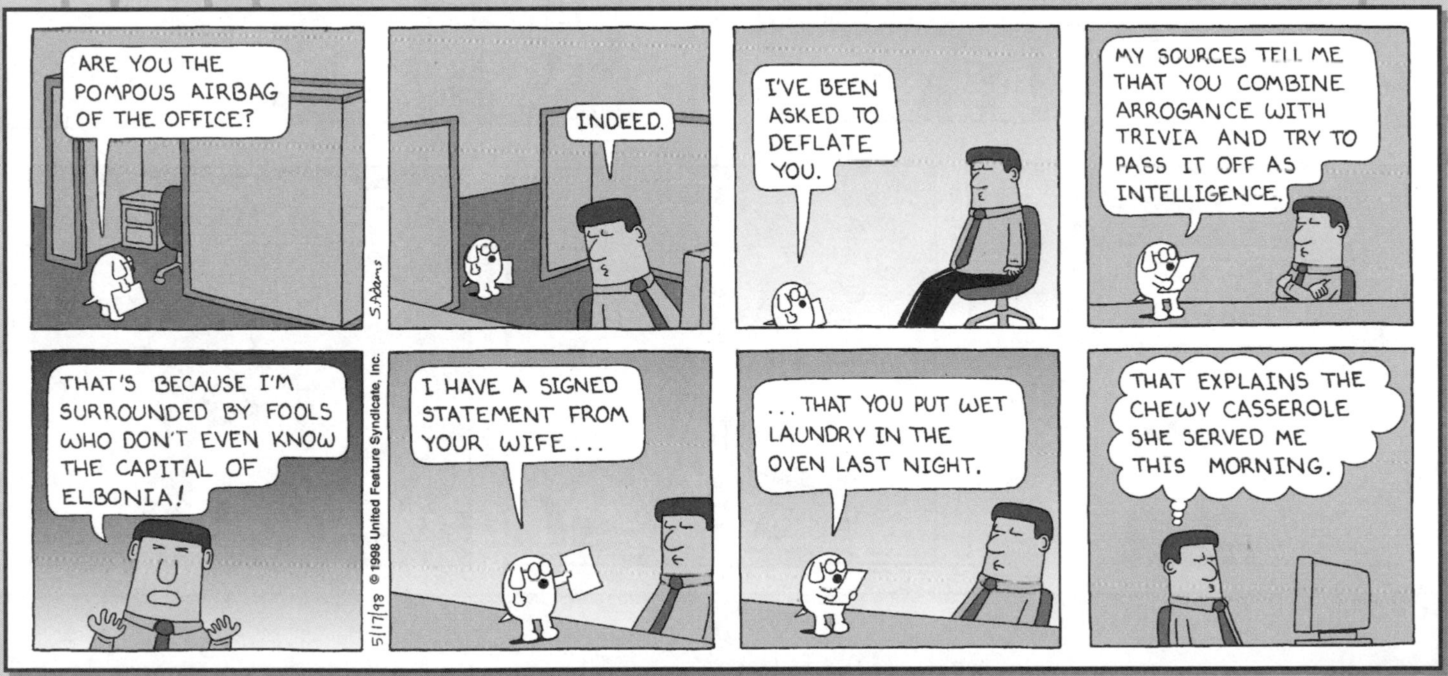
ARE YOU THE POMPOUS AIRBAG OF THE OFFICE?
INDEED.
I'VE BEEN ASKED TO DEFLATE YOU.
MY SOURCES TELL ME THAT YOU COMBINE ARROGANCE WITH TRIVIA AND TRY TO PASS IT OFF AS INTELLIGENCE.
THAT'S BECAUSE I'M SURROUNDED BY FOOLS WHO DON'T EVEN KNOW THE CAPITAL OF ELBONIA!
I HAVE A SIGNED STATEMENT FROM YOUR WIFE...
...THAT YOU PUT WET LAUNDRY IN THE OVEN LAST NIGHT.
THAT EXPLAINS THE CHEWY CASSEROLE SHE SERVED ME THIS MORNING.
S. Adams
5/17/98 © 1998 United Feature Syndicate, Inc.

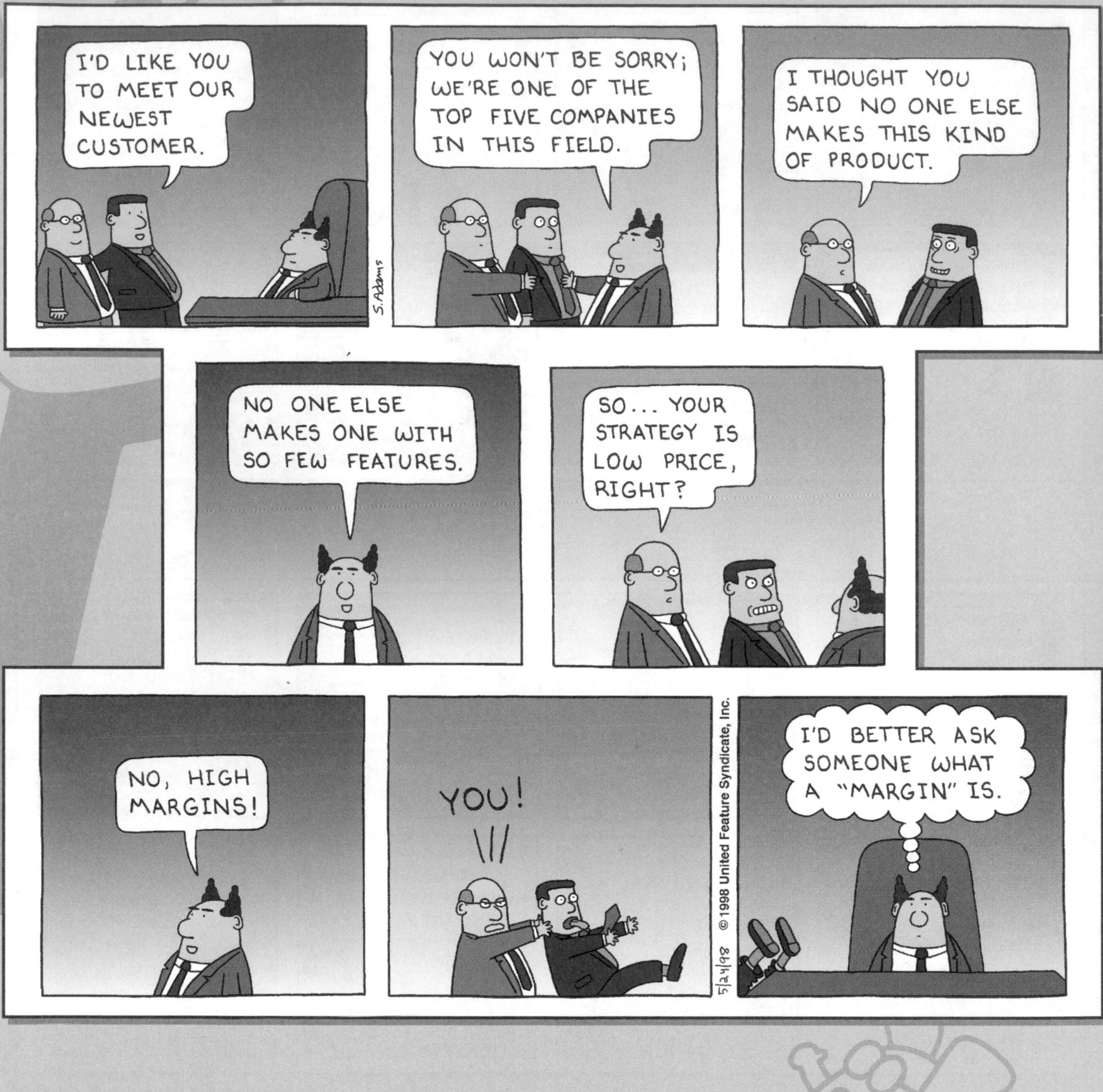
I'D LIKE YOU TO MEET OUR NEWEST CUSTOMER.
S. Adams
YOU WON'T BE SORRY; WE'RE ONE OF THE TOP FIVE COMPANIES IN THIS FIELD.
I THOUGHT YOU SAID NO ONE ELSE MAKES THIS KIND OF PRODUCT.
NO ONE ELSE MAKES ONE WITH SO FEW FEATURES.
SO... YOUR STRATEGY IS LOW PRICE, RIGHT?
NO, HIGH MARGINS!
YOU!
5/24/98 © 1998 United Feature Syndicate, Inc.
I'D BETTER ASK SOMEONE WHAT A "MARGIN" IS.

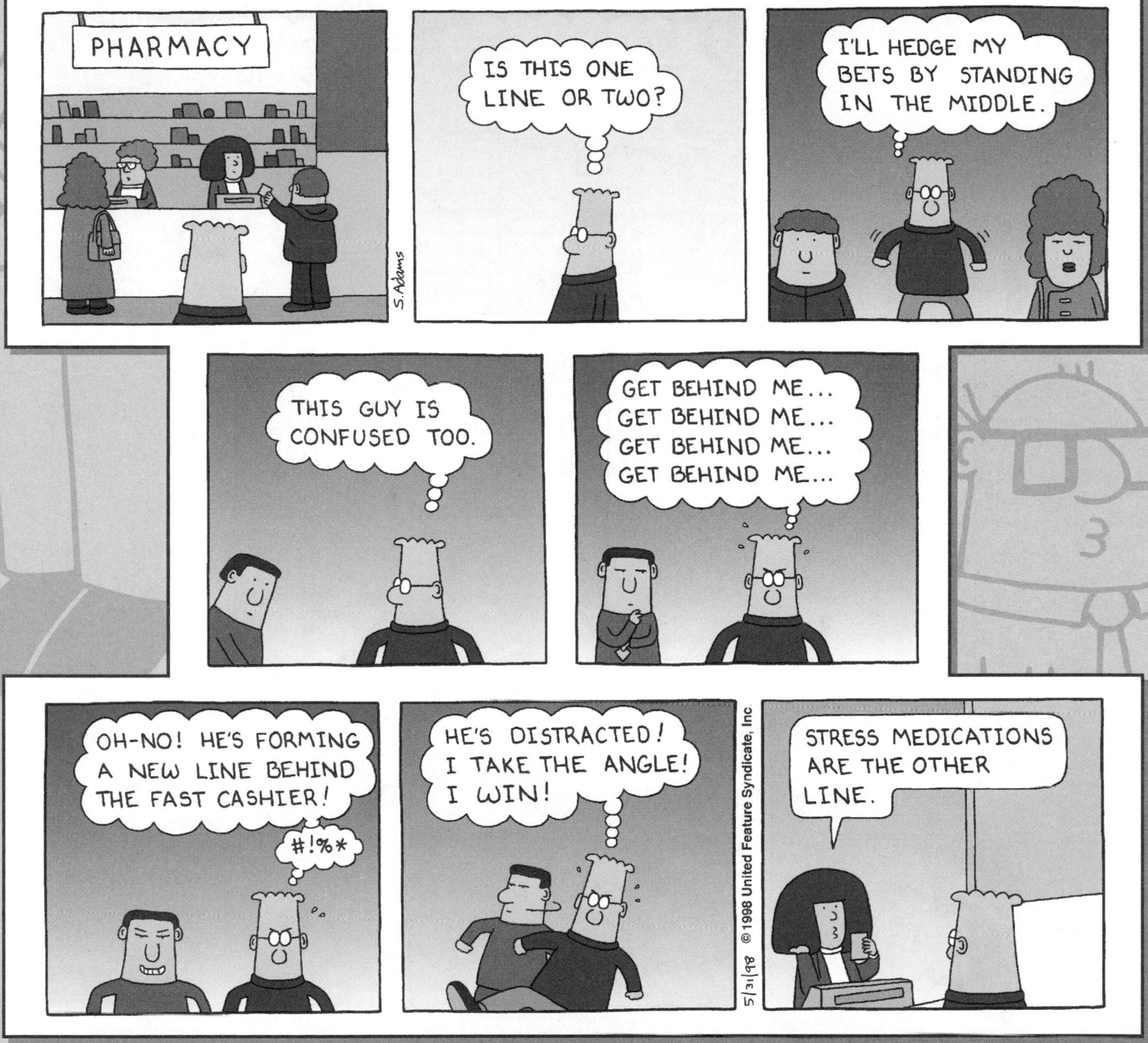
PHARMACY
S. Adams
IS THIS ONE LINE OR TWO?
I'LL HEDGE MY BETS BY STANDING IN THE MIDDLE.
THIS GUY IS CONFUSED TOO.
GET BEHIND ME... GET BEHIND ME... GET BEHIND ME... GET BEHIND ME...
OH-NO! HE'S FORMING A NEW LINE BEHIND THE FAST CASHIER!
#!%*
HE'S DISTRACTED! I TAKE THE ANGLE! I WIN!
5/31/98 © 1998 United Feature Syndicate, Inc.
STRESS MEDICATIONS ARE THE OTHER LINE.

I NEED COFFEE.
S. Adams
BUT I'M TOO TIRED TO GO GET IT.
I'M IN A DOWNWARD SPIRAL!
MY ARMS GO LIMP. THE ANTIDOTE IS ONLY YARDS AWAY BUT I AM IMMOBILE.
MAYBE SOMEONE WILL NOTICE AND BRING COFFEE.
MY CO-WORKERS FOUND ME. I'M SAVED!
6/7/98 © 1998 United Feature Syndicate, Inc.
AS THE FRENZIED MOB YANKED OFF MY TROUSERS, SOMEONE SPILLED COFFEE ON ME.
WOW, LUCKY.

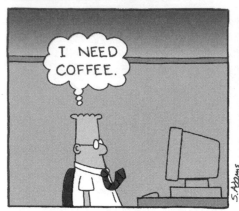

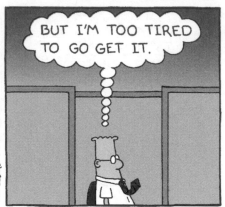

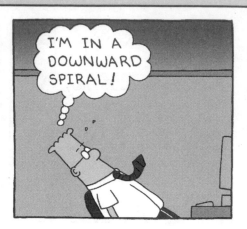

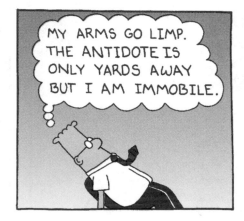

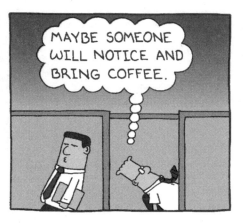

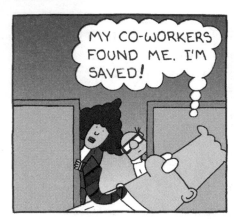

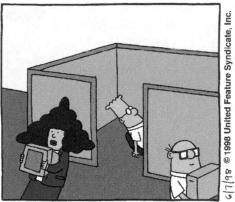

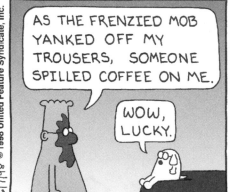

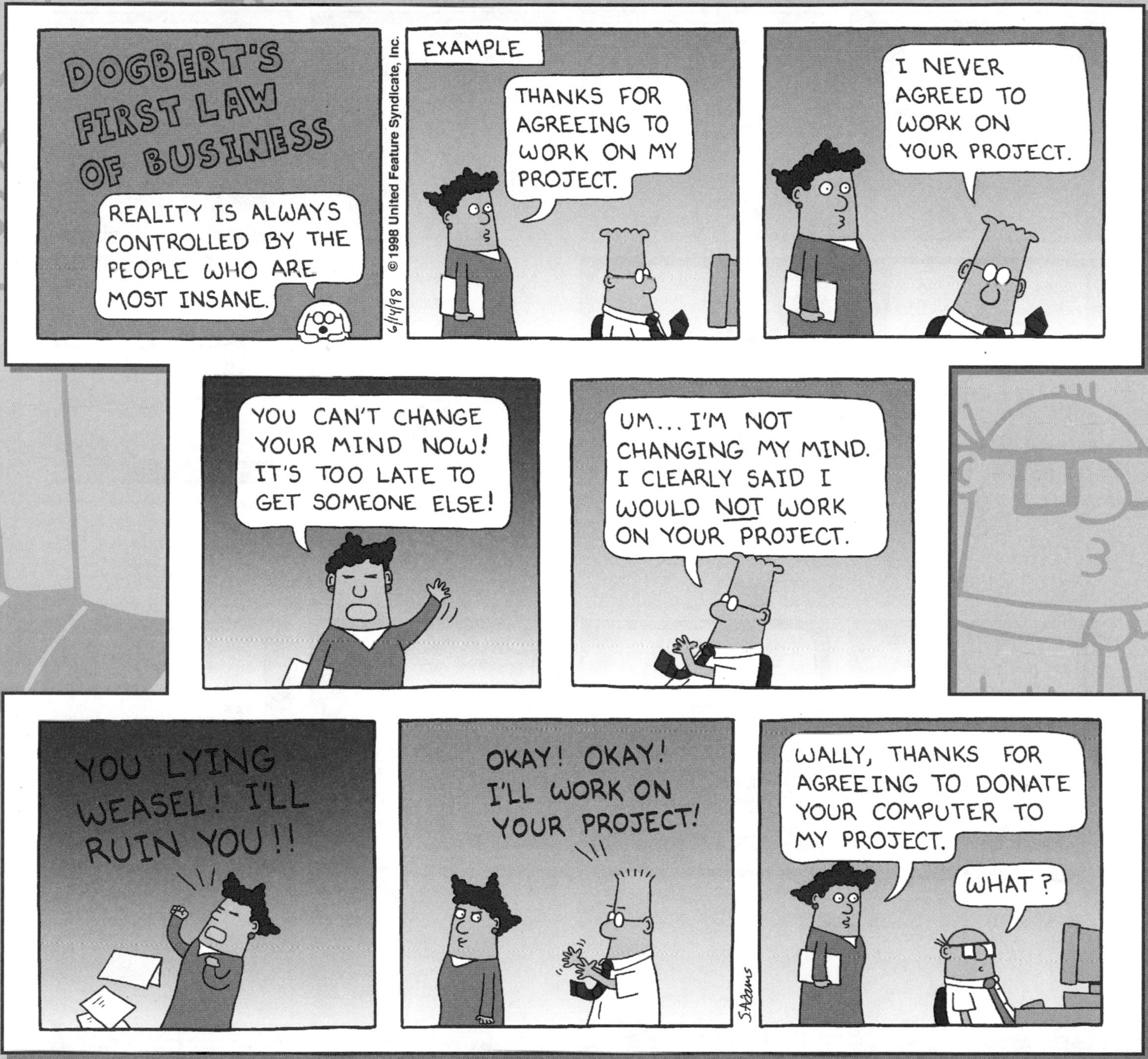
DOGBERT'S FIRST LAW OF BUSINESS
REALITY IS ALWAYS CONTROLLED BY THE PEOPLE WHO ARE MOST INSANE.
© 1998 United Feature Syndicate, Inc.
6/14/98
EXAMPLE
THANKS FOR AGREEING TO WORK ON MY PROJECT.
I NEVER AGREED TO WORK ON YOUR PROJECT.
YOU CAN'T CHANGE YOUR MIND NOW! IT'S TOO LATE TO GET SOMEONE ELSE!
UM... I'M NOT CHANGING MY MIND. I CLEARLY SAID I WOULD NOT WORK ON YOUR PROJECT.
YOU LYING WEASEL! I'LL RUIN YOU!!
OKAY! OKAY! I'LL WORK ON YOUR PROJECT!
S.Adams
WALLY, THANKS FOR AGREEING TO DONATE YOUR COMPUTER TO MY PROJECT.
WHAT?

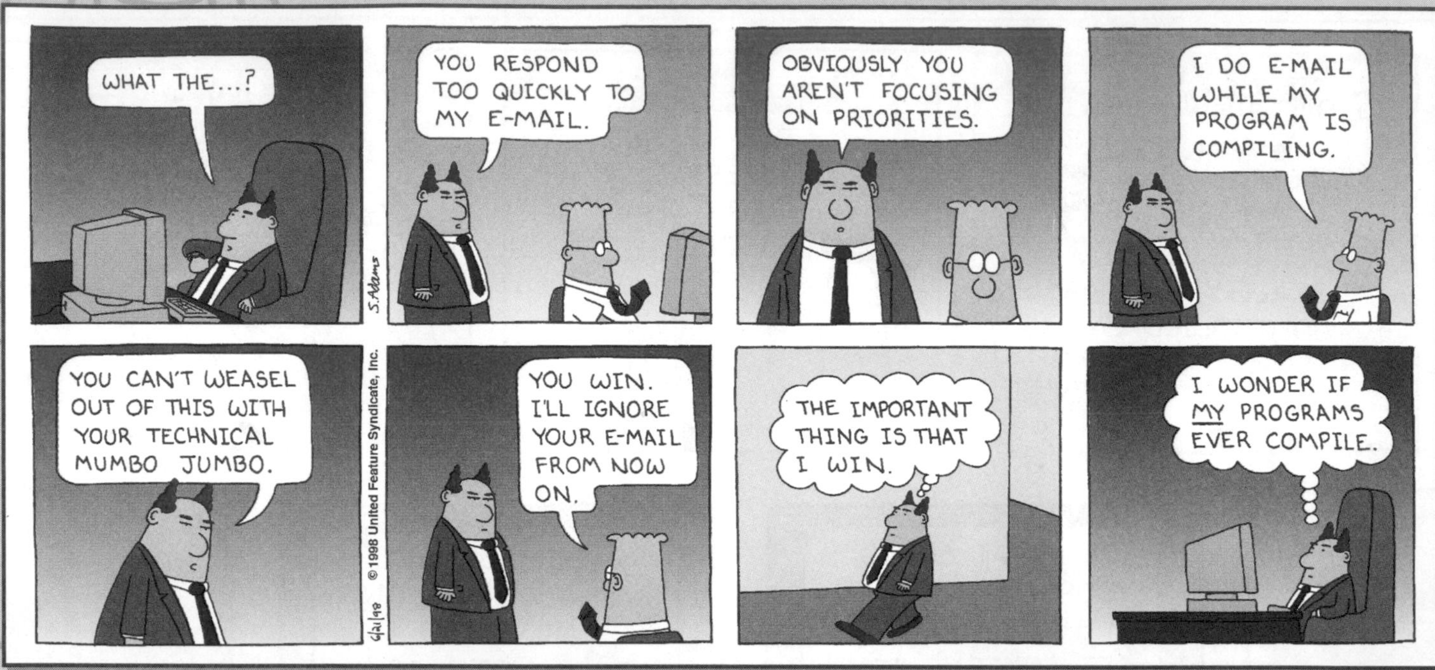
WHAT THE...?
S. Adams
YOU RESPOND TOO QUICKLY TO MY E-MAIL.
OBVIOUSLY YOU AREN'T FOCUSING ON PRIORITIES.
I DO E-MAIL WHILE MY PROGRAM IS COMPILING.
YOU CAN'T WEASEL OUT OF THIS WITH YOUR TECHNICAL MUMBO JUMBO.
6/21/98 © 1998 United Feature Syndicate, Inc.
YOU WIN. I'LL IGNORE YOUR E-MAIL FROM NOW ON.
THE IMPORTANT THING IS THAT I WIN.
I WONDER IF MY PROGRAMS EVER COMPILE.

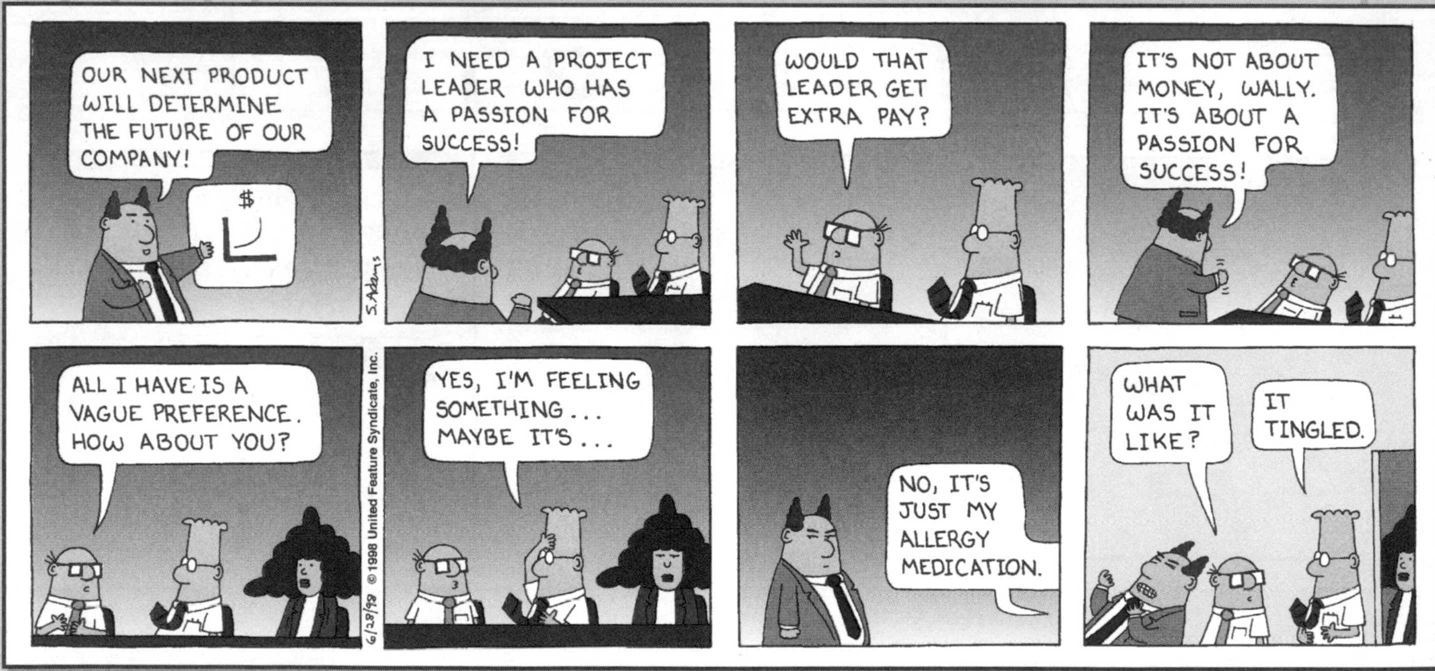
OUR NEXT PRODUCT WILL DETERMINE THE FUTURE OF OUR COMPANY!
$
S. Adams
I NEED A PROJECT LEADER WHO HAS A PASSION FOR SUCCESS!
WOULD THAT LEADER GET EXTRA PAY?
IT'S NOT ABOUT MONEY, WALLY. IT'S ABOUT A PASSION FOR SUCCESS!
ALL I HAVE IS A VAGUE PREFERENCE. HOW ABOUT YOU?
6/28/98 © 1998 United Feature Syndicate, Inc.
YES, I'M FEELING SOMETHING... MAYBE IT'S...
NO, IT'S JUST MY ALLERGY MEDICATION.
WHAT WAS IT LIKE?
IT TINGLED.

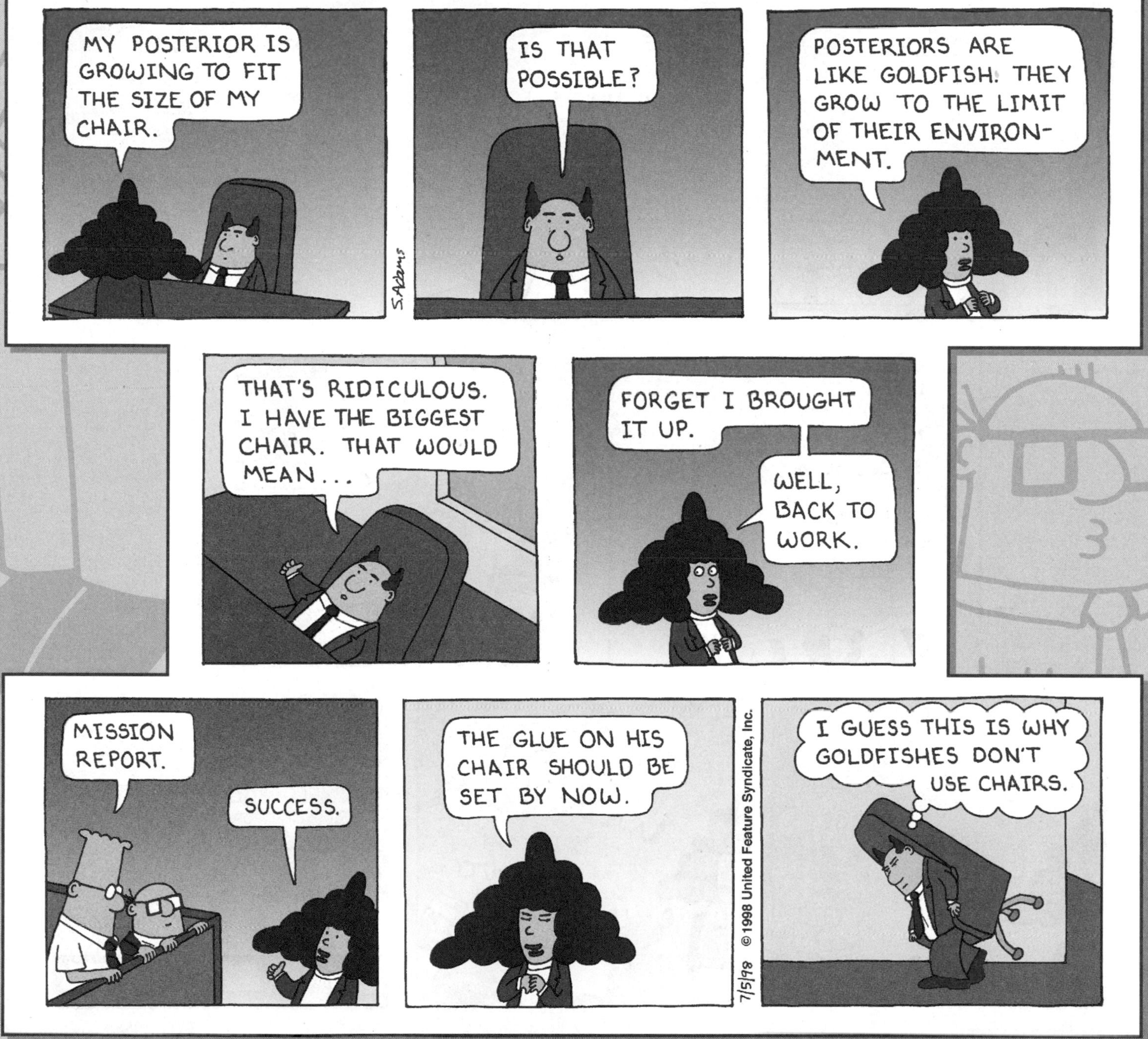
MY POSTERIOR IS GROWING TO FIT THE SIZE OF MY CHAIR.
S.ADAMS
IS THAT POSSIBLE?
POSTERIORS ARE LIKE GOLDFISH: THEY GROW TO THE LIMIT OF THEIR ENVIRON-MENT.
THAT'S RIDICULOUS. I HAVE THE BIGGEST CHAIR. THAT WOULD MEAN...
FORGET I BROUGHT IT UP.
WELL, BACK TO WORK.
MISSION REPORT.
SUCCESS.
THE GLUE ON HIS CHAIR SHOULD BE SET BY NOW.
7/5/98 © 1998 United Feature Syndicate, Inc.
I GUESS THIS IS WHY GOLDFISHES DON'T USE CHAIRS.

I CAN'T BELIEVE I GET PAID FOR THIS.
BLAH BLAH
S. Adams
THIS THING LASTS TWO MORE HOURS.
MAYBE I SHOULD FIDGET WITH MY PEN.
I'M TOO LATE. NOW I'D LOOK UNCREATIVE.
FIDGET.
I WONDER HOW LONG I CAN HOLD MY BREATH.
FIDGET.
FIDGET.
WHUMP!
7/12/98 © 1998 United Feature Syndicate, Inc.
OOH, TWO PENS. WHAT WOULD THAT BE LIKE?

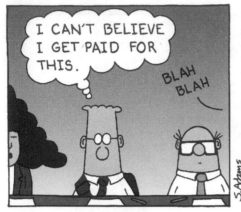

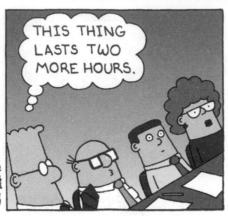

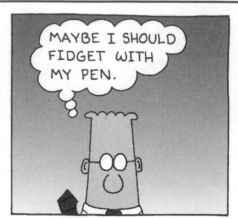

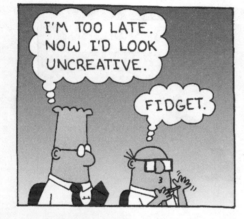

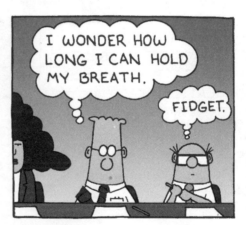

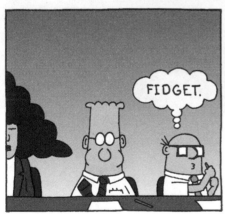

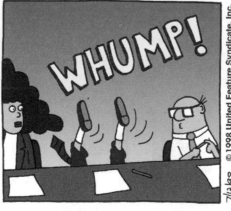

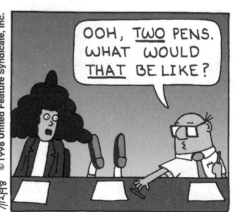

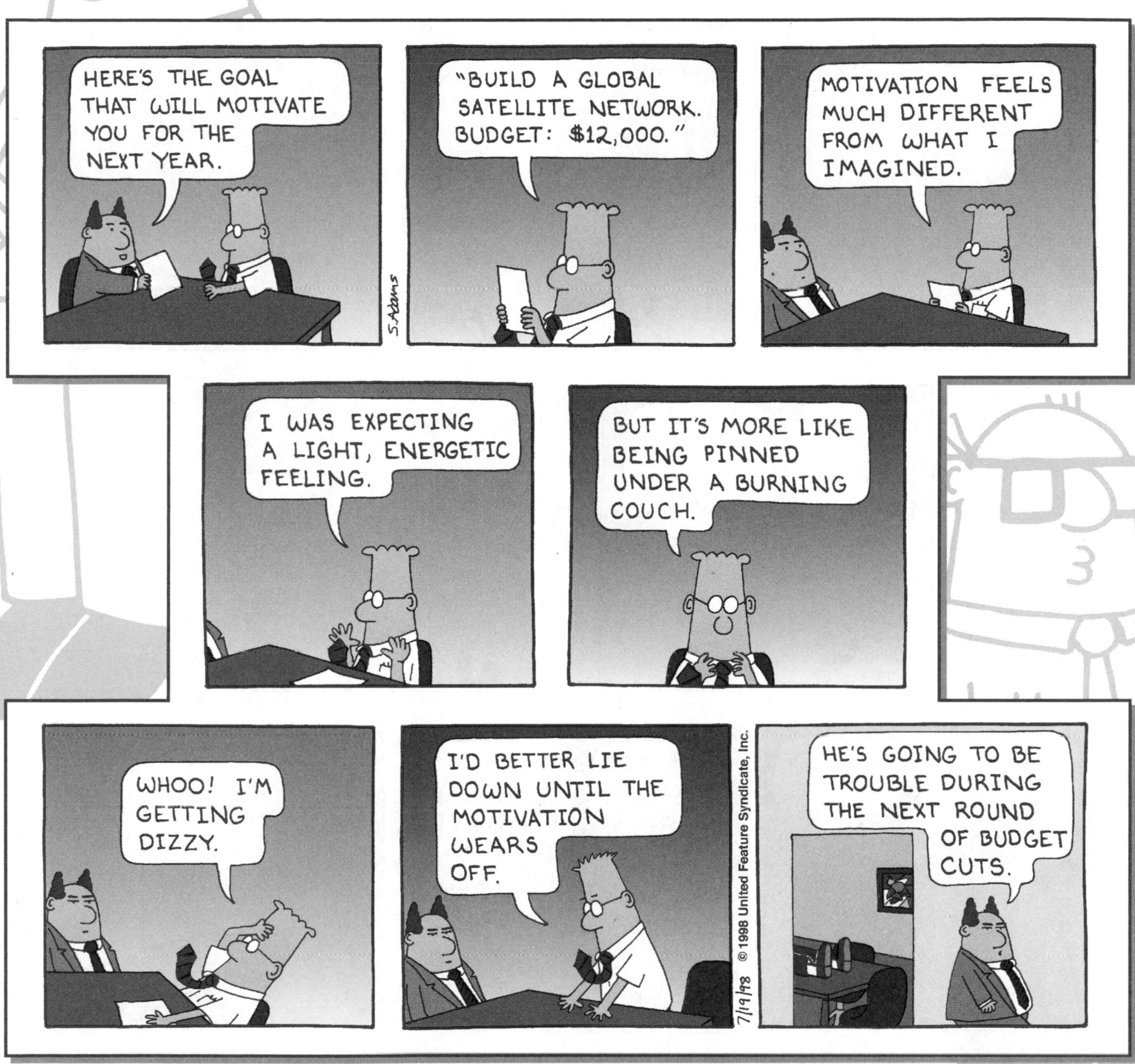
HERE'S THE GOAL THAT WILL MOTIVATE YOU FOR THE NEXT YEAR.
"BUILD A GLOBAL SATELLITE NETWORK. BUDGET: $12,000."
MOTIVATION FEELS MUCH DIFFERENT FROM WHAT I IMAGINED.
I WAS EXPECTING A LIGHT, ENERGETIC FEELING.
BUT IT'S MORE LIKE BEING PINNED UNDER A BURNING COUCH.
WHOO! I'M GETTING DIZZY.
I'D BETTER LIE DOWN UNTIL THE MOTIVATION WEARS OFF.
HE'S GOING TO BE TROUBLE DURING THE NEXT ROUND OF BUDGET CUTS.
S. Adams
7/19/98
© 1998 United Feature Syndicate, Inc.

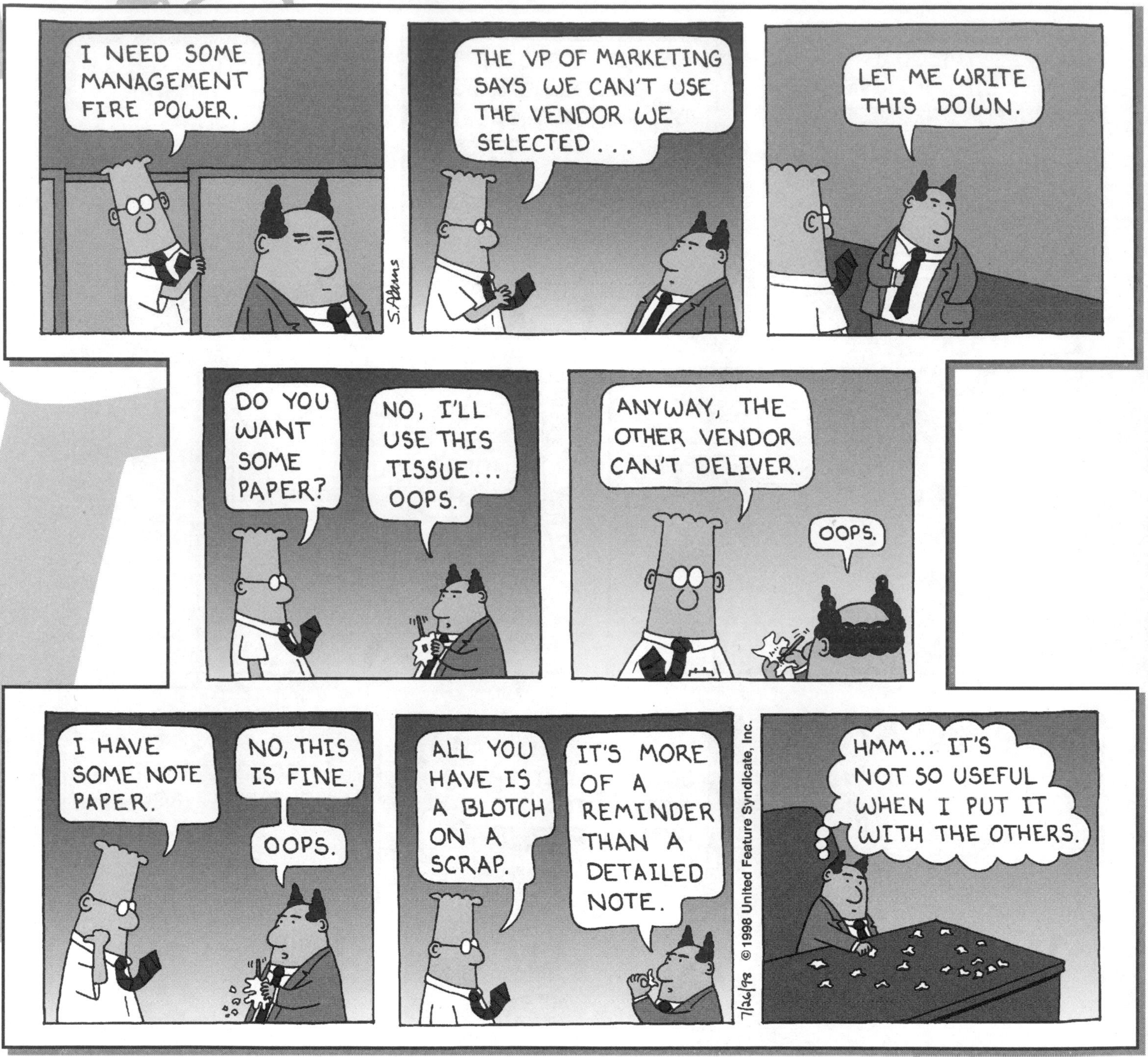
I NEED SOME MANAGEMENT FIRE POWER.
S. Adams
THE VP OF MARKETING SAYS WE CAN'T USE THE VENDOR WE SELECTED . . .
LET ME WRITE THIS DOWN.
DO YOU WANT SOME PAPER?
NO, I'LL USE THIS TISSUE . . . OOPS.
ANYWAY, THE OTHER VENDOR CAN'T DELIVER.
OOPS.
I HAVE SOME NOTE PAPER.
NO, THIS IS FINE.
OOPS.
ALL YOU HAVE IS A BLOTCH ON A SCRAP.
IT'S MORE OF A REMINDER THAN A DETAILED NOTE.
HMM... IT'S NOT SO USEFUL WHEN I PUT IT WITH THE OTHERS.
© 1998 United Feature Syndicate, Inc.
7/26/98

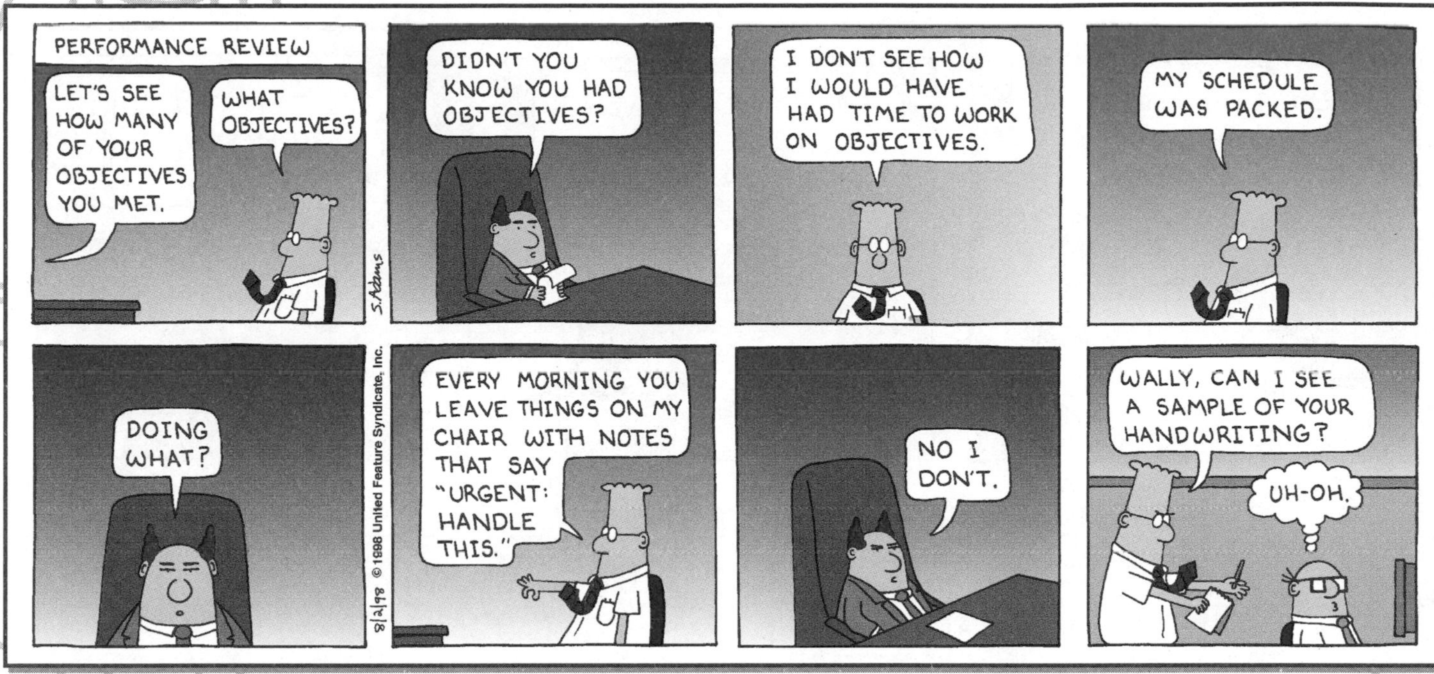
PERFORMANCE REVIEW
LET'S SEE HOW MANY OF YOUR OBJECTIVES YOU MET.
WHAT OBJECTIVES?
DIDN'T YOU KNOW YOU HAD OBJECTIVES?
I DON'T SEE HOW I WOULD HAVE HAD TIME TO WORK ON OBJECTIVES.
MY SCHEDULE WAS PACKED.
DOING WHAT?
EVERY MORNING YOU LEAVE THINGS ON MY CHAIR WITH NOTES THAT SAY "URGENT: HANDLE THIS."
NO I DON'T.
WALLY, CAN I SEE A SAMPLE OF YOUR HANDWRITING?
UH-OH.
S. Adams
8/2/98 © 1998 United Feature Syndicate, Inc.

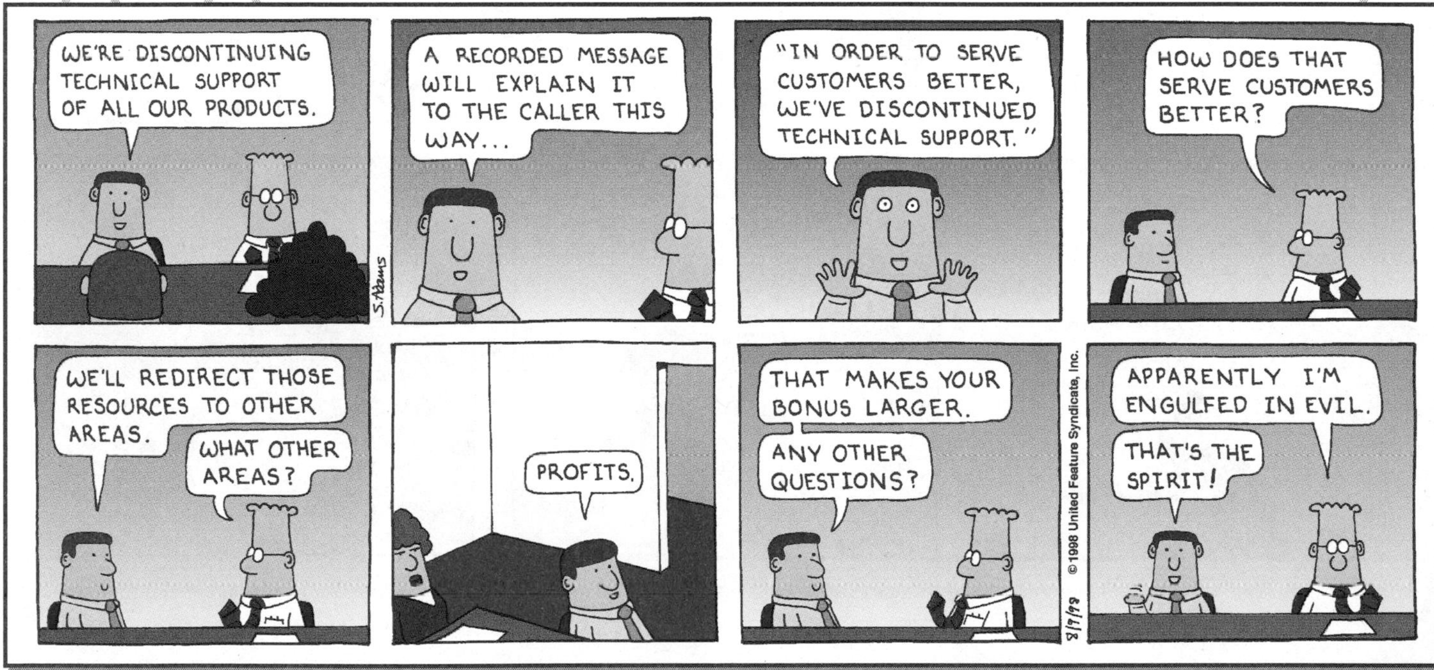
WE'RE DISCONTINUING TECHNICAL SUPPORT OF ALL OUR PRODUCTS.
A RECORDED MESSAGE WILL EXPLAIN IT TO THE CALLER THIS WAY...
"IN ORDER TO SERVE CUSTOMERS BETTER, WE'VE DISCONTINUED TECHNICAL SUPPORT."
HOW DOES THAT SERVE CUSTOMERS BETTER?
WE'LL REDIRECT THOSE RESOURCES TO OTHER AREAS.
WHAT OTHER AREAS?
PROFITS.
THAT MAKES YOUR BONUS LARGER.
ANY OTHER QUESTIONS?
APPARENTLY I'M ENGULFED IN EVIL.
THAT'S THE SPIRIT!
S. Adams
8/9/98 © 1998 United Feature Syndicate, Inc.

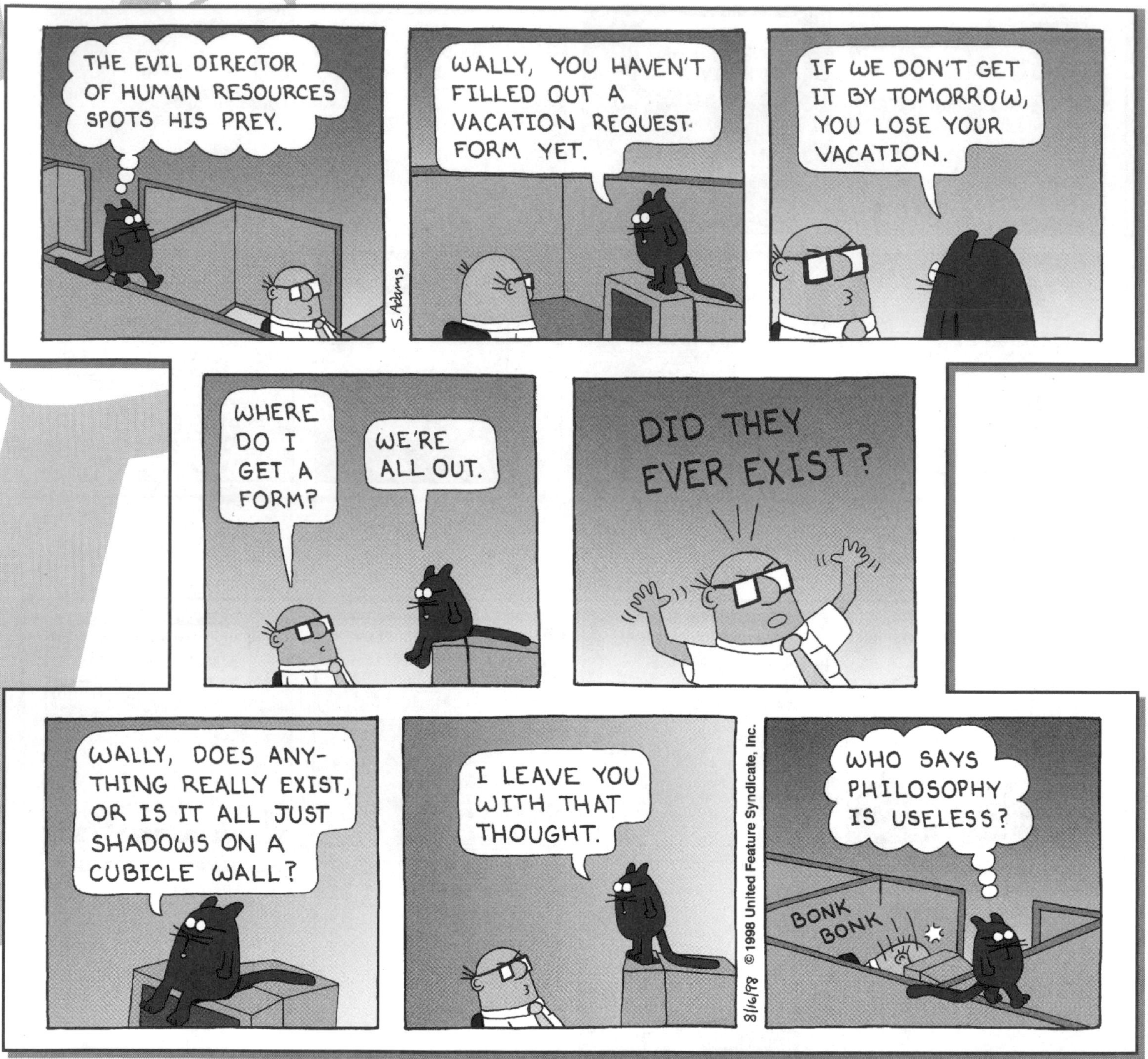
THE EVIL DIRECTOR OF HUMAN RESOURCES SPOTS HIS PREY.
S. Adams
WALLY, YOU HAVEN'T FILLED OUT A VACATION REQUEST FORM YET.
IF WE DON'T GET IT BY TOMORROW, YOU LOSE YOUR VACATION.
WHERE DO I GET A FORM?
WE'RE ALL OUT.
DID THEY EVER EXIST?
WALLY, DOES ANYTHING REALLY EXIST, OR IS IT ALL JUST SHADOWS ON A CUBICLE WALL?
I LEAVE YOU WITH THAT THOUGHT.
© 1998 United Feature Syndicate, Inc.
8/16/98
WHO SAYS PHILOSOPHY IS USELESS?
BONK
BONK

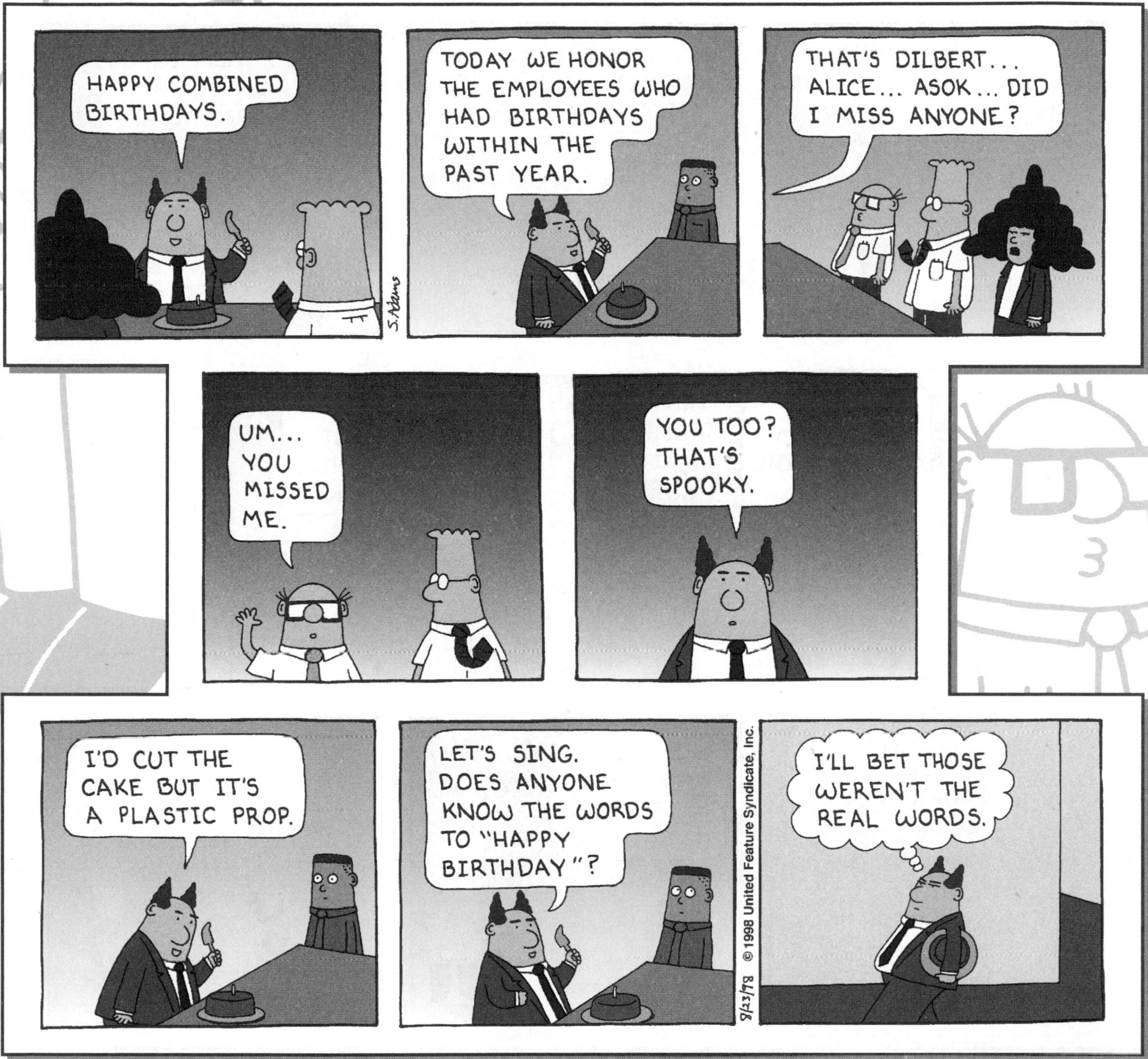
HAPPY COMBINED BIRTHDAYS.
S. Adams
TODAY WE HONOR THE EMPLOYEES WHO HAD BIRTHDAYS WITHIN THE PAST YEAR.
THAT'S DILBERT... ALICE... ASOK... DID I MISS ANYONE?
UM... YOU MISSED ME.
YOU TOO? THAT'S SPOOKY.
I'D CUT THE CAKE BUT IT'S A PLASTIC PROP.
LET'S SING. DOES ANYONE KNOW THE WORDS TO "HAPPY BIRTHDAY"?
8/23/98 © 1998 United Feature Syndicate, Inc.
I'LL BET THOSE WEREN'T THE REAL WORDS.

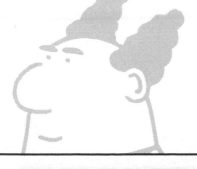

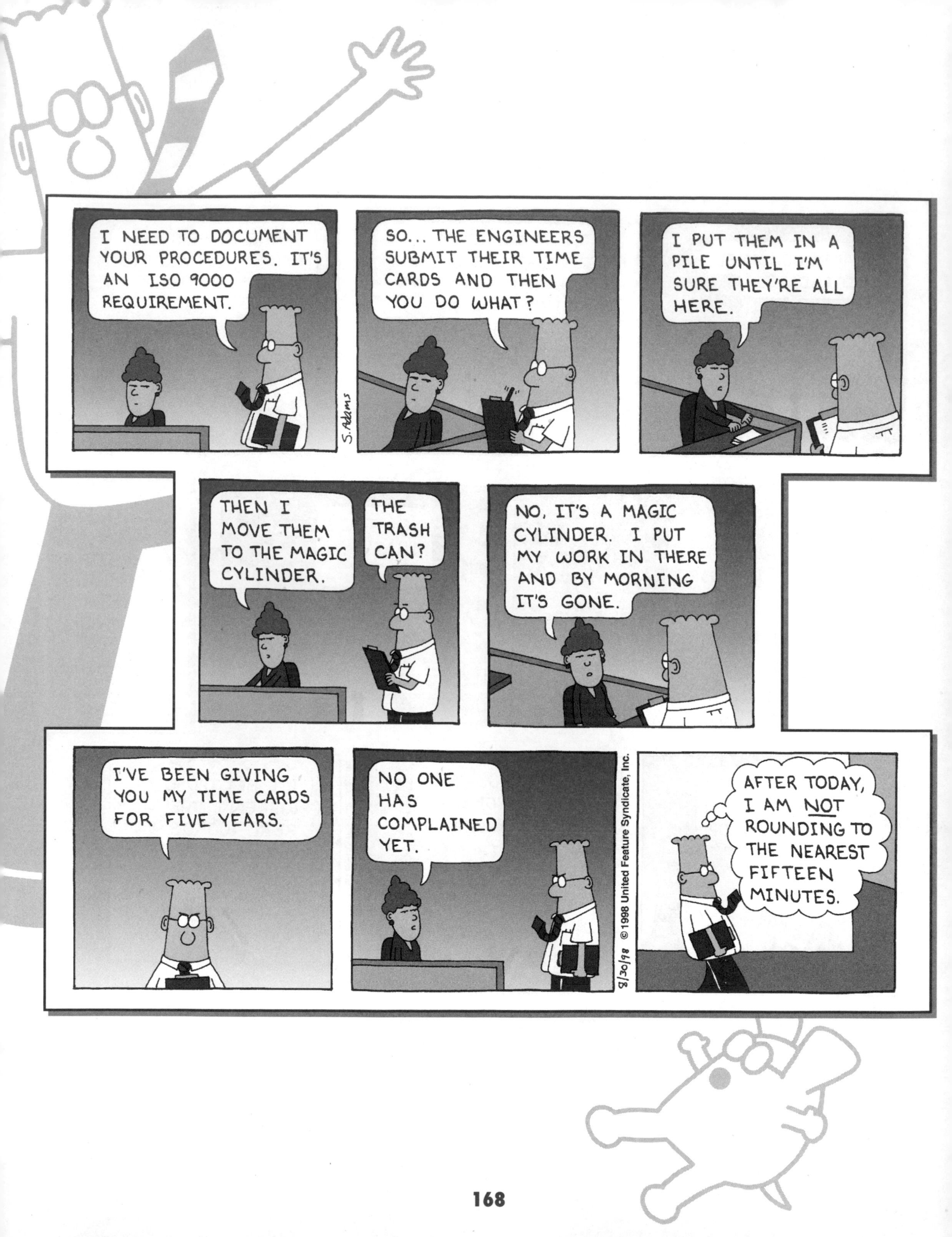
I NEED TO DOCUMENT YOUR PROCEDURES. IT'S AN ISO 9000 REQUIREMENT.
S. Adams
SO... THE ENGINEERS SUBMIT THEIR TIME CARDS AND THEN YOU DO WHAT?
I PUT THEM IN A PILE UNTIL I'M SURE THEY'RE ALL HERE.
THEN I MOVE THEM TO THE MAGIC CYLINDER.
THE TRASH CAN?
NO, IT'S A MAGIC CYLINDER. I PUT MY WORK IN THERE AND BY MORNING IT'S GONE.
I'VE BEEN GIVING YOU MY TIME CARDS FOR FIVE YEARS.
NO ONE HAS COMPLAINED YET.
8/30/98 © 1998 United Feature Syndicate, Inc.
AFTER TODAY, I AM NOT ROUNDING TO THE NEAREST FIFTEEN MINUTES.

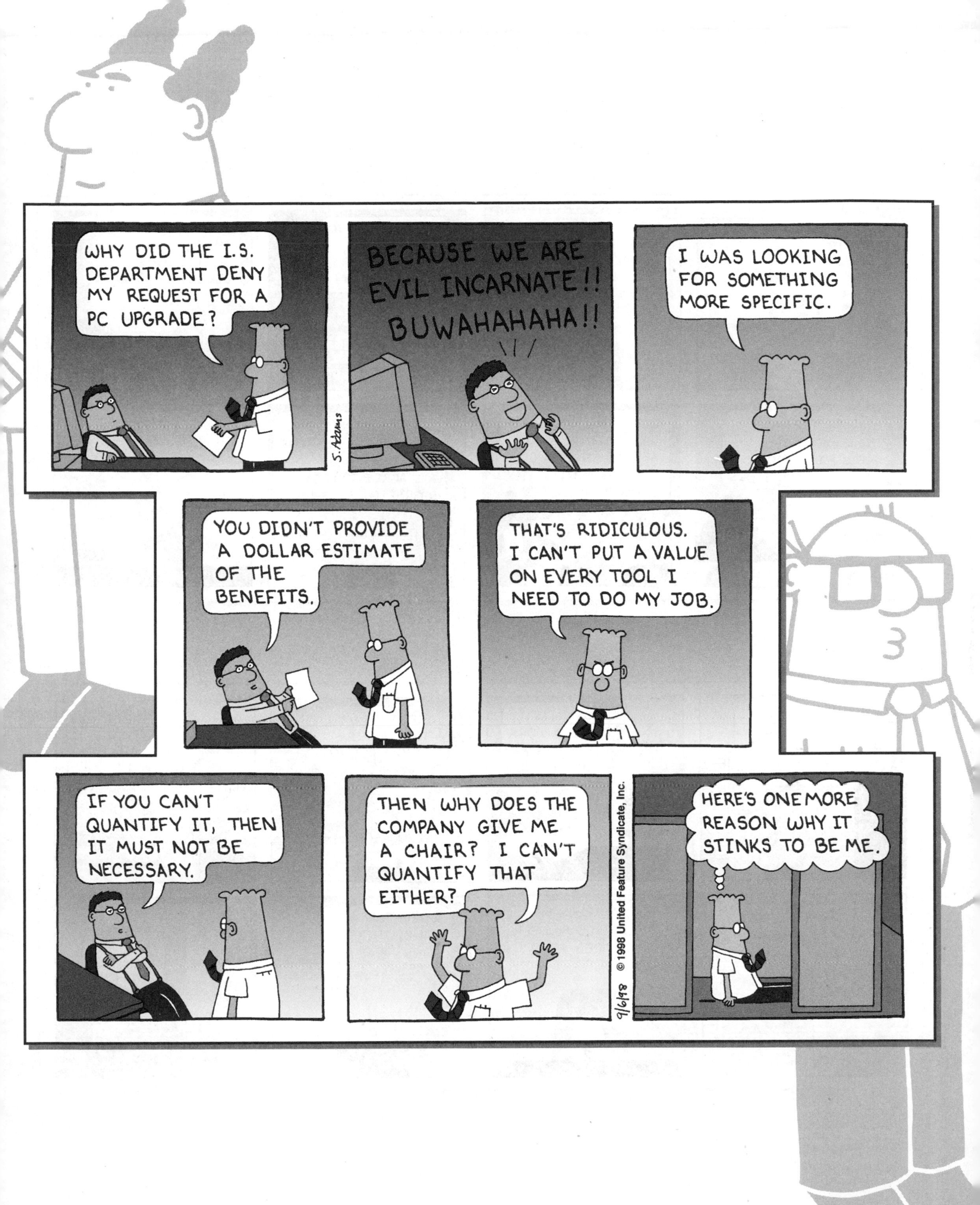
WHY DID THE I.S. DEPARTMENT DENY MY REQUEST FOR A PC UPGRADE?
S. Adams
BECAUSE WE ARE EVIL INCARNATE!! BUWAHAHAHA!!
I WAS LOOKING FOR SOMETHING MORE SPECIFIC.
YOU DIDN'T PROVIDE A DOLLAR ESTIMATE OF THE BENEFITS.
THAT'S RIDICULOUS. I CAN'T PUT A VALUE ON EVERY TOOL I NEED TO DO MY JOB.
IF YOU CAN'T QUANTIFY IT, THEN IT MUST NOT BE NECESSARY.
THEN WHY DOES THE COMPANY GIVE ME A CHAIR? I CAN'T QUANTIFY THAT EITHER?
9/6/98 © 1998 United Feature Syndicate, Inc.
HERE'S ONE MORE REASON WHY IT STINKS TO BE ME.

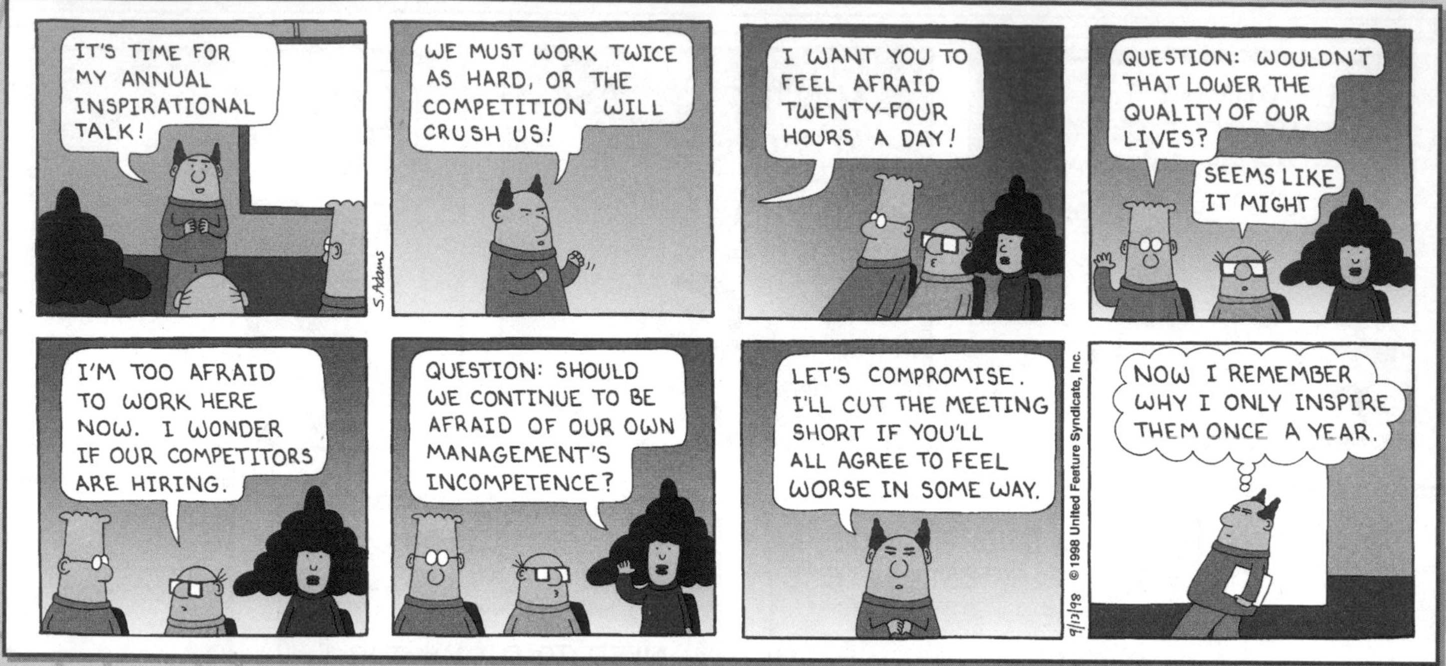
IT'S TIME FOR MY ANNUAL INSPIRATIONAL TALK!
S. Adams
WE MUST WORK TWICE AS HARD, OR THE COMPETITION WILL CRUSH US!
I WANT YOU TO FEEL AFRAID TWENTY-FOUR HOURS A DAY!
QUESTION: WOULDN'T THAT LOWER THE QUALITY OF OUR LIVES?
SEEMS LIKE IT MIGHT
I'M TOO AFRAID TO WORK HERE NOW. I WONDER IF OUR COMPETITORS ARE HIRING.
QUESTION: SHOULD WE CONTINUE TO BE AFRAID OF OUR OWN MANAGEMENT'S INCOMPETENCE?
LET'S COMPROMISE. I'LL CUT THE MEETING SHORT IF YOU'LL ALL AGREE TO FEEL WORSE IN SOME WAY.
9/13/98 © 1998 United Feature Syndicate, Inc.
NOW I REMEMBER WHY I ONLY INSPIRE THEM ONCE A YEAR.

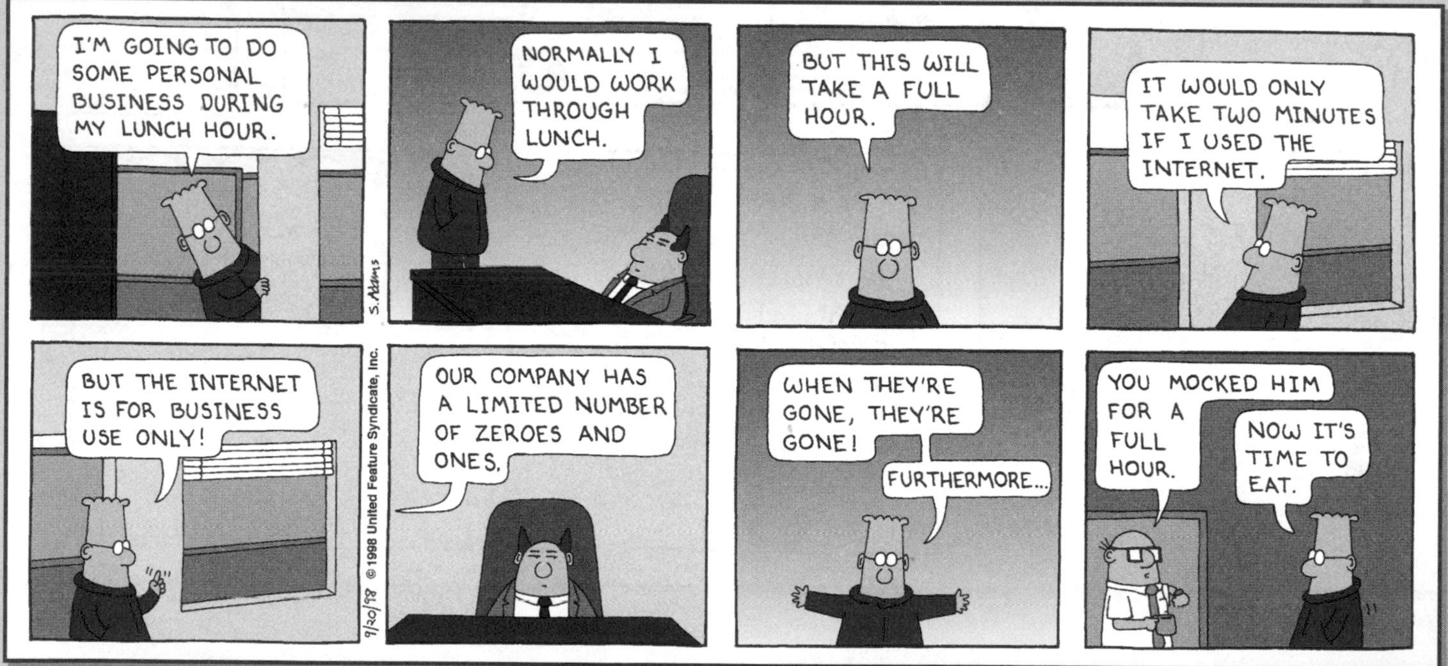
I'M GOING TO DO SOME PERSONAL BUSINESS DURING MY LUNCH HOUR.
S. Adams
NORMALLY I WOULD WORK THROUGH LUNCH.
BUT THIS WILL TAKE A FULL HOUR.
IT WOULD ONLY TAKE TWO MINUTES IF I USED THE INTERNET.
BUT THE INTERNET IS FOR BUSINESS USE ONLY!
9/20/98 © 1998 United Feature Syndicate, Inc.
OUR COMPANY HAS A LIMITED NUMBER OF ZEROES AND ONES.
WHEN THEY'RE GONE, THEY'RE GONE!
FURTHERMORE...
YOU MOCKED HIM FOR A FULL HOUR.
NOW IT'S TIME TO EAT.

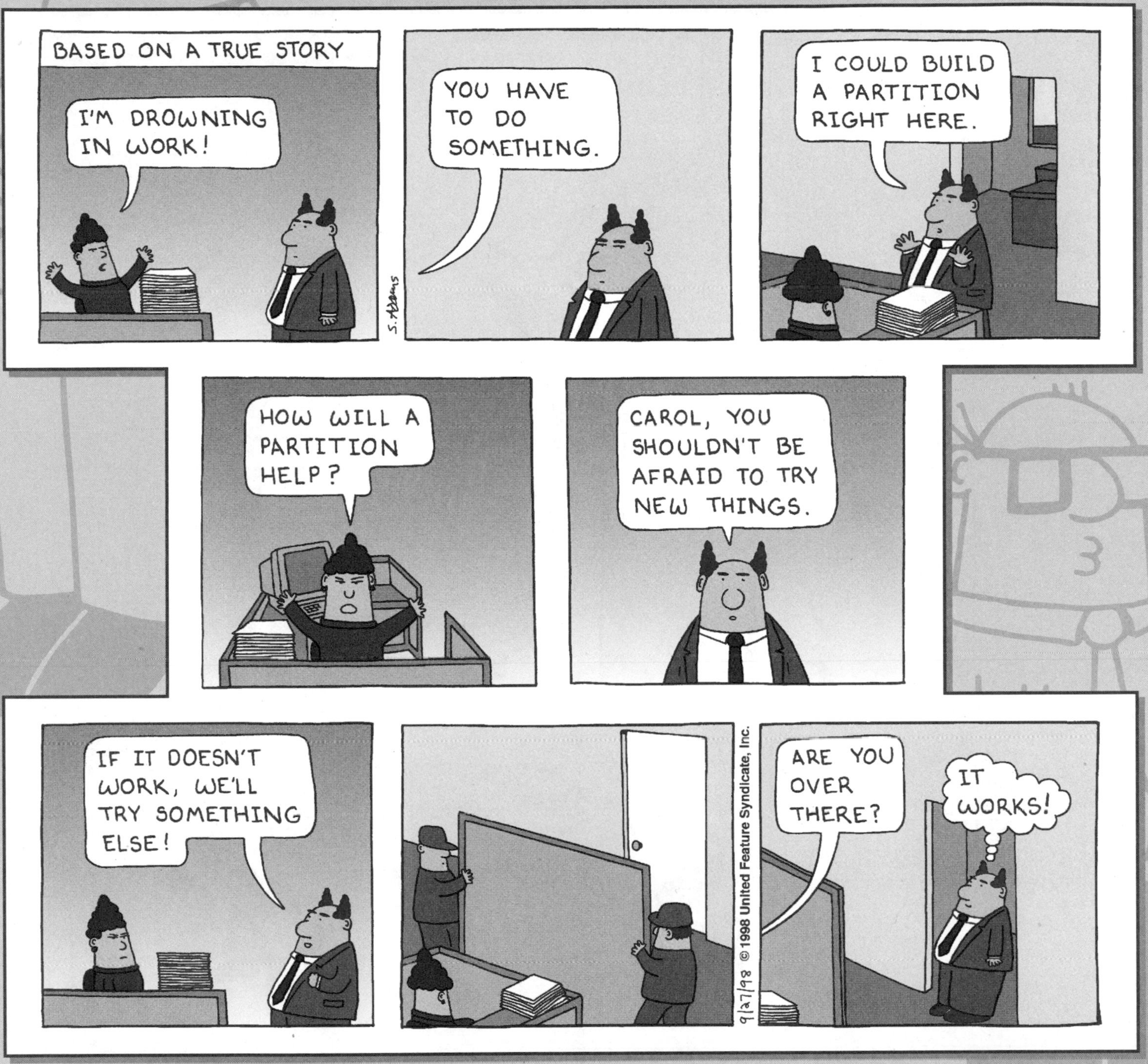
BASED ON A TRUE STORY
I'M DROWNING IN WORK!
S. Adams
YOU HAVE TO DO SOMETHING.
I COULD BUILD A PARTITION RIGHT HERE.
HOW WILL A PARTITION HELP?
CAROL, YOU SHOULDN'T BE AFRAID TO TRY NEW THINGS.
IF IT DOESN'T WORK, WE'LL TRY SOMETHING ELSE!
9/27/98 © 1998 United Feature Syndicate, Inc.
ARE YOU OVER THERE?
IT WORKS!

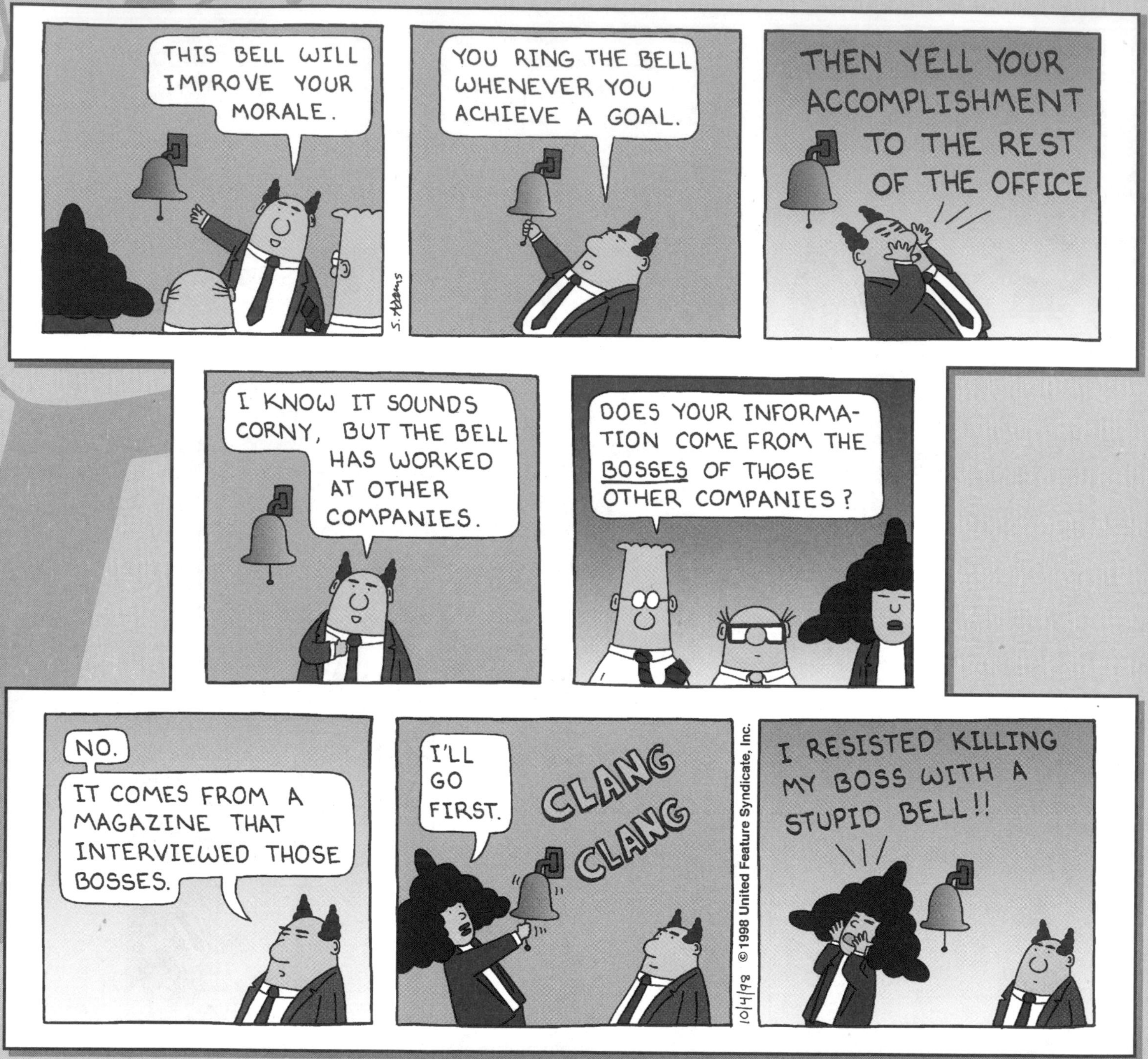

THIS BELL WILL IMPROVE YOUR MORALE.
S. ADAMS
YOU RING THE BELL WHENEVER YOU ACHIEVE A GOAL.
THEN YELL YOUR ACCOMPLISHMENT TO THE REST OF THE OFFICE
I KNOW IT SOUNDS CORNY, BUT THE BELL HAS WORKED AT OTHER COMPANIES.
DOES YOUR INFORMATION COME FROM THE BOSSES OF THOSE OTHER COMPANIES?
NO.
IT COMES FROM A MAGAZINE THAT INTERVIEWED THOSE BOSSES.
I'LL GO FIRST.
CLANG CLANG
10/4/98 © 1998 United Feature Syndicate, Inc.
I RESISTED KILLING MY BOSS WITH A STUPID BELL!!

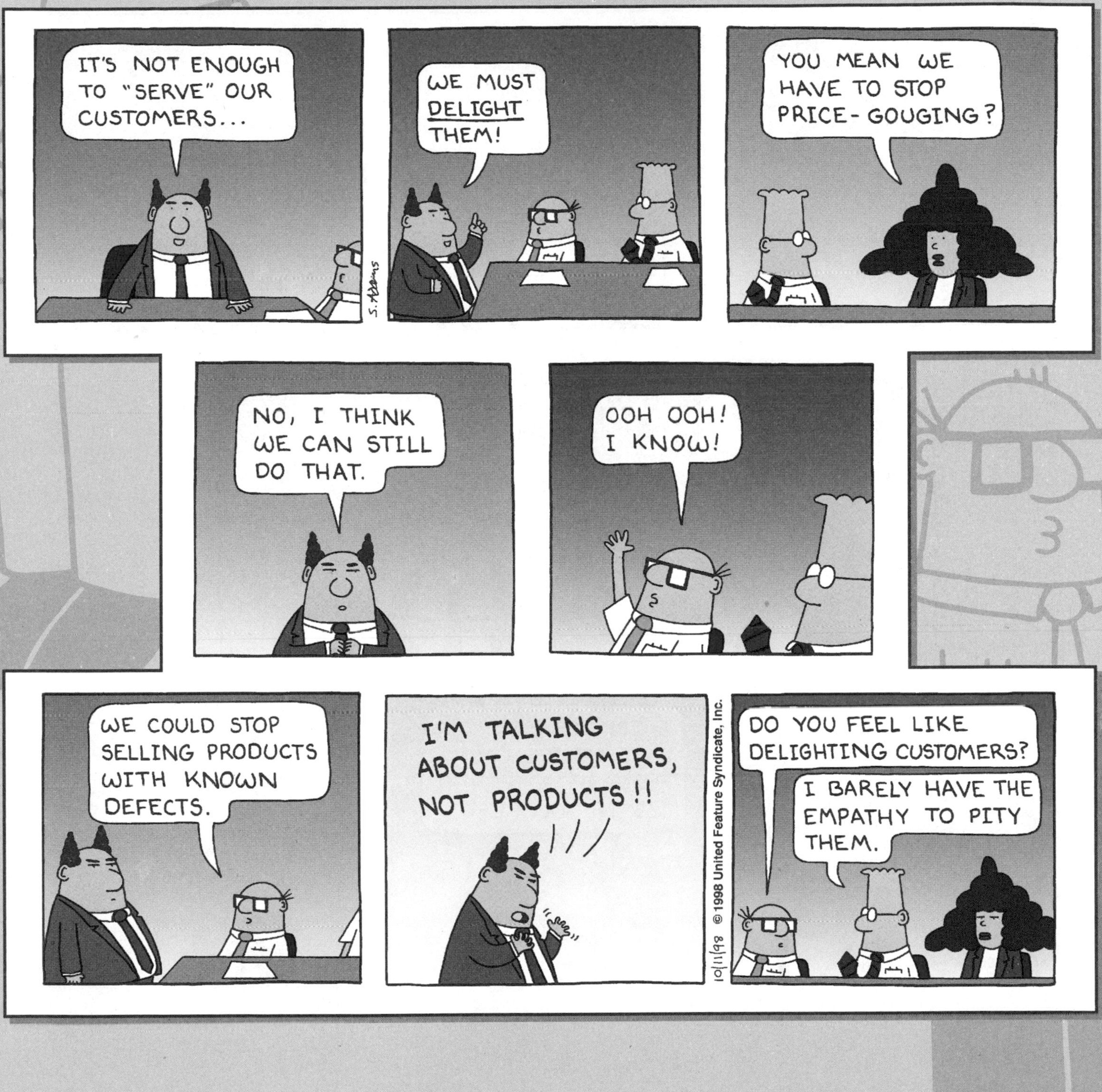
IT'S NOT ENOUGH TO "SERVE" OUR CUSTOMERS...
S. Adams
WE MUST DELIGHT THEM!
YOU MEAN WE HAVE TO STOP PRICE-GOUGING?
NO, I THINK WE CAN STILL DO THAT.
OOH OOH! I KNOW!
WE COULD STOP SELLING PRODUCTS WITH KNOWN DEFECTS.
I'M TALKING ABOUT CUSTOMERS, NOT PRODUCTS!!
10/11/98 © 1998 United Feature Syndicate, Inc.
DO YOU FEEL LIKE DELIGHTING CUSTOMERS?
I BARELY HAVE THE EMPATHY TO PITY THEM.

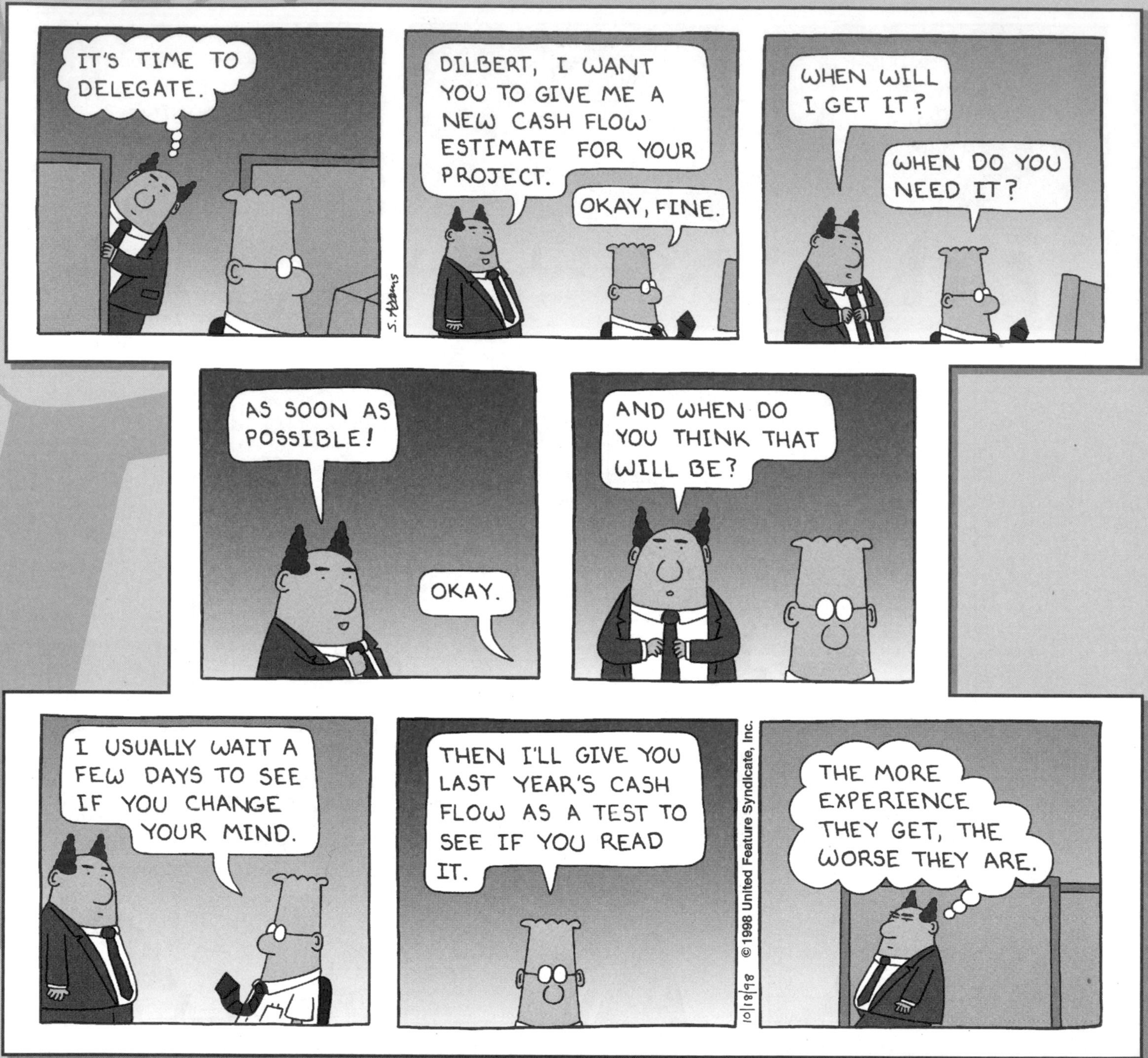
IT'S TIME TO DELEGATE.
DILBERT, I WANT YOU TO GIVE ME A NEW CASH FLOW ESTIMATE FOR YOUR PROJECT.
OKAY, FINE.
WHEN WILL I GET IT?
WHEN DO YOU NEED IT?
AS SOON AS POSSIBLE!
OKAY.
AND WHEN DO YOU THINK THAT WILL BE?
I USUALLY WAIT A FEW DAYS TO SEE IF YOU CHANGE YOUR MIND.
THEN I'LL GIVE YOU LAST YEAR'S CASH FLOW AS A TEST TO SEE IF YOU READ IT.
THE MORE EXPERIENCE THEY GET, THE WORSE THEY ARE.
S. Adams
10/18/98
© 1998 United Feature Syndicate, Inc.

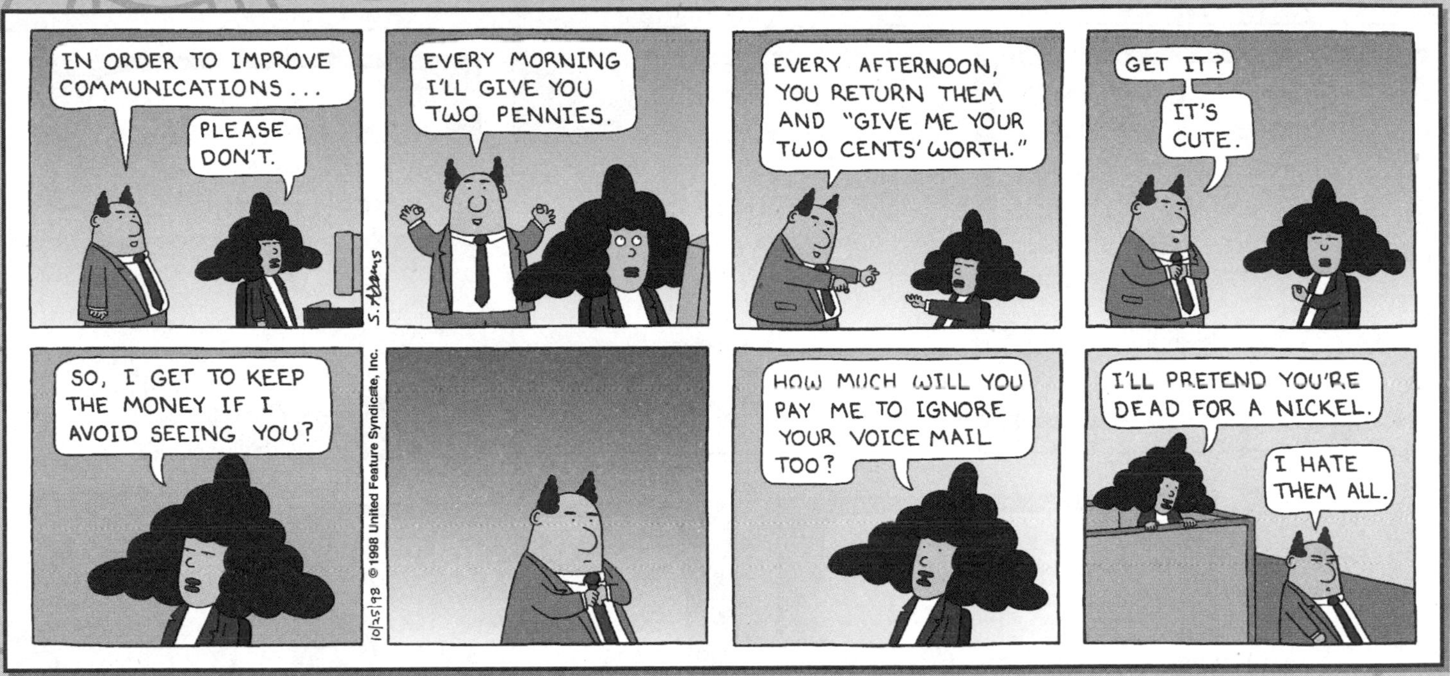
IN ORDER TO IMPROVE COMMUNICATIONS . . .
PLEASE DON'T.
EVERY MORNING I'LL GIVE YOU TWO PENNIES.
EVERY AFTERNOON, YOU RETURN THEM AND "GIVE ME YOUR TWO CENTS' WORTH."
GET IT?
IT'S CUTE.
SO, I GET TO KEEP THE MONEY IF I AVOID SEEING YOU?
HOW MUCH WILL YOU PAY ME TO IGNORE YOUR VOICE MAIL TOO?
I'LL PRETEND YOU'RE DEAD FOR A NICKEL.
I HATE THEM ALL.
© 1998 United Feature Syndicate, Inc.

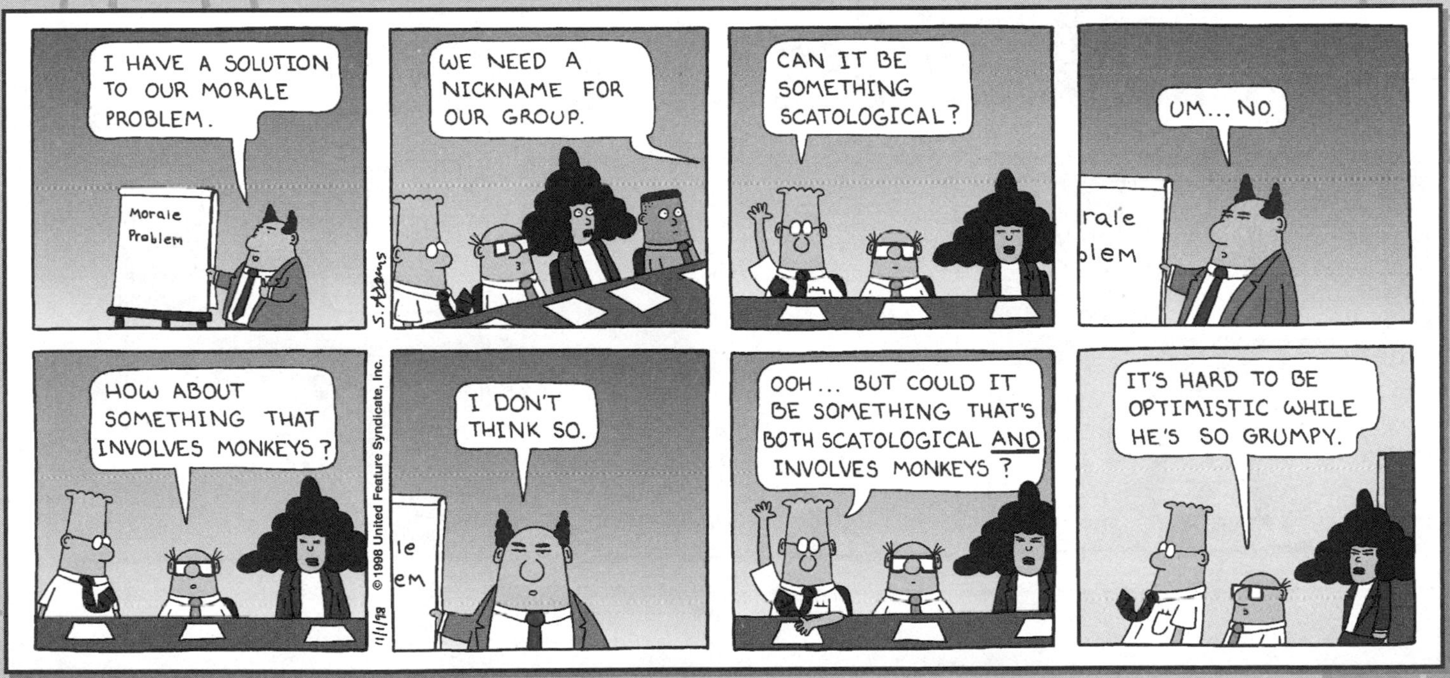
I HAVE A SOLUTION TO OUR MORALE PROBLEM.
Morale Problem
WE NEED A NICKNAME FOR OUR GROUP.
CAN IT BE SOMETHING SCATOLOGICAL?
UM... NO.
HOW ABOUT SOMETHING THAT INVOLVES MONKEYS?
I DON'T THINK SO.
OOH ... BUT COULD IT BE SOMETHING THAT'S BOTH SCATOLOGICAL AND INVOLVES MONKEYS?
IT'S HARD TO BE OPTIMISTIC WHILE HE'S SO GRUMPY.
© 1998 United Feature Syndicate, Inc.

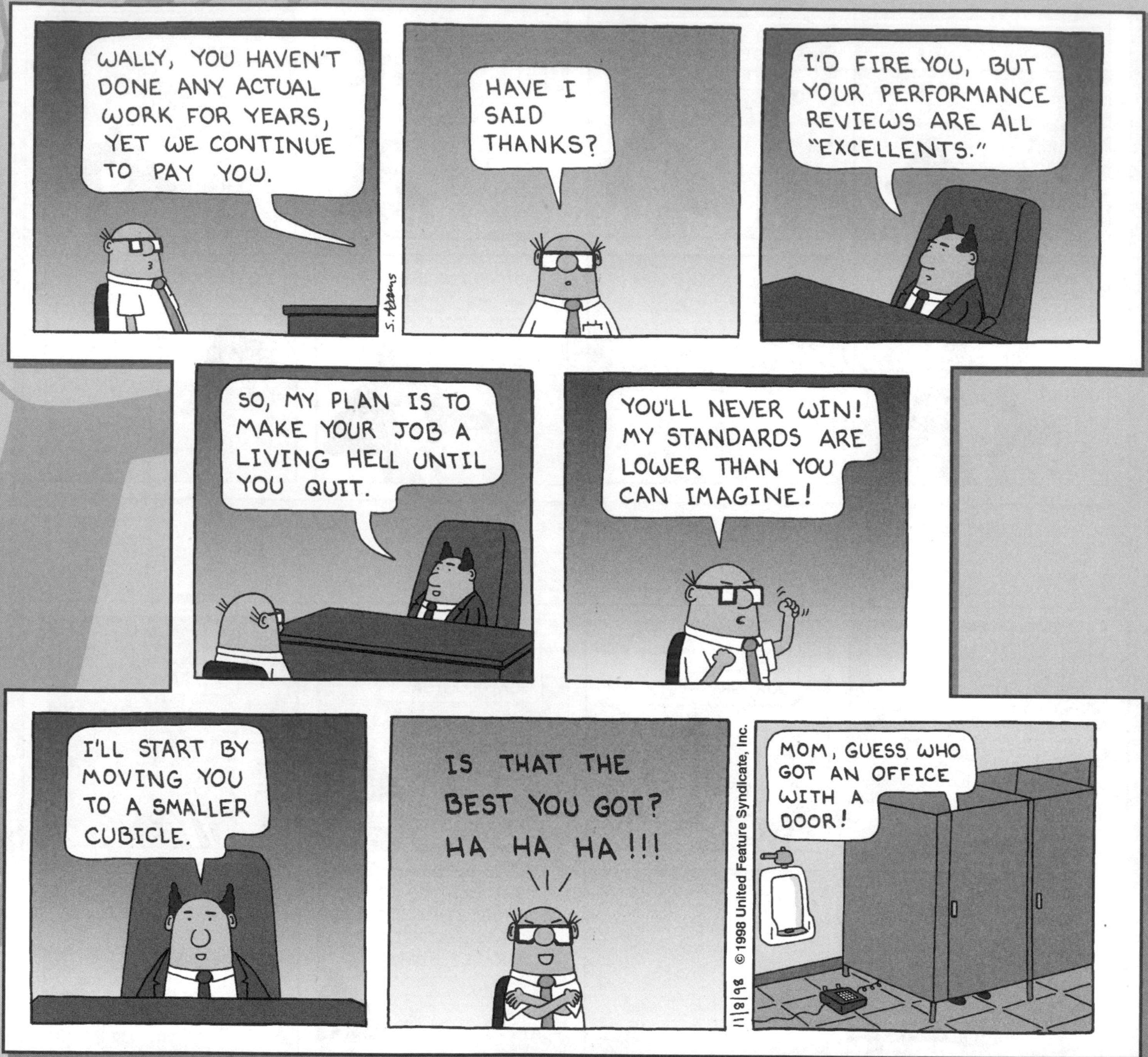
WALLY, YOU HAVEN'T DONE ANY ACTUAL WORK FOR YEARS, YET WE CONTINUE TO PAY YOU.
S. Adams
HAVE I SAID THANKS?
I'D FIRE YOU, BUT YOUR PERFORMANCE REVIEWS ARE ALL "EXCELLENTS."
SO, MY PLAN IS TO MAKE YOUR JOB A LIVING HELL UNTIL YOU QUIT.
YOU'LL NEVER WIN! MY STANDARDS ARE LOWER THAN YOU CAN IMAGINE!
I'LL START BY MOVING YOU TO A SMALLER CUBICLE.
IS THAT THE BEST YOU GOT? HA HA HA!!!
11/8/98 © 1998 United Feature Syndicate, Inc.
MOM, GUESS WHO GOT AN OFFICE WITH A DOOR!

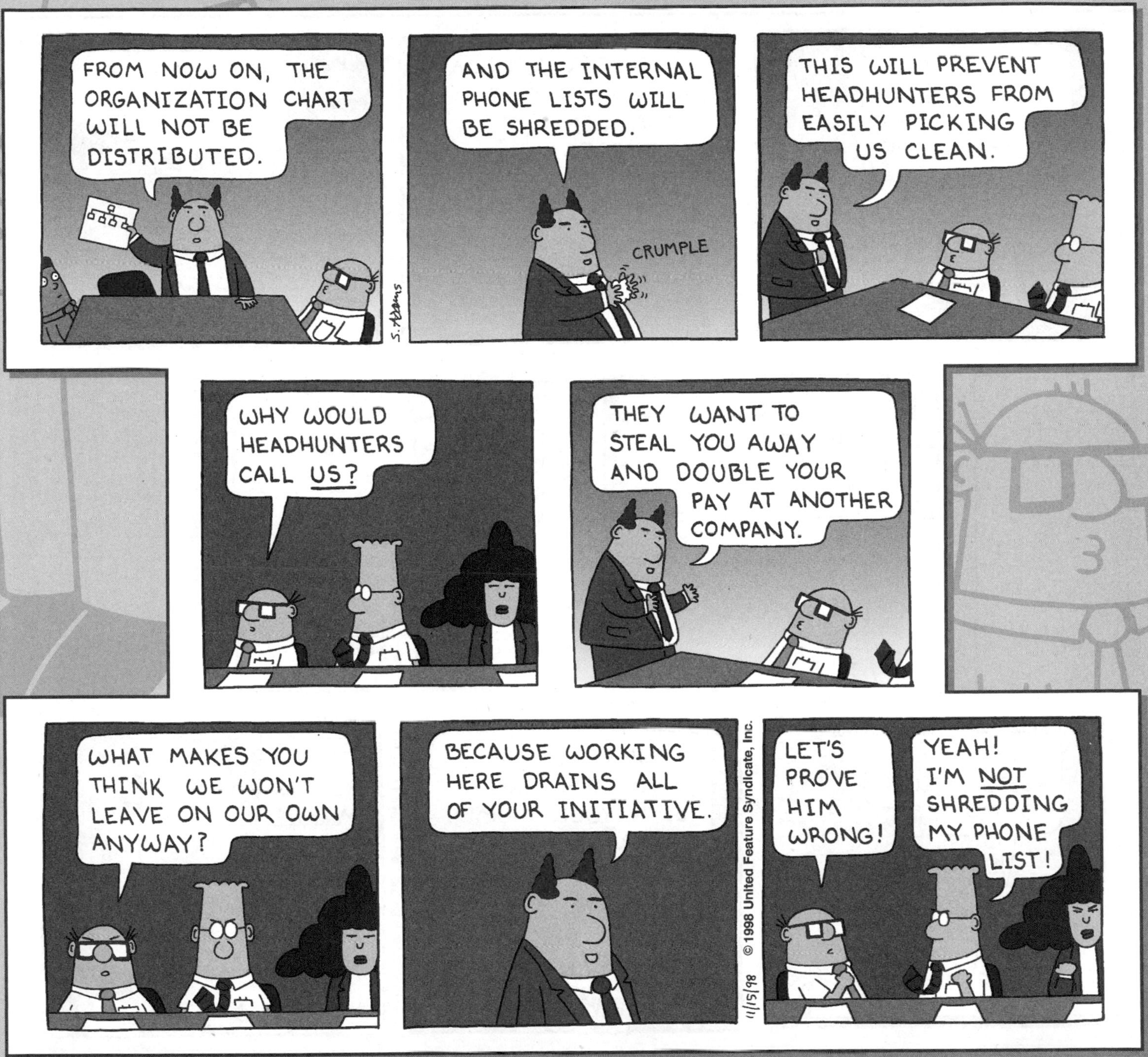

FROM NOW ON, THE ORGANIZATION CHART WILL NOT BE DISTRIBUTED.
S. Adams
AND THE INTERNAL PHONE LISTS WILL BE SHREDDED.
CRUMPLE
THIS WILL PREVENT HEADHUNTERS FROM EASILY PICKING US CLEAN.
WHY WOULD HEADHUNTERS CALL US?
THEY WANT TO STEAL YOU AWAY AND DOUBLE YOUR PAY AT ANOTHER COMPANY.
WHAT MAKES YOU THINK WE WON'T LEAVE ON OUR OWN ANYWAY?
BECAUSE WORKING HERE DRAINS ALL OF YOUR INITIATIVE.
© 1998 United Feature Syndicate, Inc.
11/15/98
LET'S PROVE HIM WRONG!
YEAH! I'M NOT SHREDDING MY PHONE LIST!

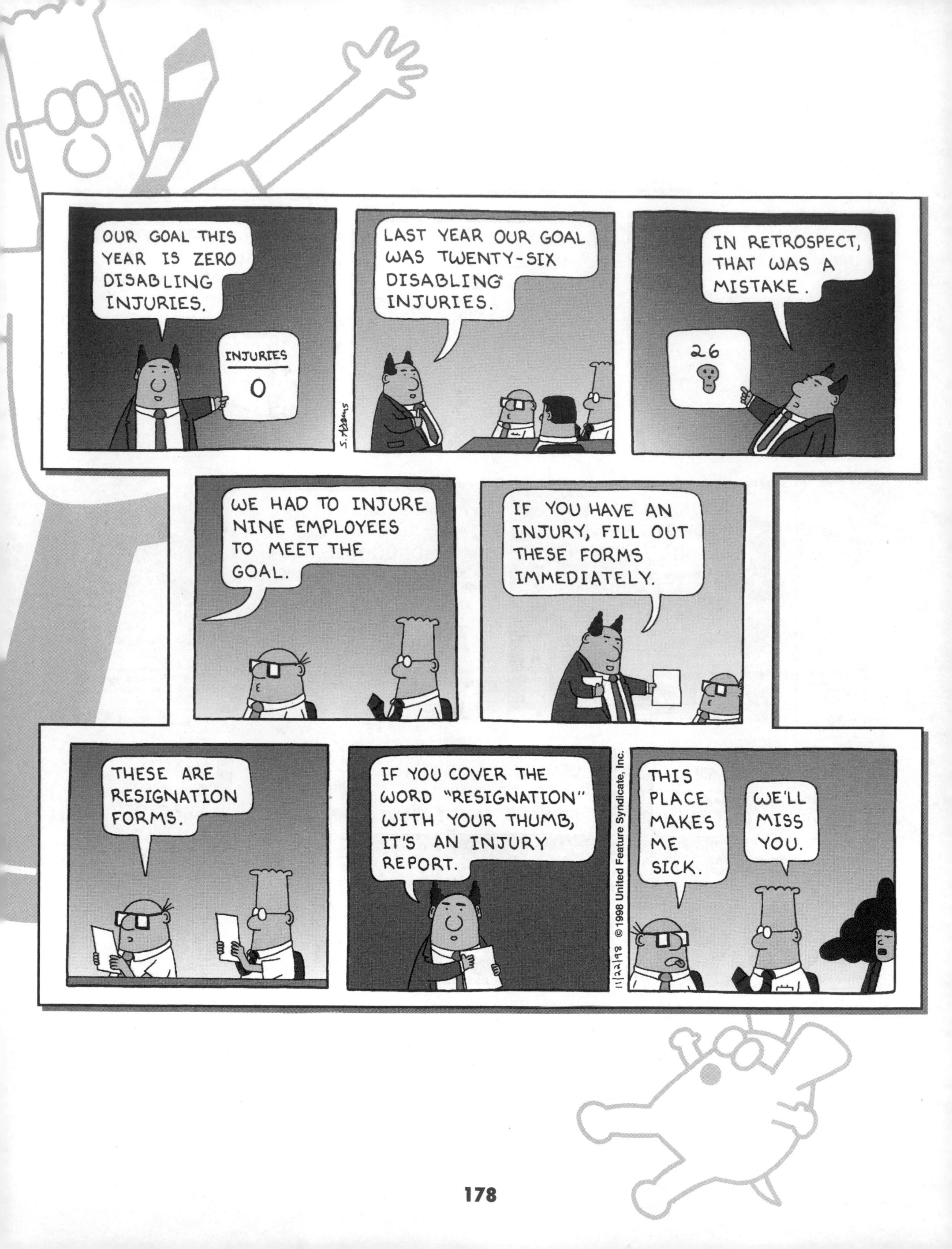
OUR GOAL THIS YEAR IS ZERO DISABLING INJURIES.
INJURIES
0
S. ADAMS
LAST YEAR OUR GOAL WAS TWENTY-SIX DISABLING INJURIES.
IN RETROSPECT, THAT WAS A MISTAKE.
26
WE HAD TO INJURE NINE EMPLOYEES TO MEET THE GOAL.
IF YOU HAVE AN INJURY, FILL OUT THESE FORMS IMMEDIATELY.
THESE ARE RESIGNATION FORMS.
IF YOU COVER THE WORD "RESIGNATION" WITH YOUR THUMB, IT'S AN INJURY REPORT.
11/22/98 © 1998 United Feature Syndicate, Inc.
THIS PLACE MAKES ME SICK.
WE'LL MISS YOU.

WELCOME TO THE MANDATORY WINDOWS NT ™ CLASS.

PERSONALLY, I'VE ONLY BEEN USING A COMPUTER FOR... HOW LONG? ANYONE?

2 WEEKS

BUT A GOOD TRAINER CAN TEACH ANY SUBJECT.

OKAY, EVERYONE STAND UP AND STRETCH!

OR SIT THERE AND GLARE AT ME.

THAT'S GOOD TOO.

I FORGOT TO RESERVE THE ROOM WITH THE COMPUTERS, SO I'LL USE THIS BOX.

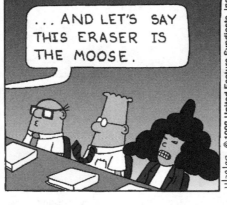

... AND LET'S SAY THIS ERASER IS THE MOOSE.

I LEFT WHEN HE TOLD US TO USE OUR TEETH AS A KEYBOARD.

OOH-YAH.

© 1998 United Feature Syndicate, Inc.

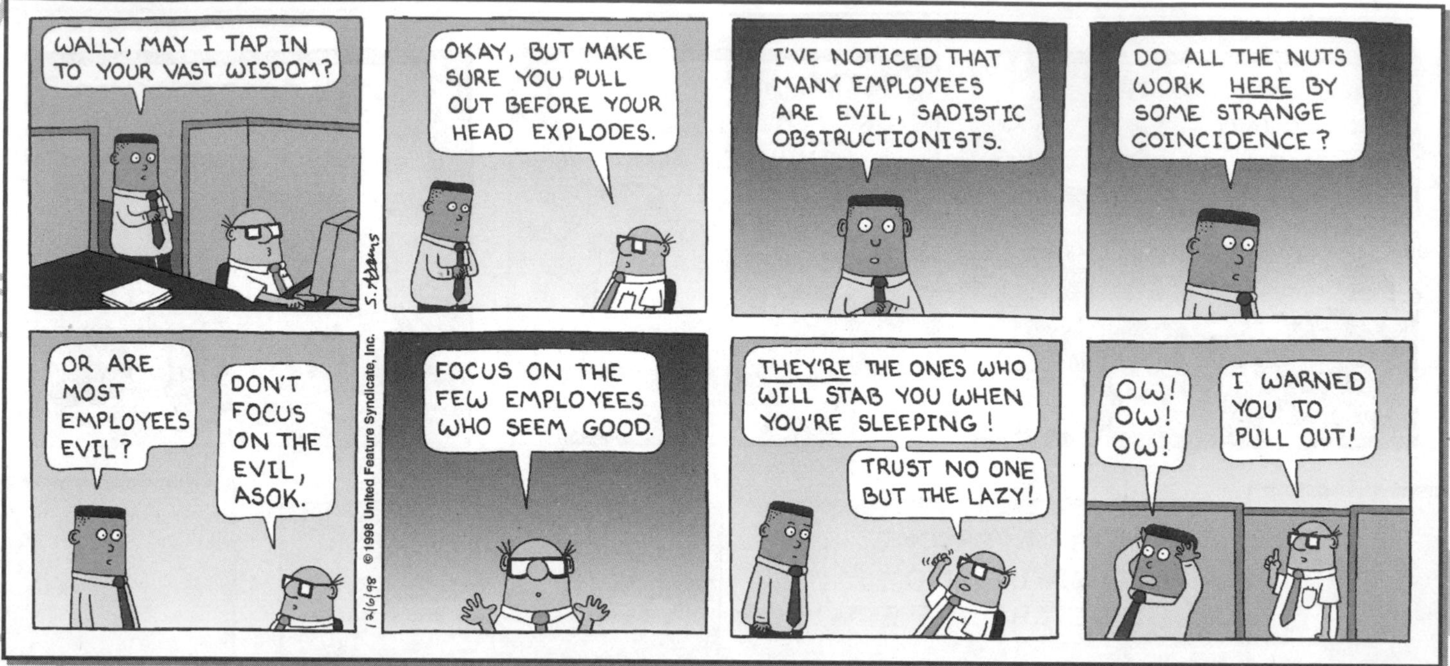
WALLY, MAY I TAP IN TO YOUR VAST WISDOM?
OKAY, BUT MAKE SURE YOU PULL OUT BEFORE YOUR HEAD EXPLODES.
I'VE NOTICED THAT MANY EMPLOYEES ARE EVIL, SADISTIC OBSTRUCTIONISTS.
DO ALL THE NUTS WORK HERE BY SOME STRANGE COINCIDENCE?
OR ARE MOST EMPLOYEES EVIL?
DON'T FOCUS ON THE EVIL, ASOK.
FOCUS ON THE FEW EMPLOYEES WHO SEEM GOOD.
THEY'RE THE ONES WHO WILL STAB YOU WHEN YOU'RE SLEEPING!
TRUST NO ONE BUT THE LAZY!
OW! OW! OW!
I WARNED YOU TO PULL OUT!
S. Adams
12/6/98 © 1998 United Feature Syndicate, Inc.

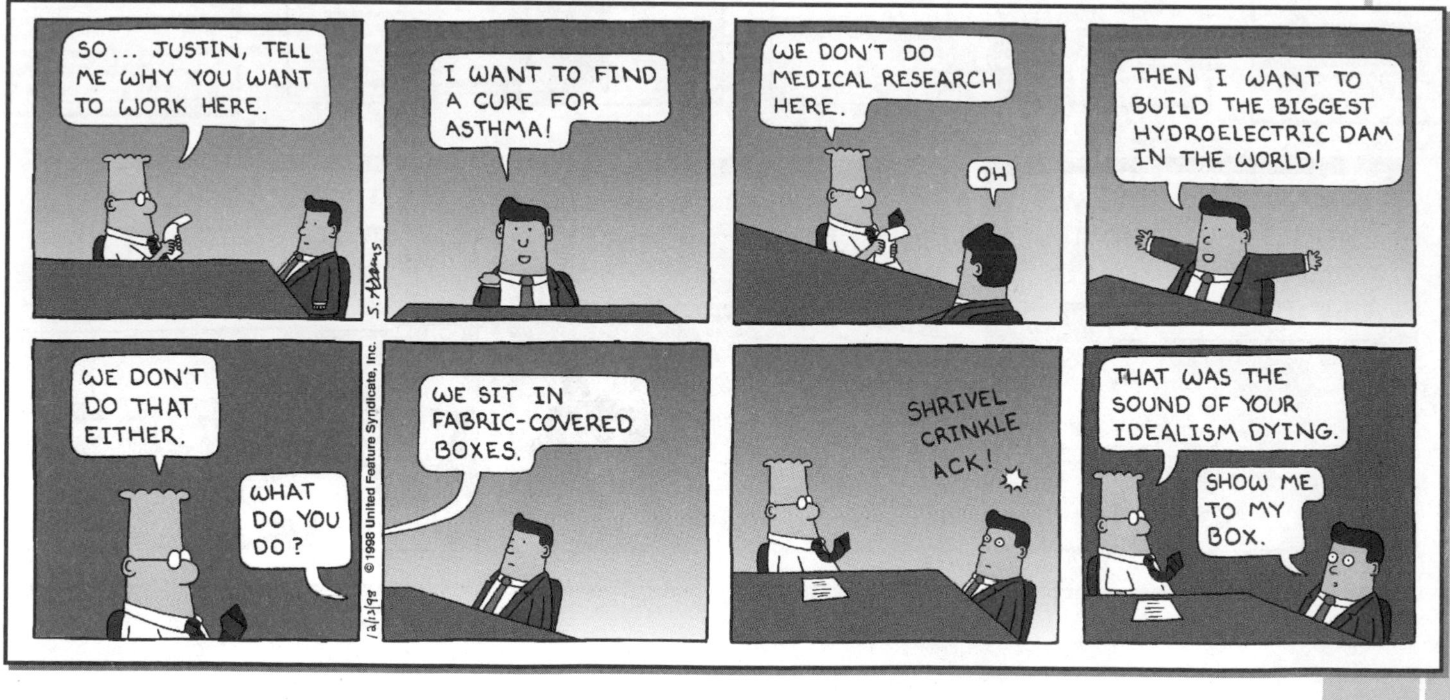
SO... JUSTIN, TELL ME WHY YOU WANT TO WORK HERE.
I WANT TO FIND A CURE FOR ASTHMA!
WE DON'T DO MEDICAL RESEARCH HERE.
OH
THEN I WANT TO BUILD THE BIGGEST HYDROELECTRIC DAM IN THE WORLD!
WE DON'T DO THAT EITHER.
WHAT DO YOU DO?
WE SIT IN FABRIC-COVERED BOXES.
SHRIVEL CRINKLE ACK!
THAT WAS THE SOUND OF YOUR IDEALISM DYING.
SHOW ME TO MY BOX.
S. Adams
12/13/98 © 1998 United Feature Syndicate, Inc.

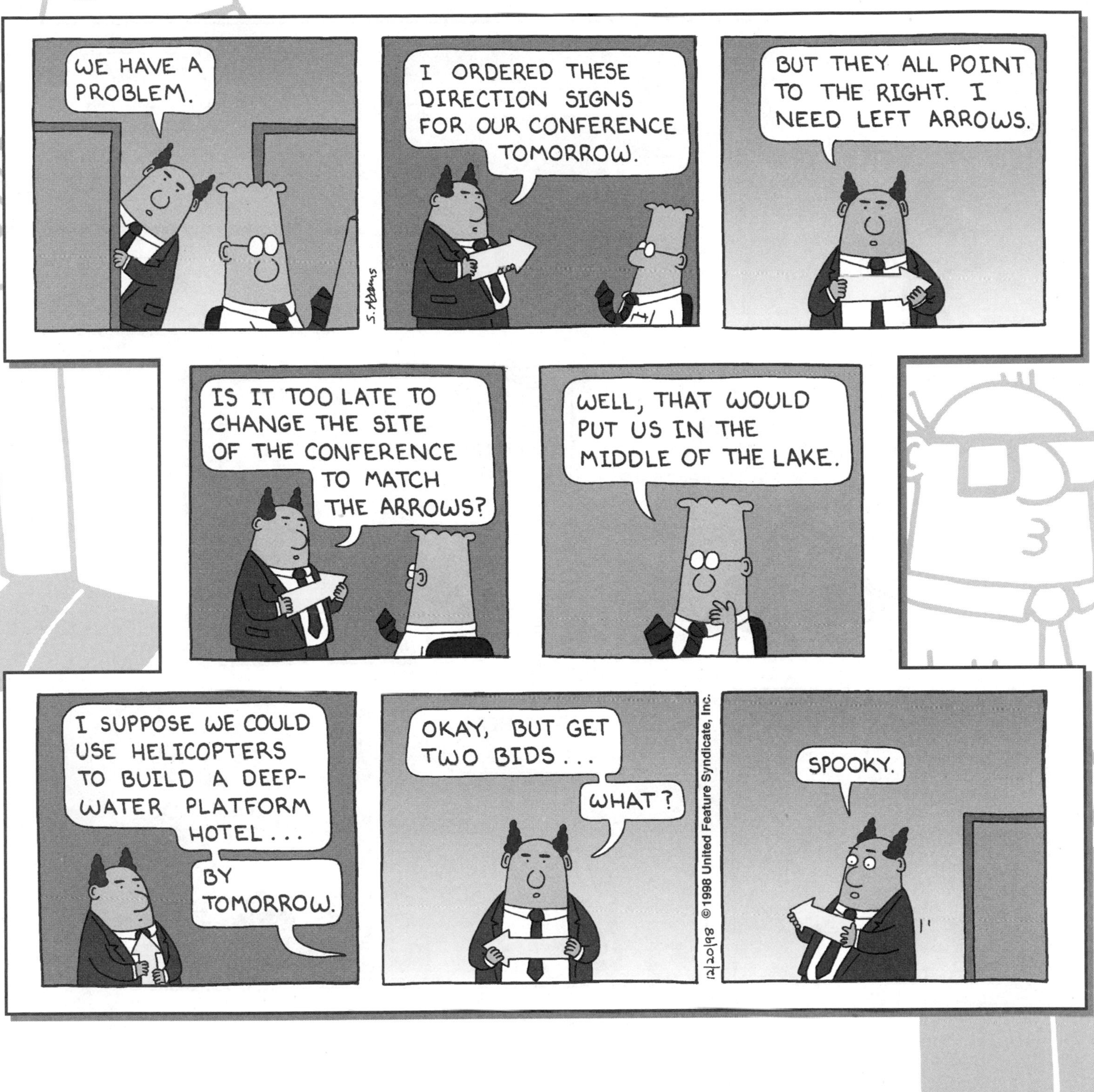
WE HAVE A PROBLEM.
I ORDERED THESE DIRECTION SIGNS FOR OUR CONFERENCE TOMORROW.
BUT THEY ALL POINT TO THE RIGHT. I NEED LEFT ARROWS.
IS IT TOO LATE TO CHANGE THE SITE OF THE CONFERENCE TO MATCH THE ARROWS?
WELL, THAT WOULD PUT US IN THE MIDDLE OF THE LAKE.
I SUPPOSE WE COULD USE HELICOPTERS TO BUILD A DEEP-WATER PLATFORM HOTEL...
BY TOMORROW.
OKAY, BUT GET TWO BIDS...
WHAT?
SPOOKY.
12/20/98 © 1998 United Feature Syndicate, Inc.

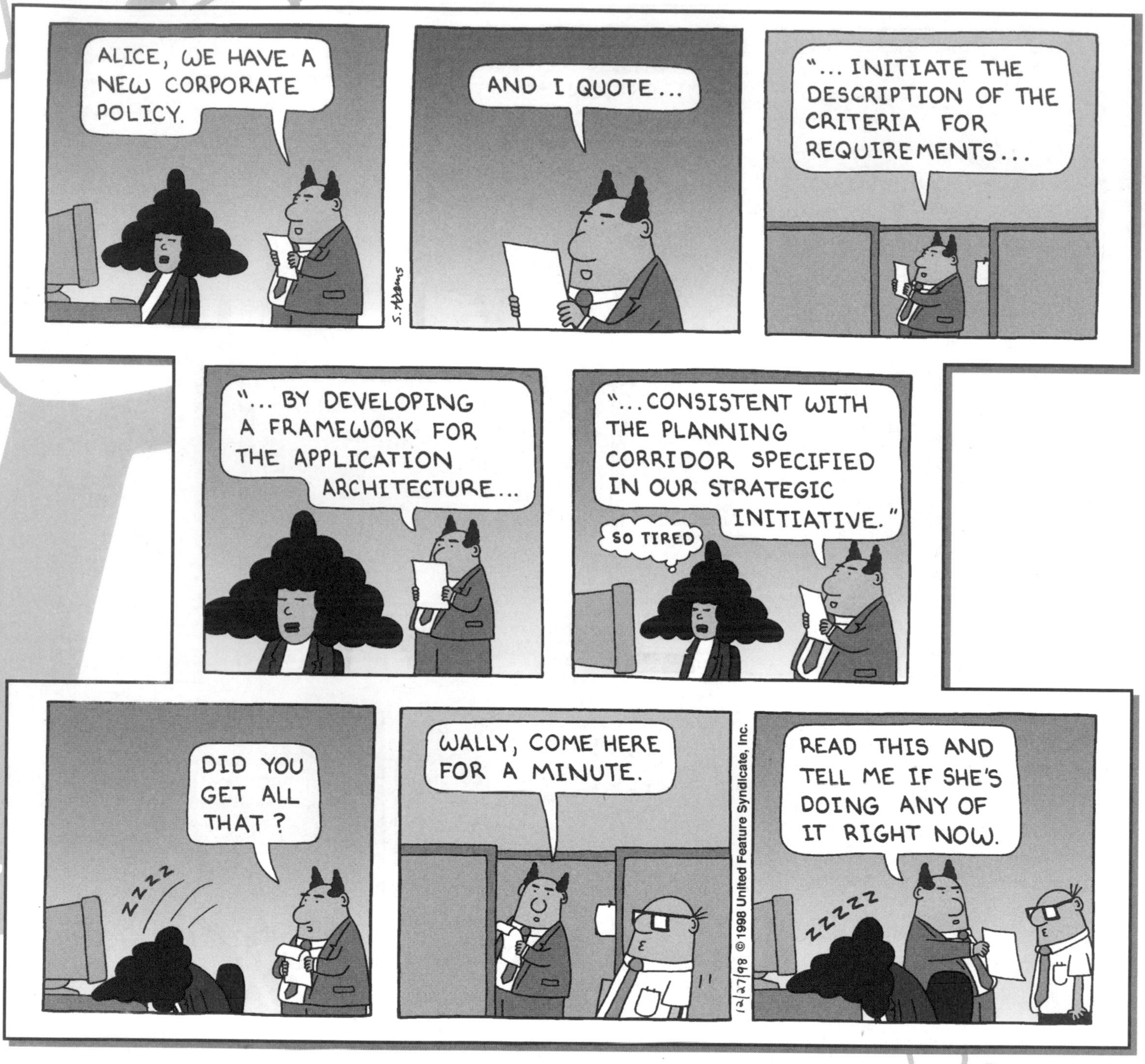
ALICE, WE HAVE A NEW CORPORATE POLICY.
S. Adams
AND I QUOTE...
"... INITIATE THE DESCRIPTION OF THE CRITERIA FOR REQUIREMENTS...
"... BY DEVELOPING A FRAMEWORK FOR THE APPLICATION ARCHITECTURE...
"... CONSISTENT WITH THE PLANNING CORRIDOR SPECIFIED IN OUR STRATEGIC INITIATIVE."
SO TIRED
DID YOU GET ALL THAT ?
ZZZZ
WALLY, COME HERE FOR A MINUTE.
12/27/98 © 1998 United Feature Syndicate, Inc.
READ THIS AND TELL ME IF SHE'S DOING ANY OF IT RIGHT NOW.
ZZZZZ

CATBERT THE DIRECTOR OF HUMAN RESOURCES

SO, YOU WANT A JOB HERE, TUBBY?

IT'S "TOBY."

DID YOU JUST CORRECT ME?

UM...

I ALONE WILL DETERMINE YOUR NAME!!

NOW, WHAT IS YOUR NAME?

TUBBY.

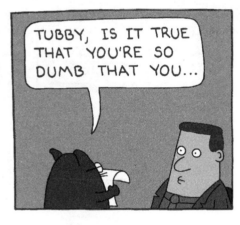

TUBBY, IS IT TRUE THAT YOU'RE SO DUMB THAT YOU...

...SENT YOUR RÉSUMÉ TO THE HUMAN RESOURCES DEPARTMENT?

DO YOU THINK THAT'S WHAT THIS DEPARTMENT DOES? LET ME SHOW YOU WHAT I DO.

I THINK I JUST BECAME AN ENTREPRENEUR.

© 1998 United Feature Syndicate, Inc.

1/3/99

I'M WRITING A COMPREHENSIVE "HOW TO" BOOK.

IN CHAPTER ONE, I TEACH PEOPLE HOW TO PICK WINNING LOTTERY NUMBERS.

CHAPTER TWO: HOW TO FIND FREE REAL ESTATE IN VERY NICE NEIGHBORHOODS.

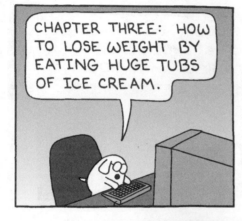

CHAPTER THREE: HOW TO LOSE WEIGHT BY EATING HUGE TUBS OF ICE CREAM.

CHAPTER FOUR: HOW TO BUILD STRONG ABS BY JOINING A GYM AND NEVER GOING.

FINALLY, HOW TO SEE ANGELS BY GIVING YOURSELF A NEAR DEATH EXPERIENCE.

THAT LAST ONE IS JUST TO GET RID OF ALL THE WITNESSES.

ON THE PLUS SIDE, I DON'T FEEL SO BAD ABOUT NOT RECYCLING.

© 1999 United Feature Syndicate, Inc.

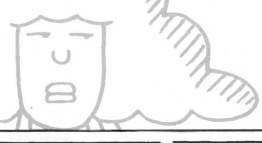

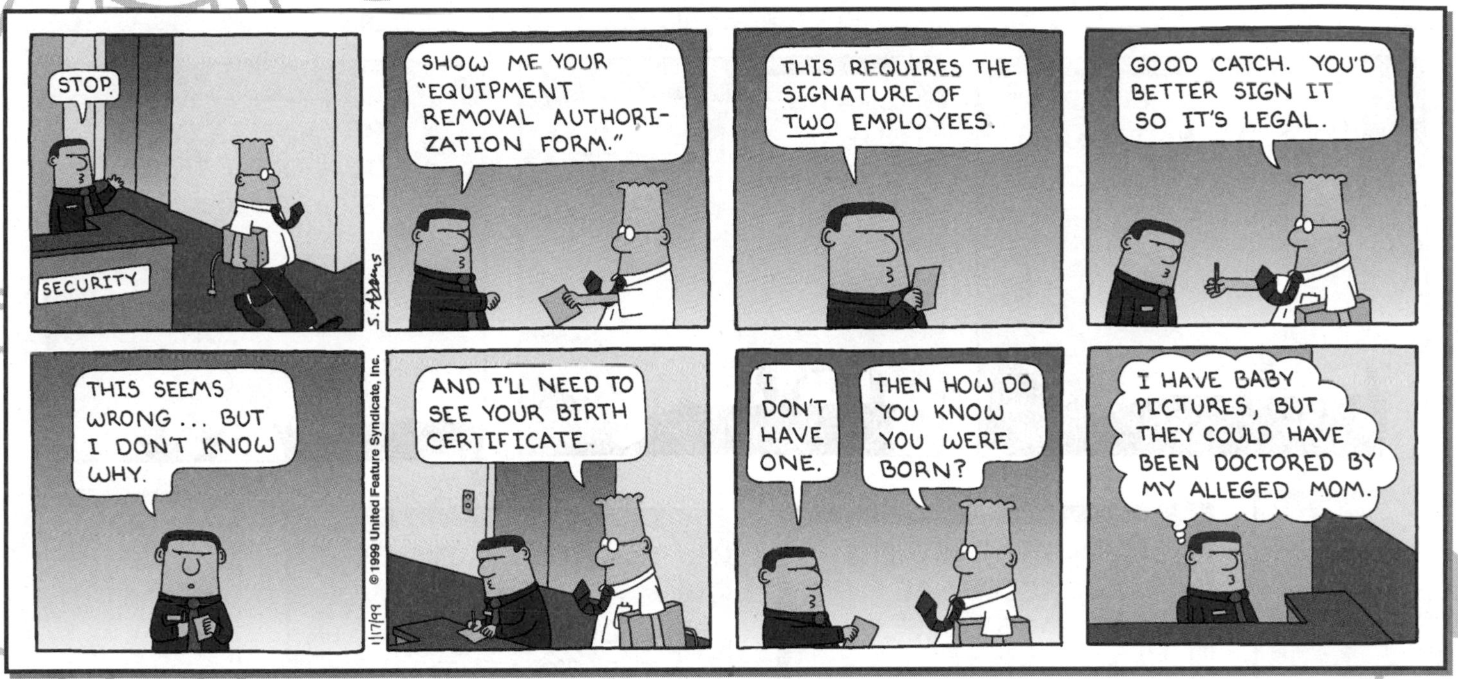
STOP.
SECURITY
SHOW ME YOUR "EQUIPMENT REMOVAL AUTHORIZATION FORM."
THIS REQUIRES THE SIGNATURE OF TWO EMPLOYEES.
GOOD CATCH. YOU'D BETTER SIGN IT SO IT'S LEGAL.
THIS SEEMS WRONG... BUT I DON'T KNOW WHY.
AND I'LL NEED TO SEE YOUR BIRTH CERTIFICATE.
I DON'T HAVE ONE.
THEN HOW DO YOU KNOW YOU WERE BORN?
I HAVE BABY PICTURES, BUT THEY COULD HAVE BEEN DOCTORED BY MY ALLEGED MOM.
S. Adams
1/17/99 © 1999 United Feature Syndicate, Inc.

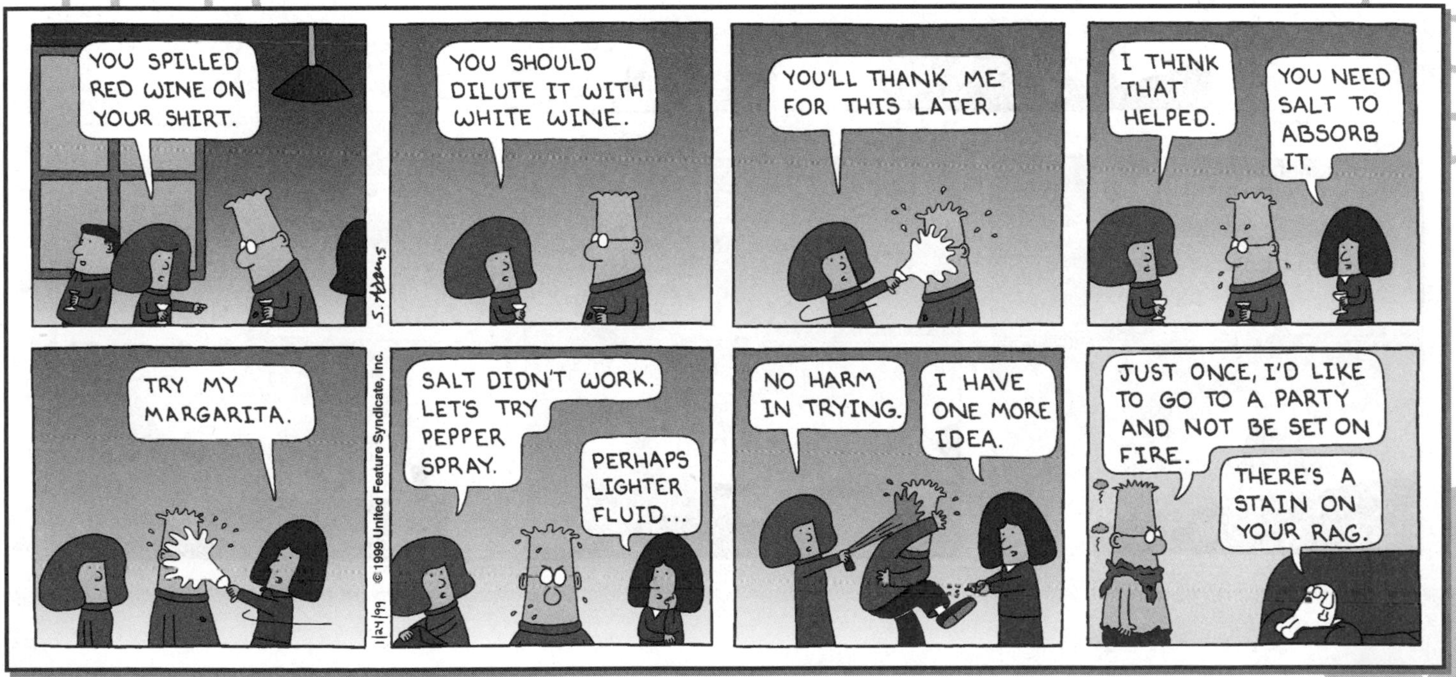
YOU SPILLED RED WINE ON YOUR SHIRT.
YOU SHOULD DILUTE IT WITH WHITE WINE.
YOU'LL THANK ME FOR THIS LATER.
I THINK THAT HELPED.
YOU NEED SALT TO ABSORB IT.
TRY MY MARGARITA.
SALT DIDN'T WORK. LET'S TRY PEPPER SPRAY.
PERHAPS LIGHTER FLUID...
NO HARM IN TRYING.
I HAVE ONE MORE IDEA.
JUST ONCE, I'D LIKE TO GO TO A PARTY AND NOT BE SET ON FIRE.
THERE'S A STAIN ON YOUR RAG.
S. Adams
1/24/99 © 1999 United Feature Syndicate, Inc.

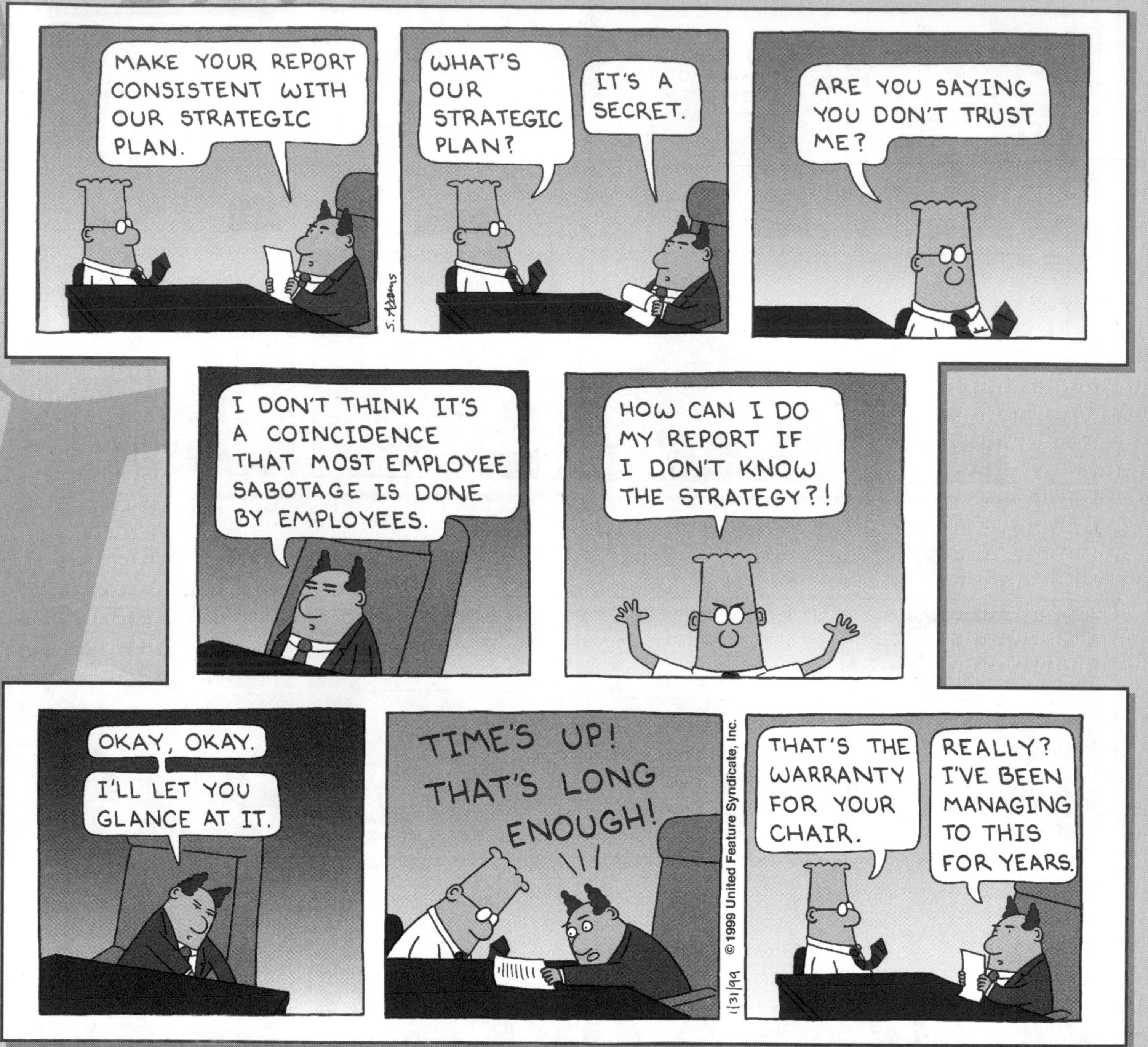

MAKE YOUR REPORT CONSISTENT WITH OUR STRATEGIC PLAN.
S. Adams
WHAT'S OUR STRATEGIC PLAN?
IT'S A SECRET.
ARE YOU SAYING YOU DON'T TRUST ME?
I DON'T THINK IT'S A COINCIDENCE THAT MOST EMPLOYEE SABOTAGE IS DONE BY EMPLOYEES.
HOW CAN I DO MY REPORT IF I DON'T KNOW THE STRATEGY?!
OKAY, OKAY.
I'LL LET YOU GLANCE AT IT.
TIME'S UP! THAT'S LONG ENOUGH!
© 1999 United Feature Syndicate, Inc.
1/31/99
THAT'S THE WARRANTY FOR YOUR CHAIR.
REALLY? I'VE BEEN MANAGING TO THIS FOR YEARS.

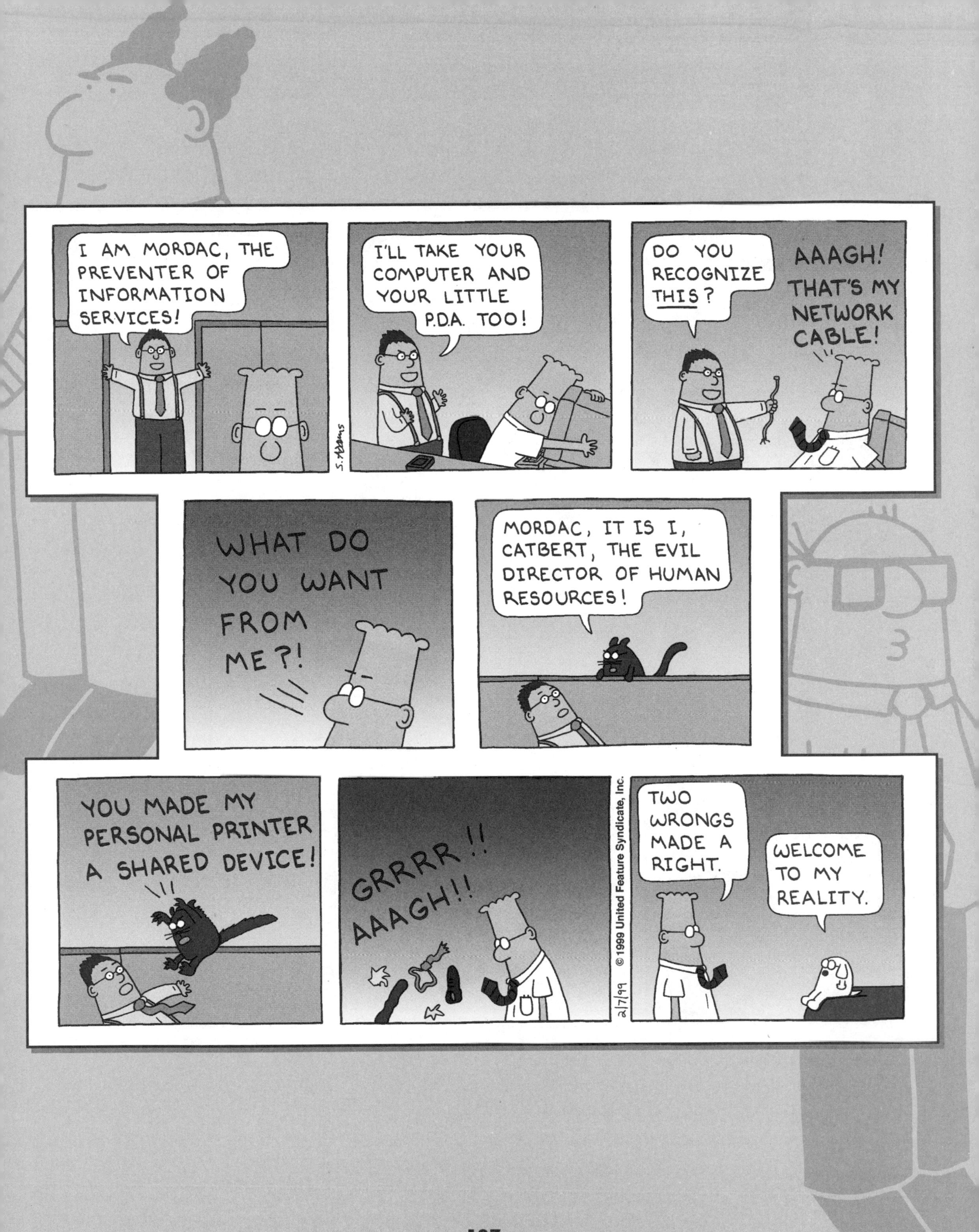
I AM MORDAC, THE PREVENTER OF INFORMATION SERVICES!
S. ADAMS
I'LL TAKE YOUR COMPUTER AND YOUR LITTLE P.D.A. TOO!
DO YOU RECOGNIZE THIS?
AAAGH! THAT'S MY NETWORK CABLE!
WHAT DO YOU WANT FROM ME?!
MORDAC, IT IS I, CATBERT, THE EVIL DIRECTOR OF HUMAN RESOURCES!
YOU MADE MY PERSONAL PRINTER A SHARED DEVICE!
GRRRR!! AAAGH!!
© 1999 United Feature Syndicate, Inc.
2/7/99
TWO WRONGS MADE A RIGHT.
WELCOME TO MY REALITY.

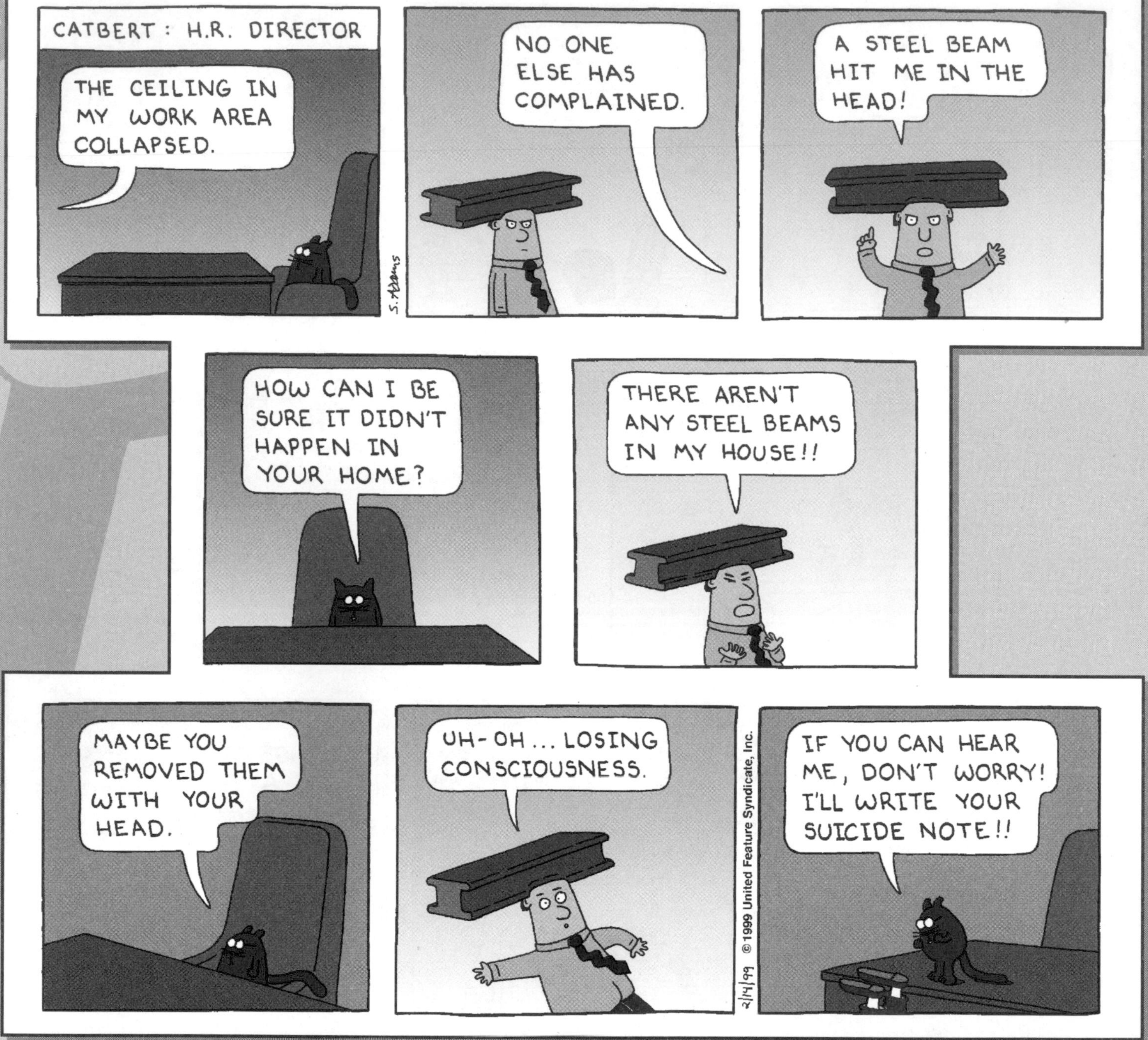
CATBERT : H.R. DIRECTOR
THE CEILING IN MY WORK AREA COLLAPSED.
NO ONE ELSE HAS COMPLAINED.
A STEEL BEAM HIT ME IN THE HEAD!
HOW CAN I BE SURE IT DIDN'T HAPPEN IN YOUR HOME?
THERE AREN'T ANY STEEL BEAMS IN MY HOUSE!!
MAYBE YOU REMOVED THEM WITH YOUR HEAD.
UH-OH ... LOSING CONSCIOUSNESS.
IF YOU CAN HEAR ME, DON'T WORRY! I'LL WRITE YOUR SUICIDE NOTE!!
2/14/99 © 1999 United Feature Syndicate, Inc.

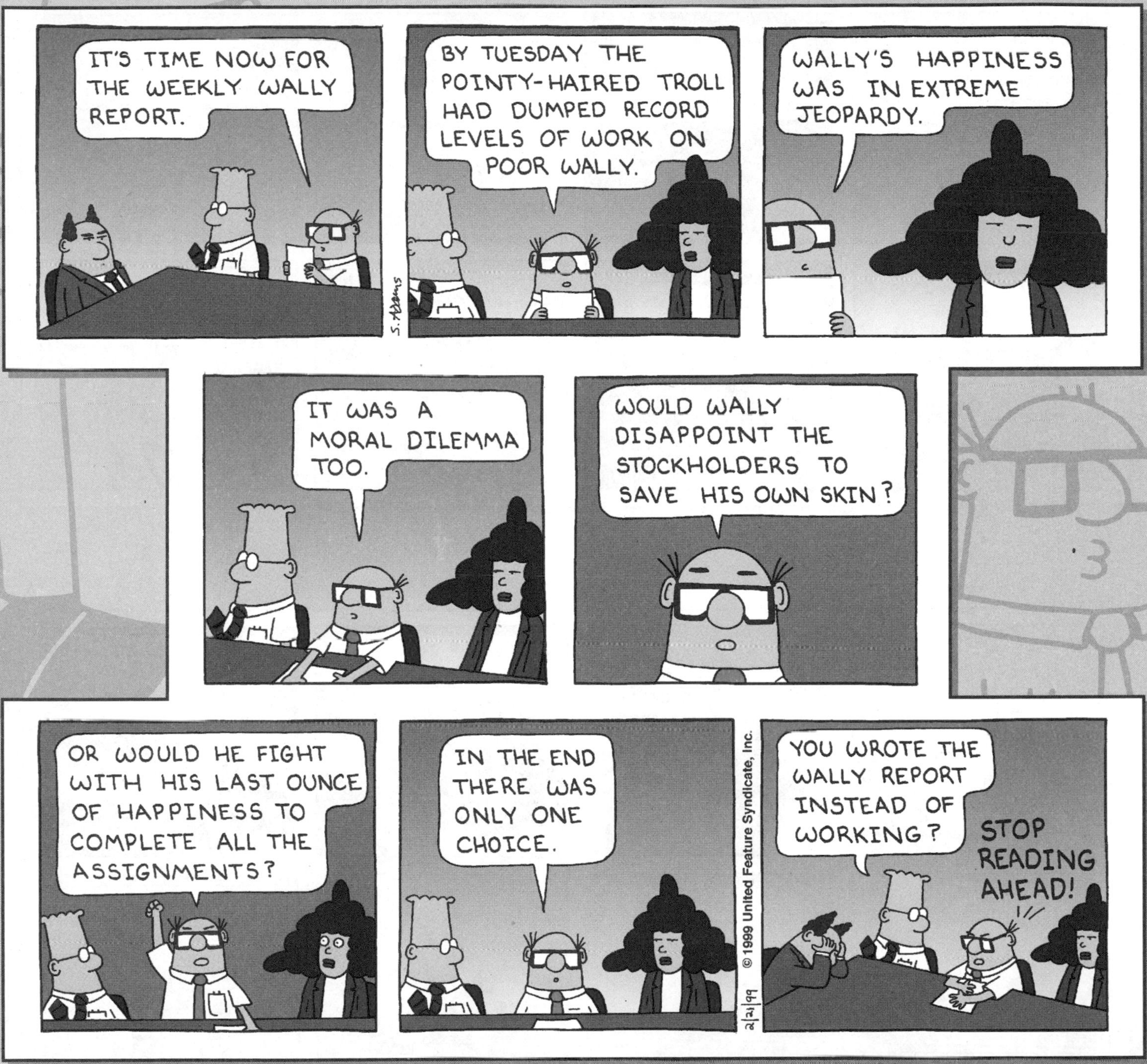
IT'S TIME NOW FOR THE WEEKLY WALLY REPORT.
S. ADAMS
BY TUESDAY THE POINTY-HAIRED TROLL HAD DUMPED RECORD LEVELS OF WORK ON POOR WALLY.
WALLY'S HAPPINESS WAS IN EXTREME JEOPARDY.
IT WAS A MORAL DILEMMA TOO.
WOULD WALLY DISAPPOINT THE STOCKHOLDERS TO SAVE HIS OWN SKIN?
OR WOULD HE FIGHT WITH HIS LAST OUNCE OF HAPPINESS TO COMPLETE ALL THE ASSIGNMENTS?
IN THE END THERE WAS ONLY ONE CHOICE.
© 1999 United Feature Syndicate, Inc.
2/21/99
YOU WROTE THE WALLY REPORT INSTEAD OF WORKING?
STOP READING AHEAD!

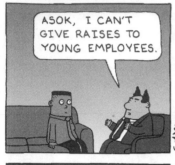

ASOK, I CAN'T GIVE RAISES TO YOUNG EMPLOYEES.
BECAUSE AS SOON AS YOU GET A FEW DOLLARS IN YOUR POCKET...
YOU BUY SMALL MOTORCYCLES AND DISAPPEAR IN THE NIGHT.
I KNOW THAT'S A GENERALIZATION.
SOME OF YOU PREFER THE CRACK COCAINE.
THE GOOD NEWS IS THAT I'M WILLING TO BE YOUR MENTOR.
AAAGH! I GOT DOUBLE EIGHT HUNDREDS ON MY SAT!!! FOR WHAT?!!
SOMETIMES WHEN I'M IN A BAD MOOD I TICKLE MY OWN FEET.
S. Adams
2/28/99 © 1999 United Feature Syndicate, Inc.

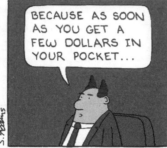

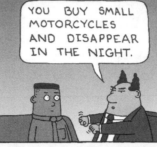

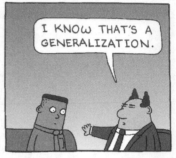

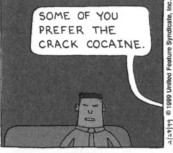

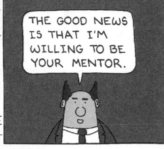

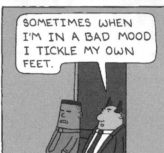

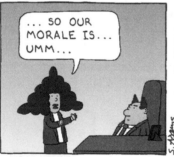

... SO OUR MORALE IS... UMM...
WHAT'S THAT ON YOUR DESK?
IT'S A FAMILY PICTURE.
I MIGHT BE WRONG, BUT I THINK IT'S ONLY A PICTURE OF YOU.
THE REST OF THE FAMILY IS HARD TO LOOK AT.
I SEE NO REASON I SHOULD SUFFER.
NOW WHAT WAS YOUR QUESTION ABOUT MORALE?
ALICE?
WE'RE SURROUNDED BY FREAKS.
S. Adams
3/7/99 © 1999 United Feature Syndicate, Inc.

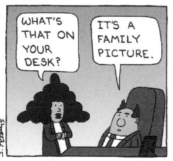

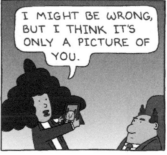

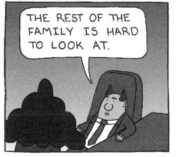

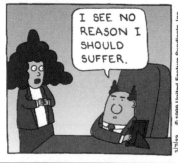

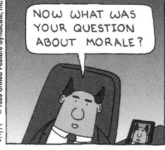

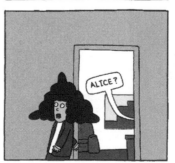

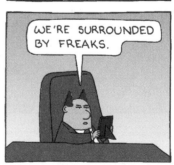

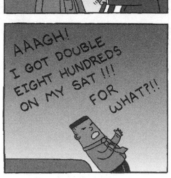

I'M FROM THE DOGBERT WRECKING COMPANY.
S. Adams
I'M RUNNING A SPECIAL ON CRUSHING YOUR BOSS'S NEW CAR IN THE PARKING LOT.
WHAT DOES IT COST?
THE FIRST ONE IS FREE.
IF YOU'RE SATISFIED, I HOPE YOU'LL CONSIDER MY MONTHLY PLAN.
IT'S THE RED ONE. HE BRAGS ABOUT IT EVERY DAY.
AND WHEN YOU SPEND THAT MUCH, THE DEALER GIVES YOU A FREE MODEL OF YOUR CAR!
BEEP BEEP BEEP
© 1999 United Feature Syndicate, Inc.
3/14/99
AND NEXT MONTH CAN YOU CRUSH THE LITTLE ONE ON HIS DESK TOO?

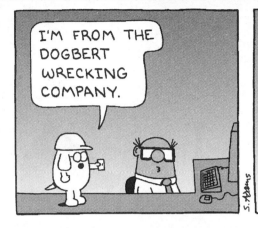

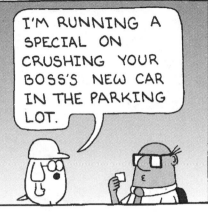

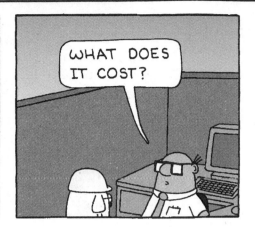

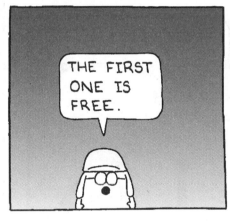

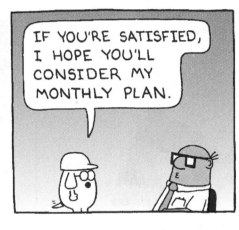

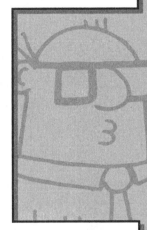

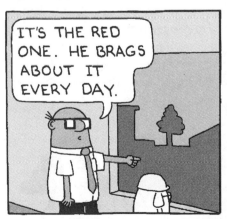

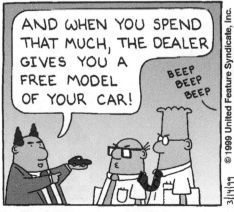

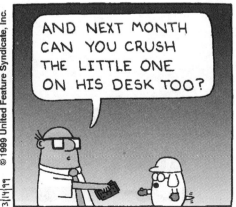

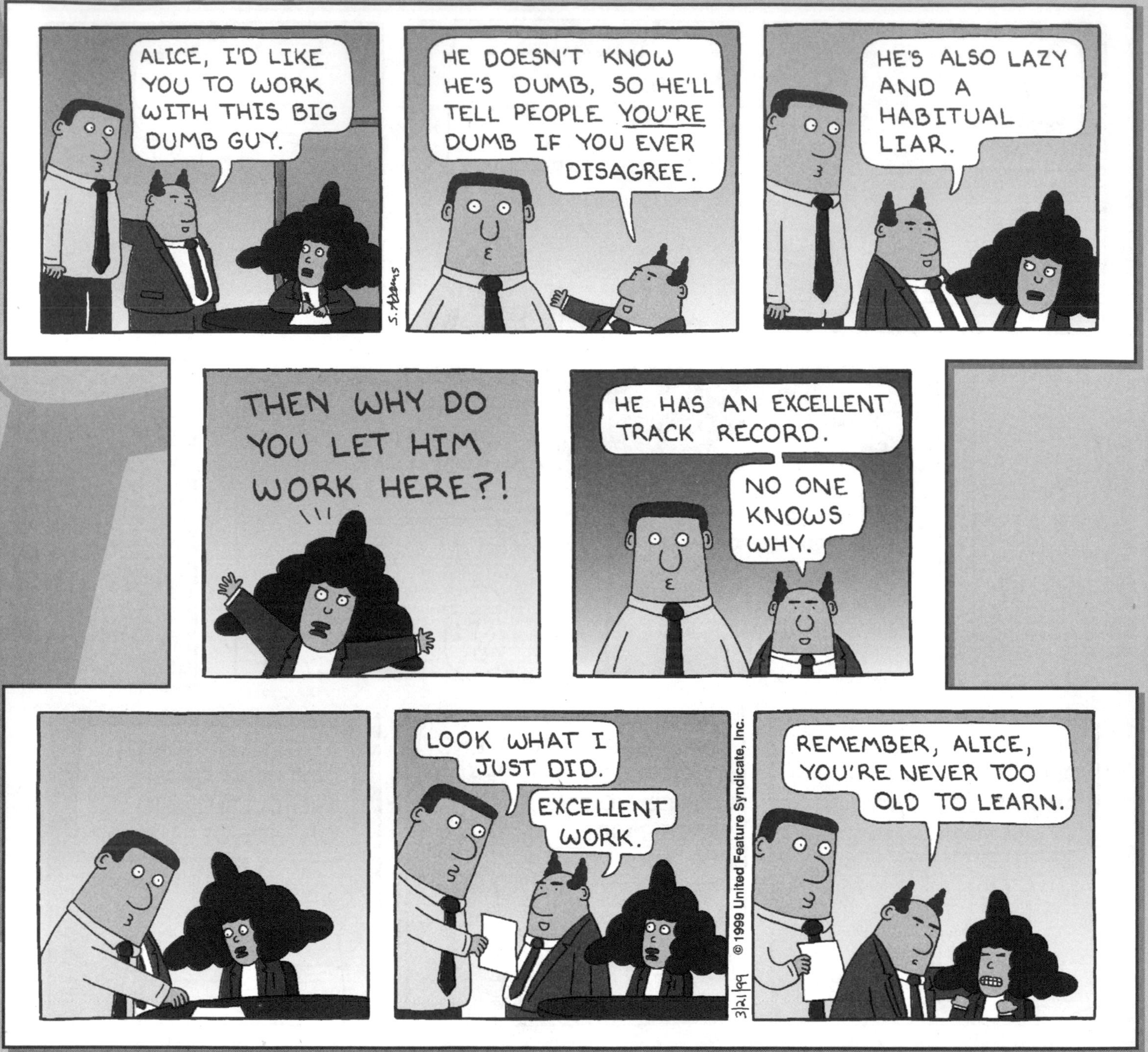

ALICE, I'D LIKE YOU TO WORK WITH THIS BIG DUMB GUY.
S. Adams
HE DOESN'T KNOW HE'S DUMB, SO HE'LL TELL PEOPLE YOU'RE DUMB IF YOU EVER DISAGREE.
HE'S ALSO LAZY AND A HABITUAL LIAR.
THEN WHY DO YOU LET HIM WORK HERE?!
HE HAS AN EXCELLENT TRACK RECORD.
NO ONE KNOWS WHY.
LOOK WHAT I JUST DID.
EXCELLENT WORK.
© 1999 United Feature Syndicate, Inc.
3/21/99
REMEMBER, ALICE, YOU'RE NEVER TOO OLD TO LEARN.

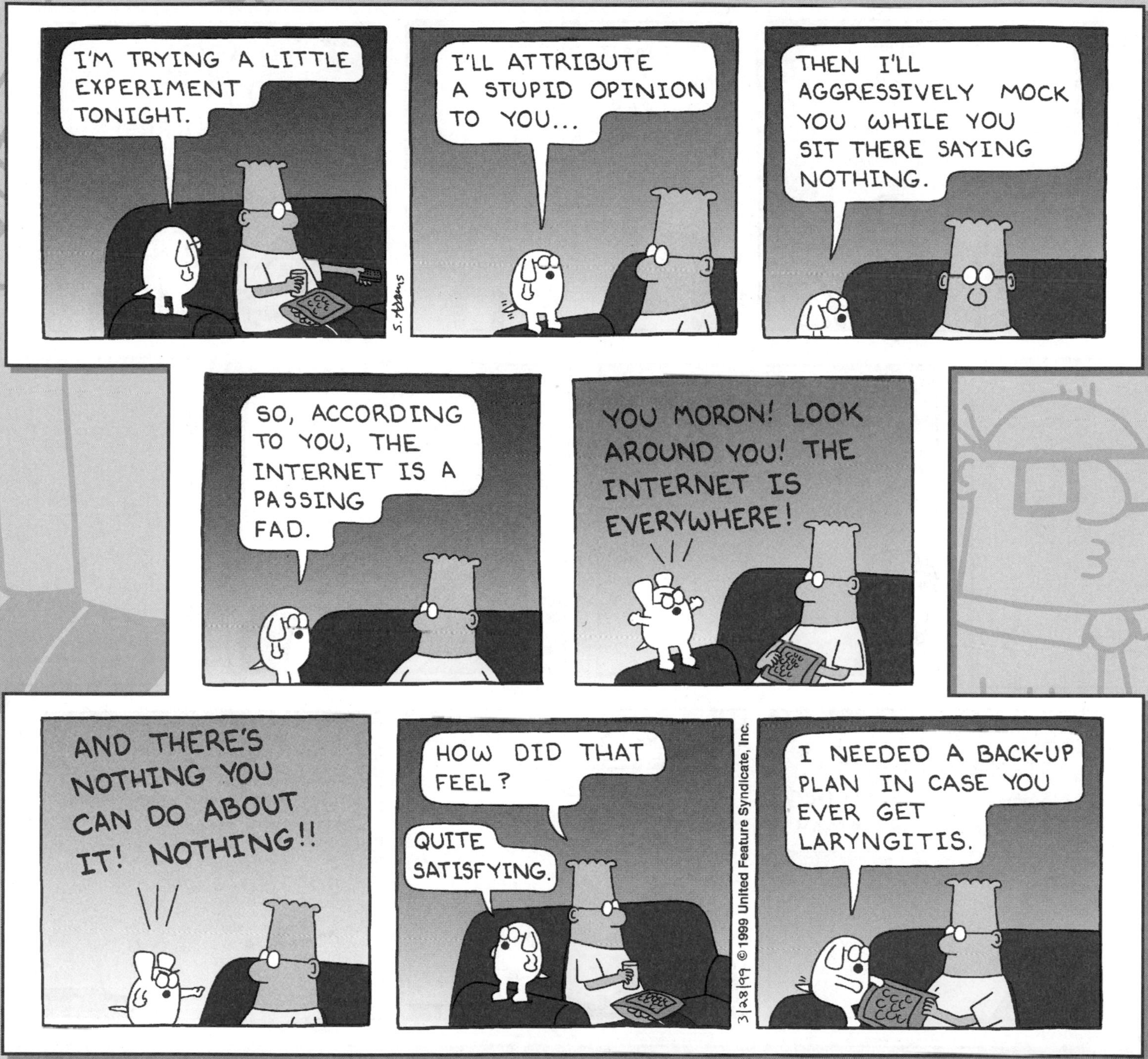
I'M TRYING A LITTLE EXPERIMENT TONIGHT.
S. ADAMS
I'LL ATTRIBUTE A STUPID OPINION TO YOU...
THEN I'LL AGGRESSIVELY MOCK YOU WHILE YOU SIT THERE SAYING NOTHING.
SO, ACCORDING TO YOU, THE INTERNET IS A PASSING FAD.
YOU MORON! LOOK AROUND YOU! THE INTERNET IS EVERYWHERE!
AND THERE'S NOTHING YOU CAN DO ABOUT IT! NOTHING!!
HOW DID THAT FEEL?
QUITE SATISFYING.
3/28/99 © 1999 United Feature Syndicate, Inc.
I NEEDED A BACK-UP PLAN IN CASE YOU EVER GET LARYNGITIS.

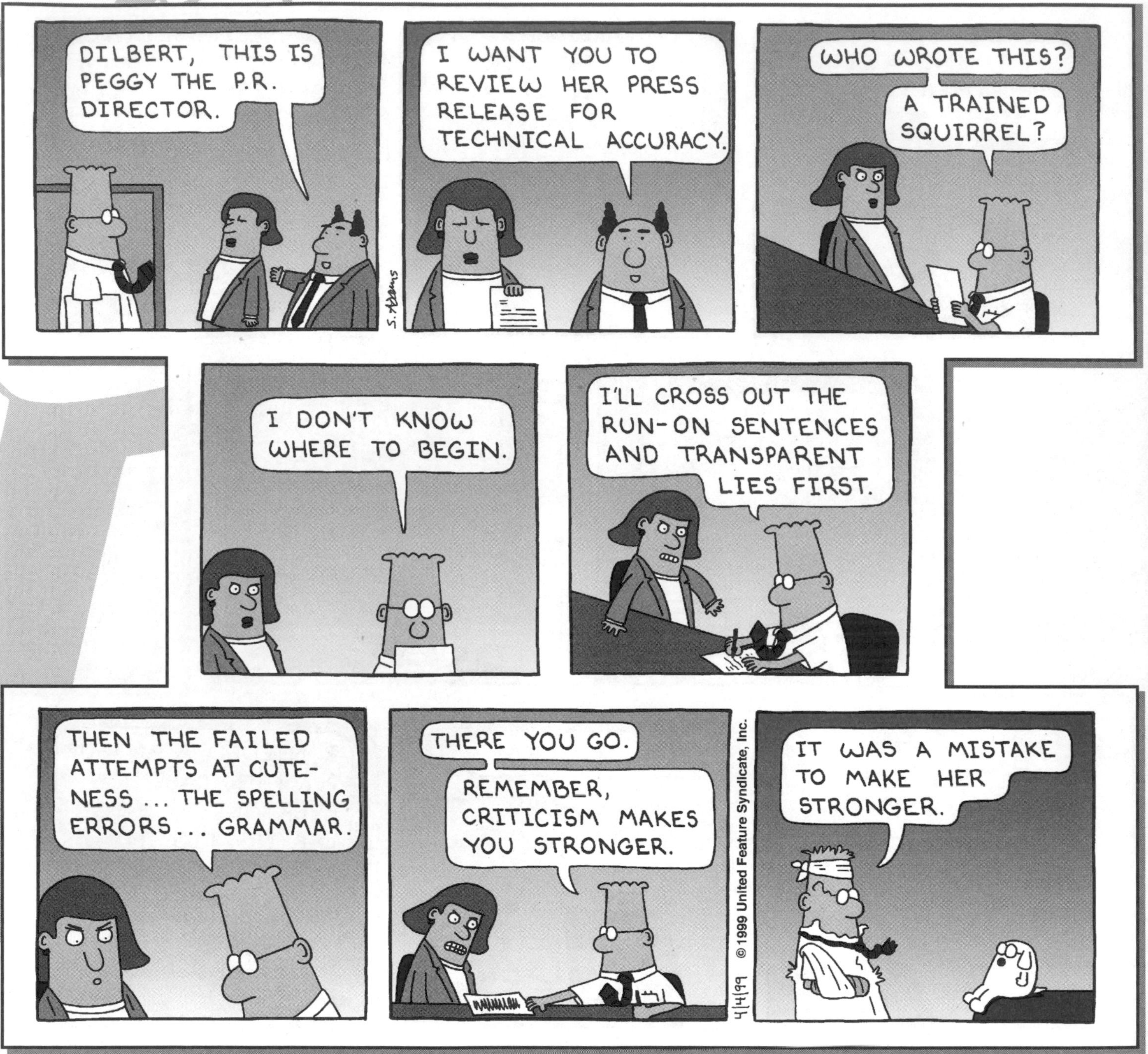
DILBERT, THIS IS PEGGY THE P.R. DIRECTOR.
S. Adams
I WANT YOU TO REVIEW HER PRESS RELEASE FOR TECHNICAL ACCURACY.
WHO WROTE THIS?
A TRAINED SQUIRREL?
I DON'T KNOW WHERE TO BEGIN.
I'LL CROSS OUT THE RUN-ON SENTENCES AND TRANSPARENT LIES FIRST.
THEN THE FAILED ATTEMPTS AT CUTE-NESS ... THE SPELLING ERRORS... GRAMMAR.
THERE YOU GO.
REMEMBER, CRITICISM MAKES YOU STRONGER.
4/4/99 © 1999 United Feature Syndicate, Inc.
IT WAS A MISTAKE TO MAKE HER STRONGER.

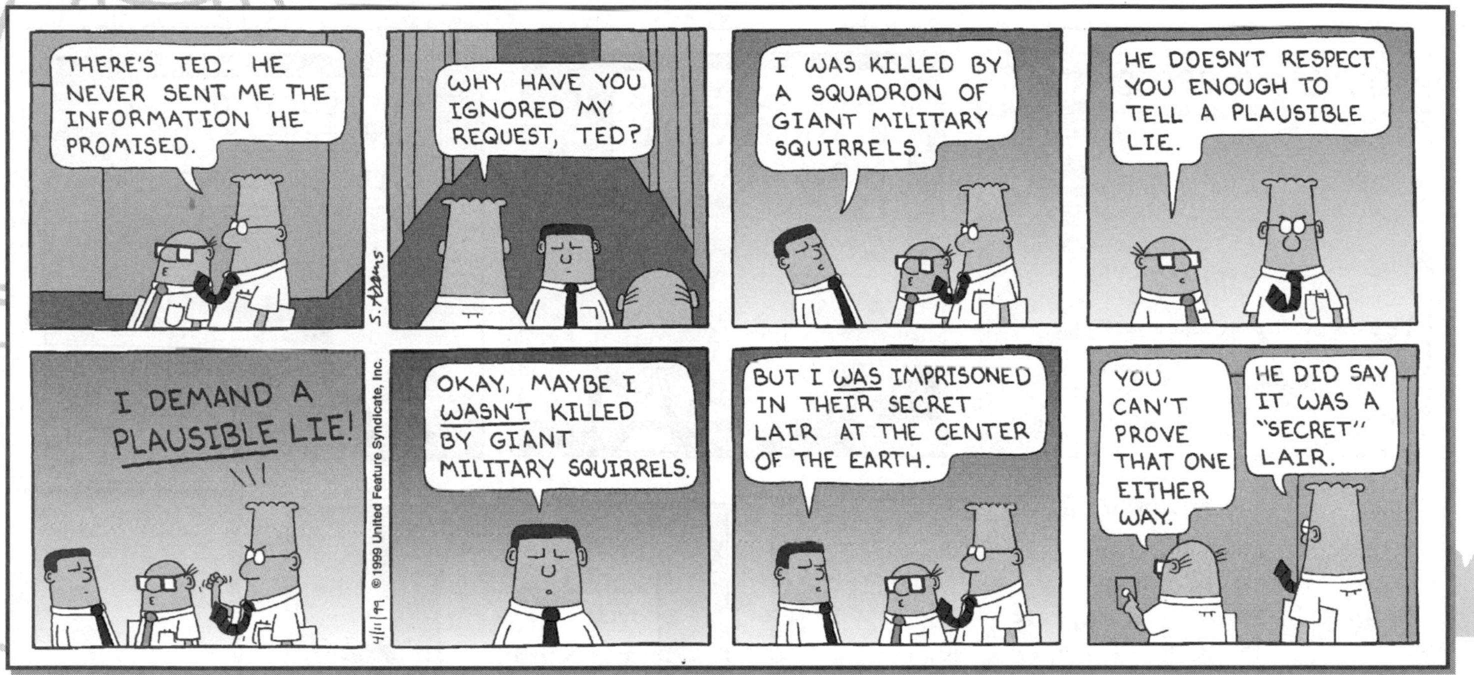
THERE'S TED. HE NEVER SENT ME THE INFORMATION HE PROMISED.
WHY HAVE YOU IGNORED MY REQUEST, TED?
I WAS KILLED BY A SQUADRON OF GIANT MILITARY SQUIRRELS.
HE DOESN'T RESPECT YOU ENOUGH TO TELL A PLAUSIBLE LIE.
I DEMAND A PLAUSIBLE LIE!
OKAY, MAYBE I WASN'T KILLED BY GIANT MILITARY SQUIRRELS.
BUT I WAS IMPRISONED IN THEIR SECRET LAIR AT THE CENTER OF THE EARTH.
YOU CAN'T PROVE THAT ONE EITHER WAY.
HE DID SAY IT WAS A "SECRET" LAIR.
S. Adams
© 1999 United Feature Syndicate, Inc.
4/11/99

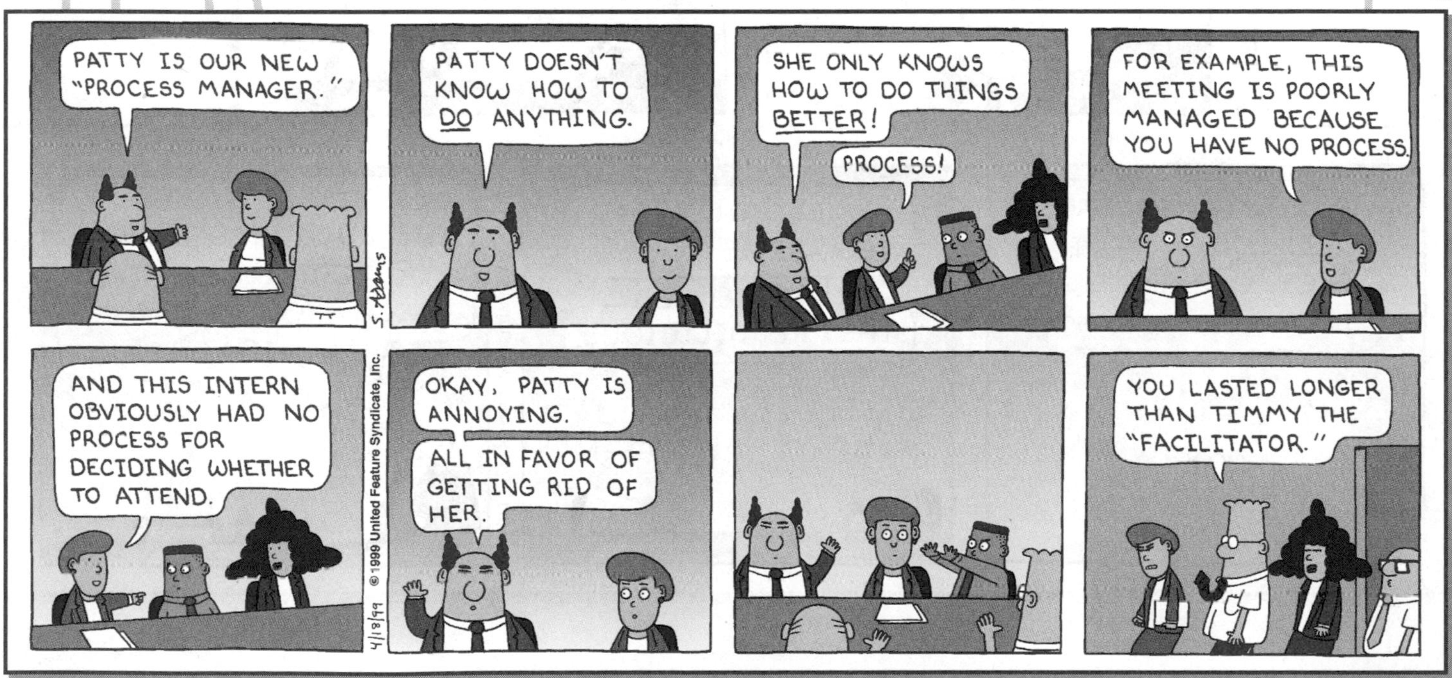
PATTY IS OUR NEW "PROCESS MANAGER."
PATTY DOESN'T KNOW HOW TO DO ANYTHING.
SHE ONLY KNOWS HOW TO DO THINGS BETTER!
PROCESS!
FOR EXAMPLE, THIS MEETING IS POORLY MANAGED BECAUSE YOU HAVE NO PROCESS.
AND THIS INTERN OBVIOUSLY HAD NO PROCESS FOR DECIDING WHETHER TO ATTEND.
OKAY, PATTY IS ANNOYING.
ALL IN FAVOR OF GETTING RID OF HER.
YOU LASTED LONGER THAN TIMMY THE "FACILITATOR."
S. Adams
© 1999 United Feature Syndicate, Inc.
4/18/99

DOGBERT PRESENTS
MANAGING BY ANALOGIES
IT'S EASY!
S. Adams
WE'LL SOLVE OUR DISTRIBUTION PROBLEM THE ESKIMO WAY.
HUH?
THE ESKIMOS GATHER ICE ALL WINTER LONG.
LATER, DURING THE LEAN SUMMER MONTHS, THE ESKIMOS EAT THE ICE THEY STORED.
WE'LL DO THE SAME THING!
BUT...THE ESKIMOS WOULD STARVE IF THEY ONLY ATE ICE.
MAYBE THEY EAT PENGUINS TOO.
THEY'RE DELICIOUS.
4/25/99 © 1999 United Feature Syndicate, Inc.
DID YOU KNOW THAT THE ZOO CAN BAN YOU FOR LIFE IF THEY CATCH YOU USING A HIBACHI?

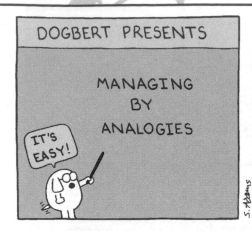

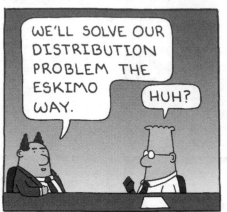

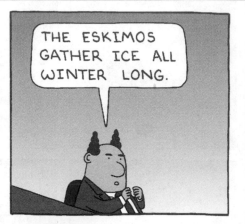

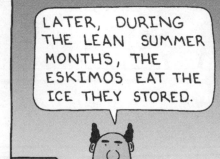

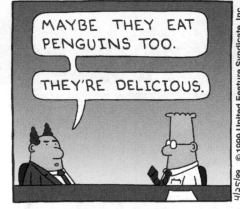

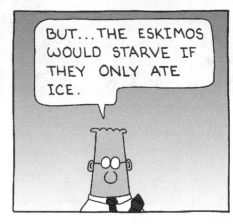

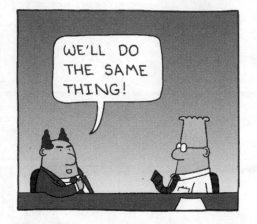

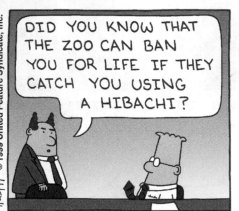

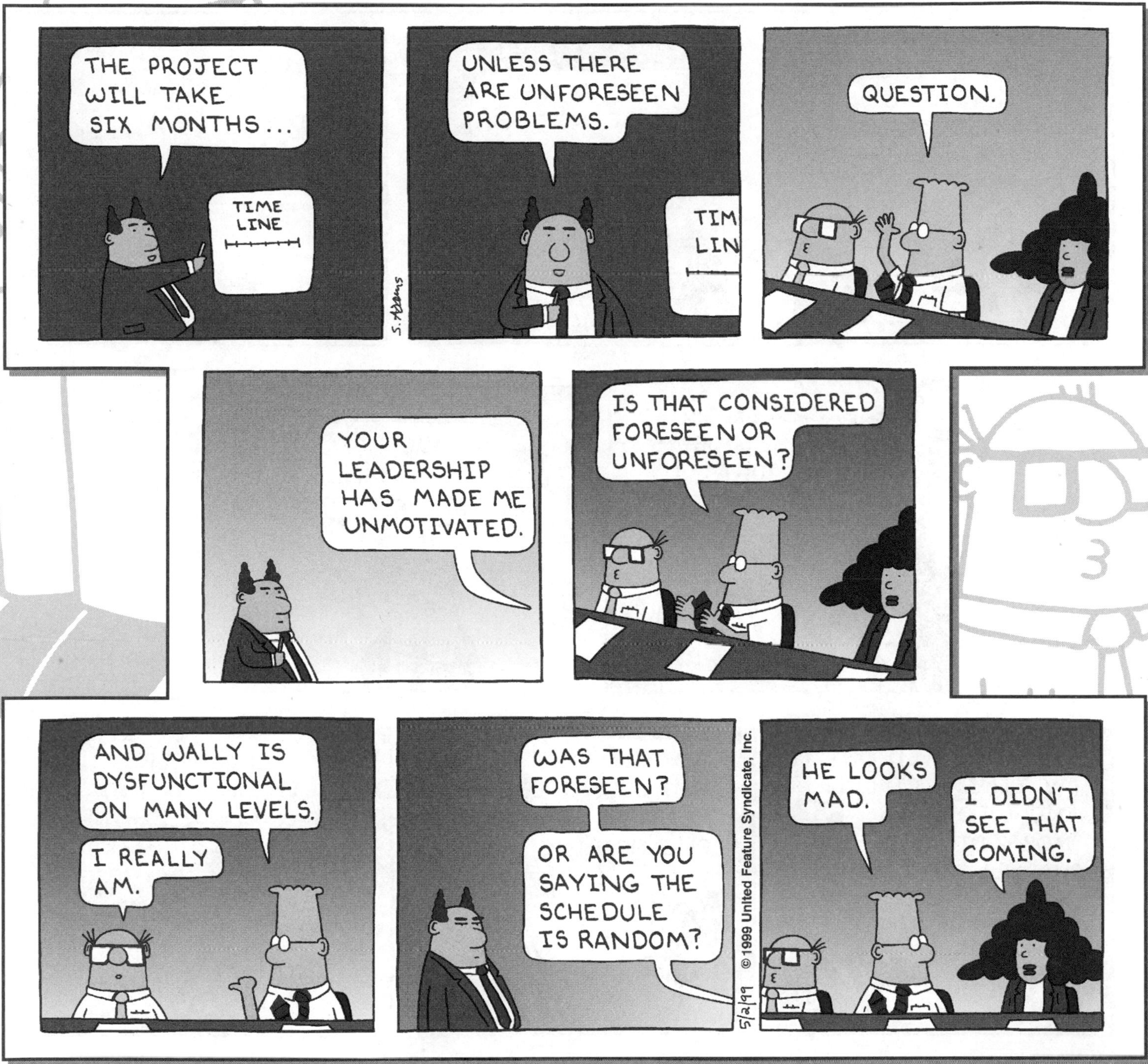
THE PROJECT WILL TAKE SIX MONTHS...
TIME LINE
S. Adams
UNLESS THERE ARE UNFORESEEN PROBLEMS.
TIM LIN
QUESTION.
YOUR LEADERSHIP HAS MADE ME UNMOTIVATED.
IS THAT CONSIDERED FORESEEN OR UNFORESEEN?
AND WALLY IS DYSFUNCTIONAL ON MANY LEVELS.
I REALLY AM.
WAS THAT FORESEEN?
OR ARE YOU SAYING THE SCHEDULE IS RANDOM?
© 1999 United Feature Syndicate, Inc.
5/2/99
HE LOOKS MAD.
I DIDN'T SEE THAT COMING.

I MADE A FEW UPGRADES TO YOUR DESIGN, ALICE.

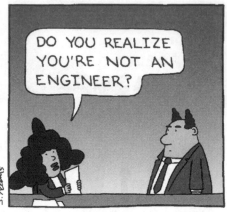

DO YOU REALIZE YOU'RE NOT AN ENGINEER?

I'M BETTER! I'M A WELL-ROUNDED GRADUATE OF A LIBERAL ARTS COLLEGE.

THE BROAD EXPOSURE TO DIVERSE TOPICS MADE ME WHAT I AM TODAY.

A MODERN RENAISSANCE MAN.

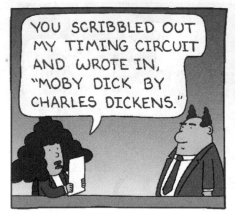

YOU SCRIBBLED OUT MY TIMING CIRCUIT AND WROTE IN, "MOBY DICK BY CHARLES DICKENS."

EXACTLY. I'LL BET YOU DIDN'T LEARN THAT IN YOUR ENGINEERING CLASSES!

POOR ENGINEERS; THEIR WORLD IS SO SMALL.

© 1999 United Feature Syndicate, Inc.

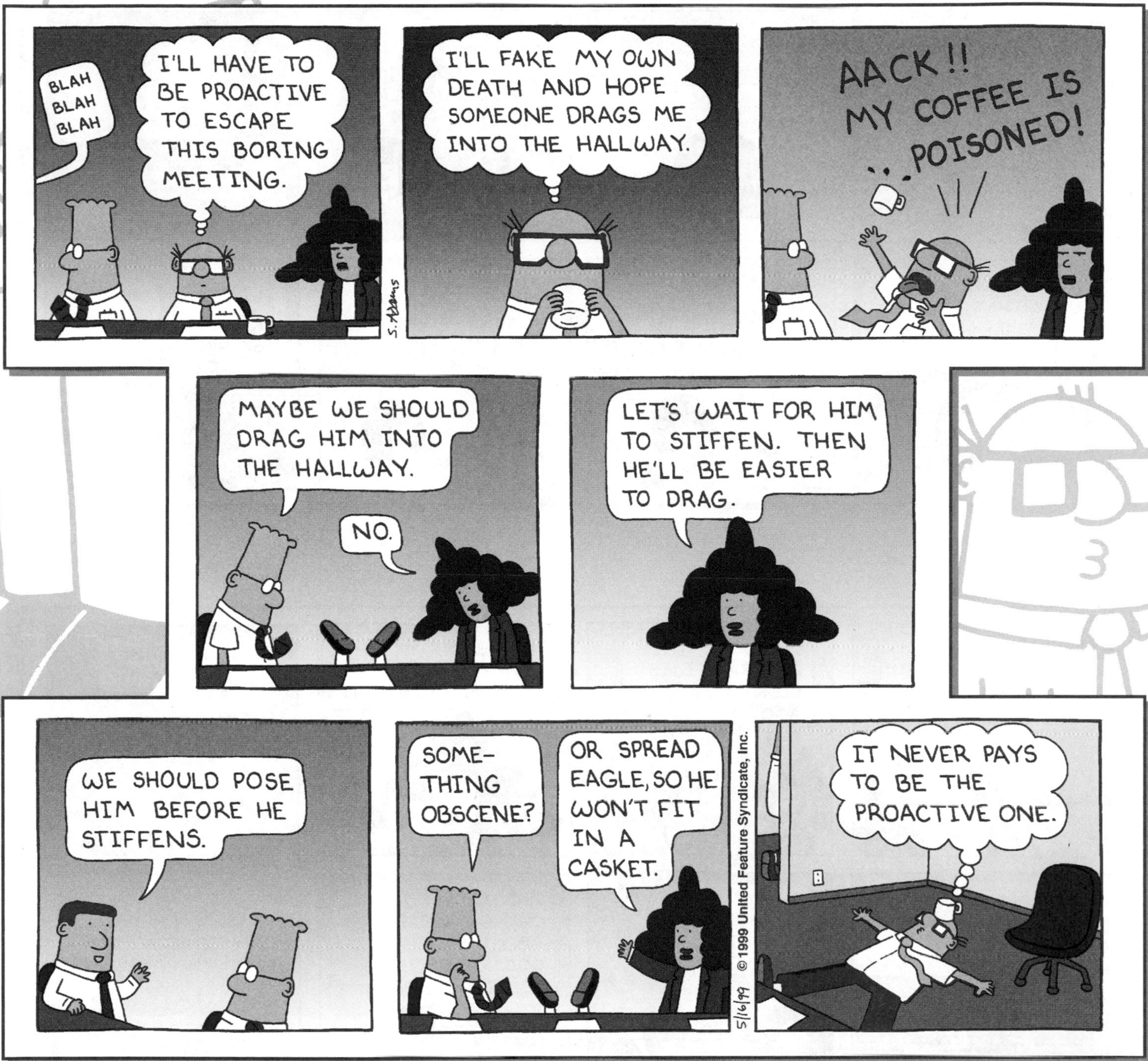
BLAH BLAH BLAH
I'LL HAVE TO BE PROACTIVE TO ESCAPE THIS BORING MEETING.
S. Adams
I'LL FAKE MY OWN DEATH AND HOPE SOMEONE DRAGS ME INTO THE HALLWAY.
AACK!! MY COFFEE IS POISONED!
MAYBE WE SHOULD DRAG HIM INTO THE HALLWAY.
NO.
LET'S WAIT FOR HIM TO STIFFEN. THEN HE'LL BE EASIER TO DRAG.
WE SHOULD POSE HIM BEFORE HE STIFFENS.
SOME-THING OBSCENE?
OR SPREAD EAGLE, SO HE WON'T FIT IN A CASKET.
© 1999 United Feature Syndicate, Inc.
5/16/99
IT NEVER PAYS TO BE THE PROACTIVE ONE.

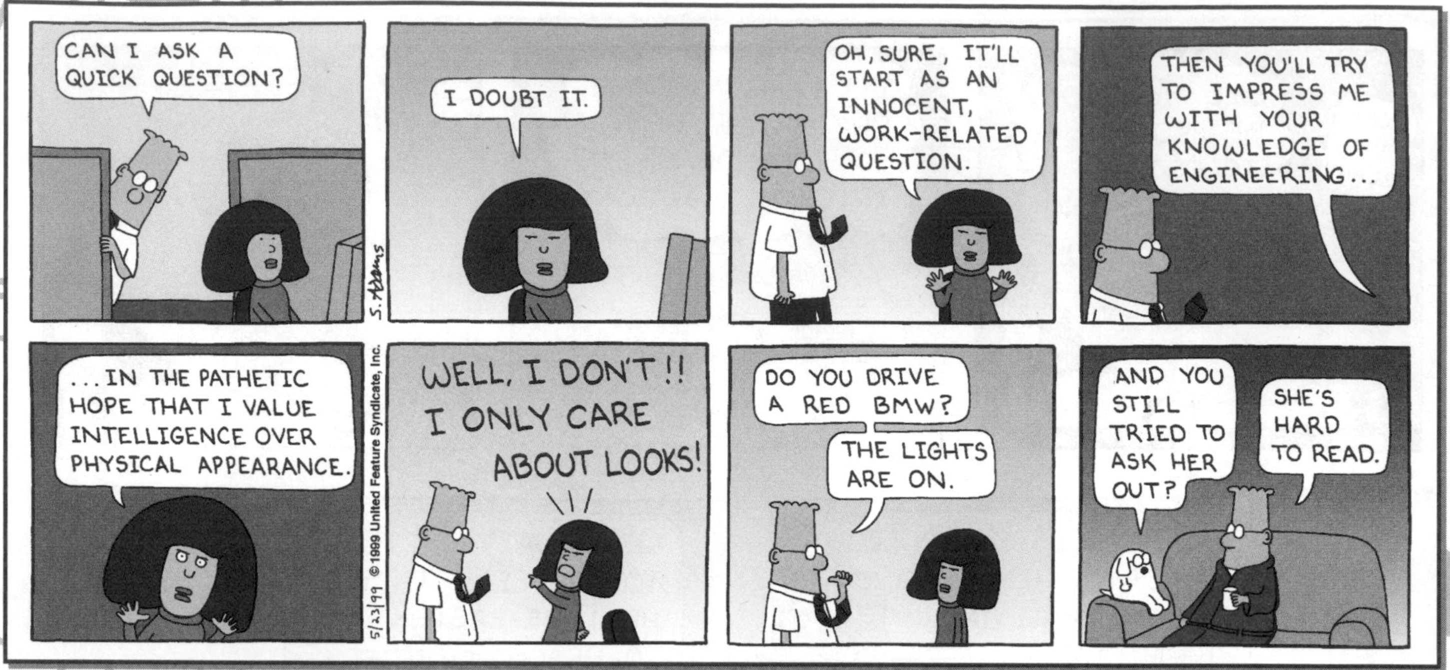
CAN I ASK A QUICK QUESTION?
I DOUBT IT.
OH, SURE, IT'LL START AS AN INNOCENT, WORK-RELATED QUESTION.
THEN YOU'LL TRY TO IMPRESS ME WITH YOUR KNOWLEDGE OF ENGINEERING...
...IN THE PATHETIC HOPE THAT I VALUE INTELLIGENCE OVER PHYSICAL APPEARANCE.
WELL, I DON'T!! I ONLY CARE ABOUT LOOKS!
DO YOU DRIVE A RED BMW?
THE LIGHTS ARE ON.
AND YOU STILL TRIED TO ASK HER OUT?
SHE'S HARD TO READ.
S. Adams
5/23/99 © 1999 United Feature Syndicate, Inc.

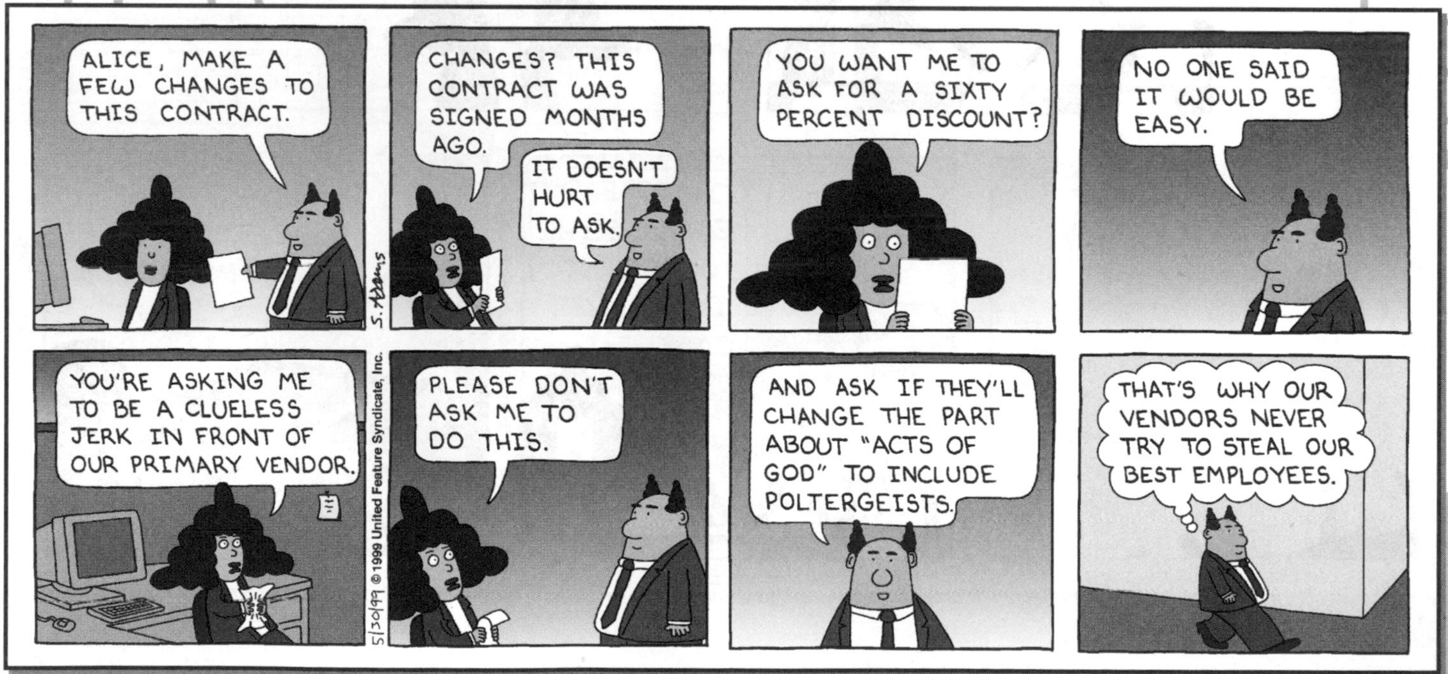
ALICE, MAKE A FEW CHANGES TO THIS CONTRACT.
CHANGES? THIS CONTRACT WAS SIGNED MONTHS AGO.
IT DOESN'T HURT TO ASK.
YOU WANT ME TO ASK FOR A SIXTY PERCENT DISCOUNT?
NO ONE SAID IT WOULD BE EASY.
YOU'RE ASKING ME TO BE A CLUELESS JERK IN FRONT OF OUR PRIMARY VENDOR.
PLEASE DON'T ASK ME TO DO THIS.
AND ASK IF THEY'LL CHANGE THE PART ABOUT "ACTS OF GOD" TO INCLUDE POLTERGEISTS.
THAT'S WHY OUR VENDORS NEVER TRY TO STEAL OUR BEST EMPLOYEES.
S. Adams
5/30/99 © 1999 United Feature Syndicate, Inc.

E-MAIL TWO COPIES TO ME WHEN YOU'RE DONE.
S. Adams
TWO COPIES?
IT'S E-MAIL.
SO?
NEVER MIND.
I'LL E-MAIL TWO COPIES.
AND FAX A COPY ON GREEN PAPER FOR MY FILES.
GREEN? IT'S A FAX!
AND BRING ME A HARD COPY OF THE INTERNET SO I CAN DO SOME SERIOUS SURFING.
MOTIVATION ... GONE ... LOSING ... CONSCIOUSNESS ...
6/6/99 © 1999 United Feature Syndicate, Inc.
HOW DID I END UP WITH ALL THE LAZY EMPLOYEES?

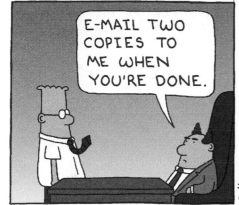

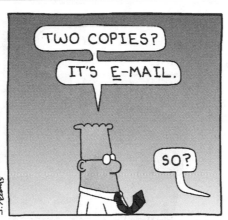

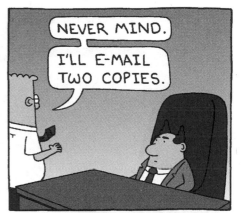

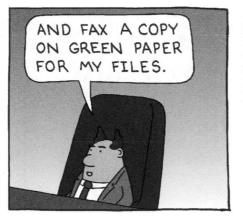

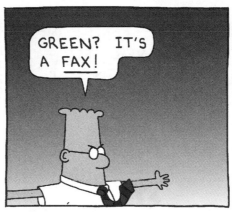

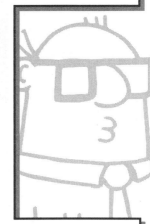

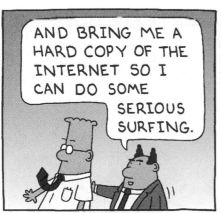

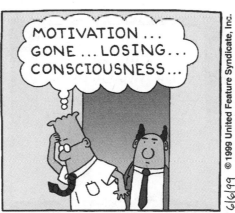

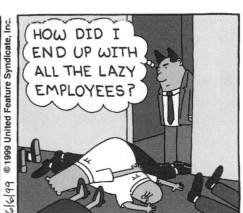

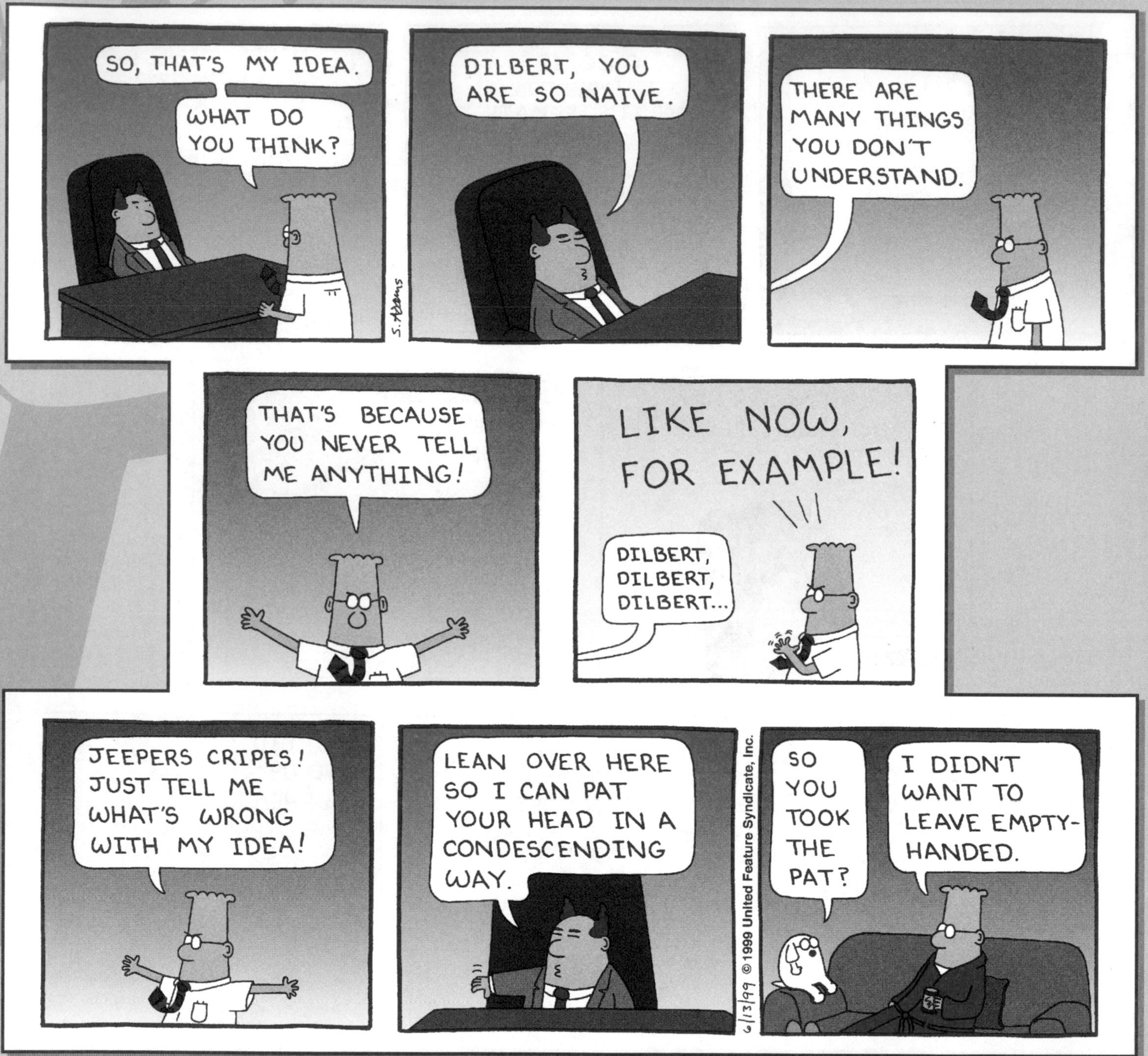

SO, THAT'S MY IDEA.
WHAT DO YOU THINK?
S. ADAMS
DILBERT, YOU ARE SO NAIVE.
THERE ARE MANY THINGS YOU DON'T UNDERSTAND.
THAT'S BECAUSE YOU NEVER TELL ME ANYTHING!
LIKE NOW, FOR EXAMPLE!
DILBERT, DILBERT, DILBERT...
JEEPERS CRIPES! JUST TELL ME WHAT'S WRONG WITH MY IDEA!
LEAN OVER HERE SO I CAN PAT YOUR HEAD IN A CONDESCENDING WAY.
6/13/99 © 1999 United Feature Syndicate, Inc.
SO YOU TOOK THE PAT?
I DIDN'T WANT TO LEAVE EMPTY-HANDED.

CATBERT: EVIL DIRECTOR OF HUMAN RESOURCES

I HIRED A NEW ENGINEER FOR YOUR PROJECT.

HE'S NEVER BEEN AN ENGINEER BEFORE.

BUT YOU'RE AN ENGINEER, SO HOW HARD COULD IT BE?

AND HE'S CHEAP! I'LL GET A HUGE RAISE FOR BEING UNDER BUDGET.

AND YOUR PROJECT WILL FAIL! HA HA HA HA!

UH-OH. I LAUGHED MYSELF FULL OF STATIC ELECTRICITY.

FUZZY. CUTE.

ZAP!

© 1999 United Feature Syndicate, Inc.

HE'S DEAD. NOW WHAT?

I GUESS YOU'LL HAVE TO DRAG HIM TO MEETINGS.

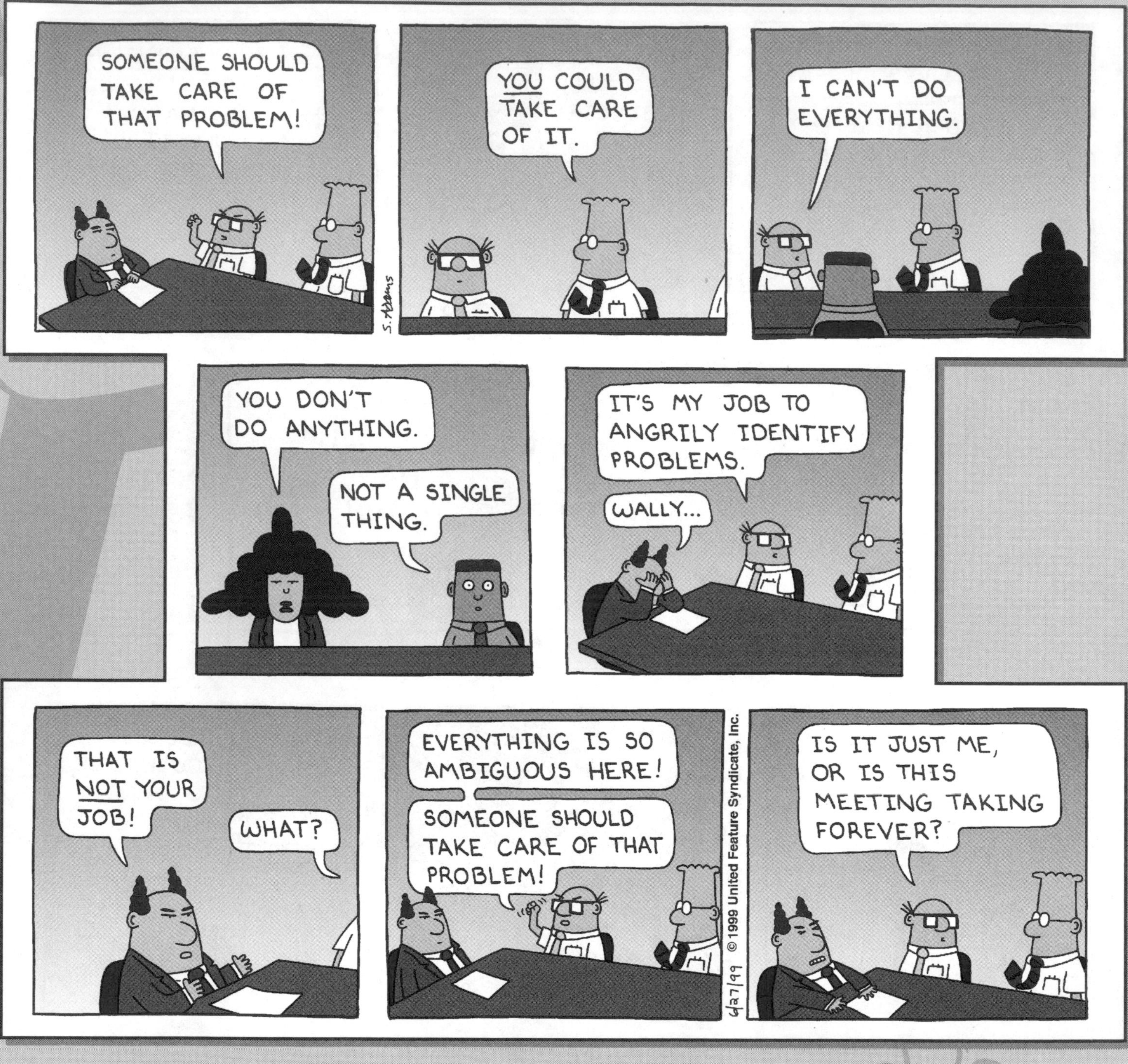

SOMEONE SHOULD TAKE CARE OF THAT PROBLEM!
S. Adams
YOU COULD TAKE CARE OF IT.
I CAN'T DO EVERYTHING.
YOU DON'T DO ANYTHING.
NOT A SINGLE THING.
IT'S MY JOB TO ANGRILY IDENTIFY PROBLEMS.
WALLY...
THAT IS NOT YOUR JOB!
WHAT?
EVERYTHING IS SO AMBIGUOUS HERE!
SOMEONE SHOULD TAKE CARE OF THAT PROBLEM!
6/27/99 © 1999 United Feature Syndicate, Inc.
IS IT JUST ME, OR IS THIS MEETING TAKING FOREVER?

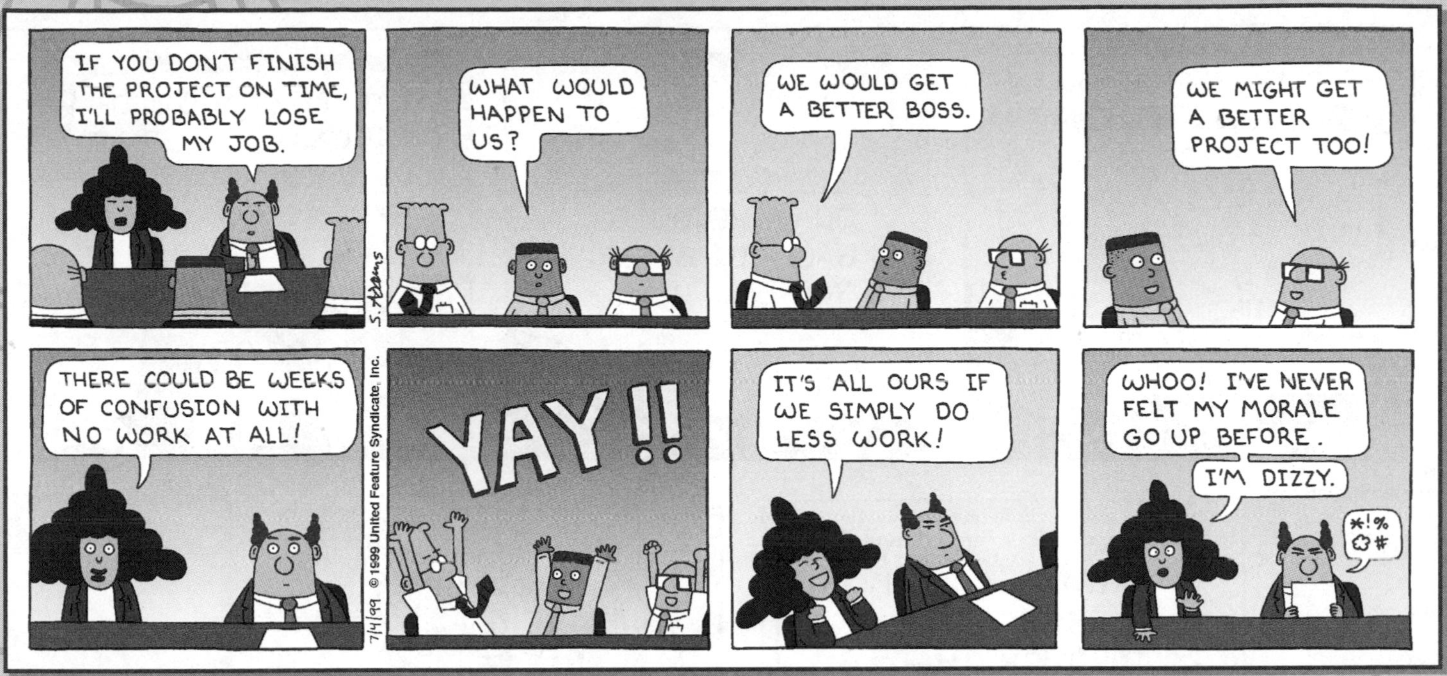
IF YOU DON'T FINISH THE PROJECT ON TIME, I'LL PROBABLY LOSE MY JOB.
WHAT WOULD HAPPEN TO US?
WE WOULD GET A BETTER BOSS.
WE MIGHT GET A BETTER PROJECT TOO!
THERE COULD BE WEEKS OF CONFUSION WITH NO WORK AT ALL!
YAY!!
IT'S ALL OURS IF WE SIMPLY DO LESS WORK!
WHOO! I'VE NEVER FELT MY MORALE GO UP BEFORE.
I'M DIZZY.
*!%
✪#
S. Adams
7/4/99 © 1999 United Feature Syndicate, Inc.

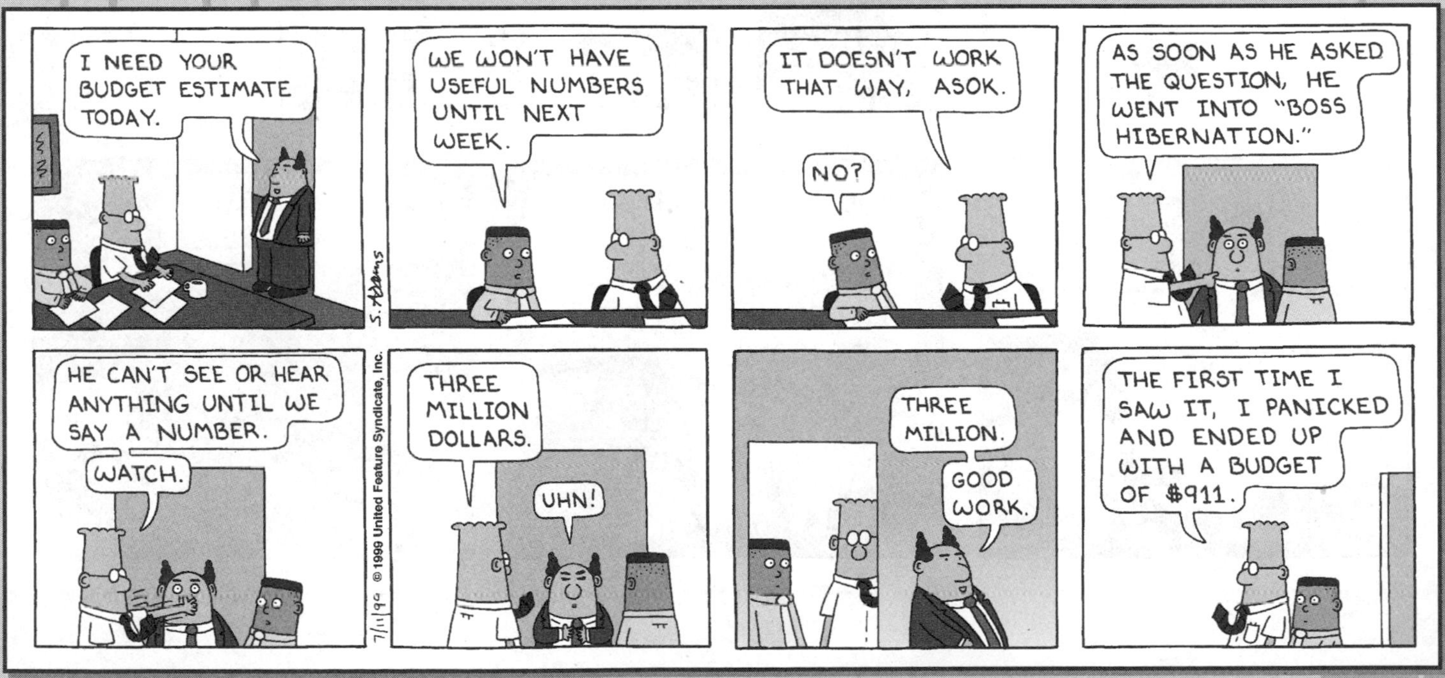
I NEED YOUR BUDGET ESTIMATE TODAY.
WE WON'T HAVE USEFUL NUMBERS UNTIL NEXT WEEK.
IT DOESN'T WORK THAT WAY, ASOK.
NO?
AS SOON AS HE ASKED THE QUESTION, HE WENT INTO "BOSS HIBERNATION."
HE CAN'T SEE OR HEAR ANYTHING UNTIL WE SAY A NUMBER.
WATCH.
THREE MILLION DOLLARS.
UHN!
THREE MILLION.
GOOD WORK.
THE FIRST TIME I SAW IT, I PANICKED AND ENDED UP WITH A BUDGET OF $911.
S. Adams
7/11/99 © 1999 United Feature Syndicate, Inc.

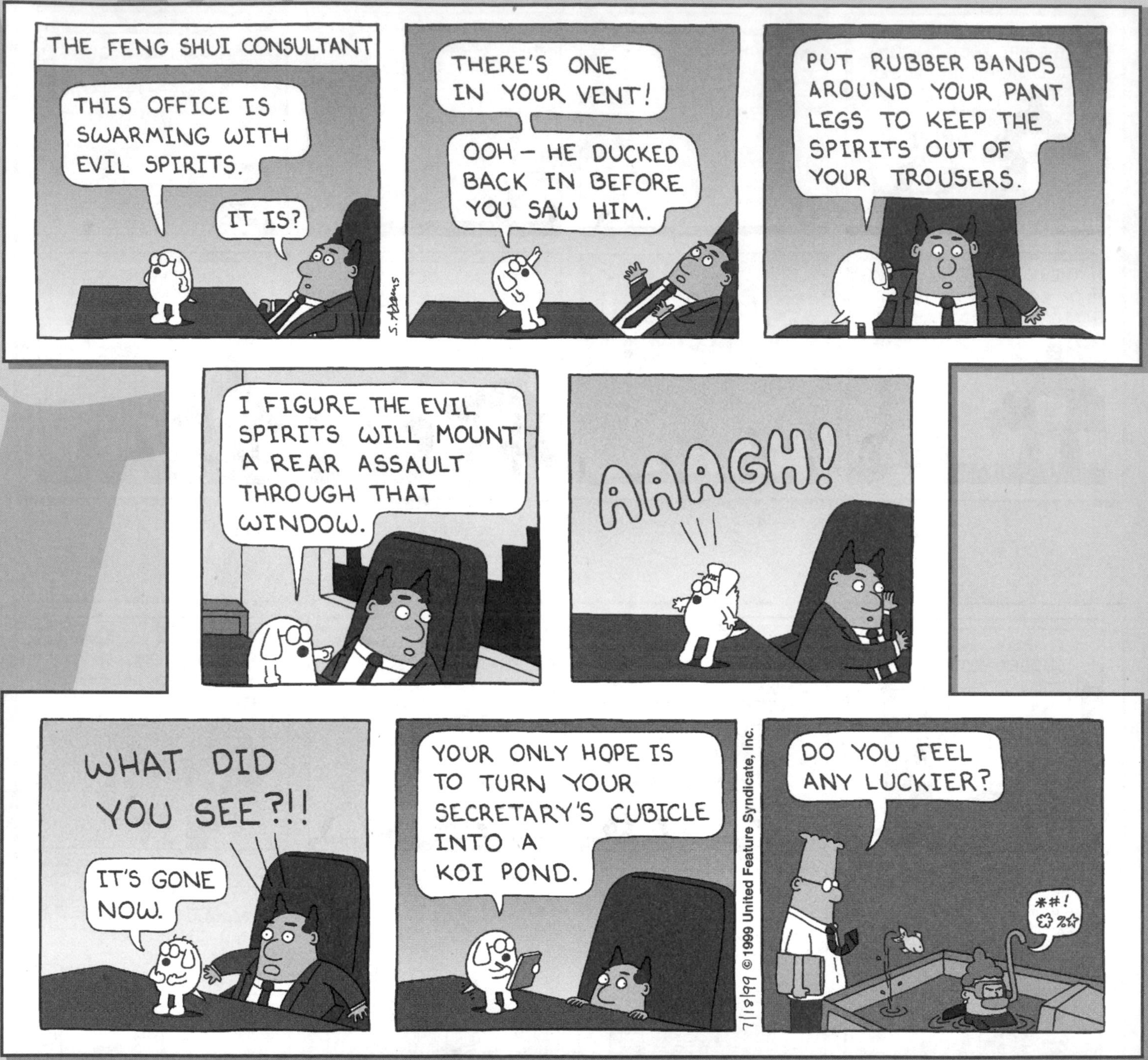
THE FENG SHUI CONSULTANT
THIS OFFICE IS SWARMING WITH EVIL SPIRITS.
IT IS?
THERE'S ONE IN YOUR VENT!
OOH – HE DUCKED BACK IN BEFORE YOU SAW HIM.
PUT RUBBER BANDS AROUND YOUR PANT LEGS TO KEEP THE SPIRITS OUT OF YOUR TROUSERS.
I FIGURE THE EVIL SPIRITS WILL MOUNT A REAR ASSAULT THROUGH THAT WINDOW.
AAAGH!
WHAT DID YOU SEE?!!
IT'S GONE NOW.
YOUR ONLY HOPE IS TO TURN YOUR SECRETARY'S CUBICLE INTO A KOI POND.
7/18/99 © 1999 United Feature Syndicate, Inc.
DO YOU FEEL ANY LUCKIER?

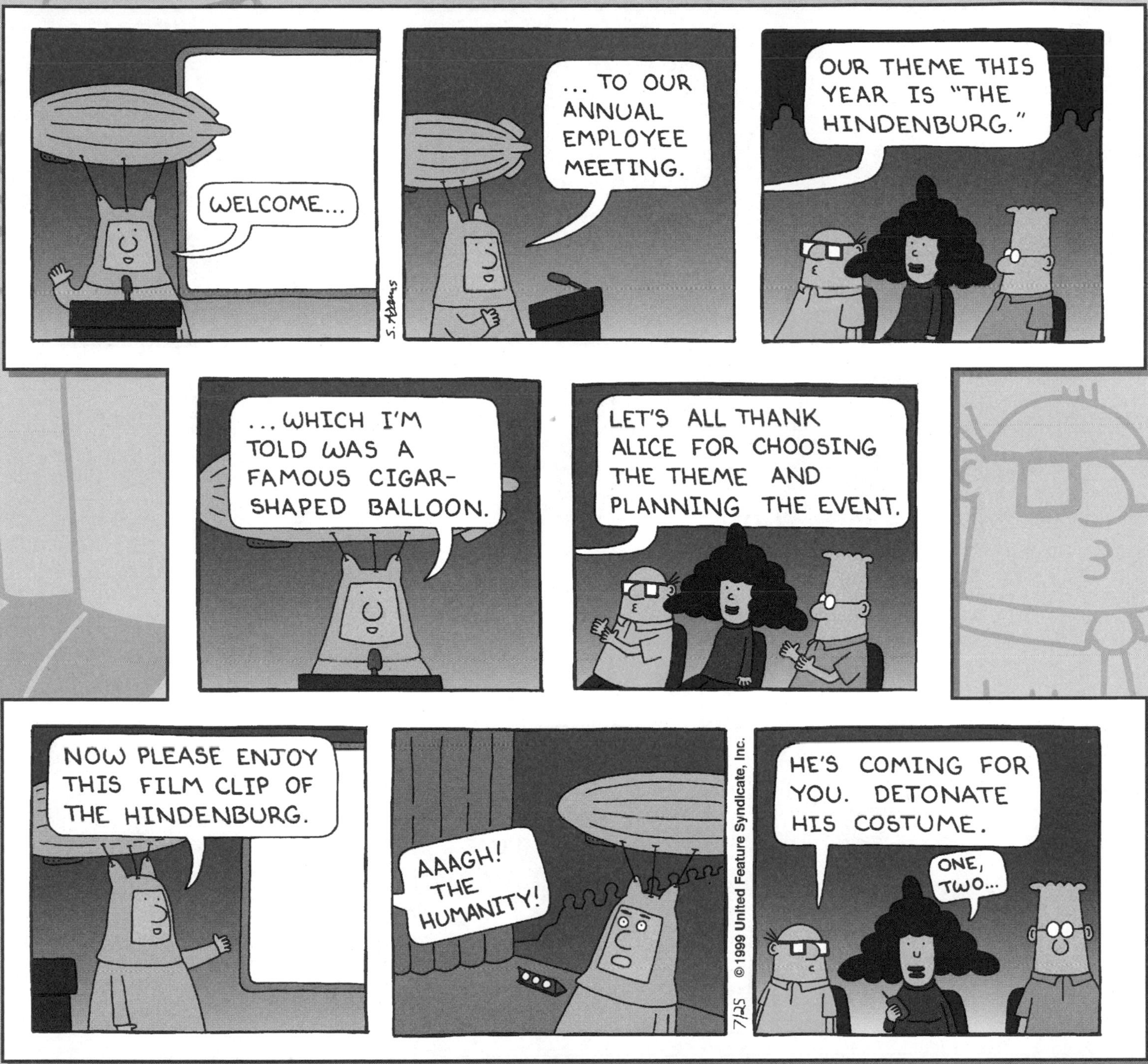
WELCOME...
... TO OUR ANNUAL EMPLOYEE MEETING.
OUR THEME THIS YEAR IS "THE HINDENBURG."
...WHICH I'M TOLD WAS A FAMOUS CIGAR-SHAPED BALLOON.
LET'S ALL THANK ALICE FOR CHOOSING THE THEME AND PLANNING THE EVENT.
NOW PLEASE ENJOY THIS FILM CLIP OF THE HINDENBURG.
AAAGH! THE HUMANITY!
HE'S COMING FOR YOU. DETONATE HIS COSTUME.
ONE, TWO...
© 1999 United Feature Syndicate, Inc.

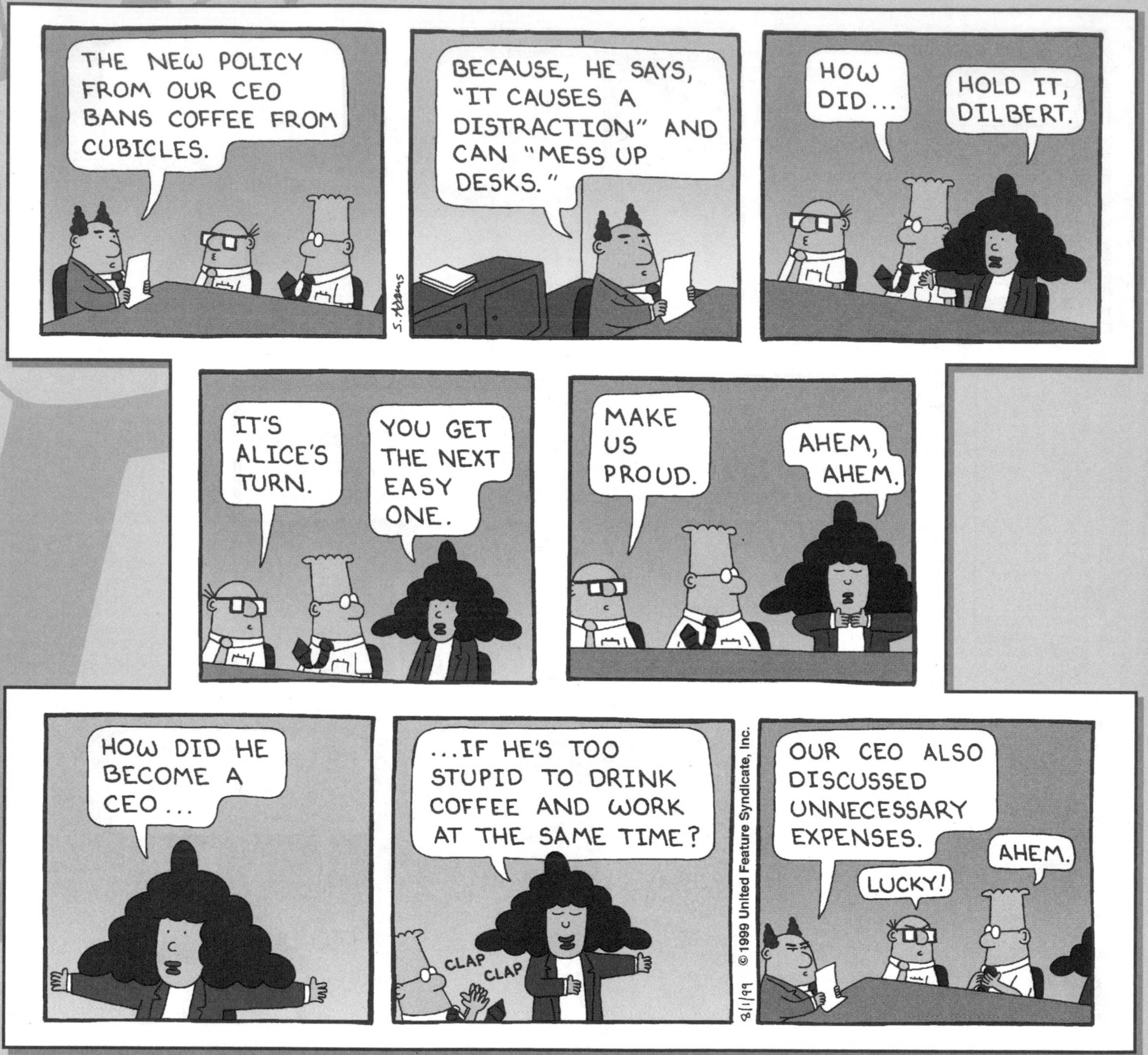
THE NEW POLICY FROM OUR CEO BANS COFFEE FROM CUBICLES.
S. Adams
BECAUSE, HE SAYS, "IT CAUSES A DISTRACTION" AND CAN "MESS UP DESKS."
HOW DID...
HOLD IT, DILBERT.
IT'S ALICE'S TURN.
YOU GET THE NEXT EASY ONE.
MAKE US PROUD.
AHEM, AHEM.
HOW DID HE BECOME A CEO...
...IF HE'S TOO STUPID TO DRINK COFFEE AND WORK AT THE SAME TIME?
CLAP
CLAP
© 1999 United Feature Syndicate, Inc.
8/1/99
OUR CEO ALSO DISCUSSED UNNECESSARY EXPENSES.
LUCKY!
AHEM.

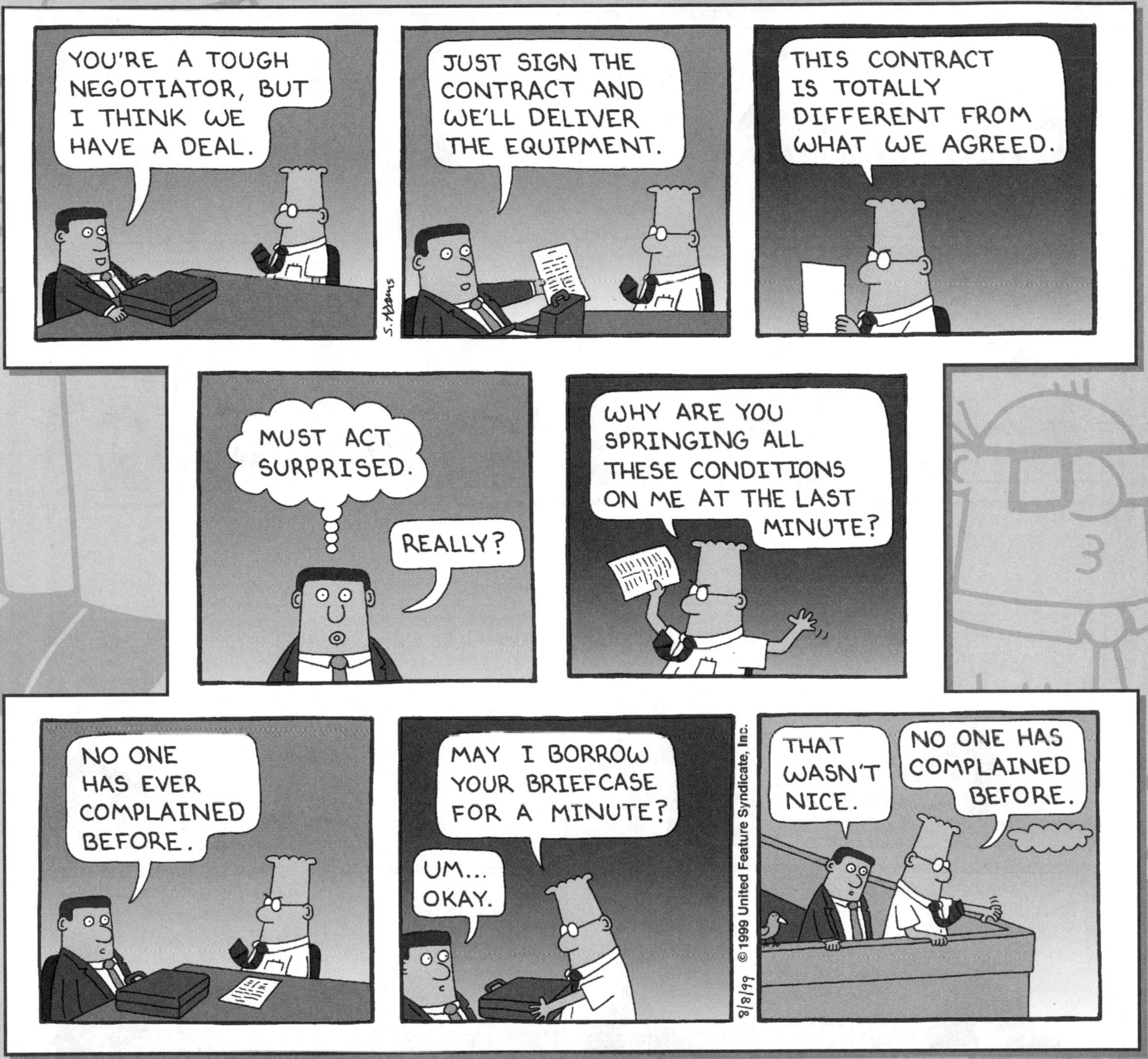
YOU'RE A TOUGH NEGOTIATOR, BUT I THINK WE HAVE A DEAL.
S. ADAMS
JUST SIGN THE CONTRACT AND WE'LL DELIVER THE EQUIPMENT.
THIS CONTRACT IS TOTALLY DIFFERENT FROM WHAT WE AGREED.
MUST ACT SURPRISED.
REALLY?
WHY ARE YOU SPRINGING ALL THESE CONDITIONS ON ME AT THE LAST MINUTE?
NO ONE HAS EVER COMPLAINED BEFORE.
MAY I BORROW YOUR BRIEFCASE FOR A MINUTE?
UM... OKAY.
8/8/99 © 1999 United Feature Syndicate, Inc.
THAT WASN'T NICE.
NO ONE HAS COMPLAINED BEFORE.

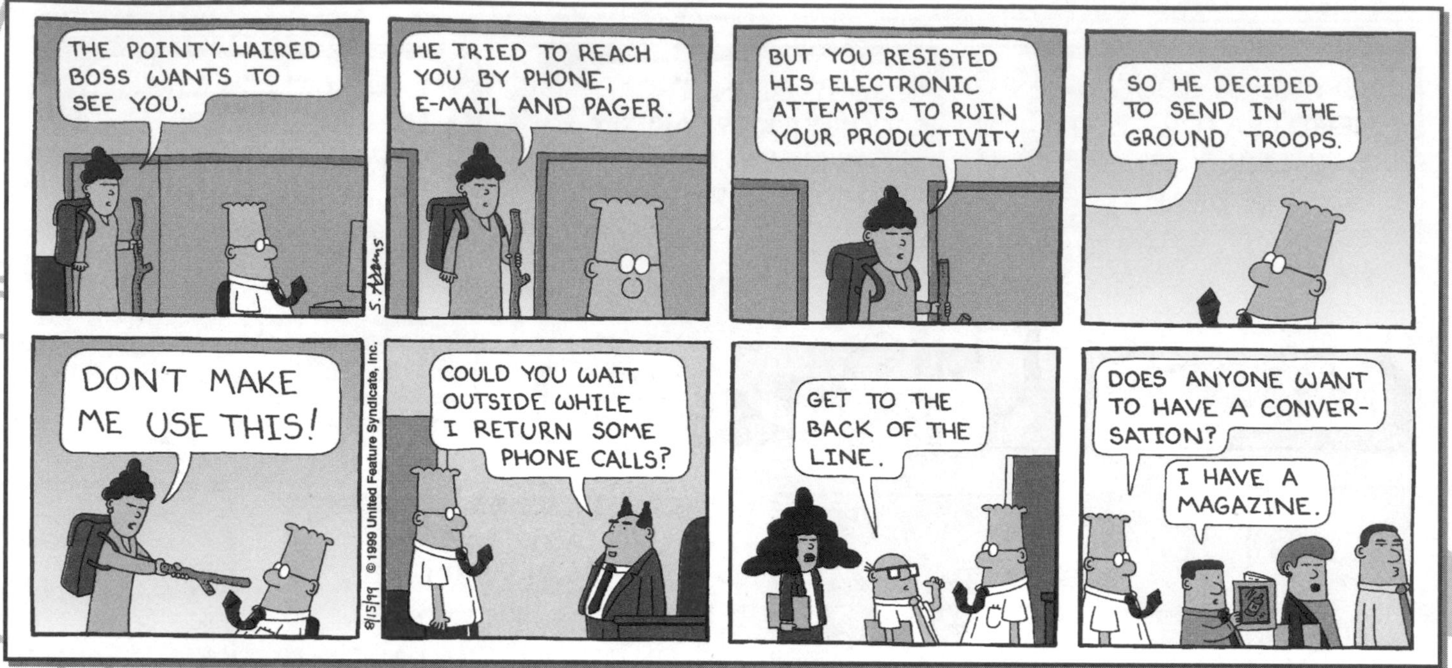
THE POINTY-HAIRED BOSS WANTS TO SEE YOU.
HE TRIED TO REACH YOU BY PHONE, E-MAIL AND PAGER.
BUT YOU RESISTED HIS ELECTRONIC ATTEMPTS TO RUIN YOUR PRODUCTIVITY.
SO HE DECIDED TO SEND IN THE GROUND TROOPS.
DON'T MAKE ME USE THIS!
COULD YOU WAIT OUTSIDE WHILE I RETURN SOME PHONE CALLS?
GET TO THE BACK OF THE LINE.
DOES ANYONE WANT TO HAVE A CONVERSATION?
I HAVE A MAGAZINE.
8/15/99 © 1999 United Feature Syndicate, Inc.

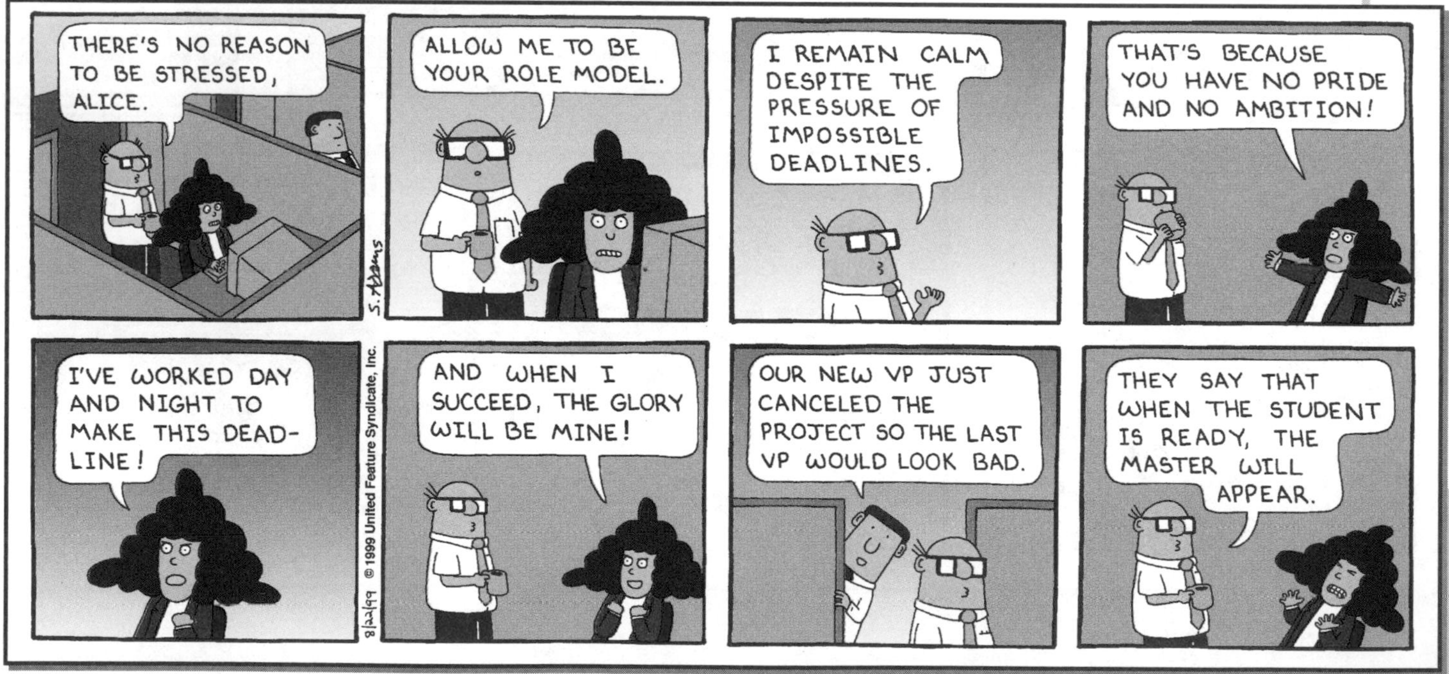
THERE'S NO REASON TO BE STRESSED, ALICE.
ALLOW ME TO BE YOUR ROLE MODEL.
I REMAIN CALM DESPITE THE PRESSURE OF IMPOSSIBLE DEADLINES.
THAT'S BECAUSE YOU HAVE NO PRIDE AND NO AMBITION!
I'VE WORKED DAY AND NIGHT TO MAKE THIS DEAD-LINE!
AND WHEN I SUCCEED, THE GLORY WILL BE MINE!
OUR NEW VP JUST CANCELED THE PROJECT SO THE LAST VP WOULD LOOK BAD.
THEY SAY THAT WHEN THE STUDENT IS READY, THE MASTER WILL APPEAR.
8/22/99 © 1999 United Feature Syndicate, Inc.

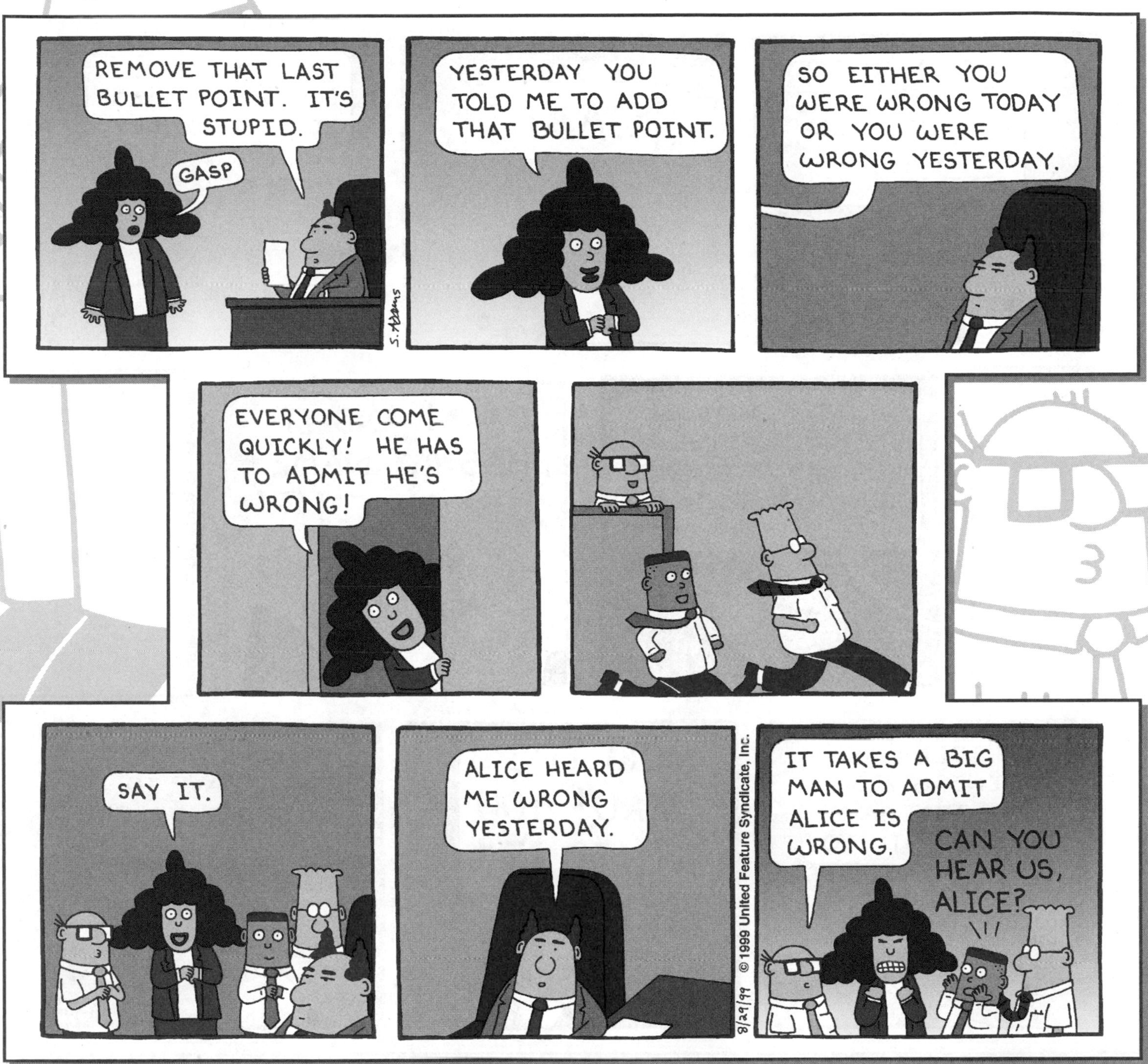

REMOVE THAT LAST BULLET POINT. IT'S STUPID.
GASP
YESTERDAY YOU TOLD ME TO ADD THAT BULLET POINT.
SO EITHER YOU WERE WRONG TODAY OR YOU WERE WRONG YESTERDAY.
EVERYONE COME QUICKLY! HE HAS TO ADMIT HE'S WRONG!
SAY IT.
ALICE HEARD ME WRONG YESTERDAY.
IT TAKES A BIG MAN TO ADMIT ALICE IS WRONG.
CAN YOU HEAR US, ALICE?
S. Adams
8/29/99 © 1999 United Feature Syndicate, Inc.

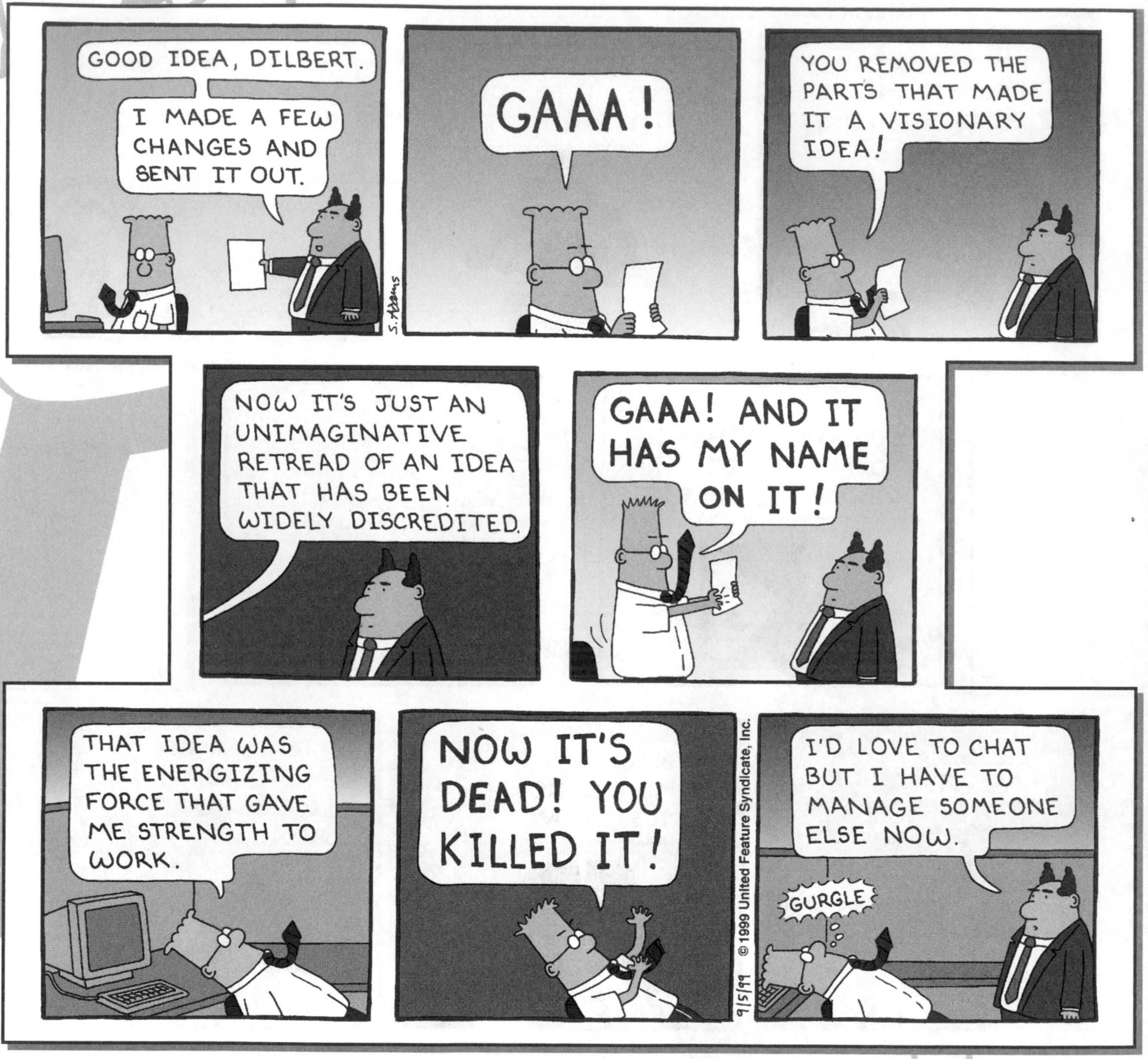
GOOD IDEA, DILBERT.
I MADE A FEW CHANGES AND SENT IT OUT.
S. Adams
GAAA!
YOU REMOVED THE PARTS THAT MADE IT A VISIONARY IDEA!
NOW IT'S JUST AN UNIMAGINATIVE RETREAD OF AN IDEA THAT HAS BEEN WIDELY DISCREDITED.
GAAA! AND IT HAS MY NAME ON IT!
THAT IDEA WAS THE ENERGIZING FORCE THAT GAVE ME STRENGTH TO WORK.
NOW IT'S DEAD! YOU KILLED IT!
9/5/99 © 1999 United Feature Syndicate, Inc.
I'D LOVE TO CHAT BUT I HAVE TO MANAGE SOMEONE ELSE NOW.
GURGLE

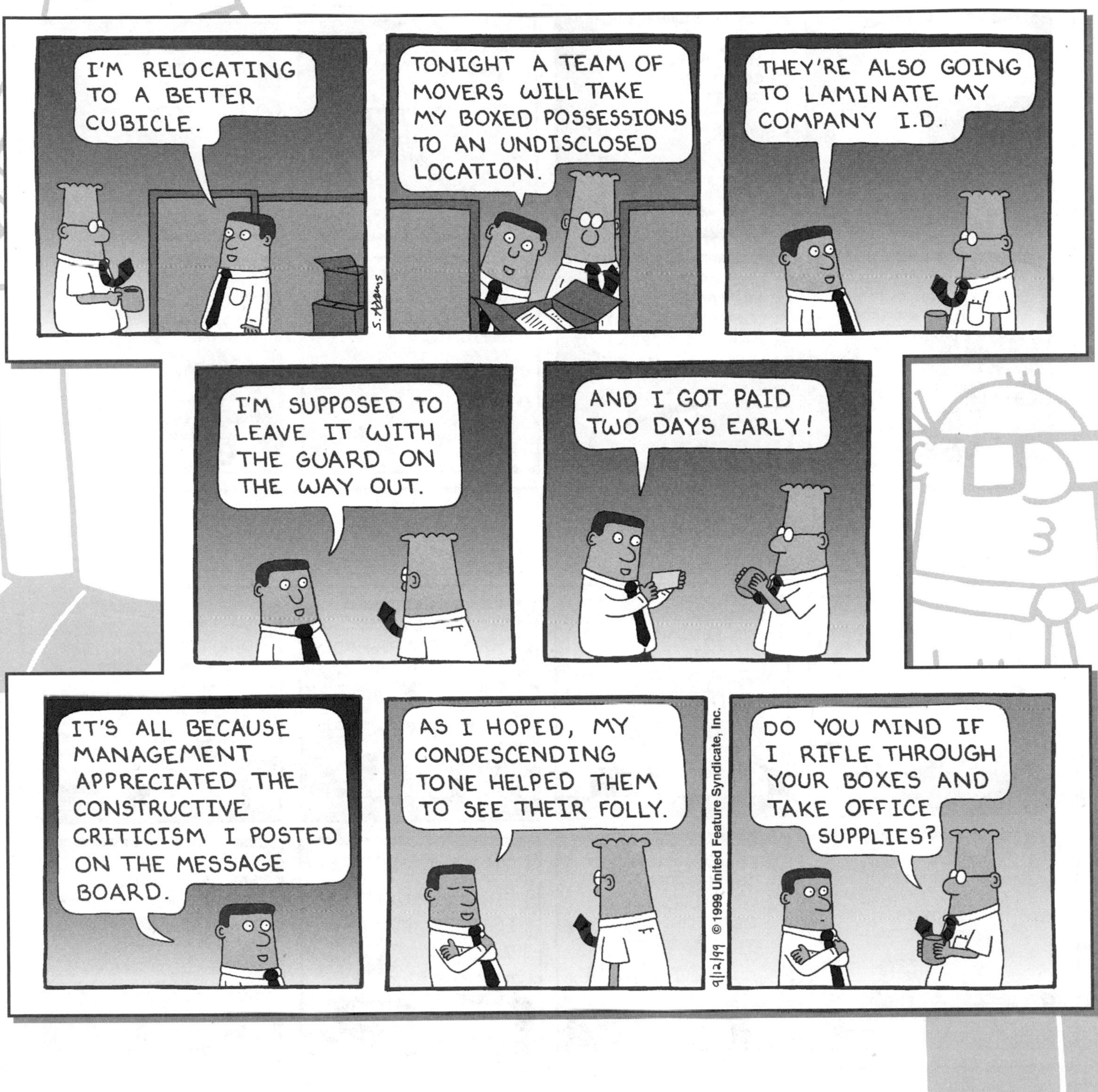
I'M RELOCATING TO A BETTER CUBICLE.
S. ADAMS
TONIGHT A TEAM OF MOVERS WILL TAKE MY BOXED POSSESSIONS TO AN UNDISCLOSED LOCATION.
THEY'RE ALSO GOING TO LAMINATE MY COMPANY I.D.
I'M SUPPOSED TO LEAVE IT WITH THE GUARD ON THE WAY OUT.
AND I GOT PAID TWO DAYS EARLY!
IT'S ALL BECAUSE MANAGEMENT APPRECIATED THE CONSTRUCTIVE CRITICISM I POSTED ON THE MESSAGE BOARD.
AS I HOPED, MY CONDESCENDING TONE HELPED THEM TO SEE THEIR FOLLY.
9/12/99 © 1999 United Feature Syndicate, Inc.
DO YOU MIND IF I RIFLE THROUGH YOUR BOXES AND TAKE OFFICE SUPPLIES?

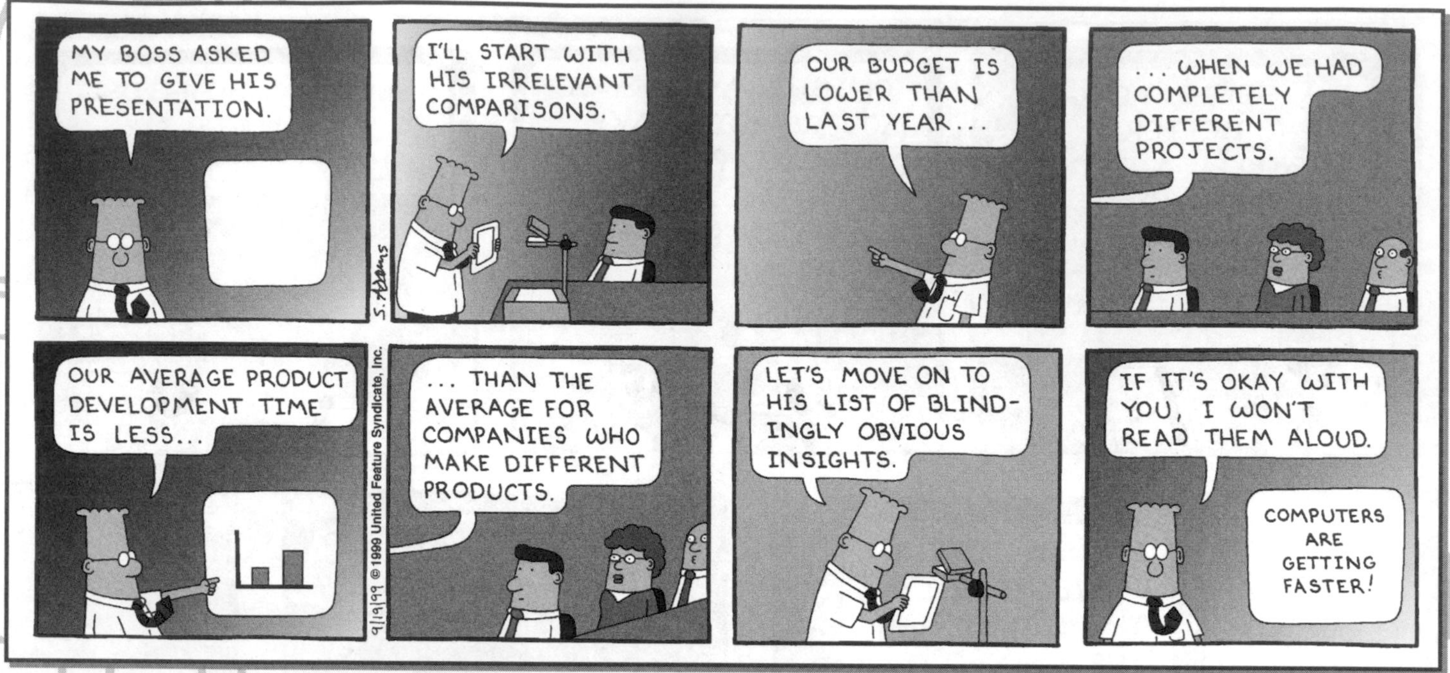
MY BOSS ASKED ME TO GIVE HIS PRESENTATION.
I'LL START WITH HIS IRRELEVANT COMPARISONS.
OUR BUDGET IS LOWER THAN LAST YEAR...
...WHEN WE HAD COMPLETELY DIFFERENT PROJECTS.
OUR AVERAGE PRODUCT DEVELOPMENT TIME IS LESS...
...THAN THE AVERAGE FOR COMPANIES WHO MAKE DIFFERENT PRODUCTS.
LET'S MOVE ON TO HIS LIST OF BLINDINGLY OBVIOUS INSIGHTS.
IF IT'S OKAY WITH YOU, I WON'T READ THEM ALOUD.
COMPUTERS ARE GETTING FASTER!
S. Adams
9/19/99 © 1999 United Feature Syndicate, Inc.

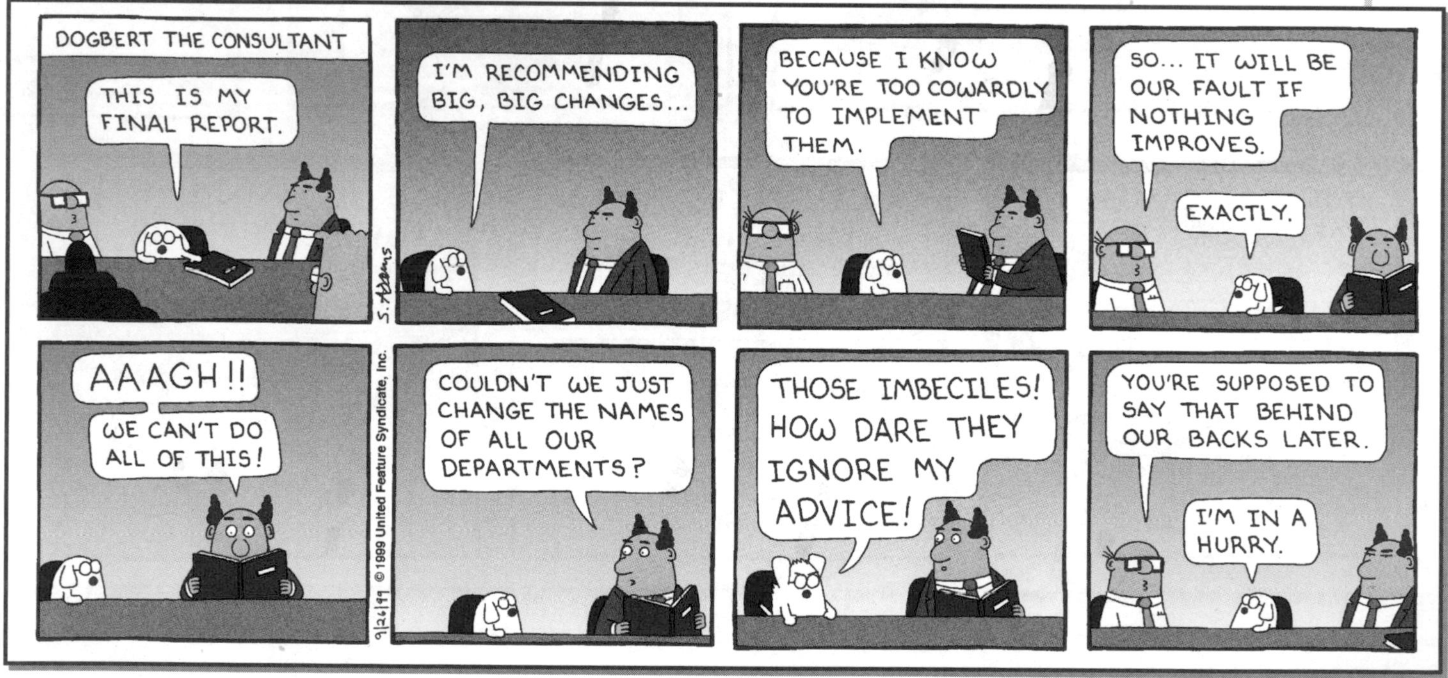
DOGBERT THE CONSULTANT
THIS IS MY FINAL REPORT.
I'M RECOMMENDING BIG, BIG CHANGES...
BECAUSE I KNOW YOU'RE TOO COWARDLY TO IMPLEMENT THEM.
SO... IT WILL BE OUR FAULT IF NOTHING IMPROVES.
EXACTLY.
AAAGH!!
WE CAN'T DO ALL OF THIS!
COULDN'T WE JUST CHANGE THE NAMES OF ALL OUR DEPARTMENTS?
THOSE IMBECILES! HOW DARE THEY IGNORE MY ADVICE!
YOU'RE SUPPOSED TO SAY THAT BEHIND OUR BACKS LATER.
I'M IN A HURRY.
S. Adams
9/26/99 © 1999 United Feature Syndicate, Inc.

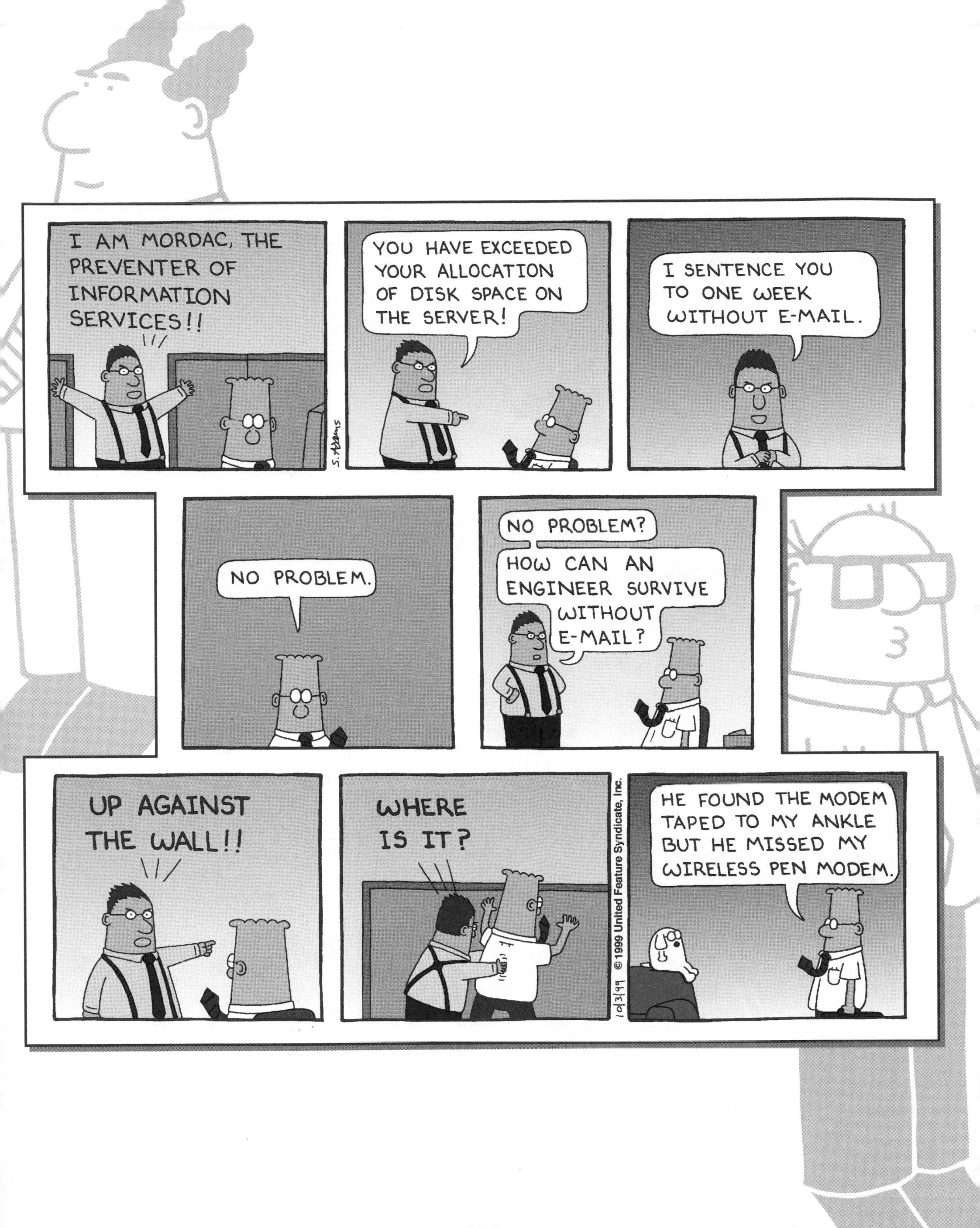
I AM MORDAC, THE PREVENTER OF INFORMATION SERVICES!!
S. Adams
YOU HAVE EXCEEDED YOUR ALLOCATION OF DISK SPACE ON THE SERVER!
I SENTENCE YOU TO ONE WEEK WITHOUT E-MAIL.
NO PROBLEM.
NO PROBLEM?
HOW CAN AN ENGINEER SURVIVE WITHOUT E-MAIL?
UP AGAINST THE WALL!!
WHERE IS IT?
10/3/99 © 1999 United Feature Syndicate, Inc.
HE FOUND THE MODEM TAPED TO MY ANKLE BUT HE MISSED MY WIRELESS PEN MODEM.

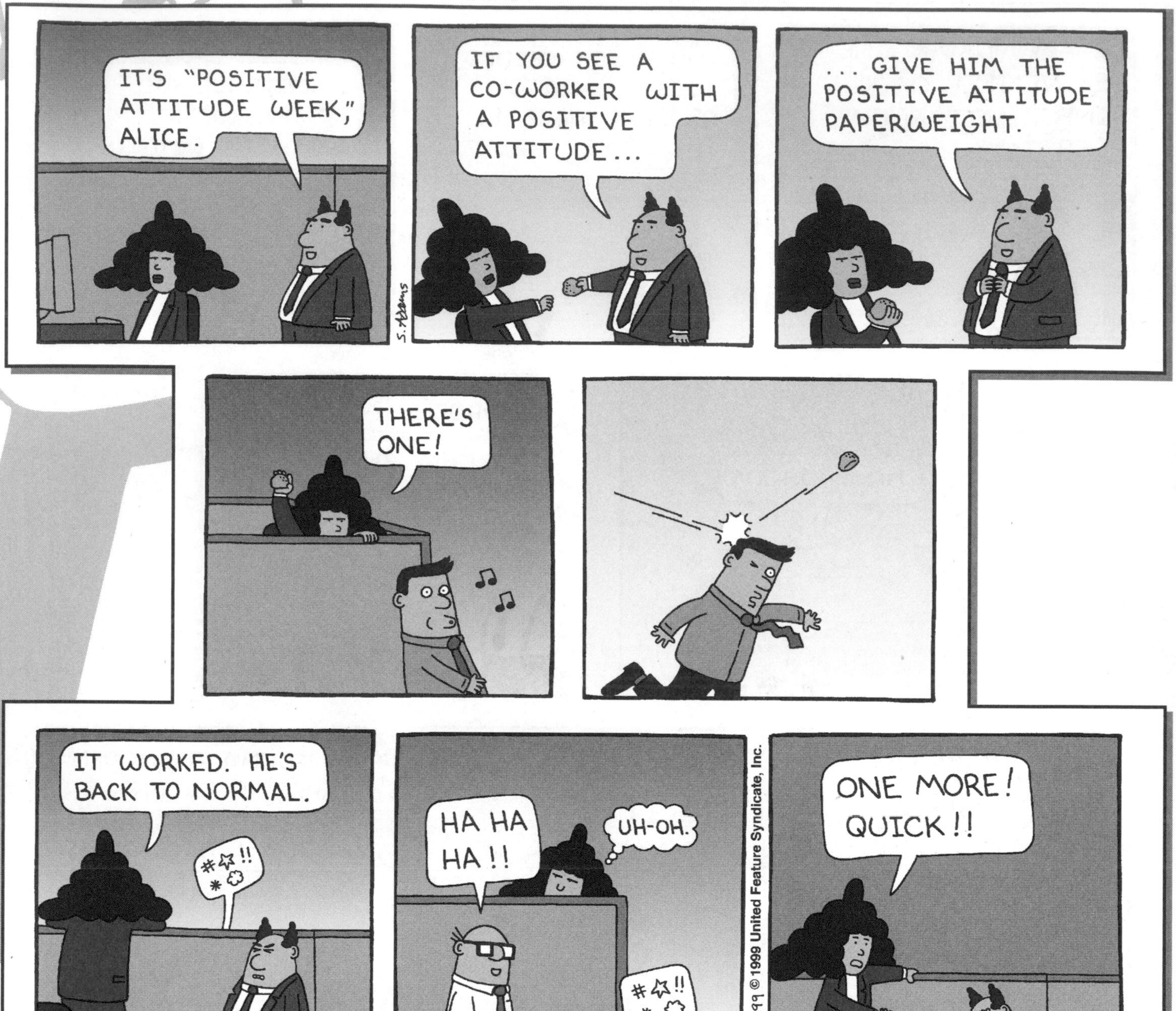
IT'S "POSITIVE ATTITUDE WEEK," ALICE.
IF YOU SEE A CO-WORKER WITH A POSITIVE ATTITUDE...
... GIVE HIM THE POSITIVE ATTITUDE PAPERWEIGHT.
THERE'S ONE!
IT WORKED. HE'S BACK TO NORMAL.
#☆!! * ✿
HA HA HA!!
UH-OH.
#☆!! * ✿
ONE MORE! QUICK!!
S. Adams
10/10/99 © 1999 United Feature Syndicate, Inc.

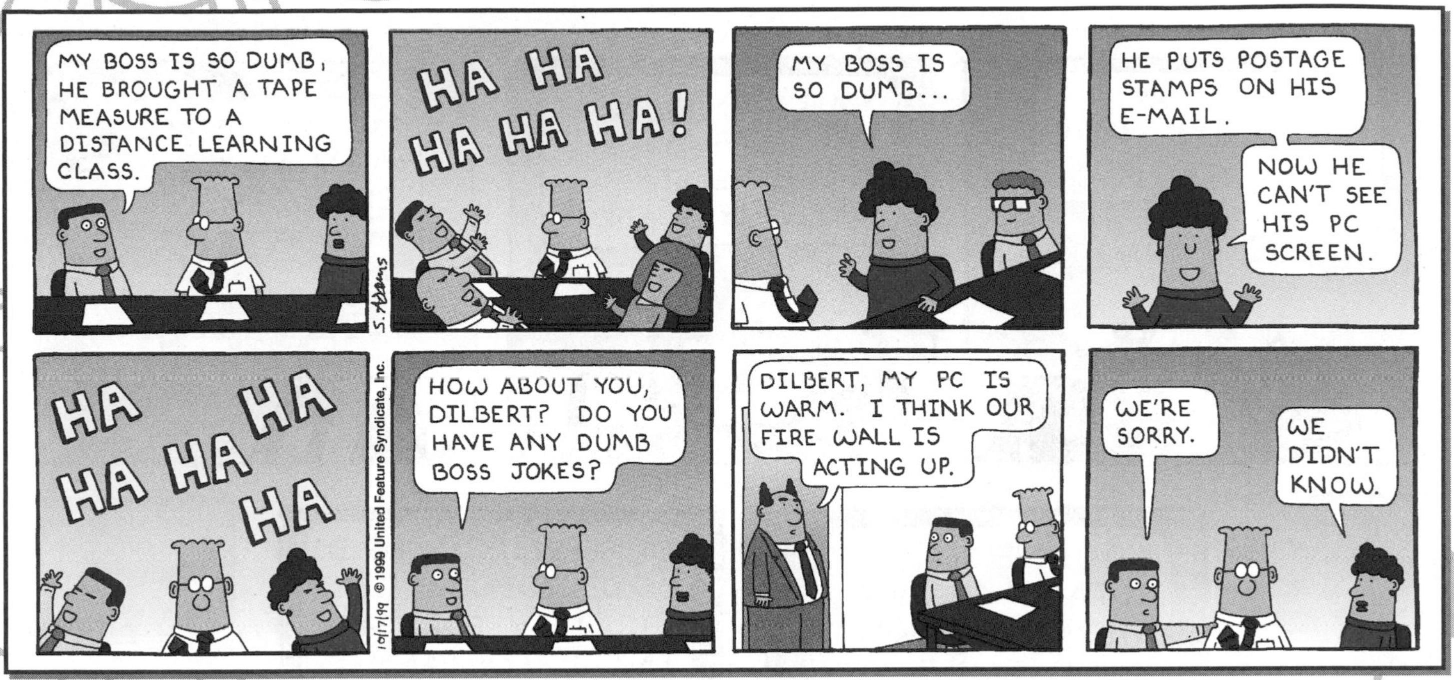
MY BOSS IS SO DUMB, HE BROUGHT A TAPE MEASURE TO A DISTANCE LEARNING CLASS.
HA HA HA HA HA!
MY BOSS IS SO DUMB...
HE PUTS POSTAGE STAMPS ON HIS E-MAIL.
NOW HE CAN'T SEE HIS PC SCREEN.
HA HA HA HA HA
HOW ABOUT YOU, DILBERT? DO YOU HAVE ANY DUMB BOSS JOKES?
DILBERT, MY PC IS WARM. I THINK OUR FIRE WALL IS ACTING UP.
WE'RE SORRY.
WE DIDN'T KNOW.
10/17/99 © 1999 United Feature Syndicate, Inc.

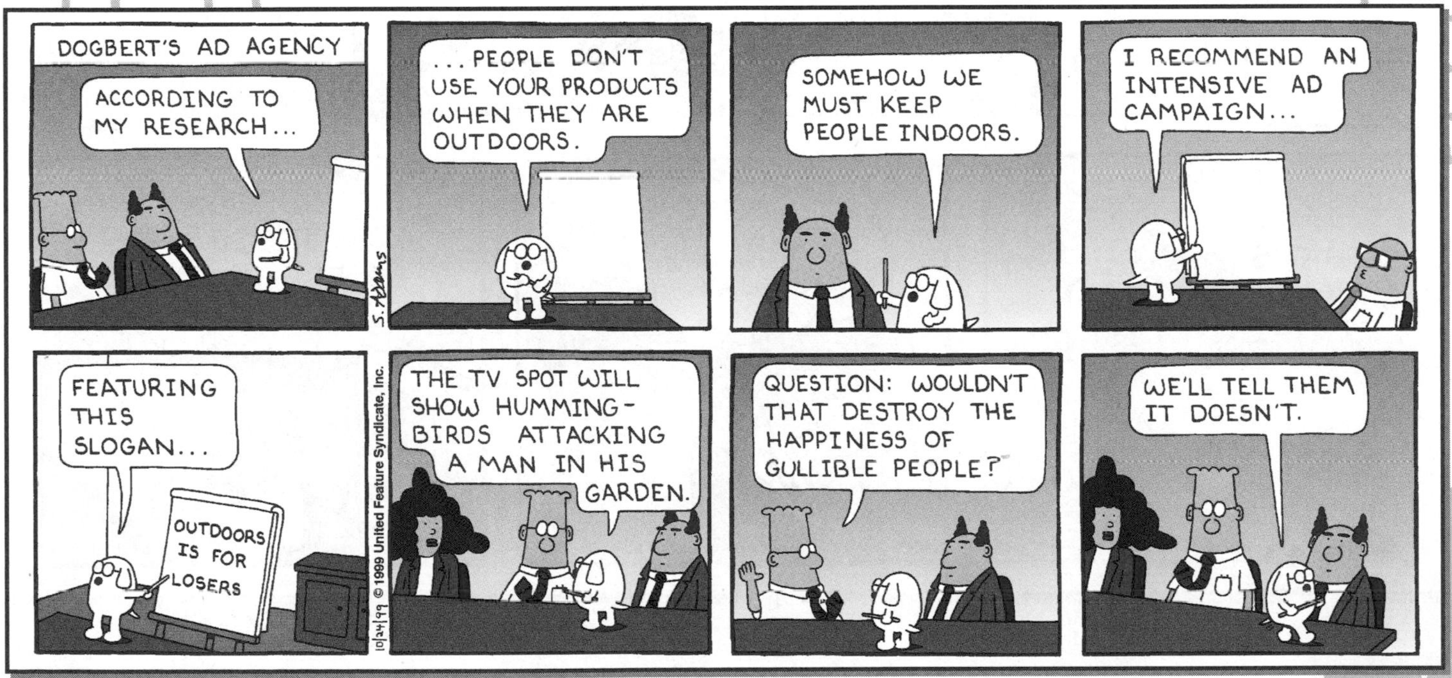
DOGBERT'S AD AGENCY
ACCORDING TO MY RESEARCH...
...PEOPLE DON'T USE YOUR PRODUCTS WHEN THEY ARE OUTDOORS.
SOMEHOW WE MUST KEEP PEOPLE INDOORS.
I RECOMMEND AN INTENSIVE AD CAMPAIGN...
FEATURING THIS SLOGAN...
OUTDOORS IS FOR LOSERS
THE TV SPOT WILL SHOW HUMMING-BIRDS ATTACKING A MAN IN HIS GARDEN.
QUESTION: WOULDN'T THAT DESTROY THE HAPPINESS OF GULLIBLE PEOPLE?
WE'LL TELL THEM IT DOESN'T.
10/24/99 © 1999 United Feature Syndicate, Inc.

HERE ARE THE STRATEGIES FROM OUR SEVEN SILO TEAMS.
S. Adams
YOUR JOB IS TO MERGE THEM INTO A COHERENT COMPANY PLAN.
THESE ARE ALL MUTUALLY EXCLUSIVE.
I'D HAVE TO TOTALLY CHANGE THEM TO MAKE THEM COHERENT.
IN EFFECT, I WOULD BE DECIDING THE STRATEGY FOR THE ENTIRE COMPANY.
THAT'S OKAY.
IT IS?
NO ONE EVER READS IT ANYWAY.
© 1999 United Feature Syndicate, Inc.
10/31/99
I FEEL SORRY FOR THOSE LOSERS ON THE SILO TEAMS.

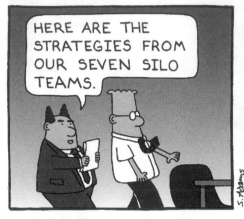

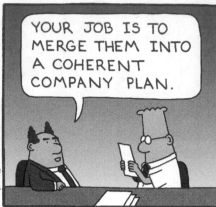

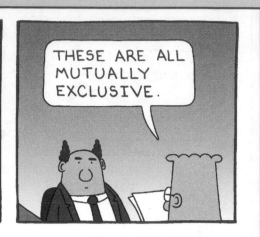

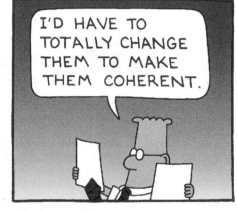

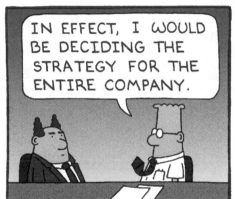

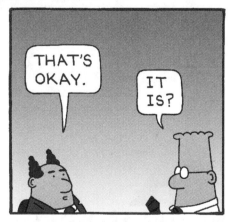

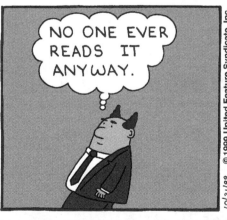

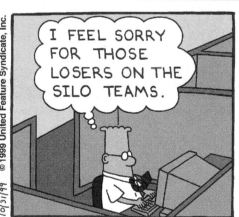

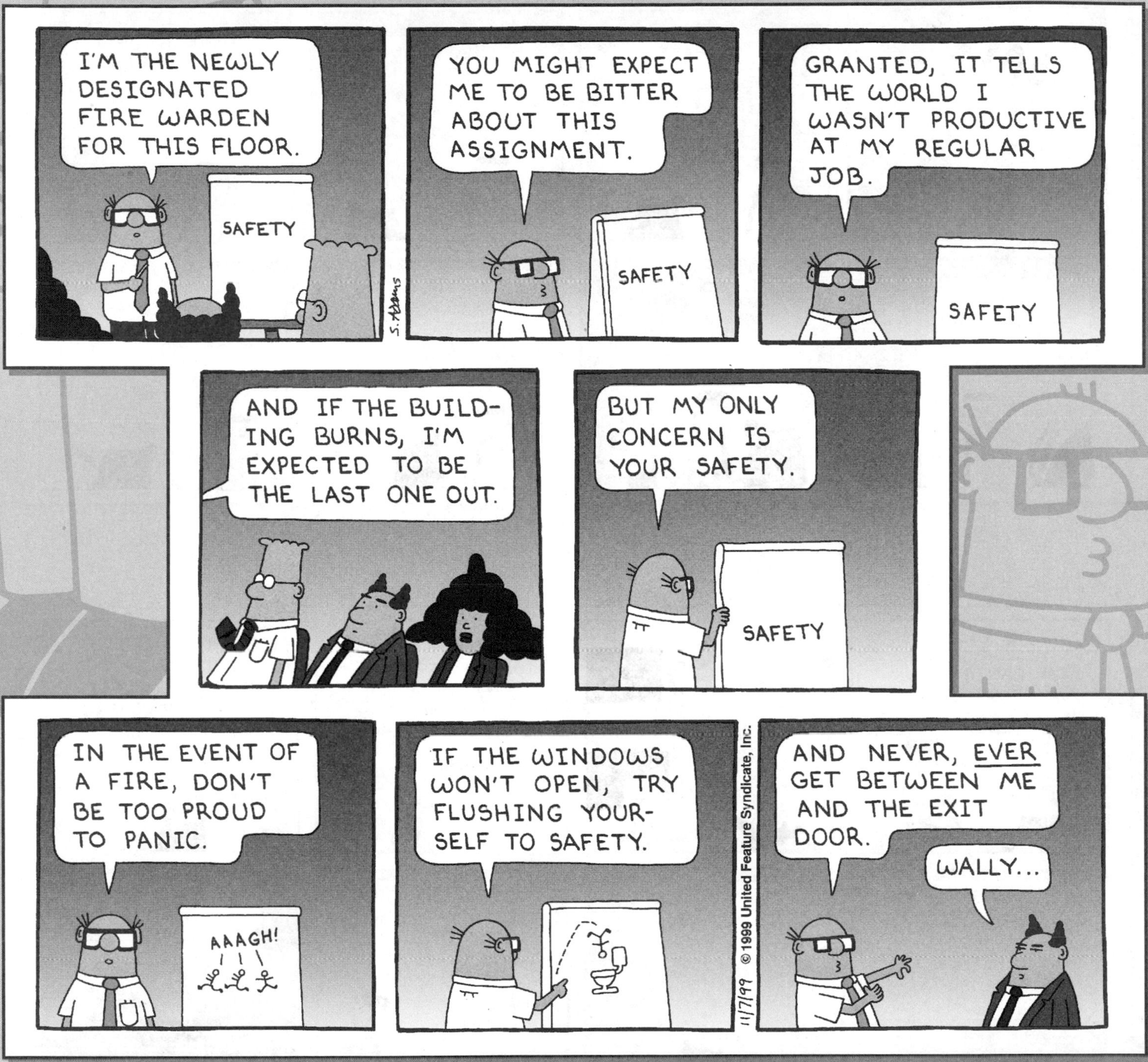
I'M THE NEWLY DESIGNATED FIRE WARDEN FOR THIS FLOOR.
SAFETY
S. Adams
YOU MIGHT EXPECT ME TO BE BITTER ABOUT THIS ASSIGNMENT.
SAFETY
GRANTED, IT TELLS THE WORLD I WASN'T PRODUCTIVE AT MY REGULAR JOB.
SAFETY
AND IF THE BUILD-ING BURNS, I'M EXPECTED TO BE THE LAST ONE OUT.
BUT MY ONLY CONCERN IS YOUR SAFETY.
SAFETY
IN THE EVENT OF A FIRE, DON'T BE TOO PROUD TO PANIC.
AAAGH!
IF THE WINDOWS WON'T OPEN, TRY FLUSHING YOUR-SELF TO SAFETY.
11/7/99 © 1999 United Feature Syndicate, Inc.
AND NEVER, EVER GET BETWEEN ME AND THE EXIT DOOR.
WALLY...

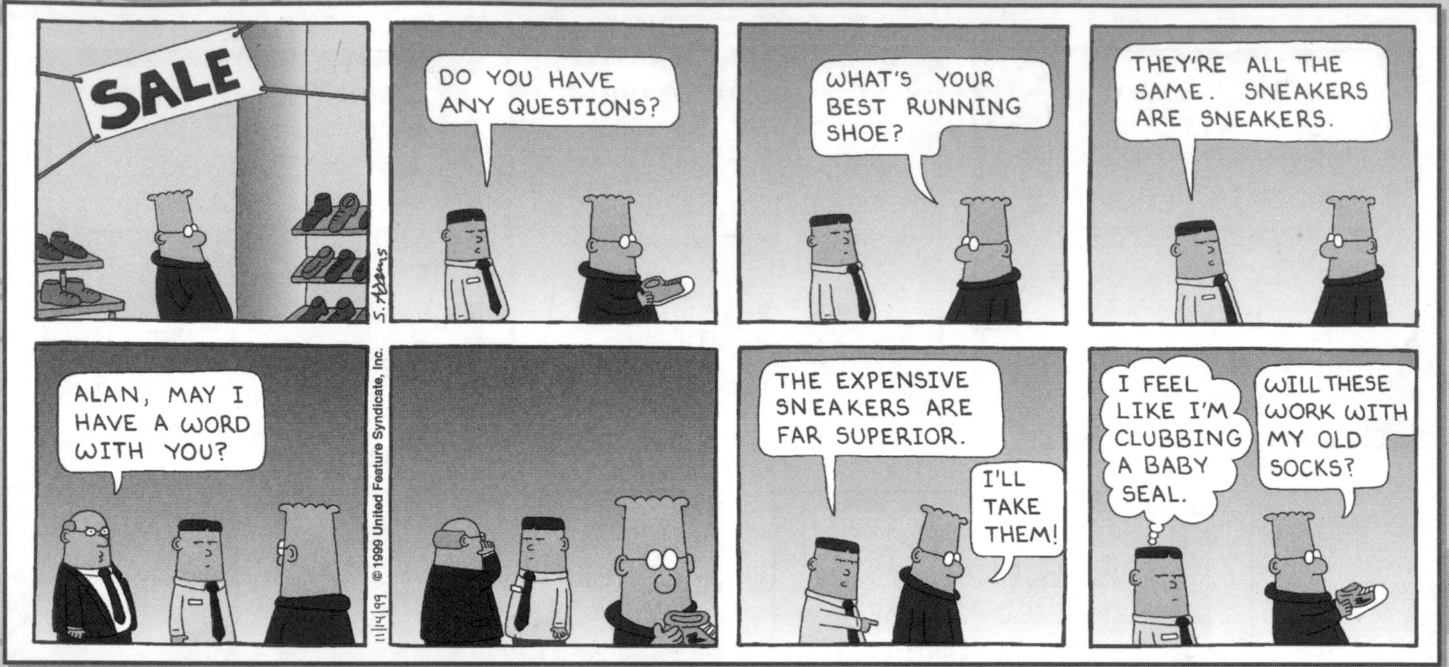
SALE
DO YOU HAVE ANY QUESTIONS?
WHAT'S YOUR BEST RUNNING SHOE?
THEY'RE ALL THE SAME. SNEAKERS ARE SNEAKERS.
ALAN, MAY I HAVE A WORD WITH YOU?
THE EXPENSIVE SNEAKERS ARE FAR SUPERIOR.
I'LL TAKE THEM!
I FEEL LIKE I'M CLUBBING A BABY SEAL.
WILL THESE WORK WITH MY OLD SOCKS?
11/14/99 © 1999 United Feature Syndicate, Inc.

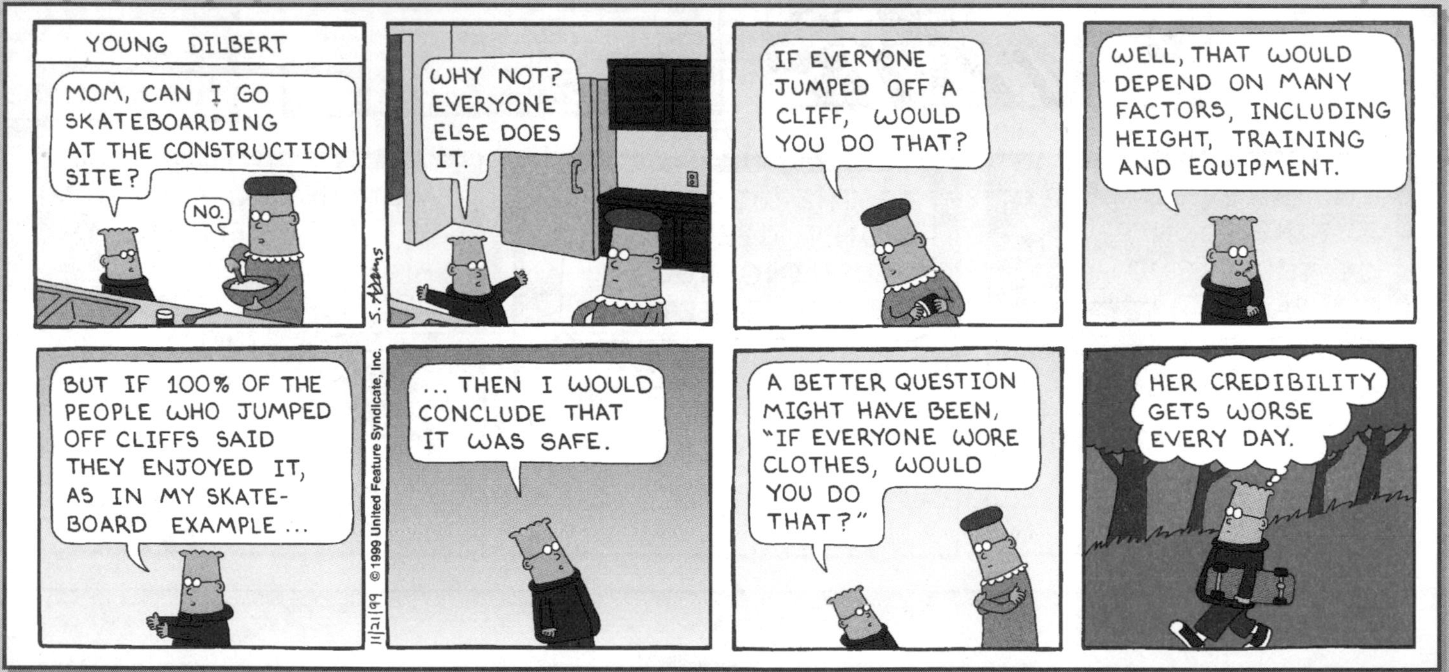
YOUNG DILBERT
MOM, CAN I GO SKATEBOARDING AT THE CONSTRUCTION SITE?
NO.
WHY NOT? EVERYONE ELSE DOES IT.
IF EVERYONE JUMPED OFF A CLIFF, WOULD YOU DO THAT?
WELL, THAT WOULD DEPEND ON MANY FACTORS, INCLUDING HEIGHT, TRAINING AND EQUIPMENT.
BUT IF 100% OF THE PEOPLE WHO JUMPED OFF CLIFFS SAID THEY ENJOYED IT, AS IN MY SKATE-BOARD EXAMPLE ...
... THEN I WOULD CONCLUDE THAT IT WAS SAFE.
A BETTER QUESTION MIGHT HAVE BEEN, "IF EVERYONE WORE CLOTHES, WOULD YOU DO THAT?"
HER CREDIBILITY GETS WORSE EVERY DAY.
11/21/99 © 1999 United Feature Syndicate, Inc.

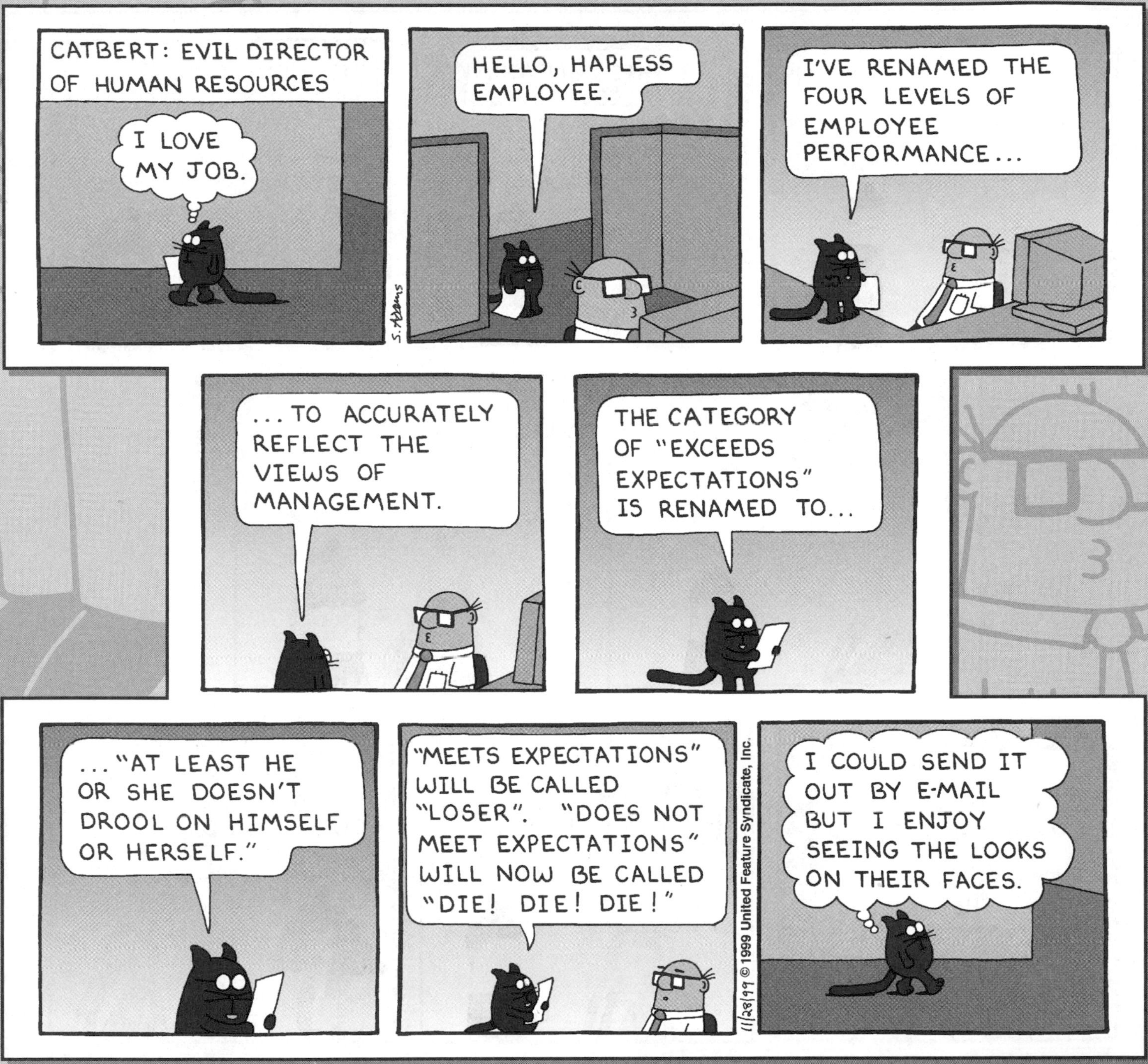
CATBERT: EVIL DIRECTOR OF HUMAN RESOURCES
I LOVE MY JOB.
HELLO, HAPLESS EMPLOYEE.
I'VE RENAMED THE FOUR LEVELS OF EMPLOYEE PERFORMANCE...
...TO ACCURATELY REFLECT THE VIEWS OF MANAGEMENT.
THE CATEGORY OF "EXCEEDS EXPECTATIONS" IS RENAMED TO...
..."AT LEAST HE OR SHE DOESN'T DROOL ON HIMSELF OR HERSELF."
"MEETS EXPECTATIONS" WILL BE CALLED "LOSER". "DOES NOT MEET EXPECTATIONS" WILL NOW BE CALLED "DIE! DIE! DIE!"
I COULD SEND IT OUT BY E-MAIL BUT I ENJOY SEEING THE LOOKS ON THEIR FACES.
S. Adams
11/28/99 © 1999 United Feature Syndicate, Inc.

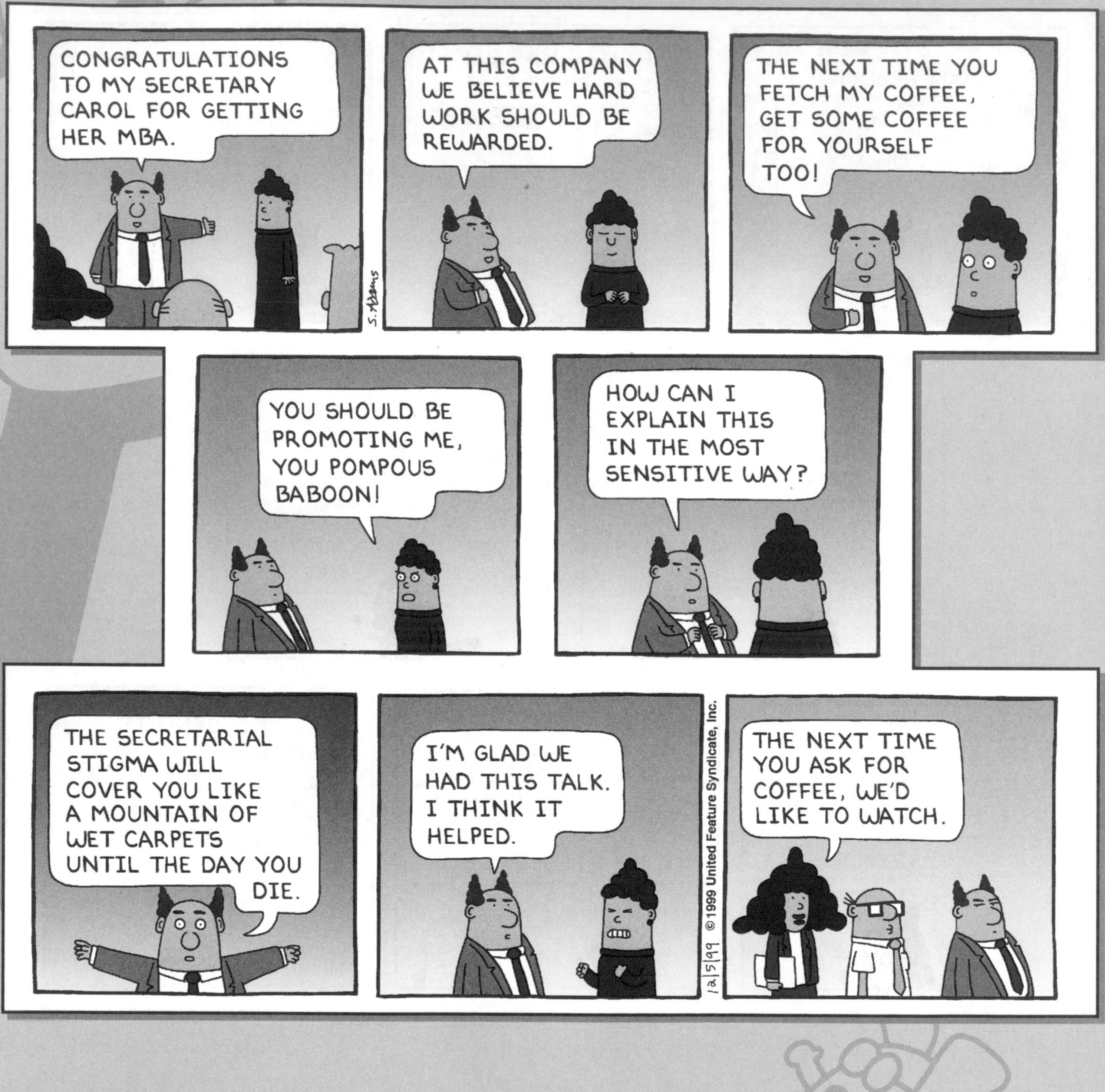
CONGRATULATIONS TO MY SECRETARY CAROL FOR GETTING HER MBA.
S. Adams
AT THIS COMPANY WE BELIEVE HARD WORK SHOULD BE REWARDED.
THE NEXT TIME YOU FETCH MY COFFEE, GET SOME COFFEE FOR YOURSELF TOO!
YOU SHOULD BE PROMOTING ME, YOU POMPOUS BABOON!
HOW CAN I EXPLAIN THIS IN THE MOST SENSITIVE WAY?
THE SECRETARIAL STIGMA WILL COVER YOU LIKE A MOUNTAIN OF WET CARPETS UNTIL THE DAY YOU DIE.
I'M GLAD WE HAD THIS TALK. I THINK IT HELPED.
12/5/99 ©1999 United Feature Syndicate, Inc.
THE NEXT TIME YOU ASK FOR COFFEE, WE'D LIKE TO WATCH.

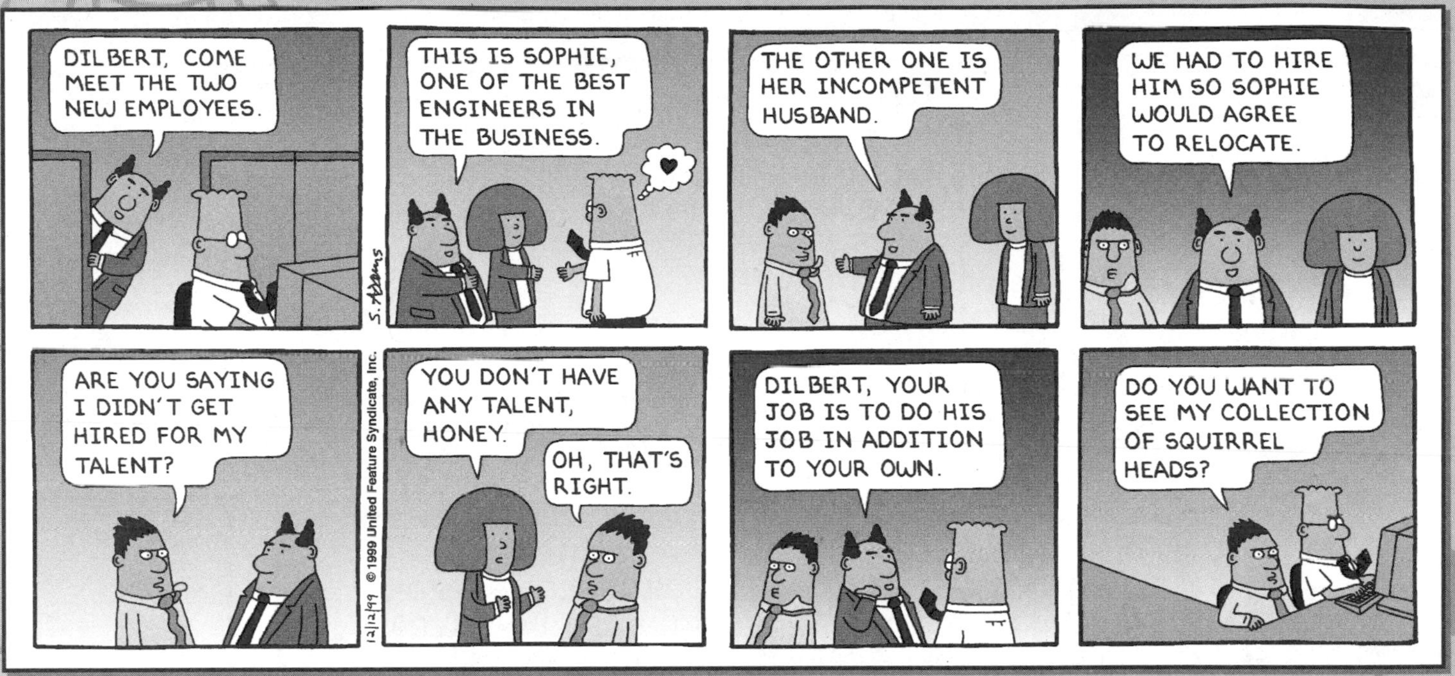

DILBERT, COME MEET THE TWO NEW EMPLOYEES.
THIS IS SOPHIE, ONE OF THE BEST ENGINEERS IN THE BUSINESS.
THE OTHER ONE IS HER INCOMPETENT HUSBAND.
WE HAD TO HIRE HIM SO SOPHIE WOULD AGREE TO RELOCATE.
ARE YOU SAYING I DIDN'T GET HIRED FOR MY TALENT?
YOU DON'T HAVE ANY TALENT, HONEY.
OH, THAT'S RIGHT.
DILBERT, YOUR JOB IS TO DO HIS JOB IN ADDITION TO YOUR OWN.
DO YOU WANT TO SEE MY COLLECTION OF SQUIRREL HEADS?
S. Adams
12/12/99 © 1999 United Feature Syndicate, Inc.


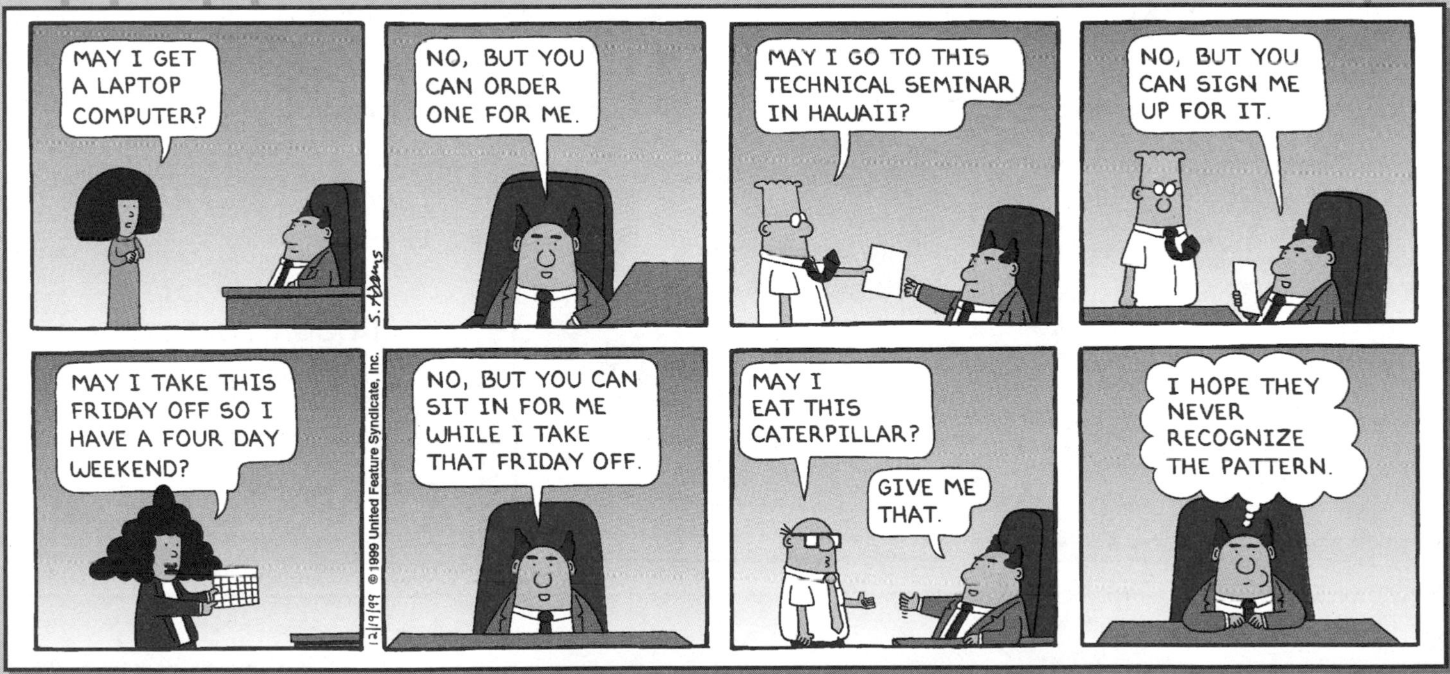

MAY I GET A LAPTOP COMPUTER?
NO, BUT YOU CAN ORDER ONE FOR ME.
MAY I GO TO THIS TECHNICAL SEMINAR IN HAWAII?
NO, BUT YOU CAN SIGN ME UP FOR IT.
MAY I TAKE THIS FRIDAY OFF SO I HAVE A FOUR DAY WEEKEND?
NO, BUT YOU CAN SIT IN FOR ME WHILE I TAKE THAT FRIDAY OFF.
MAY I EAT THIS CATERPILLAR?
GIVE ME THAT.
I HOPE THEY NEVER RECOGNIZE THE PATTERN.
S. Adams
12/19/99 © 1999 United Feature Syndicate, Inc.

YOU WERE TOTALLY CORRECT.
S. Adams
WE CAN DEVELOP THE PRODUCT ON TIME AND UNDER BUDGET.
ALL WE HAVE TO DO IS GIVE UP SOME FEATURES.
FOR EXAMPLE, THE ORIGINAL DESIGN CALLED FOR A SCALABLE WIDE AREA NETWORK SWITCH...
...WITH MULTI-PROTOCOL SUPPORT AND FULL NETWORK DIAGNOSTICS.
THE NEW DESIGN CALLS FOR A SHOEBOX FULL OF YARN.
SO WE'RE IN GOOD SHAPE.. ASSUMING YARN IS FREE.
12/26/99 © 1999 United Feature Syndicate, Inc.
YOU'RE A SERIOUS THREAT TO MY OPEN DOOR POLICY.

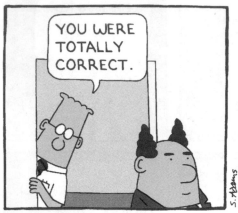

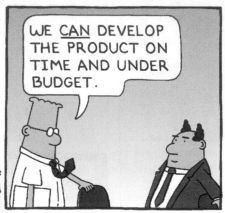

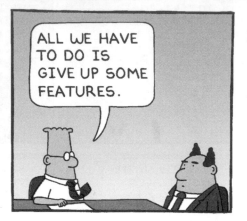

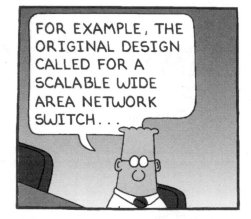

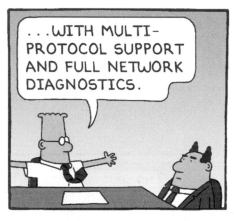

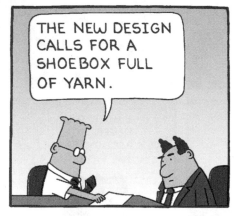

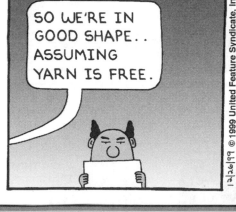

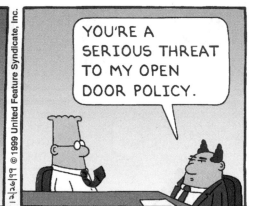